THIRD EDITION

CRISIS NEGOTIATIONS

Managing Critical Incidents and Hostage Situations in Law Enforcement and Corrections

MICHAEL J. McMAINS
Bexar County, Texas, Sheriff's Office

WAYMAN C. MULLINS
Texas State University—San Marcos

 LexisNexis®

 anderson publishing
A member of the LexisNexis Group

Crisis Negotiations: Managing Critical Incidents and Hostage Situations in Law Enforcement and Corrections, Third Edition

Copyright © 1996, 2001, 2006
     Matthew Bender & Company, Inc., a member of the LexisNexis Group

     Phone 877-374-2919
     Web Site www.lexisnexis.com/anderson/criminaljustice

Library of Congress Cataloging-in-Publication Data

McMains, Michael J.
     Crisis negotiations : managing critical incidents and hostage situations in law enforcement and
     corrections / Michael J. McMains and Wayman C. Mullins.-- 3rd ed.
          p. cm.
     ISBN 1-59345-323-X (softbound)
     1. Hostage negotiations--United States. 2. Crisis management--United States. 3. Law enforcement--
     United States. I. Mullins, Wayman C. II. Title.

     HV6598.M35 2006
     363.2'3--dc22   2006003715

Cover design by Tin Box Studio, Inc.

EDITOR Elisabeth Roszmann Ebben
ACQUISITIONS EDITOR Michael C. Braswell

Table of Contents

Chapter 4
Stress and Stress Management

153

X

Chapter 5
Hostage Dynamics

179

Chapter 10
Crisis Negotiations In Prisons and Correctional Facilities

Chapter 11
Intelligence and Intelligence Gathering

Introduction

Never give a sword to a man who can't dance.
—Celtic Motto

The best general is the one who never fights.
—Sun Tzu

Diplomacy is the art of letting someone else have your way.
—Daniele Vare

Intuitively, all good negotiators know the truth in each of the quotes above. They know that they are in a high-stakes game in which the goal is to be prepared to fight, but through the skillful use of unconventional weapons, the incident is settled without firing a shot. Each of the mottoes above reminds us of part of that goal.

The first reminds us that one needs to know what is at stake when force is an option. It is rooted in the ancient Celtic tradition of the warrior-artist. In that tradition, a man needed to see the value of life, to write about its sunrises, flowing streams, and brilliant, crystalline days before he became a warrior. He needed to be able to celebrate all that was good in life. It was through this artful appreciation of life that the warrior came to realize exactly what was at stake in battle. It encouraged the warrior to count the costs before engaging in battle, being sure that the reason for battle was worth the potential costs. It encouraged the warrior to become skilled in his art, dedicating himself to perfecting his skill. It is our experience that negotiators fit the tradition of the warrior-artist. They are keenly aware of the value of life. They know that every encounter can end in immeasurable loss. They are dedicated to refining the use of their weapons, so if life is lost, it is not due to lack of skill.

The second motto reminds us that the most effective way to win a conflict is to arrange it so the other side sees the value of not fighting. The goal in battle is not to have to go to battle. Rather, the opposition must be convinced that a peaceful resolution is their best option. Through the skillful use of both the negotiation team and the tactical team, the goal is to "bring the subject to the table, not to his knees." Through teamwork (Chapter 8), the use of unconventional police weapons such as communications/persuasion skills (Chapter 6), intelligence (Chapter 9), and special equipment (Chapter 12), negotiators convince the subject that he has more to gain and less to lose by ending the incident peacefully than he does by using force. By using their knowledge of the crisis and crisis intervention (Chapter 2), the effects of time on themselves and others (Chapter 3), and the needs of emotionally disturbed individuals (Chapter 7), negotiators do everything possible to preserve life.

The third motto reminds us that the strategies, tactics, and weapons the negotiator uses are unconventional. Rather than using a nightstick, pepper spray, or a weapon, negotiators use understanding, patience, caring, listening, and persuasion. Negotiators must develop the art of getting people to do what they want without challenging them so much that they resist or fight. It takes skill and skill takes practice. They must learn to assess risk (Chapters 7 and 9). They must work as a smooth and well-rehearsed team. Teamwork does not just happen, especially with police officers, who are used to working alone and being in control. They must develop an understanding of how they complement each other. They must be dedicated to the practice of their art as a team.

Negotiators develop an art in the use of weapons that the rest of the department frequently misunderstands. Basic classes in the academy do not train officers in negotiation skills, although some departments are beginning to see the value in all their officers having the people management skills that negotiators develop. Diplomacy is not a skill taught to most law enforcement officers. Therefore, negotiators are frequently misunderstood, especially when they go against the prevailing attitudes of the department to do their job, like the incident in Chapter 14. They must learn to care for themselves and for each other. Stress management, critical incident debriefing, and peer support are necessary for negotiators to persist in their quest to win without bloodshed.

In our experience, negotiators are the brightest and the best in law enforcement and corrections. They are the most motivated and most skilled officers in their departments. They constantly share their experiences and learn from others. It is in the spirit of that sharing that we offer this book. It was not created by us. It was created by negotiators from all over the country who have been gracious enough to share their experiences, lessons, successes, and failures. We are humbled by the trust these negotiators have placed in us. We are awed by the dedication of negotiators. We hope that what negotiators have shared with us and we share with the readers through our words will contribute to the efforts of all the warrior-artists, peaceful generals, and diplomats who practice the art of negotiation.

We cannot thank everyone who has contributed to this book. Like negotiation, it has been a team effort. We would like to thank some especially helpful people, officers and civilians, without whom we would not have been able to do this work. Many people have contributed, as well as having spent hours with us in discussions on a variety of topics important to negotiation.

Much of the material in this book is consistent with FBI teaching and practice, because many FBI agents have contributed to our thinking. They include Gary Noesner, Byron Sage, Steve Romano, and "Max" Howard, current or retired FBI agents with whom we have worked in one way or another for several years. We have also maintained a close working relationship with agents at the Critical Incident Response Group at the FBI Academy for several years. They have always been forthcoming and generous with their knowledge and information.

Many officers have contributed to our efforts. They include Joe Flores of the Carrollton, Texas, Police Department, Joe Jimenez of the Richardson, Texas, Police Department, Bill Kidd of the San Francisco Police Department, Gene Pettit of the Albuquerque Police Department, Warren Zerr of the San Marcos Police Department, and Ken Bell, Fire Marshall for San Marcos, Texas. We would especially like to thank Officer Charles Ricketts and Officer Lionel Solis of the San Antonio Police Department for their contributions to the field over the years and for their review and contributions to chapters of this book.

Recently, Bill Hogewood from the Bureau of Alcohol, Tobacco, and Firearms has been helpful. He has reviewed the training material for Mental Health Consultants and made helpful comments.

Many graduate students and staff at the Criminal Justice Department at Texas State University—San Marcos were helpful in literature searches, reviewing manuscripts, editing, and proofreading chapters. Others were instrumental in organizing and running the Annual Seminar and Competition at TSU—San Marcos, which was a significant resource for us. They include Shan Smith, who took and helped select photographs for this edition of the book, Brad Schley who researched, proofread, and wrote questions for the instructor's manual; George Guerrero, who did library searches; Amy, Jason, Lisa, Jim, Wendy, Bryce, JoDale, and all the other graduate students who helped collect research, reviewed manuscripts, and assisted in the competition.

Last, but not least, we would like to thank again all the negotiators who work without recognition or reward, other than the satisfaction of knowing they have done their job well. Thank you to all those who have taught us more than we have taught them, to all who have been friends and confidants in the hard times and the good (you know who you are), and to all who have advanced the field of crisis response management so that more may live.

To Michael Braswell, for taking the chance, we still owe you our thanks.

Finally, our thanks go to Elisabeth Roszmann Ebben, whose patience was saintly and assistance was cherished, and who made getting the book to print possible.

Hostage and Crisis Negotiations:

Development and Definitions

1

Learning Objectives

1. Understand why high-profile critical incidents forced police to consider alternatives to tactical resolution.

2. Know the principles stressed by NYPD in managing hostage incidents.

3. Know why departments began relying on negotiation in crisis situations.

4. Know which hostage incidents played a significant role in the development of hostage negotiation tactics.

5. Know how recent incidents have changed the nature of negotiations and how we can keep learning from every incident.

6. Know the importance of developing a nationwide database about hostage/crisis incidents.

7. Know about LEO, LENS, and HOBAS, and how to establish an account to access this database.

8. Know the definitions for *hostage*, *negotiations*, and *hostage situation*.

9. Understand the progression from negotiations/bargaining techniques to negotiations/crisis intervention techniques.

10. Know the types of incidents to which crisis intervention principles and techniques are applied.

Munich—1972

On September 5, 1972, 13 Arab terrorists invaded the Olympic compound that housed the Israeli Olympic athletes and took 11 hostages. The terrorists demanded the release of 200 Arab prisoners being held in Israel and free transportation to Egypt. Israeli diplomats contacted the terrorists and were advised that the threat of death to the hostages was real. Ten minutes later, the terrorists stated that if their demands were not met immediately, two athletes would be killed. If their transportation was not arranged, all of the athletes would be killed. Egypt's President, Anwar Sadat, refused to become involved. Diplomats offered alternatives to the terrorists: free passage to the Far East, payment of money, or trade of hostages for other personnel. The terrorists interpreted this as an effort to stall in order to make plans to assault. They continued to insist on the release of all 200 Arab prisoners and transportation to Egypt. Police officers observed what they thought were two dead athletes and nine bound ones. The terrorists continued to threaten to kill two hostages if transportation was not arranged for them. Plans were made to move the terrorists and the hostages to the airport. During the move to the airport, the terrorists demanded that they change from the bus to a helicopter and be flown into the airport. When they arrived at the airport, four terrorists took some of the hostages and moved toward a plane, leaving the remainder of the group in the helicopter. At 11:00 P.M., police demanded that the terrorists drop their weapons and surrender. One terrorist immediately responded by throwing a hand grenade into the helicopter. Three of the terrorists tried to escape from the area: one was killed and two were captured. The terrorists remaining in the helicopter detonated another grenade. The incident ended at 11:15 P.M. with 11 Israeli athletes, one police officer, and 10 Arab terrorists dead (Schreiber, 1973).

In the context of the close scrutiny of police practices that grew out of the 1960s, and a concern about the loss of life in hostage incidents, the international terrorist incident at the 1972 Munich Olympics described above occurred. It motivated the New York City Police Department to evaluate the effectiveness and value of forceful confrontation in hostage incident management and gave law enforcement what Roger Depue, retired Chief of the Behavioral Sciences Unit at the FBI Academy, called "its most effective, nonviolent tool."

The New York City Police Department, using the talents of Harvey Schlossberg, a detective with a Ph.D. in psychology, and then Lieutenant Frank Boltz (Schlossberg, 1979b; Boltz & Hershey, 1979; Cooper, 1978), developed tactics that led to the resolution of high-conflict incidents without the loss of life experienced in Munich. Schlossberg found that there was little literature on the use of negotiating techniques within police work. Therefore, he surveyed the psychological literature and developed principles that emphasized managing hostage incidents as though they were a crisis for the hostage taker. He and Boltz stressed:

1. The importance of containing and negotiating with the hostage taker in a hostage incident.

2. The importance of understanding the hostage taker's motivation and personality in a hostage situation.

3. The importance of slowing an incident down so time can work for the negotiator.

Schlossberg and Boltz pointed out that there were four alternatives open to the police in an incident like the one in Munich: (1) assault, (2) selected sniper fire, (3) chemical agents, and (4) contain and negotiate (Schlossberg, 1979b). The first three relied on traditional confrontational strategies. As such, they had a high probability of violence. He suggested that containing and negotiating was the safest approach for everyone. The principle of zero acceptable losses continues to be the guiding goal of negotiations today.

Understanding the hostage taker's motivation and personality is an important principle in negotiations. Schlossberg (1979a) emphasized that there is "no such thing as a 'psycho.' " Rather, all behavior is understandable, goal oriented, pleasure seeking, and problem solving in nature. To understand apparently meaningless and random behavior, the negotiator needs to understand the person's history, goals, and problem-solving abilities. For instance, the paranoid person who hears voices telling him or her to lash out at others is generally acting out of a deep-seated fear of others attacking him or her. If negotiators understand this, the "craziness" of the paranoid's hallucinations is understandable. If it is understandable, it is less frightening for those who have to deal with it. Understanding focuses attention on the problem of the person's sense of insecurity and fear rather than on the surface issue of the person's "craziness."

NYPD emphasized the importance of slowing down an incident so time can work for the negotiator. It was noted that frustration of a person's goal leads to a series of events that included arousal, problem solving, creativity, and finally aggression. When a husband is confronted with an unwanted divorce, his initial reaction will be arousal: the body energizes itself to deal with the problem and the person feels tense. He engages in some problem-solving behavior designed to reduce arousal and the feelings of discomfort. The husband may promise to change and become more considerate of his wife's requests for more attention. If his attempts at problem solving are unsuccessful and his wife still insists on leaving, further attempts at changing her mind will be made. If they are unsuccessful, tension continues to rise until aggression may be used as the final solution. At that time the wife may become a hostage.

Defusing anxiety associated with frustrated goals takes time. Therefore, the police need to respond to hostage takers in ways they do not expect: by slowing the incident down and allowing the anxiety to dissipate. Schlossberg called this "dynamic inactivity" (Schlossberg, 1979a).

The New York City Police Department established its hostage recovery program following Schlossberg and Boltz's new approach. It was the first program in the country to emphasize the soft negotiation approach to conflict rather than the hard, tactical approach.

The Williamsburg Incident

On January 19, 1973, the NYPD had the opportunity to test their new principles and the newly established Hostage Recovery Program (Boltz & Hershey, 1979; Schlossberg, 1979b; Culley, 1974). Four armed robbers entered John and Al's Sporting Goods Store in New York City. They announced a robbery and threatened employees and customers with a sawed-off shotgun and handguns. A silent alarm summoned the police, who trapped the armed robbers in the store. In the initial encounter, gunfire was exchanged and two police officers were wounded and one police officer was killed. One robber was wounded, and several officers and civilians were pinned down. Rather than storming the building in the heat of battle, the department contained the situation and began to negotiate. The hostage takers released a hostage at 8:00 P.M. This hostage was released for the purpose of taking a message to the police. The hostage takers had the released hostage tell the police that unless the hostage takers were allowed to escape, they would kill the remaining hostages. They demanded a doctor for their wounded companion. Because the robbers presented themselves as Black Muslims, several Muslim clergy were allowed to talk with them. Communications were established using a set of walkie-talkies that were not set up on the police frequencies. Food and cigarettes were given to them. A hostage was released in exchange for medical attention to the wounded robber in the store. A "think tank" was established, staffed by key department personnel, outside experts (including a psychologist), and a representative of the mayor's office. Outside agencies were contacted in the event the incident spilled over into other jurisdictions. The robbers continued to engage in sporadic gunfire throughout the incident. After the initial cover fire the police used while rescuing trapped officers and citizens, the authorities held their fire. At 12:45 P.M. the following day, the hostages escaped using a stairwell that one of the store owners knew could be accessed by breaking through the plasterboard that was covering it. The hostages, who had been in a separate room from the gunmen, had time to escape through the door that had been blocked by the store owners. To preserve life, the police continued to contain and negotiate with the gunmen, even though their leverage was gone. It took time to effect the escape. Without hostages, the gunmen lost their power. The siege ended at 4:45 P.M. when the gunmen surrendered after being "convinced" that to fight for the oppressed minorities they must first stay alive (Culley, 1974).

The Williamsburg incident was a key incident in the development of hostage negotiations. It proved the effectiveness of the "slow things down and talk things out" approach, even in the face of shots having been fired and officers having been wounded and killed. In place of the usual action-oriented approach to an incident in which emotions run high on both sides, the more controlled, slower, and less reactive approach proved successful in the sense that no other people were killed or wounded. It was a remarkable change in strategy and tactics that took immense courage, and for which the NYPD, Harvey Schlossberg, and Frank Boltz will be remembered.

Many states (and regions of the country) have professional associations dedicated to crisis negotiations. There are also many other training opportunities available for negotiators. These negotiators are at Texas State University for training and a negotiator competition. This annual event is one of the oldest negotiator training conferences in the country (going into its 17th year in 2006) and draws almost 400 police and prison negotiators from around the country. *(W. Mullins)*

FBI Hostage Negotiations Program

The New York City Police Department asked the Federal Bureau of Investigation to review the curriculum for hostage negotiation. Shortly afterward, the FBI developed a national training program for police officers who wanted to learn about hostage negotiation. The acceptance of hostage negotiation as a legitimate law enforcement strategy took a quantum leap forward when the FBI established its hostage negotiation training program at the FBI Academy in Quantico, Virginia, in 1973. In addition to training police officers from around the world in hostage negotiation, the Special Operations and Research Section of the academy brought together behavioral science experts and law enforcement personnel to develop a working relationship focused on hostage negotiation. The International Association of Chiefs of Police followed the FBI's lead by establishing a Hostage Rescue Seminar in 1976.

The FBI developed a course curriculum on hostage negotiation that has served as the basis for most local law enforcement training. Estimates are that 70 percent of trained police negotiators were trained directly or indirectly using the FBI curriculum. It has generated papers on every aspect of negotiation and has provided a model of cooperation and collaboration between law enforcement professionals and mental health professionals that is being followed today in other areas of police psychology. It published a compendium of some of their most important papers in 1998. In 1995, it organized the Critical Incident Response Group (CIRG) to plan, coordinate, and train for issues involving hostage/crisis incidents in a coordinated and proactive way.

Hostage Barricade Database System (HOBAS)

Recognizing the need for a nationwide database on hostage/crisis incidents, the Crisis Management Unit at the FBI Academy established the Hostage Barricade Database System (HOBAS) to systematically collect data from law enforcement agencies across the country. Until then, there had been no nationwide format for collecting data on hostage/crisis incidents. HOBAS is part of the LEO (Law Enforcement On-line) system developed and managed by the FBI. LEO has several specialized areas, including a bomb data center, National Academy Associates section, a joint terrorism task force section, and a Law Enforcement Negotiator Support (LENS) section. HOBAS is contained within LENS and the database serves two important purposes. First, it is a repository of information about incidents, allowing for a standardized format. It forms the basis on which research can be done and is a valuable resource for law enforcement agencies that are engaged in an active incident. Critical Incident Response Group members can draw from HOBAS profiles of similar situations and advise negotiators on others' experiences in similar incidents. Second, it collects data on both the subjects and the victims in hostage/crisis incidents, including:

1. Demographic data, including age, sex, marital status, and race of the victims and the subjects

2. Language fluency of both the victims and the subjects

3. Health actors that may have influenced the incident

4. Religious background of both victims and subjects

5. Treatment of the victims

6. Criminal history

7. Whether the subject had mental health problems

8. Prior suicide attempts on the part of the subject

9. Substance abuse before or during the incident

10. Type of weapons involved in the incident

11. Whether explosives were used in the incident

12. Movement the victims were allowed

13. Whether the Stockholm Syndrome developed

14. Relationship of subject to victims prior to the incident

15. Whether the victim was released or rescued and the types of action necessary for release or rescue

16. Outcome of the incident

17. Status of the subject at the resolution of the incident—not injured, injured, killed, etc.

Other HOBAS data includes planned/unplanned, time of day, day of week, location (for example, 53.2% of all reported incidents occurred at a private residence), whether a TPI (third-party intermediary) was used (and type of TPI), who initiated contact, how officers communicated with the subject, language negotiations conducted in, how resolved (approximately 70% resolved by negotiation strategies), tactical use of negotiators, injury and death rates, and whether violence was used by the subject, among others.

To use LENS and HOBAS, law enforcement and correctional officers need only apply by completing a short application form that the agency authorizes. Once employment is verified, the FBI provides the user with a CD containing complete information and instructions for using HOBAS. The user calls a provided number to activate their account, establish an user name and password, and install the software needed to use the system.

Table 1.1 shows a sample of HOBAS data from June 2005. It is of note that the majority of incidents were resolved without injury to the subject or the victim (79.2%). It is also important to note that more than one-half (62.5%) of the incidents reported to the FBI involved people who knew each other to some degree. Therefore, adjustments need to be made to accommodate this information. For instance, the Stockholm Syndrome does not apply to incidents in which people have a prior relationship. Negotiators need to be careful in these incidents because they are likely to be a result of the relationship, and the expressive nature of the incident increases the risk to the victim. Having major implications for policy development, negotiator selection, and training, only 4.5% of all incidents are classic hostage incidents. The rest were some type of barricade incident.

History

Hostage taking and negotiations did not start with the NYPD. It has been part of the human condition since the beginning of recorded history. In the Old Testament, both Israelites and their enemies took captives: sometimes as the spoils of war, sometimes as a means of indoctrinating the conquered nation into the ways of its captors, and sometimes to weaken the resources of the overthrown nation. These captives were used to guarantee that the vanquished nation would not wage war on its conquerors. In African nations, people were captured, held hostage, and used as slaves.

Hostage taking has involved the use of persons as guarantees of payment or as security against war. The Romans held hostages as guarantees of treaties (Call, 1999). During the Middle Ages, European nations expected that people would be held captive to assure compliance by warring nations. Merchants were taken captive to guarantee that other merchants of the same nationality would pay their debts (Souchon, 1976). During World War II, Germany took as many as two million French hostages after the division of France in 1942 to assure the cooperation and compliance of the French people. Hostages have also been used to extort payment from a second party. For instance, pirates captured hostages and demanded tribute from people who valued the hostages (Call, 1999)

The United States has been no exception. Hostage taking has been used to make a political point. Outside of law enforcement, both negotiations and tactical approaches have been used to resolve hostage incidents with varying degrees of success. Three examples of early, non-law enforcement incidents were the Barbary Coast conflict, John Brown's raid on the armory at Harper's Ferry, and Santo Tomas University.

Table 1.1
Summary of Some of the HOBAS Data Maintained by the Crisis Management Unit (CMU), Federal Bureau of Investigation, Quantico, Virginia. Data is current as of June 2005.

INCIDENT TYPE	Number	Percent		
Hostage	210	4.5		
Barricade	2300	49.1		
Barricade w/Victims	424	19.1		
Suicide	323	6.9		
Attempt Suicide	1337	28.6		
Combination	86	1.8		
INCIDENT DURATION				
0-2 Hours	1723	36.8		
2-4 Hours	1440	30.8		
4-6 Hours	743	15.9		
6-9 Hours	392	8.4		
9-12 Hours	132	2.8		
12-18 Hours	107	2.3		
18-36 Hours	105	2.2		
Over 36 Hours	38	0.8		

	VICTIMS		PERPETRATORS	
	Number	Percent	Number	Percent
AGE				
00-18	324	24.5	176	3.5
18-29	216	16.3	1389	27.8
30-45	262	19.8	2152	43.1
46-65	105	7.9	677	13.6
Over 65	37	2.8	83	1.7
Unknown	380	28.7	511	10.2
SEX				
Male	409	30.9	4510	90.4
Female	758	57.3	478	9.6
Unknown	157	11.9	0	0
MARITAL STATUS				
Married			1122	22.5
Divorced			439	8.8
Separated			276	5.5
Single			1880	37.7
Cohabitation			179	3.6
Widow/Widower			46	0.9
Unknown			1046	21.0

Table 1.1, *continued*

RACE

Nat. Amer.	27	2.0		87	1.7
Afr. Amer.	246	18.6		979	19.6
Asian	70	5.3		97	1.9
White	646	48.8		2850	57.1
Hispanic	117	8.8		431	8.6
Other	218	16.5		544	10.9

VICTIM TREATMENT

Not Mistreated	595	33.7
Phys. Abused	295	16.7
Sex. Abused	47	2.7
Verbally Abused	349	19.8
Ignored	45	2.6
Talked Freely w/Subject	132	7.5
Other	301	17.1

CRIMINAL HISTORY

None	810	13.8
Violent Crimes	1138	19.5
Hostage/Barricade	154	2.6
Other Crimes	1817	31.1
Unknown	1930	33.0

RELATIONSHIP TO SUBJECT

None	500	37.5
Family Mem.	318	23.9
Law Enf.	9	0.7
Employer	3	0.2
Spouse/Ex-spouse	131	9.8
Sig. Other	150	11.3
Friend/Co-worker	61	4.6
Other	161	12.1

PRIOR SUICIDE ATTEMPTS

None	1027	20.6
One or more	622	12.5
Unknown	3339	66.9

RELEASE/RESCUE

Released at surr.	286	14.4
Released prior to resolution	642	32.3
Negotiated release	274	13.8
Non-neg release	441	22.2
Released due health	4	0.2
Rescued by SWAT	214	10.8
Unknown	127	6.4

WEAPONS

None	1269	22.8
Blunt Object	62	1.1
Chemical	47	0.8
Handgun	1905	34.2
Knife	688	12.4
Shoulder Weapon	1241	22.3
Other	353.3	6

STATUS AT END OF INCIDENT

No Injury/Death	1049	79.2
Injured	192	14.5
Killed	78	5.9
Died	5	0.4

NOTE: This is only a sampling of the HOBAS data maintained by the CMU, FBI. For complete data contact the CMU at the FBI Academy, Quantico, Virginia.

Agencies can also contact the CMU for instructions on adding data from their incidents to the national data bank.

We gratefully acknowledge Special Agent Chris Voss and MaryAnne Bochichio for supplying this data.

Barbary Coast

Some of America's early experiences with hostage-taking demands, negotiations, and tactical actions came against the Barbary states of Algiers, Morocco, Tripoli, and Tunis. The rulers of these states owed allegiance and paid tribute to the ruler of the Ottoman Empire, the Sultan of Turkey. In turn, and to pay the Sultan, they preyed on travelers and merchants plying the Mediterranean Sea. The sea powers of Europe, Britain, Portugal, Sweden, and France paid an annual tribute to the Barbary States to keep their ships, cargoes, and crews safe. Until the American Revolution, colonial ships sailed under the protective tribute of Britain. With the coming of the war, American ships were seized, crews taken hostage, and ransom demanded. By 1785, the problem had become so severe that Congress made tribute payments part of the annual budget of the country (Beach, 1986). In that year, for example, the merchant ships *Maria* and *Dauphin* were taken by Algerian corsairs, and it cost between $1,200 and $2,900 per crewman to obtain their release (Hagan, 1991). The system of hostage taking and ransom was so sophisticated, in fact, that different ranks of crewmen demanded different ransom. Captains were much more costly than seamen.

By 1794, having had its fill of paying an annual tribute that increased every year, and still having ships and crews seized, Congress authorized the construction of six frigates: the *USS Chesapeake, Congress, Constellation, Constitution, President,* and *United States* (Beach, 1986). In 1801, the *USS George Washington* carried the annual tribute to the Dey of Algiers, who ordered the ship to carry his tribute to the Sultan of Turkey in Constantinople. As a response to this indignity, President Monroe sent a fleet of warships to the Mediterranean as a "squadron of observation." This squadron was to preserve, at whatever cost, our presence in the Mediterranean and surrounding area and was authorized to use whatever force was necessary to protect any ship traveling under U.S. naval escort.

Under conditions of increasing hostility, on October 21, 1803, the *USS Philadelphia* was run aground in the harbor at Tripoli, the crew under the command of Captain William Bainbridge was forced to surrender, and the ship was seized and converted into a Tripolian warship. On the night of February 16, 1804, Stephen Decatur Jr., commander of the *USS Enterprise* and acting in command of a captured Ottoman ketch (renamed the *Intrepid*), attacked and sank the *Philadelphia* (with no American loss of life). The fleet blockaded Tripoli and prevented any merchants from entering the country. On April 27, 1805, William Eaton, commanding seven U.S. Marines and a force of 400 seamen, and after crossing 600 miles of desert, captured the port of Derna, Tripoli, with naval support from Lt. Isaac Hull and the *USS Argus, USS Hornet,* and *USS Nautilus.* The Pasha of Tripoli sent a message to the U.S. naval commander to "recollect I have upwards of three hundred of your countrymen in my hands; and I candidly tell you that, if you persevere in driving me to the last extremity, I shall retire with them to a castle of about ninety miles in the interior of the country, which I have prepared for their confinement and my own security" (Hagan, 1991:61). The United States paid a $60,000 ransom and retired on June 10, 1805.

This last act in a history of hostage taking and of demanding ransom led the U.S. government to conclude that force could not be used to end these practices. By 1807, all American warships had been removed from the

Mediterranean, and would remain so until after the War of 1812. On March 2, 1815, at President Madison's request, Congress declared war on Algiers. On June 17, Commander Stephen Decatur Jr., aboard his flagship *USS Guerriere*, sank the Algerian *Mashouda* and achieved an unconditional peace treaty with the Dey, thus ending the Barbary Wars (Beach, 1986). The end was forced by a combination of negotiation and force. Many of the principles then employed in response to hostage taking are the same as those that are employed today.

Harper's Ferry

John Brown was a freedom fighter who first gained notoriety in the Kansas wars that preceded the Civil War. It had long been Brown's goal to strike a violent blow against slavery in the very heart of slavery, the Appalachians. As McPherson (1988) said of him; "Not for him was the Christ-like martyrdom of Uncle Tom. Brown's God was the Jehovah who drowned Pharaoh's mercenaries in the Red Sea; his Jesus was the angry man who drove money-changers from the temple." In the spring of 1858, Brown and a small group of followers moved to Chatham, Canada, and began plans for the liberation of the slaves. When he had amassed sufficient arms and money, Brown rented a Maryland farm under an assumed name and began plotting his first act of the slave revolt.

On October 16, 1858, one of the most famous of all American hostage situations began. Harper's Ferry, Virginia, was a small and somewhat insignificant U.S. armory and arsenal on a peninsula at the confluence of the Potomac and Shenandoah Rivers. On that day, John Brown and 18 of his followers captured the armory, which was guarded by only one watchman. He then ordered some of his men into the surrounding countryside to capture and return with some hostages, which they did. Brown also put out a call for slaves to leave their masters and join his band in proclaiming freedom from slavery. Only a very few joined him. The armory was then secured (McPherson, 1988).

Brown and his band captured the armory without sufficient provisions for a siege, without planning escape routes, without notifying any of the slaves he expected to join him, and without any firm demands for the government. On October 17, while the militias of Virginia and Maryland hurried to Harper's Ferry, residents of the area took up arms and began sniping at Brown's band. Three townspeople were killed, eight of Brown's men were killed, including two of his sons, and seven of Brown's men fled. Brown retreated into the fire engine house. That night, Colonel Robert E. Lee and Lieutenant J.E.B. Stuart arrived with a company of U.S. Marines. On October 18, having been ordered to avoid using firearms lest they harm the hostages, the Marines were ordered in and attacked the engine house with rams and bayonets. In a short, intense battle, the engine house was secured at the cost of two of Brown's men and one Marine. Brown and his captured men were tried by the state of Virginia and found guilty of treason, murder, and fomenting insurrection. Brown was hanged on December 2 and the other men on December 16 and March 16, 1860.

To the south, Harper's Ferry demonstrated the contentment of slaves. Because few rushed to join Brown, southerners took that as evidence of the justness of their "peculiar institution." There was also a fear among south-erners of a general uprising of slaves and a marching into the south of armed abolitionists. These fears were reduced when Brown was hung. To northerners, Brown soon became a martyr in the anti-slavery cause. Ulti-mately, Brown's actions would polarize the country and become one of the more significant acts in the long road to war.

Santo Tomas University

Surprisingly, one of the earliest recorded incidents involving hostage negotiation involved the military, not a criminal justice agency. In January 1945, General Douglas MacArthur, Commander of Southwest Pacific forces, returned to the Philippines. In Santo Tomas University, located in the heart of Manila, were 5,000 American and British civilians, captured when the Japanese first invaded the Philippines in 1942. Another 500 American prisoners were being held in the city of San Jose. MacArthur wanted the pris-oners freed as soon as possible (Costello, 1982).

Japanese defenders on the Philippines numbered 30,000 and were led by a seasoned veteran of the war, General Yamashita. Landing on Luzon unop-posed, General Griswald's XIV Corps pushed south toward Manila, while General Swift's I Corps secured the flanks and rear. Twenty-five miles inland, the XIV Corps met with heavy resistance. As the main advance began bogging down, the United States 1st Airborne Rangers and Filipino guerrillas attacked and freed the 500 Americans captive at San Jose on January 29, 1945. Upon hearing the news of the successful rescue of the San Jose captives (no American prisoners were killed), MacArthur ordered Brigadier General William Chase and elements of the 27th Infantry Division and 1st Cavalry to "Go to Manila. Go around the _____. Bounce off the _____. But get to Manila." While Swift feinted at San Manuel, and the 25th and 32nd Reserves attacked at Bagio, Chase led two flying columns of tanks and heavy armor south down Highway 5 into the heart of Manila to Santo Tomas University.

When Chase and his column arrived, the Japanese barricaded themselves in the University courtyard with the American prisoners, threatening to kill all Americans unless the Japanese were allowed to leave Santo Tomas. Thus began one of the most dramatic, if lesser known, hostage incidents of the twentieth century. Surrounded by the Japanese Army of General Yamashita and separated from the main body of the Army, General Chase engaged in three days of hostage negotiations with the Japanese. Early in the negotiations, Chase was able to provide food and Red Cross supplies for the American prisoners (Brantley, 1993). By the second day, the Japanese agreed to allow Army medical personnel into Santo Tomas to treat and remove the more seriously ill prisoners (Graydon, 1993). Other concessions were granted by the Japanese during remaining negotiations, including the release of all children (Gillooly, 1993). Finally, on February 3, Chase reached an agreement with the Japanese whereby the Japanese soldiers would be allowed to leave Santo Tomas (without any weapons) and flee into the city. As the Japanese fled the University, Chase rounded up all American prisoners and retreated to friendly lines some 13 miles outside the city of Manila. During the dash to Santo Tomas, negotiations with the Japanese and retreat to Swift's I Corps lines, Chase suffered no casualties and no American prisoners/hostages were injured or killed.

To secure the release of the Americans, Chase relied upon many of the techniques now considered standard practice in hostage negotiations. Ignoring his position deep within enemy territory, Chase used time wisely, deliberately dragging negotiations out for several days to calm the excited and frightened Japanese hostage takers. He negotiated demands, getting something for something. For example, when the Japanese demanded he move his tanks back from the front gate, Chase agreed to do so if the Japanese allowed medical personnel into the University (Irvine, 1993). He "wore down" the Japanese, keeping the Japanese commander awake for long stretches of time and then when the commander went to sleep, waking him after only an hour or two of sleep. He wisely used the threat of firepower (similar to the threat posed by SWAT officers), at one point threatening to unleash his entire column if one American was injured. In sum, he performed exactly as trained negotiators would perform. (As a postscript, the fighting to retake Manila was some of the bloodiest of the war. It took more than one month of building-to-building fighting to recapture the city. When the battle was over, more than 80 percent of the city lay in ruins, and more than 15,000 Japanese, 8,000 Americans, and 25,000 Filipinos had been killed).

Hostage taking has often been a geopolitical technique used by one nation against another. What is new in the twenty-first century is the way hostages have been used, especially in recent decades; the way the police have responded to these incidents; and the way psychological principles have been applied to the management of hostage incidents.

Development of Negotiations in Police Work—The Context

Modern police departments must handle hostage situations that are very different from the early geopolitical incidents. With the exception of the 1970s, most American law enforcement has not had to deal with hostage taking as an act of war, politics, or economics. Criminals and emotionally disturbed individuals do not take hostages to gain large-scale political or economic power;

they take hostages to force compliance with demands or to express their emotional needs. Recently, hostage taking has often been an attempt at gaining personal power by individuals caught in the commission of a crime, or by individuals who have experienced a long-standing sense of powerlessness (American Justice, 1994). Police departments have had to deal more with law violations or public safety issues when they have dealt with hostage incidents. Additionally, hostage taking in prisons and jails across the country has become commonplace. Prisoners have gained certain rights and guarantees through the courts and continually demand better treatment, better living conditions, and other privileges of prison and jail administrators. Other than legal action, the only redress prisoners may have is the taking of prison property and using hostages (usually prison staff) as bargaining chips.

Significant differences exist between the police management of hostage incidents and international-level management of hostage incidents. Although the United States' avowed policy at the international level is that it will not negotiate with terrorists, even when they hold hostages, law enforcement has generally taken the position that as long as no immediate threat to life exists, negotiations are acceptable. Following the English tradition of policing, American law enforcement emphasizes the rule of law and the rights of the individual (Walker, 1992). These elements have led to an emphasis on due process within the American legal system and have been the foundation on which much of American policing has been built. They have been the background against which negotiations have developed.

The individual's rights and the constitutional guarantees that are designed to protect those rights have led to many attempts at law enforcement reforms over the years (Walker, 1992). As early as 1933, the Wickersham Report criticized police use of force as exemplified in the "third degree." Part of the report, titled *Lawlessness in Law Enforcement,* documented the widespread abuse of citizens by police agencies. It cited examples, such as one suspect being hung by his heels from the police department building until he confessed, as abuse of citizens.

1970s

Experienced police officers report that, prior to 1973, departments faced with a person holding hostages used one of three methods to manage the incidents:

1. They relied on the verbal skills of the individual patrol officer.

2. They walked away.

3. They amassed manpower and firepower at the scene and demanded that the subject release the hostages and surrender. If compliance was not obtained within a reasonable length of time, an assault was launched (Russell & Beigel, 1979).

Typical of the first approach was the 1961 incident of a patrol officer responding to a disturbance call at a residence. Upon arrival, he found the husband and wife barricaded in their home. The husband was holding the wife at gunpoint to keep her from leaving. The officer talked with the husband through the closed door of the house. He found out that the wife wanted to leave because she was tired of the husband's coming home drunk every pay-day and beating her. The officer was able to convince the husband that it was not very manly to hold his wife at gunpoint and that there were other women in the world who would appreciate his better qualities. The officer had knowledge and experience enough not to challenge the man's coming home drunk. Rather, he encouraged the man to seek a peaceful resolution as a positive action, a strategy similar to those used by negotiators today.

There was no training in crisis management, hostage negotiation, or abnormal behavior in police departments prior to 1973. Consequently, the skill with which an individual officer handled such situations depended on the skill he or she brought to the job. The management of hostage incidents varied from officer to officer. Faced with the same situation described above, some officers simply left, saying, "It is a domestic dispute and we have no authority." Other officers would call for reinforcements, contain the situation, and demand surrender. The management of crisis incidents was not uniform or professional.

The same situation existed in prisons. When prisoners rioted and took hostages, the typical reaction of the prison administration was to use violence to regain control. Prison guards, police officers, and, in some cases, the National Guard would use nightsticks and guns to retake the prison in a military-type assault operation. Often prisoners, prison employee hostages, and members of the assault operation were injured or killed. The 1974 Carrasco incident at the Texas Department of Corrections (TDC) illustrates this approach (Stone, 2000).

Fred Carrasco was in the Walls TDC unit outside of Huntsville, Texas. He was in prison for a variety of charges, including drug dealing and the attempted murder of a police officer. Plotting escape with three other convicts, Carrasco received smuggled handguns from a trustee who worked in the prison director's kitchen (the trustee smuggled the pistols and ammunition into the prison in a hollowed-out ham). Carrasco and the other inmates entered the prison library, which was on the third floor of a multi-use building in the prison (dining halls and recreation rooms occupied the first two floors). They took a prison officer, 11 librarians, and one teacher hostage. Their plan was to use the hostages to secure escape. Their escape plot soon turned into a 10-day siege. Very few negotiations were conducted by prison officials or the police (neither of which had negotiators or a trained tactical team). One reason the incident lasted 10 days was that prison officials could not decide how to attack Carrasco's position. Plan after plan was discarded, including one plan to blow up the library building.

Finally, prison officials decided upon a plan to give the hostage takers a military armored vehicle and attack the hostage takers when they exited the library. An armored car was delivered and the hostage takers came out. They had surrounded themselves with rolling bookcases stacked with books, with the hostages tied to the outside of the "Roman Turtle." The authorities used high-pressure water hoses in an attempt to break apart the bookcase shield. When this tactic failed, officers using long fire-hook poles ran up and attempted to physically pull apart the shield. During this attempt, both sides opened fire. When the firing stopped, three hostages had been killed and several had been wounded, three hostage takers had been killed (including Carrasco), and several attackers had been wounded. It was estimated that more than 700 rounds were fired during the three-minute firefight. Not just at TDC, but also nationwide, this "attack with superior firepower" attitude was the norm.

After the establishment of specialized teams (SWAT—Special Weapons and Tactics), assaults were made by specially armed and specially trained police officers. However, their effectiveness in reducing injuries and death in violent confrontations was questionable. Schlossberg (1979a) established that in 78 percent of assaults, people were injured or killed. Police officers often sustained the casualties. Hatcher et al. (1998) point out that the SWAT approach was built on a military model in which the number of acceptable losses was part of the decision. Many departments in this era had seven-man teams so that they could take the expected casualties and still overwhelm the hostage taker.

An example of this approach was a 1979 incident in which an adolescent male shot a patrol officer when the officer stopped him outside a local high school. The officer was not fatally wounded and was able to call for help. The SWAT team was mobilized. They began a house-to-house search of the block where witnesses said the suspect had run. After surrounding the house in which they thought the suspect was barricaded, SWAT officers tried to enter the back door. The suspect burst out, shooting one SWAT officer before he was shot by patrol officers on the perimeter of the scene. The patrol officers also shot one of the SWAT officers. The incident ended with one dead suspect and three wounded officers.

The growth of psychological services within police departments was another factor that favored the development of hostage negotiation. While New York City used an officer with psychological expertise to develop the principles of negotiations, other departments began to hire civilian staff psychologists in the early 1970s (Reese, Horn & Dunning, 1991). In response to the recommendations of the President's Commission on Law Enforcement and Administration of Justice (1967), departments raised their hiring standards and increased their training in an effort to professionalize. As part of this new effort, applicants had to be certified by a mental health professional as emotionally, behaviorally, and cognitively capable of doing the job. Departments began hiring or contracting with psychologists to do pre-employment screening. This brought law enforcement and psychology into closer contact, opening the way for mental health professionals to influence departments on a number of human factors issues, including crisis intervention, management of abnormal behavior, and hostage negotiation.

Sidebar: The Early Days

Deputy William Kidd is with the Sonoma County Sheriff's Department. He retired from the San Francisco Police Department in March 2005, after 35 years of service. In 1974, he was one of the founding members of the San Francisco Police Department Hostage/Crisis Negotiation Team. Deputy Kidd holds a Master's degree in Public Administration (Justice Administration) from Golden Gate University. He is a past president of the California Association of Hostage Negotiators and is currently their administrative coordinator. A police instructor since 1976, Kidd instructs police officers in the areas of domestic violence, hostage/crisis negotiations, and sexual assault investigation. He is currently a member of the Sonoma County Sheriff's Department Crisis Negotiation Team.

Crisis negotiations—or what was known as "hostage negotiations" at the time—came west in 1973, when Harvey Schlossberg and Frank Bolz were invited to present the concept to lieutenants and above at the San Francisco Police Department. This came about despite the fact that many in American law enforcement were reticent to buy into the "radical approach" that Schlossberg and Bolz were advocating. Fortunately, however, they were invited to the Midwest to talk about their newly created team and experiences at the annual conference of the International Association of Chiefs of Police, and there they were seen by Sergeant Gerald Doane of the San Francisco Police Department.

Sgt. Doane was persuaded by the presentation made by the New York City officers and returned home to try to interest his superiors. His captain, George Eimil, agreed to have the commissioned officers of the department (San Francisco) hear Harvey Schlossberg and Frank Boltz and then make their recommendation as to whether and to what extent the hostage negotiations approach should be adopted.

As fate would have it, about two weeks after the visit by Schlossberg and Bolz, one of the students, Lieutenant Richard D. Klapp, responded at the request of another attendee, Captain James Taylor, when Taylor was confronted by an armed hostage taker in Taylor's police district. Within 90 minutes of arrival, Klapp had gotten the perpetrator to release his 18-month-old son and to surrender to Klapp and other officers.

Both Klapp and Doane thereafter became ardent supporters of the hostage negotiation model and the SFPD had an official hostage negotiations team in operation by September 1974. It was the first such team in the western United States. Klapp and Doane made numerous appearances and trained countless officers around northern California, and hostage negotiations in California was off and running. Doane soon after assembled the Basic Hostage Negotiations Course that is still conducted at San Jose State University in San Jose, California.

> I was one of the original negotiators with the 1974 team, was mentored by both Klapp and Doane and found it changed my life. Because of my fascination with and study of hostage/crisis negotiations ever since, I have been able to visit and learn from many negotiators across and from outside the United States. My career in law enforcement became twice as enjoyable and rewarding as a result, and I was able meet and learn from a host of law officers and, without a doubt, some of the finest Americans of my time. It has been an experience that has made me immensely proud to be a negotiator and a cop.

Unlike in the past, hostage takers in modern times have frequently been involved in a conflict while they are trying to force their demands on the authorities. Hostage takers often are engaged in a conflict with authorities at the same time they are making demands. This has led to unique aspects of modern hostage negotiations. For instance, the Stockholm Syndrome has been recognized as a psychological consequence of hostages and hostage takers being together in a life-threatening situation. These conflict situations are not necessarily limited to law enforcement and correctional situations. With the end of the cold war, the dissolution of the Soviet Union, the reunification of Germany, and the rise in power of Middle East dictator states, the military of the free world will be called upon to serve in conflict resolution/hostage negotiation roles. The 1989 United States invasion of Panama and the negotiations required to capture General Noriega, and the 1994 invasion of Haiti are two examples of the need for the military to understand crisis negotiation principles.

Downs v. United States: The Legal Foundation—1971

The legal foundation for the use of hostage negotiation techniques in the United States was laid by *Downs v. United States.* On October 4, 1971, FBI agents from the Jacksonville field office intercepted a hijacked aircraft that landed at Jacksonville International Airport for refueling. On board were two crew members, two hijackers, and the wife of one hijacker. The gunman and his wife were reported to have a long history of marital difficulty. Communication was established by radio with the plane's captain. The hijackers demanded fuel, an engine restarter, and the clearing of law enforcement personnel from around the plane. The fuel demand was refused. The captain reported that one gunman had 12$^{1}/_{2}$ pounds of plastic explosives on board. The copilot was allowed to leave the aircraft to negotiate for fuel. Again, the fuel was refused. A few minutes later, one gunman deplaned and asked for fuel, saying that the man left on board was extremely upset. He was arrested. The decision was made to assault the aircraft. A car was moved to block the aircraft. The Assistant Special Agent in Charge (ASAC) approached the plane, identified himself as an FBI agent, and ordered everyone in the plane to leave. Two shots were fired from inside the plane. The ASAC tried to deflate the right rear tire by shooting it, and ordered the right engine disabled by gunfire. When the engines were quieted, he approached the plane and found two dead hostages, and a mortally wounded hijacker (FBI, 1985).

The district court ruled that the FBI was not negligent in its handling of the hijacking. It ruled that the use of force was not unreasonable under the circumstances and that the agent in charge had taken the course of action that would maximize the hostages' safety.

The appeals court, however, found that there was "a better-suited alternative to protecting the hostages' well-being." It pointed out that the degree to which law enforcement officers will be excused for errors in judgment in emergency situations is "qualified by training and experience he has or can be expected to have, in coping with the danger or emergency with which he is confronted" (*Downs*, 382 F. Supp. at 752). Because the FBI guidelines on the handling of hijackings established the safety of the hostages to be of primary importance, and because there appeared to be positive (the release of a hostage and attempts to negotiate using both a hostage and one of the gunmen) rather than negative reactions from the hijackers to being delayed, negotiations were a viable alternative to force. Because the ASAC was trained on these guidelines, the court found that the district court was in error and its decision was reversed. This ruling established negotiation as a third alternative to force or escape in emergency situations.

Sveriges Kredit Bank, Stockholm: Impact on the Hostages—1973

The robbery of a bank in Stockholm, Sweden led to the development of another principle for law enforcement officers: the Stockholm Syndrome. At 10:15 P.M., a lone gunman initiated a 131-hour hostage incident at the Sveriges Kredit Bank. He demanded the release from prison of his ex-cellmate, who joined him and four hostages in the bank vault. In addition, he asked for transportation out of the country and $750,000, which the authorities refused. During the siege, the hostages came to fear the police more than the hostage takers. The hostages came to believe they knew better than the authorities what needed to be done to preserve their own lives, and they overtly sided with the hostage taker's position against the authorities. This allegiance to the goals of the hostage takers has become known as the Stockholm Syndrome (Cooper, 1978).

The Stockholm Syndrome is important in negotiations for two reasons:

1. It can be purposely developed by either the police or by the hostage to build a relationship between the hostage taker and the hostage that may save the hostage's life. For instance, when General Dossier, a U.S. Army military commander in Italy in the 1970s, was taken hostage by Communist dissidents, he developed a relationship with one of his guards. They talked about politics, family and their personal lives over a

period of days. When the Italian authorities raided Dossier's prison, this same guard turned and pointed his weapon at the General, but could not fire (FBI, 1991).

2. Negotiators need to understand that strong emotional ties develop between hostages and their captors. These ties may lead the hostages to return to the scene with hostage takers who have not surrendered. It leads to hostages downplaying the aggressiveness of the hostage taker. It sometimes leads to hostages making statements to the media favorable to the hostage taker's cause. Negotiators need to be prepared for these aspects of the Stockholm Syndrome. They need to contain and isolate the released hostages and they need to carefully evaluate any intelligence information they receive from hostages.

The South Moluccans: Success After the First Loss—1975

Another incident helped to solidify negotiation as an effective alternative to armed assault even in the most demanding circumstances. Seven members of the South Moluccan Independence Movement took over a Dutch train near the town of Beilen. Even though hostages were killed early in the incident, the patient application of hostage negotiation principles resolved the incident. The hostage takers demanded:

1. A statement by the Dutch government admitting injustice to the Moluccan cause;

2. Television time for the Moluccans to explain their cause;

3. A meeting between the South Moluccan Independence Movement and the Dutch and Indonesian governments, under United Nations auspices; and

4. The bringing of the South Moluccan cause to the United Nations by the Dutch government.

All demands were refused and a 12-day siege began. The authorities gave the hostage takers only minor concessions; food, water, blankets, and medicines. The strategy was to attend to basic survival needs and nothing else. The importance of personalizing the hostages was brought home when the terrorists chose one of the passengers to execute in order to prove the seriousness of their demands. The passenger asked to speak to his daughter and say goodbye. The terrorists changed their minds about him and chose another passenger. On December 14, 1977, the hostage takers surrendered (Cooper, 1978).

Two additional issues were illustrated by the South Moluccan incident: negotiation can be successfully pursued even after there has been violence, and hostage incidents are highly effective in publicizing situations or causes that until that time are obscure. Even though there had been shootings of the hostages during the incident, the government's refusal to give in to the terrorists' demands resulted in the eventual surrender of the subjects. Frequently, the question of when to use a tactical solution is important in hostage incidents. The usual answer is that when violence occurs, law enforcement officials have a responsibility to stop the violence. It is a logical conclusion when police responsibility for public safety is considered. The South Moluccan incident suggests that a peaceful resolution can be obtained in hostage incidents even if there has been prior loss of life.

Prior to the taking of hostages, the plight of the South Moluccans was an issue only for Holland. Most of the world had no idea where South Molucca was or what issues surrounded the conflict between South Molucca and the Dutch government. Few people knew that the Dutch had promised South Molucca its independence during World War II. However, during the incident, the world learned of the plight of the South Moluccans. Hostage incidents are effective in bringing attention to otherwise unknown causes.

Deliberate Siege

The Hanafi Muslim Incident: The Role and the Impact of the Media—1977

The Hanafi Muslims were a sect of the American Black Muslim movement that in March 1977 took over three locations in Washington, D.C. They were outraged by the murder of women and children at the Hanafis' home in Washington by a rival Black Muslim group. Even though the hostage takers had been caught, tried, and imprisoned, the Hanafi Muslims' leader, Hamaas Khaahlis, did not think they had been punished in accordance with dictates of the Koran, the holy book of Islam. He took over the headquarters of B'nai B'rith, a Jewish service organization, to gain attention to his demands. He wanted a film on the Muslim faith removed from the theaters nationwide, the murderers of his people as well as the murderers of Malcolm X brought to him, the police to reimburse him for the $750 fine levied against him for contempt of court, and all Muslim countries notified that he intended to kill Muslims and create an international incident. During the 40-hour siege, many people, including media representatives, were able to get through to the Hanafis on the telephone. The media let slip the information that one of Khaalis's bitter enemies, Wallace Muhammad, was at the Washington airport, defeating negotiators' attempts at avoiding his demands. The incident was resolved after a District Court judge agreed to allow Khaalis to remain free on bond until his trial (Miron & Goldstein, 1979; American Justice, 1994).

The Hanafi incident was important to the history of hostage negotiations because it spurred a national debate about the news media's role in the theater of hostage taking. Is the media a help or a hindrance in terrorist hostage incidents?

On one side is the media's argument that they are exercising their constitutional right to freedom of the press under the First Amendment when they do things such as telephoning the hostage taker and interviewing him. According to this argument, a free people have the right to be fully informed about matters of public safety and the media have a responsibility to report the news fully, gathering it by whatever means they think appropriate.

On the other hand, some critics point to the media's part in creating the problems of terrorism and hostage taking. They contend that part of the reason for terrorism is that otherwise powerless people are able to gain international publicity for sometimes unknown causes. In fact, this exposure is what terrorists often seek. Additionally, they argue that detailed media exposure has what social learning theorists call a "disinhibiting effect." Through watching others use violence, threats, and intimidation, an imitator is likely to see hostage taking as a legitimate and effective way to power.

The Hanafi Muslim incident brought to law enforcement's attention the need to have a working relationship with the press. It highlighted the importance of isolating the hostage taker's communications.

Additionally, the incident opened the debate on the social, economic, and political consequences of agreements made during negotiations that is still debated at the time of this writing (Miron & Goldstein, 1979; American Justice, 1994). The question of whether an agreement made during negotiations is valid has been addressed in case law. For instance, in *United States v. Crosby* (713 F.2d 1066 [5th Cir. 1983], *cert. denied*, 464 U.S. 1001 [1983]), the court ruled that the jury could not hear the portion of a negotiation tape in which negotiators promised the defendant that he would not be prosecuted if he released his hostages because it might induce unnecessary sympathy for the defendant. Similarly, in *State v. Sands*, the court ruled that a written letter of immunity signed by the local sheriff was invalid because it was signed under duress. However, the other side of the argument comes from negotiators themselves, who say that the failure to follow through on promises destroys their credibility, making it more difficult not only to negotiate with the same individual a second time but, because negotiations are a public event, making it more difficult to negotiate in good faith with anyone.

1980s

Rochester, New York: Suicide by Cop—1981

In June 1981, an incident at a bank in New York raised law enforcement's awareness of the possibility of subjects using police officers as instruments to end their own lives: suicide by cop. William Griffin, age 38, engaged the police and FBI in a three and one-half hour standoff at a neighborhood bank. He had entered the bank, ordered customers out, and taken bank employees hostage. He had the bank manager call police and tell them that if they did not "execute" him that he would start "throwing bodies out" in one half-hour. He shot and wounded two police officers who responded to the bank's silent alarm. Griffin refused to negotiate with authorities. At 3:00 P.M., he had teller Margaret More stand in front of the door of the bank and he shot her with the shotgun he had brought to the bank. He then went to the window and exposed himself to the police sniper he knew was across the street and was shot and killed. He had shot and killed his mother and a handyman and wounded his stepfather at his home prior to going to the bank. Authorities found his diary, which had a carefully worked out plan for forcing the police or sheriff to take his life. This incident brought the issue of suicide by cop, incidents in which the actor uses the police as instruments of their death, to the attention of FBI negotiators. Van Zandt (1993) used this and other incidents in the 1980s to illustrate the need for negotiators to recognize and learn to deal with this subset of suicidal people. He suggested a profile that could be used to raise officers' awareness of the potential for the subjects' forcing a violent confrontation in order to be killed. The profile included (Van Zandt, 1993):

1. The hostage taker refuses to negotiate with authorities.

2. The hostage taker has killed a significant person in his life recently.

3. The hostage taker demands that the authorities kill him.

4. The hostage taker sets a deadline for the authorities to kill him.

5. The hostage taker has recently received notice that he is suffering from a fatal disease.

6. The hostage taker indicates that he has elaborate plans for his own death.

7. The hostage taker offers to surrender in person to the person in charge.

8. The hostage taker says that he wants to "go out in a big way."

9. The hostage taker presents no demands that include his escape or freedom.

10. The hostage taker is of a low socioeconomic background.

11. The hostage taker gives the negotiators a "verbal will."

12. The hostage taker seems to be looking for a "macho" way out.

13. The hostage taker has recently disposed of his money or property.

14. The hostage taker has a criminal record that includes assaultive behavior.

15. The hostage taker has a recent history of two or more traumatic losses.

16. The hostage taker expresses feelings of hopelessness and helplessness.

The Anatomy of a Siege: Post-Traumatic Stress—1981

Wesselius and DeSarno (1983) reported an incident that illustrated the emotional and psychological impact of being a hostage. These authors reported that on a weekend morning in 1981, a 24-year-old male forced his way into the headquarters of a police agency. He took the security officer and clerical personnel hostage. He told the office personnel to continue their duties as usual. He demanded to see five police officers and a specific black chaplain with whom he had dealt before. His behavior was volatile, switching from calm to agitated with little provocation. His voice would raise in pitch, and his rate of speech would increase. He ordered food from the "best restaurant in town," and he referred to the secretary in the building as "my secretary." Clearly he was grandiose and paranoid. He released one woman early in the incident when she began to cry uncontrollably. He released three other women after a discussion with negotiators about whether he was giving up control and showing a weakness in character by doing so. Negotiators had to reassure him about his safety. He was assessed to be a paranoid schizophrenic and thought to be a threat to the hostages. The authorities decided to end the siege tactically, and a police sniper shot him when he was pointing his gun away from the hostages. Four months after the incident, the employees were interviewed by a psychiatrist, who discovered that virtually all hostages used denial to deal with the threat during the incident. They did not think it was real. However, after the denial faded, the hostages experienced a range of feelings from fear to terror, despair, abandonment, resignation, and rage. After the incident, they reported classic signs of post-traumatic stress disorder, including excessive startled reactions, emotional numbing, withdrawal from their usual activities, reliving the experience either in flashbacks or nightmares, inability to concentrate, and avoidance of situations that reminded them of the incident.

The Oakdale and Atlanta Prison Sieges: Application to Corrections—1987

Several hostage incidents have proven the utility of hostage negotiation principles in the prison setting. The largest such incident was the simultaneous rioting of Cuban immigrants at Oakdale, Louisiana, and Atlanta, Georgia, in November 1987. A total of 1,570 inmates took a total of 126 hostages at the two locations. They demanded to be heard. They thought the U.S. Government, through the Immigration and Naturalization Service, had lied to them and that the agreement between the United States and Cuba to return them to Cuba posed a serious threat to them. After nine days at Oakdale and 12 at Atlanta, the siege ended. The FBI found the following negotiation principles particularly useful (Van Zandt & Fuselier, 1989; Van Zandt et al., 1989):

1. Allowing time to pass—by giving the inmates time to present their case and by not rushing into an attempt to use force, the incident was resolved with minimal injury.

2. Negotiating with the identified leader—only after the prisoner who was making the decisions came to the negotiating table was progress made in the resolution of the inmates' grievances.

3. Negotiating in English rather than Spanish—by refusing to negotiate in Spanish, the FBI retained the ability to use their mental health consultant, to allow their command structure to monitor communications with the prisoners and to defuse the emotional implications of the Spanish language.

4. Tape-recording and reviewing negotiations—frequent review of tape recordings of the negotiations allowed negotiators to monitor the intensity of the emotions being expressed, to keep track of promises made, and to make smooth transitions when a new team of negotiators took over (negotiating teams were rotated because of the length of the siege).

5. Using mental health consultants—by using a mental health consultant familiar with the prison population, negotiators gained insight into prisoner grievances as well as into possible negotiating strategies to use with individual inmates.

6. Providing a surrender ritual—by allowing inmates to walk through an honor guard and to come to a surrender table, their honor was maintained. The details of the surrender ritual were the last issue to be negotiated.

1990s

Two landmark cases changed the face of negotiations in the 1990s: (1) the Ruby Ridge, Idaho, standoff in August 1992, and (2) the Branch Davidian Siege at Waco, Texas, in 1993. Additionally, two high-profile prison cases spurred correctional agencies to develop negotiations as an approach to conflict situations in prisons.

Talladega: Dealing with "Non-Negotiable" Incidents—1991

On August 21, 1991, Cuban detainees awaiting deportation to Cuba took over the Alpha Unit of the Federal Correctional Institution at Talladega, Alabama. They took eight Bureau of Prisons staff members, three INS staff members, and 15 American inmates hostage. A combined Bureau of Prisons and FBI negotiations team was established. The FBI brought considerable experience in negotiating both street and prison incidents, including the Atlanta and Oakdale incidents. The Bureau of Prisons negotiators had considerable knowledge about riots, correctional populations in general and the current population in particular, as well as prison management issues.

Demands were slow in developing because of the general disorganization of the inmates. When they got organized, they demanded press coverage of their plight, medical attention for inmates, and the establishment of a "commission" of prominent citizens who could plead their case to the general public. They were displeased with the outcome of the Oakdale and Atlanta incidents and wanted more than just federal involvement in the followup to their situation. When it became evident to the scene commander that negotiations were not progressing and that the safety of the hostages was threatened, he ordered a tactical entry early on August 30.

Fagan and Van Zandt (1993) reported that even though the incident was resolved tactically, negotiators were a valuable part of the overall operation. They were able to identify the more moderate leaders among the inmates and focus on negotiating through them. They tested out an approach that alternated between English and Spanish, using English when initiating negotiations and switching to Spanish later when a more complete understanding of the issues was needed. Most importantly, they found that even though the inmates would not negotiate with them, they were able to "support the entire crisis management process" by:

1. Allowing the detainees an opportunity to vent their frustrations with the system, calming them and reducing the risk to the hostages;

2. Buying time for the tactical team to gather resources, develop a unified assault team, collect needed intelligence, and develop a workable assault plan;

3. Gathering intelligence on conditions in the unit that was helpful in tactical planning;

4. Introducing changes in the situation that benefited the tactical team;

5. Lulling the detainees into a sense of safety and security, increasing the element of surprise for the tactical team.

Ruby Ridge: Third-Party Intermediaries—1992

On August 21, 1992, the United States Marshal's Service had an armed encounter with Samuel Weaver, the son of a suspected terrorist, Randall Weaver, and Randall Weaver's friend, Kevin Harris. In the incident, Marshal William F. Degan was shot and killed, as was Samuel Weaver. This resulted in a 10-day siege involving the FBI's Hostage Rescue Team, in which Randall Weaver's wife, Vicki, was shot and killed by a FBI sniper. Weaver and Harris were wounded prior to Vicki Weaver being killed. Randall Weaver was known to be an anti-government radical who did not recognize federal authority. He was considered extremely dangerous. Weaver's suspicion of federal authorities along with the assault on him and his family, led to his refusal to talk with negotiators. Consequently, negotiators used a variety of innovative techniques to try to communicate with him. They sent Weaver messages from his wife's family, not knowing that his wife was dead. They had Weaver's sister try to talk him into surrendering. Finally, they used third-party intermediaries to influence him. Bo Gritz, a retired Army Colonel who was well-known to the radical right, and Jack McLamb, a retired police officer, were used as intermediaries because Weaver said he was willing to speak with them. It was through these third parties that negotiators learned that Vicki Weaver had been killed and that Randall Weaver and Kevin Harris were wounded. Gritz and McLamb took on the role of protectors and, even under these difficult conditions, negotiations resolved the incident without further injury or death. For the negotiator's view of Ruby Ridge, see Lanceley (1999).

Branch Davidians-Waco: Coordinating Response—1993

Anticipated

In the spring of 1993, agents from the Bureau of Alcohol, Tobacco and Firearms initiated a raid on Mt. Carmel, a compound located near Waco, Texas, which housed David Koresh and his followers. The raid plan called for three teams, one of which had the job of getting between the compound and the men who were normally working away from the main structure at the hour of the raid. A second team was to enter the front door to arrest and restrain everyone in the building, particularly David Koresh. A third team was to go to the side of the compound on which the armory was located, climb ladders to the second floor, enter the armory and secure it so that members of the Branch Davidians could not use the weapons to resist. Unfortunately, the Davidians were warned and a firefight followed, leaving four ATF agents dead and 16 wounded. The FBI assumed command and control of the incident, bringing in their Hostage Rescue Team and negotiators. Using bargaining techniques, they obtained the release of many of the children by giving Koresh time to get his message out to the general public. After 56 days, the FBI-initiated actions ended in the Mt. Carmel compound being burned, with significant loss of life among the Davidians.

This incident and its tragic outcome led FBI negotiators to rethink their approach to siege incidents. It led them away from the linear approach to a parallel approach to hostage intervention, in which both the tactical teams and the negotiators work concurrently as part of a coordinated approach to resolution of the problem. The Waco siege led to the recognition that sieges are best managed through the parallel application of tactical and negotiations. A parallel approach integrates the tactics of the two elements from the start of an incident, rather than through the linear model that allows negotiators to try to resolve the incident, but if they are not successful, then use a tactical approach (Noesner, 1999).

Lucasville Prison Riot: Raising Awareness in Corrections—1993

In April of 1993, the maximum-security prison in Lucasville, Ohio, gained national attention when inmates took hostage correctional officers who were responding to another officer's distress call. Four hundred fifty inmates barricaded themselves in the L-block of the prison. Both prisoners and officers were beaten. One correctional officer and nine inmates were killed in the initial uprising. Prisoners demanded amnesty for the riot, replacement of the warden, free expression of religious beliefs for Muslim inmates, more flexible telephone and visitor privileges, that nepotism be stopped, and that forced integration of cells be eliminated. As the 11-day siege progressed, inmates organized across traditionally conflicting gang lines. They had several spokespersons. They released two hostages after being given access to the press. Before the final release of officers was agreed upon, the prisoners insisted on the media being allowed to film the surrender and that attorneys and religious leaders be present to witness the end of the siege. The negotiation techniques utilized during the siege were described as "textbook" tactics. Once again, negotiation principles were utilized successfully, even though a death had occurred in the early stages of the incident. Negotiators learned the importance of teamwork and training. The Lucasville incident, along with the Oakdale and Atlanta incidents, helped bring attention to the utility of negotiations in correctional settings.

The Freemen Standoff: Pre-incident Planning, TPIs, and Coordinated Action—1996

The FBI, concerned about the chaos after the sieges at Ruby Ridge and Waco, initiated several changes in the way they handled large-scale sieges. They included a more integrated approach to planning and responding to incidents through the Critical Incident Response Group based at the FBI Academy; systematic pre-incident assessment; greater use of third party intermediaries; a more permeable perimeter; and a lower key presence at the scene. During the 80-day confrontation with the Freemen in the spring of 1996, many of these changes were evident.

The Freemen were a group of anti-government ranchers who believed that the federal government had no authority over "sovereign" men, that people governed themselves, that America was in a decline, and that their rights to govern themselves came from the Bible, the Magna Carta, and the Bill of Rights. They had financial troubles, had lost their farm subsidy, issued bad checks, placed fraudulent liens on property, received stolen goods, and refused to vacate land they had lost in foreclosure. When federal authorities intervened, local law enforcement had limited resources and there was growing unrest in the community.

The FBI had the Freemen under surveillance for months prior to planning the arrest of two of their leaders, LeRoy Schweitzer and Daniel Peterson, at a ham radio setup on the Clark Ranch outside Jordan, Montana. The purposes of the pre-incident assessment were: (1) to take a proactive approach to planning; (2) to obtain a holistic assessment that included tactical and negotiation evaluations; (3) develop intelligence sources prior to the incident to allow sufficient time for profiling, tactical planning, and strategic planning; and (4) to help reduce the impact of the "action imperative" during the actual incident.

After the arrests of Schweitzer and Peterson, communications were attempted with the Freemen who were still at the ranch house. Because the Freemen did not recognize the authority of the FBI, they would not talk with FBI negotiators. Consequently, two types of third-party intermediaries were used to facilitate communication and influence different members of the barricaded Freemen. Family associates were used to influence their loved ones to come out, and public figures who were recognized as having some status with the Freemen were used to influence decisions that affected all Freemen.

The FBI gained the following from the Freeman standoff (Romano, 1998a):

1. Validation of the use of active listening techniques to defuse intense emotions

2. Validation of the use of the passage of time

3. The effectiveness of the parallel planning process involving both negotiators and the tactical team

4. Unreasonable positions lead to eroding support

5. The importance of surrender with dignity

Additionally, they suggested the following guidelines for the use of third-party intermediaries (TPIs) (Romano, 1998b):

1. TPI use should be carefully timed. They are best introduced after the crisis has stabilized and a thoughtful assessment of the incident, the needs of the negotiators, and the value of TPIs can be made.

2. Select TPIs that will benefit your goals. It is essential that a TPI have some specific value in advancing the goals of the negotiators in the incident. During many incidents, a number of people come forward offering to help. If there is no clear reason or goal for using them, it is not a good idea not to put them on the line "just to have something to do."

3. Script them carefully, so that the interaction is focused on the goals. Do not allow TPIs to vary from the script.

4. Use safe methods of contact.

5. Use them to help guarantee surrender.

Columbine High School: Need for Violence Prevention—1999

On April 20, 1999, Eric Harris and Dylan Klebold attacked students and faculty at Columbine High School in Littleton, Colorado, with four guns, as well as bombs. They killed 12 students and one teacher. Subsequently, they committed suicide. The compelling scenes from the tragedy and its aftermath brought to the public's awareness the importance of intervening in school violence. Because the majority of school violence incidents are over before negotiators become involved, some negotiators have taken a different approach to school violence. They have used their crisis management skills to help school authorities develop prevention programs designed to identify, assess, and manage "at risk" youth before a crisis incident occurs. Additionally, they have recognized the importance of pre-incident planning and coordination with school officials, so that the most expedient response to an actual incident can be made. The large number of hostages in these incidents and the tendency of subjects involved in these incidents to be heavily armed has led negotiators to approach these incidents with concern and caution (Feldman, 2001). A more detailed presentation of the issues involved in school violence incidents is presented in Chapter 11, Workplace and School Violence Issues.

2000s

Negotiations continue to evolve as new, noteworthy, and media-intensive incidents occur. In the post-September 11 era, crisis situations have taken on added media and public emphasis, with all eyes on responders to see how these incidents will be handled and resolved.

Lewis State Prison (Arizona Department of Corrections)

On January 18, 2004, two inmates at Lewis State Prison (south of Phoenix, Arizona) initiated one of the more notorious hostage-taking incidents in recent years. At approximately 3:00 A.M., inmates Ricky Wassenaar and Steven Coy (who were cellmates) reported for kitchen duty in their housing unit (Morey Unit). The lone officer present was attacked by Wassenaar, who took his uniform. The officer and a female civilian worker were restrained in the kitchen office. Other inmates (who refused to take part in this escape attempt) were locked in a storage area. Inmate Wassenaar changed into the officer's uniform, shaved his beard and went to the Morey Tower to get weapons. In the meantime, Inmate Coy sexually assaulted the female kitchen worker. Shortly thereafter, Coy managed to take a second correctional officer by surprise and restrained him in the office.

At about 4:55 A.M., two other correctional officers and an inmate reported to the dining hall. Coy fought with one officer, cutting him with a homemade weapon. The other officer went for assistance. Inmate Coy left the dining hall and headed toward the Morey Tower. Outside the dining hall,

Coy was confronted by other officers and staff who had arrived. He attempted to confront the staff members and was pepper-sprayed, with little effect. Meanwhile, Wassenaar had managed to fight and restrain the correctional officers in the Morey Tower and obtain an AR-15 assault rifle. Coming to Coy's aid, Wassenaar fired about 14 or 15 shots at the Lewis staff and secured Coy's release to the Morey Tower. At 5:30 A.M., the communications center at the prison was advised that a hostage incident was under way.

In the Morey Tower, inmates Wassenaar and Coy had gained control over both Tower officers—a male officer who had worked for the Department of Corrections for less than one year, and a female officer who had less than four years' experience. On the first day of the incident, both inmates sexually assaulted the female corrections officer. Ricky Wassenaar was serving 28 years for armed robbery and eight counts of aggravated assault and had been incarcerated since 1997. It is worth noting that during the armed robbery, Wassenaar wore a bulletproof vest. According to his psychological profile, Wassenaar was a sociopath. Coy was serving life for armed robbery and sexual assault. Both were in the protective segregation unit, Wassenaar because of a threat on his life, and Coy because of his having been assaulted by other inmates and almost killed. Later debriefings with Wassenaar revealed that he had been planning this escape attempt for more than three years and continually modified the plan as prison security procedures changed.

The Morey Tower was just short of 20 feet tall, with stairs leading to two enclosed floors and a roof observation deck (a total of three stories). The second level contained the control panel and had two-inch-thick Lexan safety windows all around that were tilted at 27 degrees. The first level had the restroom and was reached via circular metal stairs. The observation deck, on the third level, was accessed via a ladder through a roof hatch. The building itself was constructed of eight-inch-thick reinforced concrete. Like all prison observation towers, it was constructed to be unbreachable. As a general rule, given the actions, violence, and sexual assault committed by inmates, this incident would be a tactical team problem, not a negotiated problem. In this case, however, there was no way to tactically resolve the situation without costing the life of the two officers held hostage in the tower. Authorities were forced to negotiate.

During the course of the incident, which lasted 15 days, more than 30 negotiators were utilized. The negotiating team was a mixed team, with representatives from the Arizona Department of Corrections, the Arizona Department of Public Safety, the Birmingham FBI office, the Crisis Negotiation Unit of the FBI from Quantico, the Glendale Police Department, the Maricopa County Sheriff's Office, the Phoenix FBI Office, the Phoenix Police Department, the San Diego FBI Office, and the Tempe Police Department. In addition to the normal team functions of primary negotiator, secondary negotiator, scribe, intelligence-gatherers, and team leader, the negotiators also used a team coordinator to work with the prison command center, a profiler, a tactical liaison officer, and various advisors.

Lewis State Prison outside of Phoenix, AZ, was the site of one of the most notorious hostage situations in recent years, when two inmates took two correctional officers hostage in 2004. It took 15 days for crisis negotiators to successfully resolve the incident with no loss of life.

On the first day, Wassenaar presented an initial list of seven demands; to speak with the governor, to speak with the warden, to speak with the media, to speak to his sister, a helicopter for escape, a radio, and a handcuff key (the Arizona Department of Corrections listed handcuff keys as a non-negotiable demand). On the second day, Wassenaar requested a different negotiator (which was refused) and offered to give up a "shank" for blankets, towels, and washcloths. When negotiators tried to make substantive trades, the inmates threatened to cut off one of the hostage's fingers. On days three and four, very little progress was made on any of the issues, other than the Arizona Department of Corrections offering to drop Wassenaar's protective custody status. On day five, an interstate compact was presented, with letters guaranteeing the compact presented. A interstate compact is an agreement to transfer the inmates to a facility in another state (which both Wassenaar and Coy requested). On day six, Wassenaar offered to release a correctional officer and on day seven, the male correctional officer was released.

From the outset, Waasenaar was the leader of the inmate hostage takers. He was the "talker," decision-maker, and instigator of demand issues and other issues negotiators would have to deal with. Coy was the "doer" of the pair, the one who took orders and followed Waasenaar's lead. Their relationship was predictable and easily understandable from the perspective of having two psychopaths together (Hare, 1993). Negotiators relied on these specific behavioral and personality characteristics to negotiate with them.

The only significant movement on days eight, nine, and ten were the introduction of a TPI (Wasseneer's sister in a tape-recorded message). Also, on day ten, the negotiators delivered several small items to the inmates as a rapport-building technique. During this period, other than the Interstate Compact Agreement, the only demands were small items of food and personal comfort. As one negotiator put it, the inmates asked for items as though they were walking down the aisle of the prison commissary (Dubina & Ragsdale, 2005). And that is all they wanted. On day 12, Waasenaar's sister and Coy's uncle were introduced as live TPIs (versus tape-recorded), and the Director of the Arizona Department of Corrections was presented as a guarantor of the Interstate Compact Agreement. On the thirteenth day, there was a split in the hostage takers, with Waasenaar telling the negotiators they needed to kill Coy. Not much progress was made on day fourteen, other than the negotiators taking a "hard line" (hanging up the phone, turning off the power, etc.). Finally, on day 15, February 1, 2004, the inmates surrendered to federal custody and the remaining hostage was freed. Authorities kept their end of the agreement. Coy was transferred to a prison in Maine and received seven life sentences for his role in the Lewis Prison incident. Waasenaar was taken into federal custody. In May 2005, while acting as his own defense attorney, Waasenaar was found guilty by a jury on 12 of 20 charges and was sentenced to 16 life sentences plus 25.75 years. As of September 2005, no decision has been made on whether to send him out of the state of Arizona.

There were numerous significant lessons to be garnered from the Lewis Prison incident (Dubina, 2005; Dubina & Ragsdale, 2005). The chain of command presented a unique set of problems. Most negotiators and tactical officers were not law enforcement or corrections officers. Other than the prison warden, incident commanders and decision-makers had no corrections or law enforcement experience. The Director of Corrections in Arizona was a political appointee and was awaiting senate confirmation. Her boss, and ultimate authority, was the governor of Arizona. This is not to imply that either made bad decisions, but only to say that both had to be "educated" about issues specific to the critical incident process and negotiations. If law enforcement officers are negotiating (and/or serving as tactical officers) in a prison situation, they need correctional advisors on the team to bring them up to speed on correctional issues (language, terms, non-negotiable demands, prison policies, etc.). Prisons are an alien environment to law enforcement officers and present some unique challenges to negotiators. To avoid mistakes in the negotiation process, correctional advisors are a must. Third, care must be taken in selecting the Negotiation Operations Center (NOC). At Lewis, the NOC was selected by law enforcement negotiators and selected using subjective criteria they would likely use at a law enforcement situation. Thought was primarily given to the incident being rather short in duration, so space issues were neglected. It soon became apparent that the NOC was much too small for a protracted incident (but by then was established and could not be changed).

Fourth, it is crucial that negotiators establish prior working relationships with other negotiators in their geographical area. At Lewis, more than 10 agencies were brought in and more than 30 primary negotiators alone were used. Many team members were strangers when they were thrown together to resolve a crisis incident. Fifth, early on, work schedules have to be established and adhered to. Sixth, be flexible, able, and willing to modify the negotiation team structure to meet the unique demands of the situation. Early into negotiations, a team coordinator position was added to facilitate communications with the command structure. Seventh, use the power of the team. Each contact should be carefully planned for (issues to cover and avoid, what to say, how to say it, questions to ask, intelligence to gather, etc.). Brainstorming sessions are invaluable for communication planning as well as problem-solving, handling demand issues, and team building. Eighth, negotiations do not occur in a vacuum. The prison facility still has to operate. Even though Lewis Prison was locked down for the duration of the incident, inmates still need to be fed, maintained, and cared for. Staff still have their normal functions to perform and the facility has to be maintained. Only a small portion of the total facility can be isolated and cleared. Negotiators have to realize the unique demands of operating a prison and what is involved. Unlike a law enforcement situation (at an apartment building, for example), the prison cannot be evacuated and cleared, streets closed, etc. The overall environment has to continue to operate.

Finally, the Lewis Prison incident reinforced other practices of negotiators. A good scribe and running log of negotiations are necessary. Negotiations should be recorded and the tapes listened to by on-coming negotiators (and duplicating equipment should be available for dubbing tapes). Good situation boards are necessary and help to keep mistakes from being made. Intelligence gathering and dissemination is an ongoing process and cannot be devalued just because the prison has complete inmate files. Do not forget to involve a tactical liaison officer to maintain ongoing and error-free communications with the tactical element. Expect rumors and have a plan and person in place to deal with rumors (i.e., press liaison officer). Finally, remember that, every job is important. No task or job is too small or unimportant. Every person and every job assigned is important and helps lead to the success of negotiations.

Definitions

Before studying the principles of hostage negotiations, it is important to have a working definition of the terms *hostage*, *negotiate*, and *hostage incident*. Without a common starting place, people with the same map may not arrive at the same location. Therefore, definitions are important. They help to develop a common starting place.

Hostage

The American Heritage Dictionary (1980) defines *hostage* as: "A person held as a security for the fulfillment of certain terms."

Several points need to be emphasized when considering this definition. First, it is important to understand the implications of the involvement of a person. A living being, not an inanimate object, is at risk. Inanimate objects can be used in extortion, but it takes a living person to make an incident a hostage incident. The goal of hostage negotiation is saving lives, not preservation of property. In discussing the Williamsburg incident, one authority said, "The primary consideration in such circumstances is to secure the lives and safety of threatened hostages, the police officers, innocent bystanders, and the criminals themselves." (Schlossberg, 1979a). This makes hostage negotiations consistent with the public safety responsibility of the police, which includes aiding individuals in danger of physical harm, assisting those who cannot care for themselves, and resolving conflict (American Bar Association, 1980).

The emphasis on saving human life does two things for the negotiator:

1. It increases negotiator stress, because of the high cost of failure.

2. It attracts political and public relations attention due to the drama of a life-death confrontation.

In most hostage incidents, the explicit threat is to the hostage's life. It is not the loss of property, status, or belonging to a community that is at stake. Life itself is at stake. The cost of failure in such an incident places significant stress on negotiators. The recent recognition of the impact of traumatic stress on emergency service personnel, police officers involved in shootings (Nielsen, 1986; Solomon & Horn, 1986; Somodevilla, 1986; McMains, 1986; Reese, Horn & Dunning, 1991), and military personnel is ample evidence that loss of life can create significant stress. Negotiators need to plan for this stress.

Incidents that involve life and death have a sense of the dramatic (Keen, 1991). There is rarely a hit television show or film about the adventures of a certified public accountant; there is no life-and-death struggle. However, hostages are different. There is the threat to life; therefore, there is high drama. Terrorists understand and play on this drama. The media, neighbors, family members, and friends are attracted to such incidents. Negotiators and police departments should anticipate this attraction and plan for the management of this audience. All this attention makes negotiation incidents high-visibility and potentially high-liability situations. Because of this public interest, many units of the police department may be needed at the scene. Because of the potential liability, the department's crisis response teams need to be well trained and well rehearsed.

Second, it is important to understand that the person is "held." The hostage is not there voluntarily. The holding may be physical or psychological; the impact on the person is the same. A person is traumatized because of his or her lack of control and is made to feel powerless and dependent on the hostage taker. The former points to the need for victim debriefing. The latter sets the stage for the Stockholm Syndrome. Negotiators need to know how to recognize and manage both trauma and the Stockholm Syndrome.

Knowledge of traumatic stress has led some police departments to expand the use of their negotiators to crisis debriefing in situations other than hostage incidents. That is, some departments have used their negotiators to help search-and-rescue workers manage the emotional impact of their work. Some have used them to debrief crime victims (McMains, 1988).

Third, the person has utility. The person is being held as security—as a guarantee. The hostage is the hostage taker's currency, his or her power. The hostage is not a person, and has no value to the hostage taker as a person (Schlossberg, 1979b). Part of the negotiator's job is to personalize the hostage for the hostage taker. This has to be done subtly, however. If too much attention is directed toward the hostage, his or her worth is perceived as increased. This gives the hostage taker the perception of more power. The negotiator's goal is to personalize without valuing. The negotiator needs to encourage the development of the Stockholm Syndrome.

Fourth, the person is being held as security for certain terms. This means there is an expected return—a quid pro quo for the hostage taker. The hostage taker has needs that he or she expects to be met in return for the safety, security, and/or release of the hostage. The principal job of the negotiator is to find alternate terms for the hostage taker. Goldaber (1979) has pointed out that every hostage taking is reducible to two elements: Who are the hostage takers and what do they want? Negotiation adds two more elements to the equation: What will they take and what are we willing to give? For instance, rather than the escape a gunman demands during a bungled robbery attempt, he might settle for the negotiator going to court with him to testify about his cooperation in releasing the hostage.

Negotiate

The American Heritage Dictionary (1980) defines *negotiate* as: "To arrange or settle by conferring or discussing." Cohen (1982) added to this definition by saying that negotiation is the use of information and power to affect behavior in a "web of tension." He points out that conflict is a natural part of negotiation. It always involves people wanting to maximize their gains and minimize their losses. Again, several points need highlighting:

1. **The attitudes of the people involved in a conflict contribute to the ultimate success or lack of success of a negotiation.** Fisher and Ury (1981) and Ury (1981) have stressed the importance of recognizing that there are two parts to negotiations: resolving conflict and maintaining the relationship. Attitudes influence the relationship. McMains (1988) has pointed out that police officers tend to develop three attitudes that interfere with relationships: everything is either black or white, feelings are not important, and solutions to problems need to be found immediately. Negotiators need to develop attitudes of caring, understanding, and patience to service the relationship element in negotiations.

2. **The settlement comes through "discussing or conferring."** Rather than relying on the tactical approach, negotiations depend on the use of words and people skills. In an effort to save lives, tactical options are the least effective. Assaults result in a 78 percent injury or death rate (Strentz, 1979), sniper-fire in a 100 percent injury or death rate, while containment and negotiation have resulted in a 95 percent success rate (FBI, 1991). Recent research (Butler, Leitenberg & Fuselier, 1993) has suggested that negotiating teams that have mental health consultants available are more effective than teams that use no mental health consultant. For instance, the San Antonio Police Department, which has used a mental health consultant for 14 years, has a success rate of 99 percent. In addition to developing personality profiles of the subject, a large part of the mental health consultant's job is to keep the team focused on appropriate crisis intervention and communications skills.

Negotiators must not only be good at "discussing and conferring;" they must believe in the effectiveness of negotiating. In the early years of hostage negotiation, it was thought that a good salesman would be a good negotiator. Experience has shown this to be a false assumption. People generally know when they are being "conned" and they do not react well, especially under stress. The solution to the credibility problem raised by the "salesman approach" to negotiations seems to be to have negotiators who believe in the "product"—the peaceful resolution of conflict. This "genuineness" communicates itself for negotiators, the same way it communicates itself in counseling (Carkhuff & Barensen, 1967).

Discussing and conferring requires some specific communications skills: active listening, persuasion techniques, and problem-solving skills. Active listening is the ability to hear what the other person is saying: his words, his feelings, and his expectations, and to let him know that you have heard. It requires the negotiator to pay close attention, to ask himself what all this means to the other person and to ask the person if he has heard the message correctly. It avoids advice-giving, criticism, or judgments. Active listening is essential in the early stages of every negotiation, to defuse emotions and to establish understanding. Negotiators need to develop all of these.

3. **The goal of negotiation is the settlement of an incident.** Several authors (Bolton, 1984; Covey, 1991; Goldaber, 1983) have pointed out there are three ways of settling conflict. One is a win/lose solution, in which one side must give in. Two is the avoidance solution, in which one of the sides walks away. Three is the win/win solution, in which both sides gain something. Traditionally, police conflicts have been resolved in a win/lose manner. In most conflict situations, the police have relied on having more power than the hostage taker to force

a resolution. However, the Munich incident demonstrated the limits of raw power. It showed that sometimes the other side cannot be overpowered without significant loss. Neither can the police avoid conflict. Their role as protectors of society demands that they do something if lives are threatened. Negotiation requires and represents a fundamental change in the exclusive reliance on power to handle conflicts.

Discussion alone does not necessarily solve problems, a fact to which any husband or wife can attest. Rather, the ability to arrive at an agreement with which both parties are comfortable makes negotiation effective. Fisher and Ury (1981) have suggested that a wise agreement involves three elements. Negotiators need to keep these three elements in mind, because they provide a framework in which the negotiator's skills and abilities are practiced. An agreement must:

1. **Meet the legitimate interests of both parties to every extent possible.** This principle emphasizes the point that there are usually two sides to every issue. Negotiators have to pay as much, if not more, attention to the other side's goals and needs as they pay to their own. They need to ask: "What does the hostage taker want? What do they need? If I were the hostage takers, how would I be thinking and feeling?" Without consideration of the other side, negotiations become nothing more than power struggles.

2. **Resolve conflicting interests fairly.** This element focuses on the idea that there has to be some standard by which parties involved in a negotiation can judge the fairness of an agreement. It is not just the exercise of the most power that determines the correct solution to a problem. Rather, negotiators have to be able to show how a solution benefits both parties. In a hostage incident, benefiting both parties does not necessarily mean going along with the hostage taker's initial demands. Rather, it means helping the other person expand his or her view of his or her own needs and showing him or her new options for meeting these expanded needs. For instance, the depressed person who has lost her boyfriend and takes a hostage to force the police to kill her needs to see that there are other ways of meeting her need for care and concern from others, for finding relief from the pain of the loss, and for the embarrassment of having lost the "perfect mate."

3. **Take community interests (relationships) into account.** This element recognizes that the relationship is an important issue in negotiations. Negotiators need to separate issues from relationships and demands from people (Fisher and Ury, 1981). They need to discuss them as different issues. When this is done, it is easier for the negotiator to say, " I care about you,

but I disagree with your behavior." In addition, negotiators need to understand that their actions during an incident are being viewed by the larger community. The things they do are the things the community expects them to do the next time. For instance, if, during an incident involving family members being taken hostage by an emotionally disturbed person, a negotiator agrees to take that person to a mental health clinic and then does not, the negotiator is neglecting the relationship issue. This will make it more difficult for the hostage taker to trust police in the future. This will also make it more difficult for the larger community to trust the police.

A Hostage Incident

A **hostage incident** is any incident in which people are being held by another person or persons against their will, usually by force or coercion, and demands are being made by the hostage taker. Hostages are used to gain compliance or attention in several kinds of incidents.

Traditionally, hostage incidents have been looked at from the context within which hostages are taken. These contexts include hostages taken in the commission of a crime, hostages taken by emotionally disturbed individuals, hostages taken during prison riots, and terrorist hostage taking (Soskis & Van Zandt, 1986; Goldaber, 1983; Hassel, 1975; Miron & Goldstein, 1979; IACP, 1983). Negotiators should have a working knowledge of each kind of incident, because they will need to modify their approach to accommodate each type of situation.

In looking at hostage takers' motivation and goals, Miron and Goldstein (1979) point out that incidents have both an instrumental value and an expressive value to the hostage taker. Hostage taking is both an act designed to gain compliance with demands—the instrumental nature of the incident, and an act designed to display the power of the hostage taker—the expressive nature of the relationship. An armed robber interrupted during the commission of a crime takes hostages with the primary purpose of forcing the authorities to comply with his demands for escape. His are instrumental demands. On the other hand, the terrorist who takes hostages to draw attention to his cause and who wants to demonstrate the powerlessness of the existing government is emphasizing the expressive nature of the incident.

Hostage takers can be arranged on a continuum. The continuum starts with those who emphasize the instrumental nature of hostage incidents (Miron & Goldstein, 1979). They run from the antisocial personality who wants money and transportation (at the functional end) to the emotionally disturbed hostage takers who use the incident to express their outrage, anger, or fear of a situation (at the expressive end). Terrorists are in the middle, wanting to gain both political and economic concessions and to show their power.

Understanding the differences in these motivations is important because they will determine the strategies, tactics, and skills needed in a specific incident. Hassel (1975) has pointed out that terrorists who are dedicated to their cause have the option of choosing martyrdom by getting themselves and their hostages killed. He suggests withholding media coverage, if this is a possibility, to play on their need for publicity—their expressive needs.

From Hostage Negotiation to Crisis Intervention

Hatcher et al. (1998) have discussed the changes in negotiations from 1971 to the present. They point out that negotiations have moved from concern about hijackings, terrorist acts, and political statements to incidents that are more personal in nature, i.e., domestic incidents and barricaded subjects. Along with the change in types of incidents has come a change in strategies and tactics. Negotiators in the "first generation" emphasized reducing the confrontational nature of incidents, defusing the high emotions in most incidents, negotiating small issues to set the stage for agreement on larger issues, the use of the passage of time to allow for the reduction of the hostage takers' ability to sustain the encounter, the development of the unique relationship between the subject and the victim (Stockholm Syndrome), and reaching the point in the incident in which the subjects' interests shifted from their initial demands to concern about how to end the incident safely.

In the 1980s, the emphasis among negotiators moved away from prisoners and terrorists to emotionally disturbed individuals, trapped criminals, and domestic incidents (Hatcher et al., 1998). This was "the second generation" of negotiations in which the application of crisis intervention techniques and active listening skills came into use. It recognized that although time was generally on the side of the negotiator, there were situations in which the passage of time increased the risk to the victim. A careful analysis of the relationship among the context, the perpetrator, and the hostage was necessary (Hatcher et. al., 1998).

Initially, police negotiators focused more on bargaining principles than crisis intervention techniques. One of the federal government's concerns in the early 1970s was about aircraft hijackings. Fully 10 percent of all airline hijackings between 1931 and 1989 occurred in 1969. Five hundred twenty-eight airline hijackings occurred between 1969 and 1982 (Feldman & Johnson, 1999). Therefore, negotiation/bargaining techniques were the natural focus in dealing with these incidents, in which the subjects wanted something (substantive demands). Bank robberies also were federal concerns. Frequently, bank robbers made substantive demands and bargaining was appropriate. Local departments followed suit in approaching incidents they handled using bargaining techniques.

The FBI guidelines were heavily loaded with bargaining techniques. Suggestions such as the following emphasized the bargaining aspects of crisis, as opposed to crisis intervention techniques:

1. The use of time to increase basic needs, making it more likely that the subject will exchange a hostage for some basic need.

2. The use of time to collect intelligence on the subject that will help develop a trade.

3. The use of time to reduce the subject's expectation of getting what he wants.

4. Trades can be made for food, drink, transportation, and money.

5. Trades cannot be made for weapons or the exchange of hostages.

6. The boss does not negotiate.

7. Start bidding high to give yourself room to negotiate (ask for all the hostages).

8. Quid pro quo: get something for everything.

9. Never draw attention to the hostages, it gives the subject too much bargaining power.

10. Manipulate anxiety levels by cutting off power, gas, etc.

All of these guidelines are designed to deal with bargaining issues in a negotiation. The problem was that bargaining-oriented guidelines did not always fit the incidents that arose.

The types of incidents in which municipal police agencies use negotiators are not restricted to hostage incidents. Gist and Perry (1985) found that the majority of negotiator deployments were to domestic, barricaded, or suicidal situations. Surveying major police departments on the value of negotiators and negotiator training, McMains (1988) found that departments were using negotiation skills in a variety of non-hostage incidents. Over a five-year period, 18 percent of negotiator calls in the 15 largest U.S. cities were for hostage situations. Fifty percent of the calls during this same period involved barricaded subjects who had no hostages, 17 percent involved high-risk suicide attempts (suicide attempts in which people other than the subject were placed in danger), eight percent were to debrief people who were involved in crisis situations (victims of crimes, victims of stalking, rescue workers who were involved in mass casualty incidents, etc.) and seven percent were to help manage the taking into custody of people who were being involuntarily committed to a mental health facility. It has been suggested that of the 18 percent of incidents identified as hostage incidents, some of them really did not meet the criteria of someone being held to guarantee a demand.

Research on hostage negotiations began to show that most of the people involved in them are likely to respond to crises in their lives in maladaptive ways. In reviewing 3,330 randomly selected hostage incidents occurring between 1973 and 1982, Head (1990) noted that 70 percent of the cases he reviewed involved criminals, prisoners, or emotionally disturbed individuals—populations that would be expected to be easily overwhelmed by unplanned incidents. Similarly, Butler et al. (1993) found that the majority of hostage takers in the United States were emotionally disturbed. Feldman (2001) reported on his review of 120 incidents, in which 81 were personal/domestic disputes, mentally ill patients, workplace violence incidents, alcohol or drug related, or students; all groups that are easily thrown into crisis. Of the 144 subjects in Feldman's study, 140 (97%) had psychiatric diagnoses.

At the same time that negotiation was developing in one area of law enforcement, others were exploring the use of crisis intervention principles in policing. For instance, Rosenbluh (1974), in collaboration with William Reichart and Lt. James Olney of the Louisville, Kentucky, Police Department, developed extensive training programs in Crisis Intervention for the Louisville-Jefferson County Police Academy. Their objectives were to: (1) Help intervenors set disputants and sufferers at ease; (2) Help intervenors zero in on solvable problems; (3) Help intervenors bring individuals to workable solutions to their problems; and (4) Trace the development of maladaptive responses to crisis, such as suicide. Schlossberg (1979b) emphasized the use of crisis intervention principles as he and Frank Boltz developed the NYPD program. Professionals in other areas of the country had begun applying crisis intervention ideas to a broad range of policing issues. Greenstone and Leviton (1982) suggested that most of the people with whom officers deal are in crisis and crisis intervention principles are the preferred method of managing incidents. In the late 1970s, Lanceley (1994) began to realize that police officers were infrequently asked to deal with incidents like Munich. In most of the incidents negotiators dealt with, bargaining techniques were inappropriate. He integrated crisis intervention techniques and suicide intervention into the FBI curriculum in 1983. This change led to an even wider use of negotiators in crisis situations. Currently, they are being effectively used to intervene in:

1. **Barricaded Subject Incidents**—Barricaded subject incidents are situations in which a person has isolated himself in a protected position, has a weapon that can harm others, and is threatening to use it. Some are criminals who are interrupted during the commission of a crime. The interruption of their plans is generally a crisis for these criminals. However, the majority of barricaded subjects are people who are in emotional crisis (Austin Police Department, 1990). For instance, people who have had recent losses and are threatening suicide frequently barricade themselves. They threaten others as a way of gaining attention or of getting the police to kill them.

2. **High-Risk Suicide Attempts**—High-risk suicide attempts were defined as suicide attempts in which the subject's method endangered other people. They included, but were not limited to, suicidal people who threatened to use firearms, who threatened with explosives, and even who threatened to jump from structures in highly populated areas. Although psychologically these situations are no different from other suicide attempts, the fact that others can be injured or killed makes them of particular interest to the police, who have public safety as one of their specific responsibilities. An in-depth discussion of the management of suicidal individuals will appear later in this book. Here, note that suicidal people are generally in crisis, that suicide is their way of solving what they see as an unbearable problem, and that negotiators' crisis intervention skills are particularly appropriate in managing these people.

3. **Domestic Incidents**—Negotiators are frequently called upon to resolve domestic disputes. Very often when the police are called to a domestic dispute, rather than allowing the police into the house or calming down, one spouse makes the other a hostage. Often the dispute escalates into a hostage situation because the hostage taker does not want the police to interfere with the home situation. Conversely, the responding patrol officers may believe the level of anger and potential aggression to be so high in the situation that they use the negotiators to calm the subjects.

4. **Prison and Jail Riots**—Not all prison and jail incidents are hostage situations. Prisoners often will riot and take over a section of a jail or prison and make demands for better conditions, improved privileges, improved food, more recreation hours, etc. The riot may not even be violent. The prisoners may take over the section of the facility peacefully. This situation has occurred many more times than people generally realize (not being dramatic, they receive very little press). Many jail and prison administrators are not trained to properly respond to these incidents.

5. **Mental Health Warrants**—From the beginning of hostage negotiations in the early 1970s, negotiators have been trained in the basics of emotional and psychological disorders. Schlossberg (1979a) emphasized the importance of understanding emotionally disturbed individuals. Consequently, negotiators are more comfortable with these people. Experience in both Memphis, Tennessee, and Albuquerque, New Mexico, has shown that officers who have been trained in negotiation handle emotionally disturbed people better than they did before training, even when the contact is a routine call for service. They have learned specific guidelines for communicating and managing the emotionally disturbed person as

well as crisis intervention skills that have been helpful in resolving conflict with these people. Consequently, the negotiators manage them with more skill and confidence.

6. **High-Risk Warrants**—High-risk warrants include warrants issued for dangerous felons, raids on subjects who are known to be armed and who are expected to resist, and raids on drug dealers. The arrest of a criminal is more than likely a crisis for him. He is likely to respond in ways he has used in the past to deal with crises. If that has been through the use of force, force is likely to be his first option. The use of containment and negotiation allows time to pass, emotions to be defused, and reason (problem-solving) to increase (Stratton, 1978). Consequently, some police departments have incorporated negotiators along with tactical teams in serving warrants when they have a reasonable expectation of violence. Although there is little data on the effectiveness of this strategy, the increased use of the strategy suggests that it is helpful. Texas, for instance, has recently required all of their regional, multi-agency drug task forces to develop full negotiating and tactical capability.

7. **Debriefing in Crisis Incidents**—Crisis incidents have been defined as situations that exceed the person's ability to cope (Hoff, 1995). Incidents in which people are the victims of crimes are usually outside the range of their normal experience. Consequently, they will frequently have trouble coping with being victimized. Likewise, people who find themselves in mass casualty situations—incidents in which many people die—are not usually prepared to handle the devastation of such an incident. Years after airline accidents, search-and-rescue personnel report flashbacks and nightmares about incidents in which they were involved. Some police departments have used their negotiators to debrief victims and public safety personnel.

8. **Stalking Incidents**—Many stalking situations eventually lead to violence, even though most states have now enacted laws making stalking a crime. When a stalking situation escalates, negotiators can serve a valuable function in many of the roles described above. The incident may become a high-risk suicide or a murder/suicide situation. In almost all cases, the stalker is emotionally disturbed and prone to violence. As previously discussed, negotiators are trained for and are more comfortable dealing with these subjects than are other police officers. Additionally, the negotiators can debrief the victim of the stalker (who has experienced a crisis). Feldman found that 41, or 34 percent of the incidents he reviewed, involved stalking prior to hostage taking. It was associated with personal/domestic disputes, mentally ill subjects, and workplace violence incidents.

9. **Violence in the Workplace**—The phenomenon of workplace violence is not new to society. In the past several years, however, violence in the workplace has become much more prevalent. In 1993, 2.2 million people were attacked at work, 16 million were harassed violently, and 6.3 million were threatened with violence. Fifteen percent of the total United States workforce was attacked, and one-sixth of those were attacked with lethal weapons (Janik, 1989). There are many reasons for this that need not be explored here. Workplace violence can be any of the police crises listed in this section, or any combination of those crises. Dangerous individuals in the workplace (in order of frequency) include the chronically mentally ill, angry customers, intoxicated customers, emotionally distraught customers, and employees. Feldman (in press) reported that restaurants, bars, convenience stores, and transportation facilities were the primary workplaces in which criminals took hostages. Emotionally disturbed subjects tended to take hostages in public or government facilities.

10. **School Violence**—School violence has come to the forefront of the nation's attention during the last decade. Although the mortality rates for schools are lower than for the general population, the costs and the suffering of the families in these incidents has focused a great deal of attention on the issue. Negotiators have become involved in pre-planning and preparation for school violence incidents. Feldman (in press) reported that 6.67 percent of the 120 incidents he reviewed occurred in schools.

Summary

Although the history of hostage negotiation is relatively short in police work, it has been marked with many successes. It has proven the value of an interdisciplinary approach to police problems. Both experience and a small, but growing, body of research are showing the value of crisis intervention principles in policing, as well as helping to define the limits of their use in a variety of high-conflict situations for which law enforcement is responsible. Combining the knowledge of police officers with that of the mental health profession, a set of sophisticated techniques, based on theory, research, and experience, has been developed to reduce conflict and save lives.

References

American Bar Association (1980). *Standards Relating to Criminal Justice*. Vol. 1. Boston, MA: Little, Brown and Co.

American Heritage Dictionary (1980). New York: Houghton-Mifflin Company.

American Justice (1994). "Hostages." Arts & Entertainment Television Network.

Austin Police Department (1990). "Presentation at SAPD Hostage Negotiation School." San Antonio, TX (September).

Beach, E.L. (1986). *The United States Navy: A 200-Year History*. Boston: Houghton-Mifflin Co.

Bolton, R. (1984). *People Skills*. Englewood Cliffs, NJ: Prentice-Hall.

Brantley, H. (1993). "The Women POWs." *Quiet Shadows: Women in the Pacific War Symposium*. San Marcos, TX (March).

Butler, W.M., H. Leitenberg, and G.D. Fuselier (1993). "The Use of Mental Health Professional Consultants to Hostage Negotiation Teams." *Behavioral Science and the Law* 1:213-221.

Call, J.A. (1999). "The Hostage Triad: Takers, Victims, and Negotiators." In Hall, H.V. (ed.), *Lethal Violence: A Source Book on Fatal, Domestic, Acquaintance and Stranger Violence*. Boca Raton, FL: CRC Press.

Carkhuff, R.R. and B.G. Berensen (1967). *Beyond Counseling and Therapy*. New York, NY: Holt, Rinehart and Winston, Inc.

Cohen, H. (1982). *You Can Negotiate Anything*. New York, NY: Bantam Books.

Cooper, H.H.A. (1978). "Close Encounters of an Unpleasant Kind: Preliminary Thoughts on the Stockholm Syndrome." *Legal Medical Quarterly* 2:100-111.

Costello, J. (1982). *The Pacific War: 1941-1945*. New York, NY: Quill.

Covey, S.R. (1991). *The Seven Habits of Highly Effective People*. New York, NY: Simon and Schuster, Inc.

Culley, J.A. (1974). "Defusing Human Time Bombs—Hostage Negotiations." *FBI Law Enforcement Bulletin* 43(10):1-5.

Downs v. United States, 382 F. Supp. 752 (1991).

Dubina, J. (2005) "Lewis Prison Hostage-Taking Incident." Presentation at the Arkansas Association of Hostage Negotiators annual conference. Little Rock, AR (June).

Dubina, J. and R. Ragsdale (2005). "Lewis Prison Incident Debriefing." Presentation at the annual Crisis Negotiation Conference of the National Tactical Officers Association, Nashville, TN (April).

FBI (1985). *Hostage Negotiations Seminar*. Quantico, VA (February).

FBI (1991). *Advanced Hostage Negotiation Seminar*. San Antonio, TX (August).

FBI (1992). *Hostage Negotiations Seminar*. Quantico, VA (July).

Fagan, T.J. and C. Van Zandt (1993). "Lessons from Talladega: Even in 'Non-negotiable' Situations, Negotiations Play Role." *Corrections Today* (April):132-137.

Feldman, T.B. (2001). "Characteristics of Hostage and Barricade Incidents: Implications for Negotiation Strategies and Training." *The Journal of Police Crisis Negotiation*, 1(1).

Feldman, T.B. and P.W. Johnson (1999). "Aircraft Hijackings in the United States." In Hall, H.V. (ed.), *Lethal Violence: A Sourcebook on Fatal Domestic, Acquaintance, and Stranger Violence*. Boca Raton, FL: CRC Press.

Fisher, R. and W. Ury (1981). *Getting to Yes*. New York, NY: Penguin Books.

Gillooly, E. (1993). "The Women POWs." *Quiet Shadows: Women in the Pacific Symposium.* San Marcos, TX (March).

Gist, R. and J. Perry (1985). "Perspectives on Negotiations in Local Jurisdictions: Part I: A Different Typology of Situations." *FBI Law Enforcement Bulletin* 54:21-24.

Goldaber, I. (1979). "A Typology of Hostage-Takers." *The Police Chief* 46:21-23.

————— (1983). *Hostage Rescue Operations.* San Antonio, TX: International Chiefs of Police Seminar (September).

Graydon, E. (1993). "The Women POWs." *Quiet Shadows: Women in the Pacific Symposium.* San Marcos, TX, March.

Greenstone, J. and S. Leviton (1982). *Crisis Intervention: A Handbook for Intervenors.* Dubuque, IA: Kendall/Hunt Publishing.

Hagan, K.J. (1991). *This People's Navy: The Making of American Sea Power.* New York, NY: The Free Press.

Hare, Robert D. (1993). "Without Conscience: The Disturbing World of Psychopaths among Us." New York, NY: The Guilford Press.

Hassel, C.V. (1975). "The Hostage Situation: Exploring the Motivation and Cause." *The Police Chief* (September):55-58.

Hatcher, C., K. Mohandie, J. Turner, and M. Gelles (1998). "The Role of the Psychologist in Crisis/Hostage Negotiations." *Behavioral Science and the Law* 16(4):455-472.

Head, W.B. (1990). "The Hostage Response: An Examination of the U.S. Law Enforcement Practices Concerning Hostage Incidents." Doctoral Dissertation, State University of New York at Albany. *Dissertation Abstracts International* 50:4111-A.

Hoff, L. (1995). *People in Crisis: Understanding and Helping.* New York, NY: Jossey-Bass.

IACP (1983). *Hostage Rescue Operations.* San Antonio, TX (September).

Irvine, E. (1993). "The Women POWs." *Quiet Shadows: Women in the Pacific Symposium.* San Marcos, TX (March).

Janik, J. (1989). "Fire Under Fire." Paper presented at the Annual Meeting of the Society of Police and Criminal Psychology. Madison, WI (October).

Keen, S. (1991). *Fire in the Belly.* New York, NY: Bantam Books.

Lanceley, F. (personal communication, 1994). "The Duration of Negotiated Incidents."

Lanceley, F. (1999). *On-Scene Guide for Crisis Negotiators.* Boca Raton, FL: CRC Press.

McMains, M.J. (1986). "Post-Shooting Trauma: Demographics of Professional Support." In Reese, J.T. and H.A. Goldstein (eds.), *Psychological Services for Law Enforcement.* Washington, DC: U.S. Government Printing Office.

————— (1988). "Current Uses of Hostage Negotiators in Major Police Departments." Paper presented at the Society of Police and Criminal Psychology. San Antonio, TX (October).

McPherson, J.M. (1988). *Battle Cry of Freedom: The Civil War Era.* New York, NY: Ballantine Books.

Miron, M.S. and A.P. Goldstein (1979). *Hostage.* New York, NY: Pergamon Press.

Nielsen, E. (1986). "Understanding and Assessing Traumatic Stress Reactions." In Reese, J.T. and H.A. Goldstein (eds.), *Psychological Services for Law Enforcement*. Washington, DC: U.S. Government Printing Office.

Noesner, G. (1999). "Negotiation Concepts for Commanders." *FBI Law Enforcement Bulletin* 68:6-14.

President's Commission on Law Enforcement and Administration of Justice (1967). *Task Force Report: The Police*. Washington DC: U.S. Government Printing Office.

Reese, J.T., J.M. Horn, and C. Dunning (1991). *Critical Incidents in Policing*. Washington DC: U.S. Government Printing Office.

Romano, S.J. (1998a). "The Use of Third-Party Intermediaries in Crisis Negotiations." In CIRG, *Crisis Negotiation: A Compendium*. Quantico, VA: U.S. Department of Justice.

──────── (1998b). "The Freemen Siege: The Effective Use of Third-Party Intermediaries." In CIRG, *Crisis Negotiations: A Compendium*. Quantico, VA: U.S. Department of Justice.

Rosenbluh, N. (1974). *Techniques of Crisis Intervention*. Louisville, KY: Rosenbluh & Associates.

Russell, H.E. and A. Beigel (1979). *Understanding Human Behavior for Effective Police Work*. New York, NY: Basic Books.

Schreiber, M. (1973). "An After-Action Report of Terrorist Activities, 20th Olympic Games, Munich, West Germany." Reviewed at FBI Hostage Negotiation Seminar, February, 1985.

Schlossberg, H. (1979a). Hostage Negotiations School. Austin, TX: Texas Department of Public Safety.

──────── (1979b). "Police Response to Hostage Situations." In J.T. O'Brien and M. Marcus (eds.), *Crime and Justice in America*. New York, NY: Pergamon Press.

Solomon, R. and J.A. Horn (1986). "Post-Shooting Traumatic Reactions: A Pilot Study." In Reese, J.T. and H.A. Goldstein (eds.), *Psychological Services for Law Enforcement*. Washington, DC: U.S. Government Printing Office.

Somodevilla, A. (1986). "Post-Shooting Trauma: Reactive and Proactive Treatment." In Reese, J.T. and H.A. Goldstein (eds.), *Psychological Services for Law Enforcement*. Washington DC: U.S. Government Printing Office.

Soskis, D.A. and C.R. Van Zandt (1986). "Hostage Negotiations: Law Enforcement's Most Effective Non-Lethal Weapon." *FBI Management Quarterly* 6:1-8.

Souchon, H. (1976). "Hostage Taking: Its Evolution and Significance." *International Police Review* (June-July), No. 299:168-173.

State v. Sands, 700 P.2d 1369 (Ariz. Ct. App. 1985).

Stone, W. (2000). "The Fred Carrasco Incident at the Walls Unit, Texas Department of Corrections." Personal communication.

Stratton, J. (1978). "The Terrorist Act of Hostage Taking: Considerations for Law Enforcement." *Journal of Police Science and Administration* 6:2.

Strentz, T. (1979). "Law Enforcement Policies and Ego Defenses of the Hostage." *FBI Law Enforcement Bulletin* 48:1-12.

United States v. Crosby, 713 F.2d 1066 (5th Cir.), *cert. denied*, 104 S. Ct. 516 (1983).

Ury, W. (1981). *Getting Past No: Negotiating with Difficult People*. New York, NY: Bantam Books.

Van Zandt, C. (1993). "Suicide by Cop." *The Police Chief.* 60(7):24-27 (July).

Van Zandt, C. and G.D. Fuselier (1989). "Nine Days of Hostage Negotiations: The Oakdale Siege." *Corrections Today* (July):16-25.

Van Zandt, C., G.D. Fuselier and F. Lanceley (1989). "Negotiating the Protracted Incident." *FBI Law Enforcement Bulletin* 58(7):1-7.

Walker, S. (1992). *The Police in America: An Introduction*. New York, NY: McGraw-Hill, Inc.

Wesselius, C.L. and J.V. De Sarno (1983). "The Anatomy of a Hostage Situation." *Behavioral Science and the Law* 2:33-45.

Discussion Questions

1. Do you think that the public would have allowed United States police agencies to form hostage negotiation teams before the Munich Olympic incident?

2. If you were responsible for managing the incident involving Fred Carrasco at the Texas Department of Corrections, what would you have done differently?

3. What impact do you believe *Downs v. United States* had on municipal police departments? Do you think many police departments would have formed hostage negotiation teams without this case?

4. What conditions must be fulfilled before a person is considered a hostage?

5. Does the fact that a hostage taker makes substantive demands make a difference in a hostage situation? How would you deal with the person differently if he or she made no substantive demands?

6. What are the differences between a barricade incident and a hostage incident? How would the police response be different for each?

7. In school violence incidents such as the Columbine High School incident, how do you think negotiators can be used?

8. You respond to a hostage situation in which three armed males attempted to rob a bank and were trapped inside during the robbery. Every time you contact them on the telephone, they pass the phone around so that you are continually talking to different hostage takers. What strategies could you use to convince the hostage takers to only allow the "head" hostage taker to talk on the telephone?

9. Kidnappings are not a typical hostage taking situation that would employ negotiators. For the most part, they do not fit the requirements of a negotiated situation. Assume you were called as an incident commander at a kidnapping (where the perpetrator makes phone contact with the victim's family). What could you do to make that a negotiated incident?

10. Can you think of a hostage situation in which assault would be the preferred option? Use of a police sniper? Use of chemical agents? What factors would you have to consider in the use of each of these options?

11. A prison or jail hostage incident often involves several hostage takers and a large group of hostages (inmates and jail personnel). What would be the ramifications of an assault in one of these hostage incidents? The use of a sniper? The use of chemical agents? What would be the advantages and disadvantages of each of these options?

12. Assume you are a warden confronted with a situation similar to the Lewis Prison incident. What might you do to increase your tactical options? What if you were the tactical team leader? Negotiation team leader?

Negotiation:

Crisis Intervention

2

Learning Objectives

1. Understand how incidents have both substantive and expressive dimensions.

2. Know the characteristics of a negotiable incident.

3. Understand the differences between police negotiations and other kinds of negotiations.

4. Understand how hostage negotiation skills can be used as crisis intervention techniques.

5. Understand the value of the SAFE model in determining strategy in crisis negotiations.

6. Know the stages of a crisis incident, and what occurs to people during each stage of a crisis.

7. Know the principles of crisis intervention.

8. Understand why the duration of the crisis stage is variable.

9. Understand what interventions can be used in the crisis stage and what they accomplish.

10. Understand what interventions can be used in the accommodation/negotiation stage of a crisis.

11. Recognize the signs that an incident has been defused and the negotiator can move from crisis-intervention to problem-solving.

12. Understand what interventions can be used in the resolution stage of a crisis.

13. Know how hostage negotiation skills can benefit community-oriented policing.

It was 6:30 P.M. when the robbery alarm at the convenience store was activated. The responding patrol officer made a "silent" approach and observed two men holding guns on the clerk and two others. One of the subjects saw the officer and fired a shot through the front window. He yelled at the officer to "get out of here," while his partner grabbed one of the people, holding the gun to her head and using her as a shield. The officer called for a supervisor, who requested the mobilization of the Emergency Response Team. One negotiator was called from home, where he had just sat down for dinner with his family for the first time in two weeks. The second negotiator was called away from a family disturbance call in which he needed about 30 minutes more to convince the family to go to counseling. The tactical team arrived and secured the perimeter. Negotiators contacted the subjects using the number of the pay telephone in the store. The subject who answered was agitated, threatening, and demanding. He wanted the police to leave, for someone to bring them a car with a police radio and the negotiator to bring his wife or somebody was going to die. He gave the police 30 minutes to meet the demands. By checking with the wife, police found that her husband was a convicted felon who had often said that he would die rather than go back to jail. The second subject was her husband's friend, who spent most of his time doing odd jobs and most of his money on alcohol. The family was suffering financially and she and her husband had frequent arguments about his difficulties finding and holding a job. They had argued earlier in the day and he had left, saying that he would show her how much money he could get.

Incidents like the one described above illustrate the fact that hostage incidents involve both high emotions and difficult demands. They include what Miron and Goldstein (1979) call *instrumental* and *expressive* demands. The subjects have goals in mind: things that are concrete and specific for which they are asking. Wanting the police to leave, a car with a radio and one of their wives to come to the scene are examples of instrumental demands. Expressive demands are less tangible and often not expressed openly. At the same time, there are the emotional goals the subject hopes to attain during the incident. These are the expressive demands. Asking for an arena in which they can express their frustration with their life or with the unfairness of the system without a tangible goal would be an example of an expressive demand. Most incidents are both substantive and emotional. Negotiators need skill in managing both instrumental and expressive demands. They need skill in crisis intervention and problem solving, because problem-solving techniques are helpful in dealing with instrumental demands, and crisis intervention skills are essential in managing expressive demands.

Hostage Incidents versus Non-Hostage Incidents

Recently, Noesner (1999) has drawn a distinction between incidents that involve hostages versus incidents that involve people who are potential victims. He defines a hostage incident as one in which a subject holds other people in order to force a third party to comply with his or her substantive demands. Substantive demands are those that the subject does not think he or she can obtain without the use of hostages. Therefore, the hostages are leverage in these incidents, not targets. It is only by keeping the hostages alive that the subject has leverage with the police. Demands are reasonable and goal-directed.

Non-hostage incidents involve the subject acting out of emotion, having ill-defined goals, and making no substantive demands-expressive demands (Noesner, 1999). The demands seem unrealistic—demands that no reasonable person would expect to be fulfilled. In these incidents, subjects either are barricaded, or they hold others to express their frustration, hurt, or disillusionment about events or, more dangerously, about the individuals they are holding. The people in these incidents are not hostages; they are victims. The risk to the people being held is considerably higher in non-hostage incidents than in hostage incidents.

Types of Sieges

In addition, Lanceley (1999) discusses three types of sieges in which negotiators may become involved. They are: (1) deliberate, (2) spontaneous, and (3) anticipated sieges. It is important for the negotiator to understand the differences because the types of demands made by the subject vary, the risks posed to the hostage (victim) differ as a function of the type of incident, the strategies and tactics vary as a function of the type of incident, the length of time required to manage an incident varies, and the state of mind of the subject varies.

Deliberate Sieges

In a deliberate siege, the subject or subjects initiate the confrontation. The incident is designed to bring attention to the subject's cause or point. They involve substantive demands and the people involved are hostages in the true sense of being held as bargaining chips. The subject's state of mind is usually rational and negotiation techniques are generally the strategy of choice. The Hanafi Muslims taking hostages at the B'nai B'rith headquarters in Washington, D.C., is an excellent example of a planned siege. The subjects had substantive demands that included the removal from a theater of a film on the life of Muhammad that they thought was sacrilege and the restitution of a fine.

Spontaneous Sieges

In a spontaneous siege, the subject does not want or anticipate the authority's involvement. They do something that unexpectedly draws the attention of law enforcement. The motivation is usually personal, the demands expressive, and the person held is usually a victim in the making or a hostage. The subject's state of mind is emotional. Alcohol or drugs are frequently involved. Crisis intervention techniques are the strategy of choice. Many of the incidents managed by local law enforcement agencies are spontaneous sieges. Family violence incidents that become sieges because of the intervention of law enforcement, school violence incidents in which the subject is trapped, and workplace violence incidents are examples of spontaneous sieges.

Anticipated Sieges

In anticipated sieges, the subject expects the authorities to initiate the encounter. The subjects' goals are to survive the encounter with the authorities and maintain their freedom. The demands in these incidents are generally substantive and the people involved are usually followers or family members. The motivation for subjects is political or religious and they are usually prepared with shelter, food, water, arms, and ammunition. The subjects are usually rational in their approach. A combination of active listening and bargaining techniques is the approach. The Freemen encounter in Montana and the Republic of Texas siege are examples.

A False Dichotomy

Both of these analyses draw on Miron and Goldstein's (1979) distinction between expressive and substantive demands. Expressive demands are those that involve the need to express intense emotion and substantive demands are those involving tangibles that can be traded. This distinction seems to be at the heart of the change from the first generation to the second generation of negotiators described by Hatcher et al. (1998). The change in emphasis from dealing with substantive demands to dealing with incidents that were expressive in nature marked the change from bargaining to crisis intervention in police negotiations. Though some have tried to draw a clear dichotomy between incidents that involve bargaining principles and those that require crisis intervention techniques, the dichotomy seems artificial.

The bargaining/problem solving approach to negotiation assumes that negotiation is an interchange between interdependent people—that is, neither side can accomplish its goal without the other, and interchange has rewards and costs for both sides. The goal is to maximize rewards and minimize costs. The process is one of bargaining that emphasizes quid pro quo—this for that. It is a powerful model for negotiating on instrumental demands (Hammer & Rogan, 1997).

Hammer and Rogan (1997) point out that there are limits to a pure bargaining approach to negotiations in policing. First, crisis negotiations are not like business negotiations, in which the two sides bargain in good faith and have rational, well-thought-out positions, goals, and needs. Second, crisis situations involve high levels of stress that may interfere with rational decisionmaking. Third, a majority of incidents involve emotionally disturbed subjects; therefore, there are limits to the rationality of at least one side of the bargaining process. Finally, saving face is frequently an issue in most police crisis incidents.

Call (1999) has made a similar point. He suggests that a characteristic of hostage negotiation is its "brinksmanship" nature. By this he means that the subject deliberately creates a situation of risk, designed to make it so intolerable for the opposition that they will give in to the subject's demands. The inflexible nature of most hostage takers' demands is an example. He points out that the subject tries to force the authorities into a situation in which crisis bargaining principles apply. Crisis bargaining is characterized by:

1. The use of force—both the police and the subject have force available during an incident.

2. Bargaining for high stakes—lives are threatened and failure may result in injury or death.

3. Focusing on one alternative—demands of the subject are often presented as the only options.

4. A high degree of emotional content—anger and fear are integral parts of hostage incidents.

5. A preponderance of "saving face" issues—saving face becomes a major issue when coercion, force, and threats are used in negotiations.

6. The feeling of urgency—because the stakes are high, there is a sense of pressure and stress to incidents that are negotiated at the brink.

7. A lack of complete information—early in an incident, neither the police nor the subject have complete information about the others' capabilities, resources, goals, or methods. Intelligence develops over the course of the incident.

8. The failure to work out a detailed implementation plan.

The recognition that both expressive and substantive needs are involved in every incident suggests that it is helpful for negotiators to think of an incident as involving issues of degree and not of kind. That is, both crisis intervention skills and bargaining skills are needed in every incident, because each

Early in the negotiation process, negotiators concentrate on active listening and allowing the person to ventilate in order to reduce emotions. *(S. Davis)*

incident has expressive and substantive issues in it to a greater or lesser degree and it is the negotiator's job to recognize when what skill is appropriate.

Hammer and Rogan have suggested a formulation and technology that integrates bargaining and crisis intervention, which they call the SAFE model. They suggest that in any police negotiation, it is important to track and deal with the Substantive demands made by the subject, the Affiliation needs (liking and trust) involved in the relationship, need for the subject to save Face during the incident and the need to attend to and manage the Emotions of the subject. By carefully tracking the statements made by the subject, negotiators can define which issues are leading to conflict and the dimensions that demand immediate attention—a strategizing tool that lets negotiators systematically review critical issues so that interventions can be designed to deal with the most pressing issue as defined by the subject. The invited essay below discusses the SAFE model in greater depth.

The S.A.F.E. Model: Developing Crisis/Hostage Negotiation Strategy

by Mitchell R. Hammer, Ph.D., President, Hammer Consulting, LLC and, Professor Emeritus, American University

An Incident in Bowling Green, Kentucky

It was early in 2003 when I received a telephone call from Mr. William Hogewood, Program Manager, Crisis Negotiation program, Bureau of Alcohol, Tobacco, Firearms and Explosives (ATF). He asked me if I would develop an applied training program for all ATF negotiators that would allow them to use the S.A.F.E. framework in developing strategies for negotiating critical incidents. I accepted his offer, and by early 2004, ATF became the first federal law enforcement agency to have systematically incorporated S.A.F.E. strategy into their negotiation "toolbox."

Later in 2004, a three-day standoff took place in Bowling Green, Kentucky, that tested the negotiation skills of ATF negotiators—and the usefulness of the S.A.F.E. framework in helping resolve a very difficult incident. On September 29, 2004, ATF agents attempted to serve a warrant for firearms violations to a 41-year-old male who had a long criminal history. At 4:30 P.M. he fled and in the course of being pursued by ATF agents and the Kentucky State Police, he hit a car and exchanged gunfire with officers during which time he was shot three times. The suspect then carjacked another vehicle and at 5:15 P.M., crashed into the front door of a home. The Kentucky State Police, along with ATF, surrounded the home and negotiations were initiated. Throughout the three days, the suspect fired approximately 200 rounds from the house; fortunately, no one was injured. As the incident unfolded, it became clear that the suspect desired to end his life in a gun battle with the police. At one point, after talking with his wife, she commented, "he's not coming out of that house alive. He's not going out peacefully" (*Daily News*, Bowling Green, Kentucky, October 2, 2004). However, S.A.F.E. strategies were used as part of an overall negotiation approach that validated the suspect's experiences and enabled him to reconsider his situation and surrender peacefully.

How the S.A.F.E. Model Was Developed

Since 1973, much of what has been written about crisis/hostage negotiation has focused on the various motivational or psychological characteristics of perpetrators, the effects of being held captive (e.g., the Stockholm syndrome), and the emotional responses of hostage takers. Such information has been particularly helpful in increasing understanding about the effects of high stress on both subjects and negotiators. Specific approaches for developing effective strategies in *de-escalating* crisis situations and evaluating the progress of negotiations, however, have not been as fully developed.

The S.A.F.E. model represents one important framework for developing crisis negotiation *strategy*, defined as a communication plan to influence the behavior of the subject (e.g., hostage taker, suicidal individual) to peacefully surrender or assist in a tactical resolution. The S.A.F.E. framework is based on years of behavioral science research and incorporates the valuable insights of countless crisis negotiators. It has been field tested and adopted by a number of local, state, and federal law enforcement crisis negotiation teams and identified as a critical skill for training international law enforcement agencies by the U.S. Department of State. In 2001, the S.A.F.E. model was honored as a featured contribution to public policy in the United States by the Consortium of Social Science Associations in its book: *Fostering Human Progress: Social and Behavioral Research Contributions to Public Policy*.

Applicability of the S.A.F.E. Model

The S.A.F.E. model is a practical framework for developing effective negotiation strategies to de-escalate and resolve crisis incidents. It is useful for detecting and measuring indicators of a worsening situation and for reporting progress to command. As such, the S.A.F.E. framework can be incorporated in the three core areas of a "critical incident position paper": (1) Status (where are we now?), (2) Assessment (what brought us to this point?), and (3) Recommendations (what should we continue to do—and what should we do differently?). In addition, S.A.F.E. strategies can be incorporated in incident command decisionmaking.

The model can be employed to resolve critical situations involving terrorist activities; international "ethnic conflict" incidents; prison uprisings; cult confrontations; disgruntled, potentially violent employees; suicidal individuals; domestic (e.g., spousal violence) situations; barricaded individuals; and emotionally/mentally disturbed individuals.

Four "Triggers" for De-escalating Crisis Situations

The S.A.F.E. framework assesses and tracks four key "triggers" for de-escalating crisis situations. These four elements are expressed in the behavior and dialogue that take place between the subject and the negotiator. By tracking these four dimensions, negotiation teams are better able to develop strategies for resolving the situation that do not compromise core security concerns. The four "triggers" are:

- Substantive demands: The instrumental wants/demands made by the parties (e.g., subject and negotiator)

- Attunement: The relational trust established between the parties

- Face: The self-image of each of the parties that is threatened or honored

- Emotion: The degree of emotional distress experienced by the parties

These four "triggers" function as predominant "frames" within which the subject (and negotiator) communicatively interact as a crisis incident unfolds. The basic process for negotiating these predominant frames is:

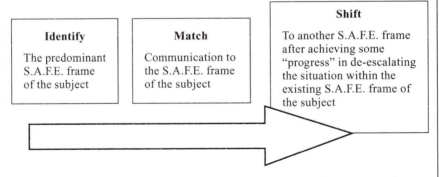

Identify	**Match**	**Shift**
The predominant S.A.F.E. frame of the subject	Communication to the S.A.F.E. frame of the subject	To another S.A.F.E. frame after achieving some "progress" in de-escalating the situation within the existing S.A.F.E. frame of the subject

Substantive Demands are the instrumental, situationally relevant wants, interests, and needs expressed by the parties. Some substantive demands are central (or primary) to the situation and some are peripheral (secondary). *When the subject is in a Substantive demand frame, the negotiator's goal is to bargain or problem-solve with the subject to achieve a peaceful surrender.* It is important to track the kinds of demands a subject makes and his or her response to the negotiator's demands and requests. In this way, appropriate and effective responses to the subject's demands can be offered. The

S.A.F.E. model highlights three Substantive demand strategies negotiators may employ when the subject is predominantly operating within the Substantive demand frame: (1) when and how to ignore or "downplay" the subject's substantive demands (in order to focus on Attunement, Face, or Emotional distress frames), (2) when and how to bargain (trade) substantive demands of the subject for central, substantive demands of the negotiator, and (3) when and how to problem-solve substantive demands with the subject. The S.A.F.E. model helps negotiators:

- Distinguish between central and peripheral substantive demands

- Determine whether the subject's demands are increasing or decreasing, hardening or softening, and whether threats made are offensive or defensive

- Track the degree to which the subject ignores/rejects or considers/accepts negotiator demands and requests

- Re-frame the subject's demands by identifying the "expressed position" versus underlying "interests" and use problem-solving strategies to negotiate the subject's underlying interests in ways that do not compromise fundamental security concerns

Attunement is concerned with the degree of trust, power, control, and relationship that is developed between the subject and the negotiator. In crisis situations, hostage takers typically experience stress and threat. Negotiators begin their interaction with subjects along these relational dimensions—not at ground zero, but at a deficit. The negotiator's goal in this area is to engage in cooperative behavior to build trust and liking (without compromising safety or security concerns.

Resolving critical incidents is often anchored in the relational trust established with the negotiator. This trust is fundamentally developed through the demonstration of *cooperative behavior*. Cooperation in a crisis incident has a cumulative effect, slowly moving a subject from a state of mistrust to a state of trust toward the negotiator. The importance for negotiators to develop a more positive relationship with subjects is critical to incident resolution and often plays a central role in the surrender ritual. The S.A.F.E. model helps negotiators:

- Inject into the negotiation systematic cooperative messages and behavior (in ways that do not compromise tactical advantage)

- Develop strategies for meeting peripheral demands in order to increase trust

- Employ persuasive strategies for building trust (e.g., the similarity principle, language, active listening skills)

Face refers to the projected self-image of the subject. Subjects are particularly sensitive to communication and behavior that may be perceived to attack or threaten their own self-image or reputation. When this occurs, subjects typically harden their positions and become more resistant to the influence of the negotiator. The negotiator's goal when the subject is in a Face frame is to validate the Face needs of the subject.

The ability of negotiators to effectively acknowledge and respond to the face needs or concerns of the subject can influence whether the situation escalates or de-escalates. When an individual's *face* is attacked or threatened, he or she is more likely to engage in more violent actions. When face is honored, the potential for violence decreases. For example, very negative statements made by the subject about his or her own face or self-esteem are common in suicide interventions. In cases in which the negotiator either does not recognize these types of statements or is not able to effectively honor or "plus up" the subject's face, suicide is a high risk. The S.A.F.E. model helps negotiators identify and develop effective responses to:

- *Face attack* behavior engaged in by the subject that is directed toward him- or herself

- *Face attack* behavior engaged in by the subject that is directed toward others

- *Face honoring* behavior engaged in by the subject that is directed toward him- or herself

- *Face honoring* behavior engaged in by the subject that is directed toward others

Emotional distress involves intense, negative emotions that compromise an individual's ability to cope with the stress of a crisis situation. It is important to track the degree to which the subject expresses positive versus negative emotions. When emotional distress compromises the subject's ability to problem-solve, a flight/fight response can emerge, increasing the unpredictability of the situation. The goal for the negotiator is to help subjects cope with their emotional distress in a way that permits them to re-assess the situation and then influence the subject toward a cooperative resolution.

The S.A.F.E. framework integrates work on emotion and stress by developing strategies of (1) empathic listening to communicate to the subject that his or her situation and emotional state is understood, and (2) influence strategies that focus on the "action tendency" of the specific emotional (distress) state of the subject. The S.A.F.E. model identifies five core emotional distress states and their action tendencies, along with specific negotiation strategies for communicating with subjects who are experiencing such emotional distress. These five key emotional distress states and their action tendencies are: (1) sadness (sense of loneliness, discouragement attached to a significant loss). The action tendency of sadness is to seek help in coping with the loss; (2) Fear/anxiety (sense of apprehension, uncertainty, danger based on a threat). The action tendency of fear/anxiety is to avoid or escape from the threat; (3) Disgust (sense of distaste, revulsion toward something or someone (typically oneself if the subject is suffering from substance abuse) who is viewed as spoiled or deteriorated. The action tendency of disgust is to get "rid of" or "wash away" the poison or cause; (4) Anger (sense of being physically or psychologically restrained and unfairly harmed by others). The action tendency of anger is to attack the offending party; and (5) shame (intensely painful sense of dejection and rejection from others, feelings of inadequacy). The action tendency of shame is to hide, disappear or die. Perhaps the most volatile emotional "cocktail" is shame combined with anger, as this produces a sense of "humiliated fury." The S.A.F.E. model helps negotiators to:

- Identify core negative emotions and their action tendencies experienced by subjects in crisis situations

- Engage in empathic communication in which emotions are accurately understood and addressed

- Employ appropriate active listening skills in dealing with the subject's emotional distress

- Use specific strategies for influencing the subject by framing the subject's behavior in terms of the action tendency of his or her predominant emotional distress state.

Using the S.A.F.E. Model

The S.A.F.E. model can be easily integrated into the team's overall critical response effort. The negotiation team or incident command should designate a "S.A.F.E. Advisor." This person should receive authorized training in the S.A.F.E. model and may be an individual whose background is in crisis intervention or conflict resolution. The S.A.F.E. Advisor can also be a member of the negotiation team or incident command structure. The primary negotiator should not, however, assume the role of S.A.F.E. Advisor. S.A.F.E. strategy should be incorporated into the decisions made by the negotiation team and by incident command. Further, negotiation strategy should be re-evaluated based on changes as the incident unfolds. The S.A.F.E. advisor should monitor and track the four "triggers" (Substantive demands, Attunement, Face, Emotional distress), maintain wall graphics to display observed patterns, and identify specific S.A.F.E. frame strategies for responding and influencing the subject. Recently, as part of S.A.F.E. training that I conduct, participants receive a copy of the *S.A.F.E. Field Guide* and *S.A.F.E. Assessment Tools*, which are helpful "on scene" as an incident develops. At appropriate times during a crisis incident, the S.A.F.E. Advisor can brief the negotiation team leader and members concerning what S.A.F.E. issues are most dominant for the subject and what kinds of strategies can be used to address these S.A.F.E. triggers.

Overall, the S.A.F.E. model offers a comprehensive approach for assessing, evaluating and developing effective response strategies to subject's behavior in crisis incidents. This model should be included in the expanded toolbox of crisis negotiation teams.[1]

---

[1]   In addition to the S.A.F.E. Field Guide and S.A.F.E. Assessment Tools, other information on the S.A.F.E. model and related work can be found in:

Hammer, M.R. (forthcoming). *A Communication Theory of Crisis Negotiation: Discourse Analysis of Hostage/Barricade Incidents.* Westport, CT: Praeger Publications.

Rogan, R.G., M.R. Hammer, and C. Van Zandt (eds.) (1997). *Dynamic Processes of Crisis Negotiation: Theory, Research and Practice.* Westport, CT: Praeger Publishing.

Rogan, R.G., and M.R. Hammer (forthcoming). "The Emerging Field of Crisis/Hostage Negotiation: A Communication-Based Perspective." In J. Oetzel and S. Ting-Toomey (eds.), *Handbook of Conflict Communication.* Thousand Oaks, CA: Sage Publications.

Hammer, M.R. and R.G. Rogan (2004). "Threats, Demands, and Communication Dynamics: Negotiating the 1991 Talladega Prison Siege." *Journal of Police Crisis Negotiations,* 4, (1),45-56.

Rogan, R.G. and M.R. Hammer (2002). "Crisis/Hostage Negotiations: A Communication-Based Approach." In H. Giles (ed.), *Law Enforcement, Communication, and Community* (pp. 229-254). Amsterdam, The Netherlands: John Benjamins.

Hammer, M.R. (2001). "Conflict Negotiation under Crisis Conditions." In W. Eadie and P. Nelson (eds.), *The Language of Conflict and Resolution* (pp. 57-80). Thousand Oaks, CA: Sage Publications.

Rogan, R.G. and M.R. Hammer (1998). "An Exploratory Study of Message Affect Behavior: A Comparison between African Americans and Euro-Americans." *Journal of Language and Social Psychology,* 17 (4), 449-464.

Rogan, R.G. and M.R. Hammer (1995). "Assessing Message Affect in Crisis Negotiations: An Exploratory Study." *Human Communication Research*, 21, 553-574.

Rogan, R.G. and M.R. Hammer (1994). "Crisis Negotiations: A Preliminary Investigation of Facework in Naturalistic Conflict Discourse." *Journal of Applied Communication Research,* 22, 216-231.

Hammer, M.R. and G. Weaver (1994; 1998; 2000). "Cultural Considerations in Hostage Negotiations." In Weaver, G.R. (ed.), *Culture, Communication and Conflict: Readings in Intercultural Relations* (Chapter 56, pp. 499-510). Needham Heights, MA: Ginn Press.

Hammer, M.R., C. Van Zandt, and R.G. Rogan (1994). "A Crisis/Hostage Negotiation Team Profile." *FBI Law Enforcement Bulletin,* 63(4):8-11.

Rogan, R.G., M.R. Hammer, and C. Van Zandt (1994). "Profiling Crisis Negotiation Teams." *The Police Chief,* 61, 14-18.

Substantive Demands

Fisher and Ury (1983) point out that one of the things that makes negotiations difficult is the tendency of both sides to use position bargaining. Position bargaining is the process that most perpetrators employ when they begin negotiations with the police. It begins with the perpetrator taking a strong position, expecting the police to take a strong position, and then gradually giving ground until an agreement is reached. The subject expects the police to take a hard line, perhaps even threatening, in return. Subjects rarely expect their initial demands to be met.

Position bargaining puts relationship and substance directly in conflict. Because taking a position interferes with the relationship, position bargaining tends to force people to choose between the relationship and the substance of the negotiations. Position bargaining either leads to conflict about positions and assaults on self-esteem, or it leads to withdrawal from conflict and avoidance of the other. For instance, if you feel attacked by another person for choosing to become a police officer, there tends to be one of two responses: you either defend yourself or you avoid the other person.

Substantive demands are generally the things the subject initially ask for. The initial position the subjects take in a negotiation is rarely where they want to end up. Generally, because they expect to engage in position bargaining, they misrepresent their actual goals, expecting to go through a lengthy process with the police taking an equally extreme position and eventually making a deal somewhere between the two positions. This is a time-consuming process that is based on deception and power. For instance, in a police contract negotiation, the officers' association took the position that all off-duty jobs available at all city facilities for law enforcement officers should be given to city officers rather than being open to any peace officer. Their goal was not to monopolize all city facilities; rather, they expected to compromise by getting exclusive rights to off-duty employment at the new sports arena. They were surprised to have the other side agree to their position without going through a lengthy process of moving from one position to another.

In dealing with substantive demands, the goal in negotiations is always to reconcile the conflicting *interests*—not the positions taken by parties. Positions have only one solution. By focusing on interests, negotiators can develop more alternatives to any conflict. Negotiators and subjects frequently have both shared interests and competing interests. For instance, most of the time, negotiators and subjects would rather not die during a confrontation. On the other hand, the subject may have an interest in not being sexually abused the way he was the last time he went to jail, while the negotiator has an interest in putting the subject in jail. The rub is that frequently, the initial position taken by the subject does not identify his true interests. The negotiator must be able to think about the problem from both his side and the subject's side.

Attunement

In any critical incident, subjects see difficulties with the relationship, because they believe that the police have more power than they do. They do not trust the police to use their power with the subjects' interests in mind, and they will have had direct or indirect experiences with the police that lead them to dislike police in general. The important point for negotiators in this analysis is that they have to be sure to take the time to build the relationship before they can expect the subject to trust them or listen to them.

One helpful skill in dealing with attunement is the ability to separate the person from the problem, Trust and liking are easier to build if it is clear that getting along with one another and solving the problem are separate issues. Fisher and Ury (1983) suggest the following guidelines:

- Separate the relationship from the substance and deal directly with the relationship.

- Put yourself in their shoes.

- Don't deduce their intention from your fears.

- Don't blame them for your problem.

- Discuss each other's perceptions.

- Look for opportunities to act inconsistently with others' expectations.

- Give them a stake in the outcome by making sure that they participate in decisionmaking.

Case Study Revisited: In the incident at the convenience store described above, several of these principles apply. For instance, negotiators started with the recognition that the subjects were not the same as the problem. They reminded themselves that the subjects had some reason for doing what they were doing that was deeper than just "getting money." It helped them from becoming overly judgmental about the "stupid" way the subjects were behaving.

Additionally, they were able to discuss the relationship by saying things like "People sometimes see the police as "jackbooted thugs," ready to kick in the door and assault the place. They may have had bad experiences with the police in the past. On the other hand, police sometimes see people as thugs, making the worst of a bad situation. If you and I think that way, we are likely to have some real problems. I don't think either of those ways of thinking is true. I think we are people who want some of the same things here today. Mainly, we both want nobody to get hurt. Right?" "We are not going to come barging in there with guns blazing and I am confident that you are going to keep things under control. We don't have to get anybody hurt, but we do need to be able to talk about what's going on. What do you think?" This approach defined the relationship as one of mutual problem solving, without the need for force.

In addition, the negotiators said, "I know you are doing what you are doing for a reason and I am not sure I understand that reason, but I am interested in why you are in the store." This focused the subjects on their needs rather than their position. It dealt with the subjects in a way that was different from what they expected. It makes the assertion of mutual problem solving more credible.

The subjects did not buy into the plan at first. They said, "Man, you must think I'm stupid. Cops who want to help. No way. Now, get my wife down here."

By replying, "You know, if I were in your shoes, I would be frustrated and confused. I probably wouldn't have expected the police and would be worried about what they might do. When they weren't as aggressive as I expected, I'd probably be more confused." The negotiator uses the reflection of feelings to challenge the subject's expectations.

The negotiators had to be aware of their own fears, anxieties, and tensions. The worst-case scenario that they developed early on was that the subject wanted the wife at the scene in order to have an audience for a suicide. This fear increased when they heard that the wife and husband had argued just before the robbery attempt and the man had said, "I'll show you. I'll do something you will remember." They had to develop a way of assuring safety and checking out their fears. They asked the wife about suicidal history and they asked the subject "You know, in the past when people have said they wanted their wife at the scene, they were thinking about killing themselves in front of her. Is this what's on your mind? I know you argued before coming down here." Both the wife and the subject denied a suicidal history or intent. They both said it was just something he said.

Hostage incidents tend not to occur on the police officer's schedule. They always interrupt something else. It is important not to blame the subjects for that interruption. One negotiator was called away from the first dinner he had eaten with his family in a week. The other was in the middle of a family disturbance call in which she thought she was 30 minutes from convincing the aggressor to go to alcohol counseling. Both were annoyed by the interruption of their plans. It was important for the negotiators to recognize that blaming the subjects for their lost opportunities would interfere with negotiations. They had to do an attitude check before contacting the subjects. They had to resist the temptation to blame the subjects for their problems.

Case Study Revisited: The negotiator's initial, accepting response of letting the subject know that he was trying to understand what he needed may well have challenged the subject's assumptions about what police are likely to do. He was building a relationship (attunement) Most people have little direct experience with police, and even fewer people, including those who have been arrested, have experience with police negotiators. Thus, to have a police officer state that he wants to be sure he understands what a person is saying challenges many assumptions subjects make about police. When the subject said, "You are damn right, I am pissed. I've been down this road before with you guys. Last time I was arrested, I was slammed against the wall and my wrist was broken." The negotiator replied "Sounds like you've had a hard time with the police. That gets me a little uptight, because I hear you saying that you think I will treat you the same way." Such a response avoids the trap of defending other officers. It shows the subject that the negotiator hears the subject's concerns and feelings. It expresses the officer's concern that he will not be given a chance to help solve things because of somebody else's actions. It utilizes many of the principles above.

Face

Face-saving, or self-esteem, issues are usually present in hostage incidents, because both the subject and the police have a reputation to maintain, either with friends, family, or associates. Everyone is playing to an audience and saving face is always an issue. Negotiators are people first. Before they become involved in a conflict, both the police negotiator and the subject were human beings, subject to the same motivations, needs, desires, and wants as any other person. This means that both the police negotiator and the subject are likely to make the same kind of negotiation mistakes for the same reasons. Foremost among negotiation mistakes is the tendency to identify your own ideas. As human beings, we all tend to think our perception of a situation is the best or even the only way to see things. Beyond that, we tend to think our ideas about an issue, a person, or a problem is who we are. Therefore, when we take a position and are challenged, we personalize it. It is not our idea that is challenged; it is our sense of self, our face. For instance, if somebody were to say to you, "It is silly for somebody as intelligent as you to think that being a cop is important work," you are likely to react poorly. That is because your idea of the importance of your work has been challenged and you do not take it as a challenge to your idea but as a challenge to who you are. You have to defend yourself.

Just as people identify with their ideas, they also tend to identify with their emotions. A challenge to the way that people feel is frequently taken as a challenge to their identity. How many times have you heard someone say "Don't tell me how to feel!" when some well-meaning person says "You shouldn't feel that way." The person is not defending his feelings; he is defending himself. Additionally, intense emotions interfere with rational decisionmaking. Emotions must be recognized and made a legitimate part of any negotiation.

The fact that people tend to identify with their thoughts and feelings means that the negotiator must approach incidents in ways that do not attack the ideas or feelings of others. To be credible, minimize conflict, and have the most influence on the subject, the negotiator must manage these issues of self-esteem. One way of doing this is to consciously separate the person from the problem. Additionally, negotiators should always take an approach that communicates respect for the subject, understanding that he or she needs to save face in every incident.

Emotions

Emotions need to be managed in negotiations. They need to be defused without challenging the other side's identity (face). To do that, Fisher and Ury (1983) suggested the following guidelines: (1) Recognize and understand emotions: theirs and yours; (2) Make emotions explicit and recognize them as legitimate; (3) Allow the other side to let off steam; (4) Don't react to emotional outbursts; and (5) Use symbolic gestures to show them that you are not going to act the way they expect. By recognizing and allowing emotions to be part of the process and by not reacting to emotional outbursts, negotiators can defuse the emotions, communicate acceptance of the person, and show that they are not like others who have tried to use their power to limit the expression of emotions.

Decisionmaking: The Action Criteria

Noesner (1999) has pointed out that commanders need to use a three-part test for making decisions about the strategies to use in a crisis/hostage incident: (1) Is the action necessary? (2) Is the action risk-effective? and (3) Is the action acceptable? The decision about the necessity of a tactical or negotiation approach to an incident will depend on the nature of the incident, whether it is negotiable, and whether it can be made negotiable. The decision about the risk-effectiveness of the action depends on the risk to life of taking an action versus the risk to life of not taking an action. Noesner (1999) points out that if the risk to victims is low, the use of a tactical approach is inadvisable and difficult to defend. On the other hand, if the risk to victims is high, the use of higher risk tactical options is easier to justify. Therefore, risk assessment and an understanding of the probability of injury or death associated with various options is essential in critical incidents. Negotiators need to be conversant with both areas in order to advise the incident commander well. Risk assessment will be discussed in depth in Chapter 7, Intelligence.

Stites (2005) has suggested that all decisions in crisis need to be weighed against two criteria: (1) Will the decision move the operation toward the mission? and (2) How does it line up with the prioritization of the value of the lives of the people who are involved in the incident? He states that the mission of SWAT and negotiators is to save lives and that the lives are ordered in importance as follows: (1) hostages/innocent citizens, (2) law enforcement officers, and (3) the suspect. All decisions should contribute to saving lives and if there is a choice of saving one life or another, hostages/citizens come first, officers second, and the subject last. Ideally, everyone should get out alive. However, an incident is not a failure if the subject poses a serious threat to others, a good faith effort has been made to save everyone, but his threat has to be neutralized.

Options Open to the Police

Several authorities (Strentz, 1979; Schlossberg, 1979a, 1979b; Boltz, 2001) suggested that there are four options available to the police when there is a negotiable situation. Each of them has strengths and weaknesses. They are:

1. An assault on the location
2. Selected sniper fire
3. Chemical agents
4. Contain and negotiate

An assault on the location—This option has the advantage of putting an end to a potentially dangerous situation. It is quick. However, it has the disadvantage of being a high-risk option. Seventy-eight percent of hostages killed are killed during an assault by police (Strentz, 1979; Schlossberg, 1979b). Additionally, an assault poses a significant risk to police officers. Some departments have organized tactical teams with more officers than they need because they expect the first two officers in the door during an assault to be killed.

Selected sniper fire—This option has the advantage of putting an end to the incident and saving lives, if the correct person is shot and if the hostage taker poses a threat to the hostages. The disadvantage is that sometimes the wrong person is shot. Hostage takers sometimes have exchanged clothing with hostages to confuse police.

Chemical agents—This option is usually used in conjunction with an assault. Sometimes it is used to disrupt a hostage taker when he is starting to do things the police do not want him to do. However, it has the disadvantage of being unreliable in its effects, of posing a health threat to some hostages (asthmatics, for instance), and of telegraphing the officers' intentions to assault.

Contain and negotiate—This option has the advantage of saving lives, projecting a good public image when police departments are dealing with sensitive situations, and protecting the department from the liability of a wrongful death lawsuit. Its disadvantages are that it is time-consuming, labor-intensive, and requires training.

The decision to negotiate is complicated. Decisionmakers need to take several factors into consideration. In addition to considering the characteristics that define a negotiable incident (see p. 69), they need to consider the political and economic climate of the community, the availability of trained personnel, the chances of the successful resolution of the incident using negotiation, and the presence or absence of an imminent threat to hostages' lives. In areas of high population density, the decision to negotiate may create an economic hardship with which the community is unwilling to live. For instance, Los Angeles cannot afford to tie up traffic on its freeway system during rush hour; therefore, they do not negotiate very long with people who are threatening to jump off overpass bridges. Rather, they use inflatable mattresses as cushions and push suicidal people off onto them (FBI, 1993).

Case Study: Keeping in mind the action criteria, the incident commander decided that because a tactical option would likely lead to injury or death (a violation of the mission), no one seemed to be at immediate risk, and because the negotiator's assessment was that negotiation was a viable option, negotiation was the strategy of choice. He instructed the tactical team to man the inner perimeter from positions of cover, but to take up positions in a conspicuous way so that the subject saw them take their positions. In this way, negotiations and tactical resources could be used in parallel to send the same message: we are willing to help, but we are capable of hurting: "Let's talk."

Incident commanders may call on negotiators to help them make a series of critical decisions. One of the first decisions to be made is, "Is it negotiable?" Strategies and tactics the commander uses come directly from this decision. Along with the tactical team, negotiators need to be prepared to advise commanders on this issue.

Characteristics of a Negotiable Incident

The FBI (1985) has suggested eight characteristics that are necessary for an incident to be negotiable. They are:

1. There must be a need to live on the part of the hostage taker.

2. There must be a threat of force on the part of the authorities.

3. There must be demands by the hostage taker.

4. The negotiator must be seen by the hostage taker as a person who can hurt the hostage taker but is willing to help him.

5. There must be the time to negotiate.

6. A reliable channel of communication must exist between the hostage taker and the negotiator.

7. Both the location and the communications of the incident need to be contained in order to encourage negotiation.

8. The negotiator must be able to deal with the hostage taker making the decisions.

There must be a hostage taker who needs to live—without the need to live, the negotiator's bottom line is removed. Mental health professionals (Glasser, 1984; Maslow, 1954) have defined the basic needs that motivate most normal people. They point out that people have a number of needs that motivate, including: the need to survive; the need to belong—to love, share, and cooperate; the need for power; the need for freedom; and the need for fun (Glasser, 1984). Needs can conflict with one another, but generally the need to survive takes priority over all the others. This priority of the survival need gives negotiators a powerful bargaining tool. An example of the power of the survival need is a hostage taker who claimed to have killed a person and then ran his family out of the house by shooting at them. He barricaded himself in the house with a "friend" and did not respond to negotiators' attempts to contact him using the telephone and a bullhorn. After five hours of not responding and after an assessment of his psychological status, he was presented with an ultimatum: either give up or the tactical team was going to assault his house and kill him. Suddenly, he asked to talk to the negotiator, claiming he did not know that the police had wanted to talk with him. He thought that the telephone that had been ringing every 30 seconds for five hours had been for somebody else. The threat to survival is a powerful attention-getter for most people.

However, people who have decided to die do not feel threatened by death. They would rather die than live with what they think of as unbearable pain. They are difficult to negotiate with because they have no desire to live. Without the need to live, there is rarely something with which the negotiator can bargain.

There must be the threat of force on the part of the authorities. Without a credible threat, hostage takers may have no reason to negotiate, because they have little to lose. In conjunction with the need to live, the threat of force always gives the negotiator leverage. However, the threat has to be believable. The authorities have to be seen as both having the force (firepower) and the will to use it. For instance, in one bank robbery, the police let the hostage taker get to the parking lot, where he took a female hostage. He started to walk around a car and was not stopped. He moved up and down the street, saying "Man, I am going to get away." He never believed that the police had the will to use their force against him. This is one of the important reasons negotiators and tactical teams need to work closely together— to provide a credible threat.

The hostage taker must make substantive demands (Noesner, 1999). Without demands, negotiators have nothing to work with. There is little that can be used to buy time; time enables negotiators to show a willingness to help. Without demands, there are no negotiations, no settling of a conflict. Depressed people will frequently demand only to be left alone, as do subjects in other types of non-hostage incidents (Noesner, 1999). The hostage taker may have any of a number of motives for taking a captive without demands: sexual exploitation, homicide, homicide-suicide, or suicide by cop. The lack of demands is one indicator of potential violence. However, without demands, there is still a strategy open to the negotiator. The negotiator can use crisis intervention goals, skills, and knowledge to manage the incident. For instance, people who are depressed sometimes make no explicit demands. However, they are communicating something—possibly a need for help of some kind. Skillful listening and an analysis of the person's motives can be helpful in resolving the incident.

The negotiator must be seen by the hostage taker as a person who can hurt the hostage taker but is willing to help him. By being both a source of harm and of help, the negotiator can maximize his or her worth to the hostage taker. By using the contrast of potentially deadly harm and a genuine desire to help, negotiators can be seen as powerful allies for the hostage taker. The contrast between the violent confrontation the hostage taker expects from the police and the understanding and help the negotiator provides makes the negotiator look like even more of an ally than he or she really is. The contrast effect is a powerful tool of influence (Cialdini, 1984).

Negotiations take time. Without sufficient time, a relationship cannot be built between the negotiator and the hostage taker, intelligence cannot be gathered, emotions cannot be defused, and problems cannot be solved. If either side is unable or unwilling to allow the time, successful negotiation is impossible. For instance, if a depressed person has a suicide plan that calls for him to shoot himself when he finishes counting down from ten to one and he is on seven, time is limited. Likewise, if a paranoid schizophrenic's delusions lead him to insist on an airplane landing in front of his house to take him to Mexico within the hour, there are limits on the time within which the negotiator has to work. Other options may be needed.

A reliable channel of communication must exist between the hostage taker and the negotiator. By definition, negotiation is the settling of conflict through conferring or discussing. Without a channel of communication, there can be no discussion. A reliable channel of communication implies that there not only must be reliable communications equipment, but there must be reliable communicators. The people must speak the same language, have a similar meaning for words, and use language consistently. Negotiators and hostage takers not only have to speak the same language, but they also have to use the same dialect. Castilian Spanish is not the same as Puerto Rican Spanish or street Spanish. The lack of a common meaning for words is one of the reasons negotiating with emotionally disturbed individuals is problematic. They frequently use language in an idiosyncratic, unique way. The negotiator must be sensitive to the personal meanings of words in order to have a clear channel of communication. It is wise to keep a log of words to which hostage takers react so the negotiator does not trip over them a second time. Finally, it is essential for the negotiator to recognize that as more people become involved in a communication, the more room there is for distortion. Negotiating through a third party opens the possibility of an unclear message because it is being interpreted and translated by an additional person. As with the children's game of whispering a message from one person to another, distortions can be introduced. Negotiators should always talk to the hostage taker directly (American Justice, 1994).

Both the location and the communications of the incident need to be contained in order to encourage negotiation. Hassel (1975) has pointed out that a successful response requires the development of team tactics, using blocking and containment techniques. The hostage taker needs to feel the limits on his freedom and on his social support. This is one reason for establishing a tight perimeter and for isolating the hostage taker's telephone lines. It forces him to deal with the negotiator and it gives the negotiator a better chance to be seen as the hostage taker's best resource for resolving his problem.

The negotiator must be able to deal with the hostage taker who is making the decisions. This does not present a problem if the incident involves just one hostage taker. However, if there is more than one hostage taker, the negotiator must identify early in the process who is the decisionmaker, so tactics can be developed for the right individual. It does little good to analyze the needs of a person and develop ways of dealing with them if the person is not the one in power.

Command and supervisory personnel should be trained in the nature of a negotiable incident so they can make informed decisions in the field. In addition, negotiators should keep a checklist of the characteristics of a negotiable incident with them so they can do a quick assessment of the negotiability of any given situation. Finally, these characteristics can be used as a guide to what needs to be done to make an incident negotiable. For instance, if no inner perimeter has been established at a scene when a negotiator gets there, a quick review identifies the need for containment. The negotiator can advise that the situation needs more containment before the hostage taker will see the sense in negotiating.

One caveat: Although helpful, categorizations are roadmaps of real life, not life itself. That is, any system shows a sketch of what goes on in real incidents, just as a roadmap shows a sketch of the cities, roads, and features of an area. Neither is complete and conditions sometimes change, so neither the roadmap nor the categorization of incidents fit exactly. Some incidents have elements of both a hostage and a non-hostage incident. Therefore, the use of any system needs to be seen as a guide, like a roadmap is a guide, not as reality or the final word. Both maps and systems are tools to be used when they fit the situation.

Case Study Revisited: The case at the beginning of this chapter illustrates the value of making an early determination about whether an incident is a hostage or non-hostage incident. The subjects caught robbing the convenience store were using the people inside as leverage. They had substantive demands, i.e., stay back, bring a car, bring my wife. These were things they could not get without the hostages. This makes the hostages valuable to the subjects and reduces the risk to the hostages. At the same time, the subjects were unprepared for the interference of the police. They reacted to the interruption of their plans with heightened emotions. This does not make the incident a spontaneous siege, because there are clear substantive demands. It means that negotiators must deal with the heightened emotions before expecting subjects to respond to attempts at solving their problems in a different way. The incident seems negotiable because the subjects do not seem to be suicidal, the threat of force is in the form of the patrol officer at first and the tactical team later, the subjects have substantive demands, negotiators are available, neither the police nor the subjects are insisting on a deadline or forcing a specific time frame, a reliable communication channel is available in the form of a telephone, the situation is contained, and the decisionmaker seems to be willing to talk with the negotiator.

Sidebar: What Is it to Negotiate?

Christopher Voss is a supervisory special agent with the FBI's Crisis Negotiation Unit (CNU). He became an FBI agent in 1983 after having been a police officer with the Kansas City, Missouri, Police Department. Voss became an FBI crisis negotiator in 1992. Prior to being assigned to CNU, he was the negotiation coordinator for FBI New York City and was also a volunteer on, and chair of the board for, Help Line, a crisis intervention hotline founded by Norman Vincent Peale. He currently oversees the FBI's negotiation response to the kidnappings of Americans internationally.

What is it to negotiate? In my father's dictionary, the colloquial definition is "to succeed in crossing, surmounting." This dictionary also tells me that to surmount is to "overcome." This is what it is to be a law enforcement negotiator—to use words to "overcome." The characteristic of what we do, the sense of it, is to use negotiation as a form of nonlethal force (negotiation may in fact be the ultimate form of nonlethal force) to overcome crisis, preserve life, and enforce justice.

The dictionary referred to is Webster's *New World Dictionary*, 1967 edition. Most of the more current definitions of negotiation often include the word "compromise." If we have four hostages, are we willing to compromise and accept preserving the lives of two? Of course not. The current definitions of negotiation simply do not apply to what hostage negotiators do.

In addition, the current perception of negotiation is that it is done more as a last resort, or if you're no longer able to "fight." Note the famous quote from Saddam Hussein as he is being pulled out of the hole in the ground in Iraq, "I am the President of Iraq and I wish to negotiate." This perception has no use for the law enforcement negotiator, and the reality of our jobs is that we often work to put our forces (SWAT, Emergency Services, etc.) in a better position to use deadly force. Negotiation is a tactic that easily complements, if necessary, lethal force. It is not either/or in our world.

Negotiation is the communication form of choice because it is effective in keeping the situation from escalating while we search for resolution options. The options we accept are those that follow the law enforcement priorities of preservation of life and enforcement of the law.

One of the great secrets of negotiation is open-ended questions. While the existence of open-ended questions as one of the tools of active listening is no secret (it is on almost every list of "active listening skills" that negotiation authors publish), its effectiveness is. It is one of the single most powerful active listening, crisis intervention, negotiation, confrontation—skills there is. Very similar to the power of emotion labeling, open-ended questions are capable of turning the tide of a negotiation. And it has been seen to work in cultures from South America to the Middle East.

Open-ended questions, by definition, are questions that begin with the words, "Who, What, When, Where, Why, or How." They are also known as interrogative questions and in counseling and therapeutic circles as guided discovery questions. Open-ended questions are what we were taught in grade school as the basics of what every story or report should answer.

In active listening terms, we are introduced to open-ended questions as a way to encourage the subject to talk; as a way of developing rapport by eliciting longer answers and making them feel listened to, that they are being heard. They are much more than that, however; they are a way of making subjects feel empowered, which has a counter-intuitive effect; it puts us in the driver's seat. We frame the question, and by framing the question we have actually set parameters on how they can answer. We have boxed them in. They never feel this because by us asking them, they feel in control. They don't realize we have burdened them with finding the solution. As a result, open-ended questions also tend to ease tension.

The issue of timing is important. We can't just plunge into open-ended questions. We have to demonstrate understanding first by the use of other active listening skills, such as paraphrasing and emotion labeling. Active listening skills have synergy; they have to be used in combination with one another.

To increase our effectiveness, several of the interrogatives can almost be eliminated. "Who," "When," and "Where" tend to have short answers and don't do us much good in terms of putting subjects in a more extended problem-solving mode. "Why" tends to make people feel accused and as a result, should be avoided. This leaves us with "What" and "How."

With practice, almost any question can be re-worked into a "What" or "How" question. And the nature of almost all cultures is the desire to respond to an open-ended question that is asked respectfully.

To draw the distinction with closed-ended questions, closed-ended questions are those that are asked seeking to be answered with a "yes" or a "no." Usually, when asked, they give the person being asked the impression that the questioner thinks there is only one correct answer. This tends to give the feeling of being forced or pushed into an answer. The phrase "loaded question" likely comes from this. An interesting aspect of this is that when the answer sought is a "yes" to something they actually want, they still feel pushed, or exposed to some hidden trap and tend to be very defensive, if not hostile.

Pushing for a "no," on the other hand, is counter-intuitive. "No" can make people feel that they have protected themselves and they often find it much easier to respond. An example of this might be "Do you want your wife to win?" You would follow this up with "What can we do to get you out of this safely?"

The "What's" and the "How's" still have to be preceded by the right amount of paraphrasing, minimal encouragers, and emotion labels. They have to be asked at the appropriate time and on the appropriate subject. It would be inappropriate to ask "How are you going to kill her?"

The ammunition of active listening comes from the things the subject has said. Open-ended questions are the tools that, when combined properly with the other tools, provide the home run hits.

Vince Dalfonzo, a member of CNU, shared this quote from Naquib Mahfouz (Nobel Prize recipient for literature, 1988) with me, "You can tell whether a man is clever by his answers. You can tell whether a man is wise by his questions." Those questions tend to be open-ended questions.

Negotiations/Crisis Intervention

Principles

Consistent with the idea that all incidents involve both substantive and expressive demands is the crisis intervention approach adopted by most police departments at this time. Both expressive and substantive issues can be accommodated by the crisis intervention model. McMains (2005) has suggested that there are several steps in crisis intervention, including: (1) check attitude, (2) gather intelligence, (3) assess risk, (4) defuse, (5) build rapport, (6) influence problem-solving, (7) resolve, and (8) debrief.

Regini (2004) has pointed out that crisis intervention as utilized by police negotiators utilizes five concepts: (1) empathy, (2) active listening, (3) boundary setting, (4) reframing, and (5) problem-solving. These models make it clear that managing substantive demands and emotional issues is a part of any incident. They both utilize active listening to defuse the incident and problem-solving skills to deal with the substantive demands.

Crisis: Definition

A crisis is defined as a situation that exceeds a person's ability to cope (Hoff, 1989). One of the fathers of crisis intervention, Caplan (1961), emphasized that a crisis occurs "when a person faces an obstacle to important life goals that is, for a time, insurmountable through the utilization of customary methods of problem-solving"—it exceeds the person's ability to cope.

When confronted with an insurmountable problem, people feel a rise in tension. They attempt to solve the problem. If that attempt is unsuccessful, there is a further rise in tension. Caplan says, "A period of disorganization ensues, a period of upset, during which many abortive attempts at solution are made." It results in what NOVA (1992) has called a cataclysm of emotions. People are overwhelmed by feelings that range from fear to panic, from anger to rage, and they experience mental confusion.

Most barricaded subjects, high-risk suicide attempts, emotionally disturbed individuals, and people who have been victimized by violent crimes are people who are facing a situation in which they are having problems coping. They can be considered in crisis. For instance, domestic disputes that erupt into violence are not usually new problems. There is frequently a history of unproductive attempts at problem-solving that cycles through the same argument time after time. In frustration, one of the partners threatens to leave as an attempted solution to the discord in the relationship. At this point, the other partner is faced with a new problem—how to keep the partner from leaving. The crisis has intensified. This is when the risk of violence increases, because the person being left has no other ways of achieving his goals. Both parties are in crisis.

Stages of a Crisis Incident

Crises can be seen as happening in stages that have different characteristics and require different skills to manage (See Table 2.1). Although different authors vary somewhat regarding the exact nature of the stages of a
crisis (Caplan, 1964; Tyhurst, 1986), each emphasizes the usefulness of viewing crisis as a process, with predictable stages through which people move.
Each stage has different issues with which negotiators must deal and requires
different skills that are valuable in dealing with the issues of that particular
stage. An understanding of the stages of an incident helps negotiators select
the right skills for what is going on at the moment, provide an organized evaluation of the incident to command and project strategies for moving to the
next stage of negotiations. The stages are:

1. Pre-Crisis

2. Crisis

3. Accommodation/Negotiation (Stabilization)

4. Resolution

Pre-Crisis Stage

The Pre-Crisis Stage is the time during which normal business is being
carried on by negotiators, hostage takers, and hostages. Emotions are under
control, stress levels are low, and both the police and the hostage takers are
thinking and planning.

During the Pre-Crisis Stage, the person going into crisis is going about
his normal routine with little sense of loss of control or emotional disruption. He may see a problem developing and begin trying to manage it. People have a general feeling that something needs to be done. The problem
seems general rather than specific. For instance, a person may see that the
economy is getting tight and may be planning a criminal act that will
involve a victim. This person is creating a crisis for the victim, but the victim is not in crisis yet, because the victim has not experienced a significant
threat to his or her ability to cope with a problem.

Practice: Negotiators are going about their regular duties. They are under
control and their emotions are in balance. During this stage, they need to do
several things that will make handling a hostage incident more successful.
They need to practice their communication skills, interpersonal skills, and
skills of persuasion. Negotiators need to educate the command structure in
the principles of negotiation and what negotiators can do at an incident. They
need to arrange for support from other agencies, both in and out of law
enforcement, and work out agreements about the functions of the police and
the other agencies. They need to plan and practice, even though there is no
immediate crisis.

Table 2.1
**Summary of the Goals, Issues, and Skills Important to Negotiators
at Each Stage of a Crisis**

Stage	Attitudes	Goals	Techniques
Pre-Crisis		Practice Planning Prevention	Public Speaking Intelligence Gathering and Analysis
Crisis/Defusing	Acceptance Caring Patience	Establishing Relationship Credibility Safety Encourage Ventilation Assess Problem Validate	Reassurance Active Listening Emotional labeling Paraphrasing Reflection of feelings Effective pauses Mimic

Adaptation/Negotiations	Acceptance
	
	Caring
	
	Patience
		Facilitate
		
		Prediction of
		  consequences
		
		Planning a
		  different action
			Open-ended Questions
			
			Problem-
			  oriented questions
			
			Persuasion and influence
			  techniques
			
			I-messages

Resolution/Surrender	Acceptance
	
	Caring
	
	Patience
		Peaceful resolution
		
		Managing increased
		  tensions
			Guided imagery
			
			Stress management
			  techniques

Source: Michael J. McMains, Ph.D. Used with permission.

Planning: In domestic violence situations, negotiators may do risk assessments, develop tactical intelligence about people and locations in the event a subject escalates, and contact the subject with an explanation of how continued harassment of the target is not in his or her best interests (San Antonio Police Department, 1997). Similarly, many departments have started coordinating, planning, and practicing with school officials and security personnel in anticipation of a school violence episode. Such planning includes gathering floor plans of schools, developing Memorandums of Understanding, and role-playing critical incidents before an incident occurs. Mental health consultants can be contacted, and profiles of potential actors can be developed before an incident occurs. The FBI performed extensive intelligence gathering and coordinated planning before the Freemen siege (Noesner, 1997).

Prevention: One of the most important activities in which negotiators engage in the pre-crisis stage and one that has become immensely important in the last decade are the prevention programs that negotiators have developed using their people management skills. Prevention means going into a potentially violent situation and doing something to prevent it from becoming violent. It is proactive and requires planning, coordination, and cooperation between agencies and people. In areas such as workplace violence, domestic violence, and the management of emotionally disturbed individuals, negotiation and crisis intervention principles have moved negotiators from a reactive to a proactive stance.

In workplace violence prevention, negotiators help employers establish a policy, develop a system for reporting threats, provide training, develop response plans, and perform threat assessments. The point of all of these activities is to make employees aware of warning signs that they can report to supervisors and managers before an incident occurs. Management can take action to prevent a workplace violence incident. Chapter 11, School and Workplace Violence, will discuss both prevention and intervention in more detail. In school violence prevention, negotiators can help school administrators employers establish a policy, develop a system for reporting threats, provide training, develop response plans, and perform threat assessments (Solis, 1999).

The Albuquerque, New Mexico, and Memphis, Tennessee, police departments' crisis intervention teams have developed a unique blend of tactics and negotiation strategies in dealing with emotionally disturbed individuals. Such approaches have led to less violent management of emotionally disturbed individuals and greater safety for patrol officers. These innovative programs have taught a specially selected and trained group of officers to manage emotionally disturbed individuals using a variety of negotiation-based knowledge and techniques, including types of mental illness, communication techniques (active listening skills and crisis intervention techniques), and de-escalation of anger. By using these approaches, the Albuquerque CIT handled 2,313 emotionally disturbed individuals in 1998 with injuries to subjects in only two percent of the cases.

In first responder and conflict resolution training, negotiators can help prepare street officers to deal with the early stages of a hostage/crisis incident. By teaching about types of critical incidents, sources of violence, characteristics of negotiable situations, the effects of time, and active listening skills, negotiators have not only raised patrol officers' awareness of the usefulness of negotiations, they have given officers skills that help defuse incidents before they become violent (Ricketts, 2000).

Threats to prominent figures in the political and entertainment arenas has been a growing concern. The focus that some negotiators have placed on stalking incidents reflects their interest in assessing the threat that stalkers pose and intervening before the incident turns violent. Such a prevention effort is founded on what Fein and Vossekuil (2000) call the Protective

Intelligence program, which has as its goals: (1) the early identification of persons who might pose a threat; (2) the assessment of the risk the person poses; and (3) the management of the case in a way that reduces the chances of the person actually acting on his or her threats. Negotiators are sometimes called upon to manage these cases.

Mohandie (in press) has suggested that it is helpful to understand four types of stalkers because they pose different levels of risk. He pointed out that the targets in stalking can be divided into Intimates and Non-Intimates and Public Figures versus Private Figures. His research revealed that stalking incidents that involved intimate relationships were the most dangerous.

Crisis Stage

The Crisis Stage is the period during which plans are interrupted, life seems out of control, emotions are high, and reason is low. A serious threat to an important need is perceived by a person and that person actively searches his or her memory in an effort to meet that need (Caplan, 1961; Glasser, 1984). The person becomes frustrated in this search and tension rises more. Although it is a crisis for the hostage taker when things do not go according to plan, it need not be a crisis for the police if they have planned for and trained to handle hostage situations.

Frequently, the Crisis Stage begins when an incident takes an unexpected turn, or when it becomes unpredictable or uncontrollable. If a robber is interrupted in the middle of holding up a convenience store by a police officer's untimely appearance, he will be thrown into crisis. If a woman who is a single parent is fired from her job without warning, she will be thrown into crisis. There is a cataclysm of emotions (NOVA, 1992) that usually range from anger to rage, from fear to panic, and that involve the loss of problem-solving ability, leading to confusion. The person in crisis searches his or her memory for a solution to the crisis that has worked in the past.

If the situation is one that the person has not encountered before, the person must develop new solutions to the crisis. Aguilera and Messick (1978) call this "productive problem-solving" because it requires the production of a new response. It depends on the person's intelligence, creativity, and experiences. The person generally tries the first thing that comes to mind to solve this problem and to regain a sense of control. For instance, the bank robber who is caught inside the bank by police may take hostages, not because it is his or her best option, but because it is the only option that comes to mind during the crisis. Prisoners who riot about poor food quality may take hostages simply because jail officers are present and available and it seems like a good thing to do.

During a crisis incident, several kinds of unplanned events may create a new crisis for an individual. They may include: a foiled escape plan, a hostage who wants to play hero and force a confrontation, hostages that develop medical problems during the incident, hostages escaping during an incident, or promises not being kept by the authorities. The negotiator needs to be alert to the possibility of a new crisis occurring during negotiations.

For people who do not take hostages, crises are precipitated by a threat to their basic needs. Many authors (Maslow, 1954; Glasser, 1984) have suggested that all of us have basic needs that include: the necessities that guarantee physical survival, i.e., air, food, water, and shelter; a secure and threat-free environment; a sense of belonging to a group; a place in a family; and the freedom, power, and control to make their own decisions. When these needs are threatened and no solution is found, a crisis is created, even in normal people. For example, the person who becomes suicidal when she finds that she has cancer seems to be acting irrationally. She is not emotionally disturbed in the sense that is used in psychiatry and psychology. Rather, she is in crisis—panicked by the threat to her life and unable to cope with this threat to her survival. In her effort to deal with the threat to her life, she threatens her life.

Like beauty, crisis is in the eye of the beholder. It depends on the person's perception. What is a crisis for one person may not be seen as a crisis by another. The person's perception of his or her ability to deal with the incident and his or her perception of the cost of failure make an incident a crisis (McMains & Lanceley, 1995). For instance, if a stockbroker loses millions of his client's money, he may see that as not only a threat to his financial security, but also to his self-esteem: he may experience a crisis. A police officer observing the stockbroker losing this money may not experience the loss of this money as having the same costs, because the officer's livelihood and professional reputation do not depend on that money. The stockbroker's perception is important, not the officer's.

When a crisis occurs, emotional arousal is intense and survival is threatened. People in crisis provide many signs of emotional arousal, signs that the incident is in the Crisis Stage. Among them are the use of words with emotional content, increased pitch and volume of speech, and emphasis on particular words. Negotiators need to be alert to all three of these clues because they help determine what skills need to be used with the hostage taker at a particular time in the negotiations. If feelings are intense, it is not a good time to try to negotiate with the subject. Rather, attention needs to be paid to helping the subject reduce the intensity of his or her feelings.

Words range in intensity of emotional meaning (Bolton, 1984). For instance, to say "I'm frustrated by being fired" is a less intense communication than "I'm enraged by being fired." Both statements refer to the same incident. However, the importance of the event for the individual is communicated by the intensity of the feeling implied in the subject's choice of words. Negotiators need to develop an ear for the intensity of the words being used by people in crisis. Bolton (1984) has suggested a rating for the intensity of meaning associated with words. His ratings are given in Table 2.2.

Table 2.2
Bolton's (1984) Ratings of Word Intensity. Feeling words are grouped according to levels of intensity. Words have slightly different meanings for different people. Most words can be moved to a higher or lower level; however, most words convey approximately the same degree of intensity to most people.

Levels of Intensity	Love	Joy	Strength	Sadness	Anger	Fear	Confusion	Weakness
STRONG	Adore Love Cherish Devoted	Ecstatic Elated Overjoyed Jubilant	Dynamic Forceful Powerful Mighty	Desolate Anguished Despondent Depressed	Violent Enraged Furious Angry Seething	Terrified Horrified Panicky Desperate	Bewildered Disjointed Confused Muddled	Crushed Helpless Done for Washed up
MILD	Affection Desirable Friend Like	Turned on Happy Cheerful Up	Effective Strong Confident Able	Glum Blue Sad Out of sorts	Mad Frustrated Aggravated	Frightened Scared Apprehensive Alarmed	Mixed-up Foggy Baffled Lost	Powerless Vulnerable Inept Unqualified
WEAK	Trusted Accepted Cared for O.K.	Bad Good Satisfied Content	Capable Competent Adequate	Below par Displeased Dissatisfied Low	Irritated Annoyed Put out Perturbed	Worried On edge Nervous Timid	Undecided Unsure Vague Unclear	Weak Ineffective Feeble

Source: Reprinted with the permission of Simon & Schuster, Inc. from PEOPLE SKILLS by Robert Bolton. Copyright © 1979 by Prentice-Hall, Inc.

Recent linguistic analyses of three hostage incidents have illustrated that the intensity of the communications in an incident varies. Rogan (1997) reported rating messages in a suicidal incident, an incident involving an emotionally disturbed individual, and a domestic hostage incident. Using a technique of rating messages on a −3.00 to +3.00 scale that estimated the subjects' deviation from neutrality, the author found that subjects in all three responded to negotiators with negative intensity shortly after being contacted, reflecting an increase in competitiveness and aggression. As the incident progressed, the three subjects began to respond differently. The suicidal subject became progressively more negatively intense up to the time the subject committed suicide. The emotionally disturbed individual, on the other hand, became increasingly more positive in intensity to the point at which he surrendered. The family disturbance incident showed an up-and-down pattern of verbal intensity.

Additionally, the author analyzed the incidents in terms of "face" messages. That is, messages that had content that suggested: (1) attack other's face; (2) attack self's face; (3) defend others; (4) defend self; (5) restore other's face; and (6) restore self's face. He found that "restoring self's face" messages were the most common in all three incidents. However, in the suicidal incident, there was a lack of "attack others" messages and a high percentage of "attack self" messages, while the other incidents were devoid of such messages, indicating that the use of self-critical messages may be an indicator that the incident is not settling down for the person who is contemplating suicide.

One of the most important skills a negotiator can possess is that of active listening. Active listening allows the hostage taker to vent emotions and frustrations, to calm down, and to engage in problem solving. *(R. Mullins)*

Elgin (1983) has pointed out that not only the content of the words used, but also the emphasis on the words in the sentence communicates feelings. For instance, to say, "I would really like you to move the patrol cars from around my house" without emphasis is generally heard as a statement that communicates a wish, but no strong desire. However, when the italicized words are emphasized in the same statement, "I would *really like* you to move the *patrol cars* from around *my* house," the message takes on more urgency. By listening for the emphasis that a person in crisis places on his or her words, the negotiator can pick up clues as to when the hostage taker is in crisis and what things are of concern to him or her.

Accommodation/Negotiation Stage

The Accommodation Stage is the period during which a person tries new solutions to the crisis, is open to suggestions, and is beginning to think through the situation. Stress may fluctuate from high to moderately high as people use the ideas that have worked for them in the past to deal with the current incident. They are engaging in "reproductive problem-solving." It depends on reproducing past successes. If they have not encountered the crisis personally before, they may go through ideas or plans they may have seen about situations close to the incident.

There are the clues that the incident is moving from the Crisis Stage to the Accommodation/Negotiation Stage. The number of emotional words may become more frequent and then less frequent due to the initial frustration of the person's attempt to solve his problem. In a similar way, as the intensity of the emotional words becomes more intense and then less intense, and as the emphasis of the communications become more neutral, the hostage taker's ability to reason increases.

Resolution Stage

The Resolution Stage is the period during which a person works out the solution to his or her problem, a new equilibrium is reached, and a variety of needs can be addressed. During this stage, new solutions may have to be invented. Creativity is necessary and problem-solving is important because the usual solutions have not worked. Aguilera and Messick (1978) call this "productive problem-solving" because the solution cannot rely on past successes; rather, a new solution must be produced. After the hostage taker tries all his ideas and finds them lacking, the Resolution Stage begins. He may find his ideas lacking because the negotiator has successfully stalled him or because the negotiator has successfully suggested to him that his solutions are not really in his best interests.

Case Study: Definition and Stages of a Crisis. The woman was 34 years old. She had called her friend in Minneapolis long distance several times during the evening. She was agitated and depressed, talking about not wanting to live. She told her friend that she had bought a gun. She was alone in her apartment.

Between phone calls, the friend called the local police department. They sent a patrol officer, who found the woman barricaded in her apartment, talking on the telephone, and threatening to shoot at the officer if he tried to get in. He called his supervisor, who evaluated the situation, determined that the woman was at no immediate risk, and called for the department's crisis response team. A limited response of two negotiators, five tactical officers, and the department psychologist was called out. When they arrived at the scene, the tactical personnel relieved the patrol officers on the perimeter, who returned to their regular duties.

The negotiators and the psychologist talked with a second friend who had arrived at the apartment after having been notified of the situation by the friend in Minneapolis. They learned that the woman had been raped two months before. She had been seeing a therapist because of the trauma of the rape. She was on medication for both anxiety and depression. She had been experiencing nightmares and "flashbacks" about the rape. She had lost her job at a local hospital because of her emotional moodiness. On the day of the incident, she was having to move in with her parents and her brother because she could no longer afford the rent on her apartment. Her brother had raped her.

Case Review. This case illustrates the nature of crises. It started with a sexual episode that threatened two of the woman's basic needs: security and self-esteem. She felt so threatened by the rape that she had spent nights in the walk-in closet so that nobody could find her. She reported feeling that she deserved the rape because she knew what her brother was like but she let him stay at her apartment anyway. The incident progressed as she made efforts to manage the crisis. First, she went to a female therapist and then she started on medication. However, her efforts at solving the problem were not entirely successful. She lost her job. Consequently, there was a rise in tension that interfered with her problem-solving ability. The only solution she could see to her financial problems was to move home, a solution that had worked for her before. This time, however, the original source of the threat, her brother, was at home. As she got closer to the day she was expected to move, her anxiety and depression increased. She felt more and more out of control and in pain. Although she did not really want to die, suicide was a solution to the problem of pain. The episode illustrates the onset of a crisis precipitated by a situation that exceeded the woman's abilities to cope. It was followed by efforts at solving the problem of her pain that were unsuccessful, leading to more tension and emotional turmoil. This was followed by worse decisionmaking and finally suicidal threats and a full-blown crisis.

Factors Affecting the Duration of the Crisis

A crisis may be short in duration or it may be long. It depends on a number of variables: the emotional reactivity of the hostage taker, the personality makeup of the hostage taker, the nature of the police response, and the presence or absence of other aggravating circumstances.

Some people are born with a high-strung nervous system. They tend to be more reactive to the stresses in their life than other people. It will take these people longer to settle down after being aroused. Tavris (1989), talking about temperament, has stated ". . . We know that adults differ markedly in their normal (resting) levels of epinephrine (adrenaline), in their output of epinephrine in response to stimulation, and in the time it takes for their epinephrine levels to return to baseline after stress." Buss and Plomin (1975) have suggested that there are four aspects to temperament that have a strong hereditary component: (1) emotionality, or the intensity of a person's reaction; (2) sociability, or the person's desire to be with others; (3) level of activity, or the person's total energy output; and (4) impulsivity, or the person's tendency to respond immediately without thinking about the consequences. A person's pattern of behavior on these dimensions tends to be constant over the person's life. The negotiator needs to assess the patterns the hostage taker has displayed over a period of time on these dimensions at home, work, school, etc., to be able to predict his or her reaction to the stress of the hostage incident. Although negotiators have no direct control over the hostage taker's temperament, they need to be aware of the differences in people on these dimensions. They need to allow reactive persons more time to calm down and to work out issues. They need to be active in consulting with command to structure an environment that reduces distractions and new irritants.

The person's temperament is related to personality type. If one thinks of personality as a fairly consistent way of seeing, thinking about, and responding to the demands of life, then personality will help define what the person sees as threatening, how chances of managing that threat are evaluated and how the person will react to the threat. For instance, paranoid people tend to be more alert, feel more threat, and react more easily than dependent people. Therefore, they will be more alert to threats, they will react more quickly to the things they think are threatening, and they will take longer to settle down after being aroused. On the other hand, depressed people tend to be less reactive and require more time to think about their situation, to respond to negotiators, and to act once they have made a decision. Negotiators need to have a working knowledge of these personality differences and to modify the pace of their work to accommodate these differences (See Chapter 7, Negotiating with Emotionally Disturbed Individuals).

A police response that emphasizes power will generally be threatening and lead to arousal in most people. The visible presence of weapons raises a normal person's anxiety level. The obvious presence of massive firepower will lead to intense anxiety in the initial stages of an incident. It is important to maintain a balance between enough threat to contain an incident and so much threat that the hostage taker panics. This means that unless there is a strategic or tactical reason for an obvious display of the tactical team's response, a low-profile approach is generally preferred in the Crisis Stage.

The intrusion of other people or agencies, the massing of an audience, and communication with the hostage taker by unauthorized or untrained people all serve to inflame crisis incidents. People feel more committed to a position when they take a public stand on an issue (Cialdini, 1984). The availability of a crowd, the media, and friends and family create a situation in which the hostage taker is forced to make a public issue of his position. Negotiators and crisis response team members need to structure an environment that reduces the audience. This is one of the psychological reasons for establishing and maintaining both an outer perimeter at the scene and a designated press area. It is also one of the strong reasons for isolating the hostage taker's communications and restricting his communications with untrained personnel.

Crisis Intervention Principles

Characteristics of Crisis Intervention

Several characteristics make crisis intervention an effective model for many situations with which negotiators must deal. They include the ideas that:

1. The people served are thought of as being in crisis rather than as having serious emotional/mental problems.

2. Intervention is focused on feelings and problem-solving.

3. Crisis management takes an active effort on the part of the crisis manager.

4. Intervention has to be delivered during crisis, so the manager has to be available 24 hours a day.

5. Intervention can be managed by non-mental health professionals with special training.

6. Intervention can be managed by a team approach. (Aguilera & Messick, 1978; Hoff, 1989)

The assumption that people are in crisis rather than suffering from serious emotional/mental problems has several implications. A popular misconception about emotionally disturbed individuals is that they are unpredictable and volatile. They are likely to "go off" without warning. Thinking of people as being in crisis rather than as emotionally disturbed reduces this sense of unpredictability, because most people can relate to having a problem they cannot solve. Additionally, not all hostage incidents involve emotionally disturbed people, much less the other incidents that negotiators manage. Experience has shown that in hostage situations, 56 percent are carried out by emotionally disturbed individuals (FBI, 1985). The majority of crisis incidents involve normal people who are temporarily confused by the intense emotions they are experiencing due to their inability to solve a problem.

In crisis intervention, the focus is on reducing the disruptive feelings the person experiences and the difficulty these feelings create for the person's problem-solving abilities. The rise in inner tension that a person experiences when his attempt at solving a problem is unsuccessful leads to anxiety and the inability to function in extended periods of emotional upset (Caplan, 1961). Frequently, the inability results in interference with the person's ability to think systematically about the nature of the problem, the possible solutions, the probable outcome of a solution, or the best method of implementing a solution, it is an interference with problem solving.

Because the person in crisis has an inability to solve his or her own problems and the anxiety has interfered with problem-solving ability, the person intervening has to take an active but subtle part in the problem-solving process. Initially, the intervenor has to help defuse the intense feelings that interfere with problem-solving. Then the intervenor has to guide the person through a systematic evaluation of the problem and the realistic solutions open to him or her. This intervenor guides the person in crisis into an exploration of the possible consequences of his or her various options and helps the person choose the one that best suits his or her long-range needs. This is an active process that requires knowledge, skill, and abilities on the part of the negotiator.

Intervention with a person in crisis is best delivered at the time of crisis. This means that the manager has to be available 24 hours a day. The referral to a community service agency that maintains regular nine-to-five office hours misses many crises. This is one reason intervention in crisis incidents has fallen to police departments. They are one of the few agencies that provide staffing 24 hours a day. The timely management of the problem-solving process by trained managers can have immediate payoffs in that it defuses a potentially violent situation. Timely management has long-range benefits in that it can frequently solve the cause of the problem, often reducing the need for return calls to the same place.

One important assumption in crisis intervention is that non-mental health professionals can effectively intervene with appropriate training. It was discovered early in the development of crisis intervention that a number of non-mental health professionals such as schoolteachers, nurses, and police officers were as effective as mental health professionals in defusing crises and in problem solving. What was required was a willingness to listen to other people's problems, an understanding of these problems, the opportunity to be present during the crisis, and problem-solving skills that could be brought to bear on the specific problem with which the person was struggling.

Finally, many crisis managers discovered the importance of a team approach to crisis management. Advantages of the team approach to crisis intervention include a more thorough assessment of the problem, the generation of more solutions, a more accurate evaluation of the outcome of the possible solutions, and more resources for carrying out the chosen solution to a problem than can be provided by only a single manager. In addition, the team approach distributes the responsibility of managing a tension-filled incident and provides for support of team members by one another; both are effective stress management techniques.

Case Study Revisited: Characteristics. The case study illustrates several of the characteristics of Crisis Intervention. First, it illustrates the importance of seeing people as normal people trying to deal with abnormal circumstances. Prior to the rape, the woman had been functioning well. She had been gainfully employed, had many friends, and had been involved in many community activities. After the rape, her behavior deteriorated as she tried to come to terms with the trauma. However, she did not have a severe emotional/mental problem as defined by psychiatry. Neither did she have a character flaw. By keeping in mind that she was an essentially normal person, the negotiators avoided the judgments that sometimes are made about suicidal people. This made it easier for negotiators to work with her because they could accept her as a normal person who was trying to cope with an abnormal situation.

Second, the incident illustrates the importance of the crisis manager being available at the time of the incident. Had a trained response team not been available, it would have been up to the woman's friends and the patrol officer to manage the situation. By being available on a 24-hour-a-day basis, the response team could help the woman calm down, consider her options, and change what had been a poor initial decision.

Third, the negotiators were actively involved both in defusing the woman's intense feelings and in rethinking the possible solutions to her problems. After recognizing her pain, they were able to point out to her that it was temporary even though at the time it might seem permanent, that the anxiety and depression both interfered with her ability to think logically so that both the decision to move to her parents' house and the decision to kill herself were only partly thought through and that there were other solutions to her problems. They focused on her feelings and on problem-solving.

Fourth, the incident illustrates the effectiveness of the team approach in crisis intervention. While the primary negotiator focused her attention on the woman in crisis, other team members worked on necessary elements. The tactical team provided security. The secondary negotiator and the psychologist gathered information, contacted friends, and brainstormed ideas that might have solved the problem. Everybody could focus on their job, without having to worry about their own survival.

Model of Intervention in a Crisis

Hoff (1989) has defined crisis intervention as "a short-term helping process. It focuses on resolution of the immediate problem through the use of personal, social and environmental resources." She suggests that there are four basic steps in crisis management:

1. Psychosocial assessment of the individual or family in crisis, including an evaluation of the risk of suicide or assault on others

2. Development of a plan with the person or family in crisis

3. Implementation of the plan, drawing on personal, social, or material resources

4. Follow-up and evaluation of the crisis management process and the resolution of the crisis

The psychosocial assessment of a person in crisis includes: (1) an assessment of the potential for danger to self or others (Is the person suicidal or homicidal?) (See Chapter 7, Negotiating with Emotionally Disturbed Individuals, and Chapter 9, Intelligence and Intelligence Gathering); (2) an assessment of the nature of the precipitating incident; (3) an assessment of the stage in the development of the crisis in which intervention is occurring; (4) an assessment of the individual manifestations and meaning of the crisis for the subject; and (5) an assessment of what interpersonal, social, or family support the individual has that are relevant to the crisis. It is called a psychosocial assessment because it includes an evaluation of the social resources available to the person as well as his or her individual resources. A suicidal person, for instance, will often feel isolated and alone because of the recent loss of a close relationship. The person is likely to be focused on the loss rather than the friends and family that he or she still has. The negotiator needs to inquire about the people that still care for the person and who can support the person as he or she is working through the crisis.

After a systematic evaluation, the development of the crisis management plan needs to involve both the crisis manager and the person in crisis. The former can facilitate the defusing of emotions and focus the subject on steps in the problem-solving process. The latter is responsible for taking a realistic look at his or her life situation, evaluating whether it is getting the person what he or she wants, and planning and carrying out changes that are more likely to get him or her what he or she wants (Glasser, 1984). For instance, a subject who took his counselor hostage at knifepoint in a mental health center informed the negotiator that he had been trying to get an appointment and medication for two days and that nobody would see him, so he brought the knife to get attention. The negotiator told the subject that he understood how frustrating it was to be ignored, that he would be angry, too. However, he wondered if holding the knife at his counselor's throat was getting him the kind of attention he wanted. Specifically, he wondered if the threat was getting him his medication. When the subject said no, the negotiator asked what else the subject could think of that might get him what he wanted without the police presence. The subject said he could have gone to the medical center or to a private physician's office. He and the negotiator discussed how he would know early that he was in need of medication and what he would do to get it before it became a crisis for him the next time. Then they agreed that he needed to let his counselor go before anybody could give him his medication now.

In the implementation of a crisis plan, it is essential that everyone understand who does what, where, when, how, and why. In implementing the plan, the timing of events is important. Frequently, people think they have an agreement in principle that is undermined by different timetables. A lack of understanding may lead to behavior that seems premature and impulsive. It may create a new crisis in an attempt to solve an old one. In the above incident at the mental health center, it was important for the officers on the perimeter to know that the subject had agreed to come out and when, so that they did not take his surrender as an aggressive act. The subject needed to understand exactly when, where, and how he was to come out of his counselor's office, and how he was to respond to the officers on the perimeter so he could keep his anxiety under control and not do anything impulsive because of his fear of the unknown.

In most crisis incidents that police manage, follow-up and evaluation of the plan is lacking. Frequently, negotiators turn the subject over to detention or mental health professionals and do not follow up on the long-range outcome. However, a systematic follow-up has several advantages: it allows the negotiator to obtain information on the effectiveness of the intervention; it gives negotiators a chance to clarify any misunderstandings; and it shows interest in the person beyond the immediate crisis, establishing police credibility with the subject in the event that they have to deal with him in the future. This is one area in which prison and jail negotiators have a distinct advantage over the police negotiator. Often, the hostage taker remains in the facility and the negotiator can conduct repeated follow-up visits.

A negative example of the importance of follow-up was seen in a recent incident involving a veteran with an alcohol problem. He fired shots into the air and then barricaded himself in his apartment. Negotiators were effective in getting the man to surrender by promising to take him to the local VA hospital. When the admitting physician was approached about the man's admission, she refused to consider it, stating that the VA had no facilities for someone who was drunk and aggressive. Rather than following up with the subject and explaining the difficulty, the negotiators let the subject be booked for aggravated assault, thinking that he would be seen in the jail the next day by the county psychiatrist. The subject was angry about what he considered the negotiator's bad faith. He told the detectives investigating the case that he was not going to go down easily the next time and that there would be a next time. Following through with an explanation of the difficulties with the admitting physician may well have reduced the possibility of future aggressive encounters.

Goals in a Crisis: National Organization of Victims' Assistance

The National Organization of Victims' Assistance has suggested that there are three major goals for crisis managers. All interventions need to be built around and evaluated in light of these general goals. They are:

1. Assuring the safety and security of the person in crisis

2. Allowing ventilation of intense feelings and the validation of those feelings to the person in crisis

3. Facilitating prediction and planning by the person in crisis

In a crisis, safety refers to physical safety of the person involved in the incident, while security means building emotional trust between the subject and the negotiator (NOVA, 1992). Both of these issues need to be addressed before people in crisis can move on to problem solving. Physical safety can be addressed by asking about the subject's well-being and reassuring him of the control the negotiator has of his side of the event. Emotional security takes longer to build and depends on the negotiator's ability to communicate understanding of the subject as well as the negotiator's ability to make good on agreements. A negotiator who reflects the person's meaning builds emotional security faster than one who cannot (see Intervention During the Crisis Stage, below). The negotiator who shows good faith early in the incident by following through on agreements demonstrates trustworthiness, helping to develop trust between the negotiator and the subject.

The process of ventilation and validation refers to the negotiator's ability to accept and encourage both the subject's story and the feelings that go along with it. Both help to defuse intense emotions and build rapport between the negotiator and the subject by giving the person the sense that he or she is heard, respected, and understood. Ventilation is encouraged by inviting the person to tell his or her story. By using simple statements that encourage the person to talk, door openers (Bolton, 1984; NOVA, 1992) such as "Tell me what happened." "How did you get into this?" and "How can I help you?" the negotiator can facilitate ventilation. Validation can be accomplished in a number of ways. An attentive silence is perhaps the simplest. Paraphrasing, reflection of feelings, and reflection of meaning are others (see Intervening During Crisis, below).

Finally, prediction and preparation in a crisis focuses on evaluating the likely outcome of the subject's options and laying out a detailed course of action. Prediction has two goals: the realization that the subject's current attempt at a solution has high costs and low gains, and that another option has lower costs and higher gains for the person. It is important to emphasize that the costs and gains of any particular solution have to be evaluated from the standpoint of the subject, not necessarily the negotiator. Preparation involves the systematic development of a detailed plan for who is going to do what, when, where, how, and why. In crisis, the preparation focuses on the near future: it is practical and it anticipates both practical and emotional issues (NOVA, 1992).

Skills in Crisis Management

The skills used by crisis managers depend on a number of factors. The appropriateness of the skills used during negotiations will depend on the stage of the crisis at the time of the intervention. For instance, the Crisis Stage will require more reassurance and active listening than will the Accommodation Stage, because emotions need to be defused and rapport needs to be built during this stage. Below are some of the skills appropriate to each stage of a crisis.

Intervention During the Crisis Stage

During the Crisis Stage, negotiators need to gather intelligence that helps them understand the subject's issues (substantive issues) personality, and motives; defuse intense emotions (manage emotions); and build a relationship (attunement) with the hostage taker.

As Hoff (1989) points out, a psychosocial assessment of the person, the person's problem, and the person's resources for solving the problem are the first steps in crisis management. Such an assessment relies on intelligence. Intelligence gathering begins when the negotiators are first notified of an incident. On the way to the scene, they can ask to have the officer who responded to the call available when they arrive. They can ask the dispatcher to check the records for the number and kinds of calls made at the location of the incident during the prior six months. If there is an identification of the hostage taker, the negotiators can ask for a records check, get in touch with other agencies who might have experience with the hostage taker, and start identifying friends and neighbors. At the scene, they can interview the responding officer, witnesses to the incident, neighbors, family, or friends of the hostage taker to get a sense of what is happening with the person.

After the preliminary assessment of the person, the negotiator needs to plan an opening that will reassure the hostage taker, allow him to tell his or her story, and build understanding. Generally, it is as simple as "Hello, I am Officer _____ from the _____ Police Department. We have everything under control out here. How can I help you?" or "How are things going in there?" The reassurance is important because most people are exposed to the police through the media, which plays up the conflict and confrontations around police work. Most people expect an aggressive confrontation. Opening with reassurance challenges that expectation and helps increase the hostage taker's sense of safety and security. Similarly, asking about his or her well-being underscores the negotiator's concern about the subject's safety and security.

After the introduction, most hostage takers will tell their story. The negotiator's job is to use effective listening skills to defuse the incident and to let the hostage taker know that he or she is being heard and understood. Listening for the emotional content, intensity, and emphasis of the hostage taker's message and reflecting it back to the hostage taker is an essential step in defusing the emotions of the Crisis Stage. It lets the hostage taker know the negotiator hears what is being said, that the negotiator hears what is important to the hostage taker, and that the negotiator accepts the hostage taker as a person. This kind of listening is called active listening, because it involves actively letting the other person know what the negotiator is hearing (Bolton, 1984).

The New York Police Department has adopted the motto "talk to me" to highlight the most important aspect of crisis intervention—getting the subject to talk. Talking helps the subject come down off the emotional high that occurs during the Crisis Stage. The negotiator can do something to encourage the subject to talk and build a relationship that will make the negotiator influential. The negotiator can listen. Active listening skills are fundamental to negotiations. They open the door for developing a relationship with the subject, they give the negotiator a non-threatening way of responding to the subject that is disarming and invites cooperation. Active listening skills include:

1. **Minimal Encouragers**—brief, well-timed responses that let the subject know the negotiator is paying attention (Noesner & Webster, 1998; Bolton, 1984; McMains & Lanceley, 1995). Most people want an audience, so showing that you are paying attention is a powerful response that generally keeps the subject talking and begins to build a relationship.

> *Use:* Minimal encouragers can be used any time during the incident to show the subject that the negotiator is listening, interested, and wants to hear more. It is a neutral, non-threatening response that can be used with any subject. If it is effective, it keeps the subject talking and leads to more information.

Example: If a prisoner says, "Get back. I want you guys out of the pod. I want to talk to the governor and I want to transfer to the Dominguez Unit."

A good minimal response would be "And?" because it opens the door for more explanation without challenging the subject.

A poor response would be "All the units are alike. Why don't you stay here?" because it is challenging, forcing the subject to defend his or her position, and is likely to lead to an increase in tension.

2. **Paraphrasing**—the negotiator repeating the subject's meaning in the negotiator's words (Bolton, 1984; Noesner & Webster, 1998). It shows that the negotiator is listening and understands the content of the subject's message. It allows the subject the opportunity to clarify the message, if it was not completely understood.

Use: Paraphrasing can be used any time the negotiator wants to be sure he has understood the subjects' message, any time he wants the subject to know that he has understood the message, or any time he needs to stall for time. It is a particularly effective way of responding to the subject's demands, because it makes it clear that the negotiator has heard the demands without agreeing to anything. It can be used with any subject, regardless of personality, because it is essentially a straightforward information exchange. It can be used in negotiations or crisis intervention.

Example: A subject who was barricaded in his apartment with his common-law wife after the neighbors called about a disturbance said, during the initial contact, "Get out of here or I am going to kill this bitch. I never did like her know-it-all smile and it is really beginning to bug me."

A good paraphrase would be, "You would like us to leave or you may hurt somebody. You are bothered by her attitude" because it shows that the negotiator has heard the message. It softens the person's statement and it invites the subject to say more. It shows interest.

A poor paraphrase would be, "I can't do anything for you when you talk like that" because it begins to set limits too early. It negates the person's message about his irritation with his wife's attitude and it communicates a lack of understanding on the part of the negotiator that will make it difficult for the subject to talk because he has to work too hard to be understood.

3. **Emotional Labeling**—the use of emotionally descriptive words to show that the negotiator understands the feelings the subject is experiencing (Bolton, 1984; Noesner & Webster, 1998; McMains & Lanceley, 1995). It is used without comment about the validity of the feelings. It helps deepen the relationship between the negotiator and the subject because feelings are more personal than content and reflecting them accurately shows a deeper understanding of the subject.

> *Use:* Emotional labeling can be used any time the subject expresses strong feelings that need to be defused. It can be used to communicate a deep understanding or to check on the negotiator's understanding of the problem. It is particularly effective with normal people who are in crisis, inadequate, borderline, dependent, suicidal, or angry people who need to be defused. It is the keystone of crisis intervention.
>
>> *Example:* A subject who was angry about her husband's wanting to leave her for another woman said, "I have the two adulterous SOBs in here and I am going to make them pay. Nobody should get away with hurting other people this way. They are going to know what it is like."
>>
>> A good use of emotional labeling would be "You sound pretty upset and hurt about being left. It doesn't seem fair" because it recognizes the feelings without judging them. It helps identify the hurt that underlies the anger.
>>
>> A poor response would be "You don't need to feel that way. If he was messing around on you, he was not worth the energy." It is judgmental. It tells the subject how not to feel. It minimizes the subject's feelings, which are a major part of who she is.

4. **Mirroring**—the negotiator repeating the last word or phrase. It communicates to the subject both that the negotiator is attending to what is being said and that the negotiator understands what is being said.

> *Use:* This technique can be used early in the negotiation to gather more information about the actor and the incident without being confrontational. It helps build rapport. It allows the subject to lead the conversation, so the issue of who is in charge is avoided. It can be used with most subjects in either negotiations or crisis intervention. It is particularly effective in the crisis stage, when the negotiator is still trying to get enough information to understand what the subject's issues are.
>
>> *Example:* A trapped armed robber in a bank might say, "I have to get out of here with the money. It's for my kid. It's not for me."

A good mirroring response would be "For your kid." To which the robber might say, "Yeah. He's got a fever and an infection and we don't have money for the pills he's supposed to take. He needs the money for the pills."

A poor mirroring response would be "You expect me to believe that it's not for you?" because it is too judgmental and misses the primary point of the subject's message.

5. **Open-ended questions**—questions that encourage the subject to talk (Noesner & Webster, 1998; McMains & Lanceley, 1995).

> *Use:* Open-ended questions are used any time during negotiations or crisis intervention when more information is needed to understand what is happening, or the negotiator needs to stall and cannot think of anything else to say, or to keep the attention on the subject. It is important to ask open-ended questions in the crisis stage to help clarify what is going on and to give the subject the impression that the negotiator is paying close attention to him or her. They can be used with any type of person.
>
> > *Example:* A local businessman barricaded himself in his apartment, threatening to kill himself when his wife showed him the credit card receipts from his affair. He said, "I just can't have it known that I had an affair. It would be too much, if people knew that my wife and I are having trouble. People have always thought we were the perfect couple."
> >
> > A good open-ended question would be "Sounds like a tough deal. Tell me how it all happened." It is non-judgmental, shows interest, and is likely to lead to more information about the man's situation.
> >
> > A poor response would be "Do you have a gun? What kind? How many bullets do you have?" because it forces the man into one-word answers, gives the impression that the negotiator is more interested in the gun than the man, and communicates a sense of urgency that will build rather than defuse tension.

6. **"I-messages"**—messages that personalize the negotiator without it becoming a personal attack (Noesner & Webster, 1998). They let the negotiator send a message about how things affect him or her without blaming the subject. It takes the form of "When _____ happens, I feel _____, because _____." (Bolton, 1984; McMains & Lanceley, 1995). They can be used to show the subject different ideas about the situation in an indirect way that does not threaten the subject or arouse his or her tendency to resist being told what to do.

Use: "I-messages" can be used toward the end of the crisis stage or during the negotiation or resolution stage, when the negotiator judges that the subject is calm enough to hear alternatives that are presented in a non-threatening way.

> *Example:* A man broke into his own home after having agreed to stay at his mother's house because of the strained relationship between him and his wife. He had been drinking and he had a rifle. He fired two rounds into the ceiling of the home. After negotiators made contact and he began to settle down, he said, "If you will just bring my wife over, I know we can work this out. We have done it before when things got rough."
>
> A good "I-message" would be "When there is alcohol involved, I get worried, because it makes people do funny things." It suggests that as long as the man is drinking, he will not be able to see his wife because the negotiator is uncomfortable, not because of something the man has done. It is non-threatening and the man does not have to defend himself.
>
> A poor response would be "As long as you are drinking, I am not going to let you see your wife because you are more likely to hurt her." It is a poor response because it puts the responsibility on the man and makes it more likely that he will feel as though he has to defend his position.

7. **Effective pauses**—periods of silence that are used to emphasize a point (Noesner & Webster, 1998) or to encourage the subject to say more (McMains & Lanceley, 1995). They can also be used to help defuse an intense emotional harangue. By being quiet and not responding to an attack, negotiators can sidestep a confrontation and allow the subject the time to vent his frustration, anger, and hurt.

> *Use:* Effective pauses are used after the subject seems to have finished saying all he has to say about a topic, or when the negotiator has made an important point. It is simply waiting 10 to 15 seconds before saying anything more or simply not responding after a temper tantrum. It can be used at any time in a negotiation or crisis intervention. It is particularly important to wait after a person who is depressed seems to have finished, because they sometimes have more to say, but process thoughts more slowly than a non-depressed person.
>
> > *Example:* In trying to assess the resources a depressed person has available, the negotiator may ask, "What did you do to feel better when you were depressed before?" but does not get an immediate response.

A good response would be simply waiting 10 seconds more, because it allows the depressed person time to respond and it uses a person's discomfort with silences to put subtle pressure on them to talk.

A poor response would be asking two more questions in that 10 seconds, because it does not give the person time to work at their pace and it exposes the negotiator's discomfort with silences and with the lack of action. It increases the stress on the person.

8. **Reflecting meaning**—the ability to show the subject that the negotiator understands the content, emotion, and implications of his or her situation. It is used to summarize understanding, to give the subject a chance to clarify any issue the negotiator does not understand, and to build rapport (McMains & Lanceley, 1995). It takes the form of "When _____ happens, you feel _____, because _____." It looks to what the subject expects to happen as a result of whatever followed "When."

Use: Reflecting meaning can be used whenever the negotiator thinks that he or she understands the subject's problems well enough to help solve them and to check on the accuracy of his or her understanding. It is generally used during the adaptation stage to help define the problem. It is effective after the subject has calmed down and is ready to focus on the issues. It can be used with any personality type.

Example: The 28-year-old subject who is angry and suicidal because his mother threw him out of the house says, "I've had it with the whole deal. I lose my job and my truck because I can't make the payments. Now, she's evicting me. I've got nowhere to go. I'll show her, she'll be sorry when I'm gone."

A good reflection of meaning would be "When you think about being out there by yourself, it's pretty scary, because you're afraid you can't make it by yourself, especially with no job and no way to get around. And, when you think about your mother wanting you to leave, you get angry and want to get back at her, because you don't think she has a right to do that." It shows attention and a depth of understanding. It clearly defines the problem for both the subject and the negotiator.

A poor response would be "Why would you want to do that? You can handle it like a man. It's time you were on your own, anyway." This response challenges the subject, is judgmental, and seems to side with the mother, with whom the subject is angry. It is not likely to build rapport.

Case Study: During the first contact with a subject who was barricaded in his house after firing shots at the neighbors, the negotiator heard:

> "Just go away. You are on their side. You've never helped me before. All those times I told you they were bugging me and you never did anything about it. I finally gave up on the police. I'll take care of this myself. To hell with you."

Using paraphrasing, the negotiator responded,

> "Let me be sure I've got this straight. You'd like me to go away because you've called several times before and have not gotten the problem solved. Is that right?"

To which the subject responded,

> "Well, I don't want you to go away so much as the police. They've just never been much help. They keep saying this whole situation is a civil matter. Those people have been harassing me for six months now and I can't get them to quit. It looks like somebody could do something."

Reflecting feelings can be used by the negotiator to help defuse the intensity of the subject's emotions and to help build rapport in relationships. By recognizing and naming the feelings the subject is experiencing, the negotiator gives the subject a way of ventilating the feelings in a controlled way. This usually reduces the intensity by allowing the subject to ventilate and it keeps his or her fear of the feelings getting out of control in check by letting the subject know that the negotiator is able to deal with emotions without fear or anger of his own.

After hearing the statement above about the subject's six months of problems with the neighbors, the negotiator said

> "It sounds like you are really frustrated since you have been trying to get something done here for six months and nothing seems to be working."

The person responded, saying

> "You're d_____ right I'm frustrated. Anybody would be. Those d_____ people keep throwing their s_____ over the fence into my yard. They come in the middle of the night and disturb my dogs, waking everybody up. They won't listen when I try to tell them to knock it off. The cops don't do s_____. Nothing's happening. At least shooting got people's attention."

Note that the message takes the form of: "When X happens, you feel Y." "When you try for six months to get the problem with your neighbors harassing you solved and nothing changes, you feel frustrated and helpless." The reflection of the frustration gave the person a chance to air his grievance in more detail. The negotiator obtained information about the nature of the problem, on some of the things the person had tried to do to solve it, and some clues as to the specific issues that needed to be solved in order to resolve the crisis.

The choice of words used to describe how the sender feels depends on the intensity of the feelings talked about and the point in the crisis at which the negotiator focuses on the feelings. Early in negotiations, when the goal is to establish the fact that the negotiator understands the other person, the feeling words need to be a fairly accurate reflection of the intensity experienced by the other person. In the above example, the negotiator would want to use "frustrated," "angry," or "p_____ off" as opposed to "disturbed" or "upset." Later in the process, the negotiator could use a less intense word, because it would help redefine the situation for the person as less serious. The negotiator can use Table 2.1 as a general guide to the intensity of feelings expressed by certain words.

Reflecting meaning communicates understanding and builds rapport by adding the subject's assumptions about the implications of the situation to the communication. It says, "I understand not only what you are saying and how you feel but I understand what you expect to happen." It brings into the open unspoken thoughts about the situation and allows for the clarification of faulty assumptions. Reflection of meaning generally takes the form of: "When X happens, you feel Y, because Z," where X again is the event that generates the feelings, Y is the feeling, and Z is the person's expectations about X.

After the man above responded by describing what he had done to try and deal with his neighbors, the negotiator said:

> "Are you saying that when you try so many things to get cooperation from your neighbors and nothing works, it is frustrating because you don't think anything will ever work?"

The man responded:

> "Yes, that's it. I don't think this thing can be solved. They won't listen to me."

During the Crisis Stage, the negotiator can start the hostage taker thinking about his situation. Problem-solving questions are helpful. Problem-solving questions raise doubts about the hostage taker's having taken hostages, having made demands, or having threatened violence, without directly challenging him. In the incident above, the negotiator might say, "Explain to me how firing your gun into the air improves your situation. How does it solve your problems with your neighbors?"

Problem-solving questions allow the person in crisis to maintain the illusion of control by putting him in the position of the teacher and the negotiator in the position of the student. At the same time, they raise doubts about the usefulness of the hostage taker's position. They move the hostage taker's prediction and planning in a direction the police want him to go.

Knowing When the Crisis Is Defused

The authors have found that one of the difficult decisions for negotiators is when to start trying to influence the subject. When is the crisis defused enough to start problem solving? Strentz (1995) has suggested that there are 10 indicators that an incident is de-escalating. They are:

1. No hostage has been killed since the incident began.
2. The threats toward the hostages have decreased.
3. The subject is spending more time talking.
4. Demands are transitioning from substantive to expressive.
5. Lower and slower tone of voice.
6. The subject starts talking about captives as people.
7. Deadlines pass without action or accident.
8. Exchanges occur without incident.
9. Captives have been released.
10. A relationship develops between the subject and the negotiator.

In addition, the authors suggest that the negotiator is not ready to switch to problem-solving until he or she is sure that they understand the subject's problem. At the very least, the negotiator should be able to answer the five "Ws" and an "H": Who is involved (not just the name but the personality of the person involved), What has happened (both before the incident and during the incident), Where it happened (and what the location means to the subject), When it happened (what the time tells you about whether the subject expected to be interrupted), Why it happened (the subject's needs) and How it happened.

Strentz (1995) points out that crises are not resolved in a linear way. That is, they do not start with high emotion and come straight down in intensity if the negotiators do everything correctly. Rather, as crises are resolved, emotions tend to fluctuate around a line that is generally decreasing in intensity. It is unrealistic for negotiators to think that emotions can be defused quickly or once and for all. They should be sensitive to the overall direction of the negotiations, rather than getting caught up in the emotions of the subject at a particular moment.

Intervention During the Accommodation/Negotiation Stage

During the Accommodation/Negotiation Stage, the person in crisis usually becomes more open to alternative solutions to his problem. He may experience frustration over his efforts to solve his problems. However, he is able to evaluate his own situation and the likelihood that his chosen course of action will get him what he wants. He will try out new ideas of his own and is more open to suggestions. The negotiator's job is to help the hostage taker come to the realization that there are better solutions to his situation than taking and threatening hostages. However, the negotiator must get suggestions to the hostage taker without raising his resistance. A key issue during this stage is guiding the negotiation in a direction the negotiator wants it to go while not challenging the hostage taker's sense of control. Any time people feel a loss of control, stress is created, judgment is impaired, and crisis occurs (Bandura et al., 1977; Glasser, 1984; Everly, 1989).

Two ways of working with the hostage taker's natural resistance to being controlled are possible. They include:

1. I messages (Bolton, 1984)

2. Embedded Statements (Elgin, 1980) (McMains & Lanceley, 1995)

I messages take the form "When X happens, I Y because Z," and they express the negotiator's concern about the validity of an idea, demand, or proposal. For instance, if the hostage taker demands $1 million in cash, the negotiator might say, "When I hear about that much money, I really feel overwhelmed because I can see a mountain of money towering over me." Such a statement does not challenge the demand or the hostage taker's idea directly. Rather, it suggests an image that says, "One million dollars will be a burden to transport." It indirectly suggests that the demand will create new problems to be solved: the problem of how to transport and manage that much money.

Embedded statements have two parts. One part assumes things to be a reality. The second part focuses the person's attention, reducing his attention to the first part. This makes it more likely that the person will accept the assumed part. After negotiations have progressed for a while, the negotiator might say, "When these things go as well as they have so far, they usually turn out good for everyone." Such a statement focuses on how well things have gone so far and implies that they will turn out well for the negotiators, for the hostages, and for the hostage taker. It sets the stage for a negotiated solution that takes everyone into account. It does not challenge the hostage taker with statements like, "We have to take everybody's needs into account before we can settle this."

At the same time, the negotiator's goal is to generate solutions that are acceptable to both the police and the hostage taker. To do this, he may have to use problem-solving skills. He can move the process into a problem-solving mode by saying something like, "We seem to be at a stalemate. I wonder if it might not be because we haven't figured out what the problem is yet? Let's back up and see if we can work through this again." This statement can help make the transition to the five problem-solving steps. Even if the negotiator cannot get the subject to go through the problem-solving steps with him, it is helpful to go through them with the negotiating team to be sure that as many alternatives as possible are considered. Those steps are:

1.   Defining the problem;

2.   Brainstorming all possible solutions;

3.   Eliminating all totally unacceptable solutions;

4.   Choosing a solution that both can live with;

5.   Planning the implementation; and

6.   Implementing the plan. (Bolton, 1984)

Defining the problem. Defining the problem requires two things: that the negotiators look at the situation from the hostage taker's point of view and that they take all of the hostage taker's needs into consideration. As Glasser (1984) has pointed out, people are motivated by a need for belonging, for control and power, for freedom, and for fun, in addition to their need for survival. Unless the negotiator considers the impact of each of these, he is not defining the problem completely. It is helpful for one negotiator to have the responsibility of thinking through the problem from the hostage taker's point of view whenever the negotiators are trying to define the problem (McMains & Lanceley, 1995).

In the example involving the frustrated neighbor, the immediate problem was the man's firing the weapon and barricading himself versus the need of the police to restore peace and order. However, looking at the situation from the perspective of the man's frustrating history, the problem can be defined as the person's need to gain some control over the situation versus the neighbors' need to maintain some control themselves. It can be broken down into a number of specific issues: for example, garbage dumping, waking a dog in the early morning hours, and the ways the neighbors deal with conflict. The solutions that need to be worked out before the police can achieve their goals are more complex than the immediate situation. Without a careful definition of the problem, a lasting solution cannot be developed.

Brainstorming all possible solutions. During this step, the goal is to develop as many ideas as possible. Therefore, no criticism is allowed. Every possible solution to the incident is put on the board. Again, it is helpful to have one negotiator play the role of the hostage taker and to come up with as many ideas as possible that reflect the hostage taker's point of view.

Returning to the barricaded subject with the aggravating neighbors, brainstorming would include generating solutions that get at all aspects of the person's problem. Ideas such as: having the subject promise to call a contact number at the police department the next time the neighbors act out rather than shooting his weapon; the neighbors bringing their dog inside at night; moving the dog house to the other side of the yard; having the negotiator sit down with both neighbors to mediate the dispute; and posting "no trespassing" and "no dumping" signs on the fence in order to generate a charge on which the police can act are all possibilities. The idea of brainstorming is to generate as many ideas as possible without criticizing them.

Eliminating all totally unacceptable solutions. Because of the different roles the hostage taker and the police play, the solutions that are acceptable to each will vary. The solutions that are unacceptable to any side are eliminated. Generally, this will leave several solutions that are acceptable to both sides.

The frustrated man may find bringing his dog inside his house is an unacceptable solution because he got the dog to alert him to intruders. He might not like posting signs, fearing that it will aggravate the situation and, although he is frustrated, he does not want to make things worse. These two possibilities are not options for him. They would be eliminated.

Choosing a solution that both can live with. Again, in considering solutions to a crisis, it is important to see the possibilities from the standpoint of the other person's needs. As the negotiating team evaluates the options that have been brainstormed, one of them needs to play the role of the subject, keeping in mind what his most important needs are in the situation. Only solutions that are satisfactory to both the police and the subject are possible. It does not have to be the perfect solution, it just has to be one that is acceptable to both sides. For instance, freedom may not always be possible for the subject. However, he may be willing to surrender when he understands that, after going to trial, people in his situation are being put on probation.

The man in the example might consider an agreement to sit down with the negotiator and his neighbor and negotiate an agreement that will prevent further escalation. Promising to not fire his weapon any more might be acceptable, if he knows that he has a contact in the police department that will respond to his phone calls. He might even be willing to be booked on a disorderly conduct charge if he knows that people booked on that charge usually are released that same day on a promise to make their court date.

Planning the implementation. As discussed above, planning has to be detailed and specific. It needs to specify who is responsible for each part of the solution, what each part involves, where each part is going to happen, how each part is going to happen, when each part will happen, and why it will happen.

Implementing the plan. Implementing the plan in most crisis incidents involves close coordination with all the elements of the police response team that are at the location. It requires coordination with the subject and with any hostages that are involved. Everyone needs to know what to expect. Communication between negotiators and the subject, between the subject and anyone he controls, and between negotiators and the rest of the department needs to be fast, timely, and accurate. The beginning of the plan needs to be communicated clearly so that everyone involved will know when the plan is happening.

Usually, this process will include the surrender and arrest of the hostage taker, the one solution acceptable to the police. The negotiator will sometimes need to be able to show the hostage taker how this alternative is in the hostage taker's best interests. It is helpful to think about all the hostage taker's needs while defining the problem. By systematically asking what needs are important to the hostage taker, rather than just assuming that only surrender is, the negotiators can get a clearer picture of the problem (McMains & Lanceley, 1995).

Prior to the beginning of the Resolution Stage, negotiators may have gone through the problem-solving steps themselves as a way of working through ideas to present to the hostage taker. When they do, it is important for one of the police officers to put him- or herself in the hostage taker's place and generate and evaluate ideas that would be acceptable to the hostage taker (Ury, 1981). This is a powerful way of keeping the face issues in focus.

Invent Options for Mutual Gain

Solving the problem in a crisis incident involves developing alternatives that solve both the negotiators' problems and the subjects' problems. Fisher and Ury (1983) point out that there are three things that make it difficult to develop mutually acceptable alternatives:

1. Premature judgment—jumping too soon to the conclusion that you understand the other side's needs, and too quickly trying to get them to buy your solution. In the authors' experience, this is the single most difficult issue for police negotiators. Learning to check the natural impulse to get things over with quickly leads inexperienced negotiators to try to solve the problems in an incident before they fully understand the nature of the problem.

2. Assuming a fixed pie—assuming that there are a limited number of solutions to the problem. Most of the time this is reflected in the "It's my way or the highway" attitude.

3. Thinking that solving their problem is "their problem"— assuming that the problem is theirs to solve tends to lead to position bargaining, greater anxiety and tension, etc. If they could have solved it, they would not have taken hostages to begin with.

To avoid the mistakes above, it is helpful for the negotiator to specifically set aside time to look at alternatives to the situation that meet as many of the subject's interests as possible, while also meeting the negotiator's interests. This involves two steps: (1) separating the inventing of options from deciding which option to pursue and (2) brainstorming.

Separating inventing from deciding—It is frequently helpful to separate trying to generate acceptable options from deciding on which option to pursue. Inventing allows for the active consideration of all the options that might be available. It allows for the generation of ideas that may not be useful but may lead to other ideas that are. Deciding involves assessing the value of each specific idea in solving the current situation. Combining the two has the potential for leading to conflict over the value of an option before all of the alternatives are on the table. Criticizing alternatives as you go shuts down creativity.

Brainstorming—Brainstorming is a process in which all possible options are put on the table without criticism. The goal is to invent as many options as possible. It needs to take the interests of both sides into consideration. See the section on crisis intervention for a more thorough discussion. It has two rules: (1) suggest anything and (2) do not criticize.

- Look for mutual gain
- Look for shared interests
- Dovetail differing interests
- Ask for their preferences

Case Study Revisited: The negotiator took the lead in suggesting options by stating "We have a lot in common. We both want this situation settled peacefully. We both know that hurting anybody, even accidentally, is only going to make the situation worse. We both want you to see your wife, even though we have some differences there: you want her to come in so you can have a private conversation, and I want her to stay out here, where it is safe, until we get things settled. How can we settle this so you can talk to your wife in private and I can be sure that she is safe?" This approach made the negotiator's needs clear, and made it clear to the subject that the negotiator understood his needs, defined the problem in a way that was inclusive rather than "your way or my way," and invited the subject to help solve the problem.

When the subject said "I could come out, but then I am going to jail and you probably won't let me see my wife, anyway," the negotiator said, "Now, on seeing your wife, I have been told that the commander will let you talk to her in a patrol car. She will be in the front seat and you in the back, to be sure that everybody stays safe. You will have 15 minutes and I will stand by to make sure nobody interrupts you two. Is that OK? Good! Now, about going to jail. I need to understand this a little better. What will happen if you go to jail?"

The subject said that the reason they did not want to go to jail was that they had been there before and his friend had had significant problems. His friend drank a lot and the last time he nearly died because he went through withdrawal while in jail and nearly died. The negotiator could then develop a plan to deal with the second subject's need to stay well.

Intervention During the Resolution Stage

During the Resolution Stage, the person's frustration may increase again. He or she will have run into a number of roadblocks and may be desperate for ideas. The negotiator may have to defuse the hostage taker through active listening, reassure him that he is safe and guide him through what to expect as he surrenders.

Case Study Revisited: Goals and Skills. The following is a condensed accounting of the intervention with the suicidal woman who had been raped. It is used to illustrate the implementation of goals and the use of specific skills as a crisis moves through the various stages.

> Negotiator: "Sue, I am Barbara. I'm a negotiator for the police department. I understand from some of the officers here that you are pretty upset. Can you tell me about it?" (quiet and attentive).

This opening accomplishes a number of things. It identifies the negotiator as somebody different from the patrol officers with whom the woman is used to working. She may not know what a negotiator does but she knows that the role is not the same as a patrol officer. Additionally, the use of a female negotiator begins the interaction with a recognition that she may not be comfortable talking with a male given the nature of the precipitating incident. Using a door opener and then being quietly attentive gives the woman a sense of control, as well as letting her know that the negotiator is interested in her and the opportunity to discuss her situation.

> Sue: "You can't help. Nobody can. He's done it before and he'll just keep doing it again. I can't get away from him. Go away. I'll take care of it myself. I'm talking with my friend. Leave me alone. "
>
> Negotiator: "Sue, you seem to think that nobody can help you. Is that right?"

Paraphrasing. It is too early in the process to reflect her feelings or meaning, even though the negotiator may be formulating some ideas. The relationship is not strong enough and more information is needed. Paraphrasing allows the negotiator to respond without getting into a struggle about going or leaving. It sends the message that the negotiator heard the main message and that she wants to know more. The negotiator does not respond to the instructions to leave, because the fact that the woman has been reaching out suggests that she really wants help.

> Sue: "Nobody's helped yet. I've seen Mischel and we've talked. The shrink put me on medications, but it doesn't help. I lost my job because I couldn't concentrate. The cops didn't keep it from happening. I'm tired. I don't want any more."

> Negotiator: "You sound pretty down: kind of hopeless, because of all the stuff you're going through. Can you tell me what happened today that makes you feel that way?"

By using reflection of feelings, the negotiator lets the woman know that she hears the depression. It validates her feelings. At the same time, the negotiator invites the woman to focus on the last 24 hours and to define the immediate situation for her. This is realistic because people who are depressed have a shortened sense of time: they get locked into the present and cannot focus well on the past or the future. In addition, it encourages ventilation.

> Sue: "I want to talk to my friends. I am on the phone. Who are you?"
>
> Negotiator: "I am Barbara. I'm here to see what I can do to help you. Your friends tell me that you were raped. I've worked with women who have been raped before. Maybe I can help. Can you tell me what happened today?'

The negotiator hears and responds to the woman's lack of trust. She does not know the negotiator. There is no reason to trust her. The negotiator tries to build a sense of trust and security by referring to the woman's friends and by sharing her previous experience with similar situations. The message is, "I've done this before and I have something to offer. You can trust me."

> Sue: "I just couldn't stand it any more today. Mischel wasn't available. The medication doesn't work. I've got to move. I'm not going. You'll have to come get me and I've got a gun. I'm not going anywhere."
>
> Negotiator: "You sound pretty desperate. We are not going to come in there. We want everybody to be safe. We will stay here to help you but we will not come in there. You are safe."

Keying on the need for safety, the negotiator reassured her.

> Sue: "You aren't coming in?"
>
> Negotiator: "Not until you say it is OK. What did you want with Mischel?"

The negotiator did not know who Mischel was, but she realized that Mischel was important to the woman. Because Mischel was mentioned in the context of what had happened during that day to precipitate the crisis, the negotiator asked about her.

> Sue: "Mischel is my therapist. I tried all day to get her. I wanted to know what to do about the move. I'm supposed to go to my parents.' I'm not leaving."

> Negotiator: "What's the problem with your parents' house?"
>
> Sue: "He is there. I can't be around him. He'll do it again. I don't know what to do."
>
> Negotiator: "You seemed confused and scared by the idea of going to your parents' house. Who is 'he'?"

Although the negotiator had already learned that the woman's brother was the rapist, she wanted the woman to say it out loud, so the conflict between her need for a place to live and her fear of her brother could be defined. Again, reflection of feelings preceded the questioning, so the woman would feel understood.

> Sue: "He is . . . I don't know if I can tell you. I guess . . . He's my brother. He's the one who did it to me. I don't . . . I can't go over there. But my folks want me to . . . they don't understand. What can I do?'
>
> Negotiator: "Sounds like the problem is that you are caught between protecting yourself and protecting your parents' feelings. You need a place to stay that is safe. You don't think your parents' house is safe because of your brother and that is scary. At the same time, you don't want to hurt your parents and you think telling them why you are having problems and why you don't want to move in with them would hurt them. The idea of hurting them is depressing you."

The negotiator used the reflection of meaning to summarize the woman's dilemma and to define the problem for both of them. It gave the woman a way of understanding the source of her anxiety.

> Sue: "That's about it."
>
> Negotiator: "Is there another way of letting them know that you won't be living there? One that will not hurt them?"

A problem-oriented question focuses the process on problem-solving:

> Sue: "I don't know. That's why I wanted to talk to Mischel. I can't decide and it helps to talk to her. But she hasn't called back all day and I have to move tonight. I'm not going."
>
> Negotiator: "Let's think of some other options . . . What would happen if you moved in with a friend and told your parents that she needed someone to take care of the house for her?"

The negotiator moves into the void left by the counselor's absence. Rather than going through the whole brainstorming process with depressed persons, it is better to ask them to focus on one option at a time. However, the option needs to offer an alternative that the negotiator believes will meet all the person's needs. Living with a friend who needs her was such an option. It allowed her a face-saving way to deal with the problem of her safety and her parents' feelings. All that remains is finding such a friend. By that time, one was at the scene.

Summary

Hostage negotiators are involved in many negotiating situations that are not hostage situations in the strictest definition of the term. Negotiators may be effectively used in situations ranging from barricaded subject incidents to stalking crimes. High-risk suicides, mental health warrants, high-risk warrants, debriefing crisis victims, and stalking are all situations in which the negotiator can be of value. In these situations, because of their unique training, special skills, and knowledge, as well as different perspective on policing, negotiators can be effectively used to resolve these situations with no injury or loss of life.

Crisis intervention is not a haphazard approach to resolving a situation. It is a process that is systematic and requires careful planning and implementation if the negotiator is to be successful. Knowing what stage of a crisis a situation is in is important for these conflict resolution decisions to be made. A negotiator will use different language and attempt to accomplish different goals in the Crisis Stage than he or she will in the Resolution Stage. Failure to understand what stage the process is in may likely result in failure to successfully resolve the crisis.

References

Aguilera, D.C. and J.N. Messick (1978). *Crisis Intervention: Theory and Methodology*. St. Louis, MO: C.J. Mosby Company.

American Justice (1994). "Hostages." Arts & Entertainment Television Network.

Bandura, A., N.E. Adams, and J. Beyer (1977). "Cognitive Processes Mediating Behavior Change." *Journal of Personality and Social Psychology* 35:125-139.

Bolton, R. (1984). *People Skills*. Englewood Cliffs, NJ: Prentice-Hall.

Boltz, F. (2001). "Intelligence Requirements in Hostage Situations." *Journal of Police Crisis Negotiations* 1(1):Spring 2001.

Buss, A.H. and R.A. Plomin (1975). *A Temperament Theory of Personality Development*. London, UK: John Wiley & Sons.

Call, J.A. (1999). "The Hostage Triad: Takers, Victims, and Negotiators." In H.V. Hall (ed.), *Lethal Violence: A Sourcebook on Fatal Domestic, Acquaintance and Stranger Violence*. Boca Raton, FL: CRC Press.

Caplan, G. (1961). *An Approach to Community Mental Health*. New York, NY: Grune and Stratton, Inc.

_____ (1964). *Principles of Preventive Psychiatry*. New York, NY: Basic Books.

Cialdini, R.B. (1984). *Influence: The New Psychology of Modern Persuasion*. New York, NY: Quill.

Elgin, S.H. (1980). *The Gentle Art of Verbal Self-Defense*. New York, NY: Dorsett Press.

_____ (1983). *More on the Gentle Art of Verbal Self-Defense*. New York, NY: Prentice-Hall.

Everly, G. (1989). *A Clinical Guide to the Treatment of the Human Stress Response*. New York, NY: Plenum Press.

Fein, R.A. and B. Vossekuil (2000). *Protective Intelligence and Threat Assessment: A Guide for State and Local Law Enforcement Officials*. Washington, DC: National Institute of Justice.

Fisher, R. and W. Ury (1993). *Getting to Yes: Negotiating without Giving In*. New York, NY: Penguin Books.

FBI (1985). "Hostage Negotiations Seminar." FBI Academy, Quantico, VA (February).

FBI (1993). "Advanced Hostage Negotiations School." San Antonio, TX (August).

Glasser, W. (1984). *Control Theory*. New York, NY: Harper and Row.

Hammer, M. and R. Rogan (1997). "Negotiation Models in Crisis Situations: The Value of a Communications-Based Approach." In Rogan, R., M. Hammer, and C. Van Zandt (eds.), *Dynamic Processes of Crisis Negotiation: Theory, Research and Practice*. London, UK: Praeger.

Hassel, C.V. (1975). "The Hostage Situation: Exploring the Motivation and Cause." *The Police Chief* (September):55-58.

Hatcher, C., K. Mohandie, J. Turner and M. Gelles (1998). "The Role of the Psychologist in Crisis/Hostage Negotiations." *Behavioral Science and the Law* 16(4):455-472.

Hoff, L.E. (1989). *People in Crisis: Understanding and Helping*. Menlo Park, CA: Addison-Wesley Publishing Co.

Lanceley, F.J. (1999). *On-Scene Guide for Hostage Negotiators*. Boca Raton, FL: CRC Press.

Maslow, A. (1954). *Motivation and Personality*. New York, NY: Harper and Row.

McMains, M.J. and F. Lanceley (1995). "The Use of Crisis Intervention Principles in Hostage Negotiations II: Stages, Skills and Objectives of Crisis Intervention." *Journal of Crisis Negotiations* 1(2):12-23.

McMains, M.J. (2005) "Negotiating with Unique Groups." Presented at The Seventeenth Annual Crisis Negotiator's Contest and Seminar. Texas State University, San Marcos, TX: January.

Miron, M.S. and A.P. Goldstein (1979). *Hostage*. New York, NY: Pergamon Press.

Mohandie, K. (2005). "Stalking and Crisis Negotiations." Presentation at New England Negotiators Association Conference. Cape Cod, MA (May).

Noesner, G.W. (1999). "Negotiations Concepts for Commanders." *FBI Law Enforcement Bulletin* 68(1):6-14.

Noesner, G.W. (1997). "Case Study: The Montana Freeman Standoff." Presented at Las Vegas Metropolitan Police Department's Crisis Management: Hostage Takers and Barricaded Subjects Seminar. Las Vegas, NV (July).

Noesner, G.W. and M. Webster (1998). "Crisis Negotiations as Crisis Intervention." In *Crisis Negotiations: A Compendium*. Quantico, VA: Crisis Negotiations Unit, CIRG, FBI Academy.

NOVA (1992). *The Community Crisis Response Team Training*. Fort Sam Houston, TX (April).

Regini, C. (2004). "Crisis Intervention for Law Enforcement Negotiators." *FBI Law Enforcement Bulletin* 73(10).

Ricketts, C. (2000). "Conflict Resolution and Negotiation Skills Training." Presented to Security, Inc., San Antonio, TX (May).

Rogan, R.G. (1997). "Emotion and Emotional Expression in Crisis Negotiations." In R.G. Rogan, M.R. Hammer, and C.R. Van Zandt (eds.), *Dynamic Processes of Crisis Negotiations: Theory, Research, and Practice*. Westport, CT: Praeger.

San Antonio Police Department (1997). "Advanced Hostage Negotiations School." San Antonio, TX (May).

Schlossberg, H. (1979a). "Basic Hostage Negotiations Seminar." Austin, TX: Texas Department of Public Safety.

_____ (1979b). "Hostage Negotiations School." Austin, TX: Texas Department of Safety.

Solis, L. (1999). "Critical Incident Management in the School Setting." Presented at TAHN Training. Austin, TX (October).

Stites, R. (2005). "Tactical Techniques for Negotiators." Presentation at Hostage/Crisis Negotiations 201. Olathe, KS (August).

Strentz, T. (1979). "Law Enforcement Policies and Ego Defenses of the Hostage." *FBI Law Enforcement Bulletin* 48:1-12.

_____ (1995). "The Cyclic Crisis Negotiations Time Line." *Law and Order* 43(3):73

Tavris, C. (1989). *Anger: The Misunderstood Emotion*. New York, NY: Bantam Books.

Tyhurst, J.S. (1986). "The Role of Transition States—Including Disasters—In Mental Illness." In *Proceedings of Symposium on Preventive and Social Psychiatry*. Washington DC: U.S. Government Printing Office.

Ury, W. (1981). *Getting Past No: Negotiating with Difficult People*. New York, NY: Bantam Books.

Discussion Questions

1. If you were the first officer arriving at the scene of the armed robbery at the beginning of the chapter, what would you do to help make the incident negotiable? What would you say to the subjects to calm them? What would you notice that might be helpful to the crisis negotiators when they got there?

2. You are a patrol officer and are sent to a domestic disturbance called in by a neighbor. The husband has been drinking and has ordered his wife out of the house, but he has two small children in the house. The wife tells you that the

conflicts have been going on for several years, that she is tired of it, and she is leaving him. When you approach the house, it is evident the husband is still in the Crisis Stage, threatening to kill the kids, to punish the wife. Is this a hostage situation? What techniques would you use to help him deal with the loss of face (self-esteem) that he is experiencing?

3. You are negotiating with a hostage taker and he looks out the window and sees SWAT officers changing locations. He thinks they are moving in for an assault. Which of the four issues that lead to conflict in the SAFE model are you likely to have to deal with (there are more than one)? How would you deal with them?

4. Which active listening skills are helpful in defusing the incident and developing trust and which are better used in problem solving? Why?

5. What can negotiators do to get the hostage taker to ventilate and validate?

6. How is saving face an important concept in negotiations? How do you help a subject save face?

7. As a brainstorming exercise, get together with at least three other people and generate as many uses for a Styrofoam cup as possible. Remember, do not criticize or evaluate the ideas as they are offered.

8. Watch the evening news, focusing on an emotional interview. Using Bolton's ratings of word intensity, assess the writer's emotional involvement in these issues. Give examples to defend your assessment.

9. List eight clues that an incident is defused (the emotions are under control) enough to move to the problem-solving phase?

10. Several factors that affect the duration of an incident were listed in this chapter. Which factors do negotiators have some control over and which ones do they not have control over? How would you minimize the negative impact of the factors over which you had control, if you were the negotiator at a school where six children were being held hostage by a fellow student in the fifth grade classroom?

Demands and the Effects of Time

3

1. Understand the difference between expressive and instrumental demands.

2. Understand the characteristics and nature of demands.

3. Understand how to prepare for and anticipate demands.

4. Learn the three theories of motivation and understand how to use those to your advantage during a barricade or hostage situation.

5. Know which demands are negotiable and which demands are non-negotiable.

6. Know how to handle and respond to demands when they are made by the hostage taker.

7. Know how (and why) to turn a demand into a sub-demand.

8. Know and understand the importance of time in negotiation situations.

9. Know how time can work for the negotiator.

10. Know what the negative effects of time are and how to mitigate those effects during a negotiated situation.

Metro Police negotiators responded to a hostage situation at Metro City Hall. A lone gunman had entered and threatened workers in the utility payment office. Witnesses stated that he was extremely angry and irate concerning his electricity being turned off for non-payment of his utility bill. Negotiators arrived before he harmed anyone. Negotiators learned that his name was Dave and that he was "fed up with the _____ paper pushers that could care less about anyone. All they were interested in was drawing a paycheck." Whenever negotiators tried to talk about resolving the electric bill in some other manner so that Dave could have electricity at his house, Dave would become agitated, emotional, and threatening, and threaten to hurt someone. When the primary negotiator asked Dave about his family, he became even angrier and more agitated. The primary figured that was a "trigger" and avoided discussing family. Several hours into negotiations with no progress being made, and Dave still becoming emotional and threatening anytime mention was made of his utility problems, intelligence officers learned that Dave's ex-wife had been able to change the divorce decree and visitation rights agreement so that Dave no longer shared custody of his two daughters. The secondary negotiator then suggested to the primary that she probe Dave's family life with him (carefully) and explore his relationship with his children and ex-wife. The primary negotiator did, and over the next couple of hours got Dave to talk about his family life, how much he missed his kids, why his wife was so vindictive, how her lawyer raked him over the coals, and other issues involving Dave and his girls. Soon, all issues concerning the utility problems were forgotten and the primary negotiator and Dave engaged in problem solving concerning how he could regain custody of his kids. About three hours later, Dave laid down his weapon and surrendered to police.

Demands in Hostage Situations

All hostage takers make demands. Without demands, there can be no hostage situation. Dealing effectively with a hostage taker's demands is a cornerstone of successful negotiation. A popular misconception regarding demands is that hostage takers make demands on the spur of the moment and negotiators react to demands. The truth is, hostage takers make demands based upon the situational milieu. The demands of the criminal hostage taker will be part of a freedom "package." Escape, no prison time, a protest of prison conditions, removal of all police, and money may all be requested as part of this package. In a domestic situation, the demands will likely center on spouse issues, visitation rights, or removing children from a family situation. The stalker who takes the victim hostage may demand love and affection from the hostage. The schizophrenic may want his delusion resolved; the depressed person may want to commit suicide. Prisoners may want improved living conditions or more fair grievance procedures from the prison administration. Terrorists may want publicity or concessions from a government (Fuselier, 1988). Regardless of whether the hostage taker has carefully constructed the demand package or whether his demands are based upon changing needs, demands are the key issue the negotiator will have to deal with before the situation can be resolved (Biggs, 1987).

Some demands may be made to satisfy immediate needs. Food, water, heat or air conditioning, cigarettes, matches, etc., all may be requested to satisfy need states. Hostage situations take time to resolve and are highly stressful. The stress and fatigue inherent in these situations can vastly increase basic need states. Demands that satisfy immediate needs are indirectly related to the freedom "package." These demands can help build rapport and trust between the hostage taker and the negotiator, ease the stress of the situation, and get hostages released.

Miron and Goldstein (1979) and Noesner and Webster (1998) describe demands as being either instrumental or expressive. Instrumental demands are physical-type demands. Escape, money, vehicles, no jail time, etc. are all instrumental demands. Expressive demands are intended to ventilate or reduce emotions. Ventilating to release frustration and anger is an expressive demand, as are shouting, demanding attention, etc. Expressive demands may also be used by the hostage taker as an expression of power. They may not be overtly stated by the hostage taker and must therefore be inferred by the negotiator. If both instrumental and expressive demands are not satisfied, the hostage situation cannot be resolved. In the 1987 Oakdale, Louisiana, prison siege, Cuban inmates went on a rampage and seized the federal prison, including 54 prison officers. The prisoners wanted several concessions from the government, including guarantees of no deportation back to Cuba and fair and impartial review of individual cases. Negotiators agreed rather quickly to these demands. To their consternation, the prisoner riot worsened—the prisoners became more violent and belligerent and, in essence, refused to accept what was offered. The negotiators had satisfied the instrumental demands of the prisoners, but had completely overlooked the prisoners' expressive demands (anger and frustration in dealing with the government). As a result, negotiation efforts were disrupted and the riot lasted nine days (Fuselier, Van Zandt & Lanceley, 1989). Borderline personalities may also verbalize instrumental demands while the real issues center around expressive demands (Borum & Strentz, 1992). The borderline individual may take coworkers hostage and demand a pay raise, better working conditions, etc. What he really wants, however, is recognition and attention (things sorely lacking in his life). The negotiator must be aware of these needs and be prepared to respond to them.

The negotiator must anticipate and predict the types of demands the hostage taker will make before they are made. Effectively dealing with demands requires knowing the type of hostage taker in the situation, having good intelligence on the situation and people involved, and knowing how to discuss and refuse demands without angering the hostage taker. Only with forethought and planning can a negotiator be proactive in dealing with demands.

Promises made to hostage takers during negotiation are not legally binding contracts (*United States v. Crosby*, 1983; *State v. Sands*, 1985). That is, if a negotiator makes a promise to a hostage taker, there is no obligation to fulfill that promise, due to the duress of the situation. In *State v. Sands*, for example, a negotiator signed a letter of leniency for the hostage taker. After arrest, the hostage taker sued the police department for not fulfilling the promise of immunity. The court ruled that the contract was not valid because it was given under duress and, as such, was unenforceable. It is against public policy to take hostages, and thus any promises made during the incident (i.e., "contracts") are unenforceable. The hostage situation is analogous to a situation in which a man hires a contract killer to murder his wife. If the contract killer fails, the husband cannot sue him or her for breach of contract. The act of murder is against public policy and such contracts are unenforceable. Neither is it necessary to Mirandize hostage takers (*New York v. Quarles*, 1984; *United States v. Mesa*, 1980; *State v. Sands*, 1985; *People v. Gantz*, 1984). A hostage taker is not considered to be "in custody" during negotiations and negotiators are not interrogating hostage takers. Any statements made by the hostage taker during negotiations are admissible evidence (*New York v. Quarles*).

Nature of Demands

Demands presented by hostage takers have several characteristics. The demands will be presented in an authoritarian "either/or" manner and are not open to negotiation. The hostage taker thinks he is making a request that provides a solution to the situation. The hostage taker has already decided what he needs in order to resolve the situation and it is the role of the police to provide that solution. A criminal who is caught in the act and takes hostages wants the assurance of freedom. In a domestic situation, the hostage taker may want increased visitation rights. To the hostage taker, demand issues are a legalistic type of contract: "You give me _____ and I will do _____." Very often, demands will be presented in such a manner that if they are not met, hostages will be injured or killed. The leverage the hostage taker has over the police is in his or her ability to harm others. The job of the negotiator is to prevent others from being harmed. This point is the key difference between hostage situations and barricaded subject situations. The police must negotiate with the hostage taker to prevent the hostage from being harmed. The police "wait out" the barricaded suspect, who has much less power in regard to demand issues.

The demand must be met as stated. To the hostage taker, there is no compromise. If a station wagon is requested, a sedan is not acceptable. Perceptually, the hostage taker knows what he or she needs. Anything else is not acceptable. When you want to purchase a pair of denim jeans, corduroy pants are not a substitute. Offering a sedan is not acceptable because the sedan does not satisfy the hostage taker's need.

Each demand has a time limit attached and this time limit is not open to compromise and must be met. In a sense, the time limit in and of itself is a demand. In most hostage situations, however, the time limit is set arbitrarily and has very little intrinsic meaning, unlike other demands. An airplane must be physically present for the hostage taker to use to leave the country. Having it by 4:00 P.M. "seemed like a good time to pick" because that gives the police enough time to get the plane.

Finally, a consequence is tied to each demand. This consequence usually involves harm to a hostage, but may involve destruction of property or even harm to the hostage taker (i.e., suicide). "If I don't get _____, people start dying" is a statement most negotiators have heard at some point. With barricaded subjects, the negotiator must assess the potential for him or her to do harm to property or commit suicide. If the barricaded subject has no consequences, the situation becomes a waiting game. This does not mean the negotiator should say, "And if we don't get _____, what are you going to do about it?" This might make the subject act out the consequence, harming a hostage or him- or herself.

On March 5, 1994, Clifford Draper entered the Salt Lake City Library carrying a bomb and a handgun. He took a group of Tibetan monks and a Salt Lake City deputy sheriff hostage. Before taking the hostages, Draper gave a written list of demands to a bystander, with instructions to give the list of demands to the first responding officer. The demands were: (1) get the National Guard on the scene and evacuate the police; (2) no attempts at "psychological manipulation"; (3) get a medical officer as a runner and provide amphetamines and sedatives; (4) no demand is negotiable and any attempt to compromise will result in the death of hostages; (5) no hostages will be permitted to leave for medical reasons; (6) secure the area from loud noises that may detonate the bomb or trigger a startled response; (7) $50,000 in currency and gold and platinum calculated on the number of years of Draper's military service; (8) the Governor of Utah is to obtain a pardon from the President; (9) immediate access to a radio station; (10) local newspapers to print Draper's explanation of the event; and (11) a 72-hour deadline. While it is somewhat unusual for a hostage taker to have a prepared list of demands, Draper's list illustrates the initial perception and belief of the hostage taker regarding demands. Negotiations lasted approximately 4½ hours, with Draper making no concessions to police negotiators. The incident was resolved when the deputy sheriff hostage shot and killed Draper.

When demands are presented, the negotiator should be prepared to respond immediately. When first presented, the negotiator should never refuse, trivialize, or say no to a demand. Initially, the negotiator should treat all requests as if they are reasonable and something that can be fulfilled if the hostage taker works with the police, behaves reasonably, and does not harm anyone. If the demand is truly non-negotiable (such as a weapon or release of prisoners) and the hostage taker is insistent, the negotiator should carefully explain why it is not going to be fulfilled and explain why. Saying no is always a last resort for the negotiator. If it becomes necessary, the negotiator should explain in a non-threatening manner that the entire package is not negotiable, but that some individual demands are negotiable and each can be discussed. The negotiator should reiterate the list of demands in such a way that the impact of non-negotiability, time, and consequences are reduced. For example, if the hostage taker wants "an empty police cruiser with a full tank of gas and $10,000 by 3:00 or hostages start dying," the negotiator should first respond as if each part of the statement is a separate entity. For example, the negotiator could focus discussions on the "police cruiser" by pointing out problems with using a police vehicle for a getaway car. Focusing on this one demand will often result in the hostage taker ignoring or even forgetting the others. If the hostage taker persists, the negotiator in turn should continue to focus on the individual components, explaining the problems associated with each. Additionally, the negotiator could ignore the demands and focus on the consequences of harm to the hostages.

The "finality" of the package can also be reduced by reiterating the demands to the hostage taker in a different, softer way. For example, using the example presented above, the negotiator could respond by saying something like the following: "So you would like a vehicle and money by late afternoon." This conveys two subtle messages to the hostage taker. First, the negotiator is willing to discuss each issue and attempt a compromise with the hostage taker. The second message being sent is that specific demands are not going to be granted and the hostage taker needs to rethink his position. One issue that extended the Fred Carrasco prison incident (discussed in Chapter 1) was that prison administrators began by telling the hostage takers that no vehicle was going to be given to them. During the 10-day incident the hostage takers kept demanding a vehicle for escape: an airplane, a helicopter, a ground vehicle, etc. Every time they demanded a vehicle, prison authorities flatly refused to provide one. It was possible that progress could have been made had the prison officials worked with the hostage taker on a vehicle, softening the demand and suggesting a compromise.

The negotiator should control discussions regarding demands and should know what the authorities will not give up (Misino & DeFelice, 2004). Controlling the discussion means anticipating and being aware of the hostage taker's needs at any particular time and manipulating those needs. That is, the negotiator should focus the hostage taker on unfulfilled basic needs and keep other issues in the background. For example, if the hostage taker is becoming anxious about a vehicle and begins to mention it repeatedly to the negotiator, the negotiator could interrupt the hostage taker and say, "Excuse me, but before we discuss that . . . My meal just arrived and I would like to eat before it gets cold. What about if you and I work on some solutions and I'll call you back as soon as I finish eating. I'll call you back in 10 minutes (hangs up telephone)." The negotiator has anticipated, deflected, and emphasized an unfulfilled basic need. The hostage taker may forget all about the vehicle and begin to think about eating. Controlling discussions regarding demands becomes easier as rapport and trust are established.

Motivation Theories

Prior to discussing negotiable and non-negotiable demands, it is necessary to understand what makes people motivated to make demands. All people make demands, not just hostage takers. Spouses make demands of their mates, as do children of their parents, employees of their supervisors and organizations, and supervisors of their employees. Understanding the context and framework within which demands are made will assist the negotiator in responding to demands. For example, understanding why a hostage taker is asking for food will help the negotiator address and resolve the demand issue and move on to more pressing and urgent demand issues that more clearly and directly lead to the resolution of the incident.

Hostage takers make demands (as do all of us) because they have a need. Understanding the context of those needs, addressing those needs, and resolving those needs is one of the key elements in resolving the incident. One theory of need satisfaction was proposed by Abraham Maslow (1954). His theory involves a five-stage hierarchical need system. A person's needs begin at satisfying biological needs, and progress in order through the need for safety, social needs, ego needs and, at the top of the hierarchy, self-actualization needs. Thus, according to Maslow's theory, a hostage taker asking for food is attempting to satisfy biological needs. Providing food satisfies that need, and the hostage taker then becomes concerned with personal safety ("get those cops out of here"). Once safety is taken care of, the hostage taker then would make demands focused on social needs ("Nobody cares about what happens to me."). Once the negotiator resolved those issues, the hostage taker would then turn to demands centered on the ego (being a good person, a loving father, etc.). At this level, the negotiator should focus on the positive qualities of the hostage taker. Once those needs are taken care of, the hostage taker would turn to self-actualization (the future). Here the negotiator could focus on a positive future for the hostage taker ("You know that once this is over, you could attend counseling for single parents that would help you become an even better parent than you are now."). Only when a lower-level need is satisfied can the individual move to the next need level. If a person is hungry and eats, for example, that person will then become concerned with safety.

Maslow's (1954) theory has been the most popular and used theory of motivation, although the research concerning the theory has not always fully supported the theory (Soper, Milford & Rosenthal, 1995). Some research suggests that there are actually fewer than five levels, and that there may be only two or three (Mitchell & Mougdill, 1976). For the purpose of negotiations, the two biggest problems are that people do not necessarily move hierarchically up the levels. They may skip levels (Aamodt, 1999) and they may not increase in levels once a need is satisfied (Salancik & Pfeffer, 1977). On the positive side, however, the level an individual is in can be easily and readily identified by a negotiator. A hostage taker shouting for the police to back off is concerned with his or her need for safety, and that can be used by the negotiators to plan strategy, direct communications, and engage in decisionmaking. Further, the negotiator can assume a hierarchy and try to move the hostage taker from the safety need level to the social needs level. The negotiator can also manipulate the need level by discussing demand issues and using time. Just because the hostage taker eats does not mean that the need is satisfied permanently. By knowing and understanding need levels, the negotiator can manipulate the hostage taker through need levels to suit the negotiators. Finally, most incidents will be resolved in the safety or social needs level. Few hostage takers will reach the ego and self-actualization needs levels.

Figure 3.1
Maslow's Hierarchy of Needs. Understanding the hostage taker's immediate need state and how to fulfill that need is a major step in resolving an incident.

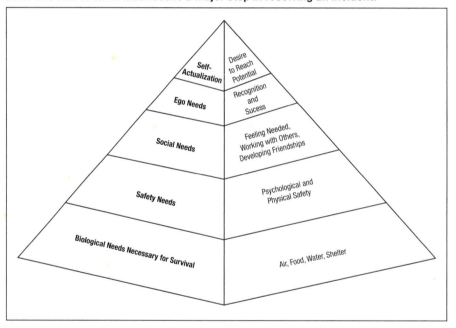

A theory of needs similar and somewhat related to Maslow's (1954) is Aldefer's (1972) ERG Theory. Aldefer proposed only three need levels; existence, relatedness, and growth (ERG). Existence needs are those that deal with biological and safety issues, relatedness needs are analogous to Maslow's social needs level, and growth needs concern an individual's ego and self-actualization. Unlike Maslow's theory, ERG Theory says people can move around and skip levels. Also, if one level becomes blocked, the person becomes frustrated and will place more emphasis on the previous level (Aamodt, 1999). The hostage taker who is alone in the world and has no friends or support networks may become fixated on personal needs such as food, shelter, not going to jail, etc. In many situations, negotiators can resolve the incident by satisfying the existence needs.

Figure 3.2
A Comparison of the Need Theories of Maslow, Aldefer's ERG, and McLelland's Theory and How They Relate to Demands

Maslow	ERG Theory	McLelland	Likely Demands
Self-Actualization **Ego**	Growth	Need for Achievement	Surrender ritual, freedom, increased visitation rights, media attention
Social	Relatedness	Need for Affiliation	Media coverage, freedom or free comrades, custody of children
Safety **Biological**	Existence	Need for Power	Food, drink, cigarettes, alcohol, transportation, money

Another theory of motivation is McLelland's Needs Theory (1961). He believed people had three needs: achievement, affiliation, and power. Further, people had either a strong or weak need in each area. For example, people who have a strong need for affiliation do not make good supervisors (because they want people to like them), but do succeed in service-oriented jobs (Smither & Lindgren, 1978). By determining which needs are most important to the hostage taker, the negotiator can focus on solving those needs and thus resolve the incident. A hostage taker who has a strong need for achievement may need to have some control over the situation and their fate. They may want to give orders concerning the delivery of food, dictate surrender terms, etc. A hostage taker with a strong need for affiliation will make demands concerning what others think of him or saving face (no picture on the news, not taken out in front of a crowd, more time with estranged family, etc.). If the hostage taker has a strong need for power, he may need to believe he "won" or that he got the authorities to do what he wanted, or that the surrender ritual be formalized, etc.

The three theories of motivation presented here (and there are others that are not addressed) are not mutually exclusive. We believe there is some of each theory at work in our personality, the way we behave and act, the way we interact with others, the way we act emotionally, and in how we communicate with others. By using the three theories together, the negotiator can manipulate and use demand issues to the advantage of the negotiators and to the disadvantage of the hostage taker. With a trained negotiator, in many incidents, the negotiator—not the hostage taker—actually dictates demand issues.

Negotiable Demands

Before considering which demands are generally negotiable and which are not negotiable, remember that each hostage situation is unique and the following discussion provides general guidelines only. Situations may arise that do not permit the police to follow these guidelines. Remember, following the educated and experienced judgment of the responding team is the only guideline set in stone.

Food. Food is probably the demand made most often by hostage takers. Hostage locations (i.e., home, apartment, business) usually have a source of water or other liquids. They generally do not have an available food supply. As time passes, the hostage takers and hostages will become hungry. If the hostage takers do not request food, the negotiator can suggest food (see, for example, the section on persuasion and suggestion in Chapter 6, Communication in Hostage Negotiations). Food can be one of the negotiator's most valuable tools in gaining the hostage taker's trust, developing the Stockholm Syndrome between hostage taker and hostages, and getting hostages released before incident resolution.

For example, if an incident has lasted several hours and little progress is being made, the negotiator could ask the hostage taker if he is getting hungry. If the response is "yes," then the negotiator could say something like; "So am I. How about me checking to see if we can get some food. If I can, will you agree to stay calmed down and in one place?" The negotiator could also ask for the release of a hostage, the dropping of a difficult demand issue, etc. What is important here is the negotiator's emphasizing "us" and using the demand to establish unity of purpose.

Negotiators stress team functioning and unity, because teamwork is how demand issues are resolved, problems are solved, and resolutions are reached. The dynamics of a hostage situation require good team dynamics. *(B. Miller)*

When food is negotiated, do not give more than absolutely necessary. Provide only a minimum amount for each hostage and hostage taker. Give each person the same food. Do not give some hamburgers, some pizzas, etc. Obtain the food in bulk and ensure it is all the same and in equal portions for all. Salt can be added to any food to increase thirst, opening the door for another possible hostage trade. Explain to the hostage taker that the food is to be divided evenly and is not all for the hostage taker, unless that was specified beforehand. In general, when food is negotiated, it should be negotiated for all parties inside the situation.

Do not include condiments (mustard, ketchup, etc.) or drinks. These items should be negotiated separately. Provide only the food, nothing else. Do not drug the food. Often in television and films a scheme is devised to drug the hostage taker. This only happens in the movies and possibly the hostage taker saw the same movie. The hostage taker will already be suspicious, and anything that may deepen that suspicion may result in harm to hostages or loss of trust with the negotiator.

In a jail or prison situation, food must be given to the hostage takers and hostages. These situations can last for several days and nobody wins when hostages starve. Although the negotiator may not get the hostage takers to release a hostage in exchange for the delivery of food, the negotiator can obtain other concessions: calming down, talking to only one of the hostage takers, etc. In a jail or prison, food should be delivered in bulk and it should be the same for everyone. Do not give the hostage takers one type of food and the hostages something else. Provide complete meals. Do not deliver food without condiments or liquids, as the use of food will not be a major tool for the negotiator. Unlike law enforcement situations in which the negotiator can use food, condiments, and liquids as separate issues, in the jail or prison situation food will likely only provide minor concessions. Additionally, the deletion of certain items might very well raise the anxiety, frustration, and aggression of the hostage takers. The small gains to be made by delivering separate parcels may not offset the long-term problems it could produce.

Cigarettes. Next to food, cigarettes are the second most bargained-for demand made by hostage takers. Cigarettes should be given one at a time and always traded for some concession, preferably a hostage. Try to make matches a separate negotiation ("I'm sorry. From the way you were talking, I thought you had a way to light your cigarette. We can provide you with something but we will need you to _____"). Be careful to not be insulting about the matches issue. You may believe that providing a cigarette without matches will insult, agitate, and anger the hostage taker. In this case, provide the matches.

The hostage taker may also need prescription medication. In addition to the benefits of getting him to make concessions, this also provides an excellent opportunity for intelligence gathering. Have the hostage taker name the medicine, dosage, reason for taking it, and doctor's name (negotiators cannot refill the prescription without the doctor's OK). The intelligence gatherer can talk to the doctor and find out a great deal about the hostage taker's history. Make sure you know the effects of the medications (including any side effects) before giving any medication.

For these smaller items, the power of suggestion can be effectively applied. One tactic that has been used is for the negotiator, while talking to a hostage taker, to inhale loudly as if he were smoking a cigarette. Inevitably, the hostage taker (if a smoker) will ask for cigarettes (see Chapter 6, Communication in Hostage Negotiations for more on suggestion techniques).

In one incident, the hostage taker asked for a particular book. The negotiator, instead of asking why he wanted the book, directed the conversation toward why he wanted that specific book. This line of conversation led ultimately to moral and ethical issues that in turn led to a resolution of the incident.

Drinks. Frequently, soft drinks, water, or other nonalcoholic beverages may be negotiated. In general, the same rules apply to drinks as to food: do not give more than requested, give only the minimum amount possible, and do not drug the drinks. The drinks should be bland, decaffeinated, low in sugar content, and somewhat salty (add salt if necessary). Make the drinks as cold as possible, as the coldness does not satisfy thirst as well as lukewarm drinks. Thirst can be fostered by shutting off the water supply to the location. Should the hostage taker question not having water, it is easy to sidestep the issue by explaining that the utility company is working on the water lines in that particular part of town and the police are trying to get the water turned back on. In addition to thirst, this tactic builds rapport, trust, and a perception of willingness to work with the hostage taker.

Alcohol. At one time, the general rule was not to negotiate alcoholic beverages. Experience has shown that in some circumstances alcohol is negotiable. If the hostage taker is highly irritable, tense, uncooperative, or excitable, small amounts of alcohol may calm him. Before giving any alcohol, the negotiating team should have good intelligence on the hostage taker and know how the alcohol will affect him. Alcohol should not be given to hostages, unless a hostage is a severe alcoholic. In this case, alcohol may be necessary for the temporary well-being of the hostage.

The hostage taker may be an alcoholic. Without moderate doses of alcohol, this type of hostage taker will be nervous, paranoid, irritable, unreasonable, and agitated. Without alcohol to calm him, the hostage taker may not be able to think clearly, may act in a somewhat irrational manner, and may harm hostages at the slightest provocation. Additionally, with time, this hostage taker may begin to experience delirium tremens (DTs), a common affliction of chronic alcoholics. Should DTs onset, negotiations will be almost impossible and the risk to hostages would increase significantly.

In some situations, the hostage taker may have ready access to large quantities of alcohol. In these situations, the negotiator should calmly and quietly attempt to keep the hostage taker from overindulging. The negotiator may appeal to the hostage taker's ability to think, point out the danger of getting drunk and passing out, and warn that in an inebriated state the hostage taker may get himself injured or killed by doing something stupid. Rarely does the negotiator want the hostage taker to drink himself into a stupor and pass out. Most hostage takers will not become this inebriated and will instead become angry, jittery, and paranoid.

Many domestic hostage incidents are precipitated by alcohol. Alcohol exacerbates the stresses present in the family situation, whether they involve arguing with a spouse or parent, or estrangement from some family members (i.e., children with the other spouse, loss of visitation rights, etc.). In these cases, the negotiator should avoid falling into the role of "counselor" and attempting to point out that many of the problems were initially caused by alcohol. The negotiator should stress the need to stop drinking during the incident, as this short-term drinking will only worsen the situation.

Media Coverage. In most situations, media coverage is negotiable. Historically, media coverage has not been a negotiable item. Negotiators were afraid that live media coverage would lead to hostages being harmed, the incident being extended, and bystanders becoming sympathetic to the hostage taker and hindering police efforts. Today, however, modern technology makes it possible for coverage to be edited instantly (even with live coverage) and anything detrimental to police efforts omitted.

In some instances, media coverage will resolve the hostage incident. In 1982, two people took a bus hostage in Jasper, Arkansas. They were members of a fringe religious cult and wanted their "message" delivered to the public. Their demand was to present their message to the media and for the message to be aired on national news. Following an interview with a media representative and the taping of their statement, all hostages were released.

If media coverage is given to the hostage taker, media members should not be put in a position in which they could be taken hostage or be harmed by the hostage taker. Before being allowed to interview the hostage taker, media representatives should be thoroughly briefed concerning the incident, who the hostage takers are, who the hostages are, what caused the situation to develop, and any other intelligence information that would not compromise negotiating efforts. If possible, and if agreeable to the media, their discussions with the hostage takers can be used to gather intelligence. If this is planned, the type of intelligence requested should be discussed with the media representatives and the media should be allowed to determine how best to obtain this information.

Additionally, the police should discuss what type of media coverage would be beneficial or detrimental to the incident's resolution. A list of possible questions to be asked may even be provided, along with a list of recommendations of what not to say. In the Jasper, Arkansas, incident, the statements and line of questioning by the media representative strengthened the resolve of the hostage takers to commit "suicide by cop" (which ultimately happened). One question the newscaster asked several times was, "Are you sure you have to do this?" The newscaster cannot be blamed for his line of questioning. He simply did not know what to ask, how to ask it, and what issues to avoid. Finally, the media may be asked to not air any conversations until the incident is resolved.

It is not advisable to have a police officer pretend to be a media representative. Police officers are not reporters and do not act like reporters. The chances are the hostage taker will readily see through a façade of this nature and all progress will be lost (at a minimum). Arrangements can be made with the hostage taker, however, to have the police accompany the media representatives. If this occurs, the police officer should be trained in negotiation and will then be able to assist the media representative in questioning the hostage taker.

In prison and jail situations, media coverage may be a critical issue to the hostage takers. They may want to talk with the media to air their grievances, or may want the media present to witness the surrender ritual, as occurred in the Oakdale and Atlanta prison situations (Fuselier, Van Zandt & Lanceley, 1989). Refusal to use the media to assist in ending the situation may result in increased violence and a breakdown in negotiations. Also, the media may be an expressive, unstated demand of the hostage takers. It is important that the negotiator pay close attention to the instrumental demands and also carefully assess what the expressive demands may be.

Negotiating media coverage is a difficult subject for the police negotiator. Dealings with the media and attempts to manipulate the media fall under First Amendment protections. However, a solid working relationship with the media should lead to their cooperation and assistance in resolving an incident successfully.

Transportation. A basic tenet of hostage negotiation is that the hostage taker be confined to one location. Transportation can, however, be negotiated to help resolve the incident. Even if there is no intent to give the hostage taker transportation, it can still be negotiated. Negotiating for transportation can wear down the hostage taker, make him see the futility of prolonging the incident, and even lead to a hostage's release. Transportation can be an effective bargaining tool and can lead to other bargaining tools. For example, if the hostage taker wants transportation, the negotiator can use this to open a discussion of other problems the hostage taker is having. The negotiator can discuss why transportation is needed, if this transportation will really solve the "problem," and additional problems that would develop if the hostage taker were to run away.

Money. As with transportation, money can be negotiated for without being given. Problems inherent in obtaining large sums of money in a short period can be used to prolong negotiations and lead to the resolution of other difficult issues. In fact, money may be given to the hostage taker as a show of good faith and to obtain the release of hostages. The hostage taker is secured and is not going anywhere, so any money given can be recovered upon resolution of the incident.

Freedom. An enduring maxim of hostage negotiations is that hostage takers are confined and will remain confined in one location and that they do not receive freedom for release of hostages. In prison incidents, freedom is non-negotiable and not open to discussion. Occasions exist, however, when the best course of action is to give the hostage taker freedom. Again, this is a decision that must be made by the on-scene response unit in conjunction with the other law enforcement officials concerned. The author is familiar with one incident in which the hostage taker was the estranged father and the only hostage was his young child. The responding unit, after several hours of negotiations, determined the father posed no further threat to himself or the child. The unit, with permission of the on-scene commander, discontinued negotiations and the next day patrol officers arrested the father on a warrant. While this situation is certainly the exception, exceptions do arise in hostage situations. If freedom is to be granted, it should only be given as a last resort and only after the safety of all hostages and other civilians has been assured. Additionally, if granting freedom, document reasons for doing so in a permanent record.

Non-Negotiable Demands

Some would argue that all demands are negotiable, even though some will not be granted regardless of the circumstances. It is our position that some demands are simply non-negotiable, and it makes no sense to enter into a discussion concerning those demands. Negotiations are a time-consuming process. There is no reason to waste time negotiating issues that have no potential to help resolve the situation. Discussing non-negotiable demands is more likely to worsen than improve the situation. If, for example, the hostage taker wants illegal drugs and the negotiator gives the impression that these might be forthcoming at some point and then tells the hostage taker that the drugs are not going to be provided, this could stop the development of trust and rapport, anger the hostage taker, or lead to hostages being harmed. Conversely, by making it known up front that illicit drugs are not going to be given, the hostage taker does not develop false expectations and the negotiator can then work on other issues.

Weapons. Additional weapons are not negotiable. The threat of violence gives the hostage taker power. This threat initially requires a weapon. If the hostage taker had no weapon, hostages would just walk away and no incident would have occurred. Even in a domestic incident, in which the hostage taker has no object (i.e., knife, gun, club), the threat of a physical beating is a "weapon." In many domestic hostage situations, there is a history of family violence and abuse by the hostage taker, so the threat is real, not perceived. Simply negotiating a weapon gives the hostage taker the perception of having power in the situation. If presented as a demand, make clear immediately that weapons are not negotiable.

Drugs. Non-prescription, illicit drugs are not negotiable. Many hostage takers have a drug habit or dependency (physical and/or psychological). They may request marijuana, cocaine, heroin, amphetamines, or barbiturates. With time, the desire for these drugs may become critical and cause the hostage taker to forget other demands and issues. The focus of the entire scenario may become satisfying a need for one or more illicit drugs. Most of the illicit drugs, however, may produce paranoia and psychotic episodes, reduce rationality and increase emotionalism, and increase unpredictability and violent behavior (Poythress, 1980). Unlike with alcohol, there is almost no probability of the hostage taker ingesting these drugs and calming down or "passing out."

Release of Prisoners. As with weapons, make clear immediately that the release of prisoners is non-negotiable, regardless of whether for political or social reasons. We are fortunate in the United States to have very few terrorist or political hostage-taking situations. The request for prisoner release is thus an uncommon demand. Occasionally, a hostage taker will ask that a friend or criminal acquaintance be released from prison. When this demand is made, the negotiator may resolve the demand relatively easily.

In prison hostage situations, the same rule about the release of prisoners applies. The prison negotiator should make it clear up front that prisoners are not going to be released. One of the issues at Attica Prison in 1971 (see Chapter 10, Hostage Negotiations in Prisons and Correctional Facilities, for a detailed analysis of the Attica riot) concerned airplanes for prisoners to flee the country. Negotiators made it clear up front that this was not negotiable. The prisoners ignored this issue and focused on their other demands. Attica is not the exception. Most prison hostage situations have freedom as a central issue. The Lucasville, Talladega, Oakdale, and Atlanta prison situations all had prisoner freedom as a core issue. At each incident, negotiators were very clear that freedom was non-negotiable. At each incident, prisoners accepted this and moved on to other issues.

Exchange of Hostages. Exchanging hostages is inadvisable for many reasons (Fuselier, 1986). The exchange of hostages will disrupt the Stockholm Syndrome. The Stockholm Syndrome occurs when the hostage taker and hostages come to see one another as real people, not as bartering objects (see Chapter 4, The Stockholm Syndrome, for a full discussion). The Stockholm Syndrome is extremely important in preventing harm to hostages. If hostages are traded, the new hostages will not be "people" to the hostage taker and are much more likely to be injured.

With a hostage exchange, the stress and tension levels of the hostage taker, hostages (old and new), and police rise to Crisis Stage levels, making the situation extremely dangerous. Additionally, with emotions at peak levels, the negotiating progress stalls. The "new" hostages will be in the Crisis Stage and their emotions, fears, and anxieties will be at peak levels. The hostage taker will have to expend mental energy with the hostages and will be unable to concentrate on negotiating. Exchanging hostages for relatives may be self-serving to the hostage taker.

The relative can now act as a first-person witness to the hostage taker's troubles, whether those troubles are directly or indirectly related to the hostage situation. An attitude of "See what you made me do?" may appear, and the hostage taker is likely to harm either the relative/hostage or himself. In domestic situations, the hostage taker may want a specific family member as a hostage in an attempt to serve some internal need states (i.e., power, prestige, etc.). Exchanging this relative only increases emotions and dangerousness, and stalls progress in resolving the incident. If the hostage taker gets the relative he or she wants, the hostage taker may cease negotiating. Suicide-prone individuals may want the relative present to witness the suicide.

A hostage exchange gives power to the hostage taker. Negotiations should convince the hostage taker that he or she is in a no-win situation. The hostage exchange gives not only the perception, but the reality of controlling the situation to the hostage. This will have a major influence on future negotiations with that hostage taker. The hostage taker, not the negotiator, will control negotiations.

An exchange of hostages cannot be equitable to the police. Nothing is gained in a trade of hostages. Hostage exchanges are not a zero sum game in which both sides win. Only the hostage taker comes out ahead.

Police officers are never exchanged for hostages (Wargo, 1989). Many people (including many police officers) have a "Hollywood" concept of hostage negotiations. In this view, the role of the police officer (or negotiator) is to trade places with civilian hostages. In the movies, the police officer then talks the hostage taker into surrendering. Unfortunately, this outcome only occurs on the silver screen. The police officer/hostage, by virtue of being a police officer, may feel compelled to take action and attempt to resolve the situation. Either the police officer/hostage or hostage taker will be injured or killed. Also, the hostage taker may perceive more prestige in killing a police officer than a civilian. The probability of a hostage being harmed increases if the hostage is a police officer. Thus, the stress and pressure on the part of the negotiators increases significantly if a police officer is a hostage (Russell & Zuniga, 1986). One of the strengths of the negotiator is the ability to negotiate from an impartial basis. The negotiator loses impartiality if a police officer is a hostage. Accordingly, the other responding police officers' tension increases if a fellow officer is hostage. They may feel unnecessary pressure to rush and resolve the incident. Mistakes are more likely to be made, decisions are biased, and force may be used unnecessarily to resolve the incident.

There are many reasons to not trade hostages. No added benefit results from exchanging hostages. In all respects, the hostage taker is the only party who benefits in a hostage trade. Exchanging hostages gives the hostage taker control.

Handling Demands

Dealing with any demand is the cornerstone of successful negotiations. The skilled negotiator can handle a myriad of demands. This negotiator cares little whether the demands are instrumental or expressive, small or large, realistic or grandiose. The skilled negotiator treats every demand the same way: important, to be used to build rapport and trust, as a solvable problem, and as a potential solution. There are several general principles to follow when considering demands from a hostage taker.

Avoid asking for demands. Many times a negotiator feels pressure from superiors or other officers to rush resolution. It is human nature, especially for the police officer, to want "just the facts," as Joe Friday in the old *Dragnet* television series used to say. The skilled negotiator will not force issues or bring demands. Rather, he or she will anticipate and prepare for demands, then wait patiently for the hostage taker to make his demands known and react to those demands. Newer negotiators sometimes slip and say something like, "What do you want?" or "What can we do for you?" These types of statements put the hostage taker in control of the discussions and give him the perception of control of the situation. By reacting to demand issues, the negotiator is showing control of the situation.

Avoid offering anything. The negotiator is caught in a bind. On the one hand, the negotiator is attempting to gain the hostage taker's trust. To establish trust, the negotiator may engage in some give-and-take. This involves trades of information, property, or personal information. The negotiator is in the awkward position of having to make trades without initiating trades. The negotiator must wait for the hostage taker to make a demand, and then change the tenor from an absolute to an equitable swap. Furthermore, the trade must appear to be the hostage taker's idea. If the negotiator were to say something like, "I'm getting ready to eat. How about if I get you something?" the negotiator has just placed him- or herself in a position of indebtedness and giving something for nothing. The hostage taker could take the food offer and see no reason to trade (i.e., "You offered the food. I didn't ask for food. Why should I release a hostage?").

As mentioned previously, the negotiator should not give anything not specifically asked for and should not give more than absolutely necessary to fulfill the agreement. If the hostage taker wants a cigarette, he should receive one cigarette, without matches. If the hostage taker then wants to light the cigarette, he should be given only enough matches to light that cigarette. If the hostage taker wants a drink of water, he should be given the absolute minimum necessary to facilitate the trade. The negotiator must give the minimum without offending, irritating, or insulting the hostage taker. For example, if the hostage taker asks for something to drink and the negotiator provides a "thimbleful," the hostage taker will feel ridiculed and may do something to retaliate (i.e., harm hostages). On the other hand, if the negotiator provides a case of soda, the hostage taker will not want to negotiate because his needs will have been completely satiated. The key is finding the balance in which the needs of the hostage taker are partly, but not completely, fulfilled. Chain smokers, for example, may want a cigarette. Providing a regular-length (not a 100mm), low-nicotine cigarette will satiate the hostage taker for only a short period (20-30 minutes). An unfiltered, strong, or 100mm cigarette will satiate the hostage taker for a longer period. The amount of the item given can itself work to manipulate the hostage taker's need states.

Never give anything without getting something in return. Handling demands involves making trades. These trades should be perceived as equitable by the hostage taker, but in reality should favor the police. A cigarette for a hostage, turning on the heat for a hostage, or food for a hostage are trades that may appear fair to the hostage taker, but are skewed to the police. Trades may not always involve the exchange of hostages. A promise to remain in one specific room, use one particular telephone, or to remain calm and keep talking to the negotiator are also trades that may be made.

There is an exception to this guideline. As will be discussed in Chapter 10, Hostage Negotiations in Prisons and Correctional Facilities, negotiators had to violate this guideline in dealing with the Cuban hostage takers at the Oakdale and Atlanta federal prisons. The Cuban culture is one in which negotiated trades are not conducted simultaneously. One person is given something by another person, and at a later time, the first person reciprocates. Negotiators at these prisons had to first give something, and then at a later time, the hostage takers fulfilled the trade. In one instance, negotiators turned the water back on and the next day the inmates released some hostages. Other cultures may be similar in terms of granting favors and making concessions. Negotiators should always understand the cultural context of their hostage takers and negotiations.

Avoid dismissing any demand as trivial. People have different pleasures, priorities, and objectives in life. One person's definition of a perfect evening may be sitting on the couch watching a baseball game. Another person may think baseball the most boring sport in the world. While the negotiator may feel silly talking to a hostage taker who only wants one extra weekend a month in child visitation rights, this may be a significant goal for the hostage taker. The skilled negotiator can put him- or herself in the emotional shoes of the hostage taker and see the world from his perspective. This negotiator can feel the pain of the hostage taker because the hostage taker never gets to see his children, and can understand his fear of jail, and the embarrassment at having his story printed on the newspaper's front page. People have different needs, wants, and desires, and what may be important to one person may seem trivial to another. The negotiator must not fall into this trap.

The negotiator should ignore deadlines, and should not set deadlines for the incident's resolution. When a hostage taker sets a deadline, one of the negotiator's duties is to talk through the deadline and get the hostage taker to forget or ignore the deadline. The negotiator should not allow artificial deadlines to be set for incident resolution. On-scene commanders are often concerned with such issues as overtime, inconvenience to the department and citizens, and other peripheral issues. This may influence their judgment, causing them to desire a rapid resolution. The negotiator should tactfully ignore these artificial deadlines and let the dynamics of the incident determine the deadlines for resolution.

In one incident, the negotiator worked out a trade of food for the release of a hostage. The negotiator told the hostage taker, "The food's on the way and will be here within 10 minutes." Unfortunately, the officer getting the food was delayed because his car battery died. The delivery of the food was delayed almost 20 minutes. By the time the food arrived, the hostage taker had reneged on the trade because the time deadline was not met. The negotiator was not able to ignore the deadline, because he set the deadline and the hostage taker was holding him to his promise. Fortunately, the incident was later resolved successfully and the negotiator learned a lesson he has never forgotten.

The negotiator should first negotiate for sick or injured hostages. This may at times involve the negotiator suggesting demands. These suggestions should be for minor items such as food, cigarettes, or even emotional well-being ("Wouldn't you feel a lot better if you didn't have to worry about that person with the heart condition?"). By gaining these early con-

cessions, the negotiator accomplishes several goals. Sick and injured hostages are released so they can receive medical treatment. The negotiator establishes trust and rapport, shows that he or she cares about the hostage taker, and establishes a position of power. The hostage taker is put at a disadvantage by showing that he is willing to negotiate and make concessions. Later, if the hostage taker becomes stubborn, the negotiator could say, "What's the matter? You were willing to work with me earlier and we did some good things together. Have I

Negotiators must constantly brainstorm, review progress on demand issues, plan for meeting the hostage taker's need states, and offer solutions to problems. Team interaction and team communication are the cornerstone for effectiveness in resolving high-intensity events. *(A. Hanna)*

done something to offend you or make you mad?" The hostage taker is placed in a position in which he has to reciprocate and make some concessions.

During a hostage situation many demands will be made. These typically start as grandiose (i.e., cars, planes, large sums of money, etc.), and become more realistic as the incident progresses (i.e., food, water, cigarettes, the promise of no harm). The last demand made is the only important one. By monitoring the type of demands made, the negotiator can determine the negotiation's progress. If the demands are being reduced in scope, this indicates that negotiations are progressing and the hostage taker is being "worn down." If, on the other hand, demands remain grandiose or even increase in scope, the hostage taker has the perception of control and power, and the negotiator should attempt to reduce this perception. When discussing demands, the negotiator should avoid discussing those presented earlier. The negotiator should focus and concentrate on the last demand and ignore previous demands.

The negotiator should assess the personality type of the hostage taker based on the types of demands made. A full discussion of personality typology and demands by typology is given in a later chapter. Basically, the negotiator should determine whether the hostage taker is a schizophrenic, psychotic, depressed, inadequate personality, or antisocial personality, based on the types of demands being made. The paranoid schizophrenic will make ridiculous, unrealistic requests (i.e., the government to quit inundating him with mind control rays, for the space creatures to leave, etc.). These demands will be part of his delusional system and to him, all are legitimate. The negotiator must treat them as such. Depressed persons will make no demands or demands that pertain to family (i.e., get my parents here so they can see what they did to me). The inadequate personality will make outlandish demands (i.e., vast sums of money, a 747 airplane to fly him to the French Riviera). The antisocial personality will make reasonable, moderate demands (i.e., money to pay rent for a year, no jail or prison time). Thus, the pattern of demands made by an inadequate person will revolve around personal recognition (media, wants the world to know, etc.), while the demands made by the antisocial person will be demands to satisfy him or herself only.

Making Demands Into Sub-Demands

Anyone who has been a negotiator in several incidents is familiar with the following scenario: the hostage taker makes a demand (let us assume, for simplicity's sake that the demand is for a vehicle with which to escape). The negotiator responds that the request will have to be "approved" by someone at the top of the hierarchy, and they are not available (but are being sought). A short time later, the hostage taker questions the status of the demand and the negotiator informs him "they are working on finding the commander, chief, warden, etc." A short time after that, the hostage taker again asks about the status of his vehicle and is once again told "we are working on it." Yet again, the hostage taker asks about his vehicle and is told "we are working on it." Each time the demand was mentioned by the hostage taker, he was stalled and the demand was not given (which is the correct approach for the responders). However, stalling tells the hostage taker "no, what you want is not going to be given," which elevates his emotions and anger. At some point, his frustration level may be elevated enough that he does something drastic in order to get what he wants. He may harm a hostage, attempt to harm a responding officer, or harm himself.

Rather than simply stall the hostage taker and deflect the demand issue, a better approach would be to break the demand into its component parts, or sub-demands, and tell the hostage taker how much is being done for him (Null, 2003). That is to say, using the above situation, if responders were going to provide a vehicle to the hostage taker, what is involved in providing that vehicle? There are likely 12 to 15 steps (or more) in acquiring and providing a vehicle for escape. Responders: (1) have to get approval from the commander, who has to (2) get approval from the chief, who has to (3) get approval from the city council, mayor, etc. (4) Once approval is given, a vehicle has to be located that satisfies the demand. (5) An off-duty officer has to be located to retrieve the vehicle (everyone on duty is tied up at the incident). (6). That off-duty officer has to go to the station and get dressed. (7) That officer has to be escorted to where the vehicle is located). (8) The owner of the vehicle has to be contacted. (9) The owner has to go to the location of the vehicle. (10) The officer then has to take the vehicle and (11) make sure it has fuel. (12) The officer then has to drive the vehicle to the scene. (13) Once the vehicle has arrived, the tactical element has to develop a plan for delivering the vehicle (14) after it has been inspected and "cleared." (15) Next, an officer has to drive the vehicle into position for the hostage taker. Other steps could be included. If the vehicle is an airplane, then proper clearances, FAA approval, and airport facility issues could be added, driving the total of subdemands close to 100.

Then, when the hostage taker asks about his vehicle, rather than stalling, the negotiator can use this as an opportunity to educate (regarding the complexity of the demand) and to build rapport by describing how much has already been done. Instead of the hostage taker's frustration level increasing, the negotiator can reduce emotions and build rapport by describing how much has been done for him. "Joe, you understand that your request for a vehicle is an extremely complicated process that involves the following steps . . . I want to let you know that we are actively working on obtaining that vehicle. Over that last two hours, we have taken your request to the commander, who has agreed and taken the request to the chief, who also signed off on the request. He went to the city manager and was turned down by her. The chief argued for you and finally got her to change her mind. So you can see, Joe, we are trying to get that vehicle for you but it is going to take some time. As I've shown, we are working on it." Later, when Joe brings up the vehicle again, the negotiator can show that other subdemands have been met and the responding authorities are working with the hostage taker and trying to get him what he wants.

Any demand the hostage taker makes can be broken into subdemands. In a prison, if a hostage taker demands to be moved to another facility, the process for accomplishing this may take several dozen steps. Some of those are small and simple (warden approval, collecting inmate possessions, transport officer, transport vehicle, etc.), while others may be time-consuming and cumbersome (agency approval, proper paperwork completed, facility to agree to take the inmate, etc.) One of the negotiation strategies the negotiators at Lewisburg Prison in Arizona used was to make the inmates aware of the complexity of moving them to another state, the various steps involved in such a move, and the time required to meet the demand. When the inmates questioned the status of their demand to be transferred, negotiators explained the process and the subdemands required to meet the transfer demand. Doing so helped defuse emotions, calm the hostage takers, and educate them in the process. Making use of subdemands also helped build rapport and trust between the negotiators and hostage takers (Dubina, 2005; Dubina & Ragsdale, 2005).

This approach can be used just as effectively with barricaded subjects and high-risk suicides as with hostage takers. Even with demands such as "Go away and leave me alone," or "I'm going to come out and make you kill me," the negotiator can turn these into sub-demands that deflect emotions, stall for time, and lead to problem-solving issues.

It is beneficial to have the team brainstorm an itemized list of sub-demands during negotiations. The primary and secondary negotiator are concentrating on communicating with the hostage taker. The rest of the team can develop a list of subdemands, rank-order the list, and even provide estimated timelines for the completion of each subdemand.

Summary

The demands made by the hostage taker will reflect the fluid nature and dynamic flow of the hostage situation. Demands can range from the impossible (a Lear Jet to fly to Barbados) to the mundane (a match for a cigarette). Regardless of the type, it is an important need to the hostage taker and should be treated as such. The negotiator should not press for demands, nor make special efforts to fulfill demands, but instead should let the situation dictate his or her response. At times, the negotiator will have to spend an inordinate amount of time discussing a seemingly trivial issue, while at other times will be able to dismiss a demand out of hand.

Once a demand has been made, the negotiator must be able to assess whether it is important to discuss and what can be gained by fulfilling that demand. Some can be fulfilled easily with valuable concessions gained from the hostage taker, while others can be virtually ignored by the negotiator.

The negotiator should use demands as an indication of the hostage taker's mental state and personality type according to the type of demands being made. An agitated or irate hostage taker will make unreasonable demands and present those demands with finality. A hostage taker who is becoming tired and ready to surrender will make demands that are simplistic and will be readily influenced by the negotiator's suggestions.

The Effects of Time on Negotiations

Paul and Judith had been divorced for five months. Judith had initiated the divorce. She was tired of Paul's drinking and occasional drug use. Paul fought the divorce, arguing he still deeply loved Judith. Shortly after the divorce, Paul began attempting to see Judith (she refused to let him in the house), began calling her on the telephone several times every day, and began sending her letters. The gist of these communications was that if Paul could not have her, then no one could, and life was not worth living without her. Finally, Judith obtained a restraining order against Paul, which he repeatedly violated. On the occasions when Judith contacted the police, they refused to arrest Paul. Next, Paul began following Judith every time she left the house. He would sit at a convenience store down the road and watch her house for several hours each night. During the day, he would wait outside her business and if she came out, follow her on foot (the phone calls and letters also continued). One night, Judith had to take her daughter Linda to the hospital emergency room. While at the hospital, Paul burst into the examining room and threatened to kill Judith, Linda, and himself, saying, "There's only one way we can be together for eternity." Three hospital orderlies escorted Paul from the hospital and called the police. The responding officer told Paul to go home and sleep it off and to stay away from Judith.

The stalking continued for another two weeks. One day, Paul entered Judith's business, ran past a secretary, locked himself in the office with Judith and attempted to rape her. The secretary called the police. The responding officer knocked on the door and was told; "Get out of here and leave us alone. We're finally going to be together forever." The officer called for the special response teams.

The tactical team was the first on the scene and cleared the office building. The negotiators arrived shortly and began collecting intelligence. The negotiators conferred with the scene commander and advised her that this would be a long negotiation, because the primary strategy was to go slow in negotiation and allow time to pass. Approximately 90 minutes after the incident began, the primary negotiator called Paul on the telephone. Initially, the negotiator's communications were met with threats and emotional hysteria. Paul repeatedly threatened to kill Judith and himself. Over the next several hours, the negotiator was able to calm Paul somewhat, reduce the number of murder/suicide threats, and open a dialogue with Paul. Paul started to sober up and began rationally thinking about his situation and began asking the negotiator what his options were. Finally, after about nine hours of negotiations, Paul put down his weapon and came out. One part of the surrender agreement was arranged by Judith, who insisted upon accompanying Paul in the police car when he was taken to jail.

For the negotiator to effectively deal with demands, he or she must make good use of time. Time is one of the negotiator's most valuable tools (Lanceley, 1985; Nudell & Antokol, 1990; Schlossberg, 1979; Van Zandt, 1991). Without time, objectives cannot be achieved, strategic and tactical goals cannot be met, and the negotiator cannot negotiate. Time decreases stress levels, increases rationality, allows for rapport and trust to develop, clarifies communications, fatigues the hostage taker, increases the probability of hostages being released unharmed, and decreases the probability that police or the hostage taker will be harmed (Needham, 1976). Along with solid communications skills, time is one of the negotiator's strongest allies.

Negotiating teams often are under pressure from on-scene commanders and other police or local officials to hurry and resolve the incident for reasons of publicity (i.e., so the media will not write negatively about the police), finances (i.e., overtime pay for 20 to 60 officers), manpower needs (e.g., most of the shift is tied up at the incident), or citizen comfort (i.e., the hostage situation has closed a main thoroughfare during rush hour). The negotiators should ignore these pressures, realize that hostage situations require time to resolve and be prepared to negotiate for as long as is necessary or for as long as progress is being made (Goldaber, 1979). A hostage situation can last from minutes to several days (in the case of prisons or cult sieges, possibly weeks or months). Mirabella and Trudeau (1982) found that the average duration of a hostage incident was 12 hours. There is no need for the negotiator to hurry.

Buying time is one of the basic objectives of negotiation (Gettinger, 1983). The skilled negotiator, like any craftsman using a tool of the trade, can work and manipulate time. As with the other tools of negotiating, the negotiator must learn to use time as a tool. Time has positive and negative effects (Fuselier, 1981/1986). The negotiator must know what positive and negative effects are, and maximize the positives and minimize the negatives.

Likewise, patrol officers should learn to manipulate time. A patrol officer will very likely be the first officer at a hostage situation. The initial minutes (15-45) of a hostage situation are the most dangerous, along with the surrender (Culley, 1978; Horobin, 1978; Spaulding, 1987). The responding officer can often mean the difference between successful and unsuccessful negotiations (Dolan & Fuselier, 1989). The first responder can set the tone for the negotiator's actions, including using time to delay the hostage taker (Garner, 1998). All patrol officers should be trained in handling hostage situations and stalling for time until negotiators arrive (Noesner & Dolan, 1992; Sloan & Kearney, 1977).

Positive Effects of Time

First and foremost, time increases basic human needs. We discussed need theories of motivation previously. In many hostage situations, it is the negotiator's job to move the hostage taker through these need states to successfully resolve the incident. That is, the negotiator must assure physiological needs (food, water), safety needs (protection against danger, threat, and deprivation), social needs (belonging, association, acceptance, and friendship), ego needs (self-esteem, status, recognition, and appreciation), and finally self-actualization needs (self-development). Time allows the negotiator to do this because time produces these needs. As these needs appear, the negotiator can take steps to fulfill these needs. As the hostage taker becomes hungry or thirsty (or begins craving a cigarette), the negotiator can use his or her position to fulfill these needs and secure concessions from the hostage taker.

Physiological needs are the most basic needs. Physiological needs are basic to survival. With time, the hostage taker will want to satisfy his growing needs for food, thirst, personal relief, etc. The negotiator can utilize and manipulate these need states to gain trust, reduce anxiety, develop the Stockholm Syndrome, and gain the release of hostages.

In Paul's case, one strategy the negotiator used was to arrange for sandwiches to be sent in to Paul and Judith. The negotiator exchanged the sandwiches for Paul's promise to quit yelling and threatening everyone so frequently. The negotiator realized progress could not be made with Paul unless his basic physiological needs were met. Additionally, the negotiator believed that by satisfying both Paul and Judith's basic needs, the two would begin talking to each other more rationally.

Safety and security needs become paramount as survival needs become fulfilled. The hostage taker will need reassurance that he is going to come out of the incident alive and will come to no harm following the resolution of the incident. At this point, if no hostages have been harmed, the negotiator can reassure the hostage taker of the non-felony nature of his act. It has been our experience and that of other teams we deal with and talk to that most hostage takers are charged with a misdemeanor (assuming no hostages are harmed; this charge is independent of any other criminal violation). In a domestic situation, the hostage taker will be charged with an offense under the family violence code (most of which are misdemeanors). If the person has no hostages (i.e., barricaded suspect), he or she is usually taken to a mental hospital and no criminal charges are filed. In cases in which a felony charge is warranted, the charge will often be reduced by the prosecutor or court. For instance, if the hostage taker fires at the responding police officers (but does not hit any officers), he will initially be charged with aggravated assault on a peace officer (felony charge). Later, that charge will probably be reduced to simple assault, a misdemeanor. In the criminal justice realm, hostage taking is not a severe crime, and because of serious prison and jail overcrowding, the hostage taker will likely serve only minimal time in a jail (versus prison). To the hostage taker, however, the large police response, the SWAT team crouched outside the door, and his perceptions of the event from the media make his act seem worthy of a lifetime in prison. The negotiator can use the difference between the reality and the perception to satisfy the need for security.

One of Paul's concerns was what would happen to him when the incident ended. He was afraid to come out because of all the police officers and what they would do to him. In his mind, he had committed several serious crimes and would spend years in prison. The negotiator explained to Paul that there were several charges that would be brought against him (including criminal trespass, attempted aggravated assault, and attempted aggravated sexual assault), but that one was a misdemeanor and the others would probably be reduced in plea bargaining procedures, and at the very worst, Paul could expect to spend a short time in a county jail and not be sent to prison. The negotiator also explained that he believed Paul was not really a criminal, but that he needed counseling and the negotiator would recommend that Paul be given treatment for his problem rather than be sent to jail. The negotiator also explained to Paul that the large police presence was not an issue, it was the job of the police to help in these situations, and the large police response was not a factor in later legal considerations.

Sidebar: Detective Jose R. Flores

Detective Joe Flores is a 27-year veteran of law enforcement and has been a negotiator for 16 years with the Carrollton, Texas, Police Department. Detective Flores is an active member and a past president of the Texas Association of Hostage Negotiators. He is a two-time recipient of the Texas Association of Hostage Negotiators Member of the Year Award and in 1991 he received the Negotiator of the Year Award. He has taught Crisis Negotiations and Violence in the Workplace Issues to law enforcement officers from across the United States for several years.

There are a multitude of different levels of intensity in a crisis negotiation incident, but dealing with the matter of a subject's demands and the effects of time are no doubt two of the most sensitive and stressful components of the negotiations process. When the subject makes demands, the negotiator must, first of all, try to determine what the subject really wants. Is he trying to obtain something tangible, such as money or a getaway vehicle, or is the subject more inclined to vent his demands to state a purpose so that he may be heard (or so a family member will be brought to him)? Then there is the element of time. Does the subject make his demands deliverable in 10 minutes? One hour? Ultimately, it really does not matter how much time he gives you. What matters is how you, the negotiator, answer the demand and how you prevail over the time deadline.

One of the longest and most grueling negotiations I was ever involved in occurred a few years ago on Thanksgiving Eve. At 4:00 in the morning, a lone adult male started a 19-hour siege in and outside of his house in an upscale section of our city. The 41-year-old Viet Nam war veteran was highly intoxicated and extremely angry with the police for (in his belief) preventing him from having custody of his three-year-old granddaughter. During the early stages of this critical incident, the man fired numerous rounds into the air and into the ground from two high-powered assault rifles. As our intelligence later revealed, the man had a virtual arsenal in his home. Another important piece of information that we discovered was that the man cared very much for young children and was in fact a big financial supporter of local children's sports teams.

Initially, the man did not express any demands. He was angry because he felt that the police dealt him wrong. As time passed, the man stopped communications with me and we were at a standstill. When night fell, the man became aware of floodlights and power generators, which had been placed in front of his house by the SWAT team. The man's immediate reaction to this discovery was explosive and hostile. His demand was that if the lights were not turned off and removed in 10 minutes, he would come out of his house with two M-16s and there would be a firefight, like no one had ever seen.

In spite of several more hours of negotiations and other demands, including the man wanting me to meet him inside his house alone, he eventually came out. The mentioning of the innocent children being injured or killed was the catalyst that tipped the scale in our favor toward a successful resolution to this incident.

There is always going to be a reason a person is taking a hostage, or barricading himself, or attempting to commit suicide, and there will also always be demands that are made by that individual to the responding law enforcement entity. The trained negotiations team members must be able to ascertain the nature of the demand and provide a reasonable answer to the demand. Keep in mind that you can always say "no" to the subject's demand without actually saying "no." I was taught and I do believe that the negotiator should always be "creative" and "flexible."

A man barricaded himself inside his home with a rifle after he assaulted members of his family. In addition to demanding that all police leave, the man demanded to speak to his mother one last time. After I learned where the man's elderly mother lived in our city, I left the critical incident scene and met the woman at her residence. I explained to her that her son was in a life-and-death situation, and asked her to record an emotional message to her son on a microcassette recorder. I instructed the woman to repeatedly mention my name as a good man who was there to be of assistance to her and him. When I returned to the negotiations command post, the primary negotiator introduced me to the barricaded man. I then informed the man that his mother wanted to speak to him. The tape was played and the man's volatile demeanor rapidly diminished. Not long afterward, the man came out peacefully.

Our negotiations team believed that the man was possibly demanding his mother on the phone as an audience for suicide, and our answer to his demand was a definitive "No," but we knew that we could not reject his demand outright. Instead, we *created* a way for his mother to speak to him.

The element of time in a critical incident can be either a very positive asset for the negotiator or very disadvantageous to the negotiations. Statistically speaking, the more time that passes during the incident, the more likely it will be resolved peacefully. Unfortunately, there will be occasions when this is not the case. The negotiator should always be watchful of the subject's demeanor for sudden changes, as these changes could be a clue of what he is contemplating on doing next.

A despondent 340-pound middle-aged man was lying in his bed draped in a sheet. He was holding a large kitchen knife to his chest and ready to commit suicide as my partner, Paul Wilford, and I tried to talk him out of it. The SWAT team was in position within a few feet of the man. The man demanded to be left alone so that he could kill himself, but he never gave any deadline. After more than an hour of talking with the man, he suddenly looked at me and said, "I've heard enough. I'm killing myself in two minutes." As we looked each other square in the eye, I realized that he was serious about his time limit. Paul quietly informed the SWAT team what the man just said and also that we believed him. I continued to distract the man by talking and almost to the second of the two-minute time limit, the man did stab himself in the chest just as the SWAT team moved in to disarm him. Although the man was successful in stabbing himself, he did not die.

Over the past several years as a negotiator and as an instructor in crisis negotiations, I have learned one very significant thing—the importance of continuing training by practical application exercises. The law enforcement officer can receive hours of classroom instruction in the theory of crisis negotiations but nothing takes the place of hands-on practical applications. By challenging your learned skills through the use of role-playing exercises with your colleagues, you can become an accomplished crisis negotiator who will be better trained in handling issues such as demands and the effects of time in a critical incident.

Once safety and security needs have been fulfilled, the social needs become primary motivators for behavior. The hostage taker must feel wanted and liked by others. It is during this need state that the negotiator can really develop a relationship and trust with the hostage taker. The hostage taker is alone and perceives the whole world as being against him. The negotiator can build upon this perception and turn it to his or her advantage by becoming that friend and associate. The negotiator can identify common areas of interest (i.e., sports, hobbies, reading, etc.) and foster the sense of belonging. Hostage takers tend to have a rather morbid outlook on life. One negotiator the authors know has this same outlook. This negotiator uses his perceptions of the world to build a common bond with the hostage taker (i.e., "I know exactly how you are feeling. Let me give you some examples from my life about how the world is against me . . ."). Before long, this negotiator and hostage taker are talking like long-lost friends.

One strategy the negotiator used to gain Paul's trust was by explaining the negotiator's divorce situation from several years past. The negotiator discussed the emotional difficulty he had in dealing with the divorce. Establishing this "common ground" enabled the negotiator to become a "friend" to Paul. Later in negotiations, Judith also explained to Paul that she still loved him, but that Paul's drinking and drug use interfered with that love, and that if Paul stopped drinking and using drugs, maybe they could talk about a future together.

Once social needs have been fulfilled, attention must turn to the hostage taker's sense of self-esteem and self-worth. The negotiator must be reassuring and constantly point out that the hostage taker is not a bad person, but merely a person who got caught up in a bad situation. For example, in a domestic situation in which a father takes children hostage because he has lost visitation rights, the negotiator must reassure the hostage taker that the children still love him as their father and are not responsible for the loss of visitation rights. Further, the negotiator must point out that if the situation continues, the father stands the chance of losing the children's love and respect. The old adage that everybody needs somebody is true. The negotiator must discover who needs the hostage taker and explore that relationship in terms of self-esteem and self-worth.

At this point, the negotiator worked on the relationship of Paul and Linda—the father/daughter dynamics of relationships. The negotiator did not dwell on what would happen to Linda without her parents, but instead focused on the love Linda had for her father and what Paul meant to Linda. The negotiator also explored Paul and Judith's past family life (prior to Paul's heavy drinking). The negotiator explored how Paul and Judith came to rely on each other to build a life as partners. The negotiator further explained how many of those "life goals" were still present, but alcohol had interfered with those goals.

The negotiator must let the hostage taker know that others care about him. The negotiator can get the hostage taker to remember a time when family did something for him. The negotiator can reinforce the idea that the family acted because they love the hostage taker, not because they had to. Just as children need the reassurance of their parents that they are still loved, so does the hostage taker. The negotiator should approach this issue just as a parent does with children. If the hostage taker came from or is in a dysfunctional family situation, the negotiator could focus on non-family relationships or any other positive relationships the hostage taker may have had in the past.

Finally, the negotiator can work on fulfilling self-actualization. The negotiator must get the hostage taker to realize that he has potential and can still grow as a person, a father, an employee, etc. To do this, the negotiator can build upon past successes of the hostage taker (i.e., "You mentioned when you coached your boys in baseball. What skills did you teach them? Did they use these skills? Well, in the future you could be like a coach and teach them many other things . . ."). Using this tactic shows the hostage taker that he has a positive future and can be beneficial as a person. In Paul's case, the negotiator explored other areas of Paul's life: work, hobbies, etc. The negotiator discovered that Paul had been an Eagle Boy Scout and explored the possibility of Paul using his scouting experience to help other youth in the future. The intelligence gathering also revealed Paul had some unique work skills and had been a valuable employee to his organization before getting fired after the divorce. Paul's ex-employer had said he would take Paul back if Paul's personal problems got resolved. The negotiator mentioned this to Paul and explored what Paul would need to do in his personal life to be able to return to his former place of employment.

Moving through these need states takes time. Furthermore, the ability to balance time when moving through these need states is crucial to success. For example, if a negotiator is moving through the hierarchy and moves too slowly, the hostage taker will regress to lower need states of survival and security and the negotiator will lose any progress made. If the negotiator moves too rapidly, the negotiator will not gain the hostage taker's trust and, while the negotiator believes most states have been fulfilled, the hostage taker will in reality be at a lower need state and far from ready to surrender.

Second, time decreases emotions and increases rationality. Hostage situations can be divided into four phases. In the early phase, or Pre-Crisis Stage, emotions are controlled, the hostage taker has a plan and that plan is being executed. In the Crisis Stage, the plan has fallen apart. Emotions are high and the ability to reason is low. The hostage taker (and hostages) are experiencing a physical "high." An "adrenaline dump" occurs: large amounts of adrenaline are released into the system, resulting in a general energizing of the body. Stress levels are high, and the hostage taker is physically primed to assure his own survival. These physical responses decrease the hostage taker's mental ability to survive. The "adrenaline dump" and other physical responses to stress interfere with and inhibit his ability to think rationally, engage in problem solving, and make decisions.

In Paul's case, one of the reasons the negotiating team decided to go slow in negotiations was to allow Paul to begin sobering up. Also, the negotiating team realized that as Paul sobered up, Paul and Judith would begin talking rationally to each other and possibly, with the help of the negotiator, discuss and resolve some of their problems.

In the third phase, or Accommodation/Negotiation Stage, the "adrenaline dump" has stopped and the buildup of adrenaline in the system has had time to dissipate. Stress has been reduced and physical systems have settled down to a normal operating level. The hostage taker is able to think clearly, engage in problem solving, and make rational decisions. During the Accommodation/Negotiation Stage the negotiator can assist the hostage taker in resolving the incident. The negotiator will be able to assist the hostage taker in arriving at a solution that assures his survival.

In the final phase, or Resolution Stage, emotions again increase and problem-solving ability decreases during surrender. Stress levels increase, adrenaline is again released into the system, and there is interference with thinking and reasoning. During this stage, the negotiator must stop being a problem solver and facilitator and become a director. The negotiator must give explicit instructions to the hostage taker and tell the hostage taker exactly what to expect when surrendering. There should be no room for questions, doubts, or surprises. If, for example, the hostage taker begins to surrender and sees police officers where they are not expected (on the front porch, for example), the hostage taker is likely to make a physical, not mental, response to the police presence and react, not think. Should this occur, the incident could well begin anew. The negotiator should give explicit instructions on how to surrender as well as what to expect upon surrender: "I want you to hold your pistol by the handle and place it outside the door. Then, place both hands over your head with your fingers clasped and step out onto the porch. There will be two police officers in black uniforms who will take your arms and handcuff you. Do you understand what you are to do and what will happen to you?"

Time allows for the development of rapport between the hostage taker and hostages (Fuselier, 1986). The hostage taker will come to see the hostages as people, not objects. The hostage taker and hostages will develop a rapport and become real people to one another. This rapport will make it more difficult for the hostage taker to harm hostages. Time also allows for rapport to be built between the hostage taker and negotiator. This development is important for a successful resolution, because it allows trust to develop between the two. The hostage taker will perceive the negotiator as someone who really cares about him and wants to help him through a difficult situation.

Several hours into Paul's situation, Paul began using the negotiator's first name. At this point, the negotiator realized that rapport was developing between him and Paul. At that point, the negotiator carefully explored other areas of mutual interest; sports, movies, etc. Although Paul did not care for organized sports, he did like camping and the outdoors. The negotiator then spent time talking about camping, hiking, fishing, etc. This process strengthened the relationship between the negotiator and Paul and helped lead to some solutions to the hostage situation.

Time increases the probability of a successful negotiation. Time allows communications to be established, decision making to occur, and managerial problems to be resolved. Solutions to the hostage taker's problems can be offered, and the hostage taker can fully think through these solutions. The hostage taker can realize that the first solution is not necessarily the best solution. For example, the criminal hostage taker makes demands without thinking through the ramifications of having them satisfied. Time allows the hostage taker to fully realize the futility of these "solutions by demand." Time also gives the negotiator the opportunity to logically argue the unreasonableness of the demands. In large part, the same is true for other hostage takers who may have pre-planned the incident (i.e., prisoners, terrorists). On the police side of the situation, needed personnel can be contacted and brought in, administrative details can be resolved, and full integration of the response teams can be accomplished.

After the negotiator and Paul had established a relationship, the negotiator turned to Paul's immediate predicament. The negotiator and Paul explored the options open to Paul in getting the family back together, reviewed various options for ending the situation, and began working on a long-term care program for Paul that involved Judith and Linda. The negotiator also helped Paul realize why murder/suicide did not benefit anyone, either in the family, social life, or organizational world. After several hours, Judith began taking part in these discussions and assisted Paul in exploring future options. It was at this point that Paul decided surrender would be in his best long-term interests.

Time permits intelligence to be gathered. The more intelligence the negotiator has, the greater the probability for success. This intelligence can only be gathered if there is time to gather it. The names of hostage takers, hostages, relatives, friends, cohorts, witnesses, etc. can be obtained. Acquaintances of the hostage taker and hostages can be interviewed. This knowledge allows the negotiator to negotiate from a power position and puts the hostage taker at a severe disadvantage. There are numerous instances in which the hostage taker has refused to give his name to the negotiator. In many of these, when intelligence gathering reveals his name and the negotiator uses it, the hostage taker is so surprised and stunned, he gives up. The hostage taker rationalizes that if the police can discover his name, there is no limit to the other things they can do, and surrender seems to be the safest alternative.

In Paul's situation, the negotiators delayed in establishing initial contact with Paul. The negotiating team spent time gathering intelligence on Paul, and contacted people who might know something about him. The negotiators talked to Judith's co-workers, neighbors, Paul's former employer, the lawyers who handled the divorce, family friends, and relatives. The negotiators found that Paul had no arrest record and had never been in legal trouble. Other intelligence was gathered before telephone contact was established. Paul was surprised that the negotiator knew so much about him, and this helped calm Paul and made him more agreeable to the negotiator's requests.

Time gives the tactical team the opportunity to prepare, gather intelligence, and get in proper position for a potential assault operation. Time is more crucial to the deployment of the tactical team than the negotiators. Negotiators arrive on the scene, select a location out of the hostage taker's sight, get on the telephone (or bullhorn), and begin talking to the hostage taker. The tactical team, however, has to make decisions for a physical resolution to the incident. The assault team has to plan and prepare, snipers have to be positioned, and the rescue team has to deploy. These decisions require complete and up-to-the-minute intelligence on the hostage taker and hostages, building plans, ingress and egress routes, etc. To properly make decisions, the tactical team needs time.

Time gives police command personnel an opportunity to get organized. Commanders can assemble any special equipment or personnel required, they can receive intelligence to make sound decisions that will bring about a safe and legal resolution to the incident, and they can explore all options in detail. The negotiator can "buy" time for the command elements so only the most well-thought-out decisions are made. Time also gives the psychologist an opportunity to analyze the personality of the hostage taker and relay this information to the negotiators and tactical team.

Time also allows for obtaining search warrants or telephone warrants. Courts have ruled that just because it is a hostage or barricade situation and negotiators or police are using time as a tool, that does not negate the need to obtain a warrant to protect the person's Fourth Amendment rights (*United States v. Donlon*, 1992), nor does the crisis incident mean that there is an exigent circumstance justifying warrantless search or seizure (*O'Brien v. City of Grand Rapids*, 1994). Just because the police treat the incident as critical does not justify warrantless actions. While the arrest of a subject depends upon many factors, including level of police authority, length of contact, or restraint of the subject, technically, surrounding and isolating the subject has placed the subject under "arrest" while inside the premises and the subject is under restraint (*Dunaway v. New York*, 1979; *United States v. Azzawy*, 1985; *United States v. Maez*, 1989; *United States v. Magluta*, 1995). One question we are often asked concerns telephone warrants. To obtain a telephone warrant, your locality must have statute authority or telephone warrants cannot be obtained (Rule 41[c][2], Federal Rules of Criminal Procedure). Some states with such statutes include Arizona (Arizona Revised Statutes § 13-3914[c]), California (California Penal Code § 1526[b]), Montana (Montana Revised Codes Ann. § 46-5-202[3]), and Nevada (Nevada Revised Statutes § 179.045). Check with your local district/prosecuting attorney or state attorney general's office to find out whether your locality has such a statute.

Time reduces the hostage taker's expectations. Time gives the hostage taker the opportunity to settle down and begin thinking about his predicament. Even without prompting from a negotiator, the hostage taker has the opportunity to rationally appraise the situation. In most cases, the hostage taker will, on his own, realize the limits of his position, what can and cannot be gained, the different possible outcomes to the situation, and the outcome if he harms hostages. Frequently in hostage situations a hostage taker begins with rather grand demands and on his own reduces those demands to basic survival.

Time gives the hostages increased escape opportunities. Like everyone else involved in the situation, many hostages will analyze their predicament and plan action. Time gives the hostages the opportunity to do this. With time, the hostage taker becomes fatigued and careless, will lapse in the attention given to hostages, will ignore hostages for brief periods, and may even briefly forget about the hostages. This inattention may give one or more hostages time to escape. Escape attempts, of course, may also produce negative outcomes. Escaping hostages may be discovered and harmed or killed by the hostage taker. Escape attempts may impair negotiations, because the hostage taker may believe the police played some role in the attempt.

With time, the hostage taker may just quit. There may be many reasons for the hostage taker to make this decision, none of them really important at this point. They may simply get tired and quit (this is especially true with the hostage taker who displays schizophrenic tendencies) (Strentz, 1986). What is important is that the hostage taker give up with no expectation of something in return.

Negative Effects of Time

One of the worst effects of time is that it increases mental and physical exhaustion, both for the hostage taker and the police response units. This exhaustion increases impulsivity. People want quick resolutions to their problems. With time, there is a tendency to force a resolution simply for the sake of bringing closure. As impulsivity increases, the ability to make good decisions decreases. Fatigue reduces the ability to make decisions. As fatigue takes its toll on the hostage taker, fatigue also influences the negotiator, tactical team, and command personnel. They may make unsound decisions and want to force a resolution. One way for a negotiating team to minimize the fatigue factor is to establish, prior to an incident, a rotation schedule for negotiators (i.e., every 10 to 12 hours) and other team members. Many teams rotate every eight to 10 hours, requiring the relief personnel to show up an hour early to work with their counterparts so the relief team knows the progress of negotiations. This becomes especially crucial during prisons and siege situations, when negotiations may last for several days or weeks.

Time also decreases the ability to think objectively. The hostage taker may begin taking unnecessary chances or engaging in risk-taking behavior. Likewise, the police may begin to take precipitous actions that are unnecessary or increase the risk to police personnel. With time, boredom increases. The negotiator may tire of talking to the hostage taker and stop facilitating negotiations. The hostage taker may also become bored and push for a rapid resolution. He may become paranoid, sensitive, and surrounded. That is, he becomes attuned to the police presence and fearful that something is about to happen. At this point, the hostage taker is likely to do something rash and engage in other paranoid-type behavior. With antisocial personalities in particular, boredom becomes a major issue in negotiations (Cleckley, 1976).

Summary

While time is a valuable tool of the negotiator, it must be used wisely. Too little or too much time can be a liability rather than an asset to the negotiator. The negotiator should balance the effects of time without merely using time as an unbridled tool. It is important that the negotiator set a comfortable pace when negotiating. This pace should be comfortable to both the police response teams and the hostage taker. Like most other aspects of the hostage situation, time is a fluid commodity and must be adjusted according to situational dynamics.

There are far greater advantages to using time than there are disadvantages. Time works for the police and the negotiator and against the hostage taker. There are no compelling reasons to rush negotiations, but there are many reasons to deliberately prolong negotiations.

References

Aamodt, M.G. (1999). *Applied Industrial/Organizational Psychology*, Third Edition. Belmont, CA: Wadsworth.

Aldefer, C.P. (1972). *Existence, Relatedness, and Growth: Human Needs in Organizational Settings*. New York, NY: The Free Press.

Biggs, J.R. (1987). "Defusing Hostage Situations." *The Police Chief* 54:33-34.

Borum, R. and T. Strentz (1992). "The Borderline Personality: Negotiating Strategies." *FBI Law Enforcement Bulletin* 61:6-10.

Cleckley, H. (1976). *The Mask of Sanity*. St. Louis, MO: C.V. Mosby Co.

Culley, J.A. (1978). "Managing the Hostage Situation." In Favreau, F. and J.E. Gillespie (eds.), *Modern Police Administration*. Englewood Cliffs, NJ: Prentice-Hall.

Dolan, J.T. and G.D. Fuselier (1989). "A Guide for First Responders to Hostage Situations." *FBI Law Enforcement Bulletin* 58:9-13.

Dubina, J. (2005). "Lewis Prison Hostage-Taking Incident." Presentation at the Arkansas Association of Hostage Negotiators annual conference. Little Rock, AR (June).

Dubina, J. and R. Ragsdale (2005). "Lewis Prison Incident Debriefing." Presentation at the annual Crisis Negotiation Conference of the National Tactical Officers Association. Nashville, TN (April).

Dunaway v. New York, 442 U.S. 200 (1979).

Fuselier, G.D. (1981, revised 1986). "A Practical Overview of Hostage Situations." *FBI Law Enforcement Bulletin* 50:12-15.

_____ (1986). "What Every Negotiator Would Like His Chief To Know." *FBI Law Enforcement Bulletin* 55:12-15.

_____ (1988). "Hostage Negotiation Consultant: Emerging Role for the Clinical Psychologist." *Professional Psychology* 19:175-179.

_____, C.R. Van Zandt, and F.J. Lanceley (1989). "Negotiating the Protracted Incident: The Oakdale and Atlanta Prison Sieges." *FBI Law Enforcement Bulletin* 58:1-7.

Garner, G.W. (1998). "Before SWAT Arrives: Negotiation Skills for First Responders." *Police* 22:26-31.

Gettinger, S. (1983). "Hostage Negotiators Bring Them Out Alive." *Police Magazine* 6:10-15.

Goldaber, I. (1979). "A Typology of Hostage-Takers." *The Police Chief* 46:21-23.

Horobin, A. (1978). "Hostage Taking—Coping with a Crisis." *Police Review* 87:1438-1440.

Lanceley, F. (1985). "Hostage Negotiations Seminar." Quantico, VA: FBI Academy (February).

Maslow, A.H. (1954). *Motivation and Personality*. New York, NY: Harper & Row.

McClelland, D.C. (1961). *The Achieving Society*. Princeton, NJ: Van Nostrand.

Mirabella, R.W. and J. Trudeau (1982). "Managing Hostage Negotiations." *The Police Chief* 45:45-47.

Miron, M.S. and A.P. Goldstein (1979). *Hostage*. New York, NY: Pergamon Press.

Misino, D.J. and J. DeFelice (2004). *Negotiate and Win: Proven Strategies from the NYPD's Top Hostage Negotiator*. New York, NY: McGraw-Hill.

Mitchell, V.F. and P. Mougdill (1976). "Measurement of Maslow's Need Hierarchy." *Organizational Behavior and Human Performance* 16:334-349.

Needham, J.P. (1976). "Research Needs for Hostage Situations." *Military Police Law Enforcement Journal* 3:27-29.

New York v. Quarles, 467 U.S. 649 (1984).

Noesner, G.W. and J.T. Dolan (1992). "First Responder Negotiation Training." *FBI Law Enforcement Bulletin* 61:1-4.

Noesner, G.W. and M. Webster (1998). "Crisis Negotiation as Crisis Intervention." In Crisis Negotiation Unit (eds.), *Crisis Negotiations: A Compendium*. Quantico, VA: Critical Incident Response Group, FBI Academy.

Nudell, M. and N. Antokol (1990). "Negotiating for Life." *Security Management* 34:56-64.

Null, S. (2003). "Another Way of Looking at Demand Issues." Presentation at the Crisis Negotiation Competition. Texas State University, San Marcos, TX (Jan).

O'Brien v. City of Grand Rapids, 23 F.3d 990 (6th Cir. 1994).

People v. Gantz, 480 N.Y.S.2d 583 (1984).

Poythress, N.G. Jr. (1980). "Assessment and Prediction in the Hostage Situation: Optimizing the Use of Psychological Data." *The Police Chief* 25:34-37.

Russell, H.E. and R. Zuniga (1986). "Special Stress Factors in Hostage/Barricaded Situations When the Perpetrator is a Police Officer." In Reese, J. and H.A. Goldstein (eds.), *Psychological Services for Law Enforcement*. Washington DC: U.S. Government Printing Office.

Salancik, G. and Pfeffer, J. (1977). "An Examination of Need-Satisfaction Models of Job Satisfaction and Job Attitudes." *Administrative Science Quarterly* 22:427-456.

Schlossberg, H. (1979). "Hostage Negotiations." Presentation at the Texas Department of Public Safety's Terrorism School, Austin, TX.

Sloan, S. and R. Kearney (1977). "An Analysis of a Simulated Terrorist Incident." *The Police Chief* 22:57-59.

Smither, R. and Lindgren, H.C. (1978). "Salary, Age, Sex, and Need for Achievement in Bank Employees." *Psychological Reports* 42:334.

Soper, B., G.E. Milford, and G.T. Rosenthal (1995). "Belief When Evidence Does Not Support Theory." *Psychology and Marketing* 12:415-422.

Spaulding, W.G. (1987). "The Longest Hour: The First Response to Terrorist Incidents." *Law Enforcement Technology* (July/August):26.

State v. Sands, 700 P.2d 1369 (Ariz. Ct. App. 1985).

Strentz, T. (1986). "Negotiating with the Hostage Taker Exhibiting Paranoid Schizophrenic Symptoms." *Journal of Police Science and Administration* 14:12-16.

United States v. Azzawy, 784 F.2d 890 (9th Cir. 1985).

United States v. Crosby, 713 F.2d 1066 (5th Cir.), *cert. denied*, 464 U.S. 1001 (1983).

United States v. Donlon, 982 F.2d 31 (1st Cir. 1992).

United States v. Maez, 872 F.2d 1444 (10th Cir. 1989).

United States v. Magluta, 44 F.3d 1530 (11th Cir. 1995).

United States v. Mesa, 638 F.2d 582 (3d Cir. 1980).

Van Zandt, C.R. (1991). "Hostage Situations: Separating Negotiation and Command Duties." *FBI Law Enforcement Bulletin* 60:18-19.

Wargo, M.G. (1989). "The Chief's Role in a Hostage/Barricaded Subject Incident." *The Police Chief* 56:59-61.

Discussion Questions

1. Gary and Eva are divorced. Eva not only has custody of the two children, but she has obtained a protective restraining order against Gary. After a night of drinking, Gary went to Eva's house (while she was at work), pulled a gun on the babysitter, told her to leave the premises, and locked himself in the house with the two children. The babysitter called the police, the responding officer approached the house and Gary took a shot at him. The negotiating team and tactical team were called. You are the primary negotiator. After talking with Gary for a period of time, he made his demands known. He believes Eva is not a good mother and he wants to take the two children to another state to live with him. It is obvious that Gary has continued drinking (beer is in the refrigerator). What tactics would you employ to convince Gary to quit drinking?

2. Concerning the incident described in #1 above, suppose that Gary became morose and depressed about not being able to see his children and began threatening to kill them and commit suicide. What needs does Gary need to fulfill and what negotiation strategies would you use to fill those needs?

3. In the incident presented in this chapter from the Salt Lake City library, the hostage taker, Clifford Draper, did not know that one of the hostages was a police officer. What do you think Draper's reaction would have been had he discovered that one of the hostages was an armed police officer? Assuming Draper found that out, what could you have done to change Draper's need state to the ego state?

4. Assume you are the on-scene commander at a hostage situation. What could you do to reduce the negative effects of time on the hostage negotiation team? On the tactical team? On perimeter and command personnel?

5. William, while robbing a convenience store, was discovered and a hostage situation ensued. William has demanded that the police leave the scene, that he be given an automobile to transport him to the airport (with a police officer driver), and a plane to fly out of the country. You believe William committed the robbery because of some problems in his personal life. What kind of questions could you ask William to get him to reveal what his expressive demands are?

6. You are called to negotiate a hostage situation at the county jail. A group of seven American Indian prisoners have taken over a cell block and have 23 other prisoners hostage. The hostage takers are demanding better living conditions, better food, more recreational privileges, and seem upset about not having their own worship services. What could you do to discover their expressive demands?

7. Harry is despondent and depressed because his ex-wife Mary obtained a restraining order preventing Harry from seeing his four-year-old son. Harry has gone to Mary's house (she is not there) and taken his son hostage. When you arrive, Harry demands that the restraining order be cancelled and the visitation agreement changed, giving Harry more rights to see his son. List the potential subdemands you could use with Harry on these demands.

8. You are the on-scene commander at a major hostage-taking event. This situation occurs on the major interstate corridor on Friday afternoon during rush hour. The mayor arrives on the scene and begins pressuring you—the negotiator—and the tactical commander to resolve the situation. What could you say to the mayor to get her to realize the importance of time?

9. Develop and conduct an exercise for your team that stresses the development and presentation of subdemands. Stress the brainstorming aspects of the exercise and use it also as a team-building exercise. Make sure the primary negotiator gets practice communicating the subdemands to the hostage taker.

10. Give five examples of expressive demands. What could you do as a negotiator to get the hostage taker to reveal expressive demands?

11. In addition to cigarettes, list 10 other consumables a hostage taker might request.

12. If a hostage taker were to ask for drugs for a medical problem, how could you verify that the hostage taker really needed the drugs instead of just wanting the drugs to satisfy an addiction? What would you do to examine the potential effects and side-effects of that medication? What if the drugs were to be used illicitly (that is, they were prescription medications, but the hostage taker really did not need them for a medical problem but rather wanted them to satisfy an addiction)?

13. In a prison hostage situation, how does time work against the negotiating team? What strategies could you employ to overcome the negative effects of time? How does time work for the negotiating team? What could you do to educate the warden about the need to use time?

Stress and
Stress Management

4

Learning Objectives

1. Define stress.

2. Understand the transactional model of stress and how it applies to hostage situations.

3. Know how different personality types are affected by stress.

4. Understand how people cope with stress.

5. Know the Yerkes-Dodson Law and how stress relates to performance.

6. Understand how stress affects people physiologically, behaviorally, emotionally, and cognitively.

7. Understand how stress affects the different participants in a hostage situation.

8. Understand how to reduce stress on all participants in a hostage situation.

9. Understand specific stress mediation techniques.

10. Know how to conduct an emotional debriefing for hostage negotiators.

Because of overcrowding in the prison, racial tension had been building for several months. At 5:30 one morning, this tension erupted in violence. Two inmates (one black and one white) began a fight in the prison kitchen. Another small group of inmates began a fire in the kitchen, and a third group attacked the first two inmates, seriously injuring one and killing the other. Officers attempting to stop the riot were attacked and driven off. Four officers and seven civilian staff were taken hostage. Before the riot was five minutes old, inmates controlled the entire dining facility and were fighting among themselves. The prison tactical response team and hostage negotiating team were called in. By noon, prison authorities had secured the rest of the prison and turned their attention to the hostage situation. Inside the dining facility, inmates had divided into three groups along racial lines and were engaged in a tense truce. Intelligence revealed that one inmate was dead, several were injured (all still inside the dining facility), and one of the injured officers was the wife of the commander of the hostage negotiation team. In addition, two other hostages were wives of tactical team members. The hostage takers made it clear from the outset that they would start killing hostages (after raping and sodomizing them) if any attempts were made to enter the library building.

The incident above illustrates the impact of stress on the people who are involved in hostage incidents. The hostage takers began their actions because of the stresses of overcrowding. The prison administration was under stress because of the riot, who was involved, and injuries to some of the hostages. The tactical team was under stress because of the relationship between some of the hostages and tactical team members. The negotiation team was under stress because their commander's wife was one of the injured hostages. Finally, stress on all participants was elevated further because of statements made by the hostage takers regarding abuses of the hostages. Clearly, stress can instigate and complicate a hostage incident. Negotiators should understand stress and recognize its impact, so they can better control it, minimizing unwanted effects.

Definitions of Stress

Hans Selye (1956), the father of stress research, defined stress as "the nonspecific (physiological) response of the body to any demand made on it." His definition focuses on what happens inside people as they respond to any situation (demand). Cox (1979) points out that there are three ideas built into Selye's definition of stress:

1. A person's response does not depend on the nature of the demand. The physiological response (i.e., increased heart rate, blood pressure elevation, adrenaline release into the

system, etc.) appears in any situation that is stressful. The physiological response is automatic and is designed to protect and preserve the person's integrity as an organism. That is, stress is a defensive reaction to threat.

2. The defense reaction progresses through three stages: the alarm reaction, in which the body shows arousal to the threat. It is energized and its resistance is reduced; the resistance stage, in which the body's reaction stabilizes and the person copes with the higher levels of arousal through a series of learned coping skills; and the exhaustion stage, in which the person's body has used all the energy it has available for adaptation and shuts down.

3. If these defense states are prolonged, diseases develop that are the result of overextending the energy available to the organism. Everly (1989) points out that chronic stress results in psychological as well as physical problems.

Selye's ideas are limited as there is evidence that both the type and the intensity of the physiological response depends on the nature of the stressor (some physical conditions, such as excess heat and cold, lead to different responses) and the person's interpretation of the situation's meaning. Cox and Mackay (1976) have developed the Transactional Model of Stress, in which the person's environment, assessment of their abilities, plans for dealing with demands, and the feedback received about the effectiveness of those plans determine the amount of stress experienced. The elements in the Transactional Model are:

1. Demands—A request or requirement for physical or mental action. It involves the perception of how much time is available to meet a demand.

2. Perception—The perception of an imbalance between the demands people see and their perceived ability to deal with those demands. The person's appraisal of this situation creates greater or lesser stress.

3. Coping—The physiological, behavioral, and cognitive changes people go through in an effort to deal with demands. The physiological arousal people experience is the arousal Selye described as stress. Changes in behavior and thinking are part of coping.

4. "Feed forward"—In every effort to cope with demands there is a quick assessment of the anticipated outcome of the considered solution. The expectation of success guides the selection of one option out of all the possibilities. If people expect their attempts at coping to be ineffective, their stress increases. If they expect them to be effective, their stress decreases.

5. Feedback—information about how effective coping is or is perceived to be. If a person's attempts at solving problems are effective or ineffective, their stress level will decrease or increase respectively.

Transactional Model for Negotiators

Demands

In hostage situations there are different demands and different perceptions about the time available depending on both the stage of the negotiation and the role a person is playing. During the crisis stage, the hostage taker probably thinks the police are going to assault in the near future. The hostages may have this same perception, along with the perception that the hostage taker may hurt or kill them. The negotiators know the police are going to contain the situation and negotiate. The stress experienced by the hostage taker will be based on the perception that he has the ability to hurt or kill the hostages, police officers, or bystanders. He will not feel directly threatened but he will be aware that there is the potential for violence. The stress experienced by the hostages will be greater than that experienced by both the hostage taker and the police. The negotiator needs to keep these differences in mind. They help explain the hostages' sometimes angry response to the negotiators and highlight the importance of reassuring and defusing both the hostage taker and the hostages.

As the incident moves from the crisis stage to the accommodation stage, everyone's perception of the situation changes. The hostage taker's fears of an assault are reduced. He will believe that taking hostages has worked for him, in the sense that he is not in immediate danger as long as he has his hostages. His stress decreases. However, the value of the hostages goes up. That leads to reactions like, "Man you must be crazy, if you expect me to give those guys up; They are the only thing keeping me alive," when negotiators ask hostage takers to let their hostages go.

The hostages begin to see the hostage taker as less threatening and the police as more threatening. Their stress level begins to decrease but their attachment to the hostage taker may begin to increase. The Stockholm Syndrome begins to develop with the hostage's perception that the hostage taker is less dangerous than the police.

The police will begin to see the situation as stabilizing. Stress levels will decrease and the potential for violence will be reduced. The stress on the negotiators will lessen and they will be able to focus on persuading the hostage taker that better alternatives exist.

Perception of Abilities

A person's appraisal of his or her ability to meet demands will depend on personality, training, experience, and the role he or she plays in a hostage drama. Everly (1989) has pointed out that a person's personality is important in both his perception of demands that are likely to be stressful and on the coping strategies the person uses to deal with those demands. Following Millon's Personality Theory, he suggests that there are basic personality styles that are sensitive to different demands.

1. The Histrionic Personality describes a person motivated by a constant need for approval, affiliation with others, and support. They are often dramatic in dress and action. They are prone to emotional displays that draw attention to themselves. They believe that the best way they have of dealing with life is to ingratiate themselves to others, particularly people in power. Negotiators are likely to deal with them because they make a suicide gesture, especially when they think they are being neglected. As hostages, they are likely to be good candidates for the Stockholm Syndrome, or they may single themselves out through dramatic and emotional overreactions.

2. The Schizoid Personality is characterized by a pattern of isolation, aloofness, and withdrawal from others. They are motivated by a need to avoid being overwhelmed by excessive external and interpersonal stimulation. They tend to be loners and only become aggressive when they feel that other people are putting too many demands on them. Under the stress of being a hostage, these people would be expected to withdraw and keep to themselves. They might quit reacting to instructions because they feel overwhelmed by the incident.

3. The Compulsive Personality is motivated by a need for perfection and social acceptance. They adhere to rules and regulations. They are concrete and specific. They fear making mistakes and being seen as socially inappropriate. They rarely are involved with the police. These people can put themselves at risk by being judgmental and critical of the hostage takers.

4. The Avoidant Personality is motivated by a desire to be accepted by others. They are so afraid of rejection that avoiding others becomes a defense against this threat. They rarely come to the attention of police, but when they do, they are usually easy to persuade. They are one of the types that are the most likely to develop the Stockholm Syndrome.

5. The Dependent Personality is characterized by acquiescing to the desires of others to gain acceptance and support. They are passive and submissive. They come to the negotiator's atten-

tion when they are paired with a more assertive partner, like the antisocial person who is generally the leader. They frequently barricade themselves in a high-visibility location to draw attention to their problems and to get themselves help. As hostages, they tend to be cooperative and compliant. They are another group that is likely to develop the Stockholm Syndrome.

6. The Narcissistic Personality expects special treatment. They have trouble postponing gratification and they must be seen by others as extremely competent. They have an inability to empathize with others and they fail to bond emotionally. Narcissism is a key element in the antisocial personality. These people will single themselves out by their unusual dress or behavior. As hostages, they may have trouble because they cannot believe the hostage taker means them when he gives orders. They may be at risk because they become a management problem for the hostage taker.

7. The Aggressive Personality is motivated by the need to control others. They are vigilant and mistrustful. They fear having to rely on others, being taken advantage of and being humiliated. They assume that only the strong survive, so they are sensitive to power and power struggles. This is another major element in the antisocial personality. If unchecked, this characteristic aggressiveness will lead them to challenge the hostage taker.

Hostage takers assess their ability to survive in different ways according to their different personalities. For instance, the dependent hostage taker who has paired up with an antisocial person believes that he has to depend on this partner for survival. The antisocial hostage taker will believe that he can depend on threats and force to intimidate the authorities in the same way he has learned to intimidate others in his life. However, he will be extremely sensitive to any sign that he is losing control of the situation, while the dependent personality will be less threatened by the loss of control.

Hostages evaluate their abilities based on their personality, too. If they tend to be histrionic, they are likely to react to the threat the hostage taker poses in a dramatic and emotional way. They will feel threatened by the hostage taker's aggression and his lack of caring. Hostages who have a more aggressive personality structure may put themselves and others at risk by being too confrontational with the hostage taker. They will react to the perceived loss of control, and whether the hostage taker cares for them will never be a question. Negotiators should know something about the hostages' motivation because that helps them predict and control the hostages' behavior.

Coping and "Feed Forward"

The ability to cope with problems results from personality style, temperament, and coping skills. Coping skills are a function of experience and training. An experienced and trained negotiation team will have developed better ways of dealing with incidents than the hostage taker or the hostages. They will have thought about and planned for more of the problems that arise during an incident than the hostage taker or hostages. They will have more options and will experience less stress. This is one reason training is important. Training helps develop skills in managing a variety of situations. It is also one of the reasons a negotiating team is more effective than a single negotiator and a single hostage taker. More ideas will be available for meeting the demands of a hostage situation.

Hostage takers' ability to cope with a hostage incident also will depend on their experience and training. With the exception of terrorists who have planned and practiced their actions, most hostage takers have never been in a hostage incident before. Therefore, they do not have experience or training on which to draw. Their stress levels will be high. They will search their memories for similar situations and pick the responses they think have the greatest chance of getting them what they want (Glasser, 1984). Their ability to predict what will happen is somewhat impaired by their stress.

Hostages will go through the same process. They will search their memory for situations that are close to the hostage situation or situations that have been stressful in the

Negotiating is a stressful process. It is crucial that negotiators be trained in various stress management techniques, not only to be more effective with a hostage taker, but also so they can monitor their own stress levels. *(R. Mullins)*

past. They will be looking for guides to how they should respond. Failing to find identical incidents, they will respond using the behavior, thoughts, and feelings that have been most successful for them in the past when they were stressed. If they have a wide range of experiences, they will have a great number of coping skills on which to draw. They will feel less stress than people who have fewer experiences. Some people have virtually no training or experience on which to draw. They experience excessive stress and generally freeze up because they can see no way of surviving.

If hostages recognize that their usual style of behaving will be counterproductive, they will have to look for other responses. This will increase their stress. For instance, the normally aggressive type of person may see that confrontation and aggression is likely to get him killed. He will have to find different ways of dealing with the situation. This generates more stress. Like a driver who is stepping on the brake and the accelerator of the car at the same time, energy is building up. Eventually, the brakes will fail or the engine will quit. Negotiators need to assess the hostages' styles and suggest stress management skills to the hostages when they can.

Feedback

If the feedback that people receive about the effectiveness of their plan is positive, the problem is solved and they move on to another problem. If the feedback is negative, they go to the beginning of the process and start over. When demanding release and threatening the hostages does not work, hostage takers have to reevaluate. They still have their needs to survive and to be in control. However, their perception of their ability to achieve these ends is changed when their demands are not met right away. They may experience additional frustration and stress. The negotiator may need to defuse them, again. They will go to their second-best solution or they may increase the intensity of their demands. The negotiator needs to defuse and play for time. After several cycles through this process, the hostage taker will run out of ideas. Then the negotiator can begin to suggest alternatives. Being a source of solutions will make the negotiator valuable to the hostage taker because he will be seen as a stress reducer.

Yerkes-Dodson Law

While one task of the negotiator is to reduce stress, the negotiator should not totally eliminate stress. We need stress to function in the world. The negotiator's task is to monitor the stress of the hostage taker and hostages and to control their stress. For negotiators, one important area in stress psychology is the Yerkes-Dodson Law. Established in 1908 (Yerkes & Dodson, 1980), the Yerkes-Dodson Law relates stress to performance. As shown in Figure 4.1, if stress is either too low or too high, performance suffers significantly. When stress is moderate, performance reaches its peak. In hostage situations, stress levels will be at the upper end of the continuum, not the lower end. The job of the negotiator is to keep stress levels (hostage taker and hostages) at a moderate level so the hostage taker's performance is maximized and hostages do not become overly emotional and act irrationally. Thus, the stress levels of the negotiator and other team members must be kept at moderate levels so they can perform most effectively.

Several points about this relationship are important to negotiations. First, at the lower end of the continuum, creativity and problem-solving are the most efficient. Second, at moderate levels of stress, physical performance is most efficient. Third, at the highest levels, problem-solving and performance deteriorate quickly. (Hart, 1991).

If the negotiators want either themselves or the hostage taker to come up with new ideas, they need to reduce the stress levels as much as possible. For instance, before starting to negotiate or between contacts with the hostage taker, negotiators may need to analyze and integrate new intelligence information into their strategy and tactics. To do this, they need to be relaxed and able to explore the new data's meaning. Similarly, if they want to problem-solve, they need to be at a low level of stress. By using deep-breathing exercises or another stress management technique just before either of these activities, they will maximize creative problem-solving.

Figure 4.1
The Relationship Between Stress and Performance Characterized by the Yerkes-Dodson Law

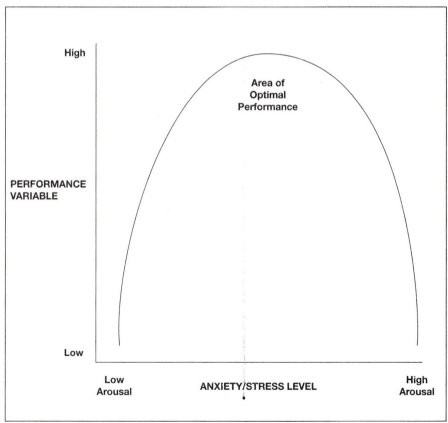

Source: W. Mullins.

If negotiators are in the process of communicating with the hostage taker, a moderate level of stress is necessary. Without it, negotiators will not stay focused and responsive to the situation. However, high levels of stress will interfere with negotiators' performance. They need to monitor their stress levels and maintain the appropriate level for their goals in negotiations. If negotiators want the hostage taker to consider new ideas that they present directly to him, they should present the ideas to him when he is the calmest. A good idea is to assign one person the task of monitoring stress levels because the person who is stressed is usually a poor observer of his or her own behavior. Usually, an outside observer recognizes the need for relaxation.

Effects of Stress

Primarily, the negotiator and others involved in the hostage situation will have elevated stress levels due to the stress of the situation, or stress that is usually referred to as acute stress (stress produced by the temporary situation). It may be the case, however, that part of the stress (especially that of the hostage taker) is the result of chronic conditions. The impact on the behavior, feelings, and thinking of people involved in crisis are the acute effects. Stress-related diseases and psychological problems are chronic effects. In addition to causing various illnesses in the long term, stress can lead to severe depression and suicide. While the data on police suicide rates is conflicting, what is clear is that police suicides are related to stress in the officer's life. D'Angelo (1999) reported that the factors related to police suicide include interpersonal and relationship problems, depression and use of alcohol/drugs, police corruption and misconduct, isolation and alienation, exposure to human misery, overbearing police bureaucracy, inconsistencies in the criminal justice system, lack of control over working conditions, social strains, physical illness, and impending retirement. Violanti (1995), one of the leading researchers into police suicide, reported that the greatest cause of police suicide is isolation; that they have no one to turn to for confidential help dealing with stress and emotional upsets. Also, Blatt (1999) reported a relationship between perfectionism and high achievement motivation to increased suicide, two attributes that have been found in abundance among negotiators.

Cox (1979) has summarized the physical, behavioral, emotional, and cognitive impact of stress.

1. *Physiological.* People under stress experience increased levels of blood sugar, catecholamines (neurotransmitter that serves, in part, to control emotional behavior), and corticosteroids (type of steroid produced by the adrenal glands that is related to emotional states. As corticosteroid levels rise, there is a rise in object loss, helplessness, depression, and a rise in aggression). There is an increase in heart rate, blood pressure, and sweating. Pupils dilate and breathing becomes difficult.

2. *Behavioral.* Acute stress leads to accident proneness, an increase or decrease in appetite, increased smoking and drinking, impulsivity, and excitability.

3. *Emotional.* People under stress experience anxiety, increased aggressiveness, boredom, fatigue, frustration, moodiness, irritability, tension, and loneliness.

4. *Cognitive.* People under stress find that their ability to concentrate and to make decisions is impaired, that they become hypersensitive to criticism, and that they are forgetful and experience mental blocks. They tend to function out of habit rather than reason. Everly (1989) points out that acute stress may lead to diagnosable psychological syndromes, including reactive psychosis, post-traumatic stress disorder, adjustment disorders, anxiety disorders, affective disorders, and some forms of schizophrenia.

Negotiators need to be particularly aware of the ability of stress to impair judgment and decisionmaking, rendering people more irritable, impulsive, and hypersensitive to criticism. All of these effects interfere with the functioning of the hostage taker, as well as the functioning of the negotiator.

Stress in the Hostage Situation

Stress affects everyone associated with a hostage situation. Hostage takers, hostages, police response units, bystanders, and acquaintances of hostages and hostage takers are all affected by stress. Physically, adrenaline is dumped into the system and body functions are on full alert. Emotions, anxiety, and fear are elevated. Thoughts are disrupted and interrupted by the stress of the situation, rationality is decreased, decisionmaking is impaired, and impulsive acts may increase.

Stress on the Hostage Taker

For the hostage taker, the situation itself produces a great deal of stress. Whether criminal, mentally disturbed, domestic, or terrorist, the hostage taker began the incident with a stressful act, but one over which he had control. In the domestic situation, for example, a disgruntled or estranged spouse makes a decision to regain control of his family or take his estranged children. He conducts some minimal planning and carries out that plan. All of a sudden, there is no plan and the situation has gotten out of his control. The situation has become highly emotionally charged, is beyond his control, and is one he has never experienced before. This newness and uniqueness adds situational stress.

The hostage taker faces an unknown future. To him, there is no positive outcome. Like an animal backed into a corner, fangs bared, he sees no safe way out. In this situation, the stress and uncertainty may overwhelm him and he may become unpredictable. In the chapter's opening scenario, the hostage takers initially engaged in their actions because of the stress of overcrowding. Once the incident began, the stress on the hostage takers exacerbated their situation, resulting in the injury and attacks on the hostages. The prisoner hostage takers engaged in unpredictable behavior.

Situational stress is also produced by having hostages. The hostage taker is now responsible for one or more people. He must use them for his safety and security. He must attempt to formulate a plan for escape, while at the same time watch over a group of people who do not want to be captive. At least perceptually, these people pose as much of a threat to him as he does to them. He must protect himself by using force to restrict their movement, he must provide for their needs, and he must deal with their emotions. The hostages may initially be fearful, confused, and disobedient. The hostage taker does not know how to deal with their behavior. All of these factors elevate stress levels of the hostage taker.

If the hostage taker is forced to harm or kill a hostage, stress will be elevated further. Now the hostage taker is confronted with the reality of having committed a serious crime. He has to deal with the injury or death, as well as with the reactions of the hostages. His situation has become more hopeless, at least in his mind.

If there are multiple hostage takers, an added source of stress is the dynamics among hostage takers. One hostage taker may want to leave, regardless of the consequences. Another may want to kill all the hostages. Another may want to "shoot it out" with the police. There may be conflict about who is to be the leader, who is to talk to the police, who is to guard hostages, etc. This tension may produce anger and frustration. The arguing and bickering among the hostage takers will add to the stress inherent in the situation.

Another source of stress on the hostage taker is the presence of the police. To the hostage taker, the police signify only one outcome: something negative. The police mean imprisonment, injury, or death. Seeing police officers with guns pointed his way elevates the hostage taker's stress level. The police also mean continued confinement and loss of immediate freedom. The police produce uncertainty. What are they going to do? Are they sneaking up right this minute? Are they going to assault and kill me? What about after the incident? All of these questions imply uncertainty and increase stress. Even talking to a police negotiator produces stress. In the opening incident, in addition to the presence of the tactical and negotiation teams, the prisoners knew that some of their hostages were related to prison officials. This only served to further elevate stress levels.

The hostage situation produces a threat to the basic needs of the hostage taker. Needs of security, safety, social acceptance, and love are all at risk in the hostage situation. The most basic need of survival is threatened by the inherently violent nature of the situation and the police response. Needs for food, drink, sleep, etc. are all affected by the situation. With time, these needs become predominant and are unfulfilled. The lack of fulfillment increases stress and anxiety. Social needs are threatened. Nobody likes the hostage taker: not the hostages, and certainly not the police. The world is against him. Even loved ones may turn against him. Family and friends may attempt to convince him to surrender. The hostage taker sees this as a betrayal and further deepens his "me against the world" perceptions. This loneliness increases stress.

Stress affects the hostage taker's decision-making skills. Stress elevates emotions, speeds physiological processes, and interferes with cognitive processing. The ability to make decisions is hindered or eliminated. The uniqueness of the situation, guarding a group of strangers, and having the guns of the police pointed at him, all work together to impair decisionmaking. The hostage taker does not have time to think with all the competing demands on his system. Not being able to think, in and of itself, increases stress.

As the situation progresses, the number of decisions that need to be made increases. This increases the demands on the system, thereby increasing stress. The need to fulfill need states interferes with decision-making ability. Hunger, fatigue, and other needs all combine to wear down the hostage taker and deteriorate decisionmaking. This leads to more frustration, which worsens decision-making skills further. This cycle repeats time and again, each time increasing stress, frustration, anxiety, and anger.

With time, the negotiator can reduce stress, calm the hostage taker, improve decision-making skills, and fulfill most need states. The hostage taker feels better and works to resolve the incident. The hostage taker finally decides to surrender. Suddenly, stress levels are back to where they were initially, with all the associated problems. The hostage taker is faced with uncertainty, his world is no longer static, he is going to give himself to the police, and fear increases. Because of the stressors on the hostage taker, the resolution phase is as dangerous as the crisis stage of a hostage situation. Emotions are high and reasoning ability is impaired.

Stress on the Hostages

The hostages are under a great deal of stress. At the onset, the hostages are confronted with loss of life, serious injury, loss of freedom, and loss of self-respect. The hostages are dealing with a person threatening to harm or kill them. They are panicky, anxious, uncertain, and fearful (Oots & Wiegele, 1985). They may feel overwhelming helplessness, existential fear, and sensory input overload (Hillman, 1981). Some may have been injured or killed, which adds to the survivors' stress. The hostages see themselves as victims of circumstance. They were going about their normal, everyday activities in an orderly world. All at once, the order of their lives has disappeared and they are facing an uncertain, and possibly short, future. More importantly, they are in a situation in which their actions, thoughts, and emotions are being controlled by someone else.

The stress confronting the hostages produces a physical arousal. This physical arousal is likely greater for the hostages than for other participants in the situation. Hostages will experience an increase in blood pressure, heart rate, neural interference, and may experience loss of muscular control (Gilmartin & Gibson, 1985). They may lose bladder control, faint, vomit, or even have heart failure, hemorrhage, or stroke. The hostage may hyper-ventilate or experience an asthma-like attack. The stress of the hostage sit-uation may cause an onset of any medical condition of the hostage (Nudell & Antokol, 1990). Diabetes, migraine headaches, gastrointestinal disorders, and other illnesses may appear. The stress may be so great, in fact, that some of the hostages may hallucinate (Lanza, 1986). Siegel (1984) reported that almost 25 percent of hostages may hallucinate. These hallucinations include sensitivity to light, difficulty in visual focusing, disorientation, preoccupation with body imagery, dissociation, geometric patterns, tunnel vision, tactile-kinesthetic hallucinations, and auditory hallucinations.

The hostages are stressed by their loss of self-respect. They perceive themselves as "bad" people because they are hostages. Their families and friends might think less of them because they allowed themselves to be taken hostage. Their perception of how others think of them may produce more stress than the stress produced by the situation. The hostages may feel guilty because they got taken hostage to begin with ("why didn't I do some-thing to get away from here?" "what did I do to deserve this?") or because they did not do something to resolve the incident (physically fight the hostage taker or reason with him). Many former prisoners of war believe they "let down their country" by being captured or not escaping captivity. Many hostages feel the same way.

As the situation progresses, the initial stress dissipates and the hostages calm down and begin dealing with the situation. After a period of time, stress begins to increase as basic needs are not met. The presence of the police pro-duces stress. To the hostage, the police are as much of a threat as the hostage taker. The hostage does not know how or if the police can differentiate them from the hostage taker and thus are as much a threat to life as is the hostage taker.

The resolution phase produces a threat to hostages. By the resolution phase, the hostages have settled into a routine and become familiar with their situation. The resolution produces uncertainty and anxiety. They realize the hostage taker may become irrational and let his fear overcome his ability to act in a rational manner. As they are released, the hostages are treated as crim-inals by the police.

In domestic situations, there is a special stress on the hostage/spouse. The hostage knows the hostage taker intimately and knows what the hostage taker is capable of. Additionally, the spouse/hostage feels some responsibility to assist the hostage taker to resolve the incident successfully (i.e., not only get out of the situation alive, but also to not go to jail). In these situations, the hostage feels a responsibility to assist in resolving the incident as well as the stress produced regarding his or her own survival.

In prisons, hostages also have the additional stressors of knowing their captors. Unlike the domestic situation, however, the hostages are aware of the violence their captors are capable of. Often, people are injured before they become hostages. All the hostages know that if the authorities do not fulfill demands and resolve the situation, the hostage takers will injure or kill the hostages. The hostages know the hostage takers hate the hostages and would, in some cases, be glad to harm the hostages. In jail and prison situations, the nature of the relationship between the hostages and hostage takers in and of itself significantly increases stress on the hostages.

Stress on the Negotiator

The stress faced by the hostages may have severe behavioral consequences. They may do things that get them killed. They may argue, fight, or resist the hostage taker. They may not follow instructions or become overly compliant. They may not obey instructions from the police.

The police are under a great deal of stress. The police, in fact, may be under more stress than the hostage taker. The negotiators know they are talking to a person who may kill people. The negotiator is faced with role ambiguity. He is expected to uphold the law, arrest criminals, and protect the public. As a negotiator, he is expected to be able to talk with and become friendly with a criminal. He must set aside his values and beliefs and operate from a different belief structure. There is an associated role conflict for negotiators. Instead of arresting and jailing a criminal, the negotiator is negotiating for the freedom (perceptually) of the hostage taker. The negotiator is not a police officer "cleaning the streets"—the negotiator is talking and compromising with the criminal. The hostage negotiator is dealing with someone who does not recognize the authority of the negotiator. The negotiator is accustomed to having people obey his or her commands. The hostage taker not only rejects the negotiator's commands, but may give orders to the negotiator, a situation not familiar to a police officer.

The negotiator realizes that every word said, every action taken, and every decision made may cost lives. The negotiator is in a critical role and literally holds the lives of others in his or her hands. One mistake, one miscue, one poor decision may cost lives: of the hostage taker, the hostages, or police officers. This fear can significantly increase stress. The negotiator may even go into denial ("this cannot be happening to me," Bohl, 1992b). To make matters worse, the negotiator must internalize these feelings. The negotiator cannot let the fear show, either to fellow officers or the hostage taker. Containing and hiding these emotions further increases stress.

The physical dynamics of the situation produces stress. The performance of the negotiator is constantly being monitored and evaluated. A move cannot be made without someone watching. The negotiator is confined in a small space for long periods and is attempting to converse with someone who may not even be listening. Basic needs may have to go unfulfilled because he or she cannot leave the telephone. The negotiator becomes fatigued, hungry, sore, and cramped.

Stress on the negotiator comes from other police officials at the incident (Davidson, 1981). Other negotiators may want them to take a different approach, or offer suggestions. The tactical team may want to assault or snipe the hostage taker. The commander may pressure the negotiator to hurry and end the situation for a variety of reasons. The patrol commander may want a quick resolution to the incident so that patrol officers may return to regular duties. When the negotiator attempts to delay further, stress increases. One of the major stressors is that other response elements (such as the tactical team, perimeter team, even command personnel) do not fully understand the role of the negotiator. Byron Sage, a retired FBI negotiator, reports that at the Davidian siege in Waco, Texas, he often received the brunt of anger from the tactical team because they did not know or understand what the negotiators were attempting or were doing. The negotiator may become angry and hostile to other police officers because of these pressures.

Stress and Stress Management

Captain Clark Morrow is the Investigations Division Commander for the Olathe, Kansas, Police Department. He maintains extra-duty assignments as an officer in charge of the Kansas City Metropolitan Major Case Squad and as a commander of his county's officer-involved shooting investigation team. He has been a police negotiator since 1995, and is a founding member and past president of the Kansas Association of Hostage Negotiators. A case study video he produced, which documented a Y2K bank robbery with hostages, has been used to train more than 1,000 police officers and bank employees across the United States.

The act of negotiating, for the negotiator, is not really about "negotiating." It's about emotional sacrifice.

It took some time for me to realize this. But over the years I've come to understand the role such sacrifice plays for the negotiator, and how closely it is intertwined with stress.

The thing about negotiators is that we *choose* to do this to ourselves. We *choose* to take emotional risks in order to help others. This emotional sacrifice takes its toll, of course; it is part of the long-term stress we carry with us and need to diffuse as much as possible.

An effective negotiator *must* make an emotional investment, he or she *must* care, and with that caring comes stress.

Without caring there is no potential loss, reward, or risk. And stress is all about risk. And uncertainty. And control—or lack thereof.

To paraphrase Dr. Kevin Gilmartin, a former police negotiator, cop stress is rooted in two factors: low control and high demands. The more I consider that concept, the more I see how it applies to negotiators.

Cops love control. It's how we operate. For most of us, when we don't have it, our stress level rises. In the typical negotiable incident, however, we can only control our own plans and actions. We can certainly guide and persuade and manipulate others (or attempt to do so), but ultimately we remain, in many ways, at the mercy of the person on the other end of the line. A person who may simply be distressed, or who may have their own secret agenda, or be mentally ill, or functioning (or not) under the influence of alcohol or drugs. The human component, the interpersonal dynamic, clings to every negotiable incident.

Then there are the high demands. The pressures. Sometimes it seems as though negotiation teams climb into a pressure box from the moment they show up on a scene. Pressure from the scene commander. From SWAT. From the hostages. From the hostage taker. From the families of the hostages or the suicidal/ barricaded person. From the media. From the community. And perhaps the greatest pressure of all is the pressure we place upon ourselves to make this a "successful" negotiation.

There is the time element, as well—more specifically, the communication opportunities that time allows.

In my city, during the past five years, we've handled two aborted bank robberies with hostages. The first lasted eight hours, and ended when the hostages (with whom we'd spent most of the day speaking) decided, without warning, to overtake the hostage taker at an opportune moment. The resulting scuffle created banging sounds over the open phone line that sounded like gunshots. I found that incident to be considerably more stressful than our second incident, which was in reality much more violent. In the second incident, not long after our arrival on the scene and following brief contact with the hostage taker over a two-way radio he sent out (to tell us to get out of his way), the hostage taker forced six hostages to disrobe, chained them together, walked them out of the bank, and loaded them into a van. When he found himself blocked in the parking lot, he shot at one of our SWAT vehicles, then directed the van (driven by a hostage) to the local airport where he attempted—with one of the hostages in tow—to steal a small airplane. He was shot outside of the airplane and the hostages, none of whom had the chance to speak with negotiators, were all rescued, unharmed.

The key as to why I found one incident more stressful than the other, I believe, lies in the fact that with the first incident I had an emotional investment in the hostages, having gotten to know them during conversations they'd had with our team's negotiators. That emotional investment could very well have been made with a suicidal or barricaded person, depending on the incident. In many cases, if not most, a successful "negotiation" is about finding the common threads that tie us together as human beings. The longer an incident lasts, the more emotional investment you are likely to have, and the more stress you are likely to feel and carry with you.

> The important point is to recognize the factors that cause stress—even if you don't recognize the stress itself, or even how it stays with you. The book you're reading is considered the "bible" by those of us in the field, and I strongly encourage you to read closely the sections on stress management and emotional debriefing. Detailed are proven techniques that may save the careers—and even the lives—of your team members.
> And maybe even you.
> I saw a documentary film some years back that profiled a group of British students as they grew up, graduated from secondary school, and matured into middle-aged adults. One of the study subjects, looking back on his life, remarked that "All lives are acts of bravery."
> As negotiators we constantly join and engage the inner battles of others; we are participants in and witnesses to such bravery. Let's not be casualties in the war.

The negotiator may experience stress due to the public and news media. The hostage situation may seriously inconvenience the public. One situation occurred in the downtown business district of a major city. The incident began shortly before evening rush hour and lasted until nearly midnight. Because of the nature of the incident, a large area had to be cordoned off (the outer perimeter was approximately four square city blocks). The inconvenienced public could not understand the need for the police to close a large section of the downtown area and kept attempting to cross police lines. City officials were pressuring the police department to hurry and reopen the downtown area. The media also may produce stress by their reporting of the incident. During the Hanafi Muslim hostage situation in Washington D.C. in the 1980s, one news reporter, in a live interview, asked the hostage takers' leader if he could trust the police. This question created doubts in the mind of the leader, and a period of time elapsed before trust could be re-established between him and the negotiator. Additionally, the media may criticize the police, bias their reporting, and perform other acts that increase the negotiator's stress.

Time produces more stress on the negotiator. The negotiator becomes fatigued and must make important decisions. Additionally, the negotiator has to deal with time demands from the hostage taker. The negotiator's commanders may interfere with or impede his or her ability to handle time demands from the hostage taker.

The negotiator will face increased stress during the resolution phase. The negotiator is responsible for the safety of all parties involved in the hostage situation. The negotiator must: (1) ensure that the hostage taker receives clear instructions on how to release the hostages; (2) communicate to the tactical team; (3) instruct the hostages on how to surrender; and (4) coordinate the actions of the police, hostages, and hostage taker. Further, the negotiator must do this while physically and mentally drained. Additionally, if the situation must be resolved tactically or if people are killed during negotiations, the negotiators may develop post-trauma stress (Mullins, 1999).

After the incident is over, negotiators continue to experience stress from the incident. They may be criticized for their actions and role in the crisis. The negotiator who had to negotiate with a person who killed a police officer, for example, may be vilified by peers for talking a "cop killer" into surrendering. In other instances, negotiators may be the recipients of anger, frustration, or criticism from the media, the public, and families of hostage takers and hostages (McMains, 1995).

Bear in mind that negotiators are under a high level of stress at the crisis situation in addition to the stressors that are in their normal lives. Like all of us, negotiators are susceptible to the stresses of family and work, in addition to some specific stressors from being on the negotiating team. Max Howard (1999, 2000) has pointed out that it is rather common for crisis negotiators to experience stress due to such factors as lack of support from administration, management issues, politics, and image maintenance.

Stress Management

The negotiator must be able to reduce stress in the hostage taker. The negotiator can employ several strategies to accomplish this goal. First, the negotiator can be calming and reassuring. The hostage taker should be allowed to ventilate and talk out problems. The negotiator can have the hostage taker slow down and take time to think and make decisions, help the hostage taker make decisions, and educate the hostage taker. The negotiator can clearly convey consequences to the hostage taker.

Second, the negotiator can reduce the hostage takers' stress by listening actively. The negotiator can focus on the feelings of the hostage taker. The negotiator can demonstrate understanding of the fear, anxiety, and anger the hostage taker is experiencing. The negotiator can show respect for the hostage taker and his position and should not be judgmental or condescending. The negotiator can empathize with the hostage taker ("I understand how you must feel. I remember a time when I felt that way"). The negotiator can restate the hostage takers' position or message. That is, he or she can summarize (using different words) what the hostage taker said. Just by having someone listen, the hostage taker's stress will be reduced.

Third, the negotiator should be non-aggressive and non-threatening to the hostage taker. Loaded words and name calling should be avoided. For example, the negotiator should avoid using words like "bub," "boy," "dude," curse words, etc. He or she should share the negotiator's feelings and stressors. The negotiator should not judge the actions of the hostage taker. This does not mean the negotiator has to agree with the hostage taker, but it does mean that the negotiator should not let disagreement be known to the hostage takers and should avoid taking sides.

The negotiator can use stress mediation techniques on the hostage taker. The negotiator can instruct the hostage taker in a simple relaxation and breathing exercise. Over the telephone, the negotiator can lead the hostage taker through this simple exercise, and then ask the hostage taker if it helped him calm down. The negotiator can assist the hostage taker in visualization exercises. For example, in the communications chapter, we discussed some techniques of suggestion. One of these techniques involves having the hostage taker visualize a less stressful time in his life. The negotiator can encourage this visualization when the hostage taker begins to become frustrated, angry, or emotional.

The negotiator can assist in reducing hostage stress. He or she can work on relaxation exercises and breathing exercises through the hostage taker. The negotiator can talk to a hostage on the telephone and use the same communicating, active listening, and stress mediation techniques used with the hostage taker. If possible, the negotiator can relay to the hostage what is occurring, why no hostages have yet been freed, and other information. It may be advisable to first tell the hostage taker what is being planned before talking with the hostages.

The police (negotiators, tactical team, and other responding officers) can use several techniques to reduce their stress during an incident. Education is one of the most beneficial and effective stress mediation techniques. Prior to an incident, negotiators should receive training about stress. This training should include education in the sources of stress during negotiations, factors that can worsen stress (children as hostages, death of a hostage, death of an officer, etc.), hostage taker factors that worsen stress (presence of alcohol or drugs, emotionally disturbed, emotional irritability, etc.), symptoms of stress (during and after the incident), long-term symptoms of stress, and stress mediation techniques. Having this knowledge is probably the single most effective stress mediation technique in the negotiator's arsenal. An empirical examination of stress education by Deffenbacher and Shepard (1989) found that education concerning stress and stress management significantly reduced the subject's general anxiety, anger, situational stress reactivity, and stress-related physiological reactions. Further, long-term follow-up on these subjects found that the positive benefits persisted over time.

The negotiator can engage in some simple progressive relaxation and breathing exercises (Nelson et al., 1989). Progressive relaxation techniques can significantly reduce physiological reactions to stress (i.e., blood pressure, heart rate) (Albright et al., 1991), anxiety, and tension, and improve cognitive functioning and decisionmaking. For relaxation exercises to be most effective, they should be practiced or used before a hostage situation. Relaxation exercises, for example, should be done daily for 10 to 15 minutes.

The most basic relaxation exercise is done as follows: The person should first sit in a relaxed position and close his or her eyes. The person should then tense all the muscles in his or her body and then force each muscle to relax. Starting at the toes and feet, the person should concentrate on making each muscle group relax. After all muscles are relaxed, the person should concentrate on thinking "relax" on each inhalation and the number "one" on each exhalation, controlling his or her rate of breathing. This exercise should be practiced each day, at different times of the day. After a brief period of using this relaxation technique, the person will find that he or she can instantly relax whenever faced with a stressful situation.

Exercise can reduce stress. The negotiator should use aerobic exercise and stretching once every hour or after a particularly difficult conversation with the hostage taker. If the negotiator cannot leave his or her chair, simple leg, arm, torso, and neck stretching exercises should be used. With arms and legs, reach as far as possible, change the plane occupied by the legs and arms, and repeat. Do this a minimum of three times. Stretch torso, shoulders, and neck as far as possible for a minimum of three times. If necessary, repeat the entire exercise.

If the negotiator can leave his or her chair, a short jog around the room, down the hall and back, or around the negotiating vehicle can be of immense benefit in reducing stress. These short jogs will allow the negotiator to remain within quick reach of the telephone. Other team members or responding police officers can take longer walks or jogs, or engage in more complex stretching and aerobic exercises. Members of the Austin, Texas Police Department negotiating team carry mats in their negotiator vehicle so team members can do aerobic exercises next to the vehicle.

Periodic time-outs can be used to reduce stress. Taking a few minutes to eat, take a coffee break, or just sit and mentally relax can reduce stress. Some negotiators keep a deck of cards handy to play solitaire. Others may draw, doodle, or engage in another mundane task. All are effective in reducing stress and improving the ability to think and make decisions. The negotiator may use a visualization technique during the time-out. Visualization is using positive mental imagery to reduce stress and clear the mind. To use visualization, sit in a comfortable position, relax, and mentally picture a pleasing scene or period in life. Vividly recalling a fishing trip, vacation, or playing with your children are effective visualization techniques.

Diet is important in controlling stress. The negotiator (and other responding police) should eat small meals and limit intake of liquids. Caffeine intake should be limited. Negotiations are not the time to drink cup after cup of coffee. Decaffeinated beverages are preferable and coffee drinking should be mixed with drinking other liquids such as water, decaffeinated sodas, or tea. Limit sugar intake. Coffee should be taken without sugar or with a sugar substitute. Sodas should be sugar free. Fatty foods should be avoided. Light meals such as salads, chicken (not fried), vegetables, etc. are preferable. Small portions should be eaten. If the negotiator gets hungry between meal periods, he or she should eat light snack foods. The responding police officers should not become overly hungry or thirsty as this increases stress and reduces the ability to think clearly and rapidly.

If the negotiator smokes, he or she should do so sparingly. Monitor nicotine intake carefully. Smoking while on the telephone with the hostage taker should be avoided. During periods of high stress, smoking should be avoided and a negotiator should wait at least 15 minutes following the stress before smoking. Nicotine stimulates the system (as does stress). The negotiator does not need the cumulative effects of stress and nicotine. The physical effects of stress should dissipate before using nicotine. When under stress, smokers use cigarettes unconsciously. They smoke without even realizing they are smoking. The stress produces a Pavlovian response of which they are not aware. Chewing on a pencil or wooden popsicle stick may fulfill the Pavlovian need to do something with one's hands and reduces the desire to smoke.

If the hostage incident is not successfully negotiated or if people are killed, the negotiator may experience some long-term stressors. These may range from a simple reaction such as an uncomfortable feeling that the negotiator did not do his or her job to a full-blown post-traumatic stress response (Mullins, 1999). Again, education can help mitigate these effects. Teaching negotiators how to focus on the positive aspects of the situation and reinforce their positive performance, and what not to do when negotiations fail (i.e., do not assign blame, do not dwell on the incident, do not feel guilt, etc.) can be one of the most effective techniques for reducing long-term stress.

Negotiators, especially following unsuccessful negotiations, should be emotionally debriefed by a mental health professional or peer support team member. This debriefing should be conducted shortly after the incident ends and be as short as possible. The debriefing should focus on: (1) information gathering—letting the negotiator describe the physical scenario and his or her role, when the negotiator arrived, who the actors were, what they did; (2) negotiator thoughts—what thoughts the negotiator had during the incident, attitudes, perceptions; (3) negotiator emotions—what emotions the negotiator experienced as the incident progressed and after the resolution; (4) physical signs of stress—what, if any, physical stress symptoms he or she is experiencing; (5) unfinished business—how any prior unsuccessful incidents influence emotions, beliefs, or attitudes concerning this incident; (6) teaching—explain post-trauma stress and explain that his or her reactions are normal, and how to properly cope with any long-term stress; and (7) summarize—answer the negotiator's questions and provide information for further assistance (Bohl, 1992a; 1992b).

A cohesive negotiator team that trains and socializes together can reduce stress in individual team members (Cox, 1991; Lazarus, 1991; McHugh & Brennan, 1992). Because negotiating units cannot be made a full-time unit within the police agency, all possible opportunities for team interaction (away from a hostage situation) should be provided. This critical interaction will build teamwork and cohesion but, just as importantly, reduce stress during an actual incident. The negotiating team will, in effect, become its own peer support team and stress reduction network. If one team member becomes overly stressed, other team members will intervene to reduce the stress.

Stress reduction also begins long before a critical incident begins. Negotiators should concentrate on reducing stress in their personal lives and at work. This means, in large part, teaching stress management and stress reduction techniques to the families of negotiators. Spouses and families often become frustrated and angry about the negotiator being called out at night, during family outings, during social events, and at other times that interrupt family activities. Families are also fearful for the life of their loved ones. Training families in the role and functions of negotiators can significantly mitigate some of these emotions (Mullins, 1998). Training negotiators to deal with family stress should be conducted. At home, negotiators must also actively listen, should take the concerns of the family seriously, and show the family a caring attitude.

Families should be taught to provide support roles for the negotiators. By talking out emotions and frustrations from the incident with family members, the family can (and should) become one of the primary supports for the negotiator. Family members should avoid second-guessing the negotiator, especially if the incident was traumatic. Do not ask questions such as, "Why didn't you . . . ?" or "Is there anything else you think you could have done?" The family should be taught to be reassuring and supportive and ask questions or make statements such as, "It sounds to me like you did everything possible to prevent his death, given the situation," "Isn't second guessing a natural part of what happens following one of these?" and "Things may look bad now, but they will get better."

To optimize stress reduction, all of the techniques discussed above should be utilized together (Buhler, 1993; McHugh & Brennan, 1992; Latack & Havlovic, 1992). Engaging in a relaxation or breathing exercise while gulping coffee or smoking a cigarette is not very beneficial. The relaxation techniques should be practiced and learned before a hostage incident. When under stress, the stress mediation techniques should come naturally and without the person having to think about them. Learning and practicing beforehand will enable the negotiator to concentrate solely on negotiating and remain calm and composed.

Summary

In any hostage incident, there are at least three groups that are affected by the stress of the situation: the hostages, the hostage takers, and the negotiators. Each will have his or her own perceptions of the demands of the situation, his or her abilities to deal with the incident, and his or her own coping styles. Each will experience different levels of stress. The negotiators need to be aware of the stress levels of all three of these groups to create the right atmosphere for negotiating. During the Crisis Stage, they will want to keep their own stress levels down and reduce the stress of others, so that the situation can be brought under control and reason can take the place of emotion. At a later time, the negotiators may want to increase the stress levels of the hostage takers, so they will use more energy or become less critical.

If they want creative problem solving, as in the resolution stage, they will want to minimize stress levels. Therefore, the negotiators must be able to recognize and manage stress.

Stress is one of the few constants in a hostage situation. Stress affects all participants in the hostage situation. Stress increases emotions, reduces the ability to think rationally, and interferes with decisionmaking. Being aware of how stress affects a person and how the system responds to stress, and learning to recognize the symptoms of stress can go a long way in controlling the negotiator's stress and that of the hostages and hostage taker. Once the sources and symptoms of stress are recognized, it is important to know how to mediate stress and control it. Making frequent use of stress mediation techniques will improve your effectiveness as a negotiator and allow you to control the stress of others.

References

Albright, G.L., J.L. Andreassi, and A.L. Brockwell (1991). "Effects of Stress Management on Blood Pressure and Other Cardiovascular Variables." *International Journal of Psychophysiology* 11:213-217.

Blatt, S. (1999). "Research Links Perfectionism in High Achievers with Depression and Suicide." *American Psychologist* 49:1003-1020.

Bohl, N.K. (1992a). "Hostage Negotiator Stress." *The Police Investigator* 3:25-27.

──────── (1992b). "Hostage Negotiator Stress." *FBI Law Enforcement Bulletin* 61:23-26.

Buhler, P. (1993). "Stress Management." *Supervision* 54:17-20.

Cox, T. (1979). *Stress*. Baltimore, MD: University Park Press.

──────── (1991). "Organizational Culture, Stress, and Stress Management." *Work and Stress* 5:1-4.

──────── and C.J. Mackay (1976). "A Psychological Model of Occupational Stress." Paper presented at Medical Research Council Meeting: Mental Health and Industry. London, UK, November.

D'Angelo, J.J. (1999). "Spirituality and Police Suicide: A Double-Edged Sword." Presentation at the FBI National Academy, Conference on Suicide and Law Enforcement. Quantico, VA (September).

Davidson, G.P. (1981). "Anxiety and Authority: Psychological Aspects for Police in Hostage Negotiation Situations." *Journal of Police Science and Administration* 9:35-38.

Deffenbacher, J.L. and J.M. Shepard (1989). "Evaluating a Seminar on Stress Management." *Teaching of Psychology* 16:79-81.

Everly, G. (1989). *A Clinical Guide to the Treatment of the Human Stress Response*. New York, NY: Plenum Press.

Gilmartin, K.M. and R.J. Gibson (1985). "Hostage Negotiation: The Bio-behavioral Dimension." *The Police Chief* 52:46-48.

Glasser, W. (1984). *Control Theory*. New York, NY: Harper & Row.

Hart, A.D. (1991). *Adrenaline and Stress*. Dallas, TX: Dallas World Press.

Hillman, R.G. (1981). "The Psychopathology of Being Held Hostage." *American Journal of Psychiatry* 138:1193-1197.

Howard, M. (1999). "Project the Message, Protect the Messenger." Presentation at the Texas Association of Hostage Negotiators. Dallas, TX (September).

_____ (2000). "Negotiator Stress." Presentation at the Texas Association of Hostage Negotiators. Dallas, TX (September).

Lanza, M.L. (1986). "Victims of International Terrorism." *Issues in Mental Health Nursing* 8:95-107.

Latack, J.C. and S.J. Havlovic (1992). "Coping with Job Stress: A Conceptual Evaluation Framework for Coping Measures." *Journal of Organizational Behavior* 13:479-508.

Lazarus, R.S. (1991). "Psychological Stress in the Workplace." *Journal of Social Behavior and Personality* 6:1-13.

McHugh, M. and S. Brennan (1992). "Organizational Development and Total Stress Management." *Leadership and Organization Development Journal* 13:27-32.

McMains, M.J. (1995). "Negotiator Stress and the Family." Presentation at the Texas Association of Hostage Negotiators. Dallas, TX (November).

Mullins, W.C. (1998). "Impact of Stress and Traumatic Stress on Domestic Violence in Policing." Presentation at the FBI National Academy, Police Officers and Domestic Violence Seminar. Quantico, VA (October).

_____ (1999). "The Relationship between Police Officer Suicide and Post Trauma Stress." Presentation at the FBI National Academy, Conference on Suicide and Law Enforcement. Quantico, VA (September).

Nelson, D.L., J.C. Quick, and J.D. Quick (1989). "Corporate Warfare: Preventing Combat Stress and Battle Fatigue." *Organizational Dynamics* 18:65-79.

Nudell, M. and N. Antokol (1990). "Negotiating for Life." *Security Management* 34: 56-66.

Oots, K.L. and T.C. Wiegele (1985). "Terrorist and Victim: Psychiatric and Physiological Approaches from a Social Science Perspective." *Terrorism* 8:1-32.

Selye, H. (1956). *The Stress of Life*. New York, NY: McGraw-Hill.

Siegel, R.K. (1984). "Hostage Hallucination: Visual Imagery Induced by Isolation and Life Threatening Stress." *Journal of Nervous and Mental Disease* 172:264-272.

Violanti, J. (1995). "The Mystery Within: Understanding Police Suicide." *FBI Law Enforcement Bulletin* 64(2): 19-23.

Yerkes, R.M. and J.D. Dodson (1980). "The Relation of Strength of Stimulus to Rapidity of Habit-Formation." *Journal of Comparative Neurology and Psychology* 18:459-482.

Discussion Questions

1. Think of a policing situation to which you have recently responded (i.e., traffic stop, domestic disturbance, burglary of a building, etc.) that produced stress. How did your perception of that event influence the stress you were under? What can you do to reduce the stress of that type of situation?

2. According the Everlys' schema, what is your basic personality style? Is this how you act when demands are placed upon you? Knowing this, how could you reduce stress in your life?

3. List five coping strategies you have developed to deal with stress. Are these strategies effective or ineffective? If they are ineffective, what coping strategies can they be replaced with?

4. Assume you are the negotiator in the opening scenario. What could you do to reduce the stress among the various groups of hostage takers? To reduce danger to the hostages?

5. Assume you are the prison administrator in the opening scenario. What would you do to reduce stress on the tactical team? On the negotiators? What would you do for the commander whose wife had been injured?

6. Jason was called into his boss's office and given his pink slip. Jason began shouting and cursing at his boss, who ordered him out of the room and picked up the phone to call security. Jason threw a heavy ashtray across the room and accidentally struck the boss in the head, killing him. He then barricaded himself in the room and the police were called. You are the primary negotiator. When you first speak to Jason, he is hysterical with fright. He has never been in trouble before (not even a traffic citation). He is afraid not only of what will happen to him, but what will happen with his family, his son who is graduating from high school and getting ready to enroll in college, and his youngest daughter, who is autistic and needs a lot of parental support. What kind of things could you say to Jason to reduce his stress, calm him down, and set the framework for successful negotiations?

7. Self-monitor your heart rate during a stressful activity. Practice the progressive relaxation technique every day for a period of two weeks. Practice about 20 minutes per day. Following this two-week period, again measure your heart rate during a stressful activity. Did you see a decrease?

8. Team up with a classmate. Ask them to recall a serious stressful event in the recent past. Conduct an emotional debriefing with them concerning this event.

Hostage Dynamics

5

1. Recognize the difference between a hostage and a potential victim.

2. Understand the ways in which different personality styles affect the way hostages react.

3. Understand what threats confront people when they are taken hostage.

4. Know why the extensive POW data set can assist us in understanding hostage behavior and reactions.

5. Know the defense mechanisms hostages employ as well as which are beneficial to survival and which are detrimental to survival.

6. Know the various adaptive and coping strategies that hostages employ during captivity. For each, know how the strategy can either help or hurt the hostage's ability to survive captivity.

7. Know Strentz's typology of Survivors and Succumbers.

8. Understand the aftereffects of captivity and how they are affected by situational variables, such as length of captivity, severity of captivity, etc.

9. Understand the process of recovery for hostages and what negotiators can do to decrease potential aftereffects.

10. Understand how to conduct an emotional debriefing with released hostages.

The man entered the bank and held the employees and several customers at gunpoint while he robbed the bank. During the robbery, the police responded to a silent alarm and the robber was not able to make his escape. Instead, he began negotiating his freedom with threats to the hostages. To show he was serious, he shot and critically wounded a hostage. After the incident, he was asked why he shot that hostage, and the robber replied, "She kept calling me 'sir' and I remembered that when I needed to shoot one." In trying to effect an escape, the robber had all the hostages undress to their underwear and tied them around him as a human shield. One hostage became highly emotional and began screaming and crying. The robber made the police negotiator talk to her. The negotiator tried to calm her by telling her to do what the robber wanted, but the hostage began screaming at the negotiator. Not making progress with the hostage, the negotiator quit talking to her and hung up the phone. When he did, the female became even more hysterical, begging and pleading with the robber to not shoot her. Finally tired of the hassle, the robber shot and killed her. The other hostages complied with the robber and surrounded him as he tried to get to a vehicle. One hostage noticed the tactical sniper and kept inserting himself between the sniper and the robber, all the while shaking his head "no" at the sniper. Before he could enter the vehicle, a second sniper shot and wounded the robber. When police closed in and untied the hostages, one took off full-speed, running down the street. A patrol officer chased her for four blocks before catching her and returning to the scene. After gathering intelligence, the police released the hostages. Three of the four bank tellers quit working at the bank within four weeks and all reported they were scared to come to work, could not sleep at night, and were having marital difficulties. Almost a year later, one of the customers committed suicide.

This case illustrates the importance of the negotiator understanding the hostage behavior, hostage emotional states, psychological reactions to being held captive, and other aspects of hostage behavior. The most critical reason for knowing this information is to know how to deal with hostage issues and keep them alive and from becoming harmed. Recognizing the potential benefits and liabilities posed by hostages and ways of managing them are necessary tools in the negotiator's tool box. Being able to deal with hostages upon completion of the incident is also critical. Negotiators should conduct an emotional debriefing with released hostages and reduce the potential for long-term effects of captivity. This chapter will look at the definitions of hostages and victims of a crisis incident, outline the kinds of people who become hostages/victims, examine what happens when people are taken hostage, explore how people adapt and cope to being held hostage, what Survivors and Succumbers are, and explain what happens to people when they are released from captivity. Guidelines for debriefing released hostages will be presented and discussed.

Hostages and Victims

One important determination to be made at the beginning of an incident is whether it is a hostage incident or a non-hostage incident. This is important because the risk of injury or death is greater in non-hostage incidents than in true hostage incidents. Noesner (1999) has pointed out that the majority of the FBI's training for commanders focuses on this issue. It is not as simple as it appears, because what you see is not always what you get in crisis situations. Sometimes people take family members or friends captive without having a substantive goal. These people can be considered "victims in the making."

Noesner (1999) defines a hostage incident as one in which *a subject holds other people in order to force a third party to comply with his or her substantive demands*. Substantive demands are those that the subject does not think he or she can obtain without the use of hostages. Therefore, the hostages are leverage in these incidents, not targets. It is only by keeping the hostages alive that the subject has leverage with the police. Demands are reasonable and goal-directed.

Non-hostage incidents involve the subject acting out of emotion, having ill-defined goals, and making no substantive demands (Noesner, 1999). The demands seem unrealistic—demands that no reasonable person would expect to be fulfilled. In these incidents, subjects either are barricaded, or they hold others to express their frustration, hurt, disillusionment about events or, more dangerously, about the individuals they are holding. The people in these incidents are not hostages; they are victims. The risk to the people being held is considerably higher in non-hostage incidents than in hostage incidents

Hostages

The American Heritage Dictionary (1980) defines *hostage* as: "A person held as a security for the fulfillment of certain terms."

Several points need to be emphasized when considering this definition. First, it is important to understand the implications of the involvement of a person. A living being, not an inanimate object, is at risk. Inanimate objects can be used in extortion, but it takes a living person to make an incident a hostage incident. The goal of hostage negotiation is saving lives, not preservation of property. In discussing the Williamsburg incident, one authority said, "The primary consideration in such circumstances is to secure the lives and safety of threatened hostages, the police officers, innocent bystanders, and the criminals themselves." (Schlossberg, 1979a). This makes hostage negotiations consistent with the public safety responsibility of the police, which includes aiding individuals in danger of physical harm, assisting those who cannot care for themselves, and resolving conflict (American Bar Association, 1980).

The emphasis on saving human life does two things for the negotiator: (1) It increases negotiator stress, because of the high cost of failure, and (2) it attracts political and public relations attention due to the drama of a life-death confrontation.

In most hostage incidents, the explicit threat is to the hostage's life. It is not the loss of property, status, or belonging to a community that is at stake. Life itself is at stake. The cost of failure in such an incident places significant stress on negotiators. The recent recognition of the impact of traumatic stress on emergency service personnel, police officers involved in shootings (Nielsen, 1986; Solomon & Horn, 1986; Somodevilla, 1986; McMains, 1986; Reese, Horn & Dunning, 1991), and military personnel is ample evidence that loss of life can create significant stress. Negotiators need to plan for this stress.

Incidents that involve life and death have a sense of the dramatic (Keen, 1991). There is rarely a hit television show or film about the adventures of a certified public accountant; there is no life-and-death struggle. However, hostages are different. There is the threat to life; therefore, there is high drama. Terrorists understand and play on this drama. The media, neighbors, family members, and friends are attracted to such incidents. Negotiators and police departments should anticipate this attraction and plan for the management of this audience. All this attention makes negotiation incidents high-visibility and potentially high-liability situations. Because of this public interest, many units of the police department may be needed at the scene. Because of the potential liability, the department's crisis response teams need to be well trained and well rehearsed.

Second, it is important to understand that the person is "held." The hostage is not there voluntarily. The holding may be physical or psychological; the impact on the person is the same. A person is traumatized because of his or her lack of control and is made to feel powerless and dependent on the hostage taker. The former points to the need for victim debriefing. The latter lends itself to the development of negotiation strategies and tactics.

Knowledge of traumatic stress has led some police departments to expand the use of their negotiators to crisis debriefing in situations other than hostage incidents. That is, some departments have used their negotiators to help search-and-rescue workers manage the emotional impact of their work. Some have used them to debrief crime victims (McMains, 2000).

Third, the person has utility. The person is being held as security—as a guarantee. The hostage is the hostage taker's currency, his or her power. The hostage is not a person, and has no value to the hostage taker as a person (Schlossberg, 1979b). Part of the negotiator's job is to personalize the hostage for the hostage taker. This has to be done subtly, however. If too much attention is directed toward the hostage, his or her worth is perceived as increased. This gives the hostage taker the perception of more power. The negotiator's goal is to personalize without valuing. The negotiator needs to encourage the development of the Stockholm Syndrome.

Fourth, the person is being held as security for certain terms. This means there is an expected return—a quid pro quo for the hostage taker. The hostage taker has needs that he or she expects to be met in return for the safety, security, and/or release of the hostage. The principal job of the negotiator is to find alternate terms for the hostage taker. Goldaber (1979) has pointed out that every hostage taking is reducible to two elements: Who are the hostage takers and what do they want? Negotiation adds two more elements to the equation: What will they take and what are we willing to give? For instance, rather than the escape a gunman demands during a bungled robbery attempt, he might settle for the negotiator going to court with him to testify about his cooperation in releasing the hostage.

The Stockholm Syndrome

A great deal has been written about a phenomenon called The Stockholm Syndrome. In 1973, Jan-Erik Olsson and Clark Olofsson attempted to rob the Sveriges Kreditbank in Stockholm, Sweden. During the robbery attempt, the police were notified and Olsson and Olofsson took four bank employees hostage. This simple robbery ended up being a hostage situation that lasted for more than 130 hours. Following the resolution of the situation (in which no one was physically injured), authorities were stunned when the hostages showed great sympathy to the two hostage takers and animosity toward the police. The hostages refused to testify at the trial of Olsson and Olafsson, spoke in public on their behalf, and even attempted to raise money for their defense fund. Several months after the incident, one of the bank employees became engaged to Olsson.

This incident gave a formal name to a psychological syndrome observed on occasion in hostage situations: the Stockholm Syndrome. Basically, the Stockholm Syndrome is an emotional reaction by people taken hostage and is an attempt, at least initially, to survive. As the hostage situation progresses, the Stockholm Syndrome becomes less of a survival reaction and more of a coping and an empathetic reaction. Even following their release, the ex-hostages can remain victim to the psychological reaction of captivity.

As described, there are three components to the Stockholm Syndrome (Ochberg 1980b; Olin & Born, 1983; Strentz, 1982). First, hostages develop positive feelings and affection toward their captors. Second, hostages develop negative attitudes toward the police. Third, following the hostage situation, hostages retain a measure of empathy and compassion for the hostage takers. Simon and Blum (1987) have pointed out that hostages are in a cognitive bind. On the one hand, they depend upon the hostage taker for their survival; on the other, they depend upon the police for their ultimate rescue. This places the hostages in a catch-22.

Etiology and Description of the Stockholm Syndrome

Shortly after the onset of the hostage situation and following the Crisis Phase, hostages will begin to develop positive feelings toward the hostage takers. Initially, there is gratitude on the part of the hostages toward the hostage takers for being allowed to live (Eitinger, 1982). If the onset of the hostage situation is one filled with violence (i.e., hostages injured or gunfire and other violence), this gratitude is even stronger (Soskis & Van Zandt, 1986). Some authors see this gratitude as a regression to childhood (Ochberg, 1980a; Strentz, 1979). The hostages become dependent upon their captors for not only their physical needs, but also for emotional security. Symonds (1983) referred to this process as Traumatic Psychological Trauma.

Quarles (1988) said that hostages become obedient, civil, agreeable, and compliant with their captors so as not to antagonize them. Over time, hostages come to know their captors as persons who have the same wants, desires, and needs as the hostages (Turco, 1987). This humanization can best be exemplified by the Gerard Vaders experience. In 1975, a group of South Moluccan radicals took the occupants of a passenger train hostage in The Netherlands. To demonstrate their seriousness, the Moluccans decided to kill Vaders. Before the execution, the terrorists allowed Vaders to say good-bye to his wife (over the telephone). After listening to the tearful farewell, the terrorists returned Vaders to his seat and selected another hostage for execution (the person was only wounded and survived). Hearing Vaders' farewell to his wife made Vaders a human being to the hostage takers, not an object to be used. Killing Vaders was not an impersonal act anymore. On the other side of the equation, to Vaders, the gunmen were no longer masked terrorists. They became people who were caught up in circumstances as much as the hostages. Following the resolution of the incident, Vaders said of his captors: "You had to fight a certain feeling of compassion for the Moluccans. I know this is not natural, but in some ways they came over human . . . I knew that they were victims, too. In the long run they would be as much victims as we. Even more . . . You couldn't help but feel a certain pity" (Soskis & Ochberg, 1982).

Finally, the stress and tension inherent in hostage situations help form the Stockholm Syndrome. The people in a hostage situation are a small group, and as such, respond as any small group would (Wesselius & DeSarno, 1983). According to the Stockholm Syndrome theory, they come to know each other, form alliances, bond, and use group problem-solving techniques to benefit the group. With time, individual autonomy disappears and is replaced by group cohesiveness. If allowed to develop (a factor of both time and treatment by the hostage takers), the police will have to deal with the group and not the individual hostage takers. Indicators that this is occurring include frequent changing of or indecision about demands, many people speaking to the negotiator (especially if earlier conversations were exclusively with one person), long delays, or hesitation in making decisions (especially if the hostage taker has to keep "getting back to you").

This issue can be particularly troublesome in jail and prison situations. When prisoners take hostages, they are already a group. All of the group dynamics discussed above are already firmly in place when the negotiator first makes contact. The first task of the negotiator becomes that of identifying the leader and talking with that person. The negotiator has to be prepared for and work within the group dynamics of the situation.

The second component of the Stockholm Syndrome that has been described is an anti-police sentiment on the part of the hostages. One part of the Kreditbank incident that is often overlooked or ignored is that one of the hostages, Kristen Enmark, called a television station and said she was more afraid of the police than of the hostage takers. She accused the police of playing with the lives of hostages and repeatedly argued for her captor's case (Cooper, 1978).

Third, the presence of the police may make the hostage taker do something rash or violent. As a rule, by the time the police response teams arrive at a hostage situation, the emotions of the hostage takers and hostages have begun to dissipate and return to somewhat normal levels. The appearance of the police negotiators elevates emotions and the hostage taker again becomes fearful, angry, and emotional. The hostages fear that the hostage taker will harm them to make a point with the negotiator.

The third component of the Stockholm Syndrome is positive feelings by the ex-hostages for the hostage takers. Ex-hostages sometimes refuse to cooperate with the police, refuse to testify against their captors, establish defense funds, and work to keep the hostage takers from being incarcerated. These after-incident positive emotions can be greatly reduced by the negotiating team in the post-incident debriefing. The aftereffects of the Stockholm Syndrome will disappear in time. Depending upon the severity of the incident, it can take weeks or months for ex-hostages to return to normal (and some have been known to experience aftereffects for years). An emotional debriefing can reduce this time to minutes in most cases.

A final component of the Stockholm Syndrome is the positive relationship that develops between the negotiator and the hostage taker. Rather than being built on fear, however, this relationship is built on trust. The hostage taker must believe in and trust that the negotiator is truly helping to resolve the incident. If this trust does not develop, the negotiator will not make progress in resolving the incident. As the negotiator/hostage taker relationship develops, the hostage taker will become dependent upon the negotiator. When this dependency develops, the negotiator can lead the hostage taker to a peaceful resolution. It cannot be stressed enough, however, that this dependency is based upon the hostage taker trusting the negotiator.

The Stockholm Syndrome Revisited

Accepted for years at face value and taught by almost every crisis negotiation instructor to almost every negotiator, The Stockholm Syndrome was used to simplify and explain complex hostage behavior. It was assumed that using the theory of the Stockholm Syndrome, negotiators could promote the safety and psychological well-being of hostages. The reality of hostage taking in the United States is somewhat different, however. In hostage events in the United States (and, as it turns out, in the rest of the world), the Stockholm Syndrome does not occur. Hostages do not come to identify with their captors, they do not help their captors at the expense of law enforcement, nor do they assist their captors against law enforcement efforts, nor do they continue to be friendly and empathize with their captors after captivity has ended. There are several reasons the Stockholm Syndrome very seldom develops or occurs. First, most hostage-taking incidents are too short in duration for hostages and captors to develop any type of relationship. It is rare for a hostage incident to last more than several hours, and when they do, it is generally a prison siege incident (and prisoners taking correctional staff hostage presents its own dynamic far removed from the Stockholm Syndrome). Second, most incidents are not intense enough. A premise of the Stockholm Syndrome is that the incident has to be of high intensity. Most hostage situations do not have this intensity. The terrorist hostage incidents that have become notorious in Iraq are certainly intense enough to meet this criteria, but even there, the few captives that have been released report no relationship with their captors or any animosity towards their military saviors. At the Moscow Theater in Russia, no released hostage spoke kindly of their captors, nor did they work against the police while captive (Dolnik, 2004). Third, in the United States, most hostage situations involve hostages and hostage takers who have a prior relationship. Domestic incidents, workplace violence hostage incidents, school hostage taking incidents, prison sieges, and others are all situations in which hostages and hostage takers have prior relationships. Behavior within the incident is predicated upon these prior relationships. The stress and intensity of the incident does not change prior dynamics. Fourth, since September 11, 2001, people have a heightened awareness of survival and self-preservation. People have psychologically steeled themselves against being victimized. They will resist what their captors do and not become psychologically attached.

This is not to say that negotiators should not try and personalize the hostages to the hostage taker. In incidents in which there is a prior relationship, the negotiator can still use some of the following suggestions to strengthen personalization. First, the negotiator should have the hostage taker give the hostages' names. The negotiator can suggest to the hostage taker that the names be given so he can inform relatives on the outside, so the negotiator knows who he is dealing with, etc. Possibly the names of the hostages can become a negotiable demand. At the outset of negotiations, the hostage taker will probably be reluctant to divulge the hostages' names. As time passes and the negotiator gains the trust of the hostage taker, the hostage taker will usually give the hostages' names. In addition to providing intelligence, knowing the names of the hostages will personalize them to the hostage taker.

Second, the negotiator could ask the hostage taker to find out whether any of the hostages has an illness or injury, if any needs medication, or other special consideration. The early stages of negotiations, in addition to building trust, should be used to personalize the relationship between the hostage taker and the hostages. If the negotiator focuses some conversation and attention on the hostages, the hostage taker will be forced to consider the hostages' needs, thereby personalizing them. The negotiator should be careful, however, to not overemphasize personalization of hostages and increase the hostage taker's perception of power.

Third, when referring to needs, include everyone. The negotiator should focus on the group situation rather than the individual situation. Send in bulk food and explain why, continue asking if everyone is okay, if anyone is hot or cold, if any relatives should be notified. Do not let the situation become "me" against "them" to the hostage taker. The negotiator is also a part of this group and should include him- or herself in the group. When food is delivered, the negotiator should "eat," when discussing air temperature the negotiator should indicate his or her personal state, etc.

Fourth, do not use the term *hostage*. Refer to the hostages as "persons," "people," or with other personalized terms. If the negotiator knows the names of some hostages, he or she should always use their names. The negotiator could ask the hostage taker to deliver messages (oral, by the negotiator) from relatives, spouses, or close friends ("Would you please tell Jane her children said they hope she is okay and can come home soon."). In domestic situations, there may be a great deal of animosity and hatred between the hostage taker and the hostages. In attempting to bring about the formation of the Stockholm Syndrome, the negotiator should focus on the past relationship between the hostage taker and hostages (i.e., "Think back to a happier time in the relationship. Tell me about your courtship, marriage."). Recounting the relationship's past positives may decrease the present-day animosity and hatred, and return long-forgotten feelings of affection.

Fifth, rely on the passage of time. The longer the hostage taker and hostages are in contact with one another, the more opportunity they will have to interact and the better the probability that the Stockholm Syndrome will develop. If the hostage taker is not interacting with the hostages, the negotiator can often force interaction. For example, if the hostages are tied and bound, the negotiator could suggest that the hostage taker untie them so permanent physical damage does not occur. Do not force the passage of time solely to develop the Stockholm Syndrome, but as with other factors related to the hostage situation, make time an ally.

Hostage Dynamics

Even without the Stockholm Syndrome, there are plenty of psychological, emotional, and physical issues confronting hostages for negotiators to be concerned with. Often at a crisis situation, because of the variety of demands placed upon negotiating teams, concern about hostages (*not* to be confused with concern *for* hostages) takes a low priority. It should not be. Hostages are central to the situation and should be afforded the highest priority during and after the incident. It is critical that negotiators understand the stresses placed upon people when taken hostage, how people react when taken hostage, how people survive captivity psychologically and physically, and what happens to captives after their captivity ends. Unfortunately, data on hostage behavior is extremely limited. There is very little data dealing with hostages per se. One excellent data source that does deal with

A negotiator must build trust and rapport with the hostage taker. Once a negotiator accomplishes this, problems can be solved and a successful resolution can be reached. *(S. Davis)*

hostage behavior comes from the literature dealing with prisoners of war and ex-prisoners of war. Much of the discussion in this chapter relies heavily on the POW data, especially that dealing with ex-POWs of the Japanese from WWII (possibly the most heavily researched and written about group in all of the POW literature). The POWs of the Japanese experienced the worst period of captivity imaginable. For POWs of WWII in the European theater, less than one percent of all United States POWs died during captivity, while in the Pacific theater, 40 percent of all United States POWs died while in Japanese prison camps or during sea transit between confinement sites (Stenger, 1992). This data does not include Navy personnel (but it is believed their death rates are comparable).

Psychological Effect of Captivity

The psychological effects of captivity begins almost immediately upon being taken hostage. First, and most obviously, is a threat to life. Many hostages initially believe their captors are going to kill them. This belief is reinforced by the emotional state of the hostage taker. During the initial hostage taking, the hostage taker is emotional, angry, shouting, aggressive, and threatening, all in an attempt to gain control of the situation and force compliance. Hostages believe this angry and emotional person will kill them. They are panicky, anxious, uncertain, and fearful (Oots & Wiegele, 1985). They may feel overwhelming helplessness, existential fear, and sensory input overload (Hillman, 1983). Some may have been injured or killed, which adds to the survivors' stress. The hostages see themselves as victims of circumstance. They were going about their normal, everyday activities in an orderly world. All at once, the order of their lives has disappeared and they are facing an uncertain, and possibly short, future. More importantly, they are in a situation in which their actions, thoughts, and emotions are being controlled by someone else.

Second, there is a threat of bodily injury. Hostages believe they will be maimed, violated, lose a limb, suffer permanent disfigurement, etc. To many, this severe bodily injury is more threatening and scary than death.

Third, there is a threat to security. People believe the world is an orderly and predictable place, that they have some control over their environment and events, and that they can plan activities and engage in routines that are safe and provide emotional security. When taken hostage, people lose this sense of orderliness and security. The world becomes random and events unpredictable. Tied in with this loss of control is the uncertainty of the future and what the future holds. Hostages question whether they are going to live, how long they will be held captive, what will happen to loved ones, etc.

Fourth, there is a threat to psychological self-image when someone is taken hostage. When people are taken hostage, they believe they did something wrong, that they let themselves down, and that they are less than good or honorable because they allowed themselves to be taken captive. For many POWs, being taken captive meant (at least at a psychological level) they let down their country, their military unit, and their buddies. As one ex-Bataan POW, J.L. "Jake" Guiles recounted, "We were ordered by General Wainwright via radio that for us the war had ended, that we were to surrender. At that time I thought surrendering was one of the most disgraceful things a person could do" (LaForte, Marcello, & Himmel, 1994).

The stress confronting the hostages produces a physical arousal. This physical arousal is likely greater for the hostages than for other participants in the situation. Hostages will experience an increase in blood pressure, heart rate, neural interference, and may experience loss of muscular control (Gilmartin & Gibson, 1985). They may lose bladder control, faint, vomit, or even have heart failure, hemorrhage, or stroke. The hostage may hyperventilate or experience an asthma-like attack. The stress of the hostage situation may cause an onset of any medical condition of the hostage (Nudell & Antokol, 1990). Diabetes, migraine headaches, gastrointestinal disorders, and other illnesses may appear. The stress may be so great, in fact, that some of the hostages may hallucinate (Lanza, 1986). Siegel (1984) reported that almost 25 percent of hostages may hallucinate. These hallucinations include sensitivity to light, difficulty in visual focusing, disorientation, preoccupation with body imagery, dissociation, geometric patterns, tunnel vision, tactile-kinesthetic hallucinations, and auditory hallucinations.

In addition to these four major psychological threats to survival, there are accompanying psychological frustrations and fears of unreality, an extreme sense of danger, a total sense of vulnerability, deep feelings of helplessness and hopelessness, sensory overload, intense feelings of defenselessness and powerlessness to fight or flee, and a lost sense of worth to themselves and others. Finally, the sense of the hostage taker being hostile, threatening, powerful, and unpredictable adds tremendously to the psychological effects of capture.

These fears can best be exemplified by the POWs themselves (LaForte, Marcello, & Himmel, 1994): William G. Adair, captured on Bataan, said, "No one I knew had made any plans to surrender or to make escape plans because they just couldn't believe it." Onnie Clem (Corregidor) said, "It was hard to realize that here you are, you've never been caged up in your life before, and all of a sudden you're caged up and somebody has the power of life and death over you." James C. Venable, captured on Wake Island, related, "We were brought into a group and lined up in a solid body, several ranks deep. Suddenly, machine-guns crews came running out, and they set up their machine guns. They lined up a number of machine guns in front of the group, and they loaded them with ammunition, they jumped down behind them, they cocked them. Then there was a deadly silence. And I recall one guy said, 'Well, this looks like it's it. So let me tell you, when they start pulling the trigger let's just jump up and get a gut full . . .' At the time it sounded like a very logical thing to do, and I was mentally prepared to do it."

Concerning the helplessness and hopelessness felt by the POWs, Albert E. Kennedy (Burma-Thailand Railway) said, "Another punishment was a case of my missing my number when counting off. I was number eight in line, and the guy that was number six said he was seven in the wrong way. I just had a blank and got the hell beat out of me. The worst part of it is the frustration of not being able to strike back." Henry Stanley (Bataan) said concerning sensory overload, "I'll never forget the surrender, but I don't know how to describe it. You just felt like you were on a boat, and the boat just went out from under you, and you were out in the middle of the ocean." Charles W. Burris (Bataan) said, "The fact is, I think, that it would have been better if we had gotten as many fliers out of there as possible—me included. Let us fight someplace else rather than let us wither on the ground there and do nothing." Dean M. McCall, who also surrendered on Corregidor, stated, "I can't recall exactly what my feelings were, but I felt sort of sorry about surrendering. I felt ashamed that we lost, I know that."

As the situation progresses, the initial stress dissipates and the hostages calm down and begin dealing with the situation. After a period of time, stress begins to increase as basic needs are not met. The presence of the police produces stress. To the hostage, the police are as much of a threat as the hostage taker. The hostage does not know how or if the police can differentiate them from the hostage taker and thus they are as much a threat to life as is the hostage taker.

The resolution phase produces a threat to hostages. By the resolution phase, the hostages have settled into a routine and become familiar with their situation. The resolution produces uncertainty and anxiety. They realize the hostage taker may become irrational and let his fear overcome his ability to act in a rational manner. As they are released, the hostages are treated as criminals by the police.

In domestic situations, there is a special stress on the hostage/spouse. The hostage knows the hostage taker intimately and knows what the hostage taker is capable of. Additionally, the spouse/hostage feels some responsibility to assist the hostage taker to resolve the incident successfully (i.e., not only get out of the situation alive, but also to not go to jail). In these situations, the hostage feels a responsibility to assist in resolving the incident as well as the stress produced regarding his or her own survival.

In prisons, hostages also have the additional stressors of knowing their captors. Unlike the domestic situation, however, the hostages are aware of the violence their captors are capable of. Often, people are injured before they become hostages. All the hostages know that if the authorities do not fulfill demands and resolve the situation, the hostage takers will injure or kill the hostages. The hostages know the hostage takers hate the hostages and would, in some cases, be glad to harm the hostages. In jail and prison situations, the nature of the relationship between the hostages and hostage takers in and of itself significantly increases stress on the hostages. Survivability and success as a hostage depends on the personality of the hostage. To some extent, negotiators can assess the personality type of the hostages and obtain a sense of how hostages will act and react to various stimuli.

1. The *Histrionic Personality* describes a person motivated by a constant need for approval, affiliation with others, and support. They are often dramatic in dress and action. They are prone to emotional displays that draw attention to themselves. They believe that the best way they have of dealing with life is to ingratiate themselves to others, particularly people in power. Negotiators are likely to deal with them because they make a suicide gesture, especially when they think they are being neglected. As hostages, they are likely to be good candidates for the Stockholm Syndrome, or they may single themselves out through dramatic and emotional overreactions.

2. The *Schizoid Personality* is characterized by a pattern of isolation, aloofness, and withdrawal from others. They are motivated by a need to avoid being overwhelmed by excessive external and interpersonal stimulation. They tend to be loners and only become aggressive when they feel that other people

are putting too many demands on them. Under the stress of being a hostage, these people would be expected to withdraw and keep to themselves. They might quit reacting to instructions because they feel overwhelmed by the incident.

3. The *Compulsive Personality* is motivated by a need for perfection and social acceptance. They adhere to rules and regulations. They are concrete and specific. They fear making mistakes and being seen as socially inappropriate. They rarely are involved with the police. These people can put themselves at risk by being judgmental and critical of the hostage takers.

4. The *Avoidant Personality* is motivated by a desire to be accepted by others. They are so afraid of rejection that avoiding others becomes a defense against this threat. They rarely come to the attention of police, but when they do, they are usually easy to persuade. They are one of the types that is the most likely to develop the Stockholm Syndrome.

5. The *Dependent Personality* is characterized by acquiescing to the desires of others to gain acceptance and support. They are passive and submissive. They come to negotiators' attention when they are paired with a more assertive partner, like the antisocial person who is generally the leader. They frequently barricade themselves in a high-visibility location to draw attention to their problems and to get themselves help. As hostages, they tend to be cooperative and compliant. They are another group that is likely to develop the Stockholm Syndrome.

6. The *Narcissistic Personality* expects special treatment. They have trouble postponing gratification and they must be seen by others as extremely competent. They have an inability to empathize with others and they fail to bond emotionally. Narcissism is a key element in the antisocial personality. These people will single themselves out by their unusual dress or behavior. As hostages, they may have trouble because they cannot believe the hostage taker means them when he gives orders. They may be at risk because they become a management problem for the hostage taker.

7. The *Aggressive Personality* is motivated by the need to control others. They are vigilant and mistrustful. They fear having to rely on others, being taken advantage of and being humiliated. They assume that only the strong survive, so they are sensitive to power and power struggles. This is another major element in the antisocial personality. If unchecked, this characteristic aggressiveness will lead them to challenge the hostage taker.

Once the initial psychological shock of being captured wears off, hostages begin settling into a psychological routine of adaptation and coping to endure their captivity. It is crucial to realize that at this point many hostages can start to psychologically deteriorate (and in intense captivity, even die) from their captivity. Surviving hostages begin to use beneficial and successful adaptation and coping strategies to survive their captivity, while others do not or cannot adapt and cope. As one ex-POW, Louis B. Read, said (LaForte, Marcello, & Himmel, 1994), "If I had to single out one thing, I would say it would have to be adaptability—ability to change with the environment. In my term as a prisoner, I've seen hundreds of guys—many of whom were personal friends of mine—sit down and die for no good reason because they could not adapt to circumstances."

It is known from extensive POW literature that the non-adapters and non-copers could not be forced to adapt and cope, even with the urgent assistance of other POWs. It is well-documented that adaptation and coping strategies employed in captivity are largely a function of one's background, family situation, lifestyle, education, age, experience in the world, and other historical and behavioral variables, and that if one is not prepared in a historical sense when taken captive, one will not learn the necessary psychological tools for survival during captivity. That is one of the reasons that high-risk employers, such as correctional institutions, military, State Department, etc., offer hostage survival training. It is hoped that this training will either develop or reinforce the appropriate adaptation and coping strategies.

Defense Mechanisms

Adaptation is the use of different behaviors, responses, and strategies to reduce stress and maximize chances of survival during captivity (Mullins, 1988). To adapt, a person relies on psychological defense mechanisms and coping strategies. Defense mechanisms are those unconscious psychological responses that reduce danger and anxiety during captivity and they are largely a function of a person's personality.

Typically, during captivity, a hostage relies on one or a combination of several defense mechanisms to withstand the psychological conditions of captivity. One beneficial defense mechanism is intellectualization. This is a defense mechanism whereby the hostage removes the emotional components of captivity, and uses reason and logic to understand what is happening, what might happen, and what is likely to happen in the future. Intellectualization enabled the hostage to attempt to ascertain the facts of captivity and not dwell on the fear and dread. One of the best examples of use of intellectualization as a defense mechanism occurred among crewmen of the *USS Pueblo* when it was captured by the North Koreans in 1968. Most crewmen were subjected to severe physical beatings by their captors. Several days into the physical torture sessions, one crewman realized they would soon be released because all of the beatings were designed to show no physical marks or injuries. Once this knowledge was shared, most crewmen had a significant change of attitude, realizing their lives were not in real danger, and the North Koreans were merely engaging in a barbaric form of psychological torture (Bucher & Rascovich, 1970).

A second beneficial defense mechanism employed by hostages is that of creative elaboration, or the use of fantasy. The use of creative elaboration allows the hostage to psychologically escape the conditions of their captivity, including the brutality and abuse, starvation, torture, and deprivation for short periods and regain a sense of sanity in their world. For example, Melford L. "Gus" Forsman, recounted in a book on the Death Railway (LaForte & Marcello, 1993) that: "I talked to myself all day long. Asked myself questions, counted the bricks and counted the cracks in the bricks, got a fly and pulled his wings off so he couldn't fly away, and talked to him and played with him. I had an odd cell. It had 437 bricks on one wall and 435 on the opposite wall . . . Sometimes I'd try to remember things. I tried to remember a book. I read all the sequences of the book. I tried to remember when I was a kid and studied catechism and was confirmed. I tried to remember mechanics—the parts of a carburetor, what made it work. I just tried to occupy my mind."

Humor is a third beneficial defense mechanism hostages use. Humor, usually bizarre, helps the hostage escape the psychological realities of captivity and move into a land of his or her own making. The more bizarre the humor, the better an escape mechanism it is. Hostage takers are given names befitting caricatures or cartoon figures. Horrors are laughed at in a grisly sort of way. The worst conditions experienced became fodder for a humor that borders on the macabre. Often, the worse the conditions, the greater the humor.

Some hostages attempting to psychologically adapt select inappropriate defense mechanisms—methods that hasten rather than stave off psychological deterioration or death. One of these detrimental defense mechanisms is a counter-phobic reaction. Hostages using this defense mechanism give behavioral responses opposite to basic survival instincts. For example, when threatened by the hostage taker, instead of looking sullen, castigated, and ashamed (necessary behaviors for immediate survival), the hostage may return the threat, argue with, or challenge the captor. This can mean physical abuse or death for the hostage. This detrimental action is not done consciously, but is done as a psychological survival mechanism over which the hostage may have no control. It is a function of personality and prior learning.

A second detrimental defense mechanism is that of denial reaction, or the hostage's refusing to believe they are really captive. The hostage using this defense mechanism functions as if everything in the world was normal, that they are not subjected and enslaved to a threatening and hostile captor. They continue to attempt to act as they did in the free world. They ignore orders and directives from the hostage taker and attempt to continue whatever course of action they were engaged in when the incident began. In a bank situation, for example, the customer may tell the hostage taker to get in the back of the line and then try to tell the teller to finish the transaction.

A third detrimental defense mechanism is reaction formation, or the hostage adopting attitudes and beliefs in opposition to their true attitudes and beliefs. Emotional anger becomes mental respect, fear becomes defiance. That is, the hostage might quiver in fear, but would tell their fellow hostages to let the hostage taker to "take his best shot." The use of this defense mechanism can best be summed up by Crayton R. Gordon, who related, "A lot of things were psychological. Like I said before, you know, venting your anger on a dead man. It helped you out. You'd think, 'The son-of-a-bitch died to get out of this, and now I've got to bury him' " (LaForte & Marcello, 1993).

Another detrimental defense mechanism is identification, now commonly known as the "Stockholm Syndrome." Hostages who use this defense mechanism are not really becoming psychologically close to their captors, they are more likely using a faulty set of behaviors and perceptions to attempt to survive captivity (see below for more on coping and surviving captivity). To again reinforce the idea that the Stockholm Syndrome very seldom occurs, two examples are in order. First, in the Japanese prison camps of WWII, there is almost no recorded instance of a U.S. military POW associating with (or even being civil toward) his captors, nor with the neighboring civilian populace while captive in Japan. Fujita (1993) describes one POW who interacted with the Japanese (virtually the only recorded account of this occurring). This POW, how-

For a variety of reasons, hostages are under more stress than any other person during an incident. To many, this stress can carry over and last long after the incident has been resolved. It is incumbent that negotiators know how to deal with hostages both during and after an incident to help them get past the emotional effects and return to a normal life. *(Enforcement Technology Group, Inc.)*

ever, was not using identification. He was a traitor who openly worked for the Japanese during the war. He was later tried and convicted for sedition (but later released on appeal). A second example comes from prison hostage-taking incidents in the United States. Ex-hostages do not report using identification during captivity, nor show empathy and concern for their captors afterwards. In fact, the common experience is anger and desire to exact justice or revenge.

Coping Mechanisms

In addition to relying on beneficial defense mechanisms to adapt to captivity, hostages also rely on psychological coping mechanisms for survival. Coping is the case in which the hostage uses innovation to continually shift and alter their behavior, adjusting to the situation as it evolves and develops (Mullins, 1988). There are several coping mechanisms practiced by hostages.

First is the psychological strategy of *Relinquishing Control* to one's captors. Accepting that the hostage taker is totally in charge and adjusting one's behavior and emotional state accordingly is not a sign of weakness among hostages, but is a coping mechanism of survival. Hostages who attempt to fight their captors, whether physically or psychologically, may be killed for their efforts. Additionally, not relinquishing control makes the psychological ramifications of capture unendurable, in and of themselves, and can result in excessive psychological stress or death. Relinquishing control means physical control as well as mental control. The hostage must control their physical behavior and posture as well as their psychological posture.

Another coping strategy is *Rationalization*. Similar to intellectualization, rationalization is the strategy by which hostages remove the emotional content of captivity and exist purely on rational and logical thought. Even more than intellectualization, however, rationalization requires hostages to completely suppress any emotions concerning their fellow hostages, friends they have seen killed, and/or families. The hostage must eliminate fear and anxiety, reduce emotions, and take a cognitive look at the circumstances of their captivity, motivations of the hostage taker, and other issues concerning their captivity.

A third coping strategy is *Controlling Emotions*. Hostages who are able to firmly grasp their fear, anger, dismay, emotional turmoil, etc. are hostages who survive their captivity, psychologically and physically. Conversely, hostages who let emotions control them are hostages who do not survive. Natalie Crouter (1980) was a civilian internee of the Japanese in the former Filipino Constabulary Camp Holmes near Baguio during WWII. Taken captive and held for the majority of the war, Natalie wrote in her diary, "The response (to the Commandant's orders) is instantaneous, wholehearted. Far underneath is fear, anxiety, hope, speculation but no waver of intention to support Carl and the committee and the Commandant. Now that we all face facts and a crisis, the tension has begun to ease . . . Feeling their black depression which was once ours, I find no hate within me, only a strange sympathy and a recent understanding, a sadness that we all had to meet in the great psychosis of war (1980)." Controlling emotions did not involve denying emotions (rationalization). Emotions were acknowledged but ignored.

A fourth coping strategy is *Creating Diversions*. Physical diversions, such as playing cards and games, reading, and sports—in short, any activity that focused the mind on the activity and off captivity—increases the chances of the hostages surviving. Any diversion a hostage can create benefits him or her, whether the diversion is psychological, as in trying to rebuild an engine in the mind, to physical, such as reading, playing cards, racing bugs or covertly trying to assemble a radio. During the South Moluccan incident, Gerard Vaders and his fellow seatmates on the train wrote a book. Each would write a sentence, pass the book to the hostage next to them, who would write a sentence and pass it to the next person, etc. This diversion helped pass the time, removed them mentally from captivity, and was a mental respite in a time of absolute emptiness.

Role Rehearsal is another coping strategy used successfully by hostages. That is, coping hostages can look beyond their immediate future and try to foresee and predict the future, examine various options concerning what the hostage taker might do, and how they should react to that change. Attempting to predict the future is only a part of role rehearsal, however. A more valuable component, at least as far as survival is concerned, is planning on how to react for future change. Merely knowing that the future will be different is not sufficient, in and of itself. For the coping strategy to be successful, the hostage has to plan how he or she would change their behavior to accommodate that change.

A sixth coping strategy is *Humor*. Much as with the adaptive defense mechanism of humor, this coping strategy turns the negative emotions associated with captivity into a positive emotion, at least temporarily. Humor allows the hostage to temporarily escape from the overwhelming fear and anxiety that is a part of their daily existence. For example, one POW of the Japanese, John W. Wisecup, at Bicycle Camp (West Batavia, Java), Changi (Singapore), Kanchanaburi, and other camps along the Death Railway, drew cartoons (LaForte, Marcello, & Himmel, 1994). Others bet on *benjo* (bathroom) runs by dysentery-affected POWs. In short, anything that could enliven a dreary existence was used by coping POWs.

A seventh beneficial and important coping strategy is *Gathering Information*. In addition to rationalization and other coping mechanisms, coping and surviving hostages will attempt to gather information on what the future intentions are of the hostage takers, think of future work assignments, food situations, and perhaps most importantly, information concerning what progress is being made by police negotiators. Hostages do not know the length of their captivity, but from gathering information, they can estimate when their release may occur. Also, if negotiations are breaking down and the hostage taker is becoming ever more agitated, they can step in and take over negotiations (a drastic last resort, but one that can save their life).

Maintaining a Daily Routine is an eighth coping strategy that is essential for survival. Establishing and maintaining a personal routine gives hostages an anchor on reality and reduces the surrealness of the experience. In many terrorist and POW situations, captors recognize adaptive and coping strategies and try to remove them from the hostages. They may blindfold or separate hostages, move hostages around, take away writing or reading material, refuse to allow showers, etc.

The coping hostage will develop a *Daily Routine*. A daily routine does not have to be elaborate. It may be as simple as standing up at the same time each hour or day. It may just be sleeping at the same time, or taking a bathroom break at the same time. As most readers know from personal experience, days off work can be disconcerting to a small degree because they break one's regular routine. Establishing a routine is one of the best, and simplest, things a hostage can do to restore psychological order to their world.

Religion and Prayer can be important coping strategies to most hostages. The old military saying, "There are no atheists in foxholes," can be retranslated to the hostage experience as, "There are no Atheist hostages." Religion provides a concrete pillar for the hostage that eases the fear of captivity. Religion does not necessarily mean the worship of God. Religion can be an enduring faith and belief in the U.S. government, the military, the police or other crisis responders, or in oneself.

The next two coping strategies, *Positive Bonding with other Hostages* and *Forming Relationships with other Hostages*, are interrelated coping strategies. Hostages need, especially in a psychological sense, the assistance and support of their fellow hostages. Gavin Daws (1994) spoke of the immense importance of "tribes" among the various nationalities of POWs in Japanese camps. While tribes were one facet of bonding and relating, the coping strategies were much more than tribal alliances. These coping strategies were rooted in the deep, personal, one-on-one relationships a POW would form with another POW. As went the fate of one, often went the fate of the other. Tribal bonding occurred in groups of two, three, but seldom more than four POWs. Not only did these bonds provide physical comfort and relief, as in the sharing of food, cigarettes, and minor material goods, but the utility of the bonds was in the sharing of the psychological hope of survival. Members of the small peer group bolstered other members in emotional ways that were immeasurable toward ultimate survival. J.L. Guiles (LaForte, Marcello, & Himmel, 1994), interned in Cabanatuan on Luzon in the Philippines, said, "In fact, a buddy and I got together because your chances of survival were much better than it was earlier when it was every man for himself. You needed somebody you could depend on or somebody who could help you." There was a definite strength of survival in small numbers.

Another coping strategy seen among the coping hostages is the strategy of *Cooperation with Captors*. Cooperation does not mean the hostage assists, helps, or provides information to his or her captors. Cooperation is merely accepting a psychological deference that the hostage taker is in charge. If a hostage taker says "sit," the hostage sits (not overly or noticeably confrontational).

One of the most intangible, but most important, of all coping strategies is the development of a *Purpose for Survival*. Almost every ex-POW and ex-hostage mentions repeatedly that early in captivity he or she developed a deep, psychological need for survival, although most could not define what it actually was. Paul Papish, a prisoner of the Japanese, related, "About that period was when your thought of survival came in. I felt that in no way was I going to succumb to anything, or no way was I going to let anything get me down. I was going to do the best I could and live the longest I could under the circumstances" (LaForte & Marcello, 1993). Most hostages and POWs who rely on any positive coping skills almost universally include Purpose for Survival as one of the positive coping mechanisms. Although there is no way to establish an exact number, a significant number of POWs of the Japanese died of what is referred to as "non-deliberate death." That is, these POWs developed no purpose for survival and just simply "gave up living." Account after account tells of POWs who died of non-deliberate death. In LaForte and Marcello (1993), for example, almost every POW describes fellow POWs who died in this manner. Edward Fung said; "Some men gave up on life. I remember the classic example distinctly. I didn't believe him at the time. He was a little Dutchman, a native of Holland. He said in 1942 that if he wasn't free by a certain date in 1943 that he wouldn't live anyway, and so he killed himself. Now, of course, he had a self-fulfilling prophecy." Roy M. Offerle related, "They tried everything in the world to save them, but some would quit eating and just give up. They would box them and slap their ears, cuss them, threaten them—everything to try to get them to eat or to make them mad or to give them an incentive to live. But some never gave up, and some would just give up. It was pitiful, but they would do it because we'd been prisoners for so long, and the weather was so bad, and the conditions were so terrible that some of them just didn't have any will or reason to live. So they just gave up."

Hostages who do not cope will do the exact opposite of those who cope. The non-coping hostage, for example, does not relinquish control to their captors. They may argue, become belligerent, or even try to give orders or instructions to the hostage taker. They may continue to be emotional for long periods, until eventually the hostage taker becomes angry at their emotional outbursts and harms them. They may refuse to bond with others hostages and remain loners; they may not establish any routines; they do not keep mentally occupied, instead sitting for hours dwelling on the morbidity of their situation; and they do not develop a purpose for survival. They do not believe the police will rescue and save them. Their psychological future is one of doom, gloom, and potentially death.

Survivors and Succumbers

Dr. Thomas Strentz, a retired FBI agent, spent the majority of his career studying hostages and hostage situations. He developed a typology of hostages that perfectly describes hostages and summarizes the adaptation and coping strategies employed by hostages. According to the typology developed by Dr. Strentz, hostages can be classified as either Survivors or Succumbers (Strentz, 1982, 1984; Strentz & Auerbach, 1988)).

Table 5.1 lists the factors employed by both survivors and succumbers. As can be seen in the list, survivors engage in the positive behaviors, emotions, and mental exercises that reduce fear and uncertainty, lessen anxiety, and mitigate many of the horrors of captivity as a hostage. Succumbers, on the other hand, engage almost exclusively in a range of totally inappropriate behaviors that are almost guaranteed to get one killed, either by the hostage taker or, in the event of long captivity, through ignoring internal resources.

Table 5.1
Typology of POW Survivors and Succumbers
Developed by Dr. Thomas Strentz from examining hostages in hostage situations.
This typology also ideally describes coping used by POWs of the Japanese
in World War II.

Survivors	Succumbers
1. Blend in with other captives	1. Stand out (too subservient or compliant)
2. Do not try to lead	2. Want to lead
3. Contain and hide hatred/disdain	3. Show hatred/disdain
4. Avoids religion/political, inflammatory, hostile language	4. Uses hostile language
5. Concentrates on survival	5. Concentrates on retaliation
6. Controls outward appearance and emotions	6. "Bowl of jelly," and raises everyone's attention
7. Projects confidence and self-esteem	7. Projects fear and anxiety
8. Positive mental attitude and faith in military and country	8. Forgotten by outside world
9. Uses fantasy and daydreaming	9. Dwells on hopelessness and despair
10. Keeps to routines	10. Has no routines
11. Affiliates with other POWs	11. Loners
12. Accepts fate and adjusts	12. Constantly second-guessing
13. Uses humor and imagery	13. Dwells on seriousness and morbidity

As the old saying goes, the "proof is in the pudding." Supporting evidence for the psychological seriousness of using positive defense mechanism, adaptation strategies, coping mechanisms, and having a "survivor" personality can be seen in the death rates of POWs of the Japanese. We can ask why so many POWs died in Japanese prison camps as compared to the European prison camps? Certainly, the physical brutality and treatment by the Japanese toward the POWs played a key role. Torture, starvation, duration of captivity, tropical disease rates, inadvertent attacks by Allied military on camps, internment sites, and transport ships, as well as the code of the *bushido,* all played roles in POW death rates. But none of these factors, alone or in combination, played as great a role in POW deaths as did the psychological warfare inflicted upon the POWs by their Japanese captors. The detection and deliberate destruction of POW adaptive and coping strategies, deliberately increasing fear and anxiety over long periods of time, constantly moving the POWs and disrupting POW peer groups, and other psychological manipulations designed purposely to emotionally, mentally, and psychologically destroy the POWs, were categorically the most significant factors in the high POW death rate among all Allied POWs. Adaptive, coping, and survival strategies were systematically removed from the POWs psychological arsenal until there was no hope left.

Post-Traumatic Stress and Hostages

Like negotiators, hostages suffer from the impact of traumatic stress. During the crisis stage of the incident, when they feel that they have no power or control, hostages experience fear, tension, and panic. They try to deny reality (Ochberg, 1979; Strentz, 1987). Their cognitive processing, judgment, and decisionmaking shut down and they may experience what Symonds (1975) has called frozen fright—fear so intense that they are overwhelmed. They experience a number of the physiological effects of heightened arousal (increased adrenaline), including dry mouth, general gastric distress, rapid heart beat, cold and clammy hands, numbness, time distortions, irritability, and a decreased sense of social concern.

All of this results from the hostages' sense of having lost control of their lives. They feel a threat to their lives, to their body, to their security, and to their sense of self. (Hillman, 1983). They feel as though all their basic needs are in someone else's hands.

As the incident settles down and is more under control, the hostages' sense of emotional arousal diminishes. They move into an adaptation stage of their own. Like the hostage taker, they have to focus on strategies for getting what they want—survival. To do that, they have to be realistic about their situation; they have to control themselves, their behavior, their feelings, and their thoughts; and they have to be subservient without giving in. Most importantly, they have to act in a way that does not draw attention to themselves but at the same time begins to personalize themselves.

Like the victims of other traumas, hostages experience the short- and long-term consequences of having their lives threatened, their freedom restricted, their person demeaned, and their worldview shaken. Research has shown that people who are held hostage for as little as four hours suffer the aftereffects of trauma (Hillman, 1983). Even though they may not rise to the level of developing Post-Traumatic Stress Disorder, it is helpful for people to know what to expect as a result of the aftermath of a life-threatening and powerful event, so that they understand that their reactions, although uncomfortable, are normal.

From research with POWs, the severity of aftereffects of captivity were predicted by severity of captivity, experience of torture, degree of biological and psychological hardship, amount of weight loss, lower pre-captivity socioeconomic status, lower military rank, and lack of social supports during captivity (Speed, Engdahl, Schwartz, & Eberly, 1989; Sutker, Bugg & Allain, 1990, 1991; Ursano & Rundell, 1990) If the impact of an incident persists for more than one month, and the following pattern is intense enough to intervene with the hostage's functioning, the problem may very well rise to level of the diagnosable problem of Post-Traumatic Stress Disorder (PTSD). The *Diagnostic and Statistical Manual-IV* (American Psychiatric Association, 1994) defines PTSD as:

1. The incident must be outside the usual range of human experience. (Certainly being held hostage, having one's life threatened, and oneself demeaned is outside the range of most human experience.)

2. It must be such that it would cause distress in most normally functioning people.

3. It must result in increased arousal.

4. It must result in blunting of enthusiasm for life.

The PTSD reaction to captivity affects the total system of the ex-hostage (Eberly & Engdahl, 1991). The aftereffects of captivity have several distinct components that affect daily functioning. There are emotional effects of captivity, cognitive functioning is impaired, behaviors are affected, physical effects are common manifestations of PTSD, and medical conditions can be elicited or exacerbated by the PTSD response. In some ex-hostages, the PTSD reaction involves a positive component as well. While the following discussion of the PTSD reaction is separated into distinct components, realize that the reactions—emotional, cognitive, physical, medical, and positive—are intertwined to produce a total systemic effect. For example, for the ex-hostage who has a great deal of unresolved anger (an emotional effect), this anger will affect cognitive functioning, behaviors, physical symptoms, and extant medical conditions.

Emotional Aftereffects

In addition to general degraded psychological functioning (Fairbank, Hansen & Fitterling, 1991) and psychological impairment (Sutker, Winstead, Goist & Malow, 1986), increased general anxiety levels are one emotional aftereffect of captivity (Ohry, Solomon, Neria & Waysman, 1994; Sutker, Allain & Winstead, 1993; Ursano & Rundell, 1990—all research with ex-POWs). The ex-hostage is unable to emotionally relax, remains fearful of the future, and becomes apprehensive, tense, and nervous, experiencing an anxiety-like attack. He or she will shake uncontrollably, experiencing unexplained fear, almost to the point of catatonia. Not only can this anxiety attack occur at unpredictable times, it intensifies when the ex-hostage is confronted with new or unique environments. This general trait anxiety, furthermore, is largely responsible for a heightened state of nervous system arousal (see section on medical effects).

Anxiety reactions are common. They are characterized by a general feeling of dread and fear for no apparent reason. The reaction is very similar to an anxiety attack, having no associated external stimulus. The person will be going about their normal, everyday routine, and suddenly, out of the blue, will be overcome by an almost paralyzing fear. Anger is an emotional aftereffect experienced by many ex-hostages. Few can find it in themselves to forgive or forget. Ex-hostages may have a deep sense of insecurity after release, rooted in a perception of losing control over their lives. All sense of personal control over one's fate was completely taken away when captured, persisting for the duration of captivity.

There may be a sense of emotional guilt, the ex-hostage believing he or she let others down, did not act admirably or how they should have, and that they were somehow a "failure" for having been taken captive. Phobias and paranoia may be present as a duo of emotional aftereffects that continue to haunt ex-hostages. They may be terrified of change in their life, of the dark, small spaces, etc. They may also display an exaggerated startle response to loud noises or sudden movement. The ex-hostage may experience severe mood swings. They will become highly elated, followed by a deep depression. Emotions will swing, with no apparent reason, between joy and sadness.

One of the most common and serious of the emotional aftereffects is chronic depression. This depression often leads to suicide (Tennant, Goulston & Dent, 1986). A quote from LaForte and Marcello (1993) more than sums up this point: "One ailment rarely spoken of but evident in reasons given for Lost Battalion members' deaths since 1945 is gunshot wounds." The leading causes of death among ex-POWs of the Japanese are accidents, homicide, and suicide (Stenger, 1992). The suicide rate among these ex-POWs is two to five times greater than the national average. Not only have the ex-POWs failed to cope with the trauma of their captivity, the lingering ramifications of that captivity are so great they cannot live with the emotional pain it has caused (Engdahl, Speed, Eberly & Schwartz, 1991). It is worth repeating at this point that these emotional aftereffects often occur in combination and, when taken together, life does not seem worth living with these emotional scars.

Cognitive Aftereffects

Closely related to the emotional aftereffects of captivity are the cognitive aftereffects. Many ex-hostages believe they "failed" themselves, co-workers, friends, and family; that somehow they are less of a person for having been taken captive. Because of their experience, they may believe their value as a functioning member of society has been diminished. Self-criticism and second-guessing are fairly common. Statements such as, "If only I had done so-and-so I wouldn't have been captured," are commonly heard. Psychosomatic ailments, diseases, and illnesses may be experienced when there is, in fact, no physical ailment present. Every scratch, cough, tic, twitch, rash, bump, bruise, and hiccup is endemic of a serious, debilitating, and life-threatening illness. A medical examination will reveal nothing wrong, but the ex-hostage refuses to be convinced, believing the doctor is wrong, missed a diagnosis, or does not understand his illness. Consultations among numerous physicians are common. Eventually, without psychological intervention, the psychosomatic ailment can become a real physical illness (e.g., a self-fulfilling prophecy).

Insecurity in one's ability to think and function in the world is another common cognitive aftereffect. The ex-hostage deems him- or herself not as smart, not as good a person, or not as valuable to himself, family, or society as he or she should be. This cognitive insecurity is closely allied with emotional insecurity. In a study of twins (one twin a combat veteran and the other twin a POW), Sutker, Allain, and Johnson (1993) found that the POW twin had deficits in visuospatial analysis and organization, planning ability, impulse control, concept formation, and nonverbal memory, as compared to the non-POW twin.

Behavioral Aftereffects

Even as there can be many internal aftereffects, there can also be many external aftereffects. The external aftereffects manifest themselves both behaviorally and physically. Behavioral aftereffects can include social and self-isolation, uncontrollable crying, an increase or decrease in aggression, poor concentration, intrusive thoughts, trouble with authority figures, an increased startle response and alcohol and drug abuse. Although perhaps self-explanatory, several behavioral aftereffects deserve further attention.

Many ex-hostages will manifest emotional aftereffects in behavioral ways. For example, unresolved emotional anger will often result in increased aggression. There need not be any real reason for this aggression: the ex-hostage will suddenly, and for no apparent reason, become aggressive. The ex-hostage will look for situations and locations to express this aggression. He or she may, for example, frequent bars where bar fights are common. He or she may show a propensity toward domestic violence, physically abusing his or her spouse and children. On occasion, the ex-hostage may look for ways to channel this aggression positively They may choose a career that allows for the expression of this aggression in legitimate ways: joining a military combat unit, becoming a police officer, or working in similar high-risk occupations.

Many ex-hostages have difficulty concentrating for periods of time. They will be engaged in some mental task (reading, studying for an exam, balancing a checkbook, etc.), and will suddenly find themselves with a blank mind. Whatever they have been concentrating on is totally forgotten and cannot be recalled. One component of this lack of ability to concentrate is having intrusive thoughts about captivity. The ex-hostage may have difficulty adjusting to the control of a boss or supervisor. Authority figures remind the ex-hostage of subjugation under a threatening and dangerous person.

An exaggerated startle response is also a common behavioral aftereffect of the hostage experience. Most people are startled by unexpected noises, people entering their visual field, and other surprising external stimuli. Most people, however, merely gasp (or do something else very innocuous) and say, "Oh, you scared me." The ex-hostage may dive behind a piece of furniture or prostrate him- or herself on the ground when startled. The normal response to unexpected stimuli becomes greatly exaggerated and severe.

Physical Aftereffects

One of the most common physical aftereffects experienced by ex-hostages is sleep disorder. For example, 50 years after the event, almost all ex-POWs of the Japanese still experienced sleep disorders (Peters, Van-Kammen, Van-Kammen & Neylan, 1990). Some cannot sleep an entire night, some sleep much more than they did before captivity, some sleep much less, some can only cat-nap, some require medication to sleep, some do not enter into Stage 4 sleep, and some very seldom engage in REM (rapid eye movement, or dream) sleep. Stage 4 sleep is the deep sleep that immediately precedes REM sleep, that deep sleep necessary for the body to replenish itself, and the stage where the greatest physiological benefits of sleep are derived. REM sleep is necessary for psychological replenishment, because without Stage 4 and REM sleep, neither the mind nor body can be renewed and revitalized. Lack of proper sleep also affects many other PTSD symptoms.

Nightmares are another common experience of ex-hostages. The nightmares include the sights, sounds, smells, tastes, physical pains and emotions of captivity. Many nightmares revolve around a common theme or a specific incident that occurred during captivity. Usually in persons suffering from PTSD, the nightmares fade with time (in both intensity and frequency). These nightmares help integrate the experience into the person's psyche. As the experience becomes integrated, the frequency and intensity of nightmares decrease. Flashbacks are another common physical aftereffect of captivity—

sensory remembrances (in an awake state) of the sensory stimuli present during the incident. Flashbacks occur in the absence of other external stimuli, lasting only for a few seconds at most, but are distressing. However, they are not dangerous. In general, flashbacks are associated with the sensory system that has the strongest memory.

Withdrawal from close personal relationships is another aftereffect. The ex-hostage may erect an invisible wall and not allow anyone inside that wall. Post-release friendships and relationships are superficial. Closely related to this aftereffect is that of sexual difficulties. Sexual relationships are the most personal of all human relationships. To keep people outside of the "wall," the ex-hostage may not engage in normal sexual practices. Eating disorders may appear. Other physical aftereffects the ex-hostage may experience include constipation, menstrual disorders, weight loss, increased irritability, general somatic complaints, and increased psychophysiological complaints. Again, these aftereffects, in some respects, are normal reactions to the conditions of captivity.

Medical Aftereffects

To the vast majority of hostages, there will be no long-term medical affects. To the very few who experience prolonged, severe, and physically abusive captivity (i.e., Iranian Embassy hostages, terrorist hostages, and maybe even prison sieges), medical aftereffects may be an issue. A database on POW captivity shows that, compared to the general population (including combat veterans), POWs have higher incidents of nutritional disorders, neuritis, peripheral nerve damage, eye disorders, gastrointestinal disorders, liver and genito-urinary disorders, diseases of the bones and joints, and heart disease. Additionally, POWs are admitted to hospitals more frequently and stay longer (Hyer, Walker, Swanson & Sperr, 1992). Eberly, Harkness, and Engdahl (1991), in fact, have theorized that many social symptoms of PTSD, such as social isolation and alcohol/drug abuse, may merely be secondary symptoms resulting from a primary symptom of stress-induced biological change.

The ordeal of captivity "resets" the nervous system to a higher level of resting potential. As a simplified illustration, if prior to captivity only one in 1,000 neurons randomly fired at any given time during periods of no activity, during captivity 100 in 1,000 neurons fired at any given time during rest periods. The general homeostasis of the entire nervous system is elevated because of the stresses inherent in the hostage situation. The elevation of the nervous system response also leads to corresponding increases in other stress response systems; elevated heart rate and blood pressure, impairment of general cognitive functioning (due to increased random neuronal nervous system activity), decreased digestion, increased stomach acidity and increased liver activity. For years it was believed that once the stress of a situation had passed, nervous system activity returned to pre-captivity levels. We now know that such is not the case, that the increased nervous system activity is one effect of PTSD. Left at this elevated state, many debilitating physiological conditions can be elicited or exacerbated by the increased nervous system activity. Heart disease, strokes, arteriosclerosis, liver damage, and ulcers are just a few of the medical conditions than may result from prolonged, elevated nervous system activity.

Positive Aftereffects

Along with the litany of negative aftereffects listed above, some ex-hostages have positive changes in their lives. Some, instead of having lowered self-esteem, have heightened self-esteem. They believe themselves to be better people for having suffered and endured under captivity, and the experience of captivity made them a stronger person. Some enjoy a heightened enjoyment of the world around them. The nearness of death for so long, seeing close friends and comrades die, and realizing just how fragile the human body is, resolved to make them enjoy every second of every day. Others, instead of refusing to allow personal relationships to form, have encouraged as many close, personal and intense relationships as possible. Because of their experience, some ex-hostages have also improved relationships with their families.

Sidebar: Hostages

Phil Andrew is a Special Agent with the Federal Bureau of Investigation assigned to the New York Office. He is a member of the NYO Crisis Negotiation Team. He joined the FBI in 1997 and was assigned to the Kansas City Division, where he supervised a Joint Terrorism Task Force. While in Kansas, Phil served as a board member of Headquarters Counseling—a regional crisis hotline. Prior to his work with the FBI, he was a prosecutor and the executive director of a public safety organization. He is a graduate of the University of Illinois and received his law degree from DePaul University. He is a recipient of a U.S. House of Representatives Award for Outstanding Courage and Heroism and several FBI Achievement Awards. Andrew has been a negotiator since 2000.

The Incident

In 1988, an emotionally disturbed woman carried out an attack (which had been planned for several months) on the Chicago suburb of Winnetka, Illinois. She prepared and distributed poisoned foods to people throughout the community, attempted to detonate a cyanide incendiary device at a school and set fire to a residence. Her attack culminated with her entry into an elementary school with three handguns and a bag of ammunition she had purchased. There she opened fire on students at point blank range, shooting six second-graders. Five were critically wounded; one was killed. She then escaped with two guns and entered a nearby home, taking three hostages. My parents were released unharmed, but I was shot and in critical condition. I was now in a race for my life.

The incident lasted one hour and 15 minutes. She announced that we were her hostages. I engaged the woman verbally, listening to the story of why she was wrapped in a trash bag, wielding two guns. She explained that she had been raped, that she had shot her assailant, and run. Now she knew the police were looking for her and she was afraid of them.

I did not completely understand the woman's story. She was clearly distraught. But the facts did not make sense. Nothing like this sexual assault was known to have happened in this affluent neighborhood, and her fear of the police seemed odd. I tried to understand her situation, to reassure her that she was safe, and to address her apparent needs. My mother and I, assuming that she would feel less vulnerable and relax, provided her with a pair of shorts to replace the plastic garbage bag she was wearing around her waist. The tactic worked to some degree, because she appeared to calm and put one gun down. I secured the weapon.

As I continued to reassure her, I convinced her to call her mother. I could hear her say, "I have done something terrible, people will not understand, I'm going to kill myself." She refused to put down the remaining gun. I was very aware of each of her erratic movements and felt the danger was growing.

Police activity increased outside the house. Playing on the subject's fear of police, we convinced her to release my mother on the pretense of keeping my sisters from coming into the house because they were likely to be escorted by the police. But the woman remained agitated and menacing, using the gun to threaten my father and me. Later, I persuaded her to let my father go if I stayed.

Relieved that my parents were out of the house and harm's way, I shifted to a more tactical option. Being physically fit, and knowing my childhood home better than the intruder and feeling only a risk to myself now, I decided to attempt to disarm her. I considered my course of action carefully, as I continued to try to reassure her. In a moment, I saw a flash and heard a pop. I knew I was being shot at and I reacted like I would have if I were evading one of my brothers in a youthful fight: I hit and ran, diving for cover in the pantry and positioned myself behind the door. It was then that I realized I had been hit.

I saw blood oozing out of my right chest and now felt constriction in my chest and was having difficulty breathing. I couldn't believe I had been shot. Initially, there was a sense of shock and then my plan changed. I knew I needed to escape and get to help. I had to get out of there. I expected to confront the subject again on the other side of the pantry door, so I mentally prepared for confrontation. When I exited the closet, she was gone. There was a sense of letdown, shock, and a little confusion.

I escaped and was taken down by police on the driveway in front of the house. It was not secure but one of them stayed with me. I later learned this officer was Detective Floyd Mohr, a heroic man. Mohr radioed for help, saying "he's turning blue—stay with me kid." He understood me.

He was my ally and was gong to help me obtain my goal. He would help save my life. I was treated at the scene about a half-hour before being transported to the emergency room. For that entire time, my goal was simple: stay conscious until told I could surrender consciousness to the professionals. Loss of consciousness meant I would die. So, I must stay awake until the experts put me out. Through the excruciating pain I controlled my breathing. I drew on my competitive swimming experience, at that time a major part of my formation. The burning, suffocating sensation in my lungs reminded me of the feeling near the end of a race. I knew I could control it and win this race. Sensing high anxiety in the faces of the responders treating me, I needed to communicate to them I was confident, tough, and disciplined so we were on the same page. I mumbled to a responder near me, "I'm a swimmer." He got the message and I was reassured.

There were other discouraging moments before arriving in the operating room, but I remained confident I could reach my goal. I believed the people around me were my allies. After awaking from many hours of surgery, I learned the full extent of my injuries (punctured lungs, pancreas, and stomach; severed esophagus; grazed pericardium) and the true mayhem caused by the subject.

Survival strategies during the incident:

Several strategies were helpful in surviving as a hostage. They included:

1. Remaining calm and assessing the subject's needs and attempting to meet them;

2. Reassuring the subject;

3. Remaining flexible by recognizing and adapting to the fact the that incident was not defusing;

4. Reducing the number of people at risk.

Survival strategies after the incident:

After surgery, it was touch-and-go for awhile. During that time and after recovery, I used several strategies:

1. Remain focused on the positives by recognizing the heroic acts of individuals who responded and limiting the contemplations of all the "what if's" that are common in reaction to traumatic events. I had to accept the incident and make something positive out of it.

2. Be goal oriented: My coaches used analogies that were meaningful and to which I could relate. For instance, in the hospital, they would tell me that I was "on the blocks,"—starting a new race, and I needed to come through again."

3. Keep a sense of humor: Never underestimate the effect of a good laugh

Lessons for Negotiators:

There are several training lessons for negotiators in this incident, including:

1. You are what you train: There is enormous carryover from life and training experiences to critical incidents. Although you may not experience exactly what you trained for, just as in athletics, training provides the discipline, context, and confidence needed to develop a successful attitude and plan in a dynamic situation. Negotiators and responders can draw on a wide array of training and life experiences to develop a successful strategy to survive.

2. Recognize that there are multiple levels of training: experience, action plan, and attitude. Training will equip you to employ each when called upon. Use imagery to fill out your planning. See it clearly and in detail. Visualize success. Even in the absence of real training time, you can practice using your own imagination, so there will be skills available when you need them.

3. Remain flexible: Critical incidents involve intense change in a short amount of time. Negotiators must remain flexible in their evaluation and response as the situation changes

4. Own your reactions: Negotiators are called on to react to highly charged emotional situations they have no control over. Outcomes can be influenced by placing our focus on positive reactions rather than the negative circumstance. In critical incidents, one of the few things we can control is ourselves, our own feelings, attitudes, and actions. Negotiators can give others an opportunity to change but, ultimately, it is their decision.

5. The Chinese have a phrase, crisis is opportunity: I have no doubt that, but for the actions of a few responders and medical professionals, I would not be alive today. As a negotiator, I think it is important not to lose sight of the fact that there are real lives and families associated with each contact—those lives, like ripples in the water, extend far beyond the critical incident.

Recovery From PTSD and The Role of Negotiators

The role of negotiators is not to be long-term caregivers, counselors, or mental health providers. Negotiators have a responsibility at the scene to provide short-term debriefings for released hostages and then to provide referral information to the ex-hostages. Police officers who work with victims of hostage incidents need to be alert for both long- and short-term symptoms, as well as the symptoms of PTSD. As people who are in positions of authority, they can be of help to the victims. By reassuring them that their reactions are normal during the early days after an incident (i.e., the first four weeks) and by suggesting that people who are experiencing symptoms like those associated with PTSD contact a mental health professional after the first month, police officers can help reduce the "secondary wound" (Symonds, 1975) that many victims experience at the hands of the authorities. Emotional and PTSD debriefings have traditionally been the role of the mental health professional on the team (Bohl, 1997; Hatcher, Mohandie, Turner & Gelles, 1998; Ricketts, 1995). They can certainly be a part of the debriefing, but other members of the negotiating team should also assist in debriefing hostages. Most negotiators have received extensive training in stress, stress management, stress-related issues, and PTSD (Allen, Fraser, & Inwald, 1990) and should put that training to use in debriefing ex-hostages.

Even before the hostages leave the scene, negotiators are in a position to minimize the traumatic impact of the incident. Mullins (1988) has suggested the following guidelines for officers who deal with hostages at the scene:

1. Interview the hostage in a comfortable, familiar surrounding.

2. Restore a sense of power to the hostage by allowing him or her to choose the debriefing site.

3. The victim should be given a warm reception.

4. Special attention should be paid to unharmed victims, so they do not feel less important than injured victims.

5. Victims should be warned about the tendency for others to "blame the victim" for their being held hostage.

6. They should be reassured that they acted properly.

7. The police should explain why they took the actions they did.

8. The victim should be allowed to ventilate, if he or she wants.

9. Officers can ask the victims what can be done to help potential hostages prepare for the experience.

10. Victims should be allowed to form a support group among themselves to discuss the incident and debrief one another.

11. The hostages' families should be kept apprised of the reasons for police decisions and the impact of being a hostage and ways of coping with the changes that will result.

Recovery from the severe stress that captivity can cause involves moving through four stages. The first two, *shock/disbelief* and *reality* (or *acceptance*)—occur during captivity. The third, *traumatic depression*, begins after release, and the hostage has to move through it to reach the fourth stage—

recovery or *resolution*. Negotiators can do several things to assist the ex-hostage in moving through Traumatic Depression and into Recovery. First, allow the person to ventilate emotions and express what happened during captivity. Second, restore a sense of power by allowing them to make small decisions (i.e., "would you like water or soda?"). This allows the person to regain control of his or her life. Third, keep communications honest and informative. Try to avoid ordering and being authoritative. Fourth, reassure the person that they acted appropriately, that they did what was necessary to survive, and that here is nothing to feel guilty about. Fifth, explain what aftereffects and long-term effects may be experienced. Let the ex-hostage know that any aftereffects experienced are normal, common, and shared by others who have been captive or exposed to extreme stress situations. Sixth, restore a sense of worth and value to the ex-hostage by asking them what can be done to help others in the future. This also allows the person to express negative experiences in a positive manner and put events in a positive context.

Another concern that negotiators need to attend to are anniversary dates. Anniversary dates are significant dates from their captivity such as day captured, day released, loved ones' birthdays missed, holidays, etc. On these days, there is likely to be an increase in the impact of negative aftereffects. Although transitory in nature, the person may feel overwhelmed by the negative effects and that he or she is regressing back into the "PTSD cyclone." Part of the rise in stress on anniversary dates comes from a sense of having been forgotten. The incident is over, people have gone home, the world has moved on, and other events have supplanted the hostages' experience. Being in the limelight for a short period and then being forgotten is stressful and distressing. A short contact with the person as an anniversary date approaches can help ward off an increase in levels of negative aftereffects and help the person to understand and prepare for what might occur. It also tells the person they are important, have not been forgotten, and that their experience was an important event.

Summary

The third leg of the crisis incident triad involves hostages. Knowing what occurs to people taken hostage, how they act inside the situation, what they are experiencing (physically and psychologically), and what they may or may not do are crucial to our ability to resolve these incidents. It is unfortunate that many negotiators, as soon as a situation is resolved, pack up and leave, paying little or no attention to hostages. As negotiators, we have a responsibility to interview, debrief, and provide long-term resources to ex-hostages. What we do as negotiators in regard to hostages can increase the probability of success in negotiating crisis incidents. We can also turn a potential enemy into an ally by paying more attention to hostages. Most hostages do not experience the Stockholm Syndrome. Any negative emotions or feelings toward response elements are generally caused by a sense of being neglected and ignored by response elements.

In addition, hostages can teach us a great deal about negotiating hostage-taking situations. Unfortunately, we have historically overlooked this source of data and have neglected to conduct extensive post-incident interviews with released hostages. By collecting data, conducting in-depth interviews, analyzing the hostage experience, and disseminating the data, we become better negotiators.

References

Allen, S.W., S.L. Fraser, and R. Inwald (1990). "Assessment of Personality Characteristics Related to Successful Hostage Negotiators and Their Resistance to Post-Traumatic Stress Disorder." In Reese, J., J. Horn, and C. Dunning (eds.), *Critical Incidents in Policing*. Washington, DC: U.S. Department of Justice.

American Bar Association (1980). *Standards Relating to Criminal Justice*. Vol. 1. Boston, MA: Little, Brown & Co.

American Heritage Dictionary (1980). NY: Houghton-Mifflin Co.

American Psychiatric Association (1994). *Diagnostic and Statistical Manual*, Fourth Edition. Washington, DC: APA.

Bohl, N. (1997). "Post-incident Crisis Counseling for Crisis Negotiators." In Rogan, R.G., M.R. Hammer, and C.R. Van Zandt (eds.), *Dynamic Processes of Crisis Negotiation*. Westport, CT: Praeger.

Bucher, L.M. & Rascovich, M. (1970). *Bucher: My Story*. Garden City, NJ: Doubleday.

Cooper, H.H.A. (1978). "Close Encounters of an Unpleasant Kind: Preliminary Thoughts on the Stockholm Syndrome." *Legal Medical Quarterly* 2:100-111.

Crouter, N. (1980). *Forbidden Diary: A Record of Internment, 1941-1945*. New York: Burt Franklin and Co.

Daws, G. (1994). *Prisoners of the Japanese: POWs of World War II in the Pacific*. New York: William Morrow and Co.

Dolnik, A. (2004). "Moscow Theater Incident." Presentation at the annual meeting of ATF negotiators. San Antonio, TX (Oct).

Eberly, R.E. and B.E. Engdahl (1991). "Prevalence of Somatic and Psychiatric Disorders among Former Prisoners of War." *Journal of Hospital and Community Psychiatry* 42:807-813.

Eberly, R.E., A.R. Harkness, and B.E. Engdahl (1991). "An Adaptational View of Trauma Response as Illustrated by the Prisoner of War Experience." *Journal of Traumatic Stress* 4:363-380.

Eitinger, L. (1982). "The Effects of Captivity." In Ochberg, F.M. and D.A. Soskis (eds.), *Victims of Terrorism*. Boulder, CO: Westview Press.

Engdahl, B.E., N. Speed, R.E. Eberly, and J. Schwartz (1991). "Comorbidity of Psychiatric Disorders and Personality Profiles of American World War II Prisoners of War." *Journal of Nervous and Mental Disease* 179:181-187.

Fairbank, J.A., D.J. Hansen, and J.M. Fitterling (1991). "Patterns of Appraisal and Coping Across Different Stressor Conditions among Former Prisoners of War with and Without Post-Traumatic Stress Disorder." *Journal of Consulting and Clinical Psychology* 59(2):274-281.

Fujita, F. (1993). *Foo: A Japanese-American Prisoner of the Rising Sun – The Secret Prison Diary of Frank "Foo" Fujita*. Fenton, TX: Univ. of North Texas Press.

Gilmartin, K.M. and R.J. Gibson (1985). "Hostage Negotiation: The Bio-Behavioral Dimension." *The Police Chief* 52:46-48.

Goldaber, I. (1979). "A Typology of Hostage Takers." *The Police Chief* 46:21-23.

Hatcher, C., K. Mohandie, J. Turner, and M. Gelles (1998). "The Role of the Psychologist in Crisis/Hostage Negotiations." *Behavioral Science and the Law* 16:455-472.

Hillman, R.G. (1983). "The Psychopathology of Being Held Hostage." In Freedman, L.Z. and Y. Alexander (eds.), *Perspectives on Terrorism*. Wilmington, DE: Scholarly Resources.

Hyer, L., C. Walker, G. Swanson, and S. Sperr (1992). "Validation of PTSD Measures for Older Combat Veterans." *Journal of Clinical Psychology* 48:579-588.

Keen, S. (1991). *Fire in the Belly*. NY: Bantam Books.

LaForte, R.S. and R.E. Marcello (1993). *Building the Death Railway: The Ordeal of American POWs in Burma, 1942-1945*. Wilmington, DE: Scholarly Resources Inc.

LaForte, R.S., Marcello, R.E., and R.L. Himmel (1994). *With Only the Will to Live: Accounts of Americans in Japanese Prison Camps, 1941-1945*. Wilmington, Delaware: Scholarly Resources Inc.

Lanza, M.L. (1986). "Victims of International Terrorism." *Issues in Mental Health Nursing* 8:95-107.

McMains, M.J. (1986). "Post-Shooting Trauma: Principles from Combat." In Reese, J.T. and H.A. Goldstein (eds.), *Psychological Services for Law Enforcement*. Washington, DC: U.S. Government Printing Office.

_____ (2000). "Critical Decision Points in Crisis Negotiations: An Intensive Case Study." Presented at the 10th Annual Crisis Negotiators' Seminar and Competition, San Marcos, TX (January).

Mullins, W.C. (1988). *Terrorist Organizations in the United States*. Springfield, IL: Charles C Thomas.

Nielsen, E. (1986). "Post-Shooting Trauma in Police Work." In Reese, J. and H. Goldstein (eds.), *Psychological Services for Law Enforcement*. Washington, DC: U.S. Government Printing Office.

Noesner, G. (1999). "Negotiation Concepts for Commanders." *FBI Law Enforcement Bulletin* 68:6-14.

Nudell, M. and N. Antokol (1990). "Negotiating for Life." *Security Management* 34:56-64.

Oots, K.L. and T.C. Wiegele (1985). "Terrorist and Victim: Psychiatric and Psychological Approaches from a Behavioral Science Perspective." *Terrorism* 8:1-32.

Ochberg, F.M. (1979). "Preparing for Terrorist Victimization." In Alexander, Y. and R.A. Kilmarx (eds.), *Political Terrorism and Business—The Threat and the Response*. New York, NY: Praeger.

_____ (1980a). "Victims of Terrorism." *Journal of Clinical Psychiatry* 41:73-74.

_____ (1980b). "What is Happening to the Hostages in Tehran?" *Psychiatric Annals* 10:186-189.

Ohry, A., Z. Solomon, Y. Neria, and M. Waysman (1994). "The Aftermath of Captivity: An 18-year Follow-up of Israeli POWs." *Journal of Behavioral Medicine* 20:27-33.

Olin, W.R. and D.G. Born (1983). "A Behavioral Approach to Hostage Situations." *FBI Law Enforcement Bulletin* 52:18-24.

Peters, J., D.P. Van-Kammen, W.B. Van-Kammen, and T.C. Neylan (1990). "Sleep Disturbance and Computerized Axial Tomographic Scan Findings in Former Prisoners of War". *Journal of Comprehensive Psychiatry* 31:535-539.

Quarles, C.L. (1988). "Kidnapped: Surviving the Ordeal." *Security Management* 32:40-44.

Reese, J.T., J.M. Horn, and C. Dunning (1991). *Critical Incidents in Policing*. Washington DC: U.S. Government Printing Office.

Ricketts, C. (1995). "Post Incident Stress for the Negotiator." *The Journal of Crisis Negotiations* (October), Vol. 1, No. 2.

Schlossberg, H. (1979a). "Hostage Negotiations School." Austin, TX: Texas Department of Public Safety.

Schlossberg, H. (1979b). "Police Response to Hostage Situations." In O'Brien, J.T. and Marcus, M. (eds.). *Crime and Justice in America*. NY: Pergamon Press.

Siegel, R.K. (1984). "Hostage Hallucination: Visual Imagery Induced by Isolation and Life-Threatening Stress." *Journal of Nervous and Mental Disease* 172:264-272.

Simon, R.I. and R.A. Blum (1987). "After the Terrorist Incident: Psychotherapeutic Treatment of Former Hostages." *American Journal of Psychotherapy* 41:194-200.

Solomon, R. & J.A. Horn (1986). "Post-Shooting Traumatic Reactions: A Pilot Study." In Reese, J.T. and H.A. Goldstein (eds.), *Psychological Services for Law Enforcement*. Washington D.C: U.S. Government Printing Office.

Somodevilla, A. (1986). "Post-Shooting Trauma: Reactive and Proactive Treatment." In Reese, J.T. and H.A. Goldstein (eds.), *Psychological Services for Law Enforcement*. Washington D.C: U.S. Government Printing Office.

Soskis, D.A. and F.M. Ochberg (1982). "Concepts of Terrorist Victimization." In Ochberg, F.M. and D.A. Soskis (eds.), *Victims of Terrorism*. Boulder, CO: Westview Press.

Soskis, D.A. and C.R. Van Zandt (1986). "Hostage Negotiation: Law Enforcement's Most Effective Non-Lethal Weapon." *FBI Management Quarterly* 6:1-8.

Speed, N., B. Engdahl, J. Schwartz, and R. Eberly (1989). "Post-traumatic Stress Disorder as a Consequence of the POW Experience." *Journal of Nervous and Mental Disease* 177:147-153.

Stenger, C.A. (1992). "A look at the Inhospitable World of the Hostage and Prisoner of War and its Impact on their Lives. " In Bird, T. (ed.), *American POWs of World War II: Forgotten Men Tell their Stories*. Westport, CT: Praeger.

Strentz, T. (1987). "A Hostage Psychological Survival Guide." *FBI Law Enforcement Bulletin* 56(11):1-8.

Strentz, T. (1979). "Law Enforcement Policies and Ego Defenses of the Hostage." *FBI Law Enforcement Bulletin* 48:1-12.

_____ (1982). "The Stockholm Syndrome: Law Enforcement Policy and Hostage Behavior." In Ochberg, F.M. and D.A. Soskis (eds.), *Victims of Terrorism*. Boulder, CO: Westview Press.

_____ (1984). "Preparing the Person with High Potential for Victimization as a Hostage." In Turner, J.T. (ed.), *Violence in the Medical Care Setting: A Survival Guide*. Rockville, MD: Aspen Press.

_____ and S.M. Auerbach (1988). "Adjustment to the Stress of Simulated Captivity: Effects of Emotion-Focused versus Problem-Focused Preparation on Hostages Differing in Locus of Control." *Journal of Personality and Social Psychology* 55:652-660.

Sutker, P.B., A.N. Allain, and J.L. Johnson (1993). "Clinical Assessment of Long-term Cognitive and Emotional Eequelae to World War II Prisoner-of-War Confinement: Comparison of Pilot Twins." *Journal of Psychological Assessment* 5:3-10.

Sutker, P.B., A.N. Allain, and D.K. Winstead (1993). "Psychopathology and Psychiatric Diagnoses of World War II Pacific Theater Prisoner of War Survivors and Combat Veterans." *American Journal of Psychiatry* 150:240-245.

Sutker, P.B., F. Bugg, and A.N. Allain (1990). "Person and Situation Correlates of Post-Traumatic Stress Disorder among POW Survivors." *Psychological Reports* 66:912-914.

Sutker, P.B., F. Bugg, and A.N. Allain (1991). "Psychometric Predictions of PTSD among POW Survivors." *Journal of Psychological Assessment*, 3, 105-110.

Sutker, P.B., D.K. Winstead, K.C. Goist and R.M. Malow (1986). "Psychopathology Subtypes and Symptom Correlates among Former Prisoners of War. *Journal of Psychopathology and Behavioral Assessmen* 8:89-101.

Symonds, M. (1975). "Victims of Violence: Psychological Effects and Aftereffects." *American Journal of Psychoanalysis* 35:19-26.

_____ (1983). "Victimization and Rehabilitative Treatment." In Eichelman, B., D. Soskis, and W. Reid (eds.), *Terrorism: Interdisciplinary Perspectives*. Washington DC: American Psychiatric Association.

Tennant, C.C., K.J. Goulston, and O.F. Dent (1986). "The Psychological Effect of Being a Prisoner of War: Forty Years after Release." *American Journal of Psychiatry* 143:618-621.

Turco, R.M. (1987). "Psychiatric Contributions to the Understanding of International Terrorism." *International Journal of Offender Therapy and Comparative Criminology* 31:153-161.

Ursano, R.J. and J.R. Rundell (1990). "The Prisoner of War." *Military Medicine* 155:176-180.

Wesselius, C.L. and J.V. de Sarno (1983). "The Anatomy of a Hostage Situation." *Behavioral Sciences and the Law* 1:33-45.

Discussion Questions

1. If you know a former prisoner of war, or know someone who knows a former prisoner of war, interview him or her about his or her experiences. Include as part of the interview any long-term effects they may be experiencing. You may have to prompt them by listing some long-term effects.

2. If possible, interview someone who has experienced a traumatic incident (i.e., car accident, burglarized home). Conduct an emotional debriefing with that person. Do you notice any symptoms common to people who experience PTSD?

3. If possible, emotionally debrief a police officer who has recently been in a traumatic incident. Are they in the recovery stage? If they are in the traumatic depression stage, what could you say to get them moving toward the recovery stage?

4. What differences would you expect in civilians, correctional officers, police officers, or military personnel who were taken hostage? Who might be the best hostage? Worst hostage?

5. What types of emotional debriefing differences do you believe there would be for police and prison officials following a hostage incident?

6. Design a training program for schoolteachers on how to act if taken hostage. What suggestions could you include for how to handle their students while in the hostage situation?

7. What types of training do you believe could be given to negotiators to minimize the emotions of a situation, especially one that has a negative outcome?

Communication in Crisis Negotiations

6

Learning Objectives

1. Understand the three principles of effective communication and how communications are interactive.

2. Know the seven components of the communication process.

3. Know the four barriers to effective communication.

4. Know what can be done to improve communication.

5. Understand the three patrol attitudes hostage negotiators must overcome.

6. Learn specific verbal tactics to be used in crisis communication:
   Concerned attitude
   Reasonable problem-solver
   Buddy—fellow traveler
   Columbo—dumb but trying
   Non-judgmental and directing

7. Understand the guidelines for determining the progress of negotiations.

8. Understand William Ury's five-step system for *Getting Past No*:
   Go to the balcony
   Step to their side
   Change the game
   Build a golden bridge
   Make it hard to say no

9. Know the techniques of influence and compliance as researched by Cialdini.

10. Know the Theories of Persuasion and how to use them in a negotiated situation.

11. Know the techniques of suggestion.

12. Know what is required for active listening and the four types of active listening.

Bob and his wife Janet were separated. Bob had been talking to Janet on a regular basis trying to "mend fences" and get back together. Janet was rather cool and distant with Bob, trying to make it evident through both verbal and non-verbal cues that she was not interested in getting back together. Bob refused to take the hint, however, and still fervently believed there was hope for the marriage. The three children (all under 5 years of age), lived with Janet. One day, a friend of Bob's told Bob he (the friend) had seen Janet on a date with another man. Bob flew into a rage, abruptly left work, and went to Janet's house. He found her at home and saw a strange car in the driveway. Believing it to be the boyfriend's, Bob grabbed a gun and stormed into the house in an even bigger rage. A neighbor saw Bob and without hesitation, called the police. The police dispatched an officer to Janet's, where Bob brandished a weapon at the officer, who backed off and notified a supervisor, who called out the Crisis Response Team.

Negotiators initiated contact with Bob, who was highly emotional, angry, and acting violent. Bob continually threatened to kill the boyfriend and Janet, and then to flee with the kids. Initial demands made by Bob were unreal and unattainable. Every time negotiators tried to talk with Bob, he would fly into a rage, begin screaming and cussing, and threatening to kill everyone he saw (inside and outside). The negotiator then changed verbal tactics and would call Bob, introduce himself, and then keep quiet. The negotiator discovered that, using the tactic of extended pauses, after about two minutes Bob would calm down and begin talking in a low tone about how messed up his life was. When he did this, the negotiator would reflect the emotional meaning of Bob's statements and then indicate to Bob he understood the emotions Bob was experiencing.

After about three hours, Bob began really talking to the negotiator and telling him what led to the breakup and how afraid he was of facing a future by himself. Recognizing that much of Bob's anger was directed at his (Bob's) future loneliness and the fear of not having anyone to share life with (the negotiator had also discovered that Bob had been abandoned by his father at a young age), the negotiator began offering suggestions on what Bob could do to find a "life partner." Initially, Bob argued with every suggestion the negotiator presented. Whenever that happened, the negotiator would be quiet, let Bob vent, and then counter Bob's argument. Over the next several hours, Bob's counter arguments got weaker. The negotiator was paying attention to the emotional content of Bob's communications. At one point, the negotiator asked Bob to come outside and meet with the negotiator to discuss one of the suggestions. Bob agreed, put down his weapon, walked outside and surrendered. No one was injured at any time during the incident.

Hostage negotiations can be summarized in one word—*communication*. The hostage negotiator is a communicator, a talker, a conveyer of ideas, a persuader (Alexander et al., 1991; Anderson & Narus, 1990; Taylor, 1983). Without communication, there are no negotiations. Whether by voice over a telephone or bullhorn, or from around a wall or face-to-face, the negotiator must be able to communicate. If the negotiator does not understand the basics of communications, crisis communications, and the ability to actively listen, he or she can have all the tools and equipment in the world and still not be effective. Communications resolve the incident (Rogan & Hammer, 1995). As Voss (2004) so aptly stated, "Crisis negotiation is a highly specialized set of communication skills designed to reduce risks and increase options in a crisis situation."

Principles of Basic Communication

The ability to communicate is not something people are born with. It is not a genetic trait passed down from generation to generation, nor is it something that "magically" appears when we reach a certain age. The ability to communicate is a skill that must be learned and practiced, just as is the ability to use a pistol or play a musical instrument. Police negotiators are not successful because they have the Midas touch. They are successful because they understand the principles of communication, practice those principles, and then apply what they have practiced to the hostage situation.

Are all negotiators who can communicate successful? No. The unsuccessful negotiator does not fail, however, because he or she cannot communicate. The unsuccessful negotiator fails because of other factors and variables that do not complement his or her ability to communicate. This negotiator may not, for example, understand the difference between everyday communication and communication in negotiations. He or she may be able to convey a message but not actively listen and understand a sent message. This negotiator may do all of the above and just not have the temperament necessary to be a negotiator. He or she does, however, understand communications basics.

Principles of Effective Communication

Effective communication involves a great deal more than merely picking up a telephone and initiating a conversation. Effective communication involves three principles. First, effective communication involves the ability to understand. Many police officers often get into difficult situations because there is a misunderstanding between them and a citizen. For example, the police officer may tell a crime suspect to "stop and spread 'em." To the police officer, this communication is very clear and concise. To the suspect, who may have had no prior police contact, the communication may mean several different things. Does this mean to finish what he is doing and then stop, to sit on his buttocks, to lie face down, to kneel, or to squat? When the suspect does what he may believe is appropriate, it sometimes is not what the police officer meant. The communications from the officer then escalate, tone and inflection increase, and the officer becomes angry and hostile. The suspect responds to this hostility in kind and a scuffle ensues. While this example is simplistic, it illustrates the basic problem in understanding communications. The sender and receiver both must understand the communication. Misunderstandings can occur for numerous reasons, including differences in religion, culture, ethnic background, geographic location, age, education, and life experiences. Words and phrases commonly used by the police are not always understood by citizens. Telling a citizen who is afraid to enter her apartment that it is "code four" means absolutely nothing to her. The negotiator, then, must communicate from the reference point of the hostage taker (Kahneman, 1992). This reference point may be cultural, religious, educational, or motivational.

Effective communication also has to achieve the desired effect. Communication has a goal that must be achieved. In hostage negotiations, the goals include reducing the emotional level of the hostage taker, keeping hostages alive and unharmed, and talking the hostage taker into surrendering. To be effective, the negotiator must begin with clearly defined goals and always be ready to change these goals and establish new ones. This means the effective negotiator must anticipate the direction the conversation will take and be ready to respond. Communications are fluid and dynamic. They change direction constantly and the unexpected often occurs. A negotiator may, for example, be discussing how the police are going to get food to the hostage taker when suddenly, out of the blue, the hostage taker demands a vehicle. If the negotiator is not prepared for this sudden change in direction, the negotiator's communications will not achieve the intended effect nor progress toward goals.

Finally, effective communication is ethical. It involves a degree of trust and respect between the communicator and receiver. This, in fact, is the first goal of the negotiator (Dolan & Fuselier, 1989). The communicator has to be sincere in what he or she is sending, and the receiver has to believe in what is being sent. If the negotiator is caught in a lie, the hostage taker will no longer communicate with that negotiator, and may in fact not communicate with any police officer (Sen, 1989). A lie may result in a depressed hostage taker committing suicide (DiVasto et al., 1992). One disturbing trend in hostage situations is repeat hostage takers. These are difficult situations for the negotiator because more often than not the hostage taker has been lied to in the past. For example, a hostage taker questions what is going to happen if he surrenders. The negotiator tells the hostage taker: "Nothing. Let the hostages go and come out and nothing will happen to you. You will be free to go on your way." If the hostage taker is a repeat offender, he knows full well that the police are going to arrest him, he is going to trial, and he may very well serve time in prison. If the negotiator were to use this fabrication, negotiations would immediately break down. Instead, if the negotiator were to say, "Provided nobody in there has been injured, you will be arrested, be able to bond out of jail as soon as you can arrange bail, and if found guilty at trial, most likely be given three months in the county jail," the hostage taker will be more likely to believe the negotiator.

Communication is a fluid, dynamic process. It is ongoing, irreversible, and unrepeatable. Once said, a communication is permanent. We have all experienced a time when we said something to someone that we instantly regretted. From experience, we know the statement cannot be taken back or undone. Should this happen in a negotiation situation, the results could be disastrous. Imagine the frustrated, tired, and irritable negotiator who says, "Listen, I've done everything I can and you're acting like a little punk by fighting . . . ah, I mean you need to work with me on this point." Chances are the hostage taker has slammed down the telephone before the negotiator has finished talking.

These points illustrate the principle that communication in negotiations is an interactive process. Research on corporate negotiations (which in many ways are similar to hostage negotiations) has shown that the largest single predictor of success in these negotiations is the parties' interaction (Alexander et al., 1991; Campbell et al., 1988; Clopton, 1984; Rubin & Brown, 1975). Communications allow the negotiator and hostage taker to exchange information, identify behavioral tendencies, determine strategy, and coordinate outcomes (Putnam & Jones, 1982).

Components of the Communication Process

Seven components make up the communication process. The first component is the source of the communication. The sender must first encode the message to be sent. The sender must decide how to convey what he or she wants to send so it can be understood and acted upon. The second component is the message itself. The message is what the receiver assigns a meaning to. Third is the channel used to convey the message. Is the message verbal or written, is it delivered over the telephone, bullhorn, or in person? The fourth component is the receiver, the person to whom the message is intended. Once received, the receiver must be able to decode the message. The fifth component is noise. Noise is anything that interferes with the message. Noise can be environmental, such as background, static in a telephone line, other people talking, or voice level. Noise can also be perceptual. That is, the sender or receiver can assign unintended meaning to a communication based upon what he or she believes the communication means, not what is actually sent. Perceptions of communication are influenced by many factors, including age, education, ethnic background, etc. The sixth component of the communication process is feedback on the communication. What is the receiver's response to the communication? The seventh component is context. What is the environment of the communication? Is the receiver ready for the communication? The negotiator who picks up the telephone and says, "Hi, my name is Joe, why don't you release those people and come out?" is not going to be very successful because the context is not appropriate for that communication.

Barriers to Effective Communication

The very act of communicating by the negotiator or hostage taker can create barriers to effective communication. The power to resolve a hostage situation depends upon language. For many reasons, language itself can be a barrier to effective communications. Many words have more than one meaning or can be interpreted to have more than one meaning. The negotiator could say to the hostage taker, "We would like to take care of you," meaning the police want to try to peacefully resolve the situation. The hostage taker, however, could interpret that statement to mean the police would like to use force to resolve the situation. To ensure that these misunderstandings do not occur, the communicator should explain and clarify meanings. The negotiator should have said, "We would like to ensure that neither you nor anyone else gets hurt and resolve this peacefully."

A second communication barrier is polarization, in which extremes are used to describe something. In the old Hollywood westerns, the good guys wore white hats and the bad guys wore black hats. The screen character had all good attributes or all bad attributes; there was no in-between. Often, people view communications the same way. This barrier may be one that influences the entire early course of negotiations and one that the negotiator has a great deal of difficulty overcoming. The hostage taker may perceive his situation to be polarized in that the only resolutions are death from the tactical team or life imprisonment (or a death sentence). Likewise, the negotiator may see the concessions from the hostage taker as all or none. No demands are met unless a hostage is released, and no other concessions are agreeable. If the negotiator talks to the hostage taker in extreme terms, no progress will be made in the negotiations.

A third communication barrier is "allness," or simplistic generalizations. "All police abuse suspects" and "all hostage takers are criminals" are two such generalizations. This cognition can defeat negotiations before they even begin. If both or even one party attempts to communicate with these perceptions dominating communications, the incident will not be resolved successfully. The negotiator has two important roles in overcoming this communications barrier. First, the negotiator must put aside his or her perceptions of the hostage taker before beginning negotiations, and second, the negotiator must overcome the hostage taker's perceptions of the police. Progress will not be made until these two tasks are accomplished.

A fourth barrier to communication is static evaluation, or communications that do not reflect the changing dynamics of the hostage situation. Initially, communications are somewhat formal. Neither the negotiator nor the hostage taker knows the other. As negotiations progress, they become more familiar with each other, know each other better as people, and become more relaxed. With time, communications become less formalized and more familiarized. This is analogous to when a person makes new friends. If your communications with that person do not grow increasingly informal you will not become friends. Likewise, if communications do not become informal in the hostage situation, the negotiator cannot make progress.

Table 6.1
Barriers to Effective Communication

Barrier	Solution
Bypassing	Use specific words—watch for multiple interpretations
Polarization	Few issues are good-bad, positive-negative
Allness Statements	Do not overgeneralize
Static Evaluation	Account for continual change
Fact-Interference Confusion	Clarify and analyze

Source: Table adapted from pp. 55-58 from *Invitation to Effective Speech Communication*, by John T. Masterson, Steven A. Beebe, and Norman H. Watson. Copyright © 1989 by Scott, Foresman and Company. Reprinted by permission of Addison-Wesley Educational Publishers, Inc.

Given that communication is often imprecise, confusing, and laden with barriers that worsen communication, can anything be done to improve communication? The answer is yes. More than anything else, feedback can be used to improve communication. Feedback is the response given concerning a communication. The negotiator must constantly provide feedback to make sure that communications are accurate, negotiations are progressing, and communications are being acted upon (Rangarajan, 1985). Feedback should be given immediately. The negotiator should immediately respond to the communication, not wait until a later time to clarify the communication. When giving feedback, the negotiator should not focus on all the details of the communication, but should summarize the general gist of the communication. Also, when summarizing the communication, the negotiator should be specific, not general. If the hostage taker wants a car, $50,000, and plans to take two hostages as security, the negotiator should summarize the conversation as: "So you want transportation, money, and you plan to take some hostages." The negotiator should not summarize by saying; "So there are some things you want." Finally, when providing feedback, the negotiator should not be evaluative, but descriptive. Instead of saying, "You mean you're trying to tell me you're not going to release any people," the negotiator should say, "I understand you to be saying that you are reluctant to release any people."

Crisis Communication

The negotiator attempts to communicate in a highly emotional situation. Stress levels are high and rationality is decreased. The crisis is caused by unpredictability and loss of control. The role of the negotiator is to defuse emotions and establish rapport, convince the hostage taker to yield his demands, release the hostages, and surrender (Nielson & Shea, 1982).

One of the most difficult tasks for the negotiator is to control his or her attitude. The negotiator must be accepting and caring, attitudes contrary to most patrol attitudes. There are three patrol attitudes the negotiator must overcome (McMains & Lanceley, 1994). The first is either/or thinking. This attitude defines people as either allies or enemies. Most police have heard the expression "there are only two kinds of people in the world, bad guys and cops." Most police have had this attitude on more than one occasion. This attitude leads to judgment and rejection. That is, "Everybody but me and my partner are bad guys and there are times I am not sure about my partner." The second patrol attitude is minimization of feelings. If an officer expresses emotions or shows any feelings, this is taken as an unprofessional and irrelevant weakness. The refusal to display emotions interferes with the ability to understand other people and leads to an attitude of "Just the facts; nothing but the facts." The third patrol attitude is that of "right or wrong, just do something." Police believe that whenever they respond to a situation, they must take immediate action. Taking immediate action leads to behavior that is not carefully planned and thought out. This behavior tends to intensify a crisis.

The primary negotiator, secondary negotiator, and mental health consultant (seated in foreground) are involved in directly speaking with a hostage taker. Standing is the team's commander (center) and primary intelligence gatherer (right). Seated to the left rear are additional team members who serve as recorders, historians, and intelligence keepers. They also plan strategy and can fill in for other team members if necessary. *(Photograph by Shan K. Smith)*

These attitudes may be warranted and necessary for most patrol situations. They can help the patrol officer survive many street situations and help remove the officer psychologically from situations he or she confronts on a daily basis. By viewing suspects as enemies rather than allies, the officer does not allow suspects to gain the upper hand or engage in combative behavior. By suppressing emotions, the officer not only insulates him- or herself from the surrounding world, the officer helps give strength to citizen contacts.

To a crime victim, for example, the officer is not only repressing pain at seeing someone else victimized, he or she is giving strength to that victim. By taking immediate action on a patrol call, the officer can defuse a situation before it becomes a crisis. It is similar to the old military axiom, "kill 'em all and let God sort 'em out." To the police it becomes, "arrest them all and let the courts decide."

These attitudes, however, are dysfunctional to the negotiator. The negotiator must develop attitudes opposite those normally developed and used by the police officer. The negotiator must be accepting of the hostage taker, must refrain from judging the hostage taker, second-guessing the hostage taker, and must not reject the feelings, emotions, and concerns of the hostage taker. The negotiator must be caring and must communicate concern for the interests, goals, and needs of the hostage taker (Froman & Glorioso, 1984). He or she must be empathetic to the hostage taker's plight. The negotiator must have patience and must think before acting and be able to use time effectively to defuse emotions and allow the hostage taker to rethink his position. The negotiator is the representative for the response team, law enforcement, the authorities, and the threat to the hostage taker (Cambria, DeFilippo, Louden & McGowan, 2002). He has become the psychological link that, to the hostage taker, can get him help or get him hurt.

When approaching a hostage situation and before beginning negotiations, the negotiator must ask him- or herself several questions and be able to respond in the affirmative to each question. Can I accept what this person is doing? Can I show this person I care about him even though I do not agree with what he is doing? Can I wait and listen long enough to help this person calm down and resolve this situation? If the negotiator answers no to any of these questions, he or she should not open negotiations because he or she will not be able to empathize with the hostage taker and work toward a successful conclusion.

The negotiator has to be non-threatening, reassuring, and facilitate ventilation and validation. By being reassuring, the negotiator can defuse anger, hostility, and control emotions. The negotiator will return some control and predictability to the situation. He will reassure the hostage taker that the situation can be brought under control and resolved satisfactorily. Consequently, the hostage taker will begin thinking and will quit acting impulsively. The hostage taker will think about his predicament and begin to rationally attempt to resolve the dilemma. The negotiator who is concerned and cares allows the hostage taker to ventilate his emotions. The hostage taker will defuse his anger and hostility by being able to tell someone his troubles. When these emotions are being discussed, the negotiator can validate these emotions ("I understand. I remember one time I was put in a similar bind and reacted the same way . . ."). This further reduces the emotional content of the situation.

Basic Patrol Officer Communications

Many police and correctional officer academies now emphasize communications for entry-level officers (patrol, correctional, etc.). We understand the importance of communications in dealing with people in stressful situations and know that good communications skills can, in almost all cases, prevent physical aggression. These same communication skills are critical for the negotiator. Cooper (1999) has identified the basic communication skills necessary for patrol officers (and correctional staff) and it is worth reviewing those basic skills prior to moving to crisis communications.

The conflict/dispute resolution skills Cooper (1999) has identified are: (1) listening actively; (2) being able to identify the key or relevant issues; (3) articulating the issues; (4) making the dispute manageable, or removing the emotions and framing the issues; (5) avoiding favoritism to any party in the dispute; (6) identifying and articulating areas of agreement; (7) using "I" rather than "you" to avoid an accusatory tone; (8) being aware of body language signals; (9) avoiding stereotypes; (10) not making statements that back people into corners; and (11) recognizing that people are emotional and allowing them to vent.

Negotiators should be flexible in using these basic skills and not have to actively think about them. The effective use of the above skills, from the first telephone conversation, makes the situation infinitely more manageable, shorter, and increases the probability of a nonviolent and successful resolution. People want to talk about their problem, have someone listen to them and understand their problem, and finally, to show them a way to resolve their problem. These communication skills do that. In the crisis situation, it often takes more active kinds of communication skills.

Verbal Tactics in Crisis Communications[1]

The negotiator can use specific verbal tactics in a hostage situation to accomplish the above objectives. First, the negotiator should display a concerned, caring, and interested attitude (Taylor, 1983). The negotiator should communicate an attitude that shows he or she has a genuine interest in the hostage taker. Examples of communications indicating these attitudes include: "Tell me what happened" "That must have been hard/sad/frightening" and "I'd really like to help you." These types of phrases work especially well with depressed, inadequate, and disoriented people.

The negotiator can also assume the role of a reasonable problem solver. When using these types of communications, the negotiator should assume the role of the leader. Examples include: "Let's work together to be sure everyone is safe" "What would you like to do about this?" and "Let's see what other solutions are possible." The negotiator should not use the reasonable problem solver role until he or she is sure that negotiations are in the Accommodation/Negotiation Stage.

The negotiator can use the role of the buddy-fellow traveler. This role is one of commiseration with the hostage taker and works well with trapped felons, impulsive people, and antisocial personalities. Examples include: "Man, I hear you. Bosses never understand." "You know how they are about _____." "That shouldn't happen to a dog."

Another tactic that produces results is the Columbo/dumb but trying persona. The negotiator does not have all of the answers but is trying to do the best he or she can. In a sense, the negotiator should appear somewhat inept at what he or she is doing. Examples include: "I know it's taking a long time, but we are trying" "Let me see what my boss says about that" "I hate it that I can't help any faster, but _____" and "What else do you think we can do?" This tactic works well with antisocials or any highly emotional hostage taker.

A final tactic the negotiator can use is that of being firm, accepting-directing, non-judgmental, and helpful. The negotiator should be compassionate but competent. This tactic is particularly good with depressed persons, disoriented or dependent people, and during the Crisis and Resolution Stages. Examples include: "You sound pretty excited. Take a couple of slow, deep breaths and relax" "Let's take this next step real slow so nobody gets hurt" "Check on your people for me, to be sure everyone is all right. I want everyone to be okay."

Like a successful business manager, the successful negotiator should use praise and reinforcement to build the hostage taker's self-esteem (Blanchard, 1991). The negotiator can elevate self-esteem in several ways. He or she should avoid minor criticism. Even an innocuous phrase like, "Don't talk so fast" may be interpreted as criticism. The negotiator should listen actively. Active listening is positive feedback and builds self-esteem, because it shows that someone is listening and cares. Finally, specific reinforcement should be given at every opportunity. The negotiator will give general reinforcement on many occasions (i.e., saying, "Yes" or "Uh-huh" when the hostage taker moves in a direction the negotiator wants). Specific reinforcement would be directed praise for specific actions or communications from the hostage taker. An example would be if the hostage taker said, "Okay, forget about _____." The negotiator might respond, "I really appreciate that. You're really working to help me out."

Like a good actor or actress, the negotiator must be able to switch between tactics, at times being concerned and caring, and at other times being firm and directing. No single tactic works during the entire situation or for a continued period of time. The negotiator must be flexible and willing to predict and change roles as the situation evolves (Abbott, 1986).

The negotiator may employ tactics that will hinder communications and sabotage flexibility and success. First, the negotiator who attempts to persuade with argument is doomed to failure. Argument will only serve to cement the resolve of the hostage taker to get his way and strengthen his resolve to maintain his position. Remember a time when someone argued with you. What was your reaction? It was likely one of entrenching yourself in your belief (even though you knew at the time your belief was wrong). You were determined not to lose because you were in a competitive situation. The same is true in a hostage situation. The hostage taker, who is on an emotional high already, will become even more emotional if the negotiator attempts to argue.

If the negotiator threatens the hostage taker or engages in a power play, negotiations will cease. Most hostage takers do not respond well to authority figures. This hostility is exacerbated in a hostage situation. The hostage taker will not only "tune out" this negotiator, he is likely to cease negotiations or even harm a hostage to show who is really controlling the situation. Along these same lines, the negotiator should avoid moralizing, diagnosing, and advising the hostage taker.

Neither will the successful negotiator be a police interrogator. As power plays alienate the hostage taker, so does "twenty questions." In patrol situations, the police interrogator role is valuable. This role gets the officer a great deal of information in a short time, puts the citizen on the defensive, and asserts the officer's position of power. This same attitude is guaranteed to doom negotiations. To the hostage taker, a police interrogator is an authority figure trying to take control away from him. In addition, the hostage taker wants solutions for his problems, not more questions and more problems. In an interrogation, the hostage taker cannot ventilate and communications are not two-way.

Negotiators have to be confident in their ability to resolve the situation. They have to appear confident to the hostage taker. This confidence is one of the key factors in gaining the hostage taker's trust. There is a fine line, however, between being confident and being overbearing and coming across like the "expert." The negotiator has to be careful to demonstrate confidence in his or her abilities, while at the same time not appearing to be cocky. The negotiator who says something like, "Don't worry about a thing, we're going to get this worked out and get you out safe," will only make the hostage taker resistant to any solutions.

An unsuccessful negotiator fails to listen to the hostage taker. Active listening is just as important as talking. Active listening is one component of effective communications and is covered in detail elsewhere.

Although there are no absolute predictors of how negotiations are or are not progressing, Soskis and Van Zandt (1986) have provided some useful guidelines that can measure the progress of negotiations. Almost all of these guidelines involve the general tone of communications between the negotiator and hostage taker. Positive signs of progress include:

1. There is less violent content in the hostage taker's conversations;

2. The hostage taker talks more often and longer to the negotiator;

3. The hostage taker speaks at a slower rate and his speech pitch and volume are lower;

4. The hostage taker talks about personal issues;

5. A deadline is talked past and there is no incident;

6. Threats from the hostage taker decrease;

7. Hostages are released; and

8. No one has been killed or injured since the onset of negotiations.

Along those same lines, Strentz (1994) has identified 13 indicators that negotiations are not progressing or could become violent. The first four indicate that the hostage taker could commit suicide. They include:

1. The hostage taker setting a deadline for his own death;

2. The subject insisting on face-to-face negotiations (i.e., provoking the police into killing him);

3. A depressed hostage taker denying thoughts of suicide (he is lying to the negotiator and setting-up "suicide by cop." As Strentz says, "A homicide looking for a victim."); and

4. The hostage taker talking about the disposition of his or her belongings.

The next five indicators deal with negotiations possibly becoming volatile and include:

5. A weapon tied to the hostage taker or to the hostage taker and hostage;

6. A history of violence of the hostage taker;

7. The hostage taker becoming angry and emotional during negotiations or negotiations becoming emotional in content;

8. The hostage taker insisting that a particular person be brought to the scene; and

9. No social outlet for the hostage taker to express his anxiety, fear, and frustration (i.e., life is him against the world).

Strentz identified two indicators related to lack of cooperation and rapport in negotiations. These are:

10. No rapport between the hostage taker and negotiator; and

11. After hours of negotiation, the hostage taker has no clear demands or his demands are outrageous.

Finally, two factors were identified related to the hostage taker's life situation. These factors are:

12. Use of alcohol or drugs by the hostage taker during negotiations; and

13. Multiple stressors in the hostage taker's life.

In a comprehensive study of the communication patterns at a high-profile prison incident (Cuban detainee siege at the Talladega, Alabama, Federal Correctional Institution, Hammer and Rogan (2004) found that when the inmates were under elevated stress levels, their communications with negotiators increased rather than decreased. They attributed this increase to the inmates wanting to make sure negotiators were not making incorrect inferences about hostage taker behavior. When stress levels were low and inmates perceived they had situational control, communications decreased. So, the amount of communications made or maintained by the hostage taker may be a clue to negotiators as to hostage taker stress levels, hostage taker perceptions, or actions that may be occurring inside the situation.

Getting Past No

William Ury, in his book *Getting Past No* (1991), provides a model for negotiating that sums up and incorporates many of the communication themes presented in this chapter. Ury's negotiation model includes five steps the negotiator should be aware of and focus on during the negotiating process. If a negotiator learns, practices, and adheres to Ury's model, the negotiator will handle the most difficult situations with confidence and success.

Go to the Balcony

Step one is "Don't React—Go to the Balcony." That is, the negotiator should view negotiations as if he or she were a third party observing what was happening. Ury (1991) uses the analogy of being an actor in a play and standing on a balcony overlooking the stage and watching the action. Very often, the hostage taker will (whether intentionally or unintentionally) say or do things to produce an emotional reaction from the negotiator. He may refuse to budge on a position (put up a stone wall), threaten some harsh consequences if the negotiator does not do what he wants (attack), or attempt to trick the negotiator into giving in to some demand. The negotiator should recognize these tactics and expect them to occur.

The natural reaction to these tactics is to strike back, give in, or break off negotiations. That is, there is a tendency to make an emotional response to these tactics. The negotiator who recognizes the tactics will be able to counter them and continue negotiating in a reasonable manner. The negotiator who does react will become emotional and lose sight of the objective. This negotiator will become engaged in a personal "war" with the hostage taker and will not negotiate objectively for incident resolution.

Ury (1991) suggests that when these tactics are used, the negotiator should "keep his or her eyes on the prize." The negotiator should focus on why he or she is negotiating, stay focused on the goal, and identify his or her BATNA (Best Alternative To A Negotiated Agreement). The BATNA is the maximum trade a negotiator can get at any one point in negotiations. The BATNA will change as the situation and circumstances change, and the negotiator should constantly assess the BATNA in light of the situation's changing dynamics.

When the hostage taker uses emotional tactics, the negotiator can do several things to reduce his or her emotional response and reduce the emotions of the hostage taker. The negotiator should buy time to think. The negotiator can do this by utilizing pauses, rewinding the tape, and taking a time-out. Rewinding the tape refers to acts such as rephrasing what the hostage taker said in non-emotional terms or writing down the conversation to slow emotions ("Excuse me, I am writing down what you said so I won't forget it"). Also, the negotiator should not make important decisions hastily. The negotiator should say, "I will need to check with my commander and get back to you." This does three things for the negotiator. First, points of information can be checked for accuracy. Sec-

Inter-team communications are just as crucial as communications between the primary negotiator and the hostage taker. *(B. Miller)*

ond, the negotiator and command personnel can think through the decision. Third, the negotiator can reflect and make sure perspective on the situation has not been lost (Fisher et al., 1991).

The negotiator should not get mad, not get even, but instead get what he or she wants. The negotiator must control his or her behavior and emotions, and dispassionately listen and converse with the hostage taker. Nothing can be taken at a personal level or the hostage taker has gained the upper hand in negotiations.

Step to their Side

Step two of the Ury (1991) system is to disarm the hostage taker and step to his side. When hostage negotiations open, the negotiator is rational and calm. The hostage taker, however, is distraught, frightened, and angry.

Before negotiating, the negotiator must help the hostage taker regain his emotional balance. Just as important, the negotiator must make the hostage taker an ally. The hostage taker must realize that the negotiator is in the situation with him, not against him. Ury suggests five strategies to reduce emotions in the hostage taker and make the hostage taker an ally.

The negotiator must listen actively to the hostage taker. The negotiator must listen to his point of view and must understand that point of view. The good negotiator does more listening than talking. The negotiator not only must listen actively, but also must demonstrate to the hostage taker that he or she is listening actively by paraphrasing and asking for corrections. The negotiator should "acknowledge the point" and recognize the hostage taker as a person (one way is to acknowledge the hostage taker's feelings, such as "I appreciate how you feel"). This does not mean or imply that the negotiator has to agree with what the hostage taker has done. The negotiator should work on finding opportunities to agree with the hostage taker and find common ground to lead into more difficult subject areas. Sports, weather, anything at all that can be shared by the two parties will set the stage for later agreements. This does not mean the negotiator has to concede to the hostage taker or agree with what the hostage taker is doing. The negotiator should accumulate yeses. Put the hostage taker in an agreeable mood and a "yes-saying" frame of mind. One good way to accomplish this is to frequently rephrase the hostage taker's statements and then ask, "Is this what you meant?" The negotiator should match the communication patterns and sensory language of the hostage taker. If the hostage taker speaks slowly, or uses local idioms, or uses "street slang" often, the negotiator should follow suit and use similar language. If the hostage taker uses "Do you SEE what I mean," the negotiator should reply in the same sensory modality ("Yes, I SEE what you mean").

The negotiator should acknowledge the person not as an adversary, but as a colleague. The negotiator can do this by first building a working relationship. The negotiator should not open negotiations by attempting to resolve issues or obtain lists of demands, but by making small talk to establish common ground and show the hostage taker that he matters as a person. The negotiator should flatter the hostage taker's ego and competence ("You seem like you are really capable of taking good care of the children.")

The negotiator should express his or her views without provoking the hostage taker. Most people negotiate with an either/or mentality. The best negotiator will use a both/and mentality. As Ury (1991) says, "don't say 'but;' say 'yes . . . and" The negotiator should not say, "I know you are getting thirsty, but we need a show of faith on your part." The negotiator should instead say, "Yes, I understand you are getting thirsty, and I want to work with you to satisfy our needs." What the negotiator should do is add to his statement. The negotiator should use "I" statements, not "you" statements. They should place a different perspective on the problem. The negotiator should recognize the differences between his or her position and that of the hostage taker (because they do have different positions), but he or she should do so optimistically ("I know this is difficult, and I know we can work it out").

Change the Game

The third step in Ury's (1991) model of negotiations is to change the game; don't reject, reframe. In hostage negotiation situations, the hostage taker often will spend a lot of time berating, belittling, or attacking the negotiator and the police. The negotiator's objective is to get past this point and have the hostage taker present the real issues and work on solutions. The negotiator must get the hostage taker to talk about the problems, not the police.

The negotiator must direct the hostage taker's focus back to the problems of resolving the hostage incident. One way for the negotiator to do this is to ask problem-solving questions: "Why?" "Why not?" and "What if?" The negotiator must determine what motivates the hostage taker and present opportunities for the hostage taker to solve the problem ("Why will taking the kids to Canada solve the problems with your ex-wife?"). If the hostage taker is reluctant to answer "why?" questions, the negotiator could rephrase the question in a "why not?" format ("What would be the problem with discussing your visitation rights with another lawyer who may be more experienced in family matters than your first lawyer?"). The negotiator could even assist the hostage taker in exploring all possible solutions to the problem ("Well, moving to Canada is certainly one option. What if, however, you were to do . . ."). The negotiator should ask open-ended questions. This makes the hostage taker think and formulate options on his own.

What if the hostage taker builds a stone wall? That is, the hostage taker makes his demands and says, "take it or leave it." The negotiator could ignore the stone wall and keep negotiating as if the ultimatum were never presented, reframe the stone wall as a positive ("We would hate to see that happen so we better quit worrying about the tactical team and get to work on solving your problem"), or test the stone wall and simply let the deadline expire, either by ignoring the deadline or talking through it.

When being attacked, the negotiator should reframe the attack into a future solution or a common problem. The hostage taker may be talking about past "injustices" suffered at the hands of the police. Rather than dwell on those, the negotiator could say, "I am terribly sorry you had experiences with a few bad apples. What can we do so that it never happens again?" The negotiator should also insert him- or herself into the problem and the solution. Change from "you" and "me" and use "we." Fisher et al. (1991) refer to deflecting personal attacks as "negotiation jujitsu." Personal attacks must be retranslated into issue problem-solving. If the hostage taker says, "I get the food before hostages are released. What's the matter? You don't think I'll live up to my word?" The negotiator might respond with the following deflection; "I appreciate your working with me on this. The issue is not about trust. The issue is the principle: Can we make the swap so both of us are satisfied? What if both happen at the same time? You have the person step to the door, pass the food in, and then leave." The negotiator has retranslated, offered a workable solution to the dilemma, and given the hostage taker the decision.

If the hostage taker attempts to use tricks, the negotiator should respond as if negotiations were progressing in good faith. The negotiator could ask clarifying questions to expose the tricks. Do not challenge the hostage taker, but rather act confused ("I'm confused. I thought I understood you to say earlier that if we provided you some food you would let one of those people go.").

Build a "Golden Bridge"

The fourth step in Ury's (1991) model of negotiating is to build the hostage taker a "golden bridge," or make it easy for him to say yes. The hostage taker may say no for many reasons. Decisions are not his idea, all his needs have not been fulfilled, he will lose face, and negotiations move too fast. The negotiator must remove these obstacles and replace them with a "bridge" of yeses.

Ury (1991) claims that too many negotiators force the hostage taker to agree, rather than getting the hostage taker on their side and then working with him to reach agreements that ultimately lead to a safe resolution. The negotiator should involve the hostage taker in the decisionmaking and make negotiations seem like a partnership. The negotiator should solicit the ideas of the hostage taker, select the most constructive of these ideas, and build upon them. The negotiator should also work with the hostage taker in criticizing those ideas and getting the hostage taker to realize the problems inherent in those ideas. ("Let's explore the idea of driving to Canada. What are the problems you see in taking that course of action?"). If the hostage taker is resistant to the negotiator's suggestions, the negotiator should ask, "Well, what problems do you see with that idea?" Finally, the negotiator could present alternatives from which the hostage taker can select.

One of the major issues at the Oakdale, Louisiana, prison siege was that the negotiators rapidly met the material demands of the hostage takers, yet the incident worsened. The negotiators did not satisfy the internal needs of the hostage takers (Fuselier et al., 1989). The negotiators moved too fast and did not recognize the emotional needs of the hostage takers. In addition to the demands the hostage taker makes, that hostage taker also has unstated needs of security, recognition, saving face, and control over his own fate. On some occasions, what the negotiator perceives to be an emotional outburst is merely the hostage taker crying out for recognition. The negotiator should view the situation from the hostage taker's perspective. If the negotiator can do this, he or she can make high-benefit, low-cost trades ("I'll back the tactical team off if you release one of those people"—low cost because the tactical team will still be in position, high benefit because a hostage is released).

The negotiator should "go slow to go fast." Negotiations are a process of small steps and frequent pauses. The negotiator cannot make one big leap and dash to the end zone. One common mistake that novice negotiators make is to open negotiations by arguing for the release of hostages (notice argue, not ask for—an important distinction). The negotiator should begin accumulating yeses by getting agreement on areas of common interest and small requests and working up to major concessions (Brett, 1991). Another common mistake that negotiators make is that they tend to rush when they sense a resolution is close. When the end is in sight, the negotiator should slow down even more, review agreements, and explain exactly what will happen during the resolution phase.

One area negotiators often do not recognize or completely ignore (and an area that can forestall or prevent resolution) is the hostage taker saving face. The hostage taker is a person who has ego needs, dignity, and a need to be respected. The resolution of the incident is where the hostage taker loses face. If a crowd of civilians is watching, or if relatives are present, or if the incident is a media event, the hostage taker may refuse to resolve the incident only because he fears losing face. The negotiator must satisfy this ego need to get resolution. Many hostage takers have surrendered, in fact, simply for a promise to not release their name to the media. Conversely, the negotiator can help the hostage taker write a "victory speech." The hostage taker may make a demand or request the negotiator cannot fulfill (and this demand or request will resolve the incident). The negotiator may tell the hostage taker: "I can't do that, but you can tell everyone I did and you refused."

Make it Hard to Say No

The fifth negotiating principle advanced by Ury (1991) is making it hard to say no, or "bring them to their senses, not their knees." When the hostage taker refuses to concede or surrender, the negotiator becomes frustrated. There is a natural tendency for the negotiator to assert authority and rely on his or her position of power (after all, this works on the street). This is when the negotiator "orders" the hostage taker to do something. In many negotiating situations, it will be necessary to negotiate from a position of power. This is acceptable, but only when power is used correctly.

The negotiator should use power sparingly, not unilaterally, and should use his or her power to educate the hostage taker. The negotiator should focus the hostage taker on the negative consequences of not agreeing or negotiating. The negotiator should do this by getting the hostage taker to realize the consequences of his lack of agreement. The negotiator can ask reality-based questions such as, "What do you think might happen if we don't work out a resolution?" "What do you think the tactical team will do if you hurt one of those people?" "What will happen to you if the tactical team assaults?" Questions of this nature are not a threat to the hostage taker; they serve to warn the hostage taker of possible consequences. The hostage taker is given the impression that he is making decisions and controlling his own fate. The negotiator may even demonstrate his or her BATNA by allowing the hostage taker to observe the tactical team preparing for an assault.

Using the negotiator's BATNA may force the hostage taker to negotiate and begin to agree on issues. The negotiator should be careful to not abuse his or her power, however. The purpose of using the BATNA is simply to show what could occur. The negotiator should use the minimum power necessary to reach agreement. This situation is analogous to a sports team "running up the score" on their opponents. They not only defeat the opposition, they embarrass, humiliate, and make enemies of the opposition. At some point, the opposing team will get revenge. The purpose of negotiation is to resolve the incident safely, not to humiliate the hostage taker.

When a hostage taker refuses to negotiate, the negotiator should continue to offer the hostage taker a way out. That is, the negotiator should leave the "bridge" open for the hostage taker to cross. The hostage taker may not realize he has a way out of his predicament (and that is why he refuses to negotiate). He may believe, for example, that the act of taking his estranged children hostage may completely ruin all visitation rights. The job of the negotiator now becomes that of convincing the hostage taker that visitation rights can be regained, but only if the hostage taker works with the negotiator. Let the hostage taker decide upon the terms of visitation ("If nobody gets hurt, you probably won't lose any visitation rights. The choice is yours, however.")

Once the hostage taker agrees to negotiate concessions, the negotiator should continue to make it hard to say no. The hostage taker, for example, could agree to surrender and at the last second get scared and refuse to come out. The negotiator should structure the agreement so any risk is minimized. Hostages should be released before the hostage taker surrenders. The negotiator can also make it difficult for the hostage taker to renege on any concessions by making it difficult to back out. One way to accomplish this is to tell others about the agreement, or have the hostage taker tell others (i.e., hostages).

At the conclusion of negotiations, the hostage taker should be as satisfied as possible. He should feel he made the choice, he is a person, his dignity is restored, and he can save face. The negotiator can accomplish this by leaving flexibility in the surrender ritual. Let the hostage taker decide how to surrender, who drives him to jail, etc. Remember, the purpose of negotiation is not to win, but to leave everyone satisfied.

Table 6.2
Summary of Negotiation Techniques.

Don't React—Go to the Balcony
No emotional response
Identify BATNA
Get what you want

Disarm Hostage Taker and Step to their Side
Active listening
Acknowledge the point
Find opportunities
Acknowledge the person
Do not provoke

Change the Game—Don't Reject, Reframe
Focus on problems, not persons
Move through stone walls
Reframe attacks
Ignore tricks

Build a "Golden Bridge"
Reach mutual agreements
Recognize unstated demands
Make small steps for progress
Save face

Bring them to their Senses, Not their Knees
Use power to educate
Do not "run up the score"
Keep the "bridge" in place
Make it hard to say no

Source: From *Getting Past No* by William Ury, copyright © 1991 by William Ury. Used by permission of Bantam Books, a division of Random House, Inc.

Advanced Communication Topics for the Negotiator

Influence and Compliance

Imagine if you had to consciously think about every behavior you performed. Breathing, for example, would become a full-time mental activity, if, for every breath you took, you had to consciously think "inhale," then "exhale." Fortunately, many responses in life are automatic and we do not have to spend time thinking about them. This is true not only for autonomic responses like breathing, blinking our eyes, etc., but also for social behaviors. When you are introduced to someone new, for example, you do not think, "extend my arm, put my fingers together with thumb apart, look the person in the eye, grasp their hand, move my arm up and down, open mouth to speak the word hello." We use shortcuts to go through life and avoid having to think about every act we perform. We perform many social functions in life in a mechanical manner that does not require active participation on our part. We are trained from birth to perform these functions without hesitation and without thinking. These automatic responses to certain trigger stimuli produce behavior of which we are barely conscious.

These automatic responses makes us particularly vulnerable to people who know how to use them. Is there anyone who has never purchased something he or she did not need or want? If you did not need or want it, why did you purchase the item? Because you encountered someone who knew about our fixed pattern of responding and was able to exploit it to take some of your money. We are all vulnerable to those who know of these fixed patterns of behavior and know how to exploit them.

Perceptual Contrast Principle

One example of how these automatic patterns of behavior work is provided by the perceptual contrast principle. If two objects are presented to us that are different from one another, they will seem more different than they really are. If we lift a light weight followed by a heavy weight, the heavy weight will seem heavier than if we had just lifted the heavy weight. The perceptual contrast principle works in numerous situations. If you go into a store to buy a new suit and a sweater, the salesperson will first sell you the suit and then sell you a sweater costing more than you initially wanted to pay. In fact, Whitney et al. (1965) found that buyers who purchased the suit first almost always spent more for accessories than those who purchased accessories first. If the salesperson attempted to sell you the sweater first, the contrast principle would work in your favor. You would spend less for the suit.

Perceptual contrast is not the only principle that triggers our automatic, stereotypical behavior. There are many others and, like the salesperson, the negotiator who is skilled in the use of the techniques of compliance and influence will be at an extreme advantage over his or her adversary, the hostage taker. Much of the following discussion on the techniques of influence and compliance come from Cialdini (1984; 1993), one of the leading researchers on how influence techniques guide our behavior. All are tools the negotiator can use frequently and effectively, and by knowing these techniques, can also prevent their use by the hostage taker. These are subtle techniques that are used on us without our knowledge. As Cialdini says, "the weapons of automatic influence lend their force to those who use them. It is not that the weapons, like a set of heavy clubs, provide a conspicuous arsenal to be used by one man to bludgeon another into submission. The process is much more sophisticated and subtle. With proper execution, the exploiter need hardly strain a muscle to get his way."

Rule of Reciprocity

One common technique is the rule of reciprocity, which states that if a favor is done for us, we feel obligated to repay that favor in the future. The negotiator might, without forewarning or prior discussion, tell the hostage taker, "I talked to my boss and got the lights left on for you." The negotiator has just done a favor for the hostage taker that the hostage taker will feel obligated to repay at a future time. It is unnecessary (and preferable) to mention that a favor has been done. Neither is it necessary that the negotiator actually do a favor—it must only be perceived by the hostage taker that a favor has been done.

The negotiator should also grant a perceived favor before the hostage taker. If the hostage taker has the opportunity to perform the first favor (i.e., "I won't hurt anybody unless my demands are not met"), then the negotiator is indebted. It is important that the negotiator perform the first favor, and grant favors early and often. Do not go overboard, however, and grant too many favors. Subtlety is the key.

There are three corollaries to the rule of reciprocity. First, the rule is overpowering. It does not depend upon the hostage taker liking the negotiator. The rule of reciprocity, in fact, often works better when the parties are strangers or do not like each other. The Hare Krishna Society is an example. While they are the subject of numerous jokes, ridicule, and scorn, they have managed to build a multi-million dollar empire by passing out flowers in airports and other public places ("Please take this as our gift to you."). After the recipient has accepted the "gift," a donation to the Society is requested and, more often than not, is given.

A second corollary to the rule of reciprocity is that it attracts uninvited debts. Reciprocity, in fact, usually works better if the favor is uninvited. Many magazines use this principle to increase subscriptions. The magazine sends you a free issue as a "gift" with no obligation on your part. Many people, however, subscribe to the magazine because they now owe the company because of the "gift." For the negotiator, uninvited favors are a powerful tool.

Third, the rule of reciprocity does not suggest that favors be of equal value. Research shows that little favors generate big returns. In certain societies, saving someone's life leaves the person saved indebted for the rest of his or her life. Leaving the power or other utilities on can be used to generate the release of hostages later. Failure to return the favor produces frustration and social ostracism. Even in a hostage situation, the hostage taker will feel pressure from the hostages to return any favors done for him. Gentle reminding by the negotiator to the hostage taker that a favor is owed can generate large concessions from the hostage taker.

Another part of the rule of reciprocity is the influence technique of reject-then-retreat. You make the recipient of the technique refuse a larger-than-wanted request and then make your true request. For example, the negotiator may ask for the release of all hostages. When this is refused, the negotiator may ask for some other concession. Not only does this technique increase compliance, it puts the hostage taker in a "yes-saying" frame of mind. The hostage taker is put in the position of perceiving himself as agreeable and willing to work with the negotiator to resolve the incident. Once this attitude develops, it will remain for the duration of the incident (unless the negotiator does something unreasonable and makes the hostage taker angry and resentful). Cialdini et al. (1975) referred to the reject-then-retreat procedure as the door-in-the-face technique.

Consistency

An example will serve to illustrate the second compliance technique discussed by Cialdini (1984). While on patrol, how many times have you vacillated regarding whether to arrest a suspect? After pondering the situation briefly, you decide to make the arrest. Just after handcuffing the suspect and placing him or her in the rear of your patrol vehicle, your sergeant drives up and asks if an arrest was really necessary. With no hesitation and no doubt in your voice, you answer, "Yes, there is no question about it." What could have changed in such a short time? Nothing in the situation changed to make you change from doubt to resolve. In fact, the only thing that happened was that the suspect was placed under arrest.

What occurred in the arrest situation is another of the automatic, fixed patterns of behavior we employ. Prior to the arrest, you were unsure of whether to make an arrest. When you decided to make the arrest, your indecision changed to confidence so your attitudes and beliefs were consistent with your behavior. You, like everyone else, do not want to appear weak-willed and indecisive. Once you decide on a course of action, even if you are unsure whether you took the correct action, you become confident of your decision and stand firmly behind that decision.

The influence technique of consistency is a powerful tool for the negotiator. The negotiator need merely get the hostage taker to make a decision or agree to do something. Consistency in the hostage situation is easy to obtain once the negotiator is able to get a commitment from the hostage taker. The negotiator should direct efforts toward getting the hostage taker to make a commitment, even if the payment for this commitment is several hours away. For example, an early promise on the part of the hostage taker to later release hostages will ensure that hostages will later be released safely. The negotiator can use several techniques to get a commitment from the hostage taker.

First, the negotiator can have the hostage taker write down any commitment. Once written, the commitment becomes more than an agreement—it becomes a promise. Putting an agreement in writing increases consistency of behavior, attitudes, and commitment to uphold the agreement. If at a later time the hostage taker is reluctant to release hostages, the negotiator can ask the hostage taker to read the agreement over the phone. The hostage taker will feel an obligation to honor his written commitment.

Second, any promise of concessions by the hostage taker can be made public (so the hostage taker knows it is public). The public being aware of the agreement increases commitment. All that need be done is for the negotiator to say something like, "Hey guys, Joe promised to release a hostage by 4:00 P.M.," and then return talking to the hostage taker regarding other matters. The hostage taker realizes he made a commitment and that the commitment has been made public. This will increase consistency and

Negotiators must be able to communicate in several directions at one time: with the hostage taker, between primary and secondary negotiators, with other team members, and with other response elements. During this communication overload, the negotiator must remain focused with and actively listen to the hostage taker. *(R. Mullins)*

commitment and increase compliance. In a classic study, Deutsch and Gerard (1955) found that when subjects in their experiment made a decision and made the decision public, even when their decision was shown to be incorrect, the vast majority of subjects refused to change their decision. Any compliance on the part of the hostage taker should be made public (to others on the negotiating team), and the hostage taker should be made aware that his or her compliance was made public. Not only does public disclosure make compliance more consistent, the hostage taker will feel compelled to follow through.

Freedman and Fraser (1966) introduced a technique to increase compliance that is referred to as the foot-in-the-door technique. The foot-in-the-door technique relies upon commitment to increase compliance by getting the person to agree to a small, inconsequential request before being hit with the real request. For example, if a negotiator wants a hostage to be released, he or she should first get the hostage taker to agree to a small request (i.e., "Would you mind staying at this telephone number while we talk?"). Further, the small request does not have to be related to the large request. Compliance with the small request changes the person's self-image. As Cialdini (1984) stated, "You can use small commitments to manipulate a person's self-image; you can use them to turn citizens into 'public servants,' prospects into 'customers,' prisoners into 'collaborators.' And once you've got a man's self image where you want it, he should comply naturally with a whole range of your requests that are consistent with this view of himself."

Further, the negotiator should try to make the hostage taker believe the compliance came from his inner self. The negotiator should make it seem like the hostage taker complied because the hostage taker is basically a good person. The negotiator might say, "You did good." Let the reinforcement for compliance be internal. That will increase compliance in the future. The hostage taker will come to see himself as someone who wants to resolve the situation in a positive manner.

Social Proofs

A third compliance technique discussed by Cialdini (1984) is that of social proofs. What others do and think guides our behavior. Behavior is correct when we see other people do it. Imagine that your department sends you to a training seminar. At each seat in the training room is a jumble of metal, screws, screwdrivers, and wrenches. You walk into the room at 8:00 and a sign on the wall says, "Class will start at 8:30 sharp. Please prepare your material for class." As you stand in front of your seat wondering what to do with the scrap metal and tools, four other people walk in, go to their seats, and begin assembling the metal into an object. What would you do? If you are like most other people, you will watch what your neighbors do with the metal and begin assembling your pile in a similar manner. You have become an example of the social proofs technique.

Further, the more similar you are to the other people, the more likely you will emulate their behavior. In the situation above, if the other students were police officers, you would be much more likely to do what they did than if the others in the class were prison inmates.

What makes the use of social proofs especially compelling to the negotiator, however, is the uncertainty principle. Social proofs are most powerful when we are unsure of ourselves and when the situation is ambiguous or unclear. How many hostage takers know how to behave in a hostage situation? The hostage taker is probably more confused and uncertain of what he should do than even the hostages. In most instances, the hostage taker is probably asking himself, "Okay, I've got hostages, the police are outside with their guns pointed at me. What do I do now?" The negotiator is in an ideal position to offer social proofs by dropping subtle hints as to how other hostage takers have acted. These hints, of course, may have little bearing on reality, but are based upon what the negotiator wants the hostage taker to do. The hostage taker may threaten to kill some hostages because a demand is not met by a deadline. The negotiator could say something similar to the following: "I understand you are upset. Most people who have been in your position have gotten upset when things did not go according to their schedule, but I really cannot remember any threatening to kill people because they were upset."

Two other aspects of social proofs are instructive in explaining why hostages act as they do and why hostage situations occur in groups. The concept of pluralistic ignorance can explain why hostages (who usually outnumber their captors) do not attempt to overpower their captors, even when given the opportunity. Pluralistic ignorance is when people wait for others to act before they act. The 1964 murder of Kitty Genovese in New York City best exemplifies pluralistic ignorance. Genovese was returning to her apartment one evening when she was attacked and killed. Her attacker actually attacked her three times during a 30-minute period. During this time, Genovese called out for help numerous times. Thirty-eight citizens witnessed the assaults and murder, yet none called for help. All were waiting to see what others would do. In a series of studies attempting to explain pluralistic ignorance, Latane and Darley (1968a; 1968b) found that in a group facing uncertainty, members of the group will wait to see what others do before taking any action. Thus, each hostage waits for another hostage to take action. Latane and Darley found that one person alone in a potential crisis situation was more likely to take action than if several people were present.

Pluralistic ignorance has implications for the tactical team if they must assault the hostage location. If tactical team members enter and shout, "Everybody down!" chances are good that no hostage will move. Each hostage will wait to see what the other hostages do. The tactical team should instead try to individually instruct each hostage as to what action to take. They may point to a hostage and say, "You—fall to your stomach." for example.

The second aspect of social proofs, known as the Werther effect, concerns why hostage situations tend to occur in clusters. Simply stated, research has shown that suicides and fatal accidents increase significantly following a well-publicized suicide. Likewise, homicide rates rise following highly publicized homicides. People are engaging in "monkey see, monkey do." Following a publicized hostage incident, other people may perceive that the same activity may resolve their problems, so they copycat.

Liking

Another influence technique the negotiator can use is *liking*. People who like each other are more likely to be compliant. In addition to helping develop the Stockholm Syndrome, liking can lead to increased compliance. Similarity can also increase compliance. The negotiator should attempt to make him or herself appear as much like the hostage taker (attitude, beliefs, etc.) as possible. Finding out about interests and hobbies can go a long way toward resolving the situation. Cooperation can increase compliance. The negotiator should work toward making the hostage taker feel that it is the two of them against the police. By cooperating with the hostage taker, the negotiator will increase compliance. This is similar to the "good cop/bad cop" interrogation technique often used on criminal suspects.

Scarcity Principle

A final technique of influence described by Cialdini (1984) is the scarcity principle, which states that opportunities are more valuable to us when they are limited. All of us have fallen prey to the sales pitch that begins, "I don't want to influence your decision, but after these are sold we will not be getting any more . . . "Some automobile manufacturers make use of the scarcity principle by limiting the production of the model and raising the price. The Corvette ZR-1 is an example. Chevrolet announced the vehicle and that only a very limited number would be made each year. Models are sold out before they go into production. How many times have you interrupted an important conversation to answer a ringing telephone? If you do not answer the telephone, the call becomes unavailable forever.

The negotiator can use the scarcity principle to his or her advantage. The negotiator might purposely limit the time allowed for a decision or the time frame for a hostage release. "I talked to my boss and he said we can deliver some food if you release one of the people. He said he needs to know your decision within five minutes or the deal is off. I had a lot of trouble getting him to agree and I don't think he'll make the offer again." Limiting the availability in this manner may increase compliance.

Table 6.3
Summary of Communication Techniques of Influence and Compliance

Rule of Reciprocity—We Repay Favors
Rule is overpowering
Invites uninvited debts
Favors do not have to be of equal value
Reject-then-retreat
Consistency—We Want to Be Consistent
Write down commitments
Make commitments public
Foot-In-the-Door
Social Proofs—We Do What Other People Do
Uncertainty Principle
Pluralistic Ignorance
Werther Effect
Liking—We Want Others to Like Us
Similarity
Cooperation
Scarcity Principle—We Want It If We Cannot Have It

Source: Mullins, W.C.

Not only are these compliance techniques powerful shapers of behavior, knowing what they are and how they work can prevent the hostage taker from using them on the negotiator. Whether we are formally aware of the techniques or not, we often use them unknowingly and have them used on us. Whether in sales situations, social settings, or relationships, we constantly attempt to influence others' behavior as they constantly attempt to influence ours. Regardless of what we might want to believe, hostage takers are not stupid individuals. While they may not know the scientific names and basis of these techniques, they do use them. Our defense against these techniques is to understand how and why they work. By knowing the hows and whys, we can counter their use as well as effectively use them to our advantage.

Behavioral Theories of Persuasion

In addition to communications, it is important that negotiators understand how behavior and attitudes are related and how one influences the other. By knowing these relationships and how they influence our actions, the negotiator can add another powerful tool to his or her arsenal. One of the oldest and most straightforward theories of persuasion is the Stimulus-Response Theory. The negotiator (who is the persuader for this discussion) wants the hostage taker to associate particular emotions with certain communications (for example, lack of fear with talk of surrendering). The negotiator must condition this new emotion and remove the old associations. The negotiator could, for example, mention surrender whenever the hostage taker is calm and then actively calm the hostage taker in the same sentence.

Attribution theory suggests that communications are understood in the perception of their intent (Woodward & Denton, 1996). How does the hostage taker see the message from the negotiator? Here it is crucial that the negotiator not appear self-serving or in a hurry, but as truly wanting to help. Communications must be perceived as sincere or they will not be effective.

Consistency theories of persuasion make the assumption that thought serves an intermediary function between stimulus and response. Balance theories, for instance, focus on how people try to reduce discrepancies between attitudes and information. How do you feel when a family member lies to you? Cognitive dissonance theory says that this situation produces discomfort and that people will change either their feelings or behavior toward the family member, depending upon which is easier to change. If one really loves the family member, it may be easiest to move farther away so you do not have to visit with that family member. On the other hand, if the relative is not close, it is probably easier to change your attitude. For the negotiator, he or she can first produce dissonance between attitudes and actions, and then offer suggestions on how to remove the dissonance ("You are a good father, but good fathers do not threaten their children, so why don't you surrender?").

Figure 6.1
Social Judgment Theory of Persuasion. Latitudes determine acceptance of communications and show how communications can produce undesirable effects. Without agreeing with the hostage taker, the negotiator should keep communications around the latitude of acceptance and slowly close the latitude of rejection.

Latitude of Acceptance	Latitude of Noncommitment	Latitude of Rejection
Anchor	Assimilation Contrast Boomerang Effects	Ego involvement expands or contracts this area

Communications of Persuasion Are:

Acceptable	Neutral	Unacceptable
Hostage taker works with negotiator	Communications can make hostage taker do opposite of what negotiator proposes	Large area during Crisis Stage, smaller during Accommodation Stage

To Expand L of A	Avoid	To Contract L of R
"I understand why you thought you had to do this."	"This doesn't solve anything."	"Think about this from (the hostage's) perspective."
"As long as you don't hurt anyone, we'll keep talking."	"I don't think you have it in you to harm any of those people."	"I want to keep SWAT out and keep everyone safe."
"You know we can't release you or your friends from prison."	"Why waste time asking for something you're not going to get?"	"Let's work on getting a surrender treaty we all can agree on."

Source: Adapted from Woodward, G.C. and R.E. Denton (1996). *Persuasion and Influence in American Life.* Prospect Heights, IL: Waveland Press Inc.

Social judgment theory is based upon the idea that the persuasiveness of communications is based upon how closely the communications relate to current beliefs (Woodward & Denton, 1996). The closer the communication to our current belief, the more likely it is to result in behavior change. According to this theory, communications need to be in line with current attitudes in order to produce behavior change. This is why telling a hostage taker that tactical officers really do not like assaulting a position often meets with derision. This statement is not consistent with the hostage taker's attitudes. The negotiator should instead introduce the idea that tactical officers want to minimize violence and then move toward the idea of not liking to assault. The negotiator should attempt to change attitudes with communications, and should attempt change one step at a time.

Suggestion Techniques

An earlier section of this chapter discussed communication techniques that rely on persuasion to get the hostage taker to comply with requests. Those techniques rely on logic and reason in getting a person to comply. The foot-in-the-door technique, for example, makes the hostage taker change his attitude about the type of person he is in order to increase compliance.

The negotiator can use another set of compliance tools that are more subtle and pervasive than the influence techniques discussed by Cialdini (1984). These are the tools of suggestibility. Suggestibility techniques embed subtle hints in statements to the hostage taker so that beliefs and/or perceptions are altered without the hostage taker being consciously aware of the alterations (Mullins, 1988).

Using persuasion, the negotiator would convince the hostage taker to surrender because the tactical team is preparing to assault the location and the hostage taker could die during the assault. Using suggestion, the negotiator would provide subtle cues as to what might happen when the tactical team assaults and let the hostage taker subconsciously determine that he might be killed during this assault.

During a hostage situation, hostage takers undergo many changes in behavior, cognitions, and emotions. They will experience sensory distortions, cognitive dissonance, and perceptual narrowing (Reiser & Sloane, 1983). Their entire focus of existence will be geared toward surviving their situation. They will be confused, emotionally and physically stressed, and their mental ability will be impaired. Emotions and perceptual distortions will interfere with the hostage taker's ability to think clearly and rationally.

This confusion and cognitive impairment can make the hostage taker more susceptible to the techniques of suggestion than might normally be the case. Suggestion can be used to force the hostage taker to concentrate all his mental energies on escape, at the expense of concentrating on demands or harming hostages. Suggestion can be used to reduce stress and emotions and get the hostage taker to think more rationally and face the predicament he is in. Suggestion can also be used to stabilize the hostage taker emotionally and physically and reduce or eliminate mood swings, settle emotions, and calm behavior.

When not talking to the hostage taker, team members must communicate with each other to brainstorm, plan strategy, and decide the goals for the next conversation with the hostage taker. *(S. Davis)*

The negotiator can use the techniques of suggestion in several ways. First, the hostage taker will try to satisfy basic need states: safety, physical, and ego (Maslow, 1970). The negotiator can identify these needs and offer suggestions that force the hostage taker to focus on those needs. With time, as the needs are not met, they become more noticeable to the hostage taker and his desire to fulfill the need becomes overwhelming. Repetitive suggestion can be used to reduce demands, gain the release of hostages, control emotion and stress levels, and even get the hostage taker to surrender. If a negotiator wants to increase or decrease a particular emotion, he or she can repeatedly use suggestion techniques geared toward that emotion. Suggestion can also be used to reinforce the hostage taker. Every time the hostage taker makes a statement that moves negotiations forward or toward resolution, the negotiator could say, "Uh huh," "Right," or "I agree." When the hostage taker says something inflammatory, the negotiator could remain silent.

Reiser and Sloane (1983; first identified by Erickson & Rossi, 1979) identify 13 techniques of suggestion that a negotiator can effectively use with a hostage taker.

1. *Binds.* Binds can be used to focus a decision by presenting the hostage taker with only one direction of behavior or action. "When would you like to release the first person?" There are no decisions to be made on the direction of the behavior, only when it will occur.

2. *Double Binds.* Double binds are similar to binds in that they provide only one direction of behavior. The difference is that double binds give the hostage taker a perception of more control. "Would you like to release a person now or wait 15 minutes?" This either/or situation, while giving no choice in the direction of behavior, does leave the hostage taker with the perception of having control and making decisions.

3. *Covering a class of responses.* This technique covers all directions of needs, emotions, or behaviors that a hostage taker may take, while at the same time forcing the hostage taker to focus on his needs. "Sooner or later you may or may not get thirsty. The important thing is that we take care of your needs."

4. *Encourage a new frame of reference.* This suggestion technique gets the hostage taker to view the situation from someone else's perspective, usually one of the hostages. By using this suggestion, the negotiator can help the hostage taker calm down, settle emotions, and most importantly, begin developing the Stockholm Syndrome between hostage taker and hostages. "The child must be really scared without her mother. If you were her, I wonder what you might be thinking?"

5. *Future Projection.* This technique can be used effectively when attempting to resolve issues or make decisions with the hostage taker. It forces the hostage taker to think about an issue and keep the hostage taker's thoughts focused on that issue. "Why don't we let this issue lie and come back to it in a few minutes?"

6. *Embedded questions.* This technique mentally and emotionally removes the hostage taker from the stress of the situation and gets him to concentrate on more positive times in his life. "Take a moment. Can you think back to a time when you were not under so much stress?"

7. *Embedded statements.* This technique forces the hostage taker to make a decision, while seemingly giving the hostage taker a choice. It will focus the hostage taker's thoughts on one issue until a decision is reached, and can be effectively used to stop the hostage taker from bouncing around from topic to topic without bringing closure to any. "You may want to find a solution to this issue so later we can move on to other issues and not waste time."

8. *Implied directive.* An implied directive is a command given to the hostage taker, but done in such a way that the hostage taker believes he is controlling the decision-making process. "When you are ready to discuss this, we'll work on it and see if we can resolve the issue."

9. *Induced imagery.* This technique focuses the hostage taker on the future consequences, either positive or negative, of his actions. "Imagine how relaxing it would be if you didn't have to worry about that sick person."

10. *Interpersonal focusing.* This technique allows the negotiator to build trust with the hostage taker and lay the foundation for the development of the Stockholm Syndrome. "Let me tell you about another situation I was able to successfully resolve."

11. *Not knowing, not doing.* This technique can be used to introduce a new idea, thought, issue, or concept to the hostage taker. "My dinner just arrived. Let me hang up and eat it before it gets cold. I'll call you back in ten minutes." This suggestion technique is very effective with any type of basic needs, whether hunger, thirst, temperature, or addiction (such as nicotine).

12. *Open-ended suggestion.* This technique allows the hostage to form a conclusion without forcing a decision. "I will take all the time necessary to resolve this issue, but you know how SWAT teams are." The negotiator has presented an idea the hostage taker will, with time, fully develop. One reason this type of suggestion is so effective is that the hostage taker will arrive at the most negative conclusion possible.

13. *Truisms.* This suggestion technique forces the hostage taker to accept the inevitable. "Sooner or later you are going to fall asleep." Not only is the hostage taker forced to confront the future, he is also forced to accept the hopelessness of his situation. The negotiator must be careful in using truisms, because the hostage taker may become angry, violent, or suicidal when he realizes the futility and ultimate outcome of his situation.

The negotiator can use all of these techniques on an ongoing basis. If one technique does not prove fruitful, leave it, go on to another, and later retry the technique. As with the techniques of influence and compliance, these techniques are to be used with care. Even more so than compliance techniques, techniques of suggestion require careful placement into the subconscious as well as room to grow. If the hostage taker is aware of what you are doing, he will become resentful, angry, and distrustful of the negotiator.

Active Listening

A final component of communication is the ability to listen. Most of us are constantly listening to our environment. There are sounds around us practically 24 hours a day. At work, there are computers, typewriters, copy machines, engine noises, other conversations, and radios. At home, we read while the television is on or the kids are playing. At night, there are ambient sounds in the background. Most of these sounds do not actively register in our consciousness. They are received by our ears and ignored by our brain. We are hearing our world, but we are not listening to it. We are passively listening; not actively listening. We spend so much of our time (more than 90%) being passive listeners that we have no skill at being active listeners. When we need to be active listeners, we do not know how.

Listening is a learned skill. It must be understood and practiced for us to be able to actively listen. Listening is nothing more than the ability to make sense of what is heard. Four components are involved in listening. First, we must be able to select the relevant stimuli in the environment. Second, we must *attend* to that stimuli, or focus on the one sound and tune all other sounds out. Third, we must understand, or assign meaning to the stimuli we are attending to. Fourth, we must be able to remember what we have heard.

There are several goals of listening. We listen to enjoy. Watching a play, a concert, a movie, or television, we are entertaining ourselves by listening. We listen to evaluate. Is the communication reliable, valid, and believable? An example presented by Masterson et al. (1989) is that of listening to a speech about beliefs radically different from ours. We listen to the speech and we do not evaluate because we are busy criticizing those views. This is an important point for the hostage negotiator. The hostage taker is going to hold beliefs and ideas that are radically different from those of the negotiator. If the negotiator mentally criticizes those beliefs, the negotiator will not be able to actively listen to what the hostage taker is saying. We also listen to empathize. We listen so other people can talk out their problems. We listen to gain information. We want to learn, so we take notes and attempt to remember the communication.

As with communicating, there are barriers to effective listening, such as the problem of information overload. There can be so much information being received that we cannot attend to it all. Also, we can be fatigued, ill, or under other stressors that interfere with our ability to concentrate. The topic or conversation can be uninteresting. Many things a hostage taker will say will not be interesting to the negotiator. The negotiator will have to make an active effort to continue to listen during these periods. Also, we sometimes become involved in personal concerns. We plan what to say next, what we are going to have for dinner, our own troubles, forgetting to turn off the stove, etc. Listening requires that we put aside these concerns. Additionally, we can become distracted by outside interruptions. Other concentrations, noise, or a commander wanting to know what is happening can all interrupt our listening concentration. Another factor is that we speak and hear at different rates. According to Masterson et al. (1989), we speak at about 100-125 words per minute. We listen at about 700 words per minute. We can listen much faster than necessary, so our mind tends to daydream and wander during the listening gaps. Finally, if the sender is presenting ideas or communications with which we do not agree, we tend to focus our attention on the messenger rather than the message. This is analogous to speaking with an attractive member of the opposite sex. Our attention is focused on him or her as a person rather than on what they are saying.

There are some strategies that can be used to improve the ability to listen, such as looking for useful ideas during a conversation. Every speaker will include useful information in the most mundane of conversations. While ranting and raving, the hostage taker will include some information that the negotiator can ultimately use. The negotiator should listen to these diatribes with the intent of uncovering that tidbit of information.

Another effective strategy is to listen for ideas, not facts. We have all heard a television newscaster say something similar to: "The Dow Jones closed today at 657.896, up 2.8 points from the previous day. Shares trades were at 7.4 million and climbing by day's end. This trend is expected to continue tomorrow, with analysts predicting a rise of 1.3 points on the Dow index, 3.4 points on the S & P, and share trading to increase by 0.36 million." Very few of us pay any attention to the data. We pay attention to the idea that the stock market is healthy and expected to stay healthy. When the hostage taker presents a long list of demands (especially if political), attempt to gather the ideas behind the specific demands. Let the secondary negotiator focus on and write down the specific demands. Later, when the conversation is over, you can memorize the specific demands.

Negotiators should not be distracted by emotions, arousing words or phrases, or inflammatory statements. Realize that the sender is in an emotional situation and this will be reflected in their communications. Ignore these statements as part of the communication process. You can use these emotional communications as an index of how negotiations are progressing and whether the hostage taker is becoming less emotional and more rational.

Adapt to the speaker. The negotiator should make sure that his or her listening behavior reflects the sender's speech patterns and habits. Force concentration on the message, not the messenger.

Adapt also to the environment of the speaking situation. If the speaker is speaking too softly or too loudly, ask that speaker to modulate his or her voice. Ask the speaker to slow the speech rate if necessary. Try to negotiate from a quiet place. Many negotiation teams isolate the primary and secondary negotiator so they will not be distracted by the confusions inherent in a teamwork situation. It is difficult to listen to a hostage taker if several people are in your ear asking questions.

Determine what your objective is in listening. What are your goals from the conversation? Each conversation with the hostage taker might have different goals. Determine what the goals for that particular conversation are and listen with those goals in mind.

Sidebar: Active Listening

Lieutenant Bob Ware has been with the Kansas Highway Patrol since 1986. When a special response team was formed in 1997, members of the team approached Ware to participate as lead negotiator. Since that time he has been lead negotiator, and coordinates training for team negotiators. The team offers assistance statewide and has been involved in numerous call-outs across the state of Kansas. In addition to his duties and responsibilities with the Kansas Highway Patrol, Ware teaches topics related to crisis negotiations to recruits and other law enforcement agencies. He is also a founding member of the Kansas Association of Hostage Negotiators, and is in his second term as director of training.

Listening to someone is one of the most powerful things you can do for him or her. It is a learned skill—one has to work hard to be a good listener. Listening is nothing more than making sense of what has been said. You have to concentrate and focus on the conversation by eliminating distractions when possible and keeping the distractions to a minimum.

When a person wants to excel at something, I think they must have a good understanding of the basics with a good foundation or knowledge base. You should understand the components of listening to become a good listener. There are three components of listening: attention, reception, and perception. The first component of listening is attention, which can be defined as the act of applying the mind to an object or sense of thought. The second component is reception, which is the act of receiving information. The third component is perception, one's understanding of a situation. I think understanding perception is key to being a good communicator. It is very important to understand not only *my* perception, but the perception of the person I am communicating with. It helps to understand what that person thinks and understands so I know how to communicate with them. This includes recognizing and labeling the emotions you hear and listening to the message you might hear.

Communication is one of the most important ingredients in any relationship. Whether it is husband to wife, parents to children, supervisor to subordinate, or among friends. A key to better active listening skills is to practice. One does not have to wait to practice until one negotiates in a critical incident. You can practice listening at home by concentrating on what is being said. Have you ever come home at the end of a long day needing to share your day with your spouse? As you start to tell about how horrific your day has been, you partner gets up, starts for the utility room, peeks their head around the door and says, "Go ahead, I can hear you," as you talk to an empty room. Take time to listen to your partner before you fill the dishwasher or put a load of clothes in the washing machine.

Have you ever been reading the newspaper while your teenager is talking to you and the conversation stops? Were you a part of the conversation or did they give up on you? Put down the newspaper when your teenager is trying to talk to you. You might even turn off the television when listening to a family member trying to share their day. Sharing their day with you is the most important thing at that moment, not seeking advice or wanting to be told how to address a problem. When you listen sincerely, you make yourself available to be a part of other people's lives. If you are not genuine, you may not get another opportunity. These suggestions seem basic, but they are grossly overlooked. We live in a fast-paced society, where multitasking is required to accomplish all the perceived tasks that we think must be completed. Taking time to listen to someone when they need to be heard is one of the best things you can do for that person. This does not mean offering advice or trying to problem solve. This means "shutting up and listening."

Problem solving is a trap that a communicator should avoid. When communicating with a family member, we sometimes take on the role of "the problem solver." We feel compelled to fix problems and give unsolicited advice. As police officers, we are paid problem solvers. During investigations, we solve other peoples' problems. On traffic stops, we tell the violator why we stopped them, request certain documents, issue a ticket, and go on to the next stop. We are taught to stay in control of the situation, fix the problem, and move on to the next one. When dealing with a person in a critical incident, you must establish a rapport before being able to help solve the problem.

The concept of active listening is difficult for some negotiators to grasp. They want to become a negotiator because they "can talk to anyone." They believe they are good communicators and have very little to learn. I want new team members to learn to listen and understand the techniques of active listening. A constant struggle for us is to get a negotiator to actively listen and not problem solve. To build rapport, first you have to engage in active listening. As noted above, the bottom line is "shut up and listen."

> I have witnessed veteran negotiators miss opportunities to respond with active listening techniques by using problem-solving approaches and questions. This usually invites confrontational conversation or a sarcastic response from the barricaded subject or hostage taker. I urge you to refer to the techniques of active listening when negotiating. These techniques will help build rapport and trust in a person who has no trust.
>
> Another concern I have is when the primary negotiator depends entirely on background information to "interview" the barricaded subject or hostage taker. By using active listening skills, such as open-ended questions, you can establish trust and rapport by allowing the person to feel as though you are sincerely trying to understand and listen to them. Additionally, a key element to successful negotiations is for the secondary negotiator to keep the primary negotiator on track with listening techniques as well as supplying ideas.
>
> Aside from concentrating on the techniques of active listening, I stress to our team the importance of understanding the components of listening. We focus on perception—not only our understanding of the situation, but the perception of the person involved in the critical event. I also stress knowing when to actively listen and when to problem-solve, the importance is in understanding the difference. Finally, we focus on preserving dignity or "saving face." In my experience, preserving dignity often times generates voluntary compliance.
>
> I'd like to leave you with this final thought: "Listening is a learned skill." You have to want to be committed to hard work and concentration to improve your skills. Once you have accomplished this, you will see how powerful and rewarding listening can be.

Anticipate the sender's next point. If the hostage taker presents a list of demands, you might anticipate that the next point to be presented will be the deadlines. This anticipation helps you remember the communication and helps you concentrate more by filling in the listening gaps.

Identify how the main ideas are presented. Some people will "beat around the bush" before getting to the main point. Others will present the main point up front and then fill in with idle conversation. Still other people will use different styles. Determine which communicating style the hostage taker is using and adjust your listening behavior to match that style. If the hostage taker rambles before presenting demands, then the negotiator should plan to achieve maximum listening several minutes into the conversation.

Mentally summarize the key ideas in the communication. Which demands are most important to the hostage taker? Which part of the oratory is most relevant?

Most importantly, practice active listening skills. Negotiators practice sending communications—they rarely practice receiving communications. Listen to boring speeches, practice summarizing main points, practice gathering ideas, practice remaining focused in the face of distractions.

Table 6.4
Listening Skills and How They Are Applied

Improving Listening Skills	Bad Listener	Good Listener
Listen for important information	Tunes out	Looks for opportunities
Listen for ideas, not just facts	Listens for facts	Listens for central themes
Not distracted by emotion-arousing words	Easily distracted	Not distracted
Adapt to speaker	Tunes out	Judges content
Adapt to situation	Easily distracted	Concentrates
Practice listening	Avoids difficult listening	Wants difficult information
Determine listening objective	No listening goals	Establishes goals
Anticipate speaker	No active involvement	Stays ahead of speaker
Identify speaker's supporting material	Does not listen for clarifying ideas	Identifies clarifying ideas
Mentally summarize few minutes	Does not restate	Summarizes every

Source: Table adapted from *Invitation To Effective Speech Communication*, by John T. Masterson, Steven A. Beebe, and Norman H. Watson. Copyright © 1989, by Scott, Foresman and Company. Reprinted by permission of Addison-Wesley Educational Publishers, Inc.

One good exercise for both sending and receiving communications is to pair negotiators up and have them engage in an extemporaneous debate on unpopular issues. For example, have them debate the issue of legalizing drugs to making drug use a medical rather than a criminal justice problem. After 10 minutes, make them switch sides. Rebuttals have to focus on points made by the other person, not on new points. While the negotiators are debating, play a movie or radio in the background. Force them to concentrate, whether they are sending or receiving.

Active Listening: Types

Bolton described four types of active listening that negotiators can use during negotiations. Each has its own set of advantages and each is used for different purposes. Bolton (1984) has described them as:

1. *Paraphrasing*—a response in which the negotiator gives the hostage taker the essence of his message in the negotiator's words;

2. *Reflecting feelings (or mirroring)*—a response in which the negotiator mirrors back to the hostage taker the emotions the hostage taker is communicating;

3. *Reflecting meaning (or emotional labeling with emotions)*—
    a response in which negotiators let the hostage taker know they
    understand the facts and the feelings the hostage taker is
    communicating; and

4. *Summative reflections*—a response in which the negotiator
    summarizes the main facts and feelings that the hostage taker
    has expressed over a relatively long period.

Ware (2003; 2004) and others have also included others:

5. *Minimal encouragement*—Saying "yes," "OK," or other ver-
    bal indicators that the negotiator is actually listening to the
    hostage taker.

6. *Open-ended questions*—Questions directed at the hostage taker
    designed to get him to open up and give a long, verbal answer.

7. *I-messages*—The negotiator expressing his/or her emotions in
    response to the hostage taker.

8. *Effective Pauses or extended pauses*—Not saying anything
    when the hostage taker finishes talking, encouraging him to
    fill the empty or blank space with additional communica-
    tions or information.

Paraphrasing is helpful when the negotiator needs to respond to the
hostage taker, but does not know what to say. It demonstrates that the negotiator has been listening and it helps keep the conversation going. A good paraphrase does not "parrot back" to the hostage taker. Rather, it puts the
hostage taker's meaning in the negotiator's words. Otherwise it will seem artificial and forced. A good paraphrase has the following characteristics: it is
concise, it summarizes the essence of the meaning, the main point is the focus,
and it is focused on facts. The hostage negotiator's feelings are not the point.

Reflecting feelings helps develop the rapport between negotiators and
hostage takers. It moves the discussion off the factual level to the emotional
level. It helps validate the hostage taker as a person and lets them know their
concern is being heard (Gray, 2003). However, it is usually difficult for negotiators to do. Most negotiators need to work to develop their ability to talk
about and reflect feelings. The authors have asked officers in several basic
negotiation schools to brainstorm the words they know that describe meanings. The average response from a class of 25 police officers is about 12 emotional words. Compared to Bolton's list (Table 2.1), this is not a wide range
of descriptors. Most negotiators need to develop their ability to describe the
hostage taker's feelings. However, at the same time, the negotiator should not
become overly sympathetic to the hostage taker's plight. It is appropriate to
be empathetic (Misino & DeFelice, 2004). As Regini (2004) points out, empathy is the cornerstone of crisis negotiations and involves the demonstration
of listening to and understanding the hostage taker.

Bolton (1984) has described three ways of becoming more aware of feelings. They are: (1) listen for feeling words and use the list referenced above to help recognize feeling words; (2) infer feelings from the context and think about the feelings that are appropriate to the situation; (3) ask yourself what you would be feeling by using your humanness to guide you in understanding what the hostage taker is feeling.

Reflection of meaning is used to help identify the hostage taker's needs and to strengthen the relationship. It helps validate the hostage taker, and reflects the implications of a situation for the hostage taker. It involves the formula, "When _____, you feel _____, because _____." For instance, if a hostage taker says, "Get those patrol cars back, man, or somebody is going to die. It really _____ me that you guys are so close." The negotiator might say, "When the patrol cars are that close, you feel threatened, because you are not sure what's going to happen; they might attack you?" This gives the hostage taker a chance to confirm the statement. If the negotiator is right, it shows the negotiator is aware of the hostage taker's need for safety and security.

Summative reflection is used to confirm information and to solidify the relationship. It reminds the hostage taker of how far the negotiations have come and how much more under control things are now than they were at first. It is helpful in conflict, because it clarifies the issues in a concise way that serves to focus negotiators and hostage takers on the relevant issues. For instance, after a rambling dialogue by a paranoid schizophrenic that included a conversation with the President, the Chief of Staff of the Army, and a Secret Service agent, all people the hostage taker "trusted" (in his delusion—and none of whom were present), the negotiator summarized by saying, "If I understand what you are saying, it is, 'You need to talk to someone you trust, because you are afraid we are going to harm you.' " The response focused directly on the issue the hostage taker was concerned about.

Minimal encouragers are used simply to indicate that the negotiator is listening to the story or emotions behind the verbal statements, that the negotiator is engaged in listening, and that the speaker's story is being understood. Minimal encouragers can be used at any time and should be used in every conversation.

Open-ended questions encourage the hostage taker to continue talking and telling their story. Open-ended questions can be used to defuse emotions; for example, if the hostage taker is being emotional, the negotiator could ask something like; "Joe, what do you think you can do to make her move back in with you?" or "What do you anticipate will happen when you do _____?" If the hostage taker is thinking, he cannot be very emotional.

I-messages tell the hostage taker why his actions may not be leading to a solution to the situation. The negotiator may be listening to a verbal attack on him, and say to the hostage taker, "You know, I get frustrated when you yell at me." The negotiator is subtly letting the hostage taker know that the present course of verbal behavior is not helping to resolve the situation.

Extended pauses can be used for a variety of purposes. First, pauses can help reduce the hostage taker's emotions. If the hostage taker begins a tirade, when there is a break in his communications, the negotiator can remain silent. This will serve to reduce emotions and move the communications into a more rational direction. Second, the negotiator can use pauses to get the hostage taker to continue providing information or intelligence. People are uncomfortable in a conversation when a person does not respond, and they feel an obligation to fill the silence. Mostly, they will continue in the direction they have been going. Third, the negotiator can use pauses to help determine if the hostage taker is being truthful. As the hostage taker continues the communication, discrepancies will arise (in many cases).

Summary

The science of communication is difficult and much more complex than most people realize. Effective communication takes rehearsal and practice, just as any other skill does. Communication involves sending and receiving. Many people learn to be effective senders, and give no effort to becoming active listeners. Unless a person is able to do both, he or she will not be an effective communicator.

A negotiator can use numerous techniques to increase compliance by the hostage taker. These techniques are subtle, and when used judiciously by the negotiator, can bring the hostage situation to a timely and safe resolution.

Note

1   The authors are indebted to Dr. Rick Bradstreet for much of the information in this section. Through years of serving as a psychologist for hostage negotiators and his efforts in training hostage negotiators, crisis responders, and police officers, Dr. Bradstreet developed, refined, and assessed the effectiveness of the techniques discussed here. His work and experience have proven the effectiveness of these techniques.

References

Abbott, T.E. (1986). "Time-Phase Model of Hostage Negotiations." *The Police Chief* 31:34-35.

Alexander, J.F., P.L. Schuland, and E. Babakus (1991). "Analyzing Interpersonal Communication in Industrial Marketing Negotiations." *Journal of the Academy of Marketing Science* 19:129-139.

Anderson, J.C. and J.A. Narus (1990). "A Model of Distributor Firm and Manufacturer Firm Working Relationships." *Journal of Marketing* 54:42-58.

Blanchard, B. (1991). "New Communication Skills, New Roles in the 90s." *Supervisory Management* 36:1-2.

Bolton, R. (1984). *People Skills*. Englewood Cliffs, NJ: Prentice-Hall, Inc.

Brett, J.M. (1991). "Negotiating Group Decisions." *Negotiation Journal* 7:291-310.

Cambria, J., R.J. DeFilippo, R.J. Louden, and H. McGowan (2002). "Negotiation under Extreme Pressure: The Mouth Marines' and the Hostage Takers." *Negotiation Journal* (October): 331-343.

Campbell, N., J.L. Graham, A. Jolibert, and H.G. Meissner (1988). "Marketing Negotiations in France, Germany, the United Kingdom, and the United States." *Journal of Marketing* 52:49-62.

Cialdini, R.B. (1984). *Influence: How and Why People Agree to Things*. New York, NY: William Morrow and Co.

_____ (1993). *Influence: The Psychology of Influence and Persuasion*, Revised Edition. New York, NY: Quill.

_____, T.E. Vincent, S.K. Lewis, J. Catalan, D. Wheeler, and B.L. Darby (1975). "Reciprocal Concessions Procedure for Inducing Compliance: The Door-in-the-Face Technique." *Journal of Personality and Social Psychology* 31:206-215.

Clopton, S.W. (1984). "Seller and Buying Firm Factors Affecting Industrial Buyers' Negotiation Behavior and Outcomes." *Journal of Marketing Research* 21:39-53.

Cooper, C. (1999). *Mediation and Arbitration by Patrol Police Officers*. New York, NY: University Press of America.

Deutsch, M. and H.B. Gerard (1955). "A Study of Normative and Informational Social Influences Upon Individual Judgment." *Journal of Abnormal and Social Psychology* 51:629-636.

DiVasto, P., F.J. Lanceley, and A. Gruys (1992). "Critical Issues in Suicide Intervention." *FBI Law Enforcement Bulletin* 61:13-16.

Dolan, J.T. and G.D. Fuselier (1989). "A Guide for First Responders to Hostage Situations." *FBI Law Enforcement Bulletin* 58:9-13.

Erickson, M.H. and E.L. Rossi (1979). *Hypnotherapy*. New York, NY: Irvington.

Fisher, R., W. Ury, and B. Patton (1991). *Getting to Yes: Negotiating Agreement without Giving In*, Second Edition. New York, NY: Penguin Books.

Freedman, J.L. and S.C. Fraser (1966). "Compliance without Pressure: The Foot-in-the-Door Technique." *Journal of Personality and Social Psychology* 4:195-203.

Froman, L. and J. Glorioso (1984). "Applying Communications Theory to Hostage Negotiations." *The Police Chief* 51:59-60.

Fuselier, G.D., C.R. Van Zandt, and F.J. Lanceley (1989). "Negotiating the Protracted Incident: The Oakdale and Atlanta Prison Sieges." *FBI Law Enforcement Bulletin* 58:1-7.

Gray, B. (2003). "In Theory: Negotiating with Your Nemesis." *Negotiation Journal* (Octobe): 299-310.

Hammer, M.R. and R.G. Rogan (2004). "Threats, Demands, and Communication Dynamics: Negotiating the 1991 Talladega Prison Siege." *Journal of Police Crisis Negotiations* 4:45-56.

Kahneman, D. (1992). "Reference Points, Anchors, Norms, and Mixed Feelings." *Organizational Behavior and Human Decision Processes* 51:296-312.

Latane, B. and J.M. Darley (1968a). "Group Inhibition of Bystander Intervention in Emergencies." *Journal of Personality and Social Psychology* 10:215-221.

—————— (1968b). The Unresponsive Bystander: Why Doesn't He Help? New York, NY: Appleton-Century-Crofts.

Maslow, A.H. (1970). *Motivation and Personality*. New York, NY: McGraw Hill.

Masterson, J.T., S.A. Beebe, and N.H. Watson (1989). *Invitation to Effective Speech Communication*. Glenview, IL: Scott, Foresman, and Co.

McMains, M.J. and F. Lanceley (1994). "The Use of Crisis Intervention Principles in Hostage Negotiations. III: Attitudes, Communications, and Treatment." *The Journal of Crisis Negotiations* 1(2):12-23.

Misino, D. and J. DeFelice (2004). *Negotiate and Win: Proven Strategies from the NYPD's Top Hostage Negotiator*. NY: McGraw-Hill.

Mullins, W.C. (1988). *Terrorist Organizations in the United States: An Analysis of Issues, Organizations, Tactics and Responses*. Springfield, IL: Charles C Thomas.

Nielson, R.C. and G.F. Shea (1982). "Training Officers to Negotiate Creatively." *The Police Chief* 27:65-67.

Putnam, L. and T. Jones (1982). "The Role of Communications in Bargaining." *Human Communications Research* 8:262-280.

Rangarajan, L.N. (1985). *The Limitation of Conflict: A Theory of Bargaining and Negotiation*. New York, NY: St. Martin's Press.

Regini, C. (2004). "Crisis Intervention for Law Enforcement Negotiators." *FBI Law Enforcement Bulletin* (October): 1-6.

Reiser, M. and M. Sloane (1983). "The Use of Suggestibility Techniques in Hostage Negotiations." In Freedman, L.Z. and Y. Alexander (eds.), *Perspectives on Terrorism*. Wilmington, DE: Scholarly Resources.

Rogan, R.G. and M.R. Hammer (1995). "Assessing Message Affect in Crisis Negotiations: An Exploratory Study." *Human Communication Research* 21:553-574.

Rubin, J. and B.R. Brown (1975). *The Social Psychology of Bargaining and Negotiation*. New York, NY: Academic.

Sen, S. (1989). "Handling Hostage Situations." *Police Journal* 62:49-55.

Soskis, D.A. and C.R. Van Zandt (1986). "Hostage Negotiation: Law Enforcement's Most Effective Non-Lethal Weapon." *FBI Law Management Quarterly* 6:1-8.

Strentz, T. (1994). "Thirteen Indicators of Volatile Negotiations." *The U.S. Negotiator* (Winter):36-39.

Taylor, R.W. (1983). "Hostage and Crisis Negotiation Procedures: Assessing Police Liability." *Trial* (March):64-69.

Ury, W. (1991). *Getting Past No: Negotiating with Difficult People*. New York, NY: Bantam Books.

Voss, C.T. (2004). "Crisis Negotiation: A Counter-intuitive Method to Disrupt terrorism. *Studies in Conflict and Terrorism* 27: 455-459.

Ware, B. (2003). "Active Listening." Presentation at the annual Crisis Negotiation Competition/Seminar. Texas State University, San Marcos, TX (January).

Ware, B. (2004). "Active Listening for Negotiators." Presentation at the annual meeting of the Kansas Association of Hostage Negotiators. Olathe, KS (April).

Whitney, R.A., T. Hubin, and J.D. Murphy (1965). *The New Psychology of Persuasion and Motivation in Selling*. Englewood Cliffs, NJ: Prentice-Hall.

Woodward, G.C. and R.E. Denton Jr. (1996). *Persuasion and Influence in American Life*. Prospect Heights, IL: Waveland Press, Inc.

Discussion Questions

1. This is an exercise that can be done in class to illustrate the various components of the communication process. Have someone whisper a sentence to the person next to them. A good sentence for this exercise is "The large brown cow took a flying leap and jumped over the round, silvery moon." That person whispers the sentence to a third person, who whispers it to a fourth person, etc., until all students have received the message. The only rule is that the sentence can be whispered only one time. Compare the beginning message with the ending message. Is there any relation between the two messages? Have everyone write the message they received and sent and then sequentially compare the written messages. Where did communications break down and why?

2. List five everyday phrases you use that have multiple meanings. How can each of these phrases be misconstrued?

3. List five everyday polarizations you use. What can you do to avoid polarizing in those areas? Do other people polarize you (your attitudes, politics, etc.). What can you do from a communication standpoint to stop other people from polarizing?

4. What barriers to effective communications lead to racism, sexism, and gender differences? In what situations do you believe police use each and how does it hurt their effectiveness as police?

5. Engage in a debate with a friend over an emotionally charged topic (i.e., women as combat soldiers, politics, etc.). During the debate, use the patrol communication tactics of Cooper (1999). Do these tactics add to the strength of your arguments? How?

6. Negotiate with your landlord for a reduction in your rent, or with your boss for a raise in pay, or with a friend to go to a certain restaurant they do not like. Use the tactics suggested by Ury in *Getting Past No*. Compared with negotiation situations in the past, did this negotiation go more smoothly? Did you enhance your chances of getting what you wanted? Did negotiations end on a friendly note? Did you get what you wanted?

7. Spend a Saturday afternoon at a shopping mall. Go into a clothing store and unobtrusively watch a salesperson interact with customers. Watch to see whether they use the influence and compliance techniques presented in this chapter. Especially note whether they use the techniques of reciprocity, consistency, social proofs, and liking (develop a checklist and make a check each time a technique is used). Does the salesperson use the reject-then-retreat or the foot-in-the-door technique?

8. While completing question 7, when you find a salesperson who frequently uses the influence and compliance techniques, track their sales as compared to a salesperson who does not use those techniques. Who makes the most sales? What technique seems to work the best?

9. As part of question 7, compare big-ticket salespeople (appliances, stereos, televisions, automobiles) to small-ticket salespeople (clothes, books, shoes, etc.). Which salespeople most often use the influence and compliance techniques? Why do you think that is the case?

10. Volunteer your time to sell something for a charity or local organization (such as a PTA candy sale, United Fund drive, etc.). Half the time, do not use any of the influence and compliance techniques. For the other half of the time, use as many influence and compliance techniques as possible (use more than one on a hesitant customer). For which half did you make the most sales?

11. List five non-sales situations in which influence and compliance techniques would be beneficial. For each situation, describe the technique to be used and the way in which it would be used.

12. For each of the 13 suggestibility techniques, give an example (other than the ones in the book) of what a negotiator could say to a hostage taker.

13. You are probably required to take a class that is not very interesting to you. Practice the techniques of active listening for one week and then apply those techniques in that class. Wait for one week. Have a friend quiz you over material from before the active listening period and during the active listening period. Which material do you remember better?

Negotiating with Mentally Disturbed Individuals:

Recognition and Guidelines

7

Learning Objectives

1. Understand the role of early childhood experiences on a person's attitudes toward authority and how that influences negotiations.

2. Understand the increase in the types of personality/mental issues negotiators are asked to deal with.

3. Know the common types of abusive personalities that are often involved in hostage/crisis incidents.

4. Know the issues and negotiating techniques for dealing with depressed people.

5. Understand what a delusional person is and how to deal with such individuals in a crisis/hostage incident.

6. Know the negotiating techniques for dealing with paranoid hostage takers.

7. Understand what constitutes a borderline/dependent personality type.

8. Know how to negotiate with borderline/dependent hostage takers.

9. Understand what constitutes an antisocial personality.

10. Know how to negotiate with an antisocial hostage taker.

11. Know the guidelines for negotiating with a compulsive personality.

12. Know the impact of substance abuse/dependence on negotiations.

The call was to the state hospital. A schizoaffective client had become irritated when he was being questioned after coming back from a visit downtown. He had a history of bringing contraband on to the ward after a pass and the staff wanted to be sure that he had no drugs with him. During a shouting match with the nurse, staff told him that they were going to give him a shot to "calm" him down. He responded by pulling a knife from his boot and dragged the female nurse's aid into a bedroom, yelling, "leave me alone!" The staff backed off and called the hospital administrator, who called the police.

Negotiators, in reviewing his hospital records, noted that he was admitted for suicidal ideation, depression, and fighting with the police officer who made the call at his home for a family disturbance. In addition, his records revealed that he grew up in Texas, Colorado, and New Mexico. He was the younger of two siblings, having one older adopted brother. His parents were divorced when he was three months old. Subsequently, he lived with both his mother and father. He reported a transient childhood with multiple moves. He bounced back and forth between his parents because each of them would manage him for a while and get frustrated and send him back to the other one. He attended high school through the eleventh grade, making Bs, Cs, and Ds. He was not in special education placement. He left high school because he was arrested for burglary and placed in Texas Youth Commission facilities. He had multiple abusive episodes as a child, including: his mother biting a chunk out of his cheek in order to show him how it felt to be bitten; his mother's boyfriend beating on him regularly; his father's wife being abusive; and, his stepfather's daughter sexually abusing him when he was seven years old. He engaged in multiple fights over the years in school, prison, and on the streets. He was divorced with no children. He was living with his girlfriend and his mother. He had not served in the military. He had been arrested for burglary, theft, driving while intoxicated (DWI), and child endangerment. He had been incarcerated in both youth facilities and through the Texas Department of Criminal Justice (TDCJ). He was placed on probation but did not comply with the conditions of his probation. It was revoked and he spent two and one-half years in prison.

Since he was 13, he had acted out on his aggression. He started by using a blow gun on his brother, spreading soap on the bathroom tub so that his brother would slip in the tub, and picking fights in school. When hospitalized, he reported feeling worthless and like he wanted to die most of his life. He stated that he saw a psychiatrist when he was 17 because he tried to kill himself for the first time. He overdosed on imipramine. He was hospitalized in Bethesda Hospital in Denver. Later that year he was transferred to Tucson, where he was in residential treatment facility for seven months. He stated that his greatest depression was as a result of difficulty adjusting to his parole. While in the hospital, he was irritable, had difficulty sleeping, averaging three to four hours of sleep at night, experienced a lack of energy, and wanted to fight with people all the time. He had several previous suicide attempts by overdose, cutting himself, and eating razor blades while in jail. His last suicidal ideation had occurred one to two weeks earlier. At that time, he tried to overdose on Neurontin but he threw it up. He last worked three and one-half years before his hospitalization at a job he held for one month. He was fired because of his attitude and fighting with other employees.

This incident is an extreme example of many encountered by the police; an incident involving an emotionally distraught individual who is in more than crisis. He is mentally ill and is likely to respond with more intensity than others. Experienced negotiators know that a large number of incidents involve emotionally disturbed individuals: people who come from chaotic backgrounds and who have not earned to manage themselves or their lives. The nature and extent of involvement with emotionally disturbed individuals has changed since the founding of police negotiations in 1972 and it is essential that negotiators understand issues involving negotiating with a wide range of emotionally disturbed individuals.

Emotionally Disturbed People and Negotiations

Since the inception of negotiations in policing, there has been a recognition that many of the people negotiators deal with are emotionally disturbed. Schlossberg (1979) emphasized the importance of understanding emotionally disturbed people as one of his foundational pieces in the development of the NYPD's Hostage Negotiations program. In 1986, Fuselier pointed out that four groups of emotionally disturbed people are most frequently involved in hostage incidents. They were:

1. Paranoid Schizophrenics

2. Manic-Depressed Psychotics, Depressed Type

3. Inadequate (Dependent) Personality Disorders

4. Antisocial Personality Disorders

Research (Head, 1990; Butler et al., 1993; Strentz, 1985) has shown that the majority of incidents a large city police department dealt with were emotionally disturbed individuals. Estimates are that between 52 percent (Fuselier, 1986) and 85 percent (Austin Police Department, 1991) of hostage incidents involve emotionally disturbed individuals as hostage takers. Feldman (2001) found that 94 percent of 120 incidents he reviewed involved people who were emotionally disturbed. HOBAS (2005) data show that of the

4,988 subjects reported to the FBI to date, 499 (7.1%) have been committed to a psychiatric facility, 702 (10.3%) were receiving therapy at the time of the incident, and 96 (1.4%) were in a residential treatment facility at the time of the incident.

Each category has recognizable signs of emotional disturbance and each requires a modification of the usual negotiating principles to fit their issues. They have their own particular sensitivities that negotiators will want to keep in mind so that they do not inadvertently threaten them. They function out of unique ego states and require individualized approaches that take their sensitivities into consideration. For instance, in the scenario at the beginning of this chapter, the paranoid person's intense need for security and safety made the violation of his personal space a predictable problem. The sudden emotional outburst could have been avoided had the importance of the boundaries of the subject's safety and the intense threat that paranoid individuals experience when people get too close emotionally been understood.

To increase the chances of success and to decrease the uncertainty that most police officers have about managing emotionally disturbed people, it is important for negotiators to learn to recognize the kind of person they are dealing with, to understand what motivates him or her, and to modify their negotiation tactics to influence these people appropriately.

A significant change since the beginning of negotiation is the recognition of the variety of types of individuals negotiators deal with. It may be that negotiator's success has led to their being de facto mental health officers in many departments. Feldman's data (in press) illustrates that when diagnoses are available, the most common types of mental problems experienced by people involved in crisis/hostage incidents were depression, antisocial or borderline personality disorders, poly-substance abuse/dependence, alcohol intoxication, or a variety of kinds of paranoia. These results show that negotiators are dealing with more than the original four groups of emotionally disturbed individuals described by Fuselier. As one experienced negotiator put it, "You don't have to be a psychologist but you have to think like one."

Issues that are important for negotiators to understand are the ways in which the emotionally disturbed relate to authority, the issues they have with relationships, sensitive areas that can elicit aggressive responses and the motivation (needs) they have that can be effective leverage if understood and utilized by negotiators. Negotiators need to know that they are generally motivated by expressive needs, have a history of difficulty with authority figures and will respond in sometimes unique ways to even the most well-intentioned negotiators. Understanding will reduce uncertainty and surprise, helping the negotiator to function more effectively when dealing with the emotionally disturbed.

Defining the Problem versus Diagnosing the Person

An issue that is being debated by negotiators is whether it is helpful to spend time deciding on the type of personality involved in the incident or to simply deal with the behavior at hand. On the one hand, the argument is that thinking in terms of personality types is time-consuming and can be misleading. On the other side, the argument is that taking the time to understand the personality they are dealing with will allow them to predict and control the person better than just dealing with the behavior at hand. A way to conceptualize the utility of personality profiling is to think in terms of the process of understanding abnormal behavior. This process involves gathering intelligence on the person's behavior, thoughts, and feelings; analyzing the issues that these behaviors, thoughts, and feelings suggest; and developing strategies and tactics to deal with the issues. Using personality issues in negotiations is about gathering, analyzing, and planning interventions, using person intelligence to predict and control the other person. It focuses on what the person's behavior, feelings, and thoughts tell you about his or her motivations, sensitivities, and interpersonal styles. It should inform the negotiating team about which strategies and tactics are likely to work and which are risky to use.

There are two other issues implied in this one: (1) it is risky to think in terms of one type of person or another; and (2) it is risky to assume that because negotiators have had trouble using personality information that it cannot be done. The first issue is based on the fact that people are rarely pure personality types. Rather, they are frequently mixtures of types with multiple issues. For instance, a person may be primarily paranoid, suspicious, and mistrusting, yet they can also have compulsive features. In fact, it is not unusual for the compulsive personality to develop significant paranoia when overly stressed. The second point above is a reminder of one of the values of a team approach to crisis/hostage intervention. Mental health professionals have a working knowledge of a wide variety of personality types and the issues associated with them. It only makes sense to include the professionals in personality types with the professionals in public safety. Butler et al. (1993) have shown that it is this combination that is the most effective in managing crises.

Domestic Violence and Negotiations

Over the last 20 years, there has been a nationwide increase in awareness of the problem of domestic violence. Along with this increase in general awareness, there has been an increased recognition of the frequency with which negotiators must deal with domestic incidents that become crisis incidents. It is important for the negotiator to have a working knowledge of domestic violence in order to predict, control, and intervene effectively in incidents that are rooted in violent domestic relationships. They tend to be among the most volatile and potentially violent incidents negotiators must deal with.

The prevalence of domestic violence in the United States is reported to be about 12 percent of reporting couples on national surveys (Porier, 1999). Twenty-eight percent of women will be abused sometime during their life (Wilson & Daly, 1993). Feldman (in press) found that almost 31 percent of the 120 hostage/barricaded incidents on which he collected data were personal/domestic in nature. Call (1999) reported research by Head on 137 hostage incidents managed by the NYPD's Hostage Recovery Program from 1973 to 1982, in which 20 percent took place in the home of the hostage or the hostage taker, suggesting that a prior relationship existed. A recent summary of 4,988 cases reported to the HOBAS database maintained by the FBI showed that of 1,324 victims in negotiated incidents, 131 (9.8%) were spouses or ex-spouses, 318 (23.9%) were family members, and 150 (11.3%) were "significant others."

Mohandie (2005) has shown that stalkers who have had an intimate relationship with their victim use the most violence. Therefore, negotiators are well served to understand the kinds of people who engage in domestic violence.

In 1979, Walker described the classic cycle of physical violence in families. From interviewing battered women, she developed a three-stage cycle that included:

1. Tension-building, during which the abuser starts to become jealous, fearing that his spouse is planning on leaving him;

2. Violent acting out, preceded by several antagonistic interchanges in which the batterer is accusatory, engages in name-calling, pushes, and is generally provocative with the abused; and

3. Period of calm and reduced tension, during which the subject is remorseful, apologetic, and contrite, promising never to do it again, and promising to do whatever it takes to keep the relationship together.

Most relationships cycle though these stages several times, with increasing escalation of the violence. In reviewing the research on the prevalence of domestic violence, Bachman (1999) concludes that:

1. Research indicates that women are more likely than men to experience violence committed by an intimate partner.

2. Women of all races and ethnic backgrounds are equally likely to experience violence committed by an intimate partner.

3. The victimization rate of women separated from their husbands is approximately three times that experienced by divorced women and 25 times higher than married women.

4. While homicide rates against men have declined over the past decade, the rates of women killed by intimate partners has stayed the same.

Of particular interest to negotiators and of relevance for this chapter, Dutton (1995) has pointed out that not all batterers are alike. Citing the research and his 25 years of experience, he proposes that there are three distinct types of abusers:

1. The Borderline/Dependent Batterer

2. The Antisocial/Controlling Batterer

3. The Compulsive/Perfectionistic Batterer

Each type has its own motives for battering, and each has differences in the ways in which he relates to people in positions of power and authority. Therefore, it is important for the negotiator to understand each type if he or she is going to predict and control the subject's behavior.

With the results of the domestic violence research and the research from the mental health community on the mental status of subjects involved in negotiation/barricaded incidents, negotiators need to be prepared to deal with: dependent, borderline, narcissistic, antisocial, compulsive, paranoid, and depressive individuals. In addition, issues involving substance abuse will be discussed.

Generally, emotionally disturbed people fall into three groups that concern negotiators. They are personality disorders, mood disorders, and psychotic disorders. Each of these three major groups are broken down into subgroups, many of whom negotiators have had to deal with. Feldman (2001), Mohandie (2005) and the domestic violence research cited above have reported that the character and behavior disorders include antisocial personalities, dependent personalities, borderline personalities, and narcissistic personalities. The mood disorders include depression, dysthymic disorders, and bipolar disorders. Common psychotic disorders include: schizo-affective disorders, schizophrenia, and delusional disorders.

General Guidelines for Dealing with Emotionally Disturbed People

Several general principles for negotiators come from the Transactional Analysis view of emotionally disturbed people.

1. Because people develop patterns of behavior, thoughts, and feelings that help them deal with authority figures in their life at an early age and these patterns tend to be consistent over time, it is important for police negotiators to avoid acting in ways that get an automatic response from actors that are

based on their style of dealing with judgmental authority figures. Negotiators should avoid judgment, criticism, preaching, or other styles that convey disapproval.

2. The use of interpersonal styles that are not critical and judgmental will confuse the other person for a while. By responding in a nurturing way or in a matter-of-fact, rational way, the negotiator is likely to throw the communications into confusion: it will probably lead to a crossed transaction. The response negotiators can expect is confusion, heightened tension, and an effort to force the negotiator to respond like most other authorities in the emotionally disturbed person's life. Generally, when dealing with an emotionally disturbed person in a Nurturing or Reasonable style, expect increased resistance. It is playing the game by a new set of rules and the person will have to see that it is a real change. He or she will test it.

3. One major goal of negotiations is to reduce the person's habitual response when they are stressed by authority figures, so they can begin to make more intelligent, thoughtful, and better-informed decisions. Using problem-oriented questions like those discussed in Chapter 6 will help. If the negotiator does not have an opportunity to be nurturing, he or she needs to stay focused on the problem; Use the Adult state to ask problem-oriented questions.

4. In establishing rapport with emotionally disturbed individuals, the negotiator's style will depend on the kind of person with whom the negotiator is dealing, as well as what stage negotiations have reached. Use the appropriate ego state for the type of person you are dealing with.

The following section will describe the most common types of emotionally disturbed individuals who take hostages and the negotiation guidelines that have proven effective with each of these types of individuals.

Sidebar: A Prison Team

Patricia Sorrels joined the Oklahoma Department of corrections in 1985 as a correctional case manager. She served as a facilitator for the mediation program and has been a certified mediator since 1988. For the last seven years she has been a community sentencing local administrator for a five-county area in southeast Oklahoma. She has been a member of the Eastern Region Hostage Team since 1995, and has been the team coordinator since 2004. She holds a B.A. in both adult and juvenile corrections from East Central University in Ada, Oklahoma.

The Oklahoma Department of Corrections Eastern Region Hostage Negotiation Team was established by the Eastern Regional Office in 1985. The team has 15 members that represent nine multilevel security facilities and community corrections. The team membership includes one team coordinator and two assistant team coordinators, and a psychological consultant. The team members are chosen for their diverse talents and abilities. Part of the selection process includes an in-depth interview and then a psychological assessment by a psychologist using the MMPI II. When the team was first established, a negotiator's manual was developed and a mission statement included the specified the goal of the team:

> Preservation of life—through a total commitment to the negotiation approach and nonviolent resolution; and to achieve this mission by a vigorous employee education program and a constant team training process.

In accordance with our mission statement, training is a priority with the team, and each team member is required to attend eight hours of training a month, which includes hostage scenario drills at various facilities. The drills are conduced with the facility tactical teams, and also include facility administrative personnel. Forty hours of annual training are also required. This annual training includes two days of classroom instruction and two days of scenario training. Outside agencies are invited to attend the training and both federal and private prison representatives attend the training. The team also attends the annual competition and training in San Marcos, Texas, and has won the Corrections Division trophy four times.

Each year the team develops goals. One of the on-going goals has been to share the knowledge they have acquired with other staff and outside agencies. The team conducts first responder and hostage survival training for all the newly hired correctional officers in their basic training program and travels to the various facilities and conducts in-service training in these topics. Training in hostage survival was presented last year at the Oklahoma Correctional Association, and the team has had an opportunity to train with different sheriff's departments this year. Planning is in progress to train with the Oklahoma Highway Patrol.

Personality Disorders

Inadequate/Dependent Persons

With the introduction of the *Diagnostic and Statistical Manual*, Third Edition-Revised (1988), the term Inadequate Personality was dropped from the diagnostic guide. However, real-life experience has shown that there is a subset of hostage takers who function in inadequate ways. They have come to expect that the authorities in their life will be critical in a way that says they are incapable. Their parents sent the message "You cannot do what you want or what you are trying, but I love you enough to do it for you." They desperately need to belong somewhere and to be reassured of their own worth. They are generally compliant and cooperative toward authority, except when the authority requires them to be independent. They may be aggressive. A frequent example of this type of person is the spouse in a divorce who tries to force his or her partner to stay in the marriage.

At the same time, these people share characteristics with a group of people described in DSM-IV (1994) as dependent personalities. Therefore, both types of personalities will be described.

Inadequate personalities are people who as children came to believe that they were worthless and incapable. They assume that they cannot solve problems alone. They must have others' help. The paradox is that they can be ingenious, creative, and persistent in finding ways to get others to take responsibility for their lives. Fuselier (1981) has described them as having the following characteristics:

1. Throughout life they have shown ineffective responses to social, emotional, and physical stress—they tend to run from stress or quit performing when stressed;

2. Often a high school dropout;

3. A history of poor job performance, leading to firing;

4. Sees self as a "loser," someone who has always failed;

5. Hostage taking may be last attempt to prove to a significant person that he or she can do something;

6. Incident may be high point of his or her life;

7. Recognized by statements like "I'll show them I really can do something.

Dependent personalities are people who must have others make decisions for them. They decided or were taught early in life that they could not do it themselves. They are people with "Current or long-standing functioning, not limited to episodes of illness, that causes either significant impairment in social or occupational functioning or subjective distress" (DSM-IV, 1994). They are characterized by:

1. Difficulty with everyday decision making without an excessive amount of advice and reassurance from others.

2. Needing others to assume responsibility for most major areas of his or her life.

3. Difficulty expressing disagreement with others for fear of loss of support.

4. Difficulty initiating projects or doing things on their own because of lack of confidence.

5. Going to excessive lengths to obtain nurturing and support from others.

6. Feeling uncomfortable or helpless when alone because of exaggerated fear that they cannot care for themselves.

7. Urgently seeking another's care and support when a relationship ends.

8. Unrealistic preoccupation with fears of being left alone to care for themselves.

The dependent person's chief motive is to re-establish a dependent relationship with a caretaker or to prevent the loss of the person on whom he or she is dependent (Everly, 1989). They do not think they can survive alone. They are like a child who is dependent on others for their survival, so they respond to abandonment and not having someone to depend on as though their lives depended on finding someone who will take care of them. Such a pattern is seen in the person who barricades himself at a mental health clinic with a counselor who is not his regular counselor. His demand is to be seen right away by the person he has seen in the past. Dependent people fear the loss of affection and they avoid conflict as a result. All of these characteristics give the negotiator considerable power over the inadequate/dependent person. He just needs to be careful not to abuse that power by assuming a critical stance.

Managing Dependent Individuals

With inadequate/dependent people who become suicidal, negotiators can use the dependency need to their benefit by nurturing a dependent relationship. After listening to the person's story and reflecting their understanding, negotiators can begin to be more directive with the dependent person than they are with other hostage takers with whom they take a less active posture (such as paranoid individuals, who are highly sensitive about being told what to do). By showing attention, caring, and understanding, the negotiator, for all practical purposes, takes the place of the person on whom the suicidal or barricaded person has relied for help in the past. The negotiator takes a nurturing posture (Bradstreet, 1992).

With inadequate/dependent people who are involved in a crime with a partner, or who have taken the person on whom they are dependent hostage, nurturing their dependence on the negotiator does not work as well as it does if they are suicidal. They have another source on whom to rely—the person involved in the incident with them. The negotiator needs to utilize the principle of negotiating with the identified leader, rather than trying to separate the inadequate person from the other person. For instance, in one incident, a man took his estranged wife hostage at her place of employment. He threatened and postured for nearly three hours before it became clear to the negotiators that he had gotten himself into a situation he could not handle. A recurring pattern developed in which he would agree to let his wife go, he would ask for 10 minutes to think about how he wanted her to leave the building, only to frustrate the negotiators by saying he had changed his mind when the 10 minutes was up. It became obvious that his unresolved problem was that he had taken his wife hostage because he could not make his own decisions with confidence and that if he let her go, he would have to rely on his own judgment, which he did not think was good. When the negotiating team realized what was going on, they asked to speak to the wife, because she was the real decisionmaker in the incident, even though she started out as the victim. The incident was resolved when the negotiators talked her into having him put the gun down, come to the front door, and come out himself.

Because dependent persons tend to have low self-esteem, it is wise for negotiators to avoid criticism and judgment of them or their ideas. Rather, an active effort to reinforce positive behavior, thoughts, and actions needs to be made, no matter how small the successes.

With inadequate/dependent people, family members have frequently been instrumental in creating the sense of worthlessness. Therefore, it is a poor idea to permit family members to negotiate, even though they frequently insist that they can get the person to give up.

FBI guidelines for dealing with inadequate/dependent people are:

1. Provide understanding and uncritical acceptance.

2. Help him or her find a way of ending the situation without "failing again."

3. Keep parents, friends, etc. away from the scene because they may evoke strong feelings of failure or embarrassment, leading him to believe he has to do something "important" (Fuselier, 1986).

Case Study: The Inadequate Individual. At 3:00 P.M., the man walked into his counselor's office at the local community mental health center, with what looked like a bomb strapped to his chest. He yelled, "Nobody around here pays any attention. I'm going to get you, too." The secretary called the police before leaving the building. The crisis response team was mobilized immediately.

Upon arrival, the tactical team cleared the building of onlookers. This was a major task because many of the employees not only wanted to stay, they wanted to talk to the subject themselves.

The Explosive Ordinance Disposal (EOD) unit was at the location to evaluate the threat and to defuse the bomb when that became necessary.

The negotiators responding to the call recognized the person. They had dealt with him three times before. He had first come to the attention of the police when he was arrested while driving a stolen car. He had bought the car from a local service station for $50. It did not occur to him that he should not be able to buy a Porsche 944 for $50. He had a long history of poor decisionmaking, dating back to a motorcycle accident he had in the eighth grade. He had difficulty holding a job and had been discharged from the Army for unsuitability. He lived with his mother and had no social life.

The first incident in which negotiators had to deal with him was the result of the car theft charge. He had been released from jail after the magistrate heard his story and talked to his counselor about his judgment. The day after his release, he began worrying about being sentenced to prison. He tried to contact the detective who was investigating the case, as well as his counselor. Neither of them was available. He responded to this crisis by climbing a TV tower and threatening to jump to get people's attention. He left his billfold with his ID at the base of the tower so he could be identified. The negotiator talked him off the tower by listening to his story, reflecting what he heard, suggesting that he would help the man get in touch with his counselor, and asking the man to come down off the tower because the negotiator was afraid of heights. After listening to the story, it took 15 minutes for the negotiator to convince the man to come down with him.

The second incident involved the man climbing a construction crane and staying there through a thunderstorm with lightning and 50 mph winds. He was not spotted until three hours later. He took a pellet gun up the crane with him and when the female negotiator contacted him, he threatened to kill himself. Because he was known, he was not considered a serious risk. The negotiator sidestepped the suicide threat and focused on having the man tell her what led to his climbing the crane. He reported being frustrated in his attempts at getting his antianxiety medication renewed at the local hospital. Because the construction crane was being used to build a parking garage for another hospital, the negotiator could guarantee him an appointment as soon as he came down. He asked her to come to the top of the parking garage where he would meet her at the end of the catwalk leading to the crane. She went to the roof but refused to meet him as long as he had the gun. She did not know it was a pellet gun. He started to walk to the negotiator and was apprehended by patrol officers who were covering her.

The third episode was a 50-minute encounter in which the man held another counselor at the mental health clinic hostage. He had been frustrated in his attempts to get appointments, advice, and medication when he wanted them. Consequently, he took a counselor hostage at knifepoint. Negotiators talked him out of the knife by promising to get him an appointment and by offering to buy him a soft drink.

In the fourth episode, EOD personnel determined that the "bomb" was probably made of road flares and not dynamite, as the subject had said. The negotiators again got him to explain that he was frustrated with the system; that it did not treat him well and the only way he got any attention was to threaten people. They asked him if he understood that threatening people scared them. He said he had not thought about that. All he had wanted was to get an appointment. He was asked if he thought that scaring people was the best way to get what he wanted. He said, "No. In fact people will probably want to stay away from me even more, if I scare them too much." The negotiator said that was right and encouraged him to show people that he did not intend to scare anybody by putting the bomb down. He did, confirming EOD's suspicion that it was not really a bomb.

Case Review. The outstanding features of this individual were his long-standing history of poor decisionmaking, lack of insight into the effects of his behavior on others and his complete reliance on others once a relationship was established. They are clear demonstrations of the extremes to which the inadequate/dependent individual will go to have others take care of him. Their crisis usually involves the loss of the person on whom they depend. They will sometimes become threatening or even violent to regain their source of support. After they are attended to, they generally listen and are compliant with negotiators. However, bringing negotiations to an end can be difficult unless the negotiator has planned for the transfer of the dependent relationship to someone else. In the case above, the first negotiator was called several times by the subject with offers to buy lunch or dinner. He finally had to tell the person that departmental regulations forbid him from seeing anyone socially with whom he had dealt officially.

Borderline Personalities

Borderline personalities are characterized by "a pervasive pattern of instability of interpersonal relationships, self-image, and affect, and marked impulsivity that begins in early adolescence . . ." (DSM-IV, 1994).

Borderline personalities have a history of being abused, physically or sexually, as children (DSM-IV). Dutton (1995) has found that borderline batterers were shamed by their father as children. Early on, they decided that authority figures in their life were unreliable. At the same time, they decided that they were incapable of acting independently and caring for themselves. This left them in the difficult, if not impossible, position of depending on others who were frightening, unpredictable, and abusive for their very existence. This leads them to an intense fear of abandonment and a chaotic rage at the people on whom they are dependent. They generally come to the attention of the police when they are in a fight or are threatening suicide in response to the threat of abandonment by the person on whom they are dependent.

The American Psychiatric Association's Diagnostic and Statistical Manual, Fourth Edition (DSM-IV) lists the following criteria for the Borderline Personality, which are helpful to the negotiator in identifying and understanding the Borderline Personality:

1. Frantic efforts to avoid real or imagined abandonment

2. A pattern of unstable and intense relationships, alternating between extremes of over-idealization and devaluation; they are either perfect or worthless

3. Markedly unstable self-image or sense of who they are

4. Self-damaging impulsivity (reckless driving, binge eating or drinking, substance abuse)

5. Recurrent suicidal behavior or self-mutilation

6. Affective instability that includes episodes of dysphoria, irritability, and anxiety

7. Chronic feelings of emptiness

8. Inappropriate, intense anger (temper tantrums, fights)

9. Transient paranoid episodes

Managing Borderlines

In dealing with borderline personalities, it is important to remember that they are driven by emotions rather than reason. Millon (1996) has pointed out that one of the strategic goals of therapy with borderlines is to help them gain better control over their feelings and increase their capacity for reasonable problem-solving. The expressive nature of their needs means that the negotiator needs to use crisis intervention techniques to manage them. It is also important to remember that the borderline has intense ambivalence about people in positions of authority, so they may "transfer" their hostility and dependency to the negotiator (Borum & Strentz, 1992). The transference of dependency to the negotiator works to help resolve the incident when managed skillfully. However, the two come together, so the negotiator needs to be able to manage the anger that comes with the dependency. Building a relationship is difficult, because it is hard to keep from being critical in the face of the borderline's mixed feelings, especially the intense rage.

Several negotiators have suggested guidelines for managing borderline/dependent personalities (FBI, 1985; Borum & Strentz, 1992; Lanceley, 1999; McMains & Mullins, 1998). They include:

1. Use active listening skills, especially emotional labeling, to establish a relationship (Lanceley, 1999; McMains, 1998).

2. Defuse emotionality through understanding, listening, and distraction (Lanceley, 1999; McMains, 1998).

3. Use a reassuring voice (Borum & Strentz, 1992).

4. Be alert to clues of suicide or homicide (Lanceley, 1999; Borum & Strentz, 1992).

5. Stay in contact with the subject as much as possible to prevent impulsive acting out (Lanceley, 1999).

6. Reassure the subject that help is available and that you will help him or her find help.

7. Be prepared for dramatic, intense, and sudden shifts in emotion.

8. Remain alert to the sudden appearance of psychotic symptoms (Borum & Strentz, 1992).

9. Reduce the usual stimulation at the scene as much as possible (Borum & Strentz, 1992).

10. Structure the situation by sharing your experience and describing in detail what normally happens during each stage of the incident (Borum & Strentz, 1992).

11. Monitor your own stress levels or have a second person monitor them (Borum & Strentz, 1992).

12. Expect mixed feelings about males (McMains, 1998).

Lanceley (1999) has made the interesting observation that corrections officers can identify borderlines more easily than street officers, perhaps because they have to deal with borderline personalities on a daily basis. Psychologists with whom the authors have talked in the prison system have reported that antisocial personalities and borderline personalities are the most common mental disorders they encounter.

Case Study: An incident from Las Vegas illustrates many of the issues that arise when negotiating with a borderline personality. Jerry was a borderline person. He had a history of quick attachments and difficulty with abandonment. He and his wife had dated two weeks in high school when he became so attached that he cried for weeks when her mother made them "break up." Additionally, he became suicidal when they were having marital problems. His style at home was distant but suspicious. He would come home and sit without interacting with the family. He frequently accused his wife of having an affair or being interested in other men. He had been abusive on several occasions, pushing, slapping, and grabbing her. After she left him, he tracked his wife to a beauty parlor with a borrowed rifle. He intended to try and coerce her back home, or to kill himself in front of her. The shooting of the cook in the adjoining business was not intentional. When patrol officers arrived, Jerry's wife became very concerned about his safety and made a show of trying to protect him from the police. Initially, she was the one doing the talking to the patrol captain who called the shop to find out what was going on. Eventually, the captain got Jerry on the phone and reassured him that everything as going to be all right, that everybody had marital problems, and that he was sure that Jerry and his wife could work theirs out with some professional help. He reassured, minimized the seriousness of the incident, and offered hope. The negotiators took over the conversation when they arrived. Jerry kept asking that the captain get back on the phone, probably because of the borderline tendency to "split" or assign people to strict categories of "good' or "bad" with no room for anything in between. The captain had intuitively done the right things to establish a positive relationship with Jerry. The negotiators, who were seen by Jerry as less friendly and caring than the captain, were initially put in the "bad" category by him. They had to continually reassure him that they would help resolve the incident without anyone getting hurt and that they wanted to help him.

Experience has shown that borderline/dependent people become involved in crises in one of two ways: (1) They are either the weaker partner in a criminal team, the other half of which is usually an antisocial personality (see below); or (2) They are involved in a relationship that is going poorly, at which time they may become suicidal or they may take the other person in the relationship hostage. In both situations, they rely heavily on others.

Antisocial (Angry/Rebellious) Persons

Antisocial individuals are perhaps the one group of people with whom police officers are the most familiar. They populate most jails. They are the people with whom officers deal most often in their law enforcement role.

Historically, the antisocial personality has been called the psychopathic personality, the sociopathic personality, or the antisocial personality, depending on the emphasis of the author. For negotiating purposes, the distinctions are moot. All three terms refer to the same type of person, who is characterized by "a pervasive pattern of disregard for, and the violation of, the rights of others that begins in childhood or early adolescence and continues into adulthood" (DSM-IV, 1994). They are characterized by:

1. Early onset (before age 15 years) of evidence of disregard for others.

2. Deceitfulness—indicated by repeated lying, the use of aliases, or conning others for personal profit or pleasure.

3. Impulsivity and failure to plan ahead.

4. Irritability and aggressiveness as indicated by frequent assaults (especially when he does not get his way).

5. Reckless disregard for the safety of self or others.

6. Consistent irresponsibility, as indicated by a repeated pattern of failure to maintain work or to pay bills.

7. Lack of remorse as indicated by being indifferent to others or rationalizing having hurt or stolen from others.

Antisocial personalities are very much like two-year-old children. They learned early in life that others are harsh and critical, but unlike inadequate personalities, they have learned to handle their aggressive parents by being rebellious. They are angry, aggressive, and abusive. As children, they learned that temper tantrums got them what they wanted, and they continue to use this as adults to get their way. They assume that if they are powerful enough, or angry enough, others will give in. Their primary motivation is for power and control. They do not take being told "no" well. They are rebellious and angry toward authority, as is demonstrated by their history.

Hare and McPherson (1984) have pointed out that a sub-group of antisocial personalities, psychopaths, account for the majority of repeat crimes and the most planned and purposeful violent crimes. Greenstone et al. (in press) has suggested that distinguishing psychopaths from other antisocial personalities may be helpful in risk assessment. Further, the incidents of psychopathy in prisons has been estimated to be 85 percent of the population (Gacano, 1998), so an understanding of this sub-type is important for both police and prison negotiators. Finally, experience in the area of domestic violence suggests that the most violent abusers are those who are antisocial (Dutton, 1995), perhaps psychopathic.

Psychopaths differ from other antisocial personalities in that they show a cluster of traits that make it easier for them to prey on others. They are more self-centered, experience less affect, are more manipulative of others, and show less empathy or remorse than non-psychopathic antisocial personalities. At the same time, they share several traits with non-psychopathic anti-social personalities, including: impulsivity, poor behavior controls, lack of goals, irresponsibly, adolescent antisocial behavior, and disregard for rules and law as an adult.

Greenstone et al. (in press) reports the results of a study using an adaptation of the Hare Problem Checklist by negotiators in the field to assess psychopathic traits. Although the number of incidents in which the checklist was used was small, the results were promising in that they tended to validate the idea that the first cluster of traits listed above can be distinguished from the second by negotiators in the field and that this cluster had value in helping negotiators decide which cases needed to be approached with more cautious strategy and tactics.

The number of cases in Greenstone's study was small (N=14). However, the results were suggestive of a useful approach to assessing psychopathy in the field. For now, it is important for negotiators to recognize that subjects who show signs of the first cluster may pose a more serious threat of violence than others and, when in combination with depression, may raise the negotiator's concern about suicide by cop (see below). Characteristics to look for include:

1. **Superficiality,** which Greenstone describes as presenting: (1) a story that is shallow and difficult to believe; (2) emotional displays that seem insincere and ingenuine; (3) telling stories that are unconvincing; (4) making statements that are readily changed when challenged; (5) using technical jargon or language inappropriately; and (6) an engaging interpersonal style that the negotiator may tend to like.

2. **Grandiosity,** which involves a number of behaviors, including presenting: (1) self and abilities in an inflated way; (2) self-assured and opinionated; (3) he or she considers the situation the result of bad luck; (4) exaggerates status and reputation; (5) sees self as victim of the system; and (6) shows little concern for the future.

3. **Deceitful,** which shows itself through the subject's attempts to: (1) manipulate without concern for rights of others; (2) distort the truth to make self look good; (3) deceive with assurance and little apparent anxiety; (4) come across as a con man. In addition, he or she may appear to enjoy deceiving others and lacks remorse, appearing to experience no guilt or conscience; verbalizing remorse without sincerity; displaying little emotion in regard to actions and appearing more concerned more about his or her own suffering than others.

4. **Lacks empathy,** presenting to negotiators and others as: (1) cold and callous; (2) indifferent to concerns or feelings of others; (3) unable to appreciate the emotional consequences of his or her actions; (4) shallow emotionally; and (5) verbal expressions are not supported by non-verbal expressions.

5. **Does not accept responsibility,** including a number of behaviors the negotiator can observe or gather reports of from others. They include: (1) rationalizing (excusing) the significance or impact of actions; (2) minimizing effects of behavior on others; (3) projecting blame onto others; (4) maintaining own innocence or minimizing own involvement; (5) claiming to be the victim; and (6) claiming amnesia or blackouts for events surrounding the incident.

Managing Antisocial Individuals

Kolb (1982) has pointed out that the antisocial personality "refers to those chronically antisocial individuals without the capacity to form significant attachments or loyalties to others, to groups, or to codes of living. Thus they are callous and given to immediate pleasures, appear devoid of a sense of responsibility and, in spite of repeated humiliations and punishments, fail to learn to modify their behavior." Antisocial individuals primarily utilize the Rebellious Child ego state in their dealings with authorities.

For the negotiator, this means that the usual techniques of establishing rapport, of using his or her credibility as a caring person, and of purposely developing the Stockholm Syndrome between the hostage taker and the hostages will have little effect. The antisocial personality does not form attachments to other people, negotiator or hostage. Rather, he or she tends to use people to meet his or her own needs. Consequently, the negotiator's job becomes one of showing the hostage taker how violence to the hostages, a threatening posture, and impulsive outbursts are not in his best interests.

Bradstreet (1992) has suggested that there are three approaches that need to be used when dealing with antisocial personalities:

1. The reasonable, problem-solving approach that can be used in the accommodation (negotiation) stage of an incident and that is characterized by a non-critical, problem-oriented, rational approach to interactions. Questions like "How is hurting others going to help you?" and "What do you think would happen if _____?" are Adult questions that facilitate evaluating and problem-solving without getting into a power struggle.

2. The buddy approach that emphasizes the negotiator and the hostage taker sharing criticism and blaming others. Comments like, "Man you know how bosses can be. They never understand," and "You know how THEY are about that s_____," are examples of Critical Parent statements that get the negotiator and the antisocial person on the same wavelength.

3. The Columbo approach, which emphasizes playing dumb, and being caring, but inept, when the other person is angry and upset. Comments like, "I know it's taking a long time, but we are trying," and "Let me see what the boss says," are examples of the inept Nurturing Parent.

These three approaches avoid directly confronting the hostage taker. Antisocial persons generally respond to confrontation with anger. And because in a negotiation incident the negotiator is the only target available to the hostage taker, the negotiator needs to take extra care to avoid arousing the hostage taker's rage.

In addition to the points discussed above, FBI guidelines suggest the following when negotiating with an antisocial personality (Fuselier, 1981):

1. Remember that he is self-centered and will try to make things easy for himself. He will try for what he sees as his best deal.

2. Be careful about trying to trick him. He is streetwise and is used to conning others. Consequently, he is aware of others conning him.

3. Promise only what you can deliver.

4. Keep him stimulated and involved. He is easily bored. Don't let him have a chance to "create" entertainment.

Although he is rebellious and impulsive, the antisocial individual does have the capacity to think through problems. This means that he can evaluate the probable outcomes of his actions. He is able to decide what is in his best interests. He spends his life conning others, making deals, and figuring the odds. In negotiations, he will be able to utilize that same ability. It is the negotiator's job to convince him that harming others is not in his best interests, without raising his rebelliousness. The negotiator needs to engage the antisocial person's Little Professor without energizing the Rebellious Child. The indirect methods of influence and suggestion discussed in Chapter 2 are appropriate for this.

Case Study: The Antisocial Individual. The 17-year-old came home drunk with a friend on Friday night. He told a story of robbing and shooting somebody downtown that same night. When his family did not believe him, he grew angry and ran them out of the house at gunpoint. He fired at them as they were going out the door. The father called the police. He was concerned about getting back into his house and wanted officers to go in and arrest his son so he could get some sleep. Not knowing whether the "friend" was being held against his will, the officers decided to call negotiators to help resolve the situation.

One of the negotiators who responded to the call knew the individual from previous calls at the house. The teenager and his family had experienced several disturbances in the past. Frequently, some member of the family shot at houses in the neighborhood. Other times, different family members threatened neighbors for being "disrespectful." Still other times, family fights required police officers to intervene when they spilled out into the street. During one such fight, the subject had run back into the house after assaulting his sister as the officer arrived on the scene. The officer chased the subject into the house, where he quickly gave up without offering any resistance. The subject had a long history of arrests for assaults, terroristic threats, thefts, and disorderly conduct involving firearms.

Negotiators started trying to communicate with the subject by phone and then by "bullhorn." He failed to respond to either. For five hours, negotiators rang the telephone every minute for 30 seconds. Every 30 minutes, they tried to get him to pick up the phone by giving him instructions over the bullhorn.

By about 6:00 A.M., traffic along the subject's street was picking up as people began to go to work. The field commander ordered the tactical team to prepare for an assault. By this time, the subject had been evaluated and his antisocial characteristics were evident. Officers had reported his usual response to being confronted by police. Therefore, the negotiators, after consulting with the commander and the department psychologist, made one more attempt at getting the individual to respond. They used the bullhorn to say,

"_____. Look out the window. See the men in the black Ninja suits? They are the SWAT team. If we do not hear from you in five minutes, they are coming in there and they will take you down."

The subject responded immediately:

"Are you guys talking to me? I didn't know you wanted to talk to me. Let's talk." He answered the phone on the next ring and he came out of the house two minutes later.

Case Review. The antisocial nature of not only the subject, but also his entire family, was evident in their continual disregard for the rights of their neighbors to live in a safe neighborhood. The family's frequent fights, as well as their shooting at the neighbors, showed little concern for others. The father's concern for his sleep over his son's safety demonstrated antisocial qualities across two generations. Additionally, the son's poor school record, repeated arrests, and disregard for his family's safety attested to his antisocial qualities. As with most antisocial individuals, as long as he thought he had the power, he acted out in self-centered ways: he did not care where his family spent the night, nor was he concerned about shooting at them. However, when confronted with a situation in which it was clearly in his best interests to cooperate, when the alternative to communicating was SWAT, he chose the best alternative for himself. He might be rebellious, but he was insightful enough to make his best deal. This is typical of antisocial individuals. The above example is for illustrative purposes—be careful to evaluate responses before using a hard line.

Compulsive/ Perfectionistic Personalities

Obsessive-Compulsive Personality Disorders are characterized by "a preoccupation with orderliness, perfection and mental and interpersonal control . . ." (DSM-IV, 1994).

DSM-IV outlines the following characteristics:

1. Preoccupation with details, rules, lists, schedules, and organization to the extent that the main point of the activity is lost.

2. Inability to complete tasks because overly strict standards are never achieved.

3. Overly devoted to work, to the exclusion of leisure time activity (workaholic).

4. Overly conscientious in matters of morality, ethics, and values.

5. A packrat—is unable to discard old, worn-out objects that have no sentimental value.

6. Inability to delegate tasks or work with others because things are not done exactly their way.

7. Miserly in spending, either on self or others.

8. Stubborn and argumentative.

Millon (1996) reports on Schneider's observations about the anankast (compulsive) personality. Schneider observes that these personality types are "always trying to hide a nagging uncertainty, undercompensatory or over-compensatory activity, especially where the inferiority feelings are of a physical or social character. Outer correctness covers and imprisons inner insecurity."

Because this personality type has not often been reported by negotiators as someone they have had to deal with, not many authors have suggested guidelines for managing them. Feldman (2001), for instance, found no compulsive personality disorders among the 144 people involved in hostage/crisis incidents in his study. The reason for this is probably because most compulsives are too constricted and rule-bound to act out. They tend to use withdrawal, ruminations, and alcohol as ways of blunting their feelings and controlling their aggressive impulses. However, one of the authors has had the occasion to deal with three obsessive, barricaded individuals in crisis, all of whom were in law enforcement. Two incidents were resolved peacefully and one ended in the person committing suicide. The following are offered as tentative guidelines for negotiating with compulsive, perfectionistic subjects:

1. Use active listening, especially paraphrasing, minimal encouragers, and to establish initial contact and to build rapport.

2. Be respectful and competent at all times.

3. Stay problem oriented most of the time.

4. Normalize feelings—especially of uncertainty and tension.

5. Be aware of the potential for depression and suicide.

6. Expect contrition and cooperation after anger.

7. Use problem-oriented questions focused on the "big picture."

8. Provide structure by sharing what is "normally done" in crisis situations.

9. Share prior experience with successful situations to establish "expertise."

10. Minimize fault/blame.

Case Study: The sergeant was considered the "poster boy" for the department. He was always well groomed, had military creases in his uniforms, kept his shoes spit-shined, and wrote perfect reports. He was promoted early. During his seventh year on the department, he started an affair with a female officer, and left his wife and two children to move in with her. After six months, she got tired of the relationship and made him move out. She started dating another officer. The sergeant had to move into an apartment complex where he worked as a security officer when off duty. He went to the ex-girlfriend's apartment at 3:00 in the afternoon on the day of the incident, found the boyfriend's patrol car there and pounded on the door to get the two to come out. Nobody answered the door. He used his service weapon and fired multiple rounds into the patrol car. At the same time, he called the dispatcher reporting shots fired at the location and requested backup. The female officer called the shots in as well, warning officers that it was a police officer doing the shooting. The Crisis Response team responded. The sergeant was found pacing back and forth in front of the house. He challenged responding officers and told them to stay away. He was assessed to be a high-risk individual, primarily for suicide, because he had multiple losses, including his wife, children, career, and face. Negotiators initiated contact from a position of cover. None of them had worked for the sergeant. They used his rank in the initial contact to show respect. Initially, he did not respond to their overtures. They kept calling out to him, until he responded, saying that it was over for him. He reported the losses noted above, was agitated and anxious. Negotiators reflected his anger and stated that it was understandable. They said that they had handled several incidents in which men were "jilted" by a woman and that they were all angry. The reflection seemed to calm him a little, but he continued to pace. The negotiators asked if he had talked to his wife since he had been in the apartment and he said no, that he was too ashamed. Negotiators suggested that it was to be expected that somebody who was as good a police officer as he was would be upset and embarrassed by what he had gone through and that they needed to decide how to help him. They needed his help doing so. They asked what they should tell his wife and children about the incident. That they were sure that his family would worry about him. They asked about times in the past that they had been worried about him and how they showed their love for him. As they talked about the family and the times they had been concerned about him in the past, he paced for a few more minutes and then visibly slumped as he sat on the bumper of the patrol car. He let the weapon slide from his hand.

Paranoid Personality

The most outstanding feature of paranoia is the person's sense of threat from others. Early in life, they assume a position that says, "Other people are unreliable, unpredictable, and dangerous." Their Child learns that the adults in their life cannot be trusted; the Child becomes fearful and resentful, expecting danger, and is ready to defend him- or herself at all times. They filter their experiences through this assumption, becoming hypersensitive to potential threats and excluding evidence that the world is safer than they think.

Paranoia usually develops because the child experiences harsh, threatening, and often inconsistent proscriptions from critical parents. They adopt a defensive, hypervigilant posture that allows them to survive. It contaminates their thinking in the sense that it predisposes them to select experiences that reinforce their assumption that the world is a dangerous place, feeding the person's paranoia without being updated by subsequent experience.

When the person's beliefs become unyielding and permanent, they can be said to be a delusion. Delusions are fixed beliefs that a person holds onto in spite of evidence to the contrary (American Heritage Dictionary, 1980). Paranoid individuals have fixed beliefs of being persecuted and about being special or having special knowledge. For example, Carol was a 28-year-old white female who believed she was being hunted by the Mafia. They wanted to kill her because she would not join. It did not matter that the Mafia had no female members. She was going to be the first. Carol was recruited from a ward at the state mental hospital because she was so talented. She had both delusions of persecution and delusions of grandeur.

Frequently, law enforcement agencies become unknowing conspirators in the paranoid person's delusion of persecution. Paranoid individuals see police as being in league with the people who are plotting against them. Officers are seen as agents of the persecutors. For instance, Harvey believed that the people he knew were behind the assassinations of Robert Kennedy, John F. Kennedy, and Martin Luther King, Jr., and they were directing the police department to assassinate him. When a patrol officer came to his door to investigate a neighborhood disturbance, he barricaded himself in his apartment and fired shots at the officer, trying to defend himself against the imagined threat.

For the negotiator, a paranoid person's delusions mean two things:

1. They need to introduce themselves simply as negotiators rather than as police negotiators. Using titles, rank, or other symbols of authority evoke a paranoid person's life-long ambivalence (fear and anger) toward authority. Ambivalence increases tension, and tension leads to greater reliance on their contaminated functioning.

2. They need to avoid arguing with the paranoid person about the reasonableness of their delusion: by definition, paranoid individuals are not going to change their beliefs through logical argument. Fuselier (1986) has suggested that negotiators accept their delusions as true for them.

Several types of people with emotional problems show signs of paranoia. They range from relatively mild disorders to seriously disabling disorders; from people who have paranoid parts of their personality that do not interfere with their functioning to schizophrenics who are severely impaired.

People with delusional disorders are those whose daily functioning in most areas of life is within normal bounds. It is only in the areas of their delusions that they have problems. For instance, recently, a man negotiators had to deal with was gainfully employed, had been a success in the military, was college educated, and had a family. His conflict was with the pastor of his church. He believed that the minister had convinced the mental health community that he was "crazy" and was trying to get him committed to a mental institution. Consequently, he appeared at the church with a jar of liquid that he claimed was gasoline, threatening to burn the church building and everybody in it.

Their delusions are persistent in nature and they can have content involving persecution, grandiosity, or erotomania.

The persecutory type of delusional disorder is the most common. People with this disorder usually have delusions involving such themes as being conspired against, cheated or spied upon, pursued, poisoned or drugged, harassed, or kept from accomplishing a valued goal. They may exaggerate the smallest slights. They may resort to repeated legal action, seeking redress for what they imagine are injustices. They are often resentful and angry, resorting to violence against people they think are hurting them (DSM-IV, 1994). They are frequently involved in episodes of violence in the workplace, because they often believe that their boss or supervisor is persecuting or cheating them.

An example of the persecutory type was the public transportation employee who took his supervisor hostage after an average performance evaluation. He thought he deserved a higher rating and that his supervisor unjustly marked his performance down. He believed that his supervisor saw him as a threat.

The erotomanic type of person holds the unfounded belief that they are loved by another person—usually a person of higher status—such as a television personality or a superior at work. The disturbed individual usually makes an effort to contact the person who is the object of the delusion. Harassing telephone calls, letters, gifts, and visits are common. Stalking is a frequent occurrence. Males who have this delusion frequently come into conflict with the law. With the growing recognition and criminalization of stalking, it is reasonable to believe that negotiators will have increasing contact with these people.

People with the grandiose type of delusional disorder believe that they possess a special but unrecognized talent, ability, or invention. This person may believe that he or she has a special relationship with a well-known person, like the special assistant to Exxon Oil or the daughter of the President. The delusion may have a religious content, such as the person having a special calling or special relationship with God. These types often become leaders of religious cults.

The hostage standoff involving cult members may well be an example of this kind of personality. FBI negotiators were divided on the type of personality they were dealing with in David Koresh. However, the strong beliefs that he was someone special in God's eyes, that he was called to a special mission, and that the federal government was persecuting him, are suggestive of the delusions seen in the grandiose type.

Paranoid Schizophrenia

Mohandie and Duffy (1999) have reported that incidents of violence among schizophrenics is five times higher than those with no disorder. In particular, individuals with active hallucinations or delusions are more likely to be aggressive than are the general population. One of the hallmarks of paranoid schizophrenics is their hallucinations, which frequently tell them to act out violently, and their delusions that others are out to get them. These characteristics bring paranoid people to negotiators' attention and make it important for negotiators to understand paranoia.

Paranoid schizophrenics are the most seriously disturbed of the group of people suffering from paranoid delusions. They are described by others as being "out of touch with reality" because they see or hear things that others do not see or hear (hallucinations). When actively psychotic, schizophrenics are characterized by:

1. At least two of the following:
   a. delusions
   b. hallucinations
   c. disorganized speech
   d. grossly catatonic behavior
   e. flat or inappropriate affect

2. Social/Occupational Dysfunction—for a significant period of time, since the onset of the illness, the person functions below his prior level of organization at work, in his interpersonal life, or in his ability to care for himself (DSM-IV, 1994).

Managing Paranoia

Building rapport and establishing a relationship are generally the first steps in negotiation. The way the negotiator does this varies somewhat with the kind of person the hostage taker is. The paranoid person generally lacks trust and is interpersonally distant. Because of their fear of hurt (Sullivan,

1954a; DSM-IV, 1994), they are excessively suspicious of people who get emotionally close. Because of their fear of intimacy, building rapport is difficult. Therefore, the following guidelines are helpful in establishing an atmosphere in which to negotiate:

1. Start in a logical, unemotional, factual way. Stay in the Adult ego state. Keeping your voice calm and even, ask for the person's view of their situation.

2. Paraphrase what you have heard without comment or criticism, and without emotional content.

3. Expect rejection and anger—respond in the Adult or Nurturing Parent manner by asking for clarification, by paraphrasing what is heard, or by reassuring the individual that as a negotiator you are different from others and that you want everybody to be safe (Bradstreet, 1992).

4. Stay on your side of the physical and emotional boundaries—getting too close too fast is frightening for them.

5. Allow ventilation, if it reduces anger and fear. If ventilation does not reduce emotional intensity, distract the person by changing the subject.

6. Show respect and interest.

7. Sidestep delusions (Fuselier, 1986). Do not argue, because it tends to elicit a Rebellious Child response; discuss other topics, which are reality based, to build rapport.

8. Build a sense of security and safety by reassuring the person of your desire to help and by gradually shifting from an exclusive language to an inclusive language—"you" to "us."

9. Focus negotiations on "problem solving," being careful not to criticize (Fuselier, 1986). Although paranoid individuals have areas of pathology, as a group they are intelligent and capable of problem-solving. Their Adult is not completely contaminated. They need to be focused on real problems, in the here and now, rather than being allowed to let their imaginations run wild.

Case Study. The call came out as a routine neighborhood disturbance at an apartment complex. The patrol officer responded to the manager's office, where he was informed that one of the tenants was complaining about another residence's music being too loud. The officer went to the complainant's door and knocked. He could hear loud music coming from the apartment next door. The subject peeked through an opening in the drapes. Seeing the police officer, he yelled, "Go away and leave me alone." The officer sensed that something was not right, because the instructions came from the man who had lodged the complaint with the apartment manager. He knocked again. Shots were fired through the front window. The officer withdrew and called for a supervisor. Closer questioning of the apartment manager revealed that the subject was a mental patient who had frequent encounters with his neighbors. He was thought to have a cache of firearms and ammunition along with a supply of water, food, and emergency lighting and bedding in his walk-in closet. The manager said, "It looks like he is prepared for a siege." More shots were fired and some went through the wall of the neighboring apartment. The residents were not injured. They evacuated the residence. The supervisor notified the deputy chief on duty, who in turn mobilized the department's crisis response team. He hoped to settle the incident without injuries.

The tactical team established a perimeter around the apartment, which included observers on all four corners and a bulletproof van immediately in front of the subject's windows. The van began to take fire almost immediately.

Other tactical officers evacuated the apartments above and around the subject's.

Negotiators began gathering intelligence on the subject. This proved to be fairly easy because the department's psychologist had worked at the local state hospital and had encountered this person on his ward. The subject was a paranoid schizophrenic who had been discharged six months previously, stabilized on medication. He had been scheduled for follow-up appointments with the outpatient clinic of the local community mental health center. He had stopped going to his appointments six weeks before. He was believed to have stopped taking his medication at that time. During the last six weeks, he had made calls and visits to the FBI and Secret Service, claiming to have information about the assassination of John F. Kennedy, Robert Kennedy, and Martin Luther King, Jr. He believed there was a conspiracy involving powerful, shadowy figures who had paid for the assassinations of all three people and who wanted him killed because of what he knew. He had this information because he was a special messenger from God. His job was to declare the coming of the new messiah to the world. He was rewriting the New Testament to bring it in line with his perception of God's new plan.

When the negotiator called him on the telephone, he identified himself as John Jones, a negotiator with the city. He said that the apartment manager had called and asked for help with a dispute between neighbors and that he was wondering how he could help. The subject responded, "You can take your assassination squad and get out of here. You have no business here. I did not call you and I do not want you. Go away."

In an even tone, the negotiator said, "Nobody's going to leave 'til we're sure everyone is safe. I only want to help. Can you tell me what happened to get this thing started?"

The subject responded, "Are you stupid? I said get out of here. I know why you are really here and I'm not letting you get a shot at me."

Negotiator: "Again, Mr. _____, I am here to help. I came at the request of Ms. _____, the manager. You know her don't you? (Pause to let subject answer). She said you had been having trouble with your neighbors. I'm here to see what we can work out. Nobody's going to get hurt. Tell me what happened."

Subject: "I checked it out with the President. You know those cops didn't come here to help. They have their truck right up against my window and they are looking right at me. They hate me. I can tell by their look (at which time he fired more rounds at the tactical van)."

Case Review. In the first few interactions, the subject shows his paranoia. He is agitated and aggressive. He refers to his delusions of persecution by suggesting that the police were there to kill him, not to help him. He demonstrated the need for an expanded interpersonal space by shooting at the people who were "staring" at him, invading his space. He hinted at hallucinations by suggesting that the President was in the apartment with him.

Collateral intelligence showed that he had been becoming more and more persistent in his delusions of grandeur: he had special knowledge because of his special calling from God. He had most likely stopped taking his medication at the same time he stopped going to his clinic visits. He had been getting more belligerent with the neighbors.

The negotiator utilized several of the principles discussed above: (1) He avoided identifying himself as a police officer; (2) He utilized the Nurturing Parent by asking how he could help; (3) He recognized the Contaminated Child who believes the police are going to kill him and responded quietly and calmly, using both the reassurance of Nurturing Parent and an Adult request for information; (4) He stayed focused on the immediate, reality-based problem.

In summary, several elements of paranoia were present. The subject seemed so disturbed by his delusions that they took on a reality of their own, independent of the reality of his surroundings. He was "out of touch" with reality, living more in his contaminated views than in the present. He was actively schizophrenic.

Paranoid individuals have been described as having an exaggerated emphasis on their own autonomy and a hypersensitivity about their sexual identity (Kolb, 1982). These lead to struggles about power and control as well as a sense of threat about intimacy with a person of the same sex. They try to distance themselves by threatening others. Their comfort zone, for instance, is three times that of the average person. They do not allow people to get too close, physically or emotionally. It is too threatening. This means that the negotiator cannot expect to use the emotional rapport he would use with others to establish his credibility with a paranoid person. He would be better served by adopting a dispassionate, analytic attitude. The Adult ego state is the most appropriate mode to take with paranoid individuals, especially in the beginning of a negotiation. It is not a good idea for the negotiator to get too close in a face-to-face negotiation. Finally, because of this need for distance, it would be inadvisable for the negotiator to suggest that anyone else violate the subject's personal space.

Their exaggerated need for autonomy makes paranoid individuals argumentative. They tend not to accept criticism or suggestions well. Therefore, the negotiator needs to be careful about power conflicts, sidestepping them and using indirect suggestions whenever possible.

It is important for the negotiator to remember that paranoid individuals are motivated by: (1) threats to their survival, and (2) threats to their self-esteem. As a result of their belief that people are out to kill them, they should be reassured, the threat of force should be minimized, and critical remarks on the part of the negotiator should be avoided. Some departments have used tightened perimeters, annoying stimuli (like loud music), and high visibility threats (like making the SWAT team's presence obvious) against paranoid individuals. These tactics only serve to increase the paranoid person's anxiety, leading to a reduction in logical thinking and problem solving.

Case Study: Establishing the Relationship. From the first interaction, the negotiator started building the relationship. Through his even tone of voice, reassurance and requests for information, he hoped to begin building the subject's sense of safety and security. By showing consistent concern for the person, he emphasized his care. By avoiding criticism, he kept away from the subject's ambivalence toward authority. By not responding directly to the subject's comments about assassination and the presence of the President, the negotiator sidestepped the delusions and hallucinations—rather, he tried to refocus the subject on the current problem by asking for information.

The presence of the tactical van was particularly agitating to the subject. He fired rounds at it several times. The negotiator focused on this issue as a problem to be solved. He explained the department's concern that the subject was firing his gun out the window where the van was located. It was pointed out in a matter-of-fact, calm way that he had been shooting prior to the arrival of the van and that one of the reasons the van was there was to keep his bullets from hitting anybody who happened to be walking by. The negotiator explained that even a small caliber weapon like a .22 carried for up to a mile. So the van was a way of making the area safe for others. He wondered if there were any other ways of making it safe?

By focusing on the immediate threat to the subject and by explaining the dilemma faced by the police, the negotiator did several things: he got the subject focused on a current problem, which did not allow him time to ruminate on his delusions; he engaged the subject's Adult problem-solving skills; and he reinforced the message that the police did not want anybody hurt.

The subject suggested that the van be moved, then he would not need to shoot. When asked about the shooting he had done before the van's arrival, he said that it had been because of the police officer threatening him. Rather than challenging his assertion, the negotiator asked him to agree to hold his fire, if the van were moved. He agreed and the van was moved.

The negotiator considered the subject's solution and asked about his own concerns. He established that there were two sides to any argument and that his legitimate concerns needed to be considered by the subject in any solution. At the same time, he showed an understanding of the subject's concerns. Although he was taking a risk, his acceptance of the subject's solution established an atmosphere of mutual respect and compromise that was the foundation for future agreements.

Unfortunately, two things happened about 22 hours into the incident that led to a renewal of shooting. The new incident commander insisted on moving the tactical van back to the front of the apartment and the negotiator got sarcastic with the subject. The former was done "to show him who is in charge here," in spite of the fact that the subject had honored his agreement not to fire for 12 hours. The latter was done because the negotiator was trying to "joke" with the subject, assuming an intimacy he did not have. When the negotiator asked the subject why he did not come out and talk with him face to face, the subject responded by asking, "Do you know the story of the three little pigs?" (perhaps alluding to the danger he saw in coming out of his 'house of bricks'). The negotiator was confused and responded, "Yeah and I know 'Mary had a Little Lamb,' too." This was taken as sarcasm, which implied criticism. The subject was immediately angered and began shooting.

After the incident, the psychologist interviewed the subject. He explained that he had felt both threatened by the van and demeaned by the one-sided decision to renege on the original agreement. Additionally, he felt that the negotiator was ridiculing him, not showing him respect. He started firing to show that he still had power.

When the subject started firing, the commander decided that it was time for a tactical resolution. He ordered tear gas fired into the apartment. The subject tried to come out when the gas filled the apartment, but the door was blocked. He asked the negotiator to get the police officers outside the apartment to help him out. He was instructed to go to the window with his empty hands up and to do what the officers said. He was warned that the officers would be dressed in black combat gear and would be pretty intimidating. However, he was reassured that they would help him (he was not told that the tactical officers "will not hurt you" because "hurt" was seen as a trigger word that would probably raise his fear). He surrendered.

It is important to note that even though the subject was clearly schizophrenic, he was not always "out of touch." There was a part of him that worked on rational problem-solving in the midst of the gas attack. During the part of the incident that was the most threatening, he was able to assess his situation, consider his options, and choose a plan that maximized his chances of survival.

Depression

A depressed mood or loss of interest in activities that were previously pleasurable for the person is basic to all depressive disorders. Like paranoia, depression is a symptom that cuts across a variety of types of people, from adjustment disorder through dysthymic personality disorders to a major depressive disorder (DSM IV, 1994). For simplicity's sake, the general features of depression will be described below.

Depression is characterized by a pattern of feelings and thoughts that include dejection, gloominess and joylessness, self-blame, self-doubt, inadequacy and low self-esteem, worrying, negativism, fault finding, pessimism, and guilt or remorse (DSM IV, 1994). There is a sense of hopelessness and helplessness in the person's view of the world (Seligman, 1991). These people have learned that nothing they do will affect their lives, so they assume that they can do nothing.

From the Transactional point of view, depressed people have a well-developed Compliant Child and a well-developed Critical Adult. They believe that they have no power to get things done, that they must go along with other more powerful people and that the authorities in their life are critical and judgmental. They are rarely outwardly rebellious, assuming it is too dangerous to face all-powerful others. They are motivated by the need for self-esteem and power, even though they do not believe they can have either. They treat authority figures with a moody deference, expecting them to be condemning.

Depression can range from a temporary state that has its origins in a recent loss in the person's life to a chronic condition that is due to a chemical imbalance and has been a lifelong problem for the person. Most depressive crises that law enforcement officers encounter are temporary in nature.

Adjustment Disorder with a Depressive Mood

An adjustment disorder is a temporary state. It is a reaction to a specific life circumstance and it lasts only as long as the circumstance exists in a person's life. It is a maladaptive reaction that interferes with the person's functioning in work, family, or social life. It is usually a reaction to the stressors of life and is characterized by:

1. Depressive moods. Depressive signs and symptoms include:

    a. Behavior such as: sleep disturbance (sleeping too much or too little); chronic fatigue; decreased effectiveness, activity, and/or productivity at work; withdrawal from usual social life; slowed speech and movement; tearfulness and crying.

    b. Emotions such as irritability and anger; lethargy.

    c.   Thinking characterized by decreased attention or con-
centration on things going on around them; pessimism
about the future; recurrent thoughts of suicide.

2.   Tearfulness and crying.

3.   A sense of hopelessness and helplessness.

An example of a depressed person in crisis is the 23-year-old male who barricaded himself in his parents' apartment after he broke up with his wife. He was afraid that he would never see his two-year-old daughter again. He had not eaten or slept for two days and nights. He had not been to work because he just did not have the energy. He had been drinking and he was threatening to kill himself, using the shotgun in the apartment. When the negotiator contacted him, he was crying, slowly stating, "I've ruined it all. If it hadn't been for my drinking, she wouldn't have left and taken Genny (the daughter). It's my fault."

Mood Disorder

People who have a mood disorder have a prolonged feeling of hopelessness that interferes with their functioning. In early hostage negotiation literature they were referred to as manic-depressives. Essentially, they exhibit severe forms of depression. Sometimes they alternate with markedly energetic phases in which they seem grandiose, hyperactive, and impulsive. They may have a history of encounters with both the legal system and the mental health system. They are usually treated with medication, but they frequently refuse to take it.

Managing Depressed Individuals

This process assumes, of course, that a relationship has been established with the hostage taker. In building a relationship with someone who is depressed, negotiators need to take a somewhat different approach than they do with paranoid individuals. Generally, they need to take a nurturing parent stance. The following are guidelines to establishing a working relationship with depressed people:

1.   Start off like a nurturing parent (Bradstreet, 1992)—show an attitude of caring, warmth, and concern.

2.   Start slowly and pick up the pace of the conversation over time—depressed individuals are frequently slowed cognitively. It takes them longer to process information. Give them time.

3. Ask open-ended questions and be ready for long pauses.

4. Be ready to be more direct in questioning if the person does not respond to open-ended questions.

5. Reflect their feelings—their depression is usually masking pain and anger. It is helpful to recognize these feelings, to show them that the negotiator can handle their real feelings.

6. Be reassuring as often as is necessary (Greenstone et al., in press)

7. Expect a slow response (Greenstone et al., in press; Lanceley, 1999)

8. Beware of a sudden improvement in mood (Greenstone et al., in press; Lanceley, 1999)

9. Be alert for the possibility of suicide by cop (Lanceley, 1999; DiVasto, 1997)

10. Discuss concrete, real-world issues rather than abstract principles (Lanceley, 1999)

11. Postpone suicidal actions (Lanceley, 1999)

Often the motivation of depressed people is to decrease pain they feel about a major loss in their life. The depression closes down their Adult, so they have trouble processing information about their situation or about their options. Negotiators may have to guide the person through an analysis of his or her situation, acting as a surrogate Adult. They may need to ask questions like, "Remember when your moodiness, your down feelings, began. Were there any changes in your life at that time? Big or small, any kinds of changes?" Such a question helps the person focus on losses he or she might not remember, because it causes too much pain. The questions help engage the individual's Adult.

Similarly, the negotiator may have to focus the depressed person's attention on past successes and happier times to engage her Adult. By saying things like, "Tell me about the first time you recall feeling good. What was different? What needs to change so you can feel good like that again?" Negotiators both remind the person that feelings change (they can change from bad to good as well as from good to bad) and help him or her focus on solving the problem of his or her pain in a different way. It is an effort to shift the focus from hurt Child to problem-solving Adult.

Depressed people who take hostages are generally looking for help. The hostage taking can be seen as a "cry for help." However, sometimes negotiators have to deal with a person who is depressed and wants to die but does not want to kill himself. Rather, he is setting up a situation that will force officers to do what he cannot. This is the "suicide by cop" incident (Van Zandt, 1993) and it will be discussed in detail in this chapter. Negotiators need to be aware of this possibility when dealing with a depressed person. They need to make a careful assessment of the individual to assess the risk of suicide by cop (see below).

Another general principle that negotiators need to be aware of when dealing with depressed individuals is that they experience sudden shifts in mood. When a person becomes calm and collected after a period of agitated depression, it may signal a decision to commit suicide. If the negotiator senses that there has been such a change, he or she needs to ask if the person is thinking about harming himself. Such a question will not suggest the act of suicide, rather it will tell the person it is all right to talk about the possibility. Because slowed thought processes are a characteristic of a depressed person, negotiators need to expect to take more time with the person than normal. Patience is required as the person thinks through questions, comments, and his answers.

When depressed, people have a pessimistic, moody outlook that is constricting. They think their problems are never going to end, that they will ruin the person's whole life, and that the problems are all their fault. As Seligman (1990) describes it, the depressed person feels that problems are permanent, persuasive, and his personal responsibility. Negotiators need to help evaluate each of these assumptions. Cognitive therapists (Beck, 1976; Ellis, 1979; Seligman, 1991) have suggested several systematic steps in changing individuals' thinking about their situation. They include:

1. Identification of relationship between beliefs and depression—It is helpful to educate people directly about the relationship between their beliefs and their feelings. For instance, people who hold the belief that their problems will go on forever tend to feel more hopeless than those who believe that there will be an end to them. By pointing out the connection between thoughts and feelings in a firm and gentle way, negotiators can help the depressed person see that he or she has some control of things.

2. Exploration of beliefs—In exploring the depressed person's beliefs, it is important to listen for his Critical Parent. Statements like, "I'm to blame for it all" suggest a stringent Parent that is being accepted without criticism. The negotiator needs to identify such statements, even when they are unspoken, and gather evidence that they are not true.

3. Challenge beliefs with evidence—By asking for proof of statements like "It is all my fault," the depressed person's Adult is mobilized. He begins to examine the validity of beliefs he had previously accepted at face value.

4. Identification of overgeneralization—Words like *always, forever, everything*, and *nothing* reflect overgeneralizations and either/or thinking on the part of the depressed person. Both of

these thinking styles need to be identified and then challenged in a gentle, supportive way (as a Nurturing and Competent Parent, Bradstreet [1992]).

5. Identification of either/or thinking.

6. Challenge of these situations—Challenging the generalizations and either/or thinking with questions like "How much of the time do you feel depressed?" "If you were to put a percentage on the amount of your life that has been ruined by this, what would it be?" "When was the last time you were not depressed?" and "What did you do to get out of your depression the last time?" engages the Adult and leads to an evaluation of the assumptions. They remind the person that his prior depression was temporary and suggests that this one will be temporary also.

Case Study: A Depressed Individual. The subject had called the dispatcher at 3:00 P.M., threatening to commit suicide. He had lost his job and could not make his house payment. He had to move in with his mother, who criticized his lack of work and he was pawning his belongings to buy drugs (amphetamines). He reported having a shotgun that he planned to use on himself. The dispatcher had the telephone number traced and got an address. She sent patrol officers, who were threatened with the shotgun when they approached the house. They withdrew, established a perimeter, and called for a supervisor. The supervisor asked for the crisis response team.

The tactical team took the patrol officers' places on the inner perimeter. Their job was to prevent the subject from leaving the house, to provide surveillance, and to prepare for an assault, if that became necessary, to prevent the subject's suicide. They were equipped with ballistic shields, flak vests, and helmets that would protect them from a shotgun if they had to move on the subject. They could assault without having to fire.

Negotiators gathered intelligence from the man's best friend. They learned that the subject had been employed as a chef at a local, upscale motel until two weeks before the incident. He lost his job because of his use of drugs at the workplace. His friend reported that the subject claimed that he had tried to stop using but that he "just got too down." Since losing his job, the subject had been lethargic and unmotivated. He had not been looking for a job, even though he was skilled. He had slept a lot, lost weight, and claimed that there was no point in trying; he'd just lose any other job that he might get. His chief activity was trying to buy drugs.

The incident that precipitated the crisis this day was that the subject and his friend had spent the morning looking for a dealer from whom they could buy "uppers." They had been unsuccessful. Upon returning home, the subject found a notice that his truck was going to be repossessed. He realized that he had missed an appointment for a job interview and he expected his mother to "give him s____ for not getting a job." His girlfriend had broken up with him the week before. He had told both the dispatcher and his friend that his life was ruined, "It ain't s ___" and, "it ain't getting any better."

Case Review. The subject had sustained recent losses typical of depressed individuals. He had lost his job, his girlfriend, his home, and was on the verge of losing his car. On top of this, there was some suggestion that he had been using amphetamines for some time to self-medicate: he may have been chronically depressed, using them as a method of coping.

His social support had become more and more limited. He was no longer in contact with friends from work or with his girlfriend. His mother was literally a critical parent and even his friend had spent the day telling him that he needed to give up drugs.

He had classic signs of depression. He was dejected and hopeless. He was withdrawn, sleeping more than usual, and not eating well. He was pessimistic, seeing little hope of getting a job. Consequently, he did not try to find work, making his pessimism self-fulfilling.

A quick assessment of his suicide potential suggested that he was a moderate risk. He had sustained recent losses. He had made threats and had a rudimentary plan involving a lethal method. However, the plan was not detailed or thought through. It involved threats to people who had the power to intervene (the police). Despite recently losing his job and apartment, he had a fairly successful history. He had been employed at the same job for three years before losing it. He was recognized as a talented chef. He had graduated from high school with above average grades. He had been gainfully employed most of the time after graduation. He had no record of prior contacts with police or mental health officials. Until recently, he had been socially active and he had dealt with his critical mother by accepting her and by not personalizing her criticisms.

Intervening with the Depressed Individual

With the depressed individual above, the negotiator started by introducing himself and asking how he could help. Then he quietly listened as the subject slowly said, "Man. I'm tired. I'm tired of trying. I can't get it together. Now they want to repossess my truck. My mom will have a fit when she finds that out. How can I get a job without a truck. I just don't know any more. I can't even score."

Negotiator: "Man. It sounds like everything's falling apart right now. Tell me what's been going on. If I understand it better, I can help you."

Subject: "Nothing's going right. I lost my job, my girl left and they want my truck. My mom's on my back. Nobody understands. Even my best friend doesn't want to hang around with me anymore."

Negotiator: "Could you tell me more? When did all this start? What was going on?"

Subject: "Well, I think it started about two weeks ago. That was when they let me go from work. Said I couldn't get there on time. (Getting more animated, energized) I was the best chef they had. They even said so. I could do the job. What was the big deal about being late?"

Negotiator: "I think I'd be mad if they fired me for not getting to work on time, especially if I was the best. It just doesn't seem fair."

Case Review. The negotiator used several of the principles discussed above. For instance, he: (1) matched the slowness of the subject's speech pattern during the first interaction; (2) reflected the subject's sense of loss of control (reflecting feelings); (3) phrased his or her words in a way that suggests that the subject's problems are temporary; (4) at the same time, the negotiator maintains an encouraging, Nurturing Parent stance, emphasizing his or her desire to help; (5) he or she also asks the subject to be more detailed to engage his Adult; (6) Reflecting the anger he sensed under the depression, the negotiator was using active listening to show understanding and support; (7) note that he reinforced the message that the subject was the best chef, building self-esteem on what the person actually said.

Challenging Beliefs. After several rounds of showing understanding and support, of being a nurturing parent and reassuring the subject about his safety, of using active listening to facilitate ventilation and validation, the negotiator can challenge the person's beliefs more directly. In the case above, he explained:

"You know, a lot of what you are going through is the usual result of a lot of losses, all at the same time. Most people, including what I hear from you, feel depressed about their losses. Unfortunately, the depression causes them to think funny and the funny thinking gets them stuck in the depression. When I hear you say things like, 'It's never going to get better,' I hear the funny thinking of depression. You don't really know that it's not going to get better. It just feels like it is going on forever, sometimes. In fact, you already told me that there have been times since losing your job that you felt better than at other times. You have experienced changes in the way you feel. It is your telling yourself that it will never get better that gets you down now. And, you know what, you don't have to believe the funny thinking of depression. How else do you think that depression makes you think funny?"

Such a statement by the negotiator illustrates several things. It normalizes the person's experiences. It says that almost everyone gets depressed. It makes the connection between the person's feelings and his beliefs, pointing out that he can control his thoughts, thereby controlling his feelings. It illustrates the distortion in the person's sense of permanence and it offers evidence from the person's own experience that counters the assumptions. It challenges overgeneralization and either/or thinking. It also focuses the subject on the task of finding new ways that his thinking is affected by the depression. This distracts him from a critical examination of the ideas presented to him.

Subject: "Yeah man, you're right. I've felt bad for a while and then I've felt good for a while. And, sometimes it was without being f____'d on drugs. I guess the feelings do come and go. I might feel better again. I guess another thing I've been telling myself is that nobody cares. My uncle has asked about getting together a lot in the last two weeks, but I haven't wanted to. It seems like he cares, even though it hasn't felt like it."

Negotiator: "Yeah man. That idea nobody cares is another funny way that depression screws you up. In fact, lots of people care. Your uncle has tried to get with you. The dispatcher was concerned enough to call us and I am here with you. We all care. In a funny way, even your mother cares when she's on your back. If she didn't care, she wouldn't bother to jump your case."

After several rounds of reassurance and re-evaluating, the subject agreed that he had skills he could use to get a job, that the things he was experiencing were temporary, that going to a doctor for a prescription would be less expensive and perhaps more effective than self-medicating by using drugs and that he would come out and talk with his uncle, who had been brought to the scene and who agreed to mediate between the subject and his mother. He agreed to a referral to the local mental health clinic for follow-up. He agreed to give up the shotgun, until he and his doctor agreed that he was emotionally capable of managing it again. He agreed to call his uncle, whom he felt cared for him, if he got desperate and confused in the future. His uncle, who was a deputy sheriff in the county, agreed to give him a pager number to which the uncle responded 24 hours a day.

Alcohol Dependence and Abuse

It is essential that negotiators stay alert to the possibility of alcohol and alcohol dependency in hostage/crisis incidents, because subjects who are involved in hostage/crisis incidents often have drinking problems. Research has found that of the 4,988 subjects on the HOBAS database, 28.4 percent had a history of alcohol abuse and 28.6 percent were intoxicated at the time of the incident. In addition, Feldman (in press) found that of the 1,544 subjects involved in the incidents he tracked, 6.43 percent had a primary psychiatric diagnosis of alcohol intoxication and 33.3 percent of the 63 subjects who had a secondary diagnosis were diagnosed as alcohol abusers/dependents.

Additionally, negotiators need to be aware of the use and/or presence of alcohol in an incident because alcohol has been shown to increase the risk of both suicide and violence. In large studies, alcohol has been more predictive of violent acting-out than mental illness. DSM-IV (1994) defines alcohol dependence in much the same way that it defines dependence on other substances, including:

1. Evidence of having developed a tolerance to the effects of alcohol that may include having to drink more and more to achieve the same effect.

2. Evidence of withdrawal symptoms when the person stops drinking that may include two or more of the following: autonomic hyperactivity (sweating, or elevated pulse rate), increase in hand tremors, insomnia, nausea and vomiting, transient hallucinations or illusions, psychomotor agitation, anxiety, and grand mal seizures.

Acute alcohol intoxication, or the use of alcohol during the incident, may create several problems for the negotiators. It may impair the subject's thinking and judgment, increase aggression, decrease coordination, and impair memory: all effects that make negotiations difficult. The most important impact of acute intoxication is the impairment of thinking and emotion that results. Negotiators need to plan for these. Slatkin (2000) suggests the following for managing acute intoxication:

1. Discourage drinking during the incident but do not try to be a counselor.

2. Never negotiate for alcohol.

3. Speak slowly to allow the subject time to understand.

4. Repeat words.

5. Use simple, brief sentences.

6. Avoid accusations.

7. Give the subject the illusion of choice.

8. Use indirect suggestions.

9. Allow ventilation, expecting anger.

10. Be alert to increased risk of suicide.

In addition to alcohol, other substances that should concern negotiators because of their effects are: amphetamines, caffeine, cocaine, crack cocaine, DMT, ephedrine, ketamine, LSD, Ecstasy, methamphetamine, morning glory seeds, PCP, and phenylpropanolamine. When confronted with substance users/abusers, negotiators need to:

1. Obtain expert consultation.

2. Decide whether to encourage discontinuance of the substance during the incident on the basis of the anticipated effects of that discontinuance on the person's emotional, mental, and behavioral reaction.

3. Try to get agreement from the subject on securing any weapons while negotiations are going on, to ensure everyone's safety.

4. Be aware of the effects of withdrawal or intoxication during the incident and have a plan developed with tactical for dealing with the effects of withdrawals, should it be necessary.

5. Stay alert to the increased risk of suicide/homicide when there is substance abuse, and plan accordingly.

Substance Dependence/Abuse

The characteristic feature of substance dependence is the continued use of the substance in spite of clear evidence that it is causing problems for the subject. It will show up as cravings for the substance, the development of tolerance, and withdrawal symptoms (DSM-IV, 1994). Changes in thinking, feelings, and behavior occur both when the person is intoxicated and when he or she is withdrawing from the drug. The degree of impairment depends on the specific substance being used. Negotiators are well-advised to become familiar with the effects of intoxication and withdrawal from the major categories of dependence-inducing drugs. Two resources for this information are the *Diagnostic and Statistical Manual*, Fourth Edition (DSM-IV), chapter on Substance-Related Disorders; and Worledge et al. (1997), *The Negotiator's Guide to Psychoactive Drugs*, published by the Critical Incident Response Group—Crisis Management Unit of the FBI.

Substance abuse is the repeated use of the substance in spite of the recurring problems it generates for the person. However, tolerance, withdrawals, and compulsive use of the substance are not present when the person stops using the substance (DSM-IV, 1994). The subject can stop, he or she just does not want to. The person may be intoxicated at work, at home, or other places where he or she has responsibilities that he or she cannot perform because of the intoxication. The intoxicated person may repeatedly place him or herself or others in danger while he or she is intoxicated. Many domestic incidents that negotiators must deal with are the result of substance abuse.

Summary

The majority of the people negotiators encounter are emotionally disturbed. Because of their problems, they have unique ways of behaving, feeling, and thinking. Through a careful analysis of the type of person negotiators are dealing with, appropriate tactics can be developed, pitfalls can be avoided, and the chances of success can be enhanced. The analysis of the personality structure of the hostage taker is usually the domain of the Mental Health Consultant (MHC) on the negotiating team. However, in the absence of the MHC, it is essential for negotiators to have a working knowledge of this area. Additionally, when the MHC is present, negotiators will more easily understand and use the advice of the MHC at the scene.

References

American Heritage Dictionary (1980). New York, NY: Houghton Mifflin Company.

American Psychiatric Association (1994). *Diagnostic and Statistical Manual*, Fourth Edition. Washington, DC: APA.

Austin Police Department (1991). "Communication Skills." Presented at SAPD Basic Hostage Negotiations School. San Antonio, TX (September).

Bachman, R. (1999). "Epidemiology of Intimate Partner Violence and Other Family Violence Involving Adults." In Ammerman, R.T. and M. Hersen (eds.), *Assessment of Family Violence: A Clinical and Legal Sourcebook*. New York, NY: John Wiley and Sons.

Beck, A.T. (1976). *Cognitive Therapies and the Emotional Disorders*. New York, NY: New American Library.

Borum, R. and Strentz, T. (1992). "The Borderline Personality: Negotiation Strategies." *FBI Law Enforcement Bulletin* 61(8):6-10.

Butler, W.M., H. Leitenberg, and G.D. Fuselier (1993). "The Use of Mental Health Professional Consultants to Police Hostage Negotiation Teams." *Behavioral Science and the Law* 11:213-221.

Bradstreet, R. (1992). "Communications: Getting on the Right Wavelength." Presented at SAPD Basic Hostage Negotiations School. San Antonio, TX (September).

Call, J. (1999). "The Hostage Triad: Takers, Victims, and Negotiators." In H. Hall (ed.), *Lethal Violence: A Sourcebook on Fatal Domestic, Acquaintance and Stranger Violence*. Boca Raton, FL: CRC Press.

DiVasto, P. (1997). "Suicide: Assessment and Intervention." Paper presented at the annual Hostage Negotiation Seminar/Competition, San Marcos, TX (July).

Dutton, D.G. (1995). *The Domestic Assault of Women*. Vancouver, BC: UBC Press.

Ellis, A. (1979). *Reason and Emotion in Psychotherapy*. New York, NY: Stuart.

Everly, G. (1989). *A Clinical Guide to the Treatment of the Human Stress Response*. New York, NY: Plenum Press.

FBI (1985). "Hostage Negotiation Seminar." Quantico, VA: FBI Academy.

Feldman, T.B. (2001). "Characteristics of Hostage and Barricaded Incidents: Implications for Negotiation Strategies and Training." *International Journal of Police Negotiations and Crisis Management* Volume 1, No. 1, Spring 2001.

Fuselier, G.D. (1981). "A Practical Overview of Hostage Negotiations." *FBI Law Enforcement Bulletin* 50(6):1-11.

Gacono, C. (1997). "The Clinical and Forensic Use of the Hare Psychology Checklist—Revised." Seminar at FCI Bastrop, Texas (May).

Greenstone, J.G, D.S. Kosson, and C.B. Gacono (in press). "Psychopathy and Hostage Negotiations: Some Preliminary Thoughts and Findings." In C.B. Gacono (ed.), *Clinical and Forensic Assessment of Psychopathy: A Practitioners Guide*. Mahwah, NJ: Lawrence Erlbaum Associates, Publishers.

Hare, R.D. and L.M. McPherson (1984). "Violent and Aggressive Behavior by Criminal Psychopaths." *International Journal of Law and Psychiatry* 7:35-50.

Head, W.B. (1990). "The History Response: An Examination of the U.S. Law Enforcement Practices Concerning Hostage Incidents." Doctoral Dissertation, State University of New York at Albany. *Dissertation Abstracts International* 50:4111A.

Kolb, L.C. (1982). *Modern Clinical Psychiatry*. Philadelphia, PA: W.B. Saunders Company.

Lanceley, F. (1999). *On-Scene Guide for Crisis Negotiators*. Boca Raton, FL: CRC Press.

McMains, M.J. and W. Mullins (1998). "The Warrior Mentality: Identifying and Intervening with 'At Risk' Officers." Paper presented at FBI Conference on Domestic Violence by Police Officers, Quantico, VA.

Millon, T. (1996). *Disorders of Personality: DSM-IV and Beyond*. New York, NY: John Wiley and Sons.

Mohandie, K. (2005). "Stalking and Crisis Negotiations." Presented at: New England Hostage Negotiations Seminar. Martha's Vineyard, MA (April).

Mohandie, K. and J.E. Duffy (1999). "Understanding Subjects with Paranoid Schizophrenia." *FBI Law Enforcement Bulletin* 68(12).

Porier, J.G. (1999). "Violence in the Family." In H.V. Hall (ed.), *Lethal Violence: A Sourcebook on Fatal Domestic, Acquaintance, and Stranger Violence*. Boca Raton, FL: CRC Press.

Seligman, M.E.P. (1990). *Learned Optimism: How to Change Your Mind and Your Life*. New York, NY: Pocket Books.

Slatkin, A.A. (2000). "Negotiating Skills: Dealing with an Alcohol Impaired Hostage Taker or Barricaded Subject." *Law and Order* 48(4):123-126.

Strentz, T. (1985). "A Statistical Analysis of American Hostage Situations." Unpublished manuscript. Quantico, VA: FBI Academy.

Sullivan, H.S. (1954a). *The Interpersonal Theory of Psychiatry*. New York, NY: W.W. Norton and Company.

———— (1954b). *The Psychiatric Interview*. New York, NY: W.W. Norton and Company.

Van Zandt, C.R. (1993). "Suicide by Cop." *The Police Chief* 60(7):24-27.

Walker, L.E. (1979). *The Battered Woman*. New York: Harper and Row.

Wilson, M. and M. Daly (1993). "Spousal Homicide Risk and Estrangement. " *Violence and Victims* 8:3-16.

Worledge, J., T.J. Kane, and G.B. Saathoff (1997). *The Negotiator's Guide to Psychoactive Drugs*. Quantico, VA: Critical Incident Management Group, Crisis Management Unit, Federal Bureau of Investigation.

Discussion Questions

1. In dealing with a person who is depressed, suicide is always a concern. What are some of the obvious and subtle signs you would look for that would suggest that one of your classmates is thinking about killing himself?

2. Suicidal persons frequently have experienced recent losses to which they do not know how to respond. Why would a promotion at work generate suicidal ideas in a person?

3. How would you determine whether a person's complaint that his neighbors are harassing him is delusional or real?

4. You are negotiating with a person experiencing mood fluctuations. The hostage taker alternates between periods of severe depression and extreme elation. When are you most likely to make negotiating progress? When is the probability the greatest that this person will commit suicide?

5. Joe is a barricaded subject and is extremely depressed, feeling helpless and hopeless. He recently lost his job and does not think he can support his family. He relates to you that his wife recently left him and took his two children with her. After talking with Joe for a time, you discover that nothing matters as much in his life as his family. What are five positives about his family life you could get Joe to focus on to ease his depression and to instill hope?

6. What kind of statements could you make to avoid being discounted by a borderline hostage taker as just another cop?

7. Give specific examples of Bradstreet's suggestions for dealing with an antisocial hostage taker.

8. How could a hostage negotiator get a hostage taker to challenge the assumptions that the pain will last forever and that loss is everything?

9. Thomas is the classic "suicide by cop." He has barricaded himself inside his house and seems determined to make the police kill him. You discover that he recently lost his job and has flunked out of college. He has a history of conflicts with authorities. Part of the reason he flunked out of college was that he could not comply with the requirements of his professors. In high school, he had frequent disciplinary problems, usually involving fights with other students. What could you say to Thomas to prevent his impending death? What tactical issues do you need to consider? Why?

10. You are talking with Steven, who is extremely depressed about a multitude of negative aspects in his life. You seem to be making progress when, out of the blue, Steven interrupts you and gives you a "verbal will." What would you do at this point?

Negotiating with Suicidal Persons

8

Learning Objectives

1. Know the definition and the common characteristics of suicide.

2. Explain the six steps of suicide intervention recommended by Living Works.

3. Be able to assess suicide threat using the Surgeon General's criteria.

4. Explain the factors suggesting that negotiators may be dealing with suicide by cop.

5. Understand how to intervene in a suicide by cop incident.

6. Explain the factors that may influence incidents of negotiating with "suicide bombers."

7. Explain the difference between altruistic suicide and the type of suicidal individuals negotiators normally deal with.

8. Understand the negotiating techniques that may be helpful in dealing with a "suicide bomber."

He was a 78 year-old, retired physician who had lost his wife of 46 years to cancer six months earlier. His daughter came to visit after not hearing from him for two weeks and found him living in squalor. She asked him to come home with her and he refused, stating that, "It doesn't matter. I will be with Jean (his deceased wife) soon." The daughter did not know how to interpret his statement, thinking initially that he was saying that he was physically ill. When she called the next day, he sounded "down" and refused to let her come over stating that he had two things to do and that she needed to check the envelope he was leaving on his dining room table. She called the police to make a welfare check. The patrol officer responding to the call got no response when he knocked on the door. He looked through the window and saw the man sitting in a chair with a gun and a bottle of pills in his hands. When the subject saw the officer, he pointed the gun in the officer's direction and told him to get away from his door. The officer withdrew and called the Crisis Response Team. Negotiators interviewed the man's daughter and found out that he had a history of depression which he masked by self-medicating, usually using stimulants. His father had committed suicide when he was in medical school but he had never talked about it with family members. He talked about supporting the idea of assisted suicide for people who had no hope of recovery from terminal medical conditions and did not want to be a burden to their families. He had retired from medicine because he had diabetes and was losing his eyesight. She reported a good relationship with her father over the years and that she had two children who loved to spend time with "Pops." He had two good friends who were still practicing medicine, one of whom was his family physician. Until recently, they had gotten together for coffee several times a week. He had been a strict Catholic, attending Mass regularly until his wife died. Since then, he had become more withdrawn.

It is not uncommon for negotiators to manage incidents like the one above. In fact, some statistics suggest that up to 50 percent of calls managed by crisis response teams are people who are threatening suicide. Therefore, it is important that negotiators understand what leads people to plan to take their own lives. This chapter will focus on the definition of suicide, the characteristics of suicidal people, assessing the risk of suicide and interventions that negotiators can use to reduce the chance that a person will complete the suicidal act. It should be clear from the start that negotiators cannot expect to prevent every person they encounter from committing suicide. However, the more negotiators know, the more they can prevent.

Hogewood (2005) reported that the 2002 American Association of Suicidology statistics, which are usually several years behind, show that in the United States there were 31,655 reported suicides that year. Of those statistics, 25,409 were male, 6,246 were female. Basically, one person in the United States killed themselves every 16.6 minutes; 86.7 deaths per day. The elderly (65+), while making up 12.2 percent of the population, accounted for 17.5 percent of the suicides. Young people (15 to 24 years of age) accounted for 12.7 percent of the suicides, while making up 14.1 percent of the total population. Other than the elderly, the most at-risk group are those 35 to 54 years of age, with 15+ percent per 1,000,000. Suicide is the eleventh leading cause of death in the United States. Homicide is fourteenth. Suicide attempts, at 745,000 per year, are a frequent call-out for many crisis response teams.

Suicidal Persons

In 1999, the Surgeon General of the United States declared suicide a serious public health problem and announced a blueprint for addressing the problem that included awareness, intervention, and methodology. He pointed out that 85 Americans die from suicide daily. Suicide rates are higher than homicide and automobile accidents together. For every completed suicide there are 100 attempts that require attention from first responders, emergency room personnel, the medical community and the mental health community.

The most recent statistics set the suicide rate in America at 11.6 per 100,000. HOBAS shows that 354 of the 4,988 subjects involved in critical incidents either killed themselves or set up "suicide by cop."

Though not a separate diagnostic category (DSM-IV, 1994), suicidal persons are frequently the responsibility of negotiators. Major departments across the country have reported that 16 percent of the cases handled by their negotiation teams were high-risk suicide attempts. That is, they were suicide attempts that posed a threat to others (McMains, 1988). Most departments handle almost as many suicide attempts as hostage incidents. Therefore, it is important for negotiators to understand and be able to deal with the suicidal person.

Definition and Characteristics

Schneidman (1985) has defined suicide as a "conscious act of self-induced annihilation in an individual who defines suicide as the best possible solution to a defined problem." There are two important points about this definition: (1) suicide is a conscious act and (2) it is a solution. The former implies that the person decided to end his life, while the latter suggests that it is a decision that has a goal—to end suffering. If it is true that suicide is a conscious act, it is also true that the person can change their mind and live. If it is a solution to a problem, it implies that there are other solutions and that the goal of suicide intervention is to help the person decide on another solution to his life problems.

Schneidman (1985) points out that all suicides (suicidal people) have several things in common that are helpful if negotiators understand them:

1. Common stressors—All suicidal people have frustrated psychological needs. They frequently have recent losses that are painful for them. They may have lost a job, a relationship, status, or even their health. Regardless of the nature of the loss, it is essential for the negotiator to understand that the person sees the loss as unbearable.

2. Common stimulus—unendurable psychological pain. The losses lead to psychological pain that the individuals think is unendurable. They do not believe that they can or want to live with the pain.

3. Common purposes—a solution to the problem of pain. Suicide is seen as a solution to the problem of pain. They think it is better to cease to exist than to live with the pain.

4. Common goals—cessation of consciousness and relief of ambivalence. Ambivalence involves the wish to live but the belief that to live means to continue to suffer. Death is seen as an end to the suffering and the mixed and confusing feelings.

5. Common feelings—hopelessness/helplessness; aloneness; fear of losing control.

6. Common thinking style—constricted, focused on pain and either/or, either live with pain or die and end it. People can only see these two options.

7. Common interpersonal goals—manipulation and control of others, expression of anger, and/or escape from interpersonal distress. Frequently, the precipitating event is the loss or threatened loss of a significant interpersonal relationship through separation, divorce, or death. Suicide is a way of controlling the other person and coercing him or her into feeling guilty or changing his mind.

8. Common history—prior suicide attempts, lifelong pattern of coping through escape, and low frustration tolerance.

Case Study Revisited: The case study above illustrates these characteristics. Though a competent professional, the man had recently lost his wife (stressor) on whom he had learn to depend over the years. In addition, he had lost his profession and health. These losses generated an overwhelming pain and fear of being alone (stimulus). He had a sense of helplessness and hopelessness about ever replacing the losses (common feelings). He wanted the pain to stop (common goal) but could not imagine any way for the pain to end other than to die (constricted/either-or thinking).

Managing Suicidal Individuals

Living Works (1999), a suicide intervention training program, suggests that people who intervene in suicides need to take six steps that are helpful for the negotiator to keep in mind:

1. Engage the person who you suspect is suicidal—Explore his or her world from his or her perspective (use active listening). Give them a sense of support and acceptance and look for signs that suicide may be on their minds, including recent losses, blue mood, giving away prized possessions, withdrawal from meaningful activities, or people that were meaningful in the past, changes in appetite, sleep patterns, or health.

2. Identify the person's thoughts of suicide, if they exist—to identify the risk of the subject committing suicide, ask directly "Are you thinking about killing yourself?"

3. Inquire about the reasons suicide is being considered, estimate what stress he or she is thinking about, how the losses are connected with his or her suicidal plan, whether he or she is feeling helpless and hopeless, how alone does he or she feel, and how acceptable suicide is as a solution.

4. Estimate the risk—Assess the seriousness of the threat, the risk factors, the protective factors, and the person's potential for violence. Explore the person's resources and his or her ways of dealing with prior stresses or losses. Get a clear picture of the person's strengths and weaknesses. Get the details of the plan, especially the time frame, because this will dictate how fast and what types of intervention are necessary.

5. Contract with the individual to intervene, so as to reduce the risk of suicide.

Identifying the risk means nothing more that stopping, looking, and listening to the subject. Research has shown that most people communicate their intention to commit suicide. Suicide risk can be identified, if negotiators are looking for the possibility. Negotiators can look for several warning signs, including: depression, apathy, decreases in productivity, flat affect, slowed speech, withdrawal from friends and family, loss of interest in hobbies, giving away possessions, feelings of worthlessness, loneliness, sadness, hopelessness, or helplessness.

To establish rapport, both active listening and a straightforward, caring approach to the person are important. Negotiators need to communicate their caring and concern for the person—they need to be a nurturing parent, providing the person with a lot of face-affirming messages. Being judgmental about the person's suicide threat is counterproductive. Statements like, "I hear your pain, _____. I know you can always take your life, if you really want to. I just would like a chance to help you explore all your choices before you make any permanent decisions," show acceptance of the person while at the same time suggesting the choices he or she has not thought about. They communicate caring and concern.

Suicidal people frequently believe that they are the only one who has experienced or can understand the kind of pain they are going through. However, a clear reflection of their pain on the part of the negotiator can help them begin to see that others can understand them, thus reducing their sense of isolation. Statements such as, "Ed, it sounds to me like you are really hurting since your wife left. In fact, it sounds like you can hardly stand the pain." This type of statement lets the person know the negotiator can understand not only the person's loss but how desperate the person really is. Such a depth of understanding establishes the negotiator as an ally and friend, helping to reduce loneliness.

After the subject begins to be more open with the negotiator, after he describes his loss and after the relationship begins to build, it is important to assess the seriousness of the individual's threat. To do this, the negotiator needs to ask a transitional question that opens up the topic of suicide, gives the person permission to talk openly about his thoughts and feelings, and shows the person that the negotiator is not going to criticize or judge him. The negotiator might say something like, "You know when people are as down and as hurting as you are, they will often think about hurting or killing themselves. I wonder if you've thought about hurting yourself or committing suicide."

Estimating Suicide Potential

The Surgeon General's call for action identified 14 risk factors and seven protective factors. The risk factors are important because they help the negotiator anticipate the seriousness of the subject's threat and to structure intervention planning. For instance, the speed with which the intervention needs to be made depends on the time frame of the subject's plan. The risk factors are:

1. Previous suicide attempts

2. Mental disorders—particularly mood disorders

3. Alcohol and substance abuse disorders

4. Family history of suicide

5. Hopelessness

6. Impulsive/aggressive tendencies

7. Barriers to treatment access

8. Relational, social, work, or financial loss

9. Physical illness

10. Availability of lethal method—guns

11. Unwilling to seek help because of stigma

12. Influence of significant people who have committed sui-cide—celebrities, peers, family members, etc.

13. Cultural and religious beliefs—belief that suicide is a solution

14. Local occurrences of suicide

15. Isolation

Protective factors include:

1. Effective and appropriate clinical care for mental, physical, or substance abuse

2. Easy access to a variety of interventions

3. Restricted access to lethal methods

4. Family and community support

5. Ongoing relationship with medical or mental health care provider

6. Learned skills in problem-solving, conflict resolution, and non-violent resolution of disputes

7. Cultural and religious beliefs that discourage suicide as a way of coping with problems

The negotiator can ask about any prior suicide attempts and the details of the suicide plan (including time, place, and method). People who have made prior attempts at suicide even once are a higher risk than the person for whom this is the first attempt. Likewise, people who have a detailed plan that includes a lethal weapon and an isolated place are more serious than are people who have had vague thoughts of dying sometime. For instance, one barricaded subject with whom one of the authors dealt had lost his job, his reputation, and his marriage. His ex-wife told him she was taking their eight-year-old daughter and moving out of state. He knew that his life was over. The only person he still cared for was leaving. He developed a plan to leave his daughter his few valuables, to get drunk while he was alone in his apartment and to shoot himself in the head. He was going to do it after his daughter's last weekend visit. He was going to leave his wife a note, commenting on how she had taken from him the last thing that made his life meaningful. His plan was detailed and fatal. He posed a more serious risk than the teenager who "would just like to die" after an argument with her parents but had no plan for dying in mind.

In addition to the risk factors, the protection factors need to be explored by the negotiator, because they frequently provide information the negotiator needs for an effective intervention. A review of the protective factors gives the negotiator valuable information about the individual's resources, which can be used to develop an intervention plan. These issues need to be systematically explored by the negotiator because the constricted problem-solving ability of the suicidal person leads to his or her needing to be reminded that they do have resources on which to draw, even though they have not thought about them. For instance, an 18-year-old man was barricaded, drinking, and threatening himself with a gun because of the recent loss of a relationship. He was asked about his family and it was discovered that, over his parents' objections, he had moved in with the girl who had left him. He was working construction and had no health benefits, so even though he knew he needed help, he did not think he could afford it. He reported having been actively involved in his church, which did not approve of suicide, but that he had stopped going to church when he moved in with the girl. He was reminded/asked about the concern of his family, the way his religion views suicide, and that he had a family physician or counselor on whom he has counted in the past. In addition, it can be pointed out to him that there are effective ways of coping with loss that he may not have thought about—such as short-term counseling, which is available inexpensively through community clinics. Finally, it could be pointed out that alcohol is a depressant and makes him feel even worse, and there are programs to help people with the drinking that might offer a face-saving option for him. The systematic exploration and use of the protection factors will help negotiators intervene.

Case Study Revisited: Assessing Suicide Potential. In dealing with the barricaded subject described above, an assessment of his suicide potential was made. Using the criteria discussed above, he was assessed to have a high potential for suicide. His daughter reported the statements he made about joining his wife soon and his instructions to her to be sure and check the instructions he had left in the envelope. He clearly had the intent. His plan involved a deadly method, firearms and barbiturates that he had available. He had cut himself off from his social support. He endorsed a set of beliefs that justified assisted suicide

In addition, the protective factors were assessed. He had no access to care because he was unwilling to go to a mental health professional because of the embarrassment of being a highly regarded professional who could not care for himself. He had cut himself off from his usual health care provider and family. Though his religious beliefs may have been protective, he had quit going to Mass. He needed to get back in touch with his resources.

It is helpful for negotiators to keep a suicide assessment checklist, such as the one in Figure 8.1, to remind them of the information they need. Not only does such an assessment give them a way of keeping track of important information, it frequently helps focus the suicidal person's attention on

Figure 8.1
Suicide Potential Checklist

Suicide Checklist		
Previous Suicide Attempts	1 2 3 4 5 6 7 8 9	Notes
Suicide Plan	serious moderate gesture	_____
Lethality of Attempts	threat pills mutilation gun	_____
Lifestyle	Stable 1__2__3__4__5 Unstable	_____
Alcohol/Drug Use	1 2 3 4 5 6 7 8 9	_____
Hostility	Rage 5__4__3__2__1 Calm	_____
Personality Integration	Normal Character Neurotic Psychotic	_____
Past Psychiatric HX	Poor 5__4__3__2__1 Good	_____
Coping Abilities	Good 1__2__3__4__5 Poor	_____
Daily Activities	1 2 3 4 5 6 7 8 9	_____
Daily Functioning	Unsuccessful 5__4__3__2__1 Successful	_____
Family Life	Intimate, caring 1__2__3__4__5 Chaotic	_____
Social Life	Withdrawn 5__4__3__2__1 Active	_____
Depression	Mild Moderate Severe	_____
Anxiety	Severe Moderate Mild	_____

Strategies
1. BUILD RAPPORT
   Introduce self and ask how you can help
   Let them know that you take their threat seriously
   Listen attentively and communicate understanding
   Reflect feelings and do not argue with them about how they feel
   Do not hesitate to talk to person about suicidal plan
   Expect them to need to be reassured about your sincerity
   Offer food, drink, candy, etc. (not alcohol)
2. MAKE ENVIRONMENT SAFE
   Could you put the _____ down for now.
3. EVALUATE SUICIDE POTENTIAL (see above)
4. TRY TO GET MORE INFORMATION ABOUT PROBLEM
   Tell me what's been going on.
5. SUPPORT THE LIFE-SEEKING PART OF THE PERSON
   I know you are hurting but part of you wants to see hope
   It can get better, let's see what we can figure out.
6. FOCUS ON ONE PROBLEM AT A TIME, BEGINNING WITH THE MAIN ONE
7. EXPLORE ALTERNATIVES THE PERSON HAS TRIED TO SOLVE PROBLEMS AND OFFER OTHERS
8. TRY TO GET A NON-SUICIDE CONTRACT
9. PLAN A CONCRETE COURSE OF ACTION, INCLUDING CONTACT WITH FRIENDS AND FAMILY
10. IMMEDIATE REFERRAL TO HOSPITAL, MHMR, OR DOCTOR.
11. DEBRIEF FAMILY
12. Foster HOPE:
   Persistence
   Pervasiveness
   Personal

Source: San Antonio Police Department. Reprinted with permission.

times in the past when things were better or on similar situations the person dealt with effectively. As a checklist, it is a guide to the information that negotiators and mental health professionals need to keep in mind in estimating the person's degree of risk. It is not a systematic test of suicide potential.

Intervention

Intervention involves helping the suicidal subject find hope; helping him or her move from a focus on the past and its losses and failures, through the here and now, to look to the future, seeing options he or she does not see. It involves working toward a plan or contract with the subject that reduces the threat to life and encourages his or her desire to live. To instill hope, the negotiator needs to get the suicidal person to challenge two ideas: (1) the pain will last forever, and (2) the loss is everything. According to Seligman (1991), it is these dimensions of permanence and persuasiveness that lead to hopelessness and helplessness.

In helping people challenge their belief that the pain will last forever, their past can be used. If they have had depressive episodes in the past, it is helpful to remind them that they have been through pain before and it got better; it will get better again. Frequently, some time has already elapsed since the person's losses or frustrations. It is rare that someone is equally depressed that entire time. Their attention can be drawn to the fact that they have had times when they felt better, even since their loss. It helps them realize that feelings do change. Even the smallest change for the better can be reinforced by the negotiator.

Factual information, such as "90 percent of people get depressed and it lasts six to eight weeks," is helpful to introduce into the negotiations after a good relationship is established. Such information helps the person realize that his or her condition is temporary.

During the assessment, the negotiator can obtain information about the person's activities, family, and friends, which is helpful in challenging the assumption that the loss has ruined his whole life. Frequently, it is the social withdrawal that has made him feel that the loss has affected everything. By asking how often he has contacted his friends and family about his problems or what they think about his problem, he can be reminded that there are others in his life. It also suggests that he can reach out. For instance, one suicidal person was convinced to give life another try when the negotiator reminded him of how close he had been to his niece and how difficult it was going to be for her to understand why her favorite uncle had left her.

Additionally, Living Works (1999) has suggested that the following are components of a good intervention with people who are suicidal:

1. The plan needs to be specific—What is going to be done about the subject's needs, when it is going to be done, how it is going to happen, and when it is going to happen; all have to be clearly and specifically spelled out for them. People who are suicidal are frequently literal and need a step-by-step plan in order to feel that there is hope for them.

2. The plan needs limited objectives—It is not likely to solve all the person's problems, nor does it need to. The intervention just needs to make a start on addressing the person's concerns and showing him or her that there is help available and hope for the future.

3. The plan needs the commitment of the subject—It is important for the subject to commit to trying the plan. It does no good to develop a plan the person does not intend to stick with. Asking the person to repeat the plan and to discuss any reservations they might have about it helps the negotiator check on the degree to which the subject understands and is committed to the plan.

4. The plan needs to include crisis support in the event the plan cannot be carried out by the subject.

5. The plan needs to provide for a suicide-safe environment.

Lanceley (1999) suggests the following guidelines for managing suicidal individuals:

1. Explore feelings through active listening.

2. Let the person express anger.

3. Focus on the cause of the problem.

4. Talk openly about the reality of death.

5. Have person describe suicide as fantasized and disrupt plan.

6. Explore what the subject still finds meaningful in life.

7. Stall for time.

8. Put the plan into perspective by exploring how well it achieves its purpose.

9. Help him choose an alternative that achieves his purpose.

Case Study Revisited: After gathering enough intelligence to make an educated guess about the doctor's risk, negotiators developed a plan that focused on allowing him to talk about his losses, refining the assessed risk, reinforcing past successes and coping skills, possibly using the grandchildren as "hooks," and focusing him on the resources he had trusted in the past (his physician friends). Negotiators contacted the doctor, using the telephone in his house. He answered and the negotiator introduced himself as a negotiator with the police department and that they were asked to check on him by his daughter who was worried that she could not contact him. He told the negotiator to "leave me alone," but did not hang up. The fact that he answered was considered a good initial sign. His thinking was slowed and his speech was slurred. Therefore, the negotiator immediately stated that he understood that he had lost his wife recently and that it must be hard without her. The doctor responded that the negotiator had no idea how hard. The negotiator took advantage of the opening and said, "You are right, I don't know how hard it is for you. Tell me what you miss about your wife." He then paused to let the doctor respond. The doctor recounted several stories in which his wife had taken care of things over the years, including the children, the finances, their social schedule, and the house. He stated that he was at a loss without her. He could not seem to get organized. The negotiator responded that the doctor seemed at a loss without his wife. The doctor said, "That's it. I can't function without her. I am looking at the bills stack up and I don't know where to start on them." The negotiator noticed a slight increase in the man's rate of speech. However, still being concerned about the slurred speech, he said, "You seem to be pretty down. It has been my experience that when people are down after recent losses, they sometimes think about killing themselves. I wonder if that is what is on your mind, today?" The doctor responded with a quiet, "yes" and a sigh. Again taking advantage of what he thought was his opening, the negotiator followed up with, "How have you thought about doing it?" The doctor said, yes, he was going to overdose on the barbiturates he had in the house because he did not want his family to see him all messed up if he shot himself. The negotiator asked if the man had already taken anything and he stated that he had not. The negotiator asked when and where he was planning to die, to see how detailed the plan was and if there was a need for immediate action. The doctor said, "today, after you leave." Being concerned about the doctor's safety, the negotiator asked if he had the gun in his hand and asked him to put it on the table, so that there were no accidents while the two of them were talking. The Doctor agreed. Refocusing the discussion, the negotiator asked what things he was having particular problems organizing. The response was, "everything," to which the negotiator said, "It sounds like you are so depressed that it is hard to get anything done." The response was, "You are absolutely correct. I just don't have the energy for anything, anymore. I am so worthless." The negotiator responded with, "What would you tell a patient who told you that they were so depressed that they could not get anything done?" He said that he would reassure him and suggest anti-depressants. The negotiator asked what was keeping him from taking his own advice? He said, "It isn't worth it. Besides what would people think if they knew that I had to take antidepressants?" The negotiator replied that they would probably think that he was able to care for himself just like he had taken care of them. After several interchanges in which the negotiator pointed out that anybody who was capable of running a successful practice could learn the things that his wife had done for him and that he had family who cared for him and would support him while the was learning, the doctor agreed to consult with his friend, the family practice physician about anti-depressants. The negotiator responded with, "When? How about I take you, today?" The doctor agreed to go with the negotiator to see his friend. After he repeated the plan to the negotiator, he put the gun down and came out of the house.

Sidebar: Thoughts on Suicide
by William Hogewood

William Hogewood has been in law enforcement for 37 years, serving as a police officer with Prince George's County, Maryland and as a training program manager with the Bureau of Alcohol, Tobacco, Firearms and Explosives. During that time, he has served as a negotiator, team leader, trainer, and as a counselor to police officers.

Unfortunately, as a police officer, negotiator, mental health volunteer, and counselor with law enforcement, suicide has become a necessary topic for me to explore. For me, understanding the suicidal mind has been as important as understanding intervention skills. Along with the available research and academic studies of suicide, actual experiences and observations have also helped me further explore the suicidal mindset.

Negotiators are often called upon to deal with individuals attempting to relieve the burdens of life through suicide. These calls are generated by the suicidal individual or by others calling to have officers check on the welfare of individuals communicating a suicide attempt. Most of these attempts pose a threat to others involved. Many times the suicide communication becomes a topic in an ongoing barricade that may have started for another reason. Suspects may use suicide as a threat to keep police at bay, or maybe even as an excuse for the actions that may have caused the barricade.

Suicide, having many definitions, is certainly an act of homicide, the killing of a human being. It happens to be directed at one's own self. There are lots of instances in which suicidal persons have redirected their feelings toward authorities and have fired at the very people who have responded to help. Negotiators, or, for that matter, any responding officer, should always be aware of the suicidal person as a threat with whatever weapon being used. This may be the worst time for any face-to-face negotiations. A rule for handling suicide should be that no officer will be injured attempting to save a suicidal person. After all, it is that person's choice to use suicide as a method of dealing with an emotional or physiological crisis.

Many times negotiators struggle to talk a person out of the act, without really knowing what that person is feeling. The use of good solid communication skills are enhanced when we better understand the turmoil that is driving the person.

Following Schneidman, McMains and Mullins offer that suicide is an **escape from unendurable emotional or physical pain**. The idea of "talking someone out of dying" may not be the proper strategy when the act is not about death. Suicide seems more about not continuing to exist in deep pain. The often contemplated question in the suicidal individual's mind is, "How long can I survive in pain, or would I rather cease to exist?" It is this ambiguity that brings suicide attempters to the attention of authorities. Otherwise, without ambiguity, the act is completed.

We know that helplessness and hopelessness are key ingredients in the suicidal psyche. In a typical emotional crisis, the individual loses control of the situation and has no predictability in terms of regaining control. The bleakness of the situation, based on individual perception, is stronger than the chance for recovery. As the individual sinks deeper into all-consuming thoughts of the crisis, that hopelessness and helplessness magnifies.

Motivation for completion of the act also plays a role. Often, the suicidal individual attaches blame to others for the crisis they find themselves in at the moment. They want to lash out at the person they blame, or they want the person to feel sorry for what they have done. This is especially true in romantic relationships and in co-worker and employer relationships. We know that sometimes, in situations like this, the suicidal individual may want to engage in a significant "final act" to satisfy their wrath. In any case, we do know that motivation for suicide is sometimes to punish others.

Harold Elliott and Brad Bailey, in their book, *Ripples of Suicide; Reasons for Living*, discuss a rationale for this. They explain suicide as a "Volitional act, aimed not merely at creating an effect, or even a specific effect, but also an observable effect." Basically, the suicidal person actually believes that after the act, they would be able to observe the pain, sorrow, or regret administered to the guilty parties. They also offer that, "There is a view that death is benign, a state worth working toward—a state in which the victim believes he will be, and will somehow enjoy, the peace he believes death holds." This substantiates the idea that suicide is not about death but more about the release of the burden. Ironically, the suicidal person may view death "as oblivion, but an oblivion that he somehow lives to enjoy."

As negotiators, we should not attempt to rebut that thought, but instead use it in our efforts to help the individual see for himself that it is delusional. Asking, for instance, "So what reaction do you expect from your wife?" may assist the negotiator in determining motivation and lead to discussion about other options that may satisfy that motivation.

Suicide is preceded by a loss. This could be the loss of a love interest, a job, a position, a promotion, an animal, or self-worth and self-esteem. Failure to achieve might be considered a loss. This is followed by anger or sometimes guilt, leading to depression and suicide as a way out of the depression. An open conversation that leads to discovery of the loss, responded to with empathic listening, may be very fruitful in helping the individual realize and accept the feelings surrounding the emotional depression.

Ironically, suicide is a concrete step out of the initial crisis. A specific plan might mean that the burden of the crisis has been lifted. This gives support to the euphoria many suicidal individuals may show prior to the committing the suicidal act. Anecdotal evidence does show that many times the suicidal person displays and communicates feelings of relief and joy. We are taught that crisis is time limited, that it finally goes away. One could argue that control and predictability are now restored.

Over the years, many of my teammates have shared observations with me that are worthy of consideration. One is that many attempts or completed suicides occur near or in front of a mirror. Many times the mirror has been strategically placed. Is this an attempt to see the "observable effect?" Does the suicidal person have a fascination with seeing the moment of death? Others have also noticed that often mementos of the individual's life are placed near the location of the suicidal act. Old photos, sports trophies, checks written out to significant others, and generally memories of a better life have sometimes been placed on purpose in locations near the scene. At several scenes of attempted and completed suicides, we found objects from the distant past, such as high school photos and certificates; perhaps a reminder of simpler times or of a greater sense of self-worth. One negotiator from another jurisdiction who attended one of our training programs later reported that, after the surrender of a UPS carrier, she found folded uniforms and other equipment for retrieval neatly arranged on the bed. Pictures of family were surrounding the scene. All of this was an obvious memorial to better times. Learning some of these nuances through active listening may be helpful during the negotiation process. Some of these mementos of earlier/better times may help establish rapport for the negotiators.

We often have discussed the meaning of methods of death. Is there symbolism to the method of suicide? Our experience, though not in any way scientifically proven, does beg the question.

We know that many times the suicidal individual uses a gun to the head as a method. It may mean something. Examination after the act has sometimes shown that person was struggling with doubts about identity, self-worth, validation of self, a sense of loathing of self over the inability to take care of family, and other **cognitive** issues. In other words, the method is specific aimed at the actual source of the thoughts. Often we have found this correlation in thoughts about self and the use of a gun to the head. A case in point found was an individual who thought of himself as a bad provider because he could not gain ground in his fight against growing debts. Before his death, by a gunshot to the brain, his theme was how little he thought of himself. Statements like, "I'm not good enough to have a family" or "I don't feel capable of providing for them, as hard as I try," were constant themes.

How do we explain suicides in which the individual shot themselves in the chest? For some, the emotional pain has been heartbreak over loss of relationships or something that they loved. For instance, former Chief of Naval Operations Admiral Jeremy Borda, when chastised about a medal that he was told by his staff that he could wear, eventually killed himself by a shot through the chest. Admiral Borda had risen from a Navy seaman to the highest office for a naval officer. He loved the Navy. It was a primary relationship. Evidence after his untimely death reflected his feelings that he had let the Navy down. He was brokenhearted over the criticism. This would seem to reflect a suicide over **emotional** issues. Other instances of a person shooting themselves in the heart were precipitated by broken relationships. The pain was from the heart.

Not as unusual as we would think are suicides with gunshots to areas affected by pain, such as the stomach, head, or chest when it was known that the prevailing issue was **physical**, such as brain, stomach, or lung diseases that were extremely painful and terminal.

In several suicides of police officers that I have reviewed, the gunshot was obviously directed toward the source of the pain, such as, a shot to the lung killing the lung cancer and more telling, a shot to the stomach, killing the stomach cancer. Certainly physical pain is a burden from which one might seek release through suicide.

One known suicide of a police officer involved dousing himself with gasoline and lighting himself afire. As he was burning, he shot himself in the head with his service weapon. What caused this apparent symbolic act? Old issues with Viet Nam and brothers he had lost in napalm incidents had been on his mind during the time leading to his death. He may have thought that he did not deserve to live and in order to be with his brothers, he had to feel their pain. Along with those memories, he was dealing with some known self-esteem issues. Again, this was not scientifically proven, but possibly symbolic.

So, how does this information help the negotiator? Through effective and active listening, we might gain a sense of the correlation between the method and the precipitating problems. If the source is cognitive, we will know that we will have to help restructure the way the person in crisis thinks about himself. If it is emotional, we may need to plan on taking more time to defuse the feelings. This may give us a chance to encourage ventilation, which can help guide the person through the understandable emotionality and into a state of reason.

Attempting to talk someone out of dying may not be the direction to take when in fact suicide is more about ceasing to carry a painful burden. Our focus has to be more toward helping the person see some light. To use the analogy of "light at the end of the tunnel," most of us in stable times are at the end of the tunnel where there is plenty of light. We cope and handle daily stressors as well as our support systems allow. For the suicidal person, as burdens overwhelm support systems, it's like walking backwards, losing the light, while losing control and predictability. The job of the negotiator is not to make things right, but to help the individual walk forward, even ever so slightly, until they see enough light to think more rationally.

> Negotiators possess many talents and skills. Characteristics most needed to deal with a suicidal individual might be compassion and patience. Being the primary with the suicidal person may be the biggest challenge for the negotiator. There is little bargaining available. We are dealing with intimate human emotions. Communication skills are just a part of the necessary skills to use. Understanding the person's futility and resulting feelings are as important. To be a "Nurturing Parent," the negotiator has to listen with *sincerity* and compassion. Being objective, allowing for ventilation, identifying feelings, grasping the motivation and the possible symbolism, all require a great deal of patience and emotional strength.

Suicide by Cop: Victim-Precipitated Suicide

A subset of suicidal people are those who will do something provocative to force the police to kill them. Negotiators occasionally must deal with such a person. Van Zandt (1993) has pointed out that, in addition to being suicidal, these people are frequently aggressive. In fact, they precipitate violent confrontations in order to get the police to kill them. Such a person is an unusual combination of the Rebellious Child and the Compliant Child. He expects criticism and judgment and wants to avoid responsibility for his actions in the way Compliant Children do. At the same time, he is angry and controlling like the Rebellious Child. Therefore, it is a good idea to assess the person's risk of violence along with his suicide potential.

o Prevalence: Mohandie and Meloy (2000) reviewed the research on suicide by cop and found different rates. A study of the 437 shooting cases involving officers from the Los Angeles County Sheriff's Office from 1987-1997 concluded that 13 percent of fatal officer-involved shootings and 11 percent of all officer-involved shooting were suicide-by-cop situations. The next year, the rates jumped to 25 and 27 percent for officer-involved shootings and officer-involved fatalities. A study of 240 articles about police shootings from 22 different newspapers during a period from 1980-1995 found evidence of possible or probable suicides in 16 percent of the cases. In looking at a second sample of 33 cases from 1992-1993, the researchers found evidence in 47 percent of the cases of possible suicide intent. A Canadian study found evidence of subjects posing a lethal threat to officers from British Columbia police departments in 48 percent of 58 cases studied. Whether it is a result of more sophisticated reporting or an actual increase in rates, suicide by cop is becoming an issue of great concern for negotiators. Not only does it pose a major challenge because it is generally used by subjects who have a history of the most violence, impulsiveness, and rebelliousness, but when the subject is successful, it can have a long-lasting and devastating effect on officers who have been forced to kill a subject.

Motivations: Individuals have used suicide by cop to attain both instrumental and expressive goals (Mohandie & Meloy, 2000). They may want to escape the consequences of their behavior, use a confrontation as a tool for reconciling a lost relationship, avoid the exclusionary clause for suicide in an insurance policy, avoid the moral responsibility of suicide, or force another person to kill them: all instrumental motivations. On the other hand, they may use suicide by cop to communicate helplessness and hopelessness, to make a statement about being the ultimate victim, to express their need to save face—dying rather than surrendering, to communicate their extreme need for power and control over a situation, to express pent-up rage and revenge, or to communicate something about an important personal issue, all expressive motivations.

Using a checklist like the one in Figure 8.1 in conjunction with the Suicide Assessment Checklist gives negotiators a way of evaluating the potential for a victim-precipitated suicide. The person who scores high on both the suicide assessment and the aggression assessment poses a potentially greater risk of precipitating an incident than does the person who is high on the suicide assessment but low on the aggression assessment. It is important for negotiators to evaluate the potential for both suicide and aggression, and then to communicate their estimates to both the field commander and the tactical team, so that everyone will be prepared for aggressive action on the part of the suicidal person.

In addition to a systematic assessment of the person's potential for aggression, negotiators need to be watchful for other indicators of victim-precipitated suicide. The indicators suggested by Van Zandt were listed in Chapter 1. In addition, the following factors have been associated with suicide by cop (Mohandie & Meloy, 2000):

1. Insists that "jail is not an option"

2. Threatens officers or others with a weapon

3. Attaches weapon to his or her person

4. Countdown

5. Suspect calls police on self

6. Forces confrontation with police

7. Assaults or harms victims in police presence

8. Uses "chemical courage"

Although the intervention with suicide by cop is the same for negotiators, special care needs to be taken with subjects who are suspected of entertaining the idea of suicide by cop, because they will kill others to achieve their ends. Additionally, they will threaten with deadly weapons. If officers do not have appropriate cover or if the subject is putting others at risk, appropriate force is the response of choice.

Figure 8.1
Hostage Taker's Aggression Index

AGGRESSION INDEX NEGOTIATOR _____					
1	2	3	4	5	6
1	AGGRESSION PREDICTORS		HOSTAGE NEGOTIATION UNIT		
2		VALUE	DEFINITION		
3	age	1	17-25		
4	sex	1	MALE		
5	RACE	1	BLACK, HISPANIC		
6	SOCIOECONOMIC STATUS	1	LOW		
7	SUBSTANCE ABUSE	1	ALCOHOL, STIMULANTS, OPIATES		
8	IQ	1	LESS THAN 90		
9	EDUCATION	1	DROP-OUT, LLD, ED, UNDER-ACHIEVER		
10	RESIDENTIAL STABILITY	1	FREQUENT MOVES		
11	EMPLOYMENT HX	1	FREQUENT CHANGES, UNEMPLOYED		
12	HI RISK POPULATION	1	PARANOIDS, MANIACS, PSYCHOPATHS		
13	COGNITIVE DISPOSITION	1	RATIONALIZES USE OF VIOLENCE		
14	AFFECTIVE DISPOSITION	1	HEROES, INSTRUMENTAL USE		
15	HX ARREST	1	VIOLENT OFFENSES		
16	CONVICTED	1	VIOLENT OFFENSES		
17	MENTAL COMMITMENTS	1	DANGER TO OTHERS		
18	JUVENILE RECORD	1	VIOLENT CRIMES		
19	FAMILY VIOLENCE	1	VICTIM, PARENTAL IDENTIFICATION		
20	HX. ARSON	1	MORE THAN TWO		
21	SIMILAR SITUATION	1	PRECIPITATING=CURRENT EVENT		
22	HX. HI INTENSITY	1	PROGRESSIVE INCREASE		
23	^ IN 2 WKS.	1	INCREASE IN # OF EVENTS		
24	> 2 MIN. EP.	1	DURATION > 2 MINUTES		
25	HX. SADISM	1	> EPISODE WITH ANIMAL		
26	RELIGION	-1	MORAL/ETHICAL TRAINING		
27	EMPATHY	-1	NEEDS, CONVERSATION, HOODS		
28	ATTRIBUTION SUCCESS	-1	SEES LITTLE CHANCE OF SUCCESS		
29	NON FAULT	-1	DOES NOT PERSONALIZE EVENT		
30	TOTAL				
31					
CONFIDENTIAL CASE # _____					

Source: San Antonio Police Department. Reprinted with permission.

Suicide Bombers

Recent events in London have underlined the fact that not all suicide bombers die. English authorities arrested 28 people believed to be involved in the two bomb attacks in London subways in 2005. Israeli officials have reported negotiating with suicide bombers who have not completed their mission. It is not out of the realm of possibility for crisis management teams to have to negotiate with suicide bombers in the United States. Therefore, it is important for negotiators to give some thought to the similarities and differences between the usual suicidal subject and suicide bombers that are involved in a political or religious cause. This section will explore some thoughts on managing incidents involving these people.

The father of Suicidology, Emile Durkheim, pointed out a century ago that there were people who sacrificed themselves for others or for a cause greater than themselves. He called these people "altruistic suicides." The soldier in war movies who throws himself on the live grenade to save his buddies is the most common image of this kind of suicide in our culture. The point is that there are people who kill themselves for reasons other than those discussed above and it benefits negotiators to understand these people, to the degree that is possible.

Altruistic suicides are motivated by an over-identification with a group and the group's needs. It is a choice by individuals who see self-sacrifice as giving their life meaning. The goal is to benefit the group, further the cause, and enhance the general good, rather than decreasing personal pain. People in this class are acting out of a sense of duty. Durkheim (1951) cited soldiers and religious martyrs as examples of altruistic suicides. Their hope is in the cause and not in ending personal pain.

Hoffer (1950) wrote on the motivation of mass movements. He used fascism and communism as models, but his analysis could just as easily apply to religious fundamentalists. He pointed out that people who are attracted to mass movements are, in some ways, broken people. They have a fundamental sense of worthlessness, disenfranchisement and powerlessness for which they make up by joining groups that have dramatic, world-changing missions. It is the group's mission that gives the person's life meaning. They have a disregard for reality, as it exists, and want to rebuild it, either as it used to be or as it should be. In the case of Fascists, it is looking back to better times that serves as the goal. In the case of Communism, it is looking to the future that gives the person meaning.

Osterman (2002) stated that an important cultural consideration that negotiators needed to consider was the difference in self-concept between our culture and others. She points out that being independent and self-sufficient are seen as ways of caring for the group. In other cultures, it is the survival of the group that assures the well-being of the individual. Thus, sacrifice for the group is seen as a way of helping the self. Hammer (2002) has made a similar point about the allegiance that Muslims feel toward their family and religion.

Strentz (1981) described the profile of the terrorist cell as being made up of three personality types:

1. the ideological thinker who is the philosopher of the group;

2. the general, who plans and leads the field activities of the group, and;

3. the soldier who is the follower and carries out the plans of the other two.

He believes that there are identifiable personality styles in theses three groups. For instance:

1. The idealist tends to be intellectualized, a black-and-white thinker who is compartmentalized and rigid in his or her thinking.

2. The general tends to have characteristics like the antisocial personalities we are used to working with. They are impulsive, action-oriented, and have problems living within society's rules.

3. The soldier is much like the inadequate personalities with whom we work. They look to others for leadership and care.

Sullivan (1954a) suggests that obsessive personalities and inadequate personalities are formed in people who have had to learn to deal with overbearing, over-controlling, authoritarian personalities in the significant others in their lives. Could it be that terrorists come from such environments?

West German psychologists found that there was no psychopathology as such in the groups of terrorists. Rather, the terrorists shared the following characteristics:

1. Disenfranchised, rebellious people who had unhappy childhoods.

2. Came from highly structured, authoritarian, middle-class homes.

3. Were educated but not successful in their chosen field.

4. Felt repressed and mistreated by society.

5. Thought that they were acting to defend themselves.

6. Would tolerate no doubts about the cause.

7. Engaged in either-or thinking.

8. Embraced the radical destruction and rebuilding of society based on a utopian notion of how things should be.

Terrorists may well come from a background that makes them susceptible to mass movements, just as Hoffer describes.

Hammer (2002; 2005) and Ostermann (2002) have suggested that recent suicidal acts have to be understood in the context of their culture. In Islam:

1. There is a high value placed on not shaming the family.

2. People tend to look to the past as a model for how to live now.

3. The average man relies on religious authority for guidance.

4. Obligations are not based on contracts but on relationships.

5. Emotions are openly expressed to convince people you are serious.

6. There is a prohibition against taking life, your own or others, except under tightly defined conditions.

7. A religious edict called a *Fatwa* is needed to justify killing.

8. *Jihad* means both a justified war in which a person who loses his or her life is considered a martyr and a personal, internal, spiritual, struggle.

9. Even in a Jihad, noncombatants and innocent bystanders cannot be killed.

An understanding of these issues may provide some leverage when working with Muslim suicide bombers, an issue to which we will return.

All is not bleak in negotiating with suicide bombers of the type we have been discussing. Some principles are the same as other negotiations: build rapport, raise doubts, and suggest alternatives to the actor through indirect suggestions and problem-oriented questions.

The specific recommendations for negotiations that flow from the above are:

1. In Rapport Building, use and expect different verbal tactics.

   a. Expect and consider using emotional expressions. If a position is logically presented, without passion, Muslims do not think you are serious. They look at your action as a guide to your real intent. Your actions must support your real position. Our usual approach of staying calm, controlled, and expecting to defuse emotions is not likely to work in a culture that values emotional expressions.

   b. Validating cause without validating actions allows you to deal with the person and increase your interpersonal worth to the individual without accepting his or her suicidal behavior. Like other negotiations, the suicide bomber can be validated. Their need to derive meaning from their past can be recognized. The legitimacy of their need for self-rule can be honored. Whatever their issues, it can be validated without legitimizing suicide and or murder as a way of achieving their ends. This is particularly important in reaching the soldiers who are in the field carrying out the bombings.

2. Raising doubts and getting the actor to question his or her suicidal actions can be facilitated by using several ideas from Islam They include:

a. *Fatwa*—a religious document that legitimizes war and killing to defend the faith. It has to be issued by a high-ranking religious official and without it, an act is not considered just. It is interesting to note that the Shi'ite Muslims who attacked the Marine barracks in Beirut did not have the blessing of their religious authorities.

b. Jihad—a holy war that is sanctioned by a *Fatwa*. The term refers to either an actual act of war or the spiritual war that occurs in the person as he or she struggles to become more holy. The actor can be asked which meaning of the term applies to his situation and whether he has a *Fatwa* approving his participation.

c. Murder of innocents—Islam prohibits the murder of innocent bystanders. Even when assassination was sanctioned, the assassin was expected to take pains to avoid killing household members or even bodyguards. He was expected to sacrifice his own life rather than kill innocents. One strategy may be to get the actor to recognize that there are innocents involved in the incident and play on Islam's prohibition in this area.

d. Family shame—the thing that makes Muslims capable of altruistic suicide may also be a way of raising doubts in their minds. The importance of the group over the individual starts with the family. The negotiator may make progress by asking the actor to consider how his or her suicide will affect the family. Will it bring honor or shame?

3. Suggestion

a. Story telling—some cultures communicate through the use of stories to make a point. The communication is indirect and metaphorical. Negotiators in our culture need to be prepared to deal with that. Finding stories in the actor's tradition and history that emphasizes the peaceful resolution of conflict may help establish your relationship with him or her and they may suggest solutions in an indirect way.

In addition, Ostermann (2002) recommends the following guidelines based on understanding cultural differences:

- Respect family and group
- Be sensitive to face issues
- Utilize suggestion and indirect communications
- Recognize that oaths and promises do not count as much as relationships

- Be aware that deadlines are less important
- Expect others to change topics frequently
- Be prepared for a fatalistic viewpoint

Summary

In conclusion, a caveat and a note of optimism. The caveat is that we are all "feeling our way" in the arena of fanatical suicide bombings. None of us have enough experience with them to be considered experts. Take what makes sense to you, think through your approach, set up training scenarios, and prepare the best you can. No one can ask any more. And stay hopeful that people are more alike than they are different. People tend to rise or sink to the level you expect. Expect the best and you just may get it, even when you have to deal with the unlikely.

References

Durkheim, E. (1951). *Suicide: A Study in Sociology*. New York: Free Press.

Hammer, M. (2002) "Cultural Factors in Negotiating with Suicidal Terrorists." Discussion at: California Association of Hostage Negotiators' Conference (May).

Hammer, M. (2005). Personal communication.

Hoffer, E. (1955). *The True Believer*. New York: Harper-Row.

Hogewood, W. (2005). "Post-Incident Debriefing/Emotional Survival for Negotiators." Presentation at Hostage/Crisis Negotiations 201. Olathe, KS (August).

Lanceley, F. (1999). *On-Scene Guide for Crisis Negotiators*. Boca Raton, FL: CRC Press.

Mohandie, K. and J.R. Meloy (2000). "Clinical and Forensic Indicators of 'Suicide by Cop.'" *Journal of Forensic Sciences* (March):384-389.

Osterman, B.M. (2002). "Cultural Differences Make Negotiations Different: Intercultural Hostage Negotiations." *Journal of Police Crisis Negotiations* Vol.2, No. 2.

Schneidman, E. (1985). *A Definition of Suicide*. New York, NY: John Wiley and Sons.

Seligman, M.E.P. (1991). *Learned Optimism*. New York, NY: Alfred A. Knopf.

Strentz, T. (1981). "The Terrorist Organizational Profile: A Psychological Role Model." In Alexander, Y. and J.M. Gleason (eds.), *Behavioral and Quantitative Perspectives on Terrorism*. New York: Pergamon.

Strentz, T. (1988). "A Terrorist Psychosocial Profile: Past and Present." *Law Enforcement Bulletin* 57, No. 4, 1988, 11-18.

Sullivan, H.S. (1954a). *The Interpersonal Theory of Psychiatry*. New York, NY: W.W. Norton and Company.

_____ (1954b). *The Psychiatric Interview*. New York, NY: W.W. Norton and Company.

Surgeon General of the United States (1999). *The Surgeon General's Call to Action to Prevent Suicide*. Washington, DC: U.S. Public Health Service.

Van Zandt, C.R. (1993). "Suicide by Cop." *The Police Chief* 60(7):24-27

Discussion Questions

1. One loss that leads people to think about suicide is the loss of health—a 38 year-old man is diagnosed with renal failure and told he has to go on a dialysis machine but non are available for two weeks. What would make him consider suicide as a real option in his life?

2. Part of the definition of suicide is that it is a conscious act: people decide and can re-decide on death as an alternative. This position makes it a rational decision and not a mental health issue. Do you agree that it is a rational decision? How can a negotiator create conditions in which a person might re-decide about killing himself?

3. One way of assessing the person's risk of suicide is to assess their current plan, their prior attempts, and the resources they think are available to them. Group each of the Surgeon General's risk factors under one of these headings and explain the reasons for your placement.

4. Refer to the case study examined in this chapter. List the issues used by the negotiators in developing their intervention. Discuss other issues you, as the primary negotiator, could use in developing your plan.

5. In reviewing the intervention by the negotiators, which elements of the plan do you think were the most effective in resolving the incident? Choose three.

6. Compare the similarities and differences between altruistic suicide and the usual suicidal person negotiators encounter. How do these differences affect your approach as a negotiator?

7. When people are suicidal, they usually are not focused on their strengths, and their self-esteem (face) is low. They tend to withdraw from others who care about them. How does the withdrawal from others benefit negotiators? How would you intervene to help a suicidal person regain his or her sense of self-esteem?

Team Structure, Roles, and Command

9

Learning Objectives

1. Know the definition of team and how a team can be built to manage crisis incidents.

2. Understand the functions needed at any crisis/hostage incident.

3. Know the responsibilities of the Field Commander.

4. Understand the importance of briefing commanders at the scene on the issues using the FBI's necessary conditions for negotiations.

5. Know the role of the Tactical Supervisor.

6. Know the role of the Negotiator Supervisor.

7. Know the role of the Public Information Officer at the scene.

8. Understand how the principles of redundancy and clarity of communications aid in managing a crisis incident.

9. Understand the composition of and roles of members of the negotiating team.

10. Understand how negotiators should be selected.

11. Understand the importance of the team concept in managing critical incidents.

12. Understand the role and responsibilities of the mental health consultant.

13. Know how to construct training plans for negotiations teams.

The officer was shot at 2:00 P.M. during a traffic stop. The subject barricaded himself in a laundromat with three women. Patrol contained the location and called for the Crisis response Team. By the time the Team arrived at the scene, there were several dozen officers at the location, many milling around, but some were trying to contain the crowd that had gathered. As time passed, more officers arrived, including homicide detectives, internal affairs officers, two deputy chiefs, and the patrol shift commander. Most of the "brass" gathered at the makeshift command post to discuss what to do. Officers continued to mill around. Intelligence gathering was difficult because the first responding officers were still holding down the perimeter. The press arrived soon, as did representatives from the District Attorney's office, to monitor the incident because it involved an officer and was high profile. Toward evening, the mayor came to the scene, volunteering to talk with the subject. After the 5:00 news, people came to the scene claiming to be related to the subject. They had seen his car on the news and recognized it.

The brief scenario above reminds us that to successfully manage a crisis/hostage incident, many elements within the police department and the public and private sector must develop a quick and effective working relationship. They must have clear and effective channels of communication, and they need an agreed-on "game plan." There has to be a team approach to managing crises. This chapter will look at a definition of teams, identify problems during incidents that are related to team issues, and describe the roles and structures of response teams that will help overcome the problems that have developed in the team management of crisis incidents.

Definition of Team

Katzenbach and Smith (1993) have defined a team in a way that is helpful for both police decisionmakers and negotiators. They say that a team is "a small group of people with complementary skills who are committed to a common purpose, performance goals, and approach for which they hold themselves mutually accountable."

A group of 10 to 12 is considered a small group. Limiting the size of a group is important in building a team, because a smaller group allows better communication, better handling of logistical problem, and more effective problem-solving than a larger group (McMains, 1995). Because most departments have fewer than 10 negotiators, limiting the size of the negotiating team is not difficult. However, when the incident is high profile, of political interest, or attractive to the press, it may require a response that involves much more than just negotiators. It requires the presence of tactical officers, command officers, traffic control officers, and public information officers. The total number of people involved can quickly grow beyond 10 or 12. To the degree that it does is the degree to which communications, control, and problem solving become more difficult.

✱ Team members have complementary skills. That is, team members are selected for their contribution to the purpose and goals of the team. Not all team members are alike, because there are many tasks to be performed in managing a critical incident. There need to be tactical, negotiators, command. ☞ Each has different skills, but the different skills must contribute to the team achieving its goals. The incident at the Talladega Federal Correctional Institution in 1991 illustrated the value of using team members with different, complementary skills. Both the FBI and Bureau of Prisons (BOP) had negotiators and tactical officers on the scene. The negotiators complemented each other, because the FBI had personnel who were experienced negotiators, while the BOP negotiators were familiar with riots, prison management, and specific information about detainees. They were assigned to teams that worked eight-hour shifts and included both FBI and BOP negotiators working together to utilize their respective strengths (Fagan & Van Zandt, 1993).

✱ Teams need to be committed to a common purpose, to common performance goals, and to common approaches to the problem. It is the purpose and goals that give the team direction. They answer the question "Why does the team exist?" It helps define success, because success is accomplishing the purpose or goal. They help define progress. Generally, in crisis/hostage incidents, the purpose and goals are understood to be saving lives and resolving the incident as safely as possible (Stites, 2005).

At a critical incident, there are in fact several teams that must come together as one working team or at least must overlap in their purpose, goals, and approaches. There is the Crisis Management Team, which is made up of the departmental, city, political, and support personnel who are responsible for managing crises in a particular jurisdiction. There is the Crisis Response team, which is responsible for managing critical incidents for the police department. There is the tactical team, which is responsible for bringing assault capabilities, containment capabilities, and deadly force options to the incident. There is the negotiating team, which is responsible for the peaceful resolution of the incident.

challenge A major issue in the team approach is that there are really several different teams that have to come together during a crisis, each with different purposes, goals, and approaches to solving the problem. The tactical team and the negotiation team may agree on the goal of a peaceful resolution, but not agree on the idea that there are no acceptable losses. Negotiators and tactical personnel have different tools or approaches to bringing the incident to an end. Similarly, if supervisors are more concerned about overtime costs than peaceful resolution of the incident, they will be working at cross-purposes with the negotiators and tactical teams. The team approach in police crises requires an integration of several teams. Without prior dis-

cussions and practice, the purposes, goals, and approaches may generate ineffective actions at the scene.

A second issue is whether the decisionmakers at an incident have the
same purpose, goals, and approach to the incident. Historically, negotiators
have identified the incident commander's lack of understanding and training in negotiation principles as a problem for the team (FBI, 1993). The FBI's
Negotiations Concepts for Commanders course was developed as a result of
the commanders at Waco, Texas, receiving sound advice from the negotiators, but not following the advice due to their lack of understanding of the
crisis negotiations perspective (Noesner, 1999). Such a lack of understanding of negotiation concepts makes it difficult, if not impossible, for the
crisis management team to respond to the crisis in a well-coordinated, efficient, and effective way. It reflects the lack of a team approach, in that
even though there may be a common goal, if there is not an understanding
and acceptance of a common approach, things are likely to become confusing,
with elements of the crisis response team working against each other. A
mutual understanding of each element of a crisis response team's way of
thinking and acting is essential for the development of coordinated strategies and tactics that maximize the chance of a peaceful resolution to crises.

Noesner (1999) has pointed out that one of the significant shifts in command principles for crisis/hostage incidents since Waco has been the shift from
a linear decision-making model that said "Try talking them out first and if
that does not work, try using force to make them come out," to a synchronized
model that emphasizes the coordinated, simultaneous application of tactical
and negotiations approaches. The synchronized approach includes both
negotiators and tactical team members in every decision made by the commander at an incident. The planning is based on what the best option is at the
time, and how both tactical and negotiators can send the same message.
This emphasis makes the issue of teamwork extremely important. Synchronized decisionmaking must have real teamwork in order to be effective.

The answer to the problem of bringing different teams together, focusing them on a common purpose, common goals, and common approaches is
cross-training of all crisis response personnel and crisis management
teams—from the mayor down to the patrol officers who respond to
hostage/crisis incidents.

Crisis Management Team

Figure 9.1 shows the general organizational structure of a typical hostage
incident. With so many elements involved, an incident requires communication, command, coordination, and control. Communication between the disparate elements of an operation is essential to guarantee that all elements are
working toward the same goals. Clear, effective, and timely communications
are necessary to ensure that critical intelligence, tactical information, and

command decisions are available to the relevant personnel when they are needed. Control is essential so that no one acts on impulse or does anything that will inflame the situation, making it more difficult to resolve. The immediate control of the negotiating team, the tactical team, and the support elements (patrol/traffic/communications) is in the field. The political control is in the chief's and mayor's offices. In incidents that draw public attention, control will fluctuate between the field commander, the chief, and various politicians. These shifts in responsibility need to be coordinated. The primary decisionmaker needs to be clear to everyone at all times. Control is essential to guarantee a coordinated response that maximizes the saving of life, as well as making the most efficient and effective use of resources.

Figure 9.1
General Organization of a Typical Hostage Negotiation Incident

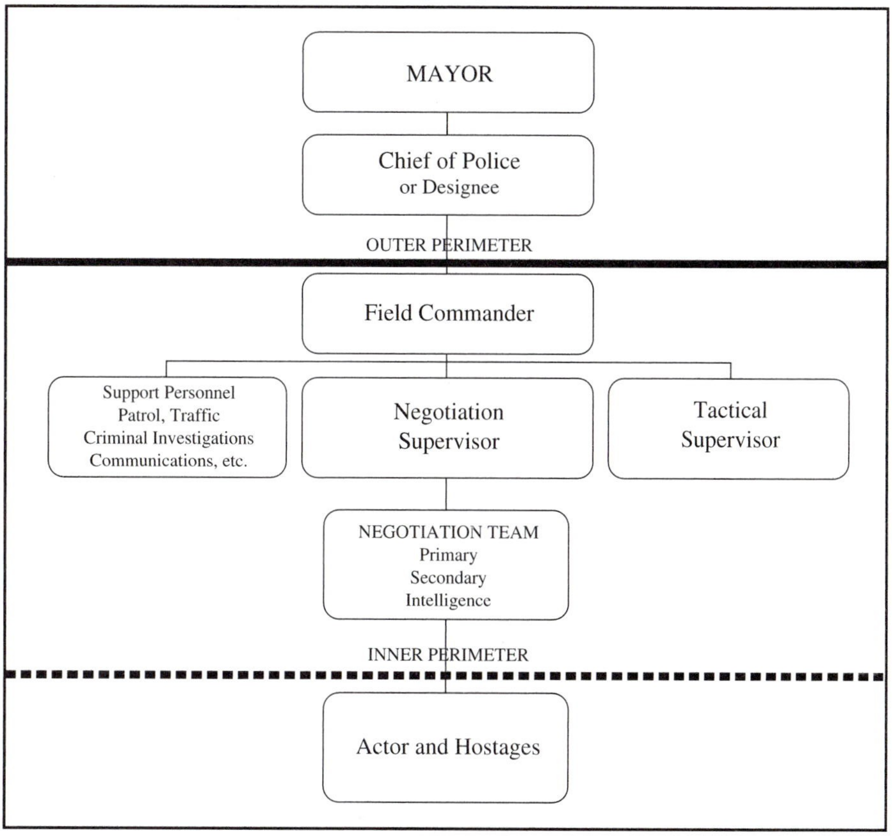

Source: McMains, M. Basic Hostage Negotiation School, San Antonio, 1984.

The degree of involvement of upper echelon personnel will depend on the politics, the economics, and the public relations consequences of a particular incident. For instance, an incident that occurs at city hall during the noon hour will have more political or public relations implications than one that happens at 3:00 A.M. in a lower middle-class neighborhood. The former is likely to receive the personal attention of the mayor and the police chief, while the latter is likely to involve only the usual command structure.

The people who make decisions, whether they are the mayor, the police chief, or the shift supervisor, must know the capabilities of their crisis response teams. Many supervisory personnel are not involved in the training and daily functioning of tactical officers and negotiators. They frequently do not know what negotiators can do. The FBI (1993) has found that a common problem in negotiations is that commanders do not train with their teams. A briefing at the beginning of the incident for decisionmakers who are not normally involved in training is helpful.

The Crisis Response Team

The Crisis Response Team for the department should be made up of the key personnel necessary to respond to a negotiation incident. It may vary in makeup and number depending on the nature of the incident. For instance, a suicide attempt by a barricaded person will receive less of a response than a hostage taker who shot a police officer and took a hostage during an aborted robbery. However, there are basic functions that are necessary in any situation.

1. The hostage taker needs to be contained and tactical options need to be worked out, if they become necessary. There is the need for a tactical element, which can make the threat of force real. Such an element may range in makeup from patrol officers who are designated as a containment and arrest team at the scene, to a fully trained and armed tactical unit. The makeup of the tactical response will depend on the resources of the specific department.

2. Communications need to be established with the hostage taker. There is a need for a negotiator element. Because the communication skills and conflict management skills used by a negotiator are different from those normally employed by patrol officers, it is important for departments to have trained negotiators. A team of negotiators requires at least two officers who can respond to a scene together.

3. Information needs to be gathered. There is a need for an intelligence element. A specific officer can be designated as responsible for gathering intelligence at the scene. He or she needs to focus on information about the incident, the people involved, and the tactical needs.

4. The situation needs to be free of bystanders, rubberneckers, and curiosity seekers. A security element is needed. Security should make provisions for managing both the public and the press. Both vehicle and foot traffic must be blocked by

security so that there is no unauthorized intrusion in the area between the inner and outer perimeters.

5. The media needs to be taken into consideration. An area needs to be established where they have access to information without putting themselves at risk. They need frequent updates on what is happening, to the extent that the information does not compromise the tactics of the incident.

6. Overall control of the situation must be maintained. A command element is necessary. The designated commander needs to assume overall command. He or she is the final approving authority for operational decisions and is responsible for ensuring that the other elements function as they should. The commander is responsible for the well-being of personnel.

7. In the last 10 years there has been a growing recognition in some departments that the hostages/victims need to be serviced beyond what the average officer or even average negotiator can do. Therefore, many departments are including victim services in their planning for crisis incidents.

Command Post

To facilitate communication, problem solving, and control of an incident, a command post needs to be established. A commander who is not in a specific location is difficult to find, keep updated, and communicate with when a decision is needed. A specific location for the command post can be established as soon as the field commander arrives at the incident. The command post should have sufficient room to accommodate the following personnel:

1. The field commander

2. A tactical supervisor

3. A negotiator supervisor

4. A traffic/patrol supervisor

5. An intelligence/recorder/communications officer.

6. A public information officer

The location of the command post should be in close proximity to the negotiators, tactical team, and representatives of other agencies, but not commingled with those other units. This will allow the commander to monitor negotiations without distracting the negotiators, keep updated on intelligence, coordinate tactical issues, resolve disputes between team members, and coordinate with other agencies. Figure 9.2 shows an example of a command post organization.

Figure 9.2
Command Post Organization

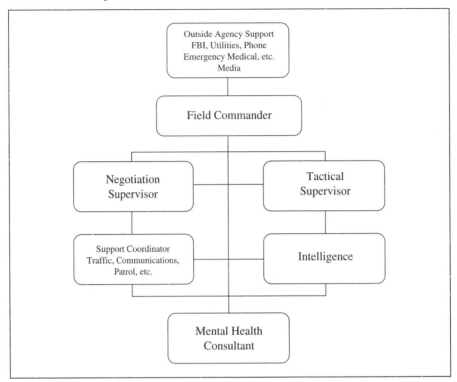

Source: McMains, M.

Field Commander

The field commander (incident commander) must understand the key negotiation concepts so that they can make the best use of their resources during an incident. Negotiators need to be aware that not all incident commanders know the capabilities of their negotiators, nor do they understand the principles on which negotiations are founded. One of the authors has participated in two major training exercises, including a SWAT school, which were resolved by negotiations before the scripted tactical assault could occur. In both incidents, the incident commanders tellingly asked, "How did that happen?" exposing their lack of understanding of the capabilities of their negotiators. The negotiator may need to educate the commander on the scene. Noesner (1999) has outlined the following as the important concepts for decisionmakers in a crisis incident:

1. The difference between a hostage incident and a non-hostage incident

2. The dynamics of a hostage and a non-hostage incident

3.   The strategies that apply to hostage and non-hostage incidents

4.   The decision-making criteria

5.   The necessity of a team in crises

6.   The importance of a unified strategy in crises

7.   Indicators that progress is being made

8.   Risk factors

9.   Tactical role of negotiations

10.   What constitutes success?

Usually, the field commander is the ranking police officer at the scene of a hostage incident. He or she is responsible for strategic management of the incident. The specific responsibilities of the field commander include:

1.   Establishing a command post at the scene in an area that is safe from confrontation.

2.   Establishing communications with and briefing the chief or the chief's representative.

3.   Ensuring the establishment of both inner and outer perimeters.

4.   Having a specific radio channel designated as an emergency channel and having all incident personnel use only the designated channel.

5.   Ensuring evacuation of any civilians inside the inner perimeter, when possible.

6.   Ensuring that only necessary manpower is on the scene.

7.   Making decisions and ensuring control and coordination of tactical and negotiating teams.

8.   Designating a press representative.

9.   Periodically, he or she needs to check on the welfare of his or her officers. (NYPD, 1973a, 1973b)

The field commander is in overall charge of the operation. He or she is there to ensure that the incident is controlled, that reasonable decisions are made, that departmental policies are followed in regard to critical incident management, and that the chief or chief's representative is informed, when necessary. The field commander needs to keep a checklist of relevant questions that might include:

1.   Is this an appropriate incident for negotiations, crisis intervention, or a tactical solution?

2.   What are the relative risks of the negotiation, crisis intervention, or tactical intervention?

3. Is the plan an integrated plan with clearly defined roles for all operational elements? Does the plan make clear how tactical and negotiators complement each other?

4. Is it negotiable? Are all the elements of a negotiable incident in place? Can they be put into place?

5. Is the situation secured? Have both inner and outer perimeters been established?

7. Have the appropriate personnel been notified?

8. Is the command post set up at a central location?

9. Are communications established between operational elements?

10. Is intelligence flowing?

11. Is the incident criminal, emergency, or mental health in nature?

12. Have the chief and other key city staff people been alerted?

13. As the incident progresses, have officers' needs for food, drinks, and restrooms been considered? Have officers manning posts been relieved periodically?

14. Has the risk changed?

15. Are the tactical and negotiator supervisors keeping me informed?

Case Study: The Field Commander. The call came in as a man with a gun in a doctor's office. Responding officers met employees from the office in the building next door. They were told that the man was the estranged husband of a fellow employee and that he had been harassing her all week. He had run everyone out of the office at gunpoint, threatening to shoot the woman if the police were called. The officers made an unobtrusive approach to the office. They could see a man with a gun and a woman inside the building. They called for a supervisor.

When the deputy chief arrived on the scene, he observed patrol officers walking around in front of the building. Citizens were talking to them. Traffic was moving past the location, through the field of fire. No perimeter or command post had been set up. He could not find the patrol lieutenant at the scene.

His first concern was establishing the safety of citizens and police officers at the scene. He ordered the exposed officers to take cover, established a perimeter into which no civilians could go, and had traffic officers block the flow of traffic past the office.

His second concern was establishing control of the situation. He ordered the field supervisor to report to his location, which he designated the command post. He assigned supervisory responsibility for maintaining the outer perimeter to the patrol lieutenant at the scene. He designated a communications channel on which the critical incident response team could operate.

His third concern was an evaluation of the situation. He obtained preliminary information about the man's identity from the responding officers. A quick records check showed that the man had three aggravated assault arrests and that he had served 18 months in the state penitentiary for one of them. The victims had all been female members of his family, including the woman he was currently holding hostage. His preliminary assessment was that the man had the potential for violence but that he was not an immediate threat to the woman. He decided that immediate action was not necessary and he called for the department's Crisis Response Team.

Tactical Supervisor

The tactical supervisor is responsible for the mobilization of the tactical team, deployment of the containment team, development of the tactical plan, and operation of the assault and arrest teams. He or she needs to be in close touch with the field commander and with the negotiator supervisor. Access to updated intelligence should be provided so that his or her planning can meet the ever-changing tactical situation at an incident. Questions the tactical supervisor should ask are:

1. Is the team necessary?

2. Has the team been mobilized?

3. Is the appropriate equipment available?

4. Are there sites at the scene that allow adequate observation of all sides of the scene, while providing sufficient cover or concealment for the observers?

5. Are the observers and containment team deployed?

6. Are communications established between the observer/containment team and the command post, intelligence officer, and negotiators?

7. Is there a feasible, integrated tactical plan that develops a coordinated use of tactical and negotiation?

8. Is there a place to practice an assault, if it becomes necessary?

9. Has the commander been briefed?

10. How can we complement the overall strategy and the negotiators?

Case Study: The Tactical Commander. The call was about a man barricaded in a house with a shotgun and his common law wife. He was threatening to kill her and himself. Patrol had responded. One officer had taken the couple's three-week-old baby from the mother because the man gave the officer six seconds to get the child or he would kill it. Subsequently, the officer returned to the scene and was pinned down by fire from the man's shotgun.

The tactical team commander began alerting his response team when he was notified of the incident. He paged his team members, asked them to monitor their emergency radio channel, and had them get their personal gear ready. He designated one officer as the equipment manager to retrieve their team gear from the police station (sniper rifles, shotguns, spotter scopes, tear gas, flash-bang grenades, shields, etc.).

Upon arriving at the scene, he checked in at the command post. The scene commander briefed him. He was asked for his evaluation of the situation and for the tactical options available. His first concern was about the safety of the personnel at the scene. He checked on the cover and concealment available to officers at the scene. He suggested that there was a need for a tighter perimeter and for the extraction of the pinned-down officer from the suspect's field of fire. He recommended replacing the patrol officers on the inner perimeter with tactical officers and that the armored vehicle used by the tactical team to rescue people be brought to the scene.

His second concern was how to neutralize the actor if he became an immediate threat to the woman, citizens, or officers. The subject was agitated and drunk. The commander recommended that the tactical team use snipers to set up cover for the officers close to the subject and that the containment and arrest teams be brought to the scene so they could be deployed, if that became necessary.

His third concern was setting up adequate communications for his team. He asked that tactical operations be switched to the designated radio channels used in crisis incidents: one channel for tactical team use and one for overall communications between elements of the crisis.

His fourth concern was the development of an assault plan. He assigned an officer to obtain a floor plan of the house from the children who had been run out of the house by the actor. He made a quick reconnaissance of the house, checking for cover and concealment, likely approaches, obstacles, and fields of fire. He considered a number of options—assaults, sniper fire, the use of gas, and the advantages and disadvantages of flash-bag grenades as a distraction. He began to lay out plans that his team could practice when they arrived.

Case Review. The role of the tactical supervisor is important on two counts in the early stages. He is responsible for assessing the risks and tactical options and for coordinating the tactical team's response with the incident commander and the negotiation team. He considers the potential for violence in a situation, the tactical resources available, and the best plans for utilizing the tactical resources. He presents his recommendations to the field commander and negotiation supervisor in joint planning sessions. He then oversees the execution of the tactical team's role in the incident plan. His is an advisory and supervisory role, not a decision-making role. The field commander makes the final decision about the course of action to be pursued in any given situation.

Negotiator Supervisor

The negotiator supervisor is responsible for the overall functioning of the negotiating team. In addition to supervisory skills, the supervisor must have leadership ability (IACP, 1983). Team members must look up to and respect this supervisor. However, the negotiator supervisor is obligated to have trained them well enough that they can function without him or her. He or she needs to be sure that the incident is negotiable, appropriate personnel are available, intelligence is gathered in a timely way, communications can be established, a negotiations strategy is worked out, an appropriate record of the negotiations is kept, and that the commander is kept informed. Questions the negotiator supervisor needs to ask at the outset are:

1. Is the incident a hostage or a non-hostage situation?

2. Is this incident negotiable?

3. What needs to be done to make it negotiable?

4. What type of siege is it? What does that mean for strategy and tactics?

5. Have the commander and the tactical team commander been briefed, and is there an integrated plan?

6. Are the right people on the job?

7. Is the proper equipment available?

8. Is intelligence about the incident being gathered?

9. Is intelligence available about the people involved in the incident?

10. Is tactical intelligence available?

11. Is there a negotiation strategy?

11. Has a threat assessment been performed/how dangerous is the hostage taker?

12. Has a profile been performed?

13. Have the primary and secondary negotiators been assigned on the basis of which negotiator can develop the best relationship with the hostage taker?

14. Has the introduction been planned and practiced by the primary negotiator?

15. As the incident progresses, has the commander been updated on progress? Are changes in the negotiations getting to the commander in a timely way?

16. Are the negotiators considering all their options?

17.   Are they periodically reviewing what they have done, and where they need to go with the negotiation?

18.   Is information continuing to flow during the incident?

19.   Are the negotiators taking periodic breaks?

Case Study: The Negotiator Supervisor. A fast patrol response had interrupted the 23-year-old male in the process of robbing a pizza restaurant. He had barricaded himself, two customers, and the manager inside. He was threatening to kill himself, although he said he did not intend to harm the other people in the restaurant. He wanted the police to leave. An on-duty negotiator with no experience had been assigned to the incident. He had begun negotiating from the dispatcher's office at the chief's insistence. The command staff was located at the scene. The negotiator supervisor was notified.

Upon arrival at the scene, he reported to the field commander and was briefed on the situation. His first responsibility was to assess the type of incident and the negotiability of the situation.

1.   Hostage incident with emotional overlay.

2.   Planned siege with emotional overlay because the plan probably did not include getting caught.

3.   The subject's need to live was somewhat in doubt. He was threatening to kill himself. The question was how serious he was about the threat. More intelligence was needed to answer that question.

4.   The department had the ability to bring a threat against the subject. In fact, a perimeter had been established.

5.   The subject was demanding only that officers kill him when he came out. Again, the seriousness of this demand needed to be assessed in more detail.

6.   The subject seemed to see department representatives as willing to help, as evidenced by his willingness to talk openly to the negotiator.

7.   There seemed to be plenty of time—even though he was talking about suicide, the man did not seem to be making active plans. In fact, asking for others to do it suggested some mixed feelings about dying.

8.   Communications were already established with the subject. However, the environment in which the negotiator was working was cluttered and distracting.

9.   The situation was contained. However, communication was not. The telephone line had not been isolated.

10.   There was only one hostage taker, so the negotiations were directed at the decisionmaker.

He advised the commander that it seemed like a negotiable situation, but that several things were needed. They included a more controlled environment for the negotiator, manpower to gather the intelligence that was needed to perform an assessment of both the man's suicide risk, his risk of aggression, and a centralized command post to facilitate communication and decisionmaking.

During the evaluation of the negotiability of the incident, the supervisor noted that even though the negotiator was inexperienced, he seemed to have good rapport, had defused the situation, and had established a degree of trust with the actor. Therefore, the supervisor recommended leaving him in the primary role and bringing in experienced negotiators and the MHC to support him.

He called the negotiators who were monitoring the incident. He had them debrief the responding officers, interview the witnesses, check local, state, and national records for prior criminal activity. None was found. Although the man had a poor work history, he was not fired. Rather, he resigned because he could not do the job. There was no history of aggression or prior suicidal behavior.

The Texas Rangers have an old saying: "One riot, one Ranger." The process of negotiating, however, requires a team. *(Photograph by Shan K. Smith)*

Case Review. Like the tactical supervisor, the negotiation supervisor is responsible for consultation with command and for supervision of the workings of his team. As he responds, he needs to think about and organize the team's response, including manpower and equipment, and he needs to assess the negotiability of the incident. He needs to advise the commander and he needs to think about tactics, including how to make transitions and what approaches to take. It is a role that requires administrative skills, management skills, assessment abilities, sound judgment and, most importantly, flexibility.

Public Information Officer

The media can inflame the public, create the perception of aggressiveness on the part of the police, and set opinions against the police by the way they report an incident. On the other hand, they can rally public opinion and they can emphasize the importance of a peaceful resolution in potentially violent situations. Gladis (1979) and others (American Justice, 1994) have underlined the helpful as well as the harmful roles the media can play in resolving hostage incidents. Media representatives have been the negotiators in incidents in which hostage takers would not talk with police. They have voluntarily withheld live coverage of hostage incidents so that the situation would not be inflamed. Television networks have developed guidelines on the coverage of hostage incidents that take the network's public safety role seriously (Gladis, 1979). The police must have a good working relationship with the media so that both agencies can do their respective jobs. In order to work effectively with the media, negotiators need to understand the media's job.

The media liaison is responsible for maintaining contacts with the media, preparing media releases during and after incidents or for assisting the media and the departmental spokesperson during an incident. During an incident, the liaison is responsible for:

1. Controlling the media's physical presence to guarantee that they do not interfere with the operation.

2. Designating a specific media area that maximizes media safety while giving them the ability to observe and photograph.

3. Preparing and disseminating written media releases with timely and accurate information.

4. Arranging interviews with the appropriate personnel during the incident if it is a long one, or after the incident if it is relatively short (TCLEOSE, 1990).

Special Needs of the Media

The way the media goes about the task of gathering the news depends on what type of media they are: print, television, or radio. They differ in the access they need to the scene, in the lead time they need to meet their deadlines, and in the verbal skills of the people they interview (i.e., an interviewee need not be as articulate for the print media as he or she might for a television interview because the print media will clean up the language while the television media will record exactly what the interviewee says).

1. Television provides headline news. They need soundbites, short quotations from people, and pictures. They can transmit live from the scene of an incident and they can break into ongoing programming. For prerecorded interviews, they need approximately two hours lead time to edit and prepare news.

2. Radio provides headline news, too. They need interviews with articulate and quotable spokespersons. They also can transmit from the scene and break into on ongoing programming, if the incident is important enough. Also, they have scheduled newscasts hourly, so frequent updates are important to them.

3. Newspapers provide more in-depth reporting than the other two media. They require more information and usually have more time to gather background information. They need media releases and printable quotations. Their deadlines are usually around midnight or noon, depending on whether they are preparing for the morning or evening edition of the paper.

With some restrictions, the department needs to be prepared to provide the media with this information. Several ways of providing this information are available. They include written media releases, interviews with departmental spokespersons at the scene, or scheduled media conferences.

A constitutional issue affects the release of information to the media. The First Amendment right to a free press conflicts with the Sixth Amendment rights of the defendant to a fair trial (IACP, 1983). Many state and federal laws restrict the kinds of information a police department may release about an incident. Before an arrest is made and a person is booked into jail, information that can be released includes (IACP, 1983):

1. A description of the exact offense.

2. The location and the time of the offense.

Information that cannot be released includes:

1. The actor's identity.

2. Witnesses' and/or victims' identity.

3. Identity of sex crime victims.

4. Identity of juveniles when restricted by state law.

5. Conjecture about actor.

6. Misleading or false information.

7. Personal conjecture about the incident or the people involved.

After an arrest and booking, more information becomes part of the public record and is subject to be released to the media. Among such information is:

1. The actor's name, age, residence, employment, marital status, and other background information.

2. The time and place of the arrest.

3. Facts and circumstances of the incident.

4. Identity of the agencies or units involved in the incident.

5. Identity of the negotiators involved unless there is some compelling reason not to release this information.

6. Disposition of the individual (IACP, 1983).

Tactical Team

The tactical team's presence is essential to successful negotiations. They provide containment and a visible threat, without which the hostage taker has no reason to negotiate. They secure the scene by establishing the inner perimeter and by evacuating any civilians who are at risk inside the inner perimeter. They observe and communicate intelligence from the scene because they are in a position to keep the hostage taker and the scene under observation. They assault or neutralize the hostage taker if that becomes necessary. They make the arrest because they are usually the first officers to contact the hostage taker when he surrenders.

Communications within the Crisis Response Team

Timely and accurate communication is essential among members of a Crisis Response Team. Intelligence information needs to flow freely from the Negotiation Team to the Field Commander and Tactical Team and vice versa. Tactical plans for both the Negotiation Team and the Tactical Team must be communicated to the Field Commander for consideration and integration. Decisions by the Field Commander should be quickly communicated to both operational teams. Input from the "think tank" and the MHC needs to flow to the Field Commander for consideration. All of this makes it essential that channels of communication are clear, responsibility for communications is designated, and all the key personnel take responsibility for ensuring effective communications.

The principle of redundancy is important in setting up communications at an incident. It is important to have different communications channels available within and among teams. Redundancy maximizes the chances of keeping effective communications flowing during the incident. Having the primary communications mode backed up will keep vital information flowing. In addition to the departmental radio net, hard telephone lines, cellular telephones, and runners can be used.

Principle of Clarity: The importance of clear, understandable, and understood communications within the Crisis Response Team cannot be overemphasized. Early in this book, the types of noise that interfere with communication were discussed. Members of the Crisis Response Team need to make every effort to reduce or eliminate this. For instance, having the tactical team assign a team member to the negotiations area to facilitate the flow of intelligence helps reduce the distortion in communication that results from information being passed along by too many people. The communication between the commander and the negotiation team can be made clear by using a speaker that allows the commander to monitor negotiations. He can then ask the negotiator supervisors about the process. The FBI uses carefully drafted written communications to provide clear communication between the negotiators, the tactical team, and the commander.

Each method of communication has advantages and disadvantages. The appropriate choice of a communication channel will depend on the communication needs at the moment. The department's radio net has the advantage of being readily available to department personnel, being staffed by trained personnel, and being familiar to department personnel. However, it has the disadvantages of being easily monitored by the press and having a limited number of available channels. Hard-wired telephones have the advantage of being difficult to monitor. However, equipment has to be bought or found; this requires an extra expense. Citizens will be inconvenienced if their telephones are used. Cellular telephones have the advantage of being mobile. However, they are expensive, can be monitored, and have limited battery life when they are not plugged into a reliable power source. Though old-fashioned, runners have the advantage of being unmonitorable. However, disadvantages are that they may distort messages if they do not write them down, they are slower than direct communications, and they require personnel.

In a negotiation incident, there are overlapping patterns of communication. Communication is nothing more than the flow of information back and forth between people who need information. Figure 9.3 is an example of the information flow and the overlap that is necessary. Note that the situation commander and the team supervisors are key to effective communications. The incident commander communicates vertically with higher command. He or she is responsible for information flow up and down the chain of command. Tactical and negotiation supervisors are responsible for the information flow between their respective teams and the command post. In addition, they are responsible for information flow between one another. This redundancy of information flow is essential so that there are no mistakes due to miscommunication.

Establishing the Negotiation Area

Because the negotiator's job is to solve problems and because excessive stress interferes with problem solving, an appropriate environment is necessary for negotiation. The environment should be designed to meet the negotiators' needs for safety and security, freedom from distractions and criticism, and control of their environment. The location should be based on the principles of separation and isolation. That is, the negotiators' area should be separate from activities at the scene that do not contribute to the performance of their job and it should have the capability of locking out all distractions during the actual negotiations. Figure 9.4 is an example of the organization of a negotiator environment that addresses these needs.

Figure 9.3
Hostage Negotiating Team Communication Flow

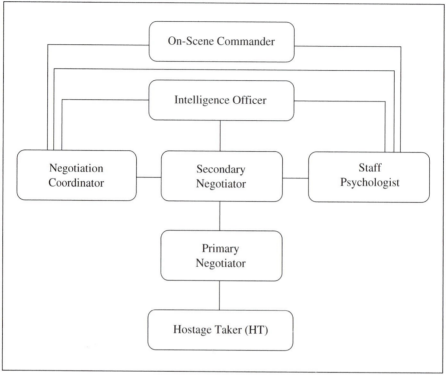

Source: McMains, M.

The location should be between the outer and inner perimeters of the operation. However, it should be out of the line of fire, so negotiators do not have to worry about their physical safety while they are trying to concentrate on the problem. It should be separate from, but close to, the commander and the command post, so the negotiator supervisor and the field commander can monitor the negotiations, coordinate with other departmental units, and coordinate with resources outside the department. It should allow the primary negotiator, secondary negotiator, and the MHC to be isolated during the actual time the hostage taker and the primary negotiator are talking. At the same time, it should allow other team members to monitor communications. It should be close to the holding area for witnesses, victims, and released hostages, so intelligence can be gathered with an economy of effort. It should also be close to the think tank, so the necessary expertise and ideas can be communicated efficiently.

Figure 9.4
**Example of a Physical Organization of the Negotiator's Environment
at the Scene of a Hostage Situation**

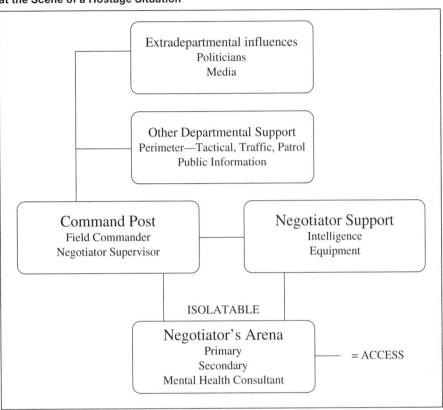

Source: McMains, M.

The Negotiating Team

One thing that distinguishes experienced negotiators from street officers is their ability to work as a team (McMains, 1992). They recognize that the successful resolution of a crisis incident requires the efforts of many people. Instead of working alone, they develop the ability to work with others, communicate with others, and solve problems with others (IACP, 1983). They learn to work as a team.

Teamwork requires several skills that must be developed systematically (IACP, 1983). They include members knowing their own role well and having a working knowledge of other team members' roles. They must be able to fill in for missing members, so that all the necessary jobs are done. They must recognize the importance of each role. Even though one role may receive more attention, each member of the team must recognize that all roles are essential to success.

Teamwork requires a joint problem-solving approach. It recognizes that in unfamiliar situations, the more people that are working on a problem, the better the solution. It recognizes the value of each individual, but it also understands that brainstorming by many generates more ideas than the efforts of a few. If it is true that two brains are better than one, it is even truer that four or five brains are better than one. There are no superstars.

However, teams do need leadership, especially in a crisis situation (IACP, 1983). One person has to take charge—not to exercise arbitrary power, but to be sure that the necessary expertise is brought to bear on the problem. The leader has oversight responsibility. He or she brings people together, assigns roles and responsibilities, and facilitates problem solving and communication.

Noesner's emphasis on a synchronized response in crises assumes that the crisis management team is well developed and functional. It assumes that elements of the team have worked, trained, and studied together enough to know each other's strengths and weaknesses. It assumes that good teamwork does not just happen—it is developed. The following are some guidelines for developing a working team (McMains, 1995; Katzenbach & Smith, 1993):

1. Limit the size of the team;

2. Select people for the skills they bring to the job;

3. Be sure all members of the team have a clear idea of the goals and are committed to them; and

4. Hold each other accountable.

Katzenbach and Smith (1993) point out the importance of eight steps in building an effective team:

1. Establish urgency and direction;

2. Select members for their skills and their potential for developing skills—not for their personality;

3. Carefully construct the first team meeting;

4. Set clear rules for behavior;

5. Set and pursue a few immediately productive tasks;

6. Challenge the group regularly with fresh facts and goals;

7. Spend lots of time together;

8. Use the power of positive feedback, recognition, and reward.

The incident at Talladega provided an example of how diverse groups can come together as an effective team in a short period. The problem was how to bring both Federal Bureau of Investigation and Bureau of Prisons negotiators together as a working team. They used a number of the principles listed above. Initially, both groups worked toward stabilizing the riot situation. The goal was clear. A counselor from BOP who had credibility and the respect of the inmates made initial contact. Three teams of negotiators, with a combination of FBI and BOP negotiators, were established, allowing a mix of experienced negotiators and prison expertise on each team. The teams were selected to complement each other. There were four coordinators—two from each agency—who resolved conflicts between team members, developed strategies, and supervised the teams in 12-hour shifts. If there were disagreements in strategy suggestions, the rules were that the commander had the final decision after hearing the suggestions from all coordinators. Each team spent eight hours a day together. At the end of each shift, they briefed the oncoming team. Additionally, they got to know each other's assets and liabilities quickly, so that by the fourth day, they were working together smoothly. Each shift was brought up-to-date through these briefings and through written situation reports that were generated periodically during the incident. These techniques kept everyone apprised of events and developments in the incident, as well as keeping the team "challenged with new facts." During the incident, the primary role was taken over by the FBI because the Talladega staff found it difficult to negotiate and talk with hostages who were friends and co-workers. The BOP staff served in a liaison role, orienting new negotiators to the facility, providing key information about subjects, and locating resources for other negotiators. This was another flexible use of the complementary skills that the combined team brought to bear on the incident.

Teamwork can be developed through experience or training. Teams that have worked together over a period of time and in many different incidents learn each other's strengths and weakness and roles. They learn to communicate and solve problems together and to compensate for one another's weaknesses. The problem with leaving the development of teamwork to experience is that sometimes teams do not work together often enough to learn these things. When an incident actually occurs, they tend to make mistakes because of their lack of knowledge of one another.

Training is the best method for developing teamwork. By having regular training sessions that require team members to work together, team functioning can be assessed and specific team-building skills can be taught. Assessment of team functioning evaluates to what degree the team shares a common vision of what they are doing, what their communications patterns are, what both individual and team motivation is for the job, the team's ability to solve problems, the team's morale, and their ability to learn from experience. Training can include both negotiator skill training and team-building exercises. The former is the type of material found in this book. The latter is the type of material taught in organizational development programs and is one of the areas with which the team's MHC can help between incidents.

The negotiating team can range in number from two to five people. The FBI (1993) recommends that a negotiating team have no fewer than two people. This is because there are too many things to do during an incident for one person to handle them all. A team solves problems better than an individual and team members provide support for one another. A negotiation team must:

1. Gather intelligence about the incident, the hostage taker, the hostages, etc.

2. Develop tactics that will defuse the incident, influence the hostage taker, and reduce the risk of loss of life.

3. Establish communication with the hostage taker.

4. Record relevant intelligence information.

5. Keep a record of the negotiations, including demands and promises.

6. Maintain equipment.

7. Coordinate and communicate with field commander and tactical team.

FBI guidelines (McMains, 1991) suggest the following organization of a negotiating team:

1. Team Supervisor. The person responsible for the assignment of team duties, for coordination with the command and tactical teams.

2. The Primary Negotiator. The person responsible for talking directly to the hostage taker, for developing verbal tactics, and for monitoring and assessing the hostage taker's level of emotional arousal, and for being alert to irrelevant information from the hostage taker.

3. The Secondary Negotiator. The person responsible for maintaining a record of contacts with the hostage taker (written log and/or audiotape of negotiations), developing verbal tactics for dealing with the hostage taker, providing moral support for the negotiator. He or she is the communication link between the negotiator and other team members, and is available to relieve the negotiator as necessary.

4. Intelligence Officer. The person who is responsible for: gathering intelligence on the personality of the hostage taker; the physical location and weapons involved in the incident; the nature of the incident; interviewing friends, family, and/or released hostages; and maintaining the status board of relevant information.

5. Mental Health Consultant (MHC). The person who is responsible for evaluating the personality of the hostage taker, recommending negotiating techniques, monitoring team stress, and consulting with command. He or she can be a psychologist, psychiatrist, or social worker who is trained and experienced in crisis intervention, conflict resolution, and negotiation principles.

Team members must understand and be able to function in multiple roles. Manpower availability may make it impossible for a department to maintain a five-person team. The different stages of an incident will require an emphasis on different roles at different times. During the early part of the Crisis stage, the initial emphasis is on intelligence gathering. All team members will function as intelligence officers, with the team leader coordinating activities. As soon as a strategy is developed and communications with the hostage taker are necessary, the team will be divided into their roles as primary negotiator, secondary negotiator, etc. Team members need to be flexible, not becoming too focused on one set of skills to the exclusion of others.

Sidebar: Lieutenant Stephen M. Pugsley (retired)

Lieutenant Steve Pugsley joined the Massachusetts State Police in 1980. He has served in a variety of positions including patrol, K-9, court prosecutor, gang unit, organized crime investigation, patrol supervisor, the legal section and barracks commander. He retired in December of 2005 as the department's crisis negotiation team commander.

Lieutenant Pugsley holds a bachelor of science degree from Boston State College (1978) and a master of arts Degree from Anna Maria College (1986), both in criminal justice. He also earned his Juris Doctor from Suffolk University Law School (1992).

Pugsley has taught at the Massachusetts State Police Academy, as well as for the Massachusetts Criminal Justice Training Council. He has extensive experience in both the development and instruction of training programs for all aspects of law enforcement including recruit training, in-service and specialty courses. Some of his subject areas have included Ethics and Integrity Leadership, Background Investigations, Interviews and Interrogations, Employee Evaluations, Civil Rights and Hate Crimes, Civil Liability, Criminal Law, and Crisis Negotiations. He has taught at international ethics conferences as well as presented at numerous crisis negotiation seminars throughout the United States and Canada. Pugsley now consults and conducts training seminars in many of the subjects he has taught through the years.

Webster's Dictionary defines a team as "a group organized to work together" and teamwork as "cooperative effort by the members of a group or team to achieve a common goal." I am sure many of us remember the days when our departments were comprised of teams without that cooperative effort or common goal. Oftentimes the tactical team had its own agenda as the negotiators were attempting to use time and rapport-building to resolve critical incidents, while the on-scene commander was watching the overtime costs and attempting to rush to a conclusion. Fortunately, most departments have adapted the "Crisis Management Triad" approach espoused by the FBI to manage and resolve crisis situations. This allows a continuous flow of intelligence and other pertinent information among the incident commander, tactical team, and crisis negotiation team. This approach not only employs sound teamwork, it lays a solid legal foundation to protect government agencies and individual officers from potential liabilities. When all entities are allowed input in a crisis situation during ongoing operational briefings, an agency is able to perpetuate, through documentation, decisions that are made.

The decisions are based on the "Action Criteria." Is the contemplated action necessary? Is the contemplated action risk-effective? Is the contemplated action acceptable? We must also answer the timing questions. Why did we take the action at this point? What conditions have changed? Finally, were less risky alternatives tried? (From the FBI's Crisis Negotiation Unit)

During a recent team call-out, we faced some of these questions and applied the decision-making formula to achieve a successful resolution. The incident began around 3:00 P.M. when the local police department requested the assistance of the State Police.

The husband had barricaded himself in the second-floor apartment after an attempt by the local department to serve him with a "domestic abuse" order to vacate the premises. It was a run-of-the-mill domestic situation in which the wife sought to have the husband removed amidst the breakdown of the marriage, which was heading toward a divorce. The subject was threatening to harm himself and any law enforcement officer who attempted to enter the residence.

Upon arrival of all entities we quickly employed the team approach. The incident commander was the major of the state police troop of jurisdiction and worked in concert with the local chief of police. The negotiation and tactical team leaders completed the Crisis Management Triad. The negotiations were conducted over a traditional hard-wired telephone. There was no cell phone in the house, which assisted in controlling the communications. Through the local service provider, we were able to change his telephone number to one that only we knew, as well as limit his outgoing service only to us. This removed the possibility of him coming into contact with anyone else.

Prior to taking control of the telephone, the subject displayed the usual rage and anger and insisted on the police killing him. There were no known weapons involved; however, he would constantly stand in front of a window and shout out for us to kill him. At one point, he broke a window and cut himself superficially on the finger. Our intelligence indicated that he did have access to a substantial amount of prescription medications, which was a concern for us.

After a short period of negotiations with the subject, the negotiators were comfortable that he would not truly harm himself and that it was just going to take time (time is our best ally). During our periodic briefings with the "Triad," it was agreed by all that we would continue to isolate, contain, and negotiate. The discussions were typical of a domestic situation (i.e., family, "the kids love you, no one will hurt you," etc.). A local officer with whom the subject had interacted positively in the past was used for a while in an attempt to resolve the situation but the subject was not "ready."

After about eight hours, the subject appeared to be ready to accept help and go to a local hospital, where he had gone in the past, for psychiatric help. He said he would come out but asked us to first contact his mother, who lived out of state, and tell her that he was going to the same hospital he had been to before and to assure her that "everything was going to be OK." We called him back and told him we had spoken to his mother. He said he needed a few minutes to get his thoughts together and then he would come out. After about five minutes, we started calling and he would not answer. We then started hailing him over speakers set up in front of the house, again to no avail. The tactical team could no longer see him, as they had been able to do throughout the incident. This was a drastic change in his behavior. We became concerned and reconvened the "Triad."

The negotiators informed the incident commander and tactical team leader that we were concerned that the subject may have used us to vicariously say goodbye to his mother before committing suicide. We were concerned he may have either cut himself or ingested the medications he had at his disposal. A plan was devised to raise the stakes in an attempt to re-establish communications. We would continue ringing the phone and hailing the subject. The tactical team would first break a few windows and if that did not work, introduce gas and then, if necessary, make entry. The "action criteria" questions were asked and the contemplated action was "necessary, risk effective, and acceptable." Next the timing questions were asked and again we could articulate what conditions had changed, why we would take the action at this point, and whether less risky alternatives had been tried. We had to implement the plan. Through a combined effort, communication was attempted, two windows were broken, gas was introduced, and then entry was made. The subject was located lying on a couch with a couple of empty prescription bottles on a table in front of him. He was barely breathing when paramedics rushed him to the hospital. He survived and remained in the hsopital for psychiatric treatment.

This incident illustrates the importance of the constant flow of intelligence and communication among all aspects of the Command Triad. The tactical team was patient throughout more than eight hours of negotiations while providing crucial on-site intelligence. When the negotiators recognized a drastic change in communications, the information was relayed in a timely manner. Throughout the incident the on-scene commanders coordinated the scene with input from all and were flexible enough to rapidly change the approach in the end. Although it was not the ideal ending with a negotiated surrender, it was considered a success because a life was saved and no one else was injured.

Selection of Negotiators

One important issue for crisis negotiation teams is that of replacing members who leave the team. In the past, many teams simply asked for volunteers and accepted anyone who volunteered. As teams have grown and the demands on them have increased, skills have become more sophisticated, and more knowledge is required, it is imperative that teams establish a set of criteria and a selection process that will allow them to select the best-qualified applicants from the volunteer pool. Teams can use the guidelines presented here as a template to assist them in developing a selection process.

For agencies that want to begin a team, the same guidelines can be used, but they need to first conduct some background research and answer some basic questions about their future team. The agency first needs to review local data to determine what the community needs may be for negotiators and what type of incidents they will respond to. The agency should review past dispatch records, EMS records, fire department calls, survey hospital emergency rooms, and talk to local women's shelters to determine the types of incidents negotiators will address. The type of person selected for the team, the training for the team, the mission of the team, policies and procedures guiding team call-outs and actions, and even the team name and identity will be established by this review of data. For example, if the majority of incidents in the community are related to domestic incidents, it does not make much sense to select negotiators for their ability to deal with hardened criminals, nor call the team a hostage negotiation team. They will be dealing with people who have elevated stress levels and are in severe crises. Negotiators should have excellent communication and listening skills, patience, and think of and perceive themselves as crisis negotiators.

Next, for the newly formed team, specific roles should be identified and filled. What do people do? Is intelligence gathering a primary and critical function for the team? What amount of equipment will be available to the team and how will it be maintained and repaired? It may be that the team needs one individual who will do nothing but make, obtain, maintain, and repair equipment. In addition to the generally accepted roles of team leader, primary negotiator, secondary negotiator, mental health consultant, intelligence officer, and scribe/historian, there may be special needs that have to be filled.

In terms of number of personnel needed, a survey by Mullins (2003) found that most law enforcement negotiator teams numbered between six and ten people, with some as small as three people, and some as large as 20 people. Prison and correctional teams averaged 16 to 26 people. Their teams were larger because they needed to prepare for siege situations with personnel rotations.

Finally, a decision should be made as to whether negotiators will be selected to perform a specific function (i.e., only as a secondary negotiator, for example) or a generalist who can perform all team functions. In terms of specialized duties, some of the advantages include: (1) training—members train for only one function and can spend more time in the specific training for their role on the team; (2) expertise—team members can become more proficient in their area of expertise because that is all they do; (3) practice—at all scenario and role-play training, team members practice only their job and no other; (4) stress management issues—team members on a call-out will be under less stress than a generalist because they will know going in what their role, job, and function will be. Some of the disadvantages of the team specialist model include: (1) time of calls—all team members have to be on constant call-out status. If the team is small, what happens if the secondary negotiator is on vacation? (2) Personnel required—the team will have to be much larger in size due to personnel being away and not on call-out status; (3) lack of team cohesiveness—team members train and operate only in their specialized job and do not interact with other team members to build team skills. Negotiation efforts are a team effort and specialization of negotiators reduces team building and unity.

Having negotiators who perform generalized duties also has advantages, most of which are the opposite of the specific duty model. Some advantages of the general model include: (1) time of calls—team members can perform all functions, so members not being available for calls presents less of a problem than the specialized model; (2) personnel required—fewer negotiators are needed as team members can "plug in" and fill the gaps; (3) knowledge of team functions—team members can build a knowledge and ability base for all functions on the team and know what everyone is supposed to do. If a team member is not doing what they should be doing, that can be addressed. Some disadvantages of the generalist model include: (1) lack of expertise—team members do not learn any one job as well as a specialist would; (2) stress management issues—team members responding to an incident do not know until they arrive what they will be doing, which raises individual stress.

Given this discussion, we believe negotiators should follow the generalist model. The disadvantages are not serious and limiting, and the advantages far outweigh the disadvantages of the specialist model. All negotiators should be able to perform all functions on the team (with the exception of the mental health consultant), including being able to fill in as team leader if needed.

Selection Model for Negotiators

Below is a proposed sequence of steps that agencies can use to select negotiators. Many departments use this sequence, some using it as outlined below, and others modifying it to fit their agency's needs.

First, negotiators should be volunteers. Making negotiations a mandatory duty assignment is neither recommended nor advised. Because of the job requirements, training requirements, and crisis response duties, team members have to be highly motivated and self-starting. One debate concerns whether persons of rank (i.e., sergeants, lieutenants, deputy wardens, etc.) should be allowed on the team. It has been our experience (and recommendation) that rank should not matter. The negotiator will not introduce him/herself as "Sergeant Mullins." They should have the ability to accept and follow orders from someone lower in rank than themselves. Team leaders are selected by experience and ability, not by rank, and many teams are led by non-ranking persons. Volunteers should not have any other special assignments. They should not be on SWAT, special investigative task forces, etc. The time demands for negotiators are high and flexible. Other duties will likely interfere with both training and call-outs. Experience in the agency should be a requirement. Most agencies require two to five years of experience before allowing personnel to join the negotiating team. The Federal Bureau of Prisons requires one year of experience in their agency (Mullins, 2000). Finally, volunteers can be selected to fill special needs on the team. If the team needs a Spanish speaker, or a female, or another specialized skill, they can ask for and fill the position with people who have that skill.

One suggested announcement for a team vacancy might be: "The _____ Police Department is seeking interested officers to serve on the Crisis Negotiation Team. Officers should have at least three years experience, have good communication skills, be willing to attend a minimum of 80 hours of training per year, be willing to be on 24-hour call for two weeks at a time, and have no other special assignments. Volunteers should also submit a letter from their supervisor recommending them for the team."

The announcement tells officers what the requirements are and, just as important, what the requirements for training and call-outs are. Also, a letter from the officer's supervisor gives the supervisor's approval for the individual being selected, assigned, and called away from regular duties for training and call-outs.

As part of the application, all interested applications should complete an interest sheet or application that asks for biographical data, work data (including complaints, grievances, suspensions, etc.), a statement as to why they are interested in the position, and other supporting documents. The interest sheet and written statement is an indicator of their communication ability.

Second, there should be a structured interview with the team leader. A structured interview means each applicant is asked the same questions, and that the answers are numerically scored and tallied. Areas to explore might include the applicant's willingness to work unusual hours, be on call, acceptance of position responsibilities, perspective of the applicant on teamwork, being in the "background" or lack of public recognition, and communication ability.

Scoring anchors can be provided for this interview. For example, if one of the questions is "How well do you communicate with other people?" scoring anchors might be: (Score of 5 – highest score)—"excellent communicator, proper use of English, no hesitation, no stuttering, ideas and thoughts clearly conveyed"; (score of 4)—"mostly uses proper English, very little hesitation, ideas and thoughts expressed very well"; (score of 3)—"average use of proper English, some hesitation, some ideas unclear, some stuttering"; (score of 2)—"ideas difficult to follow, often changed directions during a sentence or thought, poor use of English"; and (score of 1)—"no clear ideas, no proper use of English, could not understand, mumbled, did not speak to me." Anchors such as these for each question will help ensure that all applicants are assessed on the same criteria and that the potential for bias is reduced.

Third, a negotiator team interview should be conducted in which team members have the opportunity to interview and assess applicants. Although some teams use or include negotiators from other agencies to remove bias (Mullins, 2001), we believe team members should conduct these interviews. They are the ones who will have to work with the applicant. Negotiators will work hard to select the most qualified individual. Like the team leader interview, the team interview should be structured and scoring anchors should be provided.

The team interview should assess dimensions such as communication skills, adaptability, ability to think on one's feet, temperament, ability to cope with a variety of situations, team skills, reactions to crisis or unclear situations, ability to handle stress, ability to take orders, and fit with team. Some questions that may be asked include:

1. Define communications.

2. Identify your strengths and weaknesses.

3. What does the word "empathy" mean to you?

4. Tell us what your concept of "team player" means. What could you bring to the team?

5. How does crisis negotiations fit within your philosophy of law enforcement? As a police officer, what does the term "do no harm" mean to you?

6. Without using any names, think of the person you least like to work with (for whatever reason) and tell us what strategies you have used to work with that person?

7. How reliable is your first impression of people? Do you often rely on that first impression? Why or why not?

Fourth, applicants should be put through a short telephone scenario. This scenario should last about five to 15 minutes, be scripted and standardized for all applicants, and be scored by team members. One way to conduct the scenario is to complete it at the end of the team interview, using a team member as the actor. The scenario should be realistic and simple. The most commonly used scenarios involve a barricaded subject, domestic situation, depressed/suicidal individual, or an antisocial personality (Mullins, 2000).

The scenario should assess the applicant's communication skills, listening skills (communication skills and listening skills are the most critical skills to assess during the scenario), ability to adjust to changes, ability to think/talk on their feet, ability to gather intelligence information, temperament, ability to empathize, ability to handle stress, and demeanor. Regini (2002) says negotiators have to be able to maintain their voice control and have good self-control. The Tacoma Police Department includes active listening skills and establishing rapport (Griswold, 2005). Remember, however, do not expect applicants to have the same level of skill and ability as a trained negotiator. One thing the scenario is trying to assess is the applicant's ability to learn the skills and abilities necessary to be a negotiator.

One potential exercise may be a barricaded subject who is threatening to commit suicide. The subject's wife left and took their two young daughters. The suspect's drinking and gambling problems led to the wife leaving. He has never beaten the children, although on occasion he has hit his wife (although not hard enough to bruise her or do physical damage). In addition to this telephone exercise, teams may conduct a "face-to-face" or "voice-to-voice" scenario.

Some departments require a physical fitness/agility test (Hogewood, 2005). The test assesses upper body strength and stamina. Teams must sometimes carry heavy equipment or travel on foot to remote locations. Members must be able to work long periods without rest or breaks. Physical fitness/agility tests measure applicant's abilities to meet the physical demands of the job.

Some departments employ a psychological evaluation for applicants. Applicants are typically evaluated on their ability to deal with stress, anger management, stability of personality, ability to take orders and not be in charge, ability to solve problems creatively, and frustration tolerance. In a review of psychological evaluations, Logan (2004) reported that applicants are also assessed on knowledge and skill in communications, dealing with general public, verbal fluency, good self-image, reasoning ability, sensitivity to others, general characteristics (maturity, mental agility, intelligence), dependability, reliability, level of arousal, sense of morality, emphasis on cooperation versus manipulation, social withdrawal,

The role of the recorder on the team is crucial. The recorder keeps notes, logs, summarizes, disseminates info/intell, and maintains the permanent record. In long incidents where negotiators rotate, the role of Recorder is more critical, because the Recorder is responsible for providing update summaries and briefing papers to oncoming negotiators. *(S. Davis)*

and resourcefulness. We do not believe it is necessary to conduct a psychological evaluation for negotiator applicants (or team members). While it may be beneficial and necessary for tactical team members, the job negotiators perform does not lend itself to a prior psychological evaluation. In addition, in police departments, officers are given psychological evaluations when hired. Another evaluation is not necessary.

Mental Health Consultant

A mental health professional with a background in or an understanding of police work/hostage negotiations can be a valuable resource to a negotiation team (Fuselier, 1986; FBI, 1993). He or she can provide input to both the negotiators and command during the negotiation incident, as well as help to train the team and educate the command and administrative officers of the department between incidents. Generally, the mental professional has four areas of value to negotiators and to police departments during an incident (McMains, 1991):

1. The MHC has expertise in human behavior. He or she can evaluate the type of person the police are dealing with, assess the suicide and aggression potential, and help develop negotiation tactics.

2. The MHC helps reduce exposure to liability, although the department cannot be expected to allow the mental health professional to make the decisions at the scene. His or her presence and input shows a good faith effort to resolve the incident peacefully, using every available resource.

3. The MHC can enhance the police department's public image. His or her presence communicates "We are interested in doing all we can to resolve this situation in the least harmful way. We are open to non-police input and we will use every available resource—including the expertise in human relations, stress, and motivation."

4. The MHC can increase negotiation team morale by monitoring stress levels and intervening when needed, by providing emotional support and input into tactics used by the negotiating team. Decisionmaking under stress is improved when it is shared by a number of people with a variety of expertise. Including a mental health professional on the team can provide such stress reduction and morale-building functions.

Even though a mental health professional is licensed in his or her respective profession, it is no guarantee that the MHC will understand the resources of the police, the principles of hostage negotiation, or the public safety responsibility of the department. Many departments have had experiences like the one reported by Schlossberg (1979), in which the MHC simply advised the Crisis Response Team to use tear gas on the hostage taker. He made no attempt to use his mental health expertise or knowledge in defusing or managing the incident. He did not understand the fundamental principles of negotiations. However, Fuselier (1986) has suggested that mental health professionals can be of use to negotiators, if they are properly trained.

Schlossberg (1979) developed the initial principles of hostage negotiation based on the psychological perspective. It would seem that mental health professionals could learn to function on a Crisis Response Team if they are trained, just as police officers can learn to be negotiators if they are trained. The training is clearly in place to teach police about psychology. What is needed is a training program to teach MHCs about police capabilities and how psychology is applied to negotiations. Also, what are needed are mental health professionals that understand that their role is to provide knowledge and expertise within their field, not in the police field.

The research on the use of MHCs seems to show an increasing trend toward using their expertise. McMains (1988b) found that in 1985, only two percent of 20 major departments surveyed utilized a MHC at the scene. In 1988, Fuselier reported that 58 percent of the 34 departments he surveyed that have negotiating teams used a MHC. The differences in the size of the departments surveyed may account for some of the differences in usage. Fuselier reported that two of the larger departments in his sample did not use a MHC because they thought that they had sufficient experience to handle incidents without a MHC. All departments surveyed by McMains were large departments. This may have been a sampling bias. However, Butler et al. (1993) reported on a study of 300 departments that utilized negotiators to resolve conflict situations. Of those 300 agencies, 39 percent used a MHC.

The outcome of incidents in which MHCs were used is evidence of their value to negotiators. Departments using MHCs reported a higher incidence of situations ending by negotiated surrender and fewer incidents ending in a tactical resolution than departments not using a MHC. Agencies using MHCs reported fewer incidents resulting in death or injury than agencies that did not use a MHC. These results suggest that a MHC may decrease the risk of injury and death in hostage incidents.

MHCs are used in a variety of ways by negotiating teams. Fuselier (1988) found that they were used to assess the hostage taker, counsel officers after an incident, debrief the team, suggest negotiating techniques, interface with other mental health professionals, interview victims' families, and provide counseling services to victims. McMains (1988a) found that communication skills were the most valued of the skills taught in most hostage negotiation schools. These skills and their applicability to crisis management are the direct result of mental health professionals' experience and research. Another valuable role of the MHC is providing input on communications techniques. Hatcher et al. (1998) reported that there are four models for the use of psychologists in crisis intervention/hostage incidents. They are used as:

1. Consultants/advisors, which is the same as Fuselier's (1988) and McMains' (1991) descriptions.

2. An integrated team member—the psychologist functions as a psychologist and is cross-trained to function as the primary negotiator, secondary negotiator, intelligence officer, or tactical liaison officer. This model makes the MHC a full member of the team, but if he or she is used in other roles too often, the value of his or her unique knowledge, skills, and abilities is lost.

3. Primary Negotiator, a role that is not recommended. The use of the MHC to negotiate is based on the assumption that because they are experts in human behavior, they are the best people to talk to the subject. The weakness in this approach is that it is difficult for the MHC to assess the situation, the type of personality, the appropriate tactics, and the stress levels when he or she is dealing directly with the subject.

4. Primary controller of the incident. For the most part, this is not a role that MHCs in the United States have assumed, and for good reason. Just as there are few incident commanders or negotiators who are trained MHCs, there are fewer MHCs who are trained as police officers, let alone as incident commanders. It would be unethical for a MHC to assume control of an incident without the appropriate training and experience.

Figure 9.5 outlines the kinds of knowledge that MHCs have that can be helpful to negotiators and police departments.

With sufficient exposure and training, a motivated professional can learn to use his or her mental health expertise to facilitate a peaceful resolution to a high-conflict incident.

The MHC has expertise and knowledge that needs to be brought to bear before an incident begins. During the Pre-Crisis stage, a MHC can help train negotiators on active listening and persuasion techniques, principles of crisis intervention, recognition and management of personality types, threat assessment, and psychology of aggression. He or she can evaluate team functioning and design training to strengthen team development and can consult with management and command on the skills, knowledge, and abilities of negotiators, and on training to meet vicarious liability issues and management principles.

During an incident, the MHC's role is clearly defined. As part of the negotiating team, he or she evaluates the hostage taker to determine the type of personality involved, assesses the potential for violence or suicide, helps develop strategies and tactics, monitors stress levels, and recommends stress management techniques for negotiators. As part of the department's Crisis Response Team, the MHC consults with command on the potential for violence, either suicidal or homicidal, negotiability of the problem, and changing mental status of the hostage taker.

Figure 9.5
Consultation Roles for Psychologists in Hostage Negotiations.
Figure indicates knowledge necessary for the psychologist.

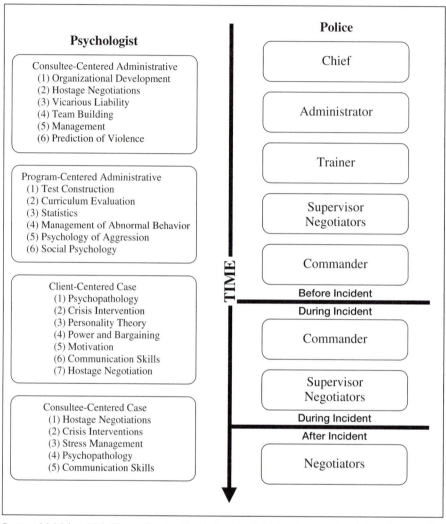

Source: McMains, M.J. "Expanding the Psychologist's Role in Hostage Negotiations." *Journal of Police and Criminal Psychology*, 4(1):2-8. Reprinted with permission.

After the incident, the MHC can help facilitate the emotional debriefing if it is necessary and can help manage the operational debriefing. He or she can help involved personnel use the incident to learn about what went well and what needs to be improved without it becoming a personal failure. The MHC can provide team building and conflict resolution management.

Selection and Training of a MHC

As with the selection and training of negotiators, selection and training of MHCs require attention to two issues: (1) the knowledge and talent of the individual, and (2) the body of knowledge he or she has or can develop about the specific area. The former deals with the issue of selection, while the latter focuses on training.

When selecting a MHC, the following must be considered:

1. Knowledge

2. Skills

3. Abilities

The MHC's knowledge can be assessed by looking at his or her education, training, licensure, and certification. In addition to having an advanced degree in their area of specialty (psychology, social work, or psychiatry), it is helpful for police departments to ask for and to review the prospective MHC's transcript and curriculum vita. They should reflect successful completion of abnormal psychology, counseling and psychotherapy, crisis intervention, suicide prevention, communications, and organizational psychology. Workshops in active listening, negotiating, problem-solving, and creativity would be helpful, although not mandatory. The MHC's course of study should be primarily clinically oriented, with emphasis on communications, crisis intervention, psychopathology, persuasion, and influence.

Other ways of checking the MHC's knowledge level would be to ask for a list of publications, workshops, or special training. It is recommended that the MHC be a licensed mental health professional. Licensure guarantees that the MHC has a minimum level of common knowledge in the field and that he or she understands the legal and ethical issues involved in the delivery of services. It also provides some protection from liability.

Finally, the MHC should be in good standing with his or her professional association or organization. In most metropolitan areas, there are local psychological associations or medical societies that can be of help in finding out about the general reputation of a particular practitioner. Smaller agencies can check with the licensing board that administers a particular mental health discipline for their state. Janik (1994) has suggested three organizations within psychology that may be contacts for agencies wanting information about psychologists with experience and expertise in police psychology, including crisis negotiations: Division 18 of the American Psychological Association, The Police Psychology Section of the International Chiefs of Police, and The Society of Police and Criminal Psychology, which in 1989 began awarding a Diplomate in Police Psychology to professionals with a demonstrated expertise in police issues.

There are several skills that are important for a MHC to possess if he or she is going to work in negotiations and in a police department. They include communication (both written and oral), teaching, diagnostic, and assessment skills. They can be assessed during the screening process, which combines an interview with a formal presentation and role-play.

A MHC must have the ability to function within a quasi-military, hierarchical organizational structure; maintain professional identity; apply knowledge to unique problems; problem-solve; and function as part of a team (Hatcher et al., 1998). He or she must have the ability to be available for training and for incidents: they need a flexible schedule and an adaptable and flexible attitude. These abilities can be assessed by reviewing the candidate's history and through role-play scenarios in which they are asked to play the part of the MHC to the department's negotiators.

Selection Process. The selection of a MHC should involve eight steps:

1. *Develop a Job Description.* Janik (1994) has pointed out that police departments need a clear idea of what they want their MHC to do for them. Do they want a full-time employee or a consultant? The decision is usually an economic one. Larger departments opt for full-time employees, because they can afford them. Smaller departments usually contract with consultants. In either case, they need a clear idea of what to expect. By developing a concrete and specific job description, police departments must focus clearly on their expectations for the MHC. A constructive approach is for the administration, command structure, and operational elements of the department to develop four or five questions they would want a MHC to answer in a crisis incident. This exercise helps clarify the expectations of each level of the organization. It also helps define areas in which the department's expectations of a MHC may be unrealistic.

2. *Advertise.* The public announcement of the need for a MHC can be done in a number of ways. Advertising in the local paper will attract local talent who may understand the culture, political issues, and local economy. Advertising in national publications focused on law enforcement or mental health will open the hiring to a broader range of skilled people, making it more likely that the agency will find qualified applicants.

3. *Review Vita and Transcripts.* Transcripts of academic training will provide an overview of the candidate's formal education. It allows the department to evaluate course content. The vita usually includes a listing of continuing professional education the candidate has had since completing his or her formal academic training.

4. *Check with Licensing Boards and Professional Associations.* Professionalism involves the application of a specific body of knowledge to defined problems. Attaining a professional

license usually involves being tested on the body of knowledge that is applied by the professional. Licensing assures a basic understanding of the knowledge of the field Therefore, the MHC should be expected to hold the appropriate license.

5. *Interview*. A person-to-person interview with MHC applicants allows a screening panel to evaluate the applicant's experience, training, philosophy, and motivation. Experienced police officers can get a feel for how well the prospective MHC will get along with the negotiating team, how well he or she can communicate, and how well he or she thinks through problems on short notice by interviewing. Their commitment and availability can be ascertained. A MHC that is not available 24 hours a day or who does not set a high priority on negotiations is not an asset to the team.

6. *Lecture and Training Block*. At the same time as the interview, prospective MHCs can be asked to prepare a lesson plan and to deliver a class on selected negotiation-related topics. For instance, he or she might be asked to prepare a lecture on the place of active listening skills in crisis negotiation. Such a task would allow the selection committee to evaluate the applicant's knowledge of communication skills, crisis intervention skills, and teaching skills.

7. *Role-Play Scenario*. To assess the applicant's ability to work as a member of a team in addition to how well he or she can apply theoretical knowledge to concrete problems, each MHC applicant should be placed in a simulated negotiation situation. The situation should be structured so that the MHC has to gather information, assess the personality of the actor, and make appropriate recommendations about the actor's dangerousness, suicide potential, and sensitive points so the team can develop appropriate strategies. The scenario needs to be "winnable" if the team and the MHC use the correct approach. All applicants should be required to deal with the same scenario and the knowledge, skills, and abilities on which they are evaluated should be determined and listed for the judges before the first applicant is interviewed.

8. *Panel Review*. A panel of experienced crisis negotiators, supervisory personnel, and command officers should interview, evaluate, and rate each MHC applicant. If one is available, a MHC with experience in crisis negotiation should be on the panel. Larger police departments have full-time MHCs who are frequently available to help structure and participate in selection procedures. In areas where no experienced police MHC is available, departments can check with hospital emergency rooms that have mental health resources, community mental health clinics, crisis telephone services, or suicide prevention centers for advice and help in selecting a MHC.

9. Training. In addition to the psychological knowledge discussed above, MHCs need specialized knowledge about law enforcement. They need to attend a basic negotiator's course in order to understand the philosophy, purpose, and techniques used by police negotiators. MHCs who work with jail and prison negotiating teams need to understand prisons. Knowledge of the jobs of prison officers, administrators, civilian staff, and trustee duties are critical to success. Additionally, the MHC should have a thorough understanding of the dynamics and psychological aspects of the prison milieu. Most police departments that have tried to use MHCs have had problems that were the result of a lack of training on the part of the MHC. They did not understand negotiating principles.

MHCs need an orientation to law enforcement, either through formal criminal justice courses, such as police systems and practices, or through exposure to patrol officers on a regular basis and voluntary participation in training activities. Janik (1994) has pointed out that police psychologists must have a clear understanding of the police worldview in order to work effectively in the organization. Such an understanding only comes through participation and exposure to the responsibilities of law enforcement.

MHCs need to study police responsibilities and discretion in issues such as arrest, search and seizure, the use of deadly force, and police ethics, to understand the legal ramifications and liability issues.

Greenstone (unpublished manuscript) has reported a growing number of inquiries from mental health professionals who express an interest in consulting with police negotiations teams. They have shown a broad range of training and experience involving law enforcement, from no experience through involvement in selection and training, to full-time employment with an agency. At the same time, a question the authors are asked at every presentation they make to law enforcement negotiators and administrators is "How do we find somebody to be our consultant in crises?" These questions from both mental health and law enforcement professionals point to the importance of selecting and training mental health consultants.

The questions asked of Greenstone (unpublished manuscript) highlight issues about which both law enforcement and MHCs need to be concerned in selecting a MHC. For instance, questions such as: "What if I am called at 2:00 A.M.?" deals with the availability of the MHC when the team needs him or her. Questions about whether the MHC should become a police officer or a reserve officer focuses on a second serious issue: How well does your mental heath consultant know the job a police officer does and how credible is he or she to the officers? Questions such as "Should I volunteer time?" deal with the commitment of your MHC. Questions such as "What is my role during an incident?" deal with how and what to train the mental health professional to do.

Most MHCs have the fundamental training and skills in areas such as active listening, emotionally disturbed people, and stress and stress management. They need orientation to see how these skills fit into crisis negotiations. They may or may not need training in suicide and crisis intervention or risk assessment. They will certainly need training in the issues that are covered on day one of the workshop discussed above. They need a clear presentation of the consultant versus decisionmaker role, culture, goals of policing, responsibilities of law enforcement in keeping the peace and keeping the public and themselves safe, as well as the strategies and tactics of crisis negotiations.

Case Study: The Mental Health Consultant. The department psychologist arrived at the scene and was briefed by the field commander. He interviewed neighbors, who reported that the subject's aunt had taken him to the mental health clinic at one of the local hospitals the week before because he was beginning to think that the aunt was conspiring to kill him. Medication was prescribed, but he refused to take it, saying that it was poisoned. The neighbors said that he had been under psychiatric care in Mexico.

The precipitating incident for the current crisis was reported to have been the aunt's taking the subject to the airport that morning to catch a plane to Mexico. It was learned from the aunt while officers were talking to both her and the subject on the porch that he had become more and more agitated as they got closer to the airport. He refused to get out of the car when they arrived at the airport. She returned home where the subject produced a knife, yelled about her wanting him dead, and dragged her into the house.

The psychologist advised the commander that, due to the subject's heightened awareness and paranoia, it was best to deploy tactical team members in an unobtrusive way, without the subject being able to see them. This message did not get to the sniper who walked in front of the house. Consequently, a crisis was created by the deployment of personnel.

The psychologist briefed the primary negotiators on the issues involved with paranoid schizophrenics. He reminded them that safety, security, and self-esteem were highly important issues for paranoid individuals and that it was important to reassure the subject that everything was under control and everybody was going to be safe. The importance of maintaining a reasonable, rational, and somewhat distant attitude was emphasized. It was pointed out that it was important to be non-judgmental, especially about the subject's delusions, so as not to challenge his self-esteem. Ways of diverting the subject when he got into his delusional context were discussed.

In developing the overall approach to the situation, the psychologist pointed out that negotiators needed to identify the subject's specific fears and to work on reassuring him about them. The working theory that the team adopted was that the idea of going back to Mexico had special meaning to him and that he could be reassured that he would not have to return. At the same time, intelligence officers were asked to check with police and mental health officials in his hometown in Mexico to see if there were specific reasons he might not want to return home. Finally, the psychologist suggested that the tactical team might be prepared to take advantage of mistakes that the subject made during the course of the incident. He pointed out that even though the subject was not well-armed, the subject still had a higher than average potential for violence because he was paranoid, not taking his medication, and from a lower-class culture that put a premium on direct action by individuals when they felt threatened. During the course of the negotiations, it was learned from authorities in Mexico that the subject had both a psychiatric and a criminal history. He had been treated for paranoid schizophrenia and he had an outstanding warrant for the attempted murder of a police officer.

Case Review. The mental health professional's role at the scene of a crisis incident is to apply his knowledge of abnormal behavior, of crisis intervention and communications principles, to the practical decisions made by commanders, negotiators, and tactical officers during the course of an incident. He needs to see himself as part of the team, not as a primary decisionmaker. His knowledge has practical application, as can be seen in the case study. However, he needs to train with the crisis response officer before the incident occurs to increase his credibility, gain a working knowledge of the team, and have a well-defined role he does not have to think about during the crisis.

Team Training Issues

Most states require negotiators to receive some initial level of training, and even where not required, the "accepted practice" in the field is that negotiators receive training and demonstrate some level of proficiency before being allowed to negotiate. Most negotiators have, at a minimum, attended a 40- to 80-hour entry-level course in crisis negotiations. There are numerous negotiator courses offered that satisfy the need for providing initial negotiator training. The FBI offers an 80-hour course, most state and regional associations offer courses of varying lengths, institutions and experienced negotiators offer courses, and some police academies offer courses. One area of concern is with ongoing training. What do negotiators do after the entry-level course is completed (the authors do not like the terms "basic" and "advanced" training for various reasons, so we try to avoid those terms whenever possible—the learning for negotiators is an ongoing, dynamic process, and even highly experienced negotiators can benefit from "refresher" training over topics covered in an entry-level course)? The learning of negotiations is not static. One introductory negotiation course does not prepare a negotiator for life. That course must be supplemented with ongoing training for the length of a negotiator's tenure.

Some states require negotiators engage in ongoing training every year. Texas, for example, requires that negotiators receive 40 hours per year of training to still be considered active in the field. Other states have differing requirements. Regardless of whether a state requires it, negotiators must continue to train, learn, refine their skills, and add to their knowledge, skill, and ability arsenal (Logan, 2004). There are various ways negotiators can continue to train and hone their skills, many can be done with their team at the local agency level.

Before discussing specific types of training for negotiators, it is important to recognize that there are some general learning principles that need to be adhered to in any learning or training environment, and some general principles that should guide negotiator training. First, training should be spread throughout the year. If the goal is to get every team member 40 hours of training per year, do not "bunch" it all into one training session. Spread the training throughout the year so team members have time to digest and integrate the training. Different agencies have different training demands (budget, workload, etc.). It is advisable that negotiators train once per month for eight hours (or one day). Second, consider individual differences in ability. Some people learn faster than other people. Make sure the training takes these differences into account and is paced so the slowest learner learns and the fastest learners do not become bored and uninterested. Third, all training should be realistic. Keep training exercises in the context of negotiations. For example, one popular training topic for negotiators concerns illegal drugs and their effects on behavior, emotions, cognitions, thought, etc. If an outside trainer is brought in to teach this topic, make sure their teaching is put in the context of negotiations and how a hostage taker or barricaded subject would be affected, how negotiators could recognize the drug the suspect may be taking, how to talk with that suspect, what the suspect may say or do, etc. Do not get a generalized lecture about drugs and their effects, or how drugs affect a person in a controlled environment (such as a hospital, clinic, rehab program, etc.). Fourth, all training should be specific. Train for what you will be negotiating. While it is exciting and interesting to conduct a scenario with terrorists taking an airplane hostage with 100 passengers, the reality is that this scenario will likely never occur in the United States (the best predictor of future behavior is past behavior, and there has never been an incident of this type in the U.S.). What negotiators will have to deal with are ex-spouses taking their children hostage and using those children as bargaining chips; they will deal with normal people having a significant event disrupt their lives and threatening suicide; they will have to deal with a mentally disturbed person climbing a radio tower and threatening to jump; they will have to deal with an inmate who is fed up with being abused by other inmates and taking a correctional officer hostage and demanding to be relocated to another facility; they will have to deal with a petty criminal needing money and deciding to up the ante and engage in armed robbery at a bank. These are the incidents that should be trained for. Fifth, joint exercises with the tactical team should be conducted at least once per year and an exercise with the full response elements (command, patrol, investigators, EMS, fire, utilities, media, etc.) once every two years. Practice operating with the tactical unit and other response elements, so everyone learns the capabilities and limitations of the other. Little else is as frustrating at an actual incident as expecting one of the response elements to do something they are not able to do. These joint exercises develop realistic expectations and reduce problems later.

Types of Training

External Training

Of the various types of training negotiators can engage in, one of the most expensive is external training, or sending team members to a negotiator conference or school. This type of training costs the most, takes officers away for their duties for an extended period (very few external schools last only one day, but there are a few), and may separate the team (that is, only one member may be able to attend a school rather than the entire team). Even with all its associated difficulties, negotiation team members should attend one external training session per year. Team members can develop new contacts and establish working relationships with other negotiators that may be valuable in the future. For example, in Chapter One the Lewis Prison incident was described. Negotiators from 10 different agencies and locations were involved in that incident. When they arrived, most knew each other from training that they had attended together. Little time was lost in introductory activities. Negotiators fell right into their team roles and had instantaneous working relationships with other negotiators.

Meeting with, interacting with, and watching other negotiators provides a different perspective on negotiations and the negotiation process. At the Hostage Negotiator Competition at Texas State University, one of the most valuable learning experiences is the opportunity to watch other teams work and observe their techniques, use of equipment, use of situation boards, etc. Almost all attendees have remarked at one time or other that being able to watch other teams operate is one of the primary benefits. This interaction is facilitated by requiring that all teams have an "open-door" policy and allow others to watch their operations.

Going to external training can give team members reinforcement that what they are doing is correct and is done by other negotiators. Interacting with and watching other negotiators can reaffirm a team's own practices, or in the worst-case scenario, illustrate what they might be doing wrong.

Finally, external training will help meet and fulfill any training requirements an agency has. Conferences and schools offer law enforcement credit for attendees through their state accreditation agency. Even out-of-state attendees can transfer credit to their state agency. For many departments, external training is the only training negotiators receive.

Internal Training

Role-Play Training. One of the most widely used types of internal training, and one of the most valuable, is role-play training. Role play training, when conducted correctly, replicates the types of situations officers will face as negotiators and allows them to prepare for those situations in a controlled, risk-free environment. Role-play exercises can be face-to-face, such as a person threatening to jump from a bridge; or voice-to-voice, such as talking with a person from outside an open window, over a bullhorn or other voice amplification system, or over a telephone.

When done correctly, there is no better situational training negotiators can receive. If done incorrectly, there is no worse training. There are some guidelines to follow and pitfalls to avoid when planning and conducting role-play training (Mullins, 2003; Null, 2001; Burrows, 2004). Prior to anything else, a goal has to be established for the training. What knowledge, skills, or abilities should the training teach? If the focus is to be on crisis intervention skills, the role-play exercise should be developed to concentrate on active listening. If the goal is personality profiling, the actors should be trained to display certain behavioral characteristics, show certain emotions, say certain things, etc. The actors have to "be in role" for a specific mental disorder. But, prior to getting to that point, it is critical to clearly define the goals of the exercise. If that is not done, the training will have no value to negotiators and may, in fact, teach the wrong lessons.

Like a movie or book, role-play exercises have to be written and scripted (Maher, 2004). Goals, a plot, characters, setting, a time period, and motivations have to be written. Imagine what watching a movie would be like if the scenes randomly skipped around, or if the personality of the characters changed in every scene, or if the background scenery did not match the action. Not only would it not be an enjoyable movie, it would be disconcerting to watch. Role-play training that is not planned and scripted is like that movie. But instead of being disconcerting, it can actually teach the wrong lessons and do more harm than good. One good source of role-play exercises is to adapt actual incidents to a training scenario (Regini, 2002).

Once the goals are established, characters in the exercise have to be developed. What is the subject doing, why is he or she doing it, what is his or her motivation, what does the subject hope to gain by engaging in this behavior, what does the subject ultimately want, and what does the subject *not* do are all issues that have to be scripted into the exercise. Hostage takers, barricaded subjects, and others in crisis, all respond in somewhat predictable ways. A paranoid schizophrenic will not ask for large sums of money, nor will a long-term methamphetamine addict speak perfect English. Hostages will not generally think rationally and calmly when faced with a threat to life. Characters in the role-play exercise have to be planned out and their actions, communications, and emotions defined according to their personality and behavioral tendencies. Intelligence sources have to be developed for the characters. Who are the family, friends, co-workers, and neighbors of the characters in the exercise and what information can each provide? A co-worker will not usually be able to speak in depth about the relationship a father has with his children, nor will a spouse be able to address how their mate interacts with co-workers. If those issues are relevant to the exercise, those intelligence sources have to be developed. Backgrounds for the characters have to be formulated. What is the context of the exercise incident? Is it at home, work, business, school? Because people are being asked to use their imaginations (actors and negotiators), the environment and location of the exercise have to be developed.

The role-play exercise has to follow a timeline. There has to be an introduction of characters, plot line, action sequence, and emotions. The script has to follow this timeline. As in real negotiated and crisis situations, emotions follow a predictable path. Subjects go through the Crisis Stage, Accommodation Stage, and Resolution Stage. The script for the role-play exercise has to follow these stages. During each stage, the actors have to act and react in certain ways. That does not mean the script has to be so tight that there is no leeway for the actors to respond to the negotiators. They have to have some flexibility. But that flexibility begins with a predictable script. Demands are made at certain time during a crisis incident and demands change based on the dynamics of the situation. The role-play exercise has to have the same demand sequence. Subjects do not begin by asking for food and cigarettes and work their way up to large sums of money and transportation out of the country. The developed script should include a timeline. Script the times when actors should be doing certain things. For example, if negotiators arrive one hour into the incident, by hour two, the actors should be moving from the Crisis Stage to the Accommodation Stage. At hour six, the subject should be getting hungry and asking for food.

If it is one of the goals of training, the environment can be written into the role-play exercise. Security access, communication problems, health hazards, the physical layout, and innocent bystanders getting involved can all be written into the exercise. For example, the negotiators could be made to negotiate the subject into a certain location so a phone could be delivered or the tactical team could deliver a phone. Negotiators could be made to negotiate the subject away from a hostage, or the subject could rearrange some furniture to assist a potential assault. Cold, heat, rain, sleet, etc. could all be part of the exercise if they are part of the goals of training.

After goals are identified and a script is prepared, actors should be trained. It is advised that whenever possible, actors not be other officers. There are several problems associated with using other officers (or co-workers). The main problem is that the negotiators know them and will recognize them, which reduces the value of the training. One problem we have experienced in hosting the Hostage Negotiator Competition for the past 16 years is that law enforcement officers, for the most part, all fall into an antisocial personality. Regardless of the script and personality of the subject, the officers rapidly become antisocial personalities and engage in yelling, screaming, and shouting matches with negotiators. We even had one exercise in which the hostage taker was a retired police chief with a terminal illness. Minutes into the exercise, actors were acting like long-term criminals. These situations will not provide the training for negotiators. Actors can be obtained from local high school drama departments, businesses (for example, if using a bank, train the bank employees to be the actors), or local community theater groups. For the most part, these people will readily volunteer and welcome the opportunity to hone their acting skills.

We have also experienced actors thinking that they knew more about negotiations than the negotiators and not following the prepared script. For this reason (and those listed above), it is recommended that "controllers" be used. These are people who have developed the script and work directly with the actors to stay true to the script. They can help the actors stay true to their personality type, stay emotionally on track, and make sure the goals of training are met. They can also assist the actors when needed and suggest responses to queries or actions by the negotiators and provide suggestions on communications. Trained and experienced negotiators should be used as these controllers. Slatkin (2001) suggested that in many cases, role-play exercises do not allow for skill practice, that they lose focus as actors begin distorting their character or become overzealous, among other things. He suggests that only a cross-section scenario be utilized so training can "focus on process and technique rather than strategy and resolution." We disagree. It has been our experience in 16 years of hosting the Negotiator Competition/Seminar at Texas State University-San Marcos that role players can stay focused and in character, that actors do not become competitive and frustrate the negotiator, that actors do not become caricatures and develop unrealistic expectations, and that full-scale scenarios should focus on strategy and outcome, The use of controllers helps give actors direction and guidance when needed, for accurate response to negotiator queries and communications.

Role-play exercises are training. It does not do any good to put your most experienced negotiator in the primary seat or your investigator in the role of intelligence gatherer. Use the exercise for training. Put the new team member on the telephone, the least experienced as intelligence gatherer, and the worst typist as recorder. Even take the team leader out of role and make someone else the team leader. Through the course of the exercise, rotate personnel. Swap the primary negotiator, recorder, intelligence gatherer, etc. Make people pick up where their successor left off. During the exercise, stop and debrief what has been happening. Evaluate the performance of the team and then continue the exercise. Make sure that the team debriefs at the end of the exercise. Include the actors in this final debriefing. For the evaluations, make sure to evaluate the goals covered. If the focus of the exercise is on active listening skills, draft an evaluation sheet for the active listening skills and evaluate according to those skills. If necessary, model the correct behaviors. Demonstrate the correct behavior or technique and then allow the team member to practice following the modeling. It is also worth taping (video or audio) the exercise so team members can observe themselves and conduct a self-evaluation (Van Hasselt & Romano, 2004).

Fishbowl Exercise. The Fishbowl exercise is a team exercise designed to build active listening skills and improve communications within the team (Burrows, 2004). In the fishbowl exercise, team members are seated in a small circle, facing each other. Two team members are selected at random, one to be the subject, the other to be the negotiator. They are seated back-to-back in the center of the circle. The subject role player is given a short scenario (pre-written and designed to achieve active listening goals) that deals with a crisis situation. The best types of scenarios to use are high-risk suicides and domestic situations, although any hostage taking or crisis situation will work. When cued, the subject says, "Hello" (assume the phone has just been answered). In talking to the subject, the negotiator is to use only active listening skills. If the negotiator gets into problem-solving, the team leader is to identify that and redirect the negotiator to stick with active listening. As the exercise progresses, the other team members are to write down every active listening skill demonstrated: what skill was demonstrated, what was said, what the statement was in response to, and any other active listening skills that could have been used. After about five to 10 minutes, the exercise is stopped.

At the conclusion, the team reviews what was said, what could have been used instead, any other active listening skills that could have been used, and how to keep using active listening skills and not problem-solving skills. To facilitate recognition of active listening skills, instead of letting team members free associate, an evaluation sheet can be provided to each team member that lists the active listening skills—team members fill in the blanks. During the critique, it is important that the critique be constructive and team members not take comments personally. The role of team leader is to facilitate the critique and make sure it remains constructive. After the critique, select two more team members and repeat the exercise until each team member has the opportunity to be both subject and negotiator.

Roundtable Exercise. One in-house exercise that is especially beneficial in building communication skills, active listening skills, as well as building a repertoire of potential responses to hostage taker comments is the roundtable exercise (Null, 2001). In the roundtable exercise, team members are seated in a circle facing away from each other. Each team member should have a notepad. The team or exercise leader stands in the center of the circle with a list of pre-written statements a hostage taker might use during a conversation with a negotiator. Some examples of these statements include; "It's not worth living anymore"; "If I can't have the kids, no one is going to have them"; "If you don't move that car back within 10 seconds, someone is going to die"; "I want a plane to Mexico in 15 minutes"; "I'm going to come out shooting and make you kill me." The team/exercise leader should have at least 10 of these prepared statements. A statement is read by the leader, and then each negotiator, working alone, writes his or her preferred response to that statement. As soon as a negotiator has finished writing a response, that negotiator raises a hand and the leader reads the next statement.

After all statements have been read, the team turns to face the center of the circle and then each response is read to each statement. The responses are discussed in terms of which is best, which one would be most/least inflammatory, which one might be most effective at reducing emotions or changing behavior, which one would make the subject pause and think, etc. One of the goals this exercise accomplishes is that each team member can build a full repertoire of responses for use during an actual incident, reduce ambiguity and hesitation, and sound more professional and assured when talking with a subject.

Case Study. Case study reviews are ideal training aids for making specific points, learning to critically evaluate actions, and reversing unfavorable trends (Howard, 2003). Case studies are detailed presentations of a specific event. It is best if the presentation is conducted by someone who participated in the events and has a multimedia presentation (i.e., lecture, audiotapes, video, etc.). Additionally, the presentation can consist of a panel of participants or firsthand witnesses. The presentation should focus on a general overview of the entire incident and then emphasize specific learning objectives from that incident. For example, if the goal of training was to learn active listening skills, the presenters should concentrate on describing the active listening skills that were used or not used. If the goal of training is to learn critical evaluation skills, audience members should be able to provide a critique of actions taken at the incident. Presenters should respond to those critics, as well as pointing out critique points that audience members missed.

One of the things to avoid when using case study training is to not focus on incidents that were not successfully resolved through negotiations. Instead, select incidents that were successfully resolved and focus on what was done to successfully resolve those incidents. For example, Jan Dubina and Robert Ragsdale have given numerous case study presentations about the Lewis Prison incident (Arizona Department of Corrections) from 2004, one of the successes of recent years. Their presentation gives an overview of the incident, and then they focus on two areas: lessons learned, and what was done correctly to peacefully resolve the incident. It is an excellent presentation that hundreds of negotiators have benefited from (see, for example, Dubina & Ragsdale, 2005). A similar presentation has been made by Jim Cavanaugh of ATF concerning a four-day incident in Kentucky in 2004 (Cavanaugh & Mills, 2005). This incident was resolved successfully. Agent Cavanaugh focuses on the actions of the negotiators and stresses the active listening skills negotiators employed to defuse emotions and reduce suicide potential.

Guest Instructor. A training day may be a classroom day conducted by a guest instructor. Team members may be assigned responsibility to provide a day of training, or a non-team member can be brought in to conduct training. Whoever conducts the training should be a subject-matter expert, should be able to instruct and manage a classroom, and should be familiar with negotiations. There is an expression that "those who cannot do, teach." Nothing could be further from the truth. Good teachers have the ability to present information clearly, concisely, accurately, and and also make it interesting. Not every subject matter expert can do this. If the audience is tuned out or not listening, the instruction is worthless. Instructors should also be familiar with negotiations so their material is directed toward negotiations. Several years ago, at the Hostage Negotiation Competition at Texas State University, an instructor was brought in to conduct a seminar in a relevant topic. The instructor was not familiar with negotiations and presented the material in a manner that made it difficult for audience members to relate it to negotiations. As a result, very few in the audience saw the relevance of the material or learned from the presentation. A good instructor will be a subject-matter expert, will keep the audience involved, and be able to relate the material to the audience. Anything less, and classroom training is wasted time.

Equipment Day. On occasion, the team should hold a training day in which the goal is to use, repair, and store equipment. As any negotiator will relate, at crisis incidents, Murphy is alive and well. Equipment days can help reduce the presence of Murphy at an actual incident. All equipment should be brought out and all team members given the opportunity to assemble and use the equipment. Any equipment in need of repair should be fixed (or assigned to a specific team member for responsibility to repair and store) and any repair needs anticipated (extra wire, fuses, tools). Team members should also practice storing the equipment correctly so it is ready for use.

The Ten Most Common Mistakes Made by Crisis Negotiators[1]

The ten most common negotiator mistakes identified by Kidd can be divided into three categories: (1) negotiator skills and techniques, (2) negotiation team management, and (3) critical incident management.

Negotiator Skills and Techniques

One common mistake made by negotiators is a reluctance to analyze critically. There is a tendency to overlook problems if there are no deaths or injuries, or to downplay the importance of the hostage taker's problems and emotions. Because the offender surrendered and no one was injured, there is a perception that negotiators were successful and things went well. From these incidents, negotiators take away the wrong lessons by not critically analyzing their performance, communications, intelligence gathering/dissemination, decisionmaking, and other facets of the negotiation operation.

Another mistake negotiators often make is an ineffective or incorrect assessment of the hostage taker. Negotiators fail to assess, search for, and try to understand the hostage taker's motivations and goals. Because things are going well, negotiators do not focus on using the active listening skills, and concentrate on bargaining/decision making instead of building rapport and trust. Negotiators not making a correct assessment of the hostage taker's motives do not distinguish between instrumental (hostages are tools for freedom, hostages are not integral to criminal conduct, or there is a demand for escape) and expressive demands (hostages are integral part of hostage taker's conduct or motivation—escape may not be desired).

A third mistake negotiators tend to make is to ignore or mistreat hostages when we might need their cooperation or have to actually negotiate through them. Negotiators tend to assume that the hostage's situation and well-being are tactical concerns. When this happens, negotiators tend to focus too much on the hostage taker and fail to adequately protect hostages or ignore a possible tactic to negotiate through the hostages.

Negotiation Team Management

A common management mistake often made by team leaders is the failure to recognize, practice, or use the "dualistic approach." The resolution to a negotiated incident requires a parallel application of crisis response assets (versus a linear approach). Often, team leaders become locked into the idea that negotiators can resolve an incident without the support and use of other elements, most notably tactical. The team leader motivates negotiators to focus on the overt negotiator skills such as empathy, helpfulness, emotional understanding, and rapport building. The team leader thus tends to de-emphasize negotiators covertly communicating the need for the hostage taker to engage in problem-solving, resolution-based, and objective-based negotiations.

Teams, team leaders, and agencies may not adequately stress the need for established criteria for negotiator selection. When adequate criteria are not developed and a comprehensive selection system is not used, negotiators are not selected based on the knowledge, skills, and abilities necessary for negotiating an incident. Communication skills are overlooked, interviewing skills are devalued, and attributes of patience and understanding are not considered. Instead, officers are selected subjectively, based more upon knowledge of who the person is, rather than what they can bring to the team.

Another common mistake made by team leaders is failure to know or monitor the philosophies of the tactical commander and/or overall incident commander. This translates at the scene of an incident into a tendency of the team leader to not attempt to educate or train the other commanders in negotiator practices, abilities, or capabilities. Instead, the team leader attempts to badger, argue, or even propagandize with the other commanders to get them to see things the "negotiator way." This also usually means that the team leader does not develop a contingency plan when the incident commander emphasizes practices that are contrary to accepted practices (or does not attempt to educate the incident commander).

Another mistake often seen in team leaders is a tendency to downplay the importance of the secondary negotiator. Instead of putting their "best other negotiator" with the primary negotiator, team leaders assign new negotiators or inexperienced negotiators to the secondary negotiator role as an opportunity to learn.

Critical Incident Management

Incident commanders can be guilty of failing to maintain or pursue knowledge necessary to adequately manage incidents. In 2005, the state of crisis response was that incident commanders had the least amount of training of any of the response personnel. There is sometimes a perception in incident commanders that if they can manage a patrol shift, an investigative division, a prison cellblock, they have adequate training to manage a crisis incident. This is simply not true. Commanders need training and practice to learn how to manage crisis incidents. These incidents have a unique set of problems and challenges. Commanders must be trained in these issues, practice that training (with other response elements), learn from others who preceded them, and learn from the significance of past incidents. All too often, incident commanders do not receive input from the tactical and negotiator team leaders (Vecchi, 2002).

Commanders can also fail to follow standard practices. Lack of experience, training, and practice (in scenarios) can lead to commanders failing to mobilize sufficient resources to resolve a crisis incident, having inadequate staffing on hand, and disregarding prior experiences. Many watched the aftermath of Hurricane Katrina on the Louisiana coast. One of the largest mistakes made by FEMA managers was failing to adequately prepare, deploy, and allocate resources and staffing in the aftermath of the storm. As a result, many people did not receive needed assistance until days after the incident. Failures in Louisiana were due to failures of incident command.

A third common mistake made by incident commanders is violating the balanced triad of crisis response. Commanders may rely too much on the use of tactical elements and ignore negotiators, or conversely, rely too much on negotiators and ignore the tactical element. This is a violation of the parallel application of force doctrine. Without force, the hostage taker will not negotiate. Without the use of negotiators, people may become injured unnecessarily. One role of the incident commander is also to resolve conflicts between team commanders and build a working relationship (Vecchi, 2002). The incident commander is responsible for reducing conflict between team leaders and teams. In many instances, incident commanders fail to realize that while the goals of tactical and negotiators are the same, different methodologies are employed to achieve those goals. The incident commander who fails to realize this will unwittingly promote competition between teams rather than cooperation.

Figure 9.6
The Ten Most Common Mistakes Made by Crisis Negotiators

Negotiator Skills and Techniques
Reluctance to Critically Analyze Situations
Ineffective or Incorrect Assessment of Hostage Taker
Ignoring or Mistreating Hostages

Negotiations Team Management
Failure to Recognize or Practice a Dualistic Approach to Negotiations
Inadequate Criteria and Selection System for Negotiators
Not Knowing or Monitoring Philosophies of Tactical or Incident Command
Insufficient Focus on or Use of Secondary Negotiator

Critical Incident Management
Unwillingness to Maintain or Pursue Highest Level of Knowledge
Failure to Follow Standard Practices
Ignoring or Violating the Critical Incident Response Triad

Very often, these mistakes do not occur in isolation. Several may be made at one incident. While any one particular incident may be successfully resolved, mistakes continue to accrue and build across incidents until the team has an unsuccessful incident in which officers, hostages, or the hostage taker is injured or killed. The team then has a tendency to wonder why this particular incident ended badly and what went wrong. They fail to see the accumulation of mistakes and errors over a long period that led to this incident. Operational debriefings do not necessarily prevent the accumulation of mistakes unless all response personnel are open and brutally honest with themselves and with each other during the debriefing. Teams also have to critically question, analyze, and assess their performance at every incident and training scenario. It is recommended that teams develop some type of evaluation form to use for evaluation and assessment. A standardized evaluation process will assist in reducing these mistakes.

Summary

The police response to a hostage incident is a multifaceted response, requiring the coordination and cooperation of patrol, the tactical team, the negotiating team, and department supervisors. The incident may involve the participation of units such as criminal investigation, public relations, and other specialized units within the department. The key to this police response is prior planning, preparation, and training. Of these, training is the most important. Prior to an incident, the department as a unit should participate in exercises designed to simulate hostage incidents, so that when an actual event does occur, planning and preparation will be in place. The department should prepare for the pressures and intervention of non-police factors at an incident. City officials, politicians, and other parties may respond with the police department. If not prepared, these outside parties may hinder the negotiation effort. Clearly delineated policy and procedure statements may preclude the interference of these parties at an incident.

Communication between the police response units is clearly vital for the successful resolution of the hostage incident. Clear lines of communication must be established and adhered to by the department's various response units. Commanders, the tactical team, and the negotiating team must be kept completely informed with clear, up-to-date, and complete information throughout the incident. Any breakdown in communications may seriously hinder efforts to resolve the incident peacefully.

Note

1   The information contained in this section was developed by William Kidd over a number of years and refined through numerous public presentations at negotiator conferences, seminars and meetings, such as the California Association of Hostage Negotiators, the Hostage Negotiation Competition/Seminar at Texas State University (San Marcos, TX) the Kansas Association of Hostage Negotiators, the Texas Association of Hostage Negotiators, and many others. Our thanks go to Officer Kidd for allowing us to include this information.

References

American Justice (1994). "Hostages." Arts and Entertainment Television Network.

Burrows, S. (2004). "Negotiator Team Training." Presentation at the annual convention of the Texas Association of Hostage Negotiators, Austin, TX (November).

Butler, W.M., H. Leitenberg, and G.D. Fuselier (1993). "The Use of Mental Health Professional Consultants to Hostage Negotiation Teams." *Behavioral Science and the Law* 1:213-221.

Cavanaugh, J. and J. Mills (2005). "Hostage Standoff in Bowling Green, Kentucky." Presentation at the Annual Convention of the Arkansas Crisis Negotiators Association, Little Rock, AR (June).

Dubina, J. and R. Ragsdale (2005). "Lewis Prison Incident Debriefing." Presentation at the annual Crisis Negotiation Conference of the National Tactical Officers Association, Nashville, TN (April).

Fagan, T.J. and C.R. Van Zandt (1993). "Lessons from Talladega: Even in 'Non-negotiable' Situations, Negotiations Plays an Important Role." *Corrections Today* (April):134-137.

Federal Bureau of Investigation (1993). "Advanced Hostage Negotiations Seminar." San Antonio, Texas.

Fuselier, D. (1986). *A Practical Overview of Hostage Negotiations*. Quantico,VA: FBI.

——— (1988) "Hostage Negotiation MHC: Emerging Role for the Clinical Psychologist." *Professional Psychology: Research and Practice* 19:175-179.

Gladis, S. (1979). "The Hostage/Terrorist Situation and the Media." *FBI Law Enforcement Bulletin* 48(9):10-15.

Greenstone, J. (unpublished manuscript). *How to Be a Mental Health Consultant to a Police Hostage and Crisis Negotiations Team, or, Should I or Shouldn't I?*

Griswold, D. (2005). "The Tacoma Police Department Hostage Negotiator Selection Process." *Western States Hostage Negotiator Association Journal* XXX:1-3.

Hatcher, C., K. Mohandie, J. Turner, and M. Gelles (1998). "The Role of the Psychologist in Crisis/Hostage Negotiations." *Behavioral Science and the Law* 16:455-472.

Hogewood, W. (2005). "ATF's SRT Negotiation Team." *NTOA Crisis Negotiator Journal* 5:1-3.

Howard, M. (2003). "Effective Techniques for Teaching Crisis Negotiation." Presentation at the Annual Convention of the Texas Association of Hostage Negotiators, Addison, TX (November).

International Association of Chiefs of Police. (1983). "Hostage Rescue Seminar." San Antonio, Texas.

Janik, J. (1994). "Desirable Characteristics in a Police Psychologist." *Journal of Police and Criminal Psychology* 10(2):24-31.

Katzenbach, R. and D.K. Smith (1993). *The Wisdom of Teams*. New York, NY: Harper Business Books.

Logan, M. (2004). "Selection and Training of Crisis Negotiators in Policing." *Crisis Negotiator Journal* Fall:5-7.

Maher, J.R. (2004). "Role-Play Training for Negotiators in Diverse Environments." *FBI Law Enforcement Bulletin* 73(6):10-12.

McMains, M.J. (1988a). "Uses of Hostage Negotiators in Major Police Departments." Paper presented at the Society of Police and Criminal Psychology's 17th Annual Conference, San Antonio, TX.

——— (1988b). "Expanding the Psychologist's Role in Hostage Negotiations." *Journal of Police and Criminal Psychology* 4:1:2-8.

——— (1991). "Psychologists' Roles in Hostage Negotiations." Presentation at FBI Advanced Hostage Negotiations Seminar, San Antonio, TX.

——— (1992). "Psychologist's Role on a Hostage Negotiations Team." Basic Hostage Negotiations School. San Antonio, TX: San Antonio Police Department.

——— (1995). "Developing Teams for Crisis Negotiations." *Journal of Crisis Negotiations* Vol. 1, No. 1. (Spring):17-26.

Mullins, W.C. (2003). "Negotiator Practices: Resuls of a Survey Assessing Selection Practices." Presentation at the annual Hostage Negotiation Competition, Texas State University, San Marcos, TX (January).

Mullins, W.C. (2001). "Negotiator Team Selection." Presentation at the annual Hostage Negotiator Competition/Seminar, Texas State University, San Marcos, TX (January).

Mullins, W.C. (2000). "Hostage Negotiator Team Formation and Selection." Presentation at the annual meeting of the Texas Association of Hostage Negotiators. San Antonio, TX (November).

Noesner, G.W. (1999). "Negotiation Concepts for Commanders." *FBI Law Enforcement Bulletin* 68(1):6-14.

Null, S. (2001). "Team Training Issues." Presentation at the annual Hostage Negotiation Competition, Texas State University, San Marcos, TX (January).

New York Police Department (1973a). "Policies and Procedures for Hostage Rescue." Reviewed at SAPD Hostage Negotiation Training, August 1978.

New York Police Department (1973b). *Polices and Procedures for Hostage Rescue.* New York, NY: Author.

Regini, C. (2002). "Crisis Negotiation Teams: Selection and Training." *FBI Law Enforcement Bulletin* 71(11):1-5.

Schlossberg, H. (1979). "Basic Hostage Negotiations Seminar." Austin, TX: Texas Department of Public Safety.

Slatkin, A.A. (2001). "Structured Role-Play for Negotiators." *Law and Order* 49(3):74-76.

Stites, R. (2005). "Tactical Techniques for Negotiators." Presentation at Hostage/Crisis Negotiations 201. Olathe, KS (August).

TCLEOSE (1990). "Texas Basic Hostage Negotiations Course, Course No. 3002." Revised: January 1, 1990. Austin, TX: Texas Commission on Law Enforcement Officer's Standards and Education.

Vecchi, G.M. (2002). "Hostage/Barricade Management: A Hidden Conflict within Law Enforcement." *FBI Law Enforcement Bulletin* 71(5):1-6

Van Hasselt, V.B. and S.J. Romano (2004). "Role-Playing: A Vital Tool in Crisis Negotiation Skill Training." *FBI Law Enforcement Bulletin* 73(2):12-17.

Discussion Questions

1. You are the negotiating team commander at a hostage situation at the county jail. Your team has been negotiating with a barricaded inmate for two hours and he is beginning to settle down. The sheriff, who is acting as on-scene commander, enters your area and demands that you get things wrapped up in the next hour. What would you say to the sheriff to prevent his interference?

2. With a group of three others, individually rank-order the elements in the definition of a team: share your rankings and reasons for the order with the others; discuss the difference until you come to an agreement on the rankings and the reasons for the ranking.

3. You are responsible for setting up the department's first Crisis Response Team. What skills would you look for in the commander, the negotiator supervisor, and the tactical team leader? How would you assess them? What procedures would you use? How would you evaluate their leadership ability? Is there a difference between leadership and supervision? Describe this difference.

4. You want to conduct training on the following topic: The use of active listening skills in rapport building and problem solving. What training techniques would you use? Construct a lesson plan that includes skill building along with a test of whether the negotiator's skill changes.

5. How can you use your negotiation team to support the tactical team? If you decide to continue negotiating, how can you use your tactical team to support the negotiators?

6. You are selecting two new negotiators for your team. What qualities in the applicants do you think are the most important and why? How would you test the applicants for these qualities?

7. The media are almost as fast getting to the scene of a barricaded bank robbery with hostages as the police. They wander across fields of fire several times, putting themselves at risk. What do you say to them to keep them contained in the Public Information Officer (PIO) area you have established outside the outer perimeter? What can you do that will reduce their need to get closer to the action? Would you treat TV, radio, and newspaper media differently?

8. Should negotiators specialize within the police department? Why or why not? If not, what duties within the department should negotiators be assigned as their regular duties?

9. You have been asked to select a mental health consultant for the negotiating team. What would you look for when selecting this person? List and rank-order all the criteria you would use in the selection process. How would you train this person?

10. A hostage situation has occurred in your classroom building. Set up the physical arrangements for the police response. Include inner and outer perimeters.

Crisis Negotiations in Prisons and Correctional Facilities

10

Learning Objectives

1. Know the similarities and differences between hostage negotiations in prisons and hostage negotiations in the police sector.

2. Understand the various situational dynamics present in the prison situation.

3. Know the purposes of negotiating in prison situations.

4. Know what needs to be done prior to beginning negotiations in prison situations.

5. Know and understand the principles and goals of negotiating in prison situations.

6. Understand which demands are negotiable and which are non-negotiable.

7. Understand the issues of language difficulties and differences in prison situations and how to overcome those difficulties.

8. Know the process necessary for developing a prison hostage negotiation team, including:
   A. Team membership
   B. Why all prison personnel should be trained in hostage negotiation
   C. Establishment of a Victim's Assistance Team

9. Know the critical lessons learned from high-profile, high-intensity prison situations.

10. Understand the unity of cultural and racial groups in prisons.

11. Know the differences between military veteran inmates and non-military veteran inmates.

12. Understand the cultural trends among inmates, as identified by Turner and Miller (1991).

William, a white inmate and member of the Aryan Nations prison gang, was convinced by the prison staff intelligence division to provide information on the Aryan Nations gang. After about a month, William reported to the staff that he thought other inmate knew he was a "stoolie" and was afraid for his life. The investigators had heard nothing to substantiate his fears and told him he was just being paranoid. The next night, William attempted to escape. He was captured outside the fence and returned to the facility. While in a holding area, he managed to grab a correctional officer's nightstick and beat the officer. When another armed officer attempted to subdue William, the inmate overpowered the officer and took his weapon. Two other correctional officers then arrived and William took them hostage.

The facility was locked down and the crisis response team activated. Additionally, victim services personnel were mobilized to meet with the families of the correctional officers being held hostage. After about 10 hours of negotiations, William released the injured correctional officer in exchange for a promise to be transferred to another facility. What the prison administration would not agree to, however, was William serving the rest of his time in complete isolation from other inmates.

Negotiators slowed their pace and reduced the amount of time they spent on the phone with William, letting time pass and need states become more acute. After another seven or eight hours, William agreed to release the second correctional officer in exchange for some food and water. In the meantime, the facility warden spoke with his bosses and got an agreement to transfer William to a prison in another state and to give him another "identity" (name, criminal history, background, etc.). Negotiators then presented the warden's deal to William. After about four hours of continued negotiations, William agreed to the move and change in identity, released his remaining hostages and surrendered.

Police departments are not the only agencies that face hostage situations. Prisons are especially vulnerable to hostage incidents. Attica, New Mexico, Oakdale, and Atlanta prisons are part of American folklore because of the national publicity that their hostage situations generated. They are certainly not the exception, however. Prisons and jails throughout the country have dealt with hostage situations. Prisons are especially vulnerable to hostage situations due to the nature of their business: the type of people incarcerated, the number of prisoners versus the number of officers, and the physical arrangement.

One of the most famous hostage incidents in the United States occurred at New York's Attica Prison in September 1971. Tension had been building in Attica for several months, when on September 9, at approximately 8:45 A.M., a group of inmates from Cell Block A overpowered the correctional officers, broke a defective door separating their cell block from the keeplock area (master door controls for all cell blocks), and unlocked all the cell blocks. In minutes, inmates had taken control of the entire prison, holding 42 correctional officers and civilians hostage. The inmates, with their hostages, moved to the D yard and established an operations base. Inmate leaders presented a list of 32 demands to prison and state authorities, including replacement of the prison superintendent, administrative and legal amnesty to all prisoners involved in the takeover, placement of Attica under federal jurisdiction, application of New York's minimum wage law to working prisoners, religious freedom, an end to prison censorship, implementation of realistic and effective rehabilitation programs, educational and narcotics treatment programs, better diet, more recreation time, increased numbers of black and Hispanic officers, establishment of an inmate grievance procedure, expansion of work-release programs, outside doctors and dentists to visit inmates for medical and dental work (at the inmate's expense), and airline flights to other countries for any inmate who wanted to leave the United States. Over the following three days, prison and state officials negotiated with the inmates on these demands, making little progress. On Monday, September 13, New York Commissioner of Corrections Russell G. Oswald, with the concurrence of New York Governor Nelson Rockefeller, ordered the New York State Police to regain control of the prison (New York State Special Commission on Attica, 1972).

At approximately 10:00 A.M. on September 13, the State Police and correctional officers stormed the wall surrounding D yard, firing shotguns and pistols at anything in front of them. Clearing the wall, officers entered D yard and, using lethal force, quelled the prisoners and ended the siege. In just over 15 minutes, the officers had killed 39 people and wounded 80 others. Eleven of the dead and 33 of the wounded were correctional personnel. One officer and three inmates had been killed by inmates during the siege. After the retaking of the facility, several more inmates suffered serious injury in reprisal actions by officials.

Following the event, the New York State Commission on Attica (1972) reported that the authorities had erred in several areas. The intent of state officials all along had been to retake Attica by force. The assault was not planned with the intent to minimize loss of life. The choice of weapons on the part of the police was made by what was available at the time and not by situational dynamics. No safeguards were in place to prevent the excessive use of force. No controls were present to prevent firing by those who were not part of the main assault. No arrangements were made for medical care and those needs should have been anticipated. Finally, no system was in place to prevent vengeful reprisals against inmates following the siege.

The events at Attica brought about numerous changes and reforms in prisons and jails in the United States. Included in those reforms were mandates to develop tactical response teams trained in prison uprisings and to train hostage negotiators conversant in penal situations. The Attica case was just recently settled. In the aftermath of the riot, civil suits were filed on behalf of 1,281 inmates at the facility at the time. The plaintiffs originally asked for $2.8 billion. In 2000, the courts awarded the inmates $8 million from the State of New York, with an additional $4 million awarded for attorneys' fees (Chen, 2000). This settlement is the largest ever in a prisoner's rights case and demonstrates the lasting effects that mishandling an incident can have.

Other significant and noteworthy prison incidents include the New Mexico State Prison riot of 1980, in which 33 inmates were killed (two were beheaded in the Segregation Unit. Eighty-nine other inmates were injured in a 36-hour riot. Fortunately, no correctional staff were harmed. In 1987, at Oakdale Federal Detention Center, Louisiana, inmates took 26 hostages in a nine-day incident. Also in 1987, at the Atlanta (GA) United States Prison, 100 hostages were held during a 12-day incident. In 1991, at Talladega Federal Correctional Institution, inmates took 26 hostages, including 10 correctional officers and held them for nine days. In 1993, at Lucasville, inmates took over a wing of the facility and held eight people for 10 days. At St. Martinsville, Louisiana, Parish Jail in 1999, inmates took three staff members hostage (the warden and two correctional officers) and held them for five days (Sage, 2003). And in 2004, two inmates took two correctional officers hostage in a tower at Lewis Prison in Arizona and held them for 15 days. In all of these incidents except New Mexico and Talladega, the incidents were resolved through a negotiated settlement (Bazan, 2004).

One reason prison incidents tend to be so highly charged, emotional, and large-scale is the nature of the causes for the incident. At the Lewis Prison incident, for example, a state blue ribbon commission appointed by the Arizona governor, reported that problems had been building for years and that the ultimate hostage event was the result of a combination of factors, including "complacency, inexperience, lack of professionalism, inadequate staffing, vague security procedures, poor training, lack of situational awareness, premature promotions, noncompetitive pay, ineffective communication, malfunctioning equipment, high inmate-to-officer rations, bad architectural design and myriad other causes" (*Corrections Digest*, 2004). Many of these problems plague prisons across the nation, federal as well as state institutions.

This chapter will cover hostage taking in prisons. There are many similarities to the police negotiating effort, but there are some subtle differences for the prison staff or business community. These differences will be explored in detail. Note that although we discuss prisons, the discussion also applies to county and municipal jails.

Negotiations Specific to the Prison Situation

Fuselier (1988) and Needham (1977) have stated that hostage negotiations in prisons are like those faced by the police negotiator. The Office of the Attorney General of New Mexico (1980) reported that the riot at the New Mexico State Prison was resolved using standard police negotiating strategy and tactics. Fuselier et al. (1989), following the Oakdale and Atlanta riots, stated: ". . . all negotiators involved in the two sieges agreed that standard 'criminal' negotiations guidelines are applicable in protracted situations having a large number of hostage takers . . ." We agree in principle that prison and civilian hostage-taking scenarios are similar, but some differences exist that can have implications for negotiations, negotiating strategy, and incident tactics.

Negotiators with the FBI's Critical Incident Response Group (CIRG), Crisis Negotiation Unit, teach a seminar on negotiations in the correctional setting and discuss the similarities and differences between correctional and police negotiations. Much of the information presented in this section, unless otherwise cited, comes from the work done by CIRG at the FBI. Also, what is discussed here for the prison situation applies equally to jail and other correctional setting negotiations (i.e., private prisons, halfway houses, etc.)

During a prison incident, the first assessment concerns whether the situation is a contained hostage/barricade situation or whether it is a planned or spontaneous riot (Romano, 2003; Bazan, 2004). If it is a contained situation, then the general principles of crisis negotiation apply and the response units can use time in the same way police negotiation units use time. If it is a riot, a rapid tactical response is recommended if there are numerous injuries or property damage is ongoing. If a rapid tactical response is not physically possible, then the response units are forced into negotiations.

One of the more significant advantages the prison negotiator has is that the hostage takers are already known to the negotiators. The hostage takers are prisoners and the negotiators are prison staff. Negotiators have complete intelligence on the hostage takers. There are extensive background histories, medical and mental health files, psychological profiles, aggression and violence indexes, and other data available on the hostage takers. The crisis site is known, physical layouts are familiar, blueprints are on hand, and other obstacles are known to the response team. Related to this is the fact that the situation is already contained to some degree, and the issue generally becomes where to provide additional containment (that is, moving the situation to a smaller, confined area). At the very least, the response elements know the situation is going to remain inside the four walls of the facility. To the hostage takers (and unlike many hostage takers the police deal with), they realize and know they are vulnerable to tactical efforts. To the prison response team, the problem often becomes sifting through and discarding unhelpful intelligence rather than trying to gather intelligence. Additionally, the prisoners are already incarcerated and may have a history of violence and anti-authority sentiment, so negotiators already have a basic framework within which to begin negotiations.

Another difference is that hostages are usually coworkers (Miller et al., 1988). When prisoners take hostages, some of the hostages are likely to be correctional staff. This can be both positive and negative for the negotiators. On the positive side, negotiators have intelligence on the hostages and know them behaviorally and psychologically and can predict how the hostages are likely to react. On the negative side, the negotiators are acquaintances and friends of some of the hostages, which places added stressors on the negotiators and added demands on decisionmaking. This situation is analogous to a police officer being held hostage.

Also, the inmate hostage takers know the prison staff and their hostages. The treatment afforded the hostages will, in large part, be a function of how the staff treated inmates prior to the incident. Thus, the familiarity between hostage takers and hostages can either help or hurt negotiators and other response elements. In general, staff workers who are taken hostage are likely to be better treated than are correctional officers who are taken hostage.

There are some disadvantages faced by prison negotiators. First, tactical entry may be a problem (Romano, 2003). The tactical response unit may not be able to physically broach the site without loss of life (team or hostages). At the Lewis Prison incident, tactical resolution was not a viable option because of the architectural design of the physical structure. The tower was designed to keep people out. That function was fulfilled all too well. Second, the prison situation often involves group dynamics issues among hostage takers. One rather common experience among prison negotiators is the fact that a group of hostage takers is much more likely to become violent than is a single hostage taker. Third, the negotiators and other response personnel may have prior negative relationships with the hostage takers. Fourth, leadership among the hostage takers may become an issue when negotiating, especially if the hostage takers are of different races. Prison gangs share a common hatred toward correctional staff, but also share a hatred of other inmate groups and gangs. Negotiators need to determine who to direct negotiations toward, and who has the authority and influence to make decisions (Romano, 2003).

A final difference is that demands may require command personnel to involve higher government authorities in negotiating demands. State prison officials, the state prison board, or the governor may become involved at the county jail or state prison level. The Bureau of Prisons, the FBI, or State Department may become involved with federal prison hostage situations. At the Oakdale and Atlanta sieges, the highest-level State Department administrators and the President of the United States were involved in demand resolution. Obviously, stress on the negotiators and response team increased significantly.

Situational Dynamics in the Prison Situation

The basic purposes of negotiations in prison incidents are similar to negotiations in any hostage situation. They are to preserve life and re-establish control of the prison population. Negotiations attempt to save the lives of hostages, citizens (if involved), prison staff, and hostage takers, in that order. Prison staff should negotiate to regain control of the prison environment and, in order of priority, prevent escape, minimize casualties, apprehend the hostage takers, and recover property (Bazan, 2004). One may ask why preventing escape is a higher priority than minimizing casualties. There are two answers to this question. First, many of the hostage takers will be the violent population of the prison (and will be prisoners sentenced for violent crimes such as murder, aggravated sexual assault, aggravated assault, abuse of a child, etc.) and, if they are allowed to escape, pose the greatest threat to the community's safety. Second, history has shown that casualties are most likely to be other prisoners. While not devaluing the life of prisoners, we must be realistic and compare the lives of prisoners to the lives of community members. If a choice must be made between taking the life of a prisoner and freeing a convicted murderer into the community, taking the prisoner's life would be the preferred alternative. Finally, the prison negotiator must be concerned with property recovery, an objective that is not necessarily a police negotiator's concern. The prison's property is necessary for maintaining the prison population. Experience has shown that prison hostage takers destroy prison property that is necessary to the control of the population. The cost of the New Mexico Prison riot, for example, exceeded $28.5 million in damages, prison renovation, repair, and remodeling costs (Dillingham & Montgomery, 1985). At the Lucasville, Ohio, prison riot in 1993, repair costs for L-Block were $28 million (It only cost $30 million to build the entire prison in the early 1970s). Thus, one objective is to prevent the prisoners from "burning down their own house."

During the onset or crisis stage of the incident, the situation itself will be more highly charged and emotional than non-prison situations. The inmates will be trying to establish control and dominance; prison staff will be trying to protect themselves and prevent inmates from taking control; and prison staff and officials outside of the situation will be attempting to rapidly and decisively establish control and prevent other staff from being taken hostage. It is crucial that early on in the incident negotiators focus on using active listening skills. The inmates are not ready to make demands and solve problems. They are instead displaying expressive behaviors designed to ventilate emotions, anger, and frustrations. Be extremely careful about trying to move too fast and offer too much, because the hostage takers may not be emotionally ready. Instrumental, or demand-making behavior, will surface (and may have to be induced), but only with the passage of time.

As demands begin to surface, the negotiator will have to determine whether the hostage taker's demands are intended to benefit all inmates or whether they are self-serving. The Attica riot was an example of the former, the New Mexico Prison riot the latter (Mahan, 1985). The negotiator can use two factors to determine which is the case. If demands are stable over time and if property destruction is minimal, the demands are probably designed to benefit all inmates. If demands change frequently and if there is significant property damage, demands are probably self-serving.

Leadership among the hostage takers can become a significant issue for the negotiators. Many prison situations begin without clear leadership. A prison riot, for example, may involve several groups of inmates, each with a different agenda. Negotiators should be prepared to help the hostage takers get organized and build a leadership structure. There will have to be a spokesperson for the group and the negotiator can clearly assist in choosing this person. Negotiators should select a moderate and reasonable individual who has some influence among the hostage takers (Fagan & Van Zandt, 1993). This can be discovered through intelligence and knowledge of the inmates. Once identified, the leadership of this person can be developed through talking with him and making minor concessions to this person and only this person. The act of making concessions to this person reinforces his standing and status with the other hostage takers. To them, the way to make progress and have demands met is through this person. With groups of inmates joined by circumstances, the negotiators may have to help the inmates form "committees" to work under the leader to get decisions made.

Before beginning negotiations, there are several other things the negotiating team should do. We have already mentioned that the hostage takers should be contained. In many prison situations, the hostage takers have control of a building, cell block, or other large area of the prison. The prison's special response team should reduce this "freedom" as much as possible before negotiations begin. At the Lucasville riot, prisoners controlled two gymnasiums and a cell block with eight wings. The tactical team slowly took "real estate" away from the hostage takers and, when the physical area had been significantly reduced, negotiations opened. At the Lewis Prison incident in Arizona, the containment of the hostage takers produced the major problem: the tactical team could not get to them. Sealed in a tower in the Morey Unit, entry could not be made fast enough to neutralize the hostage takers before they could injure or kill the hostages, nor could the sniper be used (Dubina, 2005; Dubina & Ragsdale, 2005).

Negotiators should not open a dialogue until all possible intelligence has been gathered. In the prison situation, negotiators have a tremendous advantage over their police counterparts. Prison records will have complete information on the hostage taker and the hostages. Prior criminal history, educational history, work history, psychological profile, family history, and other significant information will be available to the negotiators. Similar information on the hostages will be available. Additionally, the negotiators can put the hostage takers at an immediate disadvantage by using this intelligence from the outset.

Additionally, in a mob or riot situation, negotiations should not begin until the situation has stabilized. Negotiating with a rioter is impossible. If the situation does not stabilize, it may be preferable to assault rather than negotiate (Saenz & Reeves, 1989). Also, it may preferable to assault before group leaders begin to emerge (Fuselier, 1981; 1986). In regard to assaults, the courts have ruled that using force to quell a riot is not unlawful unless the assault team acts maliciously and sadistically for the purpose of causing harm (*Whitley v. Albers*, 1986). If the force is wanton and unnecessary, as occurred in the aftermath of the Attica riot, prison officials may be guilty of violating the prisoners' Eighth Amendment rights (*Hudson v. McMillian*, 1992).

Many principles and goals of hostage negotiations are the same for the prison staff as they are for the police negotiator. A few are different, however. Negotiation is the preferred method of dealing with a hostage situation. As in the civilian world, fewer people will be hurt by using negotiations than other solutions. In the prison, the hostage holds no intrinsic value to the hostage taker. The hostage's only value is as a bargaining chip for demands. Prisoners riot and ultimately take hostages for either instrumental or expressive purposes. Instrumental reasons are for status and power. The hostage takers tend to be rational and have a clear slate of issues, such as to end overcrowding, improve food, improve visiting conditions, improve facilities (recreational and educational), and improve grievance procedures (Dillingham & Montgomery, 1985). Expressive violence is designed to release anger and frustration, is irrational, and is usually non-goal-oriented (Bowker, 1985). Many riots that begin as expressive become instrumental once emotions are spent. If the riot is expressive in origin, the negotiator should recognize the need for emotional release. One good indicator that the riot began as expressive venting is if demands are not well thought out, are disjointed, and are poorly presented. If that is the case, the negotiator should assume that the situation is expressive and concentrate resolution efforts on emotional issues. In general, the hostage taker does not want further violence to occur. He wants his demands to be met peacefully and to arrive at an agreeable resolution to the incident.

The goals of hostage negotiations are to open communication lines, reduce stress and tension, build rapport, obtain intelligence, stall for time, allow ventilation, and establish a problem-solving atmosphere. Time is a crucial variable for prison negotiators, possibly more so than for police negotiators. The hostage takers need time to vent their frustrations and resentment of authority. At both the Oakdale and Atlanta Prison sieges, negotiators agreed to many demands early in negotiations (no deportation and individual case review), but these concessions actually hurt negotiations. The inmates still had a need to vent frustration and anger, which these early concessions did not satisfy (Fuselier et al., 1989; Van Zandt, 1989). The prison situation needs to "mature" in order for ventilation to occur.

Because prison situations often last for a considerable length of time, Byron Sage, retired FBI Special Agent in Charge and hostage negotiator, recommends that the negotiation team make regular use of negotiation position papers (NPPs). Police teams should use NPPs as well, if it is suspected that the incident is going to last for more than a day. NPPs are summaries of what has occurred to date in the incident and serve to help the negotiators, on-scene commander, tactical commander, and others receive current information, encode that information, process the incident status, and make assessments and decisions. NPPs do not replace any oral briefings—they supplement them. For the negotiating team, NPPs help: (1) in getting everyone's input into planning and future directions, making the team proactive rather than reactive; (2) in avoiding groupthink; (3) as a briefing document for the relief teams, and to supplement situation boards, logs, and audiotapes; (4) assist in briefing anyone outside the team concerning negotiating strategy, tactics, and progress; (5) to document the team's assessments and strategy on an ongoing basis, so if there are discrepancies later on, there is a written record. Byron Sage suggests that the NPPs be set up in the following format: (1) list the number of the NPP (NPP-1, NPP-2, etc.), date, and time prepared in the upper right corner; (2) include a short introduction, giving the number of contacts and the time of those contacts the specific NPP is based on; and (3) divide the body into three parts that give status, assessment, and recommendations (Sage also adds that bullets under each part are preferable to paragraphs, as this keeps the NPP short, concise, and simple). The status section should give a short summary of the situation from recent contacts and should include names, welfare, or status of actors and hostages, any demands presented and deadlines keyed. The assessment section is for a review of motivations, behaviors, seriousness of threats and demands, rapport between negotiator and hostage taker, etc. The recommendation section is to present negotiation strategy, what is hoped to be accomplished by the negotiators, how that will be accomplished, and to request command decisions before implementing a specific strategy. NPPs should be prepared any time teams rotate or at any other times the negotiator commander recommends.

Negotiators should also be aware of the role that prescription medications can have on the hostage takers. Many inmates are on some type or combination of types of medications. The more common include anti-anxiety drugs, antidepressants, antipsychotics, and antimanics (Dennery, 2000). Negotiators should have an understanding of how these drugs affect people (behaviorally, cognitively, and emotionally), side effects, length of action, deterioration of action effects, withdrawal symptoms, and other effects of the drug (a good resource is Worledge et al., 1997). It is crucial that the team have at the very least a health care professional on-call to discuss drug effects and provide input.

The surrender may present special problems for the prison negotiator. Demands center around unfairness and living conditions, and prison authorities may concede to these demands. Before surrendering, the hostage takers may want a formalized ceremony in which documents are signed. They will likely want the media and outsiders to witness this ritual. At Oakdale, the hostage takers wanted Miami's Bishop Agustin Roman to witness the resolution agreement (Fuselier et al., 1989). The bishop was brought in and the signing ritual ended the siege.

Several demands are non-negotiable in the prison situation. Release or escape, weapons, exchange of hostages, and pardon or parole are all non-negotiable (the reasons should be obvious). All other demands are open to negotiation. Unlike the police situation, in which the police negotiator may discuss the possibility of granting non-negotiable demands, the prison negotiator should be clear up-front (if the issue arises) that the demand is not open for discussion.

Sidebar: Lewis State Prison Siege

Detective Jan Dubina is a 24-year veteran of the Phoenix Police Department. She is currently assigned as a full-time member of the special assignments unit and is a training officer with that unit. She has been a member of the special assignments unit for 16 years, beginning as a sniper. She has been a negotiator for more than 16 years and has negotiated hundreds of incidents. Jan is also the Crisis Negotiation chairperson for the Crisis Negotiator Division of the National Tactical Police Officers' Association. She began the NTOA *Crisis Negotiator Journal* and is responsible for hosting the annual National Tactical Officers' Association Crisis Negotiation Team conference.

On January 18, 2004, two inmates at the Lewis State Prison in Buckeye, Arizona, took two correctional officers hostage. Inmates Ricky Wassenaar and Steven Coy held Lois Fraley and Jason Auch inside the tower at the Morey Unit, in what turned out to be the longest siege in U.S. prison history. Jason Auch was released, in exchange for food supplies, after seven days of negotiations. The inmates finally surrendered after 15 days, releasing Lois Fraley, their final hostage.

How were two inmates able to take over an impregnable guard tower that was designed and built to keep inmates out? The culmination of three years planning by Wassenaar began at 2:30 A.M. on a Sunday. Both inmates had minded their behavior in order to keep their jobs in the prison kitchen because this is where the plan called for the escape to begin. They had manufactured shanks (homemade knives) to use as weapons until better weapons could be obtained. The lone on-duty corrections officer was confronted and overcome. Wassenaar changed into the officer's uniform, shaved his beard, and headed toward the Morey Unit tower, the next step in their escape plan. The tower was not their ultimate goal. Their ultimate goal was to escape from the prison, but in order to do that they were going to need some weapons and there were weapons in the tower.

Other inmates declined to join the escaping inmates. They were locked in a storage area. Coy remained in the office with the corrections officer and a civilian female kitchen worker. While waiting for word from his partner, Coy sexually assaulted the female. A second corrections officer, arriving early for work, was surprised by Coy with the shank. He also ended up restrained in the kitchen office.

Wassenaar, under the guise of being a fellow officer, was permitted entry into the tower where he struck Auch with a 30" metal stirring paddle to overcome any resistance. Fraley, seeing this and realizing what was occurring, sprang to her partner's assistance but was beaten into submission. Both officers were secured by the inmate as the siege began.

Meanwhile, back in the kitchen, the escape plan had been discovered by two other officers who were checking on the on-duty officer. Coy had one of the restrained officers open the kitchen door and attacked one of the two new corrections officers with the shank, cutting him. The other officer fled the dining hall to get help, pursued by Steven Coy.

The escape plan had been discovered and an alert was sounded. Coy was confronted in the yard by staff. Initially refusing commands, he was pepper sprayed and probably would have been taken into custody if not for his partner. Wassenaar had the AR-15 rifle from the tower and he fired approximately 14 to 15 rounds at the officers attempting to subdue Coy, allowing Coy to make it to the tower. The prison communications center was advised of the hostage incident at approximately 5:30 A.M. Negotiations began around 8:00 A.M. and they would continue for 15 days as authorities bargained for the lives of the officers.

The first responding tactical teams and negotiators worked 31 hours straight in an effort to end the siege. Ultimately a call was sent out for relief. The FBI's Critical Incident Response Group (CIRG), Crisis Negotiation Unit from Quantico offered the assistance of their local negotiation team. They would also send two senior CNU negotiators and a behavioral science profiler to supplement the team's effort during the course of the incident. Their assistance would be crucial in terms of experience and resources. Their efforts were supported by fellow FBI negotiators from around the country who were assigned to intelligence duties.

During the 15-day siege there would be tactical teams and negotiators from various federal, state, county, and municipal agencies. The core of the negotiation team was comprised of 30 negotiators, supported by many more officers and agents from around the country. In the end, 10 primary negotiators spoke with the hostage takers. Each negotiator was used strategically to the team's advantage.

The Phoenix Police Department and the local FBI office work as one negotiations team, helping and supporting each other as the need arises. I responded as a member of the local FBI team, part of the relief on day two of the siege. My experience had been limited to that of a police "street" negotiator If you asked me before this experience if I ever thought I would be negotiating in a prison, my answer would have been "no." Obviously I do not feel that way today. I had never worked a negotiation job in a correctional setting and thought of it only as a remote possibility, but still I had prepared myself with what was available, receiving training from the FBI—"Negotiating in a Correctional Setting," and reading about these types of negotiations in both the first and second editions of *Crisis Negotiations* by Michael McMains and Wayman Mullins. Now I would have the opportunity to experience it firsthand. It would be difficult to write about all the day-to-day negotiations so I am going to discuss and share some of the many lessons learned (from my perspective) during my time at Lewis Prison.

First, every position on the team was important regardless of your particular assignment. No job was too small or insignificant and they were treated this way. Besides the primary, secondary, and team leader, a warden was assigned to the on-duty team to provide insights into this unfamiliar culture and their assistance was invaluable. A scribe documented the on-going negotiations in real-time using a laptop computer and a commercially available crisis management program that were provided by the Arizona Department of Public Safety. This log, which ultimately consisted of 114 pages, facilitated the timely retrieval of activities and events for the negotiators and command. The daily log, position papers, briefings, and cassette recordings allowed negotiators to review not only their own negotiations, but also the activity on the other shifts.

Speaking of shifts, the FBI put the siege into perspective in terms of hours and days. During the first week the negotiators did not have a set shift or schedule, which sometimes made for some long days. In street negotiations, according to HOBAS, most barricades last less than six hours and in Phoenix that statistic holds true. Our longest incident lasted 19 hours and I used to think that was a long time. We had never been faced with a protracted incident that needed relief or rotation of manpower beyond one day. At the prison, we were faced with the possibility of an incident that could last for weeks, and this incident was consuming our every thought while on-scene, as well as occupying our thoughts in our off time. Because everybody wanted to be part of the solution, it was sometimes hard to get people to take days off. Set shifts—hours and days off—were necessary to prevent fatigue and burnout, two factors that can negatively affect the negotiation effort.

Decisionmaking at the correctional facility was very different from a police barricade. While we are used to having our commander on scene, streamlining the decisionmaking process, this was not the case at the prison. The big command center was off site and when decisions had to be made, phone calls had to be placed to the director or the governor. These decisions, depending on the nature of the request, could take a couple of hours, or all day. At times this was frustrating because it was not what I was used to. On the street our decisions are made in a matter of minutes. There was a lot of patience on the part of everybody at the scene, and it did not take long to realize this was not an ordinary barricade (if there is such a thing).

The negotiations operations center was a small administrative office adjacent to the warden's office and the main conference room. The room was too small for our six-person teams. It was also too close to the on-site command center and the warden's office. Until speakers were finally set up in the command center, personnel would open the NOC door to "see" what was going on. An attempt was made to move the NOC to a larger, more distant and more private room, but the request was denied. Remember to carefully choose a location that facilitates the negotiations process.

There are numerous benefits to recording the negotiations and these were seen at the prison and in the follow-up trial of Wassenaar; however, when you do record your negotiations, use the best equipment available. In fact, in all areas of negotiations, use the best equipment you have. At the prison we used what was readily available and on hand. For 15 days the negotiations were recorded on a hand-held cassette recorder that looked like an octopus with all the wires and cheap headsets coming out of it. This equipment in no way adversely affected the negotiations, but better equipment was available. Seven different agencies were involved in the negotiations and equipment like throw phones, headsets, cameras and quality recorders were available, but during the 15 days not one of us thought to use this equipment. Better equipment would have made the monitoring and taping of the negotiations go much more smoothly.

With all the different agencies involved, communications between the tactical and negotiations teams were difficult at times. The police radios were not universally compatible so the tactical liaison position, while always important, took on added importance in terms of updating the tactical component and also combating rumors. The Phoenix tactical team stated in our post-incident debrief that communication between the two elements could have been better and delivered in a more timely manner. If a tactical team is going to operate effectively, they must have accurate and timely intelligence.

A few more thoughts on lessons learned before I close: The intelligence and information is readily available 24/7 for a negotiations team in a corrections setting. Investigators were on hand on all shifts and the requested information would be provided in a matter of minutes. On the street, intelligence gathering, in the form of interviews and investigative follow-ups, take a lot longer and is sometimes manpower-intensive, depending upon the nature of the incident.

Finally, I would recommend to all teams that they train with other federal, state, and local agencies, as well as correctional facilities in their area. As previously mentioned, the negotiations team was comprised of 30 negotiators from seven different agencies. Almost 80 percent of the negotiators knew or recognized each other from some type of training prior to the incident. With this kind of networking, it did not take long for a six-person, multi-agency team to form into a cohesive and effective unit. The negotiation team (whether on-site or off-site) worked hard and it was an honor to work with these professionals. I think each of us walked away with a valuable learning experience that can be shared with others for years to come.

One maxim of negotiations is to "always get something for something." Never cede to a demand without obtaining a concession in return. The cultural diversity faced by the prison negotiator may require violating this tenet. The Cubans at Oakdale and Atlanta told negotiators they did not trade in Cuban culture (Fusilier et al., 1989). The Cubans wanted something for nothing and at a later time would give something for nothing. At one point, the Cubans just released some hostages. The next day, negotiators gave the hostage takers mail and turned on the water. The negotiators had to forego their training and mind-set concerning negotiations and work within the culture of the hostage takers. All negotiators may face this dilemma, but it is more likely to be experienced by the prison negotiator.

One issue that arose at the Oakdale, Atlanta, and Talladega sieges that has major implications for all prison negotiators is language. Often a large population of inmates speak English as a second language or speak only a very limited amount of English. Should negotiations be conducted in English or the other language? This question will have to be addressed by the response team at each situation. Fuselier et al. (1989) identified several factors the response team should consider when making this decision.

If negotiations are conducted in a foreign language, the negotiator will have to translate everything for the rest of the negotiating team. This will slow negotiations considerably and place an added strain on the negotiator. Additionally, the opportunities for more mistakes, errors, and miscommunications are present due to translating's additional step. The assessment process will also be slowed and incorrect assessments may be made. Many language idiosyncrasies that are used to identify specific pathologies may not be present in a foreign language or may be lost in translation.

The hostage takers might have difficulty expressing themselves in English, thereby frustrating the ventilation process and increasing stress and anxiety. The hostage takers may become frustrated and violent by their inability to speak good English. They may also be embarrassed and hesitant to speak to the negotiator. To assist in venting emotions, negotiating in the hostage taker's native language may move the situation forward. The hostage taker may also be able to more clearly articulate and express the issues if talking in their native language.

On the positive side, using English may prevent some violent-sounding dialogues. Spanish, for example, is an emotional and passionate language. Some statements and outbursts in Spanish should not be given the same attention that they might in another context. At the Atlanta siege, for example, negotiators were constantly told (following outbursts in Spanish), "Don't pay any attention to that threat; that's just the way we are" (Fuselier et al., 1989).

English can reduce the emotional content of negotiations, especially if the hostage takers are violent and highly emotional. Using English will force the hostage takers to slow down and think about what they are going to say. Merely mentally translating will reduce emotions and increase rationality. This will also tire the hostage takers psychologically and wear them down (Van Zandt, 1989).

The specific situation will dictate what language to negotiate in. The best solution may be to compromise and negotiate in both languages. When the content is emotional, it may be best to use English, then switch to the foreign language when people are calm and thinking rationally. Negotiators at the Talladega prison riot began negotiating in English and then switched to Spanish, a strategy that proved exceptionally effective (Fagan & Van Zandt, 1993).

The Prison Negotiating Team

The prison should develop its own negotiating team. Each prison will have to develop its own plan for creating a negotiation response team. All prisons should follow some general guidelines. The team should be non-management and non-officers. Wardens, deputy wardens, sheriffs, chief jailer, all correctional officers, etc., should not be considered for the negotiating team. Due to their lack of familiarity with prisons and the unique demands of prison hostage situations, law enforcement teams should not be used as primary response teams. The prison may call upon a law enforcement team to assist in negotiating, but this should be for assistance, not direction. Team members should go through a selection process. They should be volunteers, emotionally stable and mature, have good communication skills, calm under pressure, intelligent, have good listening skills, team players, in good physical condition and health, adaptable and flexible, and culturally diverse (Hazelton & Rhodes, 2000).

The negotiation team should consist, at minimum, of a team leader, a primary negotiator, a secondary negotiator, a mental health professional, and a recorder. If personnel are available, the team might include a liaison with an Emergency Response Team, an intelligence gatherer, and a communications equipment person (as with police, the negotiating team and emergency response team should be separate teams). The training and responsibilities of these team members are the same as for any negotiating team. Because hostage situations in prisons often become sieges, the prison negotiating team should receive plenty of experiential case studies (Braswell, 1985). In a hostage situation, the negotiating team should develop written summaries of significant events to date. These written summaries should include demands, pertinent intelligence, identification of leaders, observations, and recommendations. These summaries should be made available to all parties involved in the negotiating process.

One prison team issue concerns the primary negotiator and whether that person should be from the same institution or from the outside. Advantages to using a same-institution negotiator are that the negotiator knows the hostage takers, the hostages, and the institution. Disadvantages may be that the negotiator and hostage taker have a prior relationship that is negative, the hostages may be close friends and objectivity is lost; and the negotiator becomes too emotionally involved, and that following resolution of the incident, the negotiator and hostage takers will be in contact with each other (although many institutions now have a policy requiring hostage takers to be transferred to another institution). A compromise position might be for the negotiating team to use a primary negotiator from a different institution and the team performs the rest of the functions. There are, however, problems with this solution as well, including loss of team unity, or lack of relationship between the primary negotiator and hostage takers.

Strict timetables for on-duty team members and shift rotation schedules should be made and closely adhered to. Critical positions such as primary negotiator, tactical team sniper, etc. should rotate every six to eight hours. Other team members should be limited to 12-hour shifts. Typically, team members will want to violate the time limits (i.e., "We're close to resolution. I need to be here for it."). Do not allow them to violate the time limits.

All prison staff should receive basic training in hostage negotiation and hostage survival. This training does not have to teach staff how to be negotiators, but should familiarize them with the basic purposes of negotiation, negotiation strategy, and tactics. Hostage survival skills should include the "do's and don'ts" of hostage behavior, adaptation, and coping skills, survival skills, developing the Stockholm Syndrome, important intelligence needs of the response teams and how to gather that intelligence, and aftereffects on hostages. This training will help prison staff survive the hostage situation physically and mentally and, more importantly, allow the hostage staff to help the negotiating team resolve the situation. If the hostage knows how to "behave," it will make the negotiator's job much easier and keep the hostage alive.

Table 10.1
Prison Hostage Survival Skills

DO:	DON'T
Prepare for extended time	Panic
Keep up strength	Do anything stupid
Escape mentally	Be a negotiator
Limit conversation with hostage taker	Increase stress on the hostage taker
Appear neutral and non-threatening	Offer suggestions to the hostage taker
Pay attention to details	Argue with the hostage taker
Stay in sight of the hostage taker	Argue philosophy with the hostage taker
Show yourself as a person	Show emotions
Retain personal control and dignity	Pay obvious attention to ongoing crisis
Be a good listener	(draws undue attention)
Give credibility to the negotiator	
Have an emergency plan	
Remove signs of your office	
Be a group member	
Be aware of your body language	
Discuss issues with family prior to event	

ESCAPE ATTEMPTS	ASSAULT
Only try to escape if certain of success	Drop to floor with hands overhead
Review plan of action	Stay still and be calm
Do not attempt if other hostages might be injured or killed in retaliation	Obey orders of assault team
Your escape may add pressure to other hostages	

Source: Adapted from Hazelton, J. and T. Rhodes (2000). "Prison Negotiations and Hostage Survival Skills." Presented at the Hostage Negotiator Competition, Southwest Texas State University, San Marcos, TX (January).

The chain of command during a hostage situation will have to be developed by each prison. In general, the negotiating team should report directly to the warden or sheriff, work in conjunction with the emergency response team under the auspices of a situation commander, and receive support from other prison staff. The critical incident management response effort for the Federal Bureau of Prisons is shown in Figure 10.1.

One important point not faced by the police negotiator is worth mentioning at this point. Often in the prison hostage situation, one or more of the hostages will be a ranking member of the prison administration. Chances are this administrator will want to assume his or her everyday supervisory role. Under no circumstances should this be allowed to occur. Policy should be clearly written and communicated before an incident that any captive staff has no authority over any noncaptive staff (including the warden's designee if the warden is a hostage). The captive administrator will not be thinking clearly, his or her interests will not be in the situation's best interests, he or she may be under duress from the hostage takers, and he or she gives unwanted, unneeded, and unnecessary control to the hostage takers.

Figure 10.1
The Federal Bureau of Corrections Critical Incident Management Response Flow Chart for Handling Hostage Incidents

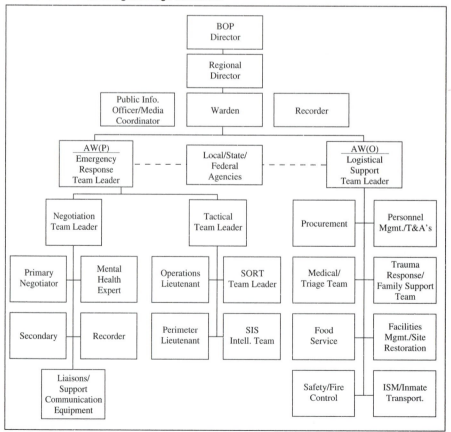

Source: Federal Bureau of Corrections.

A clear example of this occurred in a 1993 non-prison situation in Costa Rica. Two armed terrorists (who later turned out not to be terrorists but drug dealers) took the Federal Supreme Court of Costa Rica hostage and demanded the release of fellow drug dealers, money, and transportation to a safe haven. The Chief Justice of the Court, who was a hostage, insisted on being the spokesperson for the hostage takers and continually gave orders to the primary negotiator (who worked for the Federal Judicial Police and reported directly to the Supreme Court). His actions endangered the hostages, hindered negotiations and intelligence-gathering efforts, and prolonged the incident for many hours. Because of his interference, the federal police did not discover until the end of the situation that the hostage takers were not terrorists and the incident had to be resolved tactically. To the credit of the negotiator, who successfully circumvented most of the judge's interference, no lives were lost.

Because prison hostage situations usually become sieges, and because prison workers are often hostages, it is advisable to establish (prior to the incident) a victims' assistance team. This team should be trained to deal with the hostages' families. This training should, at a minimum, include stress management techniques, post-trauma stress issues and effects, emotional debriefing, and basic crisis counseling skills. When a situation occurs, the victims' assistance team should notify the hostages' families and establish a family services area. They should provide emotional support to the families, disseminate information and intelligence on the hostage situation, and shield family members from the news media (Miller et al., 1988; Squires, 1988). This team may also be used to conduct the emotional debriefing of all released hostages.

Lessons Learned From History

Based on the Lewis Prison situation (and a review of others), Dubina (2005) provides an excellent summary of issues that correctional negotiators should be aware of, prepare for, and make part of their response policies and operations. First, chain-of-command issues can be critical. At many prison situations, the ultimate incident commander may be a director of corrections (or other title) who is a political appointee and who may have little or no experience in a prison or in command of an incident. It is especially critical that wardens, associate wardens, and others who may be designated incident commanders receive incident command training. Also, it is advisable to make sure one of these trained individuals is assigned to the office of the director of corrections to advise that person on situational issues, incident dynamics, response team issues, demand issues, etc.

If negotiators are non-correctional personnel, correctional advisors should be assigned to the team and should be utilized to educate team members on correctional issues. Correctional personnel should also be brought in to assist the intelligence gatherers, tactical team, media relations people, and anyone else who does not have a correctional background. Prisons have their own language (terminology, slang, etc.), issues specific to a facility, and other special requirements that non-correctional personnel will probably not be aware of. One thing not anticipated by the police negotiators at Lewis Prison was that the prison (or Arizona Department of Corrections) had a policy that inmate hostage takers would not be given handcuff keys; they were a non-negotiable demand. Negotiators were making progress in meeting the inmate demands for a key, reached the point where a trade was imminent, and then were told that it was a non-negotiable demand. A great deal of time, effort, energy, and goodwill were expended by not being aware of this issue.

The negotiating area, or NOC (negotiation operations center), should be chosen carefully, keeping in mind that the prison negotiating team may be significantly larger than a law enforcement negotiating team, and that the incident may last for several days or weeks. In addition to adequate size, furnishings should be selected and brought in that provide a modicum of comfort. A padded swivel chair will make the job easier for the primary negotiator than sitting on a metal folding chair for 10 hours at a time.

In terms of the team, a work/rotational schedule should be established right away and negotiators made to adhere to the schedule. Rotations should be clearly indicated, people assigned to specific tasks for each shift, and personnel should leave the area when they are not on duty. The negotiating team structure may need to be modified to facilitate negotiations and communications. At Lewis Prison, for example, negotiators were assigned to the command post, a tactical liaison was maintained at all times utilizing a negotiator, and the negotiator team leader was assigned to the NOC. The entire team on duty should be utilized in some capacity. Team members should not be allowed to wait around with no job to perform. Extra personnel can be assigned to collect intelligence (and intelligence gathering and dissemination is ongoing throughout the incident), assist the scribe/recorder/historian, assigned to monitor equipment, etc. The team should also be regularly used to brainstorm and plan communications. It is critical that all communications with the hostage taker be planned. Prior to each phone conversation, the team should plan each communication and brainstorm the handling of critical issues that may arise.

Complete, concise, and accurate situation boards are a must. A good scribe and running log are necessary. The log should be time stamped and typed, and should be disseminated to all personnel on a regular schedule, especially when the team rotates. A full briefing by off-going team members given to on-coming team members using the typed log and negotiation summaries is necessary.

Negotiations should be taped and copies should be made of the tape. Any participating team member (including tactical and command elements) should have open and free access to any negotiation tapes. It is a good idea to have on-coming negotiators listen to recent taped conversations to get a sense of the flow of negotiations. This is also related to the point that equipment needs in a long-term siege should be anticipated and filled in advance. For example, it may be anticipated that tape recorders will be necessary, but will batteries for those recorders be remembered (and what if a cord breaks, electricity goes out, etc.).

Aggression Among Inmates

Prison inmates are as culturally diverse as the civilian world. Inmates, however, are much more homogeneous than in the civilian world. Cultural groups tend to coalesce and unite with one another. Interests, language, and cultural identity all may account for cultural clustering in prisons. However, cultural groups unite and close ranks primarily for safety and protection. This section presents an overview of the more common groups in prisons and provides information for possible negotiations with these groups.

Prison officials should be aware of and prepared to handle race-related issues in hostage situations. These issues had implications for Federal Bureau of Prisons personnel at the 1991 Talladega, Alabama, prison riot (Phillips, 1991). If the riot and hostage situation are race-related (or even involve one race), prisoners of that race incarcerated at other locations should be carefully monitored or even "locked down." Prisoners at other locations are likely to want to help their "brothers" achieve their goals. There is a possibility of the episode serving as the catalyst for other episodes.

It is crucial that negotiators be aware of, attuned to, and prepared for racial and cultural issues. Diversity issues in the prison may revolve around race, ethnicity, nationality, and/or religion (Pryor, 2000). Consideration should be given to economics, politics, geography, family structure, climate, technology, and education. Influences that have worked to shape the hostage taker that produce cultural and racial differences are family, personal experience, theology, and media, to a limited extent. The negotiator should be aware of these influences and differences and be sensitive to them when negotiating. Being able to deal with diversity issues is a combination of skill, knowledge, and motivation (Beebe & West, 1999). It is strongly encouraged that prison negotiators, especially, be trained in cultural diversity issues.

Whites in prisons are apt to join the Aryan Brotherhood, a right-wing organization under the umbrella of the Aryan Nations (Mullins, 1988; 1997). This far-right organization believes in white supremacy, and many members base this belief on religion. Members of the Aryan Brotherhood have been involved in many violent activities, including the killing of minority inmates and attacks on minority correctional officers. One part of the membership "contract" is that the member kill the police officer who arrested him.

Other right-wing groups that are likely to have inmate representation or recruit from inmate populations include the Ku Klux Klan; religious organizations such as the Christian Patriot Defense League (CPDL); the Covenant, Sword, and Arm of the Lord (CSA); neo-Nazi organizations (National Socialist White People's Party and American Nazi Party); and various factions of the skinhead movement. All these organizations have two factors in common: they hate all minorities and they are extremely violent.

Their violent activity in prisons will first be directed toward minorities and will be acts of perceived self-protection: individual and for all whites. If their perception of the minority threat grows, they are likely to riot and take hostages. Minority correctional staff are especially vulnerable to hostage taking and injury or death. The group's demands will revolve around issues of segregation, "white" rights, and even separate facilities for whites. They will not negotiate with minorities and may not acquiesce if the commander or prison authority is non-white. Also, if they are involved in an incident, civilian members of the far right will demonstrate at the prison and engage in activities designed to interfere with negotiations and assist their "brethren" in achieving their goals.

Blacks and Hispanics in prisons are more likely than white inmates to riot and take hostages. Blacks and Hispanics are the fastest-growing prison populations (Barak-Glantz, 1985; Irwin, 1980). Black inmates tend to be urbanized, sophisticated, and somewhat racially radical. Many will join the Black Muslim religion, a religion in which some factions (especially those in prison) advocate the rise of black supremacy through violence. This violence is directed specifically at white power structures, such as the prison administration. The black inmate also has an acute sense and mission of the civil rights struggle of the past several decades. This civil rights movement has gained momentum in the past several years, and in the prison can easily become manifest in violence and hostage taking. The religious, racially militant, black inmate is prepared to use violence to achieve his objectives (Barak-Glantz, 1985). Black inmates have a highly developed social structure that increases the likelihood of blacks leading a hostage situation. The organizational unity present in the black subculture further promotes rioting and other acts of mass violence.

As with blacks, Hispanics have a highly developed social subculture, as evidenced by the majority of Hispanic inmate membership in the Mexican Mafia and Nuestra Familia (Bowker, 1980). The Hispanic inmate, even more so than the black inmate, sees himself as an oppressed minority. When an attack (real or perceived) comes from an outside source, Hispanics will put forward a unified front to meet the challenge. In addition to resisting, the Hispanic inmate will attack the source of resistance. The attacks do not have to be physical; they can be attacks of injustice, unfairness, or control by another group. The negotiator must be acutely aware of the Hispanic hostage taker's cultural milieu and must negotiate within that framework. The negotiator must be careful in asserting authority and control over the hostage situation. More than with whites or blacks, the Hispanic hostage taker will see this authority as an insult and use it as the basis for more violence. It is important to the Hispanic to be able to maintain his respect in the eyes of others (Fuselier et al., 1991).

In recent years, black and Hispanic inmates have been heavily influenced by gang members. These young, urbanized, and organized males bring a level of aggression and violence never before seen in prison populations. These younger inmates are extremely militant, highly organized, and unusually violent. They pose a special problem to the hostage negotiator because they have very little regard for the lives of others or themselves. They are likely to kill a hostage just to show they can. They are often irrational, unpredictable, unreasonable, and uncompromising. They would rather die than concede their demands. Negotiating means getting their way. One of the few approaches open to the negotiator is to ensure that the leaders save face and concede while appearing to win. The negotiator must be very careful not to sound authoritative, but must take a deferential role and act as if the inmate hostage taker is in control. The gang member is very concerned with the gang (or group). The negotiator should emphasize the group and how the resolution will benefit the group.

Turner and Miller (1991), in a study for the Federal Bureau of Prisons, identified five factors that could result in increased aggressiveness and hostage-taking behavior among prison inmates.

1. Foreigners with less than two years in the United States before their first felony were likely to be more aggressive than other inmates. These inmates were not likely to be verbally aggressive, but would use physical aggression. If they did become physically aggressive, they would also be likely to employ verbal aggression, such as shouting and screaming. This suggests that their aggression will involve a high emotional level and they will be irrational.

2. Inmates with an eighth to tenth grade education were most likely to be violent. Inmates with a ninth to tenth grade education were also likely to be physically violent, but more often their violence was verbally directed, and employed refusal, insolence, and sarcasm. The least violent inmates were those with a college degree or those with no formal education.

3. Inmates who were raised without a father or father figure and who had the stereotypical "macho" attitude were more likely to be physically aggressive.

4. Non-citizen inmates who espoused the traditional values of their culture were more likely to be physically aggressive. Cum'Fa, Jamaican Posse, Obeah, Rastafarian, and Voudun are cultures that believe in violent problem solving. If one inmate with these values became violent, other members of that cul-

ture were likely to become involved. One exception found by Turner and Miller (1991) were Haitian Vouduns who did not practice Voudun. These inmates were very passive, superstitious, and extremely dependent upon others.

5. Type of crime predicted violence. Inmates who committed crimes for profit tended to be more verbally aggressive than physically aggressive. When they did turn to physical violence, this violence was usually preceded by verbal threats. Inmates who committed crimes of self-indulgence were the most physically aggressive.

Veterans in Prison

Military veterans in the nation's prisons and jails make up 12 percent of all inmates. Some information concerning that population segment is presented to help negotiators understand the military veteran hostage taker and to provide a negotiation framework. The information presented is summarized from a Bureau of Justice Statistics Special Report by Mumola (2000). Only about 20 percent of inmate veterans saw combat duty, with more than half serving during a period of combat. Most veterans were Vietnam War era (1964-1973), followed by the Persian Gulf war (1990-1991), Korea (1950-1953), and WWII era (1941-1945). Almost 60 percent served in the Army, followed by Navy service (14% federal, 17.2% state), Marine Corps (16.2% federal, 15.6% state), and Air Force (11.9% federal, 8.9% state). The average length of service was 45 to 48 months (for federal and state facilities, respectively).

The majority of military veteran inmates are white (49.8% federal, 52.8% state), while the majority of non-veteran inmates are black (38.4% federal, 47.8% state). Veteran inmates, on average, are 10 years older than non-veteran inmates (veterans had a median age over 40), were more likely to have been married currently or in the past (71% for veterans, 39% non-veterans), and had more education than non-veterans. In fact, 41.6 percent of federal veteran inmates and 32 percent of state veteran inmates had some college or a degree (comparatively, 24.2% and 10.7% for non-veteran inmates). Age, marital history, and education can play significant roles in negotiating with the military veteran.

Veterans were more likely to be serving sentences for violent offenses and were less likely to be drug offenders than non-veterans, although at the federal level, more than 51 percent of veteran inmates were serving time for drug offenses (most for trafficking). Robbery was the most common offense for veterans at the federal level; sexual assault and homicide at the state level. About 25 percent of federal veteran inmates were serving time for a violent offense, about 55 percent of state veteran inmates were serving time for a violent offense. At the state level, combat veterans were less likely than non-combat veterans to be serving sentences for violent offenses. Veterans were serving longer sentences than non-veterans at both the federal and state levels, and were spending longer time in prison prior to release. Pre-incarceration drug use among veterans was lower than among non-veterans. Around one-third of veteran inmates reported alcohol abuse prior to incarceration.

Among state veteran inmates serving time for violent crimes, most knew their victim (69%). Thirty-one percent victimized a friend or acquaintance, 22.4 percent a relative, 11.4 percent an intimate (spouse, boy/girlfriend, or ex), and 5.2 percent knew the victim only by sight. Thirty-one percent did not know the victim. Non-veteran inmates were most likely to have victimized a stranger (48.9%), 27.3 percent a friend or acquaintance, 9.3 percent a relative, 8.8 percent an intimate, and 7.1 percent known by sight. Thirty-six percent of the veterans victimized a juvenile, 20.4 percent a child under the age of 12 (this compares to 19.8% and 9.4% for non-veterans, respectively).

For other differences among veteran inmates, the reader is encouraged to read the full report by Mumola (2000). The issues reported here are those most significant for the prison negotiator, and can help with negotiating strategy, communication directions, and resolving demand issues.

Inmate Cultural Trends

As part of a study for the Federal Bureau of Prisons, Turner and Miller (1991) examined inmate cultural trends and offered psychological profiles of these cultures based upon the MMPI, Mental Status Examination, Rosenzweig P-F Study, and behavioral observation.

Jamaican inmates were demanding, confrontational, impulsive, macho, remorseless, sociopathic, did not conform to social demands and limitations, did not learn new coping skills, and repeatedly relied on the same coping mechanisms, exhibited machismo indicative of a poor self-concept, were initially polite but with time in prison became aggressive, and showed little concern for others and directed their frustrations toward others, using insults and threats of injury. Behavioral observations of Jamaicans inmates identified seven behavioral trends: (1) they tended to make verbal threats before becoming physically aggressive; (2) they were good at being able to judge the correctional staff and conform their behavior to the demands of the staff; (3) they placed great emphasis on time and reacted aggressively when their time expectations were violated; (4) they verbally threatened physical violence when they wanted information and that information was not forthcoming; (5) they resisted wearing others' clothing, even after it had been laundered, believing the "spirits" of others inhabited the clothing. Many wore clothing inside-out so they would not be contaminated by these "spirits;" (6) They would psychologically abuse weaker Jamaicans by telling stories of "duppies" (ghosts of people who died a violent death who roam the earth and frighten the living). These "duppy believers" would use the psychologist to exorcise the "duppies" by performing certain rituals (saying three curse words, putting water under their bed, or reciting the Lord's Prayer); and (7) they did not respect females, although they would be polite to female prison staff when face-to-face.

A second inmate population examined by Turner and Miller (1991) were Haitians. Haitians were complaining, demanding, irritable, pessimistic, rigid, exhibited poor judgment, were impulsive and unpredictable, viewed the world as dangerous, saw themselves as rejected by others, were not able to properly express their anger and were resentful, needed a great deal of attention, their interpersonal relations were plagued by defensiveness, distress, conflict, and manipulation, and they perceived themselves as being mistreated by the world, and did not take responsibility for their actions. The Haitians were easily insulted and physically countered any perceived insult; had little regard and respect for other people and perceived themselves as victims; solutions to problems were simplistic and self-serving; they were not able to handle frustration and stress (used name-calling and physical threats); and overreacted when stressed. Behavioral trends identified

The Oklahoma Bureau of Prisons East Regional Hostage Negotiation team receiving the award for 1st Place in the Prison Negotiating team at the 2004 Negotiation Competition at Texas State University. Prison teams are generally larger than law enforcement teams because prisons have to expect long sieges that require assigning negotiators to shifts. *(R. Mullins)*

included: (1) aggressiveness or passivity depending upon active participation in Voudun. Those who actively practiced Voudun tended to be the aggressive group; (2) low frustration tolerance, wanted immediate gratification of their needs, and acted without thinking; (3) cooperating better with and forming better relationships with female staff. Also, if a Haitian had formed a relationship with a staff member, he or she would be the only staff member they would go to or talk with concerning any problems; (4) being anti-Dominican, believing that Dominicans were "headhunters" looking for Haitian scalps; and (5) not associating with or relating to Hispanics.

The analysis of Hispanic inmates was more complex. Hispanic inmates included Mexican, Central American, Dominican, and Colombian inmates. Hispanics were conventional, opinionated, moralistic, moody, and restless. They had a strong need for attention and became angry when they did not receive attention. They were short-tempered, reactionary, narcissistic, and egocentric. Interpersonal relationships were formed for personal gain and were sociopathic. They often reported many physical symptoms of illness, but these illnesses were for secondary gain (i.e., to get out of work details, extra benefits, increased bunk time, etc.) and tended to be psychosomatic.

Mexican inmates were found to be apologetic, sincere, and passive. Relationships were formed for personal gain. They assigned self-blame for external difficulties and directed anger internally. For problems, the locus of control was external. Problems were the result of bad luck or fate being against them. Central Americans were abrupt and impatient with others, directed their aggression toward others, and often used verbal aggression. Colombian inmates tended to only use verbal aggression when insulted. They had a low frustration tolerance and internalized their frustration. They did not accept personal responsibility for their actions and believed themselves to be victimized by others. They often wanted attention, pity, and approval from others.

Behaviorally, the Mexican inmates caused the fewest problems. They made few demands of the staff and assisted the staff when possible. They tended to be non-aggressive, non-threatening, and polite. The Central Americans were the most aggressive and presented the most problems of the three Hispanic groups. If things did not go their way, they became aggressive and accusing, confrontational and accusatory. They attempted to recruit others in carrying their "torch," and when they did, the Central Americans would become observers and quit their participation. Inconveniences increased their aggressiveness. The Colombians were the most demanding and believed themselves superior to other inmates. They believed they were falsely imprisoned and that their troubles were the result of others being "out to get them." They were highly prejudiced against other Hispanics and blacks.

Turner and Miller (1991) also identified three groups at Oakdale that could become violent, riot, and take hostages. Members of these groups can be found in most prisons and jails throughout the United States, and deserve mention.

One group is the Rastafarians, a combination religious-political group. The Rastafarians believe Caribbean blacks to have been oppressed by white society (White Babylon). Blacks are encouraged to overthrow white rule and prepare blacks for repatriation to Ethiopia. In recognition of their kinship to Ras Tafari (former emperor of Ethiopia Haile Selassie), many use nicknames with "Prince" or "Ras" prefixes. Religious Rastafarians tend to have stable job histories, read and interpret the Bible, and have minimal achievement motivation. Crimes are usually nonviolent. In prison, they avoid trouble and are polite and cooperative with staff. Political Rastafarians involve themselves in social change, politics, and violence. Their criminal history includes violent crime. In prison they are hostile and argumentative (especially concerning prisoners' rights), rally others to protest and rebel, and become insurrection leaders.

A second group that Turner and Miller identified were the religious fetish cults. These included Cum'Fa, Obeah, Santaria, Shango, and Voudun. These cults practice both good (white) and bad (black) magic and regularly practice blood sacrifice (Obeah sacrifices by poison). In prison, they are passive and followers. They are usually not violent, but can be coerced by others to participate in riots or hostage taking.

A third group identified by Turner and Miller (1991) was the Jamaican Posse, a well-organized group tied to drug trafficking and black market weapons. They are extremely violent and reactionary. In prison, they will often ally with the political Rastafarians and assume leadership positions within the prison. They are violent and physically aggressive. Members often use intimidation and strong-arm tactics.

The Turner and Miller (1991) study was limited to the inmate population at Oakdale Federal Prison, Louisiana. There are problems with generalizing their results to other prison populations, especially state and county populations. The findings of Turner and Miller, however, provide negotiators with some basic guidelines in determining the emotional, psychological, and behavioral characteristics of prison hostage takers. State prison populations are more violent than those in federal prisons. County jails have about the same violence potential as federal prisons. At the state and county level, prison and jail populations tend to fragment into three to five distinct groupings: Caucasian, black, Hispanic, American Indian, and Asian. The one major deviation from the above discussion for county and municipal jails is that inmates are not as well organized or as cohesive as they are in prisons. Jail inmates serve less time than their prison counterparts and many are in jail waiting to go to prison.

Racism and racial protection are the underlying theme of each group. Caucasians tend to become members of the Aryan Brotherhood, blacks become Muslims, Hispanics join the Brown (or Mexican) Mafia, etc. If a hostage situation develops, the hostages at most risk (other than correctional staff) are members of other racial groups. For the negotiating team, the issue becomes one of who makes the most effective negotiator. Should the negotiator be of the same race as the hostage taker? There is no single answer to this question. In some circumstances, a same-race negotiator may be most effective, but in other circumstances, the most effective negotiator may be of a different race. White hostage takers, if members of the Aryan Brotherhood, would probably refuse to talk to a black or Hispanic officer. An Asian hostage taker, on the other hand, would be more likely to talk to a non-Asian official. If the negotiator is not making progress, the problem may very well be a race issue rather than a negotiating issue. The secondary negotiator and mental health consultant should carefully monitor the race situation and be ready to make a change at any indication of a race issue.

Summary

Hostage negotiations in prisons are comparable to hostage negotiations in the civilian world. The same basic principles apply, although there are some differences in phenomenology. A major advantage for the prison negotiator is in the amount of intelligence data available at the outset of the incident. Hostage takers are contained, and understand the potential for force to be used against them. Each prison should have a trained and prepared negotiating team ready for any situation that may arise. The negotiators should be ready to respond to emotional frustrations as well as instrumental demands. Additionally, prison negotiators should prepare for incidents of much longer duration than civilian-world incidents. Crucial training for the prison negotiator should include cultural diversity training.

References

Barak-Glantz, I.L. (1985). "The Anatomy of Another Prison Riot." In Braswell, M.C., S. Dillingham, and R.H. Montgomery, Jr. (eds.), *Prison Violence in America*. Cincinnati, OH: Anderson Publishing Co.

Bazan, V. (2004). "Negotiations in Correctional Settings." Presentation at the Hostage Negotiation Competition, Texas State University, San Marcos, TX (January).

Beebe, S. and V. West (1999). "Communication and Cultural Diversity: Bridging Differences Between Strangers." Workshop at Southwest Texas State University, San Marcos, TX (October).

Bowker, L.H. (1980). *Prison Victimization*. New York, NY: Elsevier.

———— (1985). "An Essay on Prison Violence." In Braswell, M.C., S.D. Dillingham, and R.H. Montgomery, Jr. (eds.), *Prison Violence in America*. Cincinnati, OH: Anderson Publishing Co.

Braswell, M.C. (1985). "Understanding the Dynamics of Prison Violence: An Experiential Model for Teaching and Training." In Braswell, M.C., S.D. Dillingham, and R.H. Montgomery, Jr. (eds.), *Prison Violence in America*. Cincinnati, OH: Anderson Publishing Co.

Chen, D.W. (2000). "Inmates in Attica Offered $8 Million Deal." *Austin American-Statesman* January 5:A8.

Correctional Digest (2004). "Breakdowns, Complacency are Key Problems in 15-day Arizona Takeover." *Corrections Digest* 35:1-2.

Dennery, C.H. (2000). "Psychotropic Medication Resources." Presentation at the Hostage Negotiation Competition, Southwest Texas State University, San Marcos, TX (January).

Dillingham, S.D. and R.H. Montgomery (1985). "Prison Riots: A Corrections Nightmare Since 1774." In Braswell, M.C., S.D. Dillingham, and R.H. Montgomery, Jr. (eds.). *Prison Violence in America*. Cincinnati, OH: Anderson Publishing Co.

Dubina, Jan. (2005) "Lewis Prison Hostage-Taking Incident." Presentation at the Arkansas Association of Hostage Negotiators annual conference. Little Rock, AR (June).

Dubina, J. and R. Ragsdale (2005). "Lewis Prison Incident Debriefing." Presentation at the annual Crisis Negotiation Conference of the National Tactical Officers Association, Nashville, TN (April).

Fagan, T.J. and C.R. Van Zandt (1993). "Lesson From Talladega: Even in 'Non-negotiable' Situations, Negotiation Plays An Important Role." *Corrections Today* (April):71-75.

Fuselier, G.D. (1981). "A Practical Overview of Hostage Negotiations." *FBI Law Enforcement Bulletin* 50:12-15.

_____ (1986). *A Practical Overview of Hostage Negotiations*. Quantico, VA: FBI.

_____ (1988). "Hostage Negotiation Consultant: Emerging Role for the Clinical Psychologist." *Professional Psychology* 19:175-179.

Fuselier, G.D., C.R. Van Zandt, and F.J. Lanceley (1989). "Negotiating the Protracted Incident: The Oakdale and Atlanta Prison Sieges." *FBI Law Enforcement Bulletin* 58:1-7.

Fuselier, G.D., C.R. Van Zandt, and F.J. Lanceley (1991). "Hostage/Barricade Incidents: High-Risk Factors and the Action Criteria." *FBI Law Enforcement Bulletin* 60:6-12.

Hazelton, J. and T. Rhodes (2000). "Prison Negotiations and Hostage Survival Skills." Presentation at the Hostage Negotiation Competition, Southwest Texas State University, San Marcos, TX (January).

Hudson v. McMillian, 112 S. Ct. 995 (1992).

Irwin, J. (1980). *Prisons in Turmoil*. Boston, MA: Little, Brown and Co.

Mahan, S. (1985). "An 'Orgy of Brutality at Attica' and the 'Killing Ground' at Santa Fe: A Comparison of Prison Riots." In Braswell, M.C., S.D. Dillingham, and R.H. Montgomery, Jr. (eds.), *Prison Violence in America*. Cincinnati, OH: Anderson Publishing Co.

Miller, P.L., J.R. Johnson, and J.S. Petrovsky (1988). "Lessons Learned: The Oakdale/Atlanta Riots—Interviews with BOP Wardens Johnson and Petrovsky." *Corrections Today* 50:16-18.

Mullins, W.C. (1988). *Terrorist Organizations in the United States: An Analysis of Issues, Organizations, Tactics and Responses*. Springfield, IL: Charles C Thomas.

_____ (1997). *A Sourcebook on Domestic and International Terrorism: An Analysis of Issues, Organizations, Tactics, and Responses*, Second Edition. Springfield, IL: Charles C Thomas.

Mumola, C.J. (2000). *Veterans in Prison or Jail*. Washington DC: U.S. Department of Justice, Office of Justice Programs, Bureau of Justice Statistics Special Report.

Needham, J. (1977). "Neutralization of a Prison Hostage Situation." *Criminal Justice Monographs* 8:1-48.

New York State Special Commission on Attica (1972). *Attica*. New York, NY: Bantam Books.

Office of the Attorney General for the State of New Mexico (1980). *Report of the Attorney General on the February 2 and 3, 1980 Riot at the Penitentiary of New Mexico*. Santa Fe, NM: Author.

Phillips, R. (1991). "Crisis in Talladega: How the Federal Bureau of Prisons Resolved this Summer's Dramatic 10-day Hostage Incident." *Corrections Today* 53:122-133.

Pryor, J. (2000). "Cultural Diversity Issues in Prisons." Presentation at the Hostage Negotiation Competition, Southwest Texas State University, San Marcos, TX (January).

Romano, S.J. (2003). "Achieving Successful Negotiations in a Correctional Setting." *Corrections Today* April, 114-118.

Sage, B. (2003). "Major Incidents: Lessons Learned." Presentation at the Hostage Negotiation Competition. Texas State University, San Marcos, TX (January).

Saenz, A.B. and T.Z. Reeves (1989). "Riot Aftermath: New Mexico's Experience Teaches Valuable Lessons." *Corrections Today* 51:66-70.

Squires, S. (1988). "Held Hostage: Inside the Oakdale and Atlanta Prison Uprisings: Mind Games and Survival Tactics." *Washington Post* January 12:Z15.

Turner, L. and J.H. Miller (1991). *Cultural Implications for Behavior: A Preliminary Report from the Federal Detention Center, Oakdale, LA.* Washington DC: Federal Bureau of Prisons.

Van Zandt, C.R. (1989). "Nine Days of Crisis Negotiations: The Oakdale Siege." *Corrections Today* 51:16-18.

Whitley v. Albers, 106 S. Ct. 1078 (1986).

Worledge, J., T.J. Kane, and G.B. Saathoff (1997). *The Negotiator's Guide to Psychoactive Drugs.* Quantico, VA: FBI Critical Incident Response Group.

Discussion Questions

1. You are the primary negotiator at a prison situation in which two inmates have taken a civilian nurse hostage and are locked in a closet. Both inmates are highly agitated and are threatening to rape and kill the hostage. Without having any demands presented, what could you do to reduce the possibility of violence toward the nurse?

2. Reread the hostage scenario that opens this chapter. Assume you are the state police negotiator. What kind of things could you initially say to the inmates to establish your credibility, calm the rioting, and start establishing the Stockholm Syndrome?

3. Develop a method to select hostage negotiators for a prison team.

4. You are negotiating at a federal prison where inmates have rioted and taken numerous prison staff hostage. One of the hostages is the Deputy Director of Prisons for your region. He insists upon ordering you in what to do and what demands to agree to. What would your response to that person be? What could you say to the inmates to keep him off the phone? How could you get him to relinquish control?

5. At Oakdale, negotiators quickly agreed to the instrumental demands of the inmates. What strategies could the negotiators have used to delay progress until the inmates made their expressive demands known?

6. You are called to a prison hostage situation. The prisoners are demanding two airplanes to fly inmates to another country where they can be free. This is their only demand. The inmates tell you that unless the airplanes are ready to go in 10 hours, they will start killing hostages. How would you respond to their demand?

7. Inmates at a maximum-security prison riot and take control of the prison. White inmates occupy one cell block, Hispanic inmates occupy another cell block, and black inmates occupy the third cell block (this division of inmates was done intentionally after the riot). Each group holds hostages (prison staff, different racial backgrounds) and each group has different demands. Tell how you would establish negotiations, select a leader, develop inmate committees, and what strategies you would employ with each group. Also, prepare a NPP for the on-scene commander.

8. Assume you are called upon to teach a course on cultural diversity to a group of prison negotiators. Develop an outline of your presentation.

9. This chapter discussed the similarities and differences of the prison situation as compared to the police situation. How could the advantages employed by a prison team be applied to a police negotiating team?

10. Based on the demographics and characteristics of military veteran prisoners presented in this chapter, develop a list of guidelines regarding negotiating with veteran hostage takers versus non-veteran hostage takers.

Intelligence and Intelligence Gathering

11

Learning Objectives

1. Understand and define *intelligence*.

2. Explain the eight tasks that need to be done in the process of gathering intelligence.

3. Know what a negotiator can do to facilitate intelligence work during the pre-incident phase.

4. Know the various sources that can be used for gathering intelligence and how to use those sources.

5. Understand the importance of bank robberies and the value of preplanning when managing a bank robbery.

6. Understand how to use the Structured Cognitive Interview.

7. Know how to assess the credibility of human sources of intelligence.

8. Know the importance of analyzing and disseminating information in a timely way.

> The subject was a Mexican national who had been staying with his aunt in the United States. His aunt was trying to take him to the airport to return him to Mexico when he pulled a knife on her and demanded that she take him back to her home. Neighbors saw the two fighting as they entered the house and called the police. When the patrol officer responded, the man met him at the front door with a knife at his aunt's throat. He threatened to kill her and himself. The officer secured the scene and called for SWAT and negotiators. Negotiators interviewed the neighbors and found that the man had been acting odd over the last six weeks, that his aunt had talked about his being seen at the local community mental health facility, and that she complained about his not taking the medication that was prescribed for him. Contact with the mental health agency revealed that the man had been diagnosed as a paranoid schizophrenic, that he had a mental health history in Mexico and that he had failed to come to the follow-up appointment that had been scheduled for him. Inquiries to the Mexican authorities yielded the fact that not only did he have a mental health history, but also that he was wanted in Mexico for the shooting of a federal police officer.

The incident above illustrates the importance of accurate, complete, and detailed intelligence in effective negotiations. Not only did the negotiators understand the nature of the man's problem and his motivation for not wanting to go back to Mexico, but they could develop an assessment of the risk he posed to both himself and to his aunt using intelligence that was gathered and analyzed as the incident unfolded. Useful intelligence depends on the negotiator's ability to gather information, organize it, analyze it, and make inferences about what it means to the negotiations. This chapter discusses the kinds of information that are useful during an incident, the sources of intelligence information that are available to negotiators, the interviewing skills necessary to gather the information from the sources, and cognitive skills that are important in evaluating the meaning and usefulness of the intelligence information.

Purposes of Intelligence

The purpose of intelligence in negotiations is to know ahead of time what you need to know later (Slatkin, 2002). It is prediction of behavior, thoughts, and feelings that will be helpful in accomplishing the crisis response team's mission of saving lives. By gathering, analyzing, and disseminating useful information, negotiators may be able to anticipate and plan for events before they occur. They can facilitate command decisions and decrease the stress of the situation. There are three main uses of intelligence in negotiations: (1) to understand the subject's motivation, (2) to predict the risk he poses to others, and (3) to predict the risk he poses to himself.

Intelligence: The Process

Intelligence gathering needs to be coordinated: a specific officer needs to be in charge of consulting with command, SWAT, and the negotiators in order to decide what questions need to be answered. Then he needs to gather the information needed to answer those questions, document the information, assess its implications for the questions asked, and disseminate the intelligence to all parties who need it. Like the negotiating process itself, the intelligence process is fluid; the questions change as the incident changes. Thus, intelligence work starts before the incident and progresses though the whole negotiation.

Slatkin (2002) suggests that there are eight tasks in the intelligence process. They are: (1) collecting information; (2) recording information; (3) evaluating the reliability and credibility of the source of information; (4) determining the relevance of the information to the questions asked (how does this information help us); (5) assessing the information by sifting through it; (6) selecting relevant items and integrating them into what is already known; (7) making deductions from the analyzed information about what is likely to happen; and (8) dissemination of the intelligence to key players.

Understanding Motivation

Understanding the subject's motivation helps negotiators understand the problem the subject is trying to solve and suggests solutions that may be acceptable to him. For instance, the subject's problem in the scenario above was not that he was paranoid, although that influenced the negotiations. It was that he knew he was facing life in prison if he returned to Mexico. The stress of that was driving his psychosis and it was the issue negotiators had to deal with before a peaceful resolution could be achieved. The ability to collect information from Mexico was essential in identifying the subject's motivation and to moving the negotiations along more quickly than if negotiators had to wait on the subject to volunteer the information.

Threat Assessment

Intelligence helps the negotiator assess the risk the subject poses to others and also helps the negotiator make decisions about how much force may be needed to manage the incident. The assessment of the potential for violence depends on knowing the subject's history as well as his recent behavior. Knowing how to access and understand this information is essential to effective management of the incident. For instance, the fact that the subject above had a prior violent confrontation with police suggests that he could be expected to have preconceived attitudes about police that would elevate his risk level. Negotiators would have to take this history into consideration in approaching him. They might describe themselves as merely negotiators and play down the police department connection. At the very least, they would have to work at separating themselves from other police with whom the subject had contact. They would expect that negotiations would take longer because building rapport would be more difficult than if the subject had not had confrontations with police in the past.

A second part of threat assessment is evaluating the threat the subject poses to himself—the threat of suicide. An adequate suicide risk assessment requires that the negotiators know whether there have been suicide attempts by the subject or by significant others in the subject's life. It requires that the negotiator have a sense of the subject's current plan, the subject's social resources, and the subject's usual method of coping with stress, i.e., does he usually see stressors as a challenge or something to be avoided. The answer to these and other questions related to suicide risk and intervention requires information to be gathered, analyzed, and utilized by negotiators. In short, negotiators must be able to manage and make sense of large amounts of information.

Definition of Intelligence

The *American Heritage Dictionary* (1980) defines *intelligence* as: "The capacity to acquire and apply knowledge." In negotiations, there are several issues that need to be addressed in acquiring and applying the knowledge that negotiators, tactical team members, and commanders need in order to successfully manage an incident. The capacity to acquire suggests that negotiators have the ability to obtain the information they need in an efficient and effective way. There are potentially multiple sources of information available, some of which will be readily available at the scene—such as friends, neighbors, and family members of the subject or the victims. Being aware of the value of these resources and asking them to remain at the scene while negotiators are on the way helps guarantee access to these sources. Other sources, such as medical records, probation records, and police department records, will be more difficult to obtain. Acquiring this

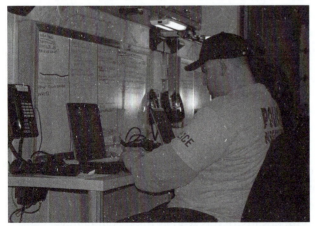

Intelligence boards do not have to be large and unwieldy. They should be concise, with crucial information listed. They should also be centrally located, so any team member can easily see them. *(R. Mullins)*

information may require agreements to be worked out with the sources prior to the incident. It is a good idea to have a designated contact person at each intelligence source the negotiator anticipates using during an incident.

A second issue is what information is needed. Law enforcement agencies have or can gain access to an overwhelming amount of information. Crisis management teams need to have specific kinds of information. Having a clear idea of what information is needed will help make intelligence more efficient because it focuses the gathering and analyzing of information.

Third, there needs to be a process for managing the information. Clear procedures for gathering information, collating and analyzing it, and disseminating the results of the analysis need to be developed and practiced before an incident occurs. This will keep negotiators from being overwhelmed by large amounts of information and will alleviate the problems of communicating the information that routinely seem to plague incidents.

Process of Intelligence Management

Managing intelligence starts before the time of the call and flows through the entire incident. It is fluid in the sense that the amount of time and energy devoted to the process changes as the situation changes. For instance, in the early stage of the incident, the majority of the negotiator's time and energy will generally go into the intelligence process. As a clearer picture of the situation emerges, a plan is developed and intervention is started, less time and energy will be devoted to intelligence work. However, intelligence work is not abandoned, and new information received later in the process can change the strategy and tactics dramatically (Boltz, 2001). For instance, a man was barricaded for eight hours in his home. He had pulled a gun and shot into the ceiling when his girlfriend refused to move in with him. On the basis of the girlfriend's information, the plan was to convince him to go to the local hospital for a mental health evaluation. The scene commander was concerned about the threat the man posed to himself and to others. Later, a negotiator interviewed the man's ex-wife and found that the subject had never been suicidal, that this was the first time he had done anything aggressive, and that he had been a deputy sheriff in New York. He knew the law and negotiator tactics. It became clear that he was not going to come out to meet the deputies. The scene commander ordered the emergency response team to disengage, because the risk levels had changed due to new intelligence. Managing intelligence involves four phases (Solis, 1997):

1. Pre-incident planning and preparation

2. At the scene: the Chaos phase

3. At the scene: the Stability phase

4. Post-incident phase

Intelligence Gathering

Pre-Crisis Phase

Intelligence on some issues can be gathered and stored well before an incident occurs. Boltz (2001) has pointed out that pre-planning will facilitate intelligence gathering. Discussing bank robberies, she notes that it is helpful to have floor plans available at another bank, so negotiators and tactical personnel can have ready access to them. Similarly, information about schools, public buildings, hospitals, and other locations that are likely targets can be gathered before an incident and a plan can be developed to have information about floor plans, employees who normally work at the location, and their hours of employment on file.

The San Antonio Police Department and the Northeast Independent School District Police developed a CD-based information file as part of their critical incident response plan that includes floor plans and utility schematics of every school in the district (Solis, 1999). Negotiators can access a wealth of tactically important information almost immediately upon being notified of an incident at a school. Such computer-based files can be kept at the dispatch office or at another location where they are readily available to the crisis response team. They need to be updated annually. Smaller departments that do not have the technical resources to use computer-based files can achieve the same result by using hard copies of plans that are readily accessible.

Another essential pre-crisis activity is the working out of agreements to access records with the custodians of a variety of records. Although there are legal limitations placed on accessibility to databases, most states allow access under exigent circumstances. Pre-crisis meetings and memorandums of understanding need to be worked out ahead of time. It is much more difficult to gain access to protected records during an incident if the custodian of the record is hearing from the negotiator for the first time.

Negotiators need to systematically train for the management of intelligence as part of any scenario they design. Just like active listening skills and crisis intervention techniques, intelligence management is a perishable skill. It is subject to the same interference by stress as other negotiator skills. Therefore, it needs to be overlearned and renewed periodically. Training is the best way to keep intelligence management skills fresh.

The initial call will give negotiators preliminary information about what, where, when, and how. Negotiators can begin thinking about whether the incident is a hostage or non-hostage incident; whether it is a spontaneous, planned, or anticipated siege; and whether it can be negotiated when he or she gets the callup. They can ask for a check of the calls for service at the location of the incident, to see whether there have been recent situations that may have some relationship to the current one. If the subject is identified, the negotiator can ask for a records check as a quick way to get an idea about the subject's propensity for violence, his or her mental health problems, involvement with people at the scene, and his or her previous suicide attempts/threats.

Boltz (2001) suggests that negotiators need to do a thorough analysis of the following questions:

1. *Who* is involved? Both the identity of the subject and the hostage/victims, as well as the nature of the relationship between them helps negotiators decide the type of incident they are dealing with and the best approach to the incident.

2. *What* has happened? This includes the nature of the incident as well as the means used to carry out the incident. The means includes information about weapons and/or explosives that may be available to the subject (Boltz, 2001).

3. *When* did the incident occur? Information about when the incident began is valuable in cases in which time limits have been imposed (Boltz, 2001). If negotiators become involved after a time limit has been given and they are not aware of it, it places them at a tactical disadvantage. Additionally, information about "when" is valuable in combination with "where" in determining what kind of incident the negotiator is dealing with. An incident at a residence or apartment at 2:30 A.M. is likely to be a domestic, involving people who have had a conflict after the bars closed at 2:00 A.M.

4. *Where* did it happen? The location would allow the negotiator to ask about prior calls at the same address that might help identify what was going on. For instance, if the call is an incident between spouses at a residence, the chances of it being a spontaneous incident requiring crisis intervention are fairly great. On the other hand, if it is at a work site, it may be a crime that was interrupted or a conflict between a supervisor and an employee, in which case more information would be needed to decide on what approach to use.

5. *How* did it happen and how did the police become aware of the incident? This includes not only how the incident occurred, but also how it came to the attention of the police (Boltz, 2001). It gives negotiators an idea of what kind of person they are dealing with, how violent he or she might be, and what his or her motives are.

6. *Why* did the incident happen? This is about the motivation of the people involved and is the key to deciding how to handle the incident. If the subject is a person who is down and out and is creating an incident to bring attention to himself and his plight, it is one thing. If he is simply expressing his rage at the machine, it is another kind of motivation and needs to be managed differently.

At the Scene: The Chaos Phase

Arriving at the scene, negotiators have to deal with the increased stress, activity, confusion, and chaos that goes with the crisis stage of an incident. Their goal in the first hour to two hours is to bring order to the chaos. They need to set up their negotiating area, the command post, and the equipment. They need to quickly develop intelligence that allows them to identify for command the type of incident, the risk to the subject and others, and the recommended strategy and tactics. They need to identify the subject, if he or she has not already been identified. They need to gather tactical intelligence and set up a clear channel of communication with tactical as well as command.

Negotiators need to talk with all available sources early in the incident. Witnesses, associates, family members, and neighbors can be valuable resources in gathering intelligence.

The first responding officer is a source of intelligence that needs to be contacted and debriefed. Mullins (1995) has pointed out that the first responder can be a valuable source of information on the location, floor plan, location of obstacles, etc. He or she can provide information about weapons. He or she may have intelligence on the subject's mental state, including intellectual level, apparent depression or agitation, whether or not the subject is intoxicated, whether he talks logically or rambles, etc.

Witnesses need to be identified and interviewed. It is important to try to reduce the effects of the chaos on witnesses. Taking them to a relatively quiet location, even the front seat of a patrol car that is off to the side of the incident will help reduce distraction and increase their concentration. They may provide descriptions and/or identifications of subjects, information about victims/hostages, history of incidents at that location, information about weapons they may have observed, and intelligence about relationships. If they work at the location, they can provide information about floor plans, obstacles, and utilities.

At a location close to both the negotiating arena and the command center, designated negotiators need to establish a status board to track relevant information. It can be organized around topics such as who, what, where, when, how, and why. It is best done in color so the different types of information are easily recognizable.

The importance of continual and instant dissemination of intelligence cannot be overemphasized. During the chaos phase, clear channels of communication among negotiators, tactical, and command need to be established so intelligence can be available in real time. Setting up monitors that allow commanders and tactical personnel to monitor negotiations is one way of facilitating communication. Another is to have both a negotiator and a tactical officer assigned to the intelligence arena. Each is responsible for monitoring the activities and information from their respective teams and making sure it is immediately posted and disseminated to the other elements of the operation.

In departments that do not have MHCs on staff, a decision that needs to be made early about "Who is this person?" "What is their mental condition?" and "Do we need MHC input?" Negotiators need to be alert for signs of emotional disturbance. Anger alone is not likely to be very helpful, because most everyone who encounters the police may show anger. However, the exception is worthy of note. People who show clear signs of depression, slowed thinking, slow talking, or distractibility should raise the depression/suicide possibility and alert negotiators to the need for professional MHC consultation. The use of alcohol or drugs is another indicator that MHC input would be helpful. Information about current functioning is important in the assessment of the personality type, motivation, and risk level. Recent changes in the person's life are frequently the precipitating factors in a hostage incident. The subject's way of reacting and coping with the changes will be reflected in his or her recent behavior and may be clues that the MHC needs to be called. Important recent changes are:

1. Recent dramatic changes in any behavior.

2. Recent changes in activity level—withdrawal or agitation.

3. Increases in drinking or drug use.

4. Changes in sleep patterns—increases or decreases.

5. Changes in eating habits.

6. Changes in feelings, especially an increase in the frequency, duration, or intensity of the feelings.

7. Disorganized or confused thinking.

8. Self-critical remarks.

9. Suicidal ideation.

10. Hypercritical of others.

11. Thoughts of others being "out to get me."

12. Thoughts of special privilege drove him (i.e., he is somehow a special person, different from everyone else).

13. Hallucinations, seeing or hearing things that others do not see; especially if the voices tell them to do things.

Stabilization Phase

After the Crisis Stage passes, the situation has stabilized. Emotions have been defused on both sides and reason and problem solving are becoming the focus. If drugs or alcohol were involved in the incident, the effects begin to wear off. Threats have diminished. The negotiator has more time to do in-depth intelligence gathering and analysis. He or she can reach out to collateral sources of information, confirming or discounting information received earlier. He can review the chronology of events, contact sources that have not yet been contacted to see whether they can add anything to the analysis of the incident. A more in-depth risk assessment can be made at this point, because the immediate threat has passed. Strategy and tactics can be reviewed and revised as needed.

Post-Incident Phase

The intelligence work is not complete when the incident ends. Negotiators need to document the incident, and record and store the records where they are accessible for future reference, but where they are afforded appropriate privacy. Documentation is important for several reasons.

Noesner (1999) has pointed out that police management of hostage/crisis incidents is coming under increasing scrutiny. To protect themselves from charges of mismanagement and negligence, negotiators need to document their actions.

Solis (1997) has pointed out that properly documented incidents are valuable training resources for negotiators. Without the case studies cited in this book and hundreds of others not cited, the field of crisis negotiations would not be nearly so advanced.

Documentation is important when negotiators have to deal with the same subject on more than one occasion. It is important for negotiators to know how the subject was handled previously, because it will set the subject's expectations about how he or she is going to be handled this time. Negotiators need to know what worked and what did not work with the subject on prior occasions so they do not spend time on tactics that were ineffective. They can benefit from the site intelligence information gained from prior incidents, if the subject is in the same location. They can use the personality assessment as a starting point for risk assessment and the development of strategies and tactics. Negotiators do not need to reinvent the wheel.

Intelligence boards need to be updated in real-time. One member of the team should be assigned to maintain intelligence boards to minimize mistakes and errors. *(R. Mullins)*

Intelligence Sources

An intelligence source is anyone or anything with information that is relevant to the management of the incident. They are the people and records that have relevant information about the incident, person, or tactical needs of the police. The sources include, but are not limited to, data banks, human informants, and records. It is frequently necessary to obtain this information from a number of sources, because in high-risk incidents, everyone's perceptions tend to be distorted.

Data banks are good sources of information about a person's history. Arrest records, for instance, can provide information about the person's history of rule violations, attitudes toward authority, and prior use of violence. Data banks can be good sources of tactical intelligence as well. They might provide floor plans, information on power sources, data on obstacles to an assault, and the location of telephones. Relevant data banks are:

1. Police records

2. Medical/mental health records

3. Military records

4. Public/personal files

5. Newspaper

6. Probation records

7. Personnel records

8. School records

9. Building maintenance records

Today, many of the data banks the police might need to review are available as computer files. Not only is criminal justice data available, but also available are business records, educational records, financial records, and government data. While the police cannot routinely access many of these data banks, a telephone call to the appropriate person and an e-mail address might provide instant access to the information. An example might be the hostage taker in a prison situation whom negotiators discover has served in the military. A question of interest would be what specialized training the hostage taker received in the military. The team could contact the U.S. Government Records office in St. Louis, Missouri, and if the team had an e-mail address, could receive the hostage taker's military records. The point, however, needs re-emphasizing. While there are many computerized data banks that hostage negotiators can rely upon for information (if the appropriate data bank manager is contacted), it is illegal for negotiators to arbitrarily access computer data banks to obtain information.

Human sources of intelligence are varied, ranging from people who know the hostage taker well to those who have only a passing acquaintance with him or her. People are good sources of both recent and historical information. However, their reliability must be assessed. Human sources of intelligence include (TCLEOSE, 1990):

- Family members
- Friends
- Co-workers
- Bosses/supervisors
- Neighbors
- Police officers
- Probation or parole officers
- Mental health workers and counselors

Types of Intelligence Information

Three general categories of intelligence are important in any negotiation incident. (SAPD, 1994). They are:

1. *Incident Intelligence.* Information about the incident necessary to establish probable cause if a warrant is necessary, exigent circumstances if emergency intervention is justified, and/or authority to intervene under the mental health laws of the state.

2. *Tactical Information.* Information necessary for the tactical team to establish an inner perimeter and to plan their options.

3. *Person Intelligence.* Information about the hostage taker necessary to understand his motivation, the degree of risk to himself or others, and his personality type, so that informed decisions about strategies and tactics could be made.

Incident intelligence includes the who, what, where, when, and how of an incident. It focuses on the primary people involved, the hostage taker and the hostages, who they are, and how they relate to one another. It establishes what happened, preferably in chronological order, and in as accurate and complete a way as possible. It defines where the incident started, the physical location where the action has taken place, and where it is now. It defines the time frame during which the incident has occurred—the "when." Finally, it describes how the incident happened, and what the action has been so far.

Tactical intelligence information needs to be gathered, analyzed, and disseminated quickly. The tactical team needs much of this intelligence to establish the inner perimeter, anticipate the type of resistance they may encounter, and plan any evacuations that may be necessary. Tactical intelligence includes two general areas: target information and hostage taker information. Target information is particularly important during the tactical team's setup. It includes:

1. Type of construction of the structure

2. Location of power, water, and gas cutoffs

3. Construction of the interior

4. Floor plan

5. Nature of security devices

6. Presence of dogs or other noise-making animals

7. Location, construction, and heights of fences or other barriers

8. Surrounding terrain, including the location of any outbuildings, storage sheds, or garages

9. Presence of security alarms

10. Chemicals, explosives, or hazardous materials at the location (TCLEOSE, 1990).

Person intelligence includes a physical description of the hostage taker and hostages. The physical description should include height, weight, hair, eye color, distinguishing marks, etc. It should include a clothing description. The purpose of the physical description is tactical. It is needed to make sure that the right person is identified if a tactical solution becomes necessary.

Case Study: Use of Intelligence. Patrol officers responded to a suicide threat at 6:23 P.M. on a Thursday. Upon arrival, they found a 24-year-old white male barricaded in a camper trailer in his backyard. He came home drunk, argued with his common law wife, and threatened to kill his wife and himself. When his wife ran to the neighbors' house for help, he barricaded himself, saying "They will never take me alive." Upon arriving at the house, patrol officers learned that he had been arrested for homicide after the wife's two-year-old child had died of blunt trauma injuries to the abdomen. He had been released from jail that same day.

Patrol supervisors decided that the only direct way to get him out of the trailer was to assault it. However, the open space around the trailer, and the narrow, single doorway made an assault particularly dangerous. Therefore, they decided to try to negotiate with the subject. In addition, they decided to mobilize the tactical team in case an assault became necessary, reasoning that SWAT was better trained and equipped for an assault than were the patrol officers.

When the tactical officers arrived, they examined the entire area. They found observation points on all four sides of the trailer that allowed observation of the trailer while providing concealment for the officers. The closest point was inside the subject's house, where the trailer could be observed through a bathroom window. The point closest to the trailer door was approximately 60 feet away behind a tool shed. Officers could approach the trailer from the side opposite the trailer door without being observed, because there were no windows on that side.

When negotiators and the psychologist arrived, they confirmed the arrest and booking on the homicide charge. They learned that the subject had been extremely upset about being jailed. He insisted that he would rather die than return to "that hell." He had been drinking since his release from jail. He had a history of alcohol abuse, including several attempts at rehabilitation. He was not employed at the time of his arrest. He had "about a dozen jobs since he left high school," usually leaving because of a "misunderstanding or conflict" with the boss. Leaving high school meant that he was expelled in the tenth grade for fighting and never returned. He had been in special programs during his entire school career. He "was always good with his hands but not so good with his words." His father and mother were divorced. Even though he and his father had gotten into violent confrontations, his father did not think he would hurt anyone and that the charges were because the police were out to get him.

From the neighbors, negotiators learned that the subject had two pistols that he frequently wore in western-style holsters as he walked around the neighborhood challenging people. At other times, he was reported to take pleasure in putting his Rottweiler (a dog frequently used for security) on the flat deck of his car and driving around the neighborhood ordering the dog to attack both adults and children.

As the incident continued, it was reported on the nightly news. Neighbors from the subject's old neighborhood arrived at the scene. They reported that the subject used to describe himself as a gunfighter and that he talked about making a stand against overwhelming odds. They, too, reported intimidating and aggressive behavior in his old neighborhood. In fact, their reason for being at the scene was that they hoped to see the subject killed by the police.

Case Review. Based on the information about the approaches to the trailer and the nature of the weapons the subject had available, the tactical team developed assault plans that called for filling the trailer with tear gas, approaching it from the blind side, and using ballistic shields for protection. They ruled out the use of a concussion grenade because of the small size of the trailer. The negotiators and psychologist decided that the chances of violence were high. They advised the field commander and the tactical commander that they thought the subject was likely to precipitate a confrontation with the goal of getting the police to kill him. They decided to approach him with the idea that his common law wife needed him and was willing to stand by him throughout the ordeal of his trial. Negotiators decided that they needed to know specifically what it was that troubled him about jail. Without that information, a major obstacle to his surrender was still in place. The intelligence gathered in the first hour of the incident was the basis on which the crisis response team built both a tactical and negotiating plan.

In addition to physical descriptions, a vital component of person intelligence is the psychological profile. The psychological profile helps put the hostage taker's actions in the context of his life. It helps the negotiators understand his motives and goals. It gives the negotiators ideas about things that the person enjoys and things that he does not like. The former is important in establishing a relationship, because people tend to feel more comfortable with other people with whom they share things in common (Cialdini, 1984). The choice of a negotiator may depend on an interest the negotiator shares with the hostage taker. The latter is to help the negotiator avoid sensitive areas early in negotiations. It is also helpful in identifying words the negotiator needs to avoid and behavior the negotiator needs to not discuss, because they touch on problem areas for the hostage taker.

The psychological description should include both historical and recent behavior, feelings, and thoughts, because both are important in assessing the hostage taker's mental status, personality structure, and dangerousness. Historical information is particularly important in assessing the person's risk to himself and others. A history of prior suicide or assaultive behavior makes the person a higher risk in the current situation. Information about the way the hostage taker handles his anger and how he deals with people who have power and authority over him are two other important patterns that need to be examined historically. Therefore, it is important to obtain:

1. History of criminal activity, including the nature of any arrests or convictions;

2. Work history, including the nature of work, the length of the time on specific jobs, and the reason for leaving any job, especially conflicts with bosses, supervisors, or co-workers;

3. Family history, including current marital status, past marriages, nature of relationship with wife and children, if there are any, and the nature of the relationship with parents and siblings;

4. School history, including achievement levels, disciplinary problems, expulsions/suspensions (and the reasons for them), grades, type of friends, and number of moves from one school to another;

5. History of violence, including prior incidents under similar situations, prior incidents under different situations, the outcome of prior incidents, and the consequences of prior incidents to the hostage taker;

6. History of prior suicide threats or attempts, including method, location, and outcome; and

7. Mental health history, including diagnosis, hospitalizations (voluntary, involuntary), therapists, doctors, medications, and outcome.

Sidebar: Sergeant Joseph F. Jimenez

Sergeant Joseph Jimenez has been a police officer with the Richardson, Texas, Police Department for more than 19 years. He has been a negotiator for 12 years and has been involved in numerous crisis incidents. He has received extensive training in hostage/crisis negotiations during his tenure as a negotiator and serves as a judge/evaluator at the North Texas State (formerly SWT) annual Negotiator Competition in San Marcos. Sergeant Jimenez received the "Negotiator of the Year" award from the Texas Association of Hostage Negotiators in 1995. He is a member of the Texas Association of Hostage Negotiators and has also served on its Board of Directors, and has assisted in the planning and in the presentation of several negotiator conferences.

As a negotiator of more than 12 years, I have had the opportunity to attend as well as instruct at numerous negotiation schools and training seminars. I have had the good fortune to train with some of the best and most experienced negotiators in the United States. Serving as a judge at SWT-sponsored seminar/competitions for numerous years has provided me with a unique insight into various tactics for gathering and prioritizing intelligence. My "backyard" informal training and instructing has included many facets of hostage/crisis negotiations. From Vacaville, California, to Seekonk, Massachusetts; from Poison, Montana, to Tickfaw, Louisiana; from Ojo Caliente, New Mexico, to Okeechobee, Florida; and from Flippin, Arkansas, to Gun Barrel City, Texas, the one thing all negotiators believe is that you have to stick to the "basics." My years of experience have taught me the value of trusting the "basics." Without them our team would rely on educated guesses to get us through fluid and often volatile incidents. This can be a fatal mistake. We have learned from both good and bad experiences and also from Dr. Mullins and Dr. McMains that an essential basic foundation in any negotiation is the gathering and prioritizing of good, solid, and verifiable intelligence. Practice and implementation of this basic skill puts us consistently on the successful side of the chart.

We live in an era of rapidly changing technology, within which the task of intelligence gathering can be almost totally completed with one "magic button." Yes, I'm talking about the Internet. Through interdepartmental and private sector cooperation we have access to all sorts of records and documents. We can find anything from a person's address, date of birth, driver's license, cars, boats, work information, military records, criminal history, family, friends, and neighbors with just a few keystrokes. Let us not forget that we have to verify this information with other sources to be sure it is correct and current.

Our team is comprised of eight negotiators and two tactical information center officers. That one-fourth of our team is dedicated solely to this task demonstrates the importance we place on this process. The TIC staff are assigned to gather all intelligence, prioritize and disseminate the intelligence information, and conduct interviews/debriefings of the first responding officer, witnesses, and friends, ensuring that the intelligence information flows both up and down the communication channel in real-time. Remember also that communication is not achieved until the information has been both given and effectively received. Be sure that the intelligence information you disseminate is complete and is acknowledged by the recipient. The same applies to the intelligence you receive. Our TIC staff are very effective in not only gathering the plethora of intelligence, but also in quickly and accurately sifting through and verifying this information. Although our T.I.C. is responsible for intelligence gathering, it is important to remember that it is also the responsibility of each team member to participate in this process to varying degrees. With the gathering of intelligence comes profiling the person in crisis. The team needs to know what they are dealing with and how to best resolve the situation. Let us not forget our tactical counterparts, though. They, too, need good and clear intelligence as quickly as possible to effectively set up and maintain the inner and outer perimeters.

Another, equally important thing to remember is that these skills we so relentlessly work to achieve and rely upon are perishable skills. It takes a lot of training and practicing to hone your negotiator skills. Just as you have to practice your active listening skills (ALS) to be effective as a primary negotiator, the same applies to the other facets of negotiating.

Working as a cohesive team, strategy planning and intelligence gathering should be practiced and continually updated through periodic training and review exercises. When we train we think about how we can do our jobs better, more effectively. Remember, there are no shortcuts to doing a job well.

Some new negotiators may wonder what we did before computers, cell phones, and all the other useful technology we have at our disposal these days. Don't forget that humankind has been "negotiating" since the beginning of time. When you get a call-out on a "jumper" for instance, and you find yourself on top of a bridge or building and the only "secondary/coach" you have is 50 to 100 feet away or, worse yet, you're in a stairwell or on scaffolding where no one else can get close enough to pass along notes, give you feedback, and provide you that comfort zone to which you had become so accustomed, what do you do then? That is the time to take a deep breath and rely on the training, experience, and skills you have been working on so religiously throughout your tenure as a negotiator. You will begin to "gather" intelligence on your own as you apply your active listening skills, build rapport, and develop trust with your person in crisis.

One of the hardest things I have ever done as a negotiator was responding to a call where a young man had been in his residence drinking heavily and firing a handgun. When my secondary and I arrived we were briefed on the situation. With the subject's mother present, we were told that the young man had HIV, was off his medication, owed his roommate a lot of money, had been laid off from work, his wife was pregnant and had left him, he was drinking heavily, his prized vehicle was being repossessed, and he had been firing a gun. His mother turns to us and says, "Don't let my son die." Our team was undaunted by the situation and proceeded to be escorted to the residence. As we arrived at the house, we were told that SWAT was "not coming" and all we had were several street cops for a perimeter and backup. I wound up negotiating from inside the house with my Secondary outside the front door. So I took my "deep breath" and began talking with the subject. The "basics" kicked in and I was able to gather, prioritize, and verify a lot of good intelligence. We were able to stabilize the situation and subsequently resolved the incident without injury to anyone. Yes, sometimes you do have to go back to the "basics." Trust the basics; they will get you through it.

Risk of Aggression

One of the most critical questions the negotiator needs to address is the hostage taker's potential for violence. If he shows a clear preference for violence and the risk to the hostages is high, a tactical resolution is the appropriate choice. It is important for the negotiator to have some guidelines for estimating the hostage taker's violence potential. In reviewing the literature on predicting violence, Monahan (1981) concluded that the following elements correlate with violence:

1. Age. Most violence is committed by 17- to 25-year-olds.

2. Sex. Males commit most violent acts.

3. Socioeconomic status. The poor tend to be more violent than the middle class.

4. Substance abuse. Alcohol and stimulants tend to contribute to impulsive violence.

5. Intelligence. People with IQs of less than 90 tend to be more violent.

6. Educational history. Dropouts, truants, and those with attention deficit disorders tend to be more impulsive.

7. Residential stability. People who make frequent moves tend to be more aggressive.

8. Employment history. The unemployed or people who make frequent job changes tend to be more aggressive.

9. Mental health history. Paranoid, manic, and antisocial individuals that have a history of arrests prior to hospitalization have a higher incidence of impulsive violence than others.

10. Cognitive disposition. Rationalizes the use of violence ("If she hadn't done _____, I wouldn't be doing this.").

11. Affective disposition. Feels release of tension through aggression.

12. History of arrests for violent offenses. Offenders who have been arrested for violent offenses such as assaults have an increased incidence of future crimes of violence. The chances of future violence increase with each arrest.

13. History of convictions for violent offenses.

14. Involuntary commitment to mental health facility for dangerousness to others.

15. Juvenile record of violence. Patterns of violence show up early. Violent offenders frequently have a pattern of violence in school and at home from an early age.

16. History of family violence. As a group, people who come from families in which violence was used as a method of solving problems or as an expression of frustration are more likely than others to use violence themselves.

17. History of two or more arsons. In studying multiple murderers, the FBI has suggested that a history of two or more arsons is one of the factors that sets these people apart from the general population.

18. Similarity of current situation to past situation in which the person became violent. Because people usually use the solutions that have worked for them in the past, people who have used violence successfully in a particular situation in the past are more likely than others to use violence in a similar situation.

19. A pattern of increasingly more intense reactions. A pattern of increasing intensity of reaction over the recent past is predictive of violence, usually because the person has become more and more violent without being challenged.

20. A pattern of increasing frequency of violent behavior during the last two weeks.

21. A pattern of aggressive episodes that are increasing in duration.

22. A history of more than one sadistic episode with animals. One of the other factors the FBI associates with multiple episodes of violence is a history of sadistic acting-out against animals as children. Most children relate to animals even when they do not relate to people, so to harm or to torture animals is highly unusual behavior for a child.

In a survey of the predictors of violence almost 10 years after Monahan's work, Brizer (1989) reiterated the importance of age, gender, prior history of violence, family history of abuse, a family history of mental illness, and alcohol abuse in predicting violent behavior. In addition, he pointed out that over-controlled individuals and people with a history of seizure disorders or brain dysfunction had a higher-than-average incidence of violence.

More recently, Mount (1995) suggested the following associated with the risk of violence: Personality factors included male; age: 15-24; history of violence; paranoid ideation, especially ideas of persecution that lead the person to believe that people are an immediate threat; below-average intelligence; psychopathic or borderline personality. Situational indicators are: Families that teach violence as a way of solving problems and dealing with frustrations; a peer group that endorses the use of violence; job instability, loss, or threatened loss; availability of deadly weapons; availability of target; alcohol or stimulant use. Biological factors: History of central nervous system trauma, infection, or disease, including seizures; major mental disorders.

In reviewing the research on violence prediction, one of the authors found the following criteria to be common to all research on indicators of violence:

1. Prior violence in current home

2. Prior violence in public

3. Alcohol/stimulant abuse

4. Availability of a weapon

5. Prior chaotic relationship with potential victim

6. Violence in home of origin

7. Neurological impairment

8. Increasing pattern of violence and

9. Loss of a relationship or job

In presenting a model of risk assessment based in part on the HOBAS data collected on negotiated incidents, the FBI (2003) suggested the following risk factors that are specific to negotiation incidents be reviewed:

1. Is the incident a hostage or a non-hostage incident? Non-hostage incidents mean increased risk.

2. Precipitating event: Incidental versus expressive—Is it emotion driven? If so, increased risk.

3. Initiation of the call: Did the subject initiate the call, suggesting that he is inviting a confrontation, or did someone else (family member, stranger, neighbor)?

4. Location of incident: Was the call to a residence? If so, it may mean a relationship-based, emotionally driven incident, and increased risk.

5. Relationship of subject and victim: Intimate partners are at risk.

6. Timing of violence: Was there violence at the beginning of the incident and/or did it continue through the episode? If so, increased risk.

7. General demeanor of subject

8. Recent and multiple losses increase the risk.

9. Prior impulsive violence increases the risk.

10. Substance abuse.

11. Demands: No demands suggest increased risk.

12. Threats: Offensive, defensive, unconditional.

13. Suicide is always possible: If threats and depression are present, it increases the risk of violence.

14. Amount of preparation: Planned, anticipated, spontaneous.

A Caveat Revisited: As was noted in the first chapter, categorizations are roadmaps, not reality. Risk factors and checklists are only tools for organizing information and raising awareness of the possibilities of violence. Recent groups of people who have used violence to solve their personal problems have not fit all the factors above. Perpetrators of school violence have generally been bright, young, and in many cases privileged; not adolescent/young adults, poor, and unintelligent (Solis, 1999). Likewise, people who engage in workplace violence are generally 35 to 60 years old, have a relatively stable work history that is threatened, and are middle class (San Antonio Police Department, Advanced Hostage Negotiation School, 1995). This is not to suggest that negotiators quit doing risk assessments. Rather, it is to warn against the mechanical approach that uses a checklist and a frequency count to try to predict violence. Checklists simply function as guidelines to the factors that need to be evaluated in performing a risk assessment.

Case Study Revisited: Potential for Violence. Using the indicators above to evaluate the subject's potential for violence and another checklist to review the variables that have been found relevant in assessing suicide potential (discussed fully in Chapter 7), the crisis response team decided that he had a higher-than-average potential for both violence and suicide. These factors, taken together, have been suggested as the elements necessary for victim-precipitated homicide or suicide by cop.

The following was the potential for violence assessment.

> Age-positive for violence because he fell within the age range that has been found to commit the most violent acts.
>
> Sex-positive because males generally have been found to act out aggressively more than females.
>
> Prior history: Employment history was positive for violence because of his pattern of aggressiveness and failure to live within the expected standards of behavior while on the job. Juvenile record of violence was positive because of his expulsion from school for repeated fighting.
>
> Escalating pattern: History of arrests for violence was positive because he had just been arrested for the death of the two-year-old.
>
> Substance abuse was positive for violence both because of his history of alcohol abuse and his current state of inebriation, which impaired his judgment and his impulse control.
>
> Neurological history was positive because of his attention deficit disorder, history of aggression in school, and poor attitude toward authority.
>
> History of family violence was positive because his mother and father divorced after a "stormy relationship" that included alcohol abuse and violence on the part of the father. Additionally, he had a history of acting out against family members.

Using the above indicators, together with the personality assessment that suggested that this subject was an antisocial personality prone to impulsive acting out, and the indicators of suicide by cop, the incident commander was advised that there was a good risk of his trying to force a confrontation with the intent of getting the police to kill him. Therefore, both the field commander and the tactical team could make contingency plans on the basis of conclusions derived from intelligence analyzed using the best predictors available to date.

Although the research on prediction of violence suggests that the validity of an assessment is limited to a relatively brief period (Monahan, 1981), such as two to three days, this is not a problem for most critical incidents, because what the negotiator needs is an assessment of how the hostage taker is likely to perform in the immediate future. The goal is to determine the potential for aggression in the present.

Keeping an intelligence checklist on each major area is helpful. This assures complete coverage of all the critical information, some of which might be lost in the stress of the incident. In addition, checklists provide a format for keeping critical information as it comes in over the course of the incident. Rather than having several hundred pieces of paper, information can be reduced to its most meaningful and concise form. Figure 11.1 is a typical intelligence checklist.

Figure 11.1
Intelligence Checklist

Negotiations Team
Intelligence Checklist

Event _____

_____

_____

_____

Aggressor: ___ Husband ___Wife ___Son ___Daughter ___Father ___Mother ___Other: _____
Victim(s): (1)   ___ Husband ___Wife ___Son ___Daughter ___Father ___Mother ___Other: _____
          (2)   ___ Husband ___Wife ___Son ___Daughter ___Father ___Mother ___Other: _____
          (3)   ___ Husband ___Wife ___Son ___Daughter ___Father ___Mother ___Other: _____
          (4)   ___ Husband ___Wife ___Son ___Daughter ___Father ___Mother ___Other: _____
          (5)   ___ Husband ___Wife ___Son ___Daughter ___Father ___Mother ___Other: _____
          Method: ___ Verbal abuse ___Physical Assault ___Weapon: Knife, Gun (Type): _____
Other Weapons

_____

_____

_____

BEHAVIOR
___ Recent Dramatic Changes: _____
___ Withdrawn: _____
___ Over-Active: _____
___ Aggressive: _____
___ Unpredictable: _____
___ Drinking: _____
___ Drug Usage: _____
___ Sleeping Problems: _____
___ Eating Problems: _____
___ Hostile: _____
___ Uncooperative: _____
___ Other: _____

FEELINGS
___GUILTY   ___GLAD   ___MAD   ___SAD   ___AFRAID   ___BLUNTED
In the last two days, has the frequency of the feelings: ___ increased, ___ decreased, ___ stayed the same.
In the last two weeks, has the frequency of the feelings: ___ increased, ___ decreased, ___ stayed the same.
In the last two days, has the intensity of the feelings: ___ increased, ___ decreased, ___ stayed the same.
In the last two weeks, has the intensity of the feelings: ___ increased, ___ decreased, ___ stayed the same.
In the last two days, has the duration of the feelings: ___ increased, ___ decreased, ___ stayed the same.

THINKING
___Disorganized: _____ ___Confused: _____ ___Self-critical: _____
___Hypercritical of others: _____ ___Grandiose: _____
___Persecutory: _____ ___Hallucinatory: _____

HISTORY
___Similar Incidents: _____ Date(s): _____
___Outcomes: _____
___Violence involved? _____
___Mental Health HX: Y N Diagnosis: _____ Dr. (Hospital): _____
___Criminal HX: Y N Type Complaints: _____ Violence: _____

Source: San Antonio, Texas Police Department. Reprinted with permission.

Interviewing Intelligence Sources

Through their own skill in interviewing, negotiators can maximize or minimize the information they obtain from their sources. The structured cognitive interview (Fisher & Geiselman, 1988, 1992) is an interview process that has been effective in gaining a great deal of accurate information in a relatively short time. It is based on principles of cognitive psychology and memory research, and uses a six-step process designed to guide the source into the most complete information in his or her memory. The steps are:

1. Motivate the person.

2. Use multisensory memories.

3. Ask open-ended questions.

4. Maintain silence.

5. Use repetition to focus attention.

6. Use follow-up questions to focus on specific details following the flow of the original report.

Basic to the structured cognitive interview is the idea that the source has the information that the interviewer wants stored in memory. Therefore, it is important for the source to be motivated to do the work necessary to retrieve the memories. The negotiator cannot do the work for the source. If the negotiator talks more than the source, the wrong person is doing the work.

The negotiator/intelligence officer needs to "prime the pump" by telling the source something like, "You know we have a life-threatening situation here. You can help us settle it without anyone getting hurt or killed by sharing with us what you know about the situation and the people involved. In fact, you are the only one that can help us in some ways, because you have a unique perspective and memory of things. We need you to work hard at remembering everything you can about the situation, the incident, and the people involved. Only you can get at what you know. Therefore, I am going to ask you one question at a time and remain quiet so you will have plenty of time to search all your memories and give me everything you remember." These instructions place the responsibility for the work of searching memory squarely on the source's shoulders. It relieves the negotiator/intelligence officer of the responsibility of searching the source's memory—an impossible mission.

The second step in the structured cognitive interview is to ask open-ended questions (Fisher & Geiselman, 1992; Bolton, 1984). These questions focus the source on his or her task, rather than on the agenda of the negotiator/intelligence officer. Open-ended questions give the source the space and time to explore his or her own memories, and if they reinforce the earlier message, the source is responsible for the work of exploring his or her own memory. After the motivating speech above, the negotiator/intelligence officer might say something like: "Now, I want you to start early in the day, before this incident began, and tell me everything you remember, no matter how important or unimportant it may seem. Most people try to edit their memories by deciding what's important enough to tell us. I'd like you not to do this kind of editing. Tell us everything that comes to mind. Everything you saw, heard, felt, smelled, thought, and did. Now start with what was happening at about 8:00 and tell me everything you remember up to the time you met me."

The sentence about everything the source "saw, heard, felt, smelled, thought, and did" is the third step in the structured interview. It capitalizes on the fact that there are multiple sensory modes with which the person experiences the world. Consequently, there are multiple memories of any given event. By asking the source to focus on all sensory modes, rather than just one or two (what he saw or heard), the negotiator can cross-stimulate memories, increasing the number of memories available to the source (Fisher, 1990; Fisher & Geiselman, 1992). In addition, there is evidence suggesting that people have sensory preferences. Some people are verbalizers, some are visualizers, some are more feeling-oriented. By asking them to focus on all modes, it is more likely that the source will use their preferred mode—leading to more detail.

The fourth step in the structured interview is to maintain silence after giving the motivating and multisensory instructions (Fisher, 1990). Bolton (1984) has pointed out that "Silence on the part of the listener gives the speaker time to think about what he is going to say and thus enables him to go deeper into himself. Silence also allows the speaker to proceed at his own pace and serves a gentle nudge to go further into a conversation." Additionally, silence makes many people uncomfortable and motivates them to work at filling the silence. By being quiet and waiting for the source to work, the negotiator lets the source's discomfort work for him. To fill the silence and to reduce the discomfort, the source has to do his job—search his memory and report what he finds.

The negotiator/intelligence officer can use the quiet time to:

1. *Attend to the source.* A negotiator demonstrates his interest in the source's communications by sitting forward, by making appropriate eye contact, and facing the source in an open posture. He focuses his attention on the source and lets the source know that he is listening.

2. *Observe the source.* Noting the source's facial expression, posture, and gestures to judge the consistency between the source's body language and message. This helps evaluate the source's credibility.

3. *Think about the source's message.* The negotiator formulates follow-up questions to focus the source on overlooked details, to explore areas of inconsistency, and to check the accuracy of his understanding of what has been said (Bolton, 1984).

The fifth step is to have the source go through memories a second time, with the negotiator/intelligence officer guiding the source's attention to details left out during the initial report (Fisher, 1990). After asking the source to go back through the memories in the same kind of detail, the negotiator might say things like, "Now that you are thinking about the person's face, please focus in on his forehead, now eyebrows and eyes. Tell me what you see." Even though the source has been asked not to edit, they may do so inadvertently. Sometimes it is necessary to focus the person on details that were overlooked due to inattention. Gentle guidance is necessary.

Finally, specific fact-oriented questions can be asked. If, after having gone over his or her memories several times and if after having been focused on specific areas, the source has not described important details, the negotiator can ask directly about those details. For instance, if the source has not described a hostage taker's eye color after several attempts at open-ended recall, the negotiator might say "Now I'd like to go back and see if we can pick up some details. Focus your attention on the man's face. Get it clearly in mind. Now focus in on his eyes. Just like one of those close-up lenses on TV, zoom in on his eyes. What color do you recall them being?"

Case Study Revisited: Cognitive Interview. Using cognitive interviewing techniques, negotiators approached the subject's father, who was already at the scene, in the following way:

> *Motivating:* "Mr. _____, we are not sure what is going on with Sam. We understand that he called you earlier about being arrested. You can help us settle this situation. In fact, you are in a unique situation since you have spoken to him today and you have known him all his life. You know more about him than anybody here does; certainly more than we do. So you can help us find a way to get him out without anyone getting hurt. We are going to need you to tell us as much as you remember about your talk with him today and later we are going to need you to tell us about his growing up. You are the only one that can do it, because you're the only one that knows him so well."

> *Open-ended Questions and Multi-sensory Instruction:* "Now, can you think back to today about noon? I know that you got here about 4:00 P.M., but it is helpful to go back earlier and tell everything that you remember about your day; everything you heard, saw, smelled, felt, thought, no matter how unimportant it seems to you now. You never know what might be important in helping Sam. So start at about noon and tell us everything you remember about the day

(starting before the event the negotiator wanted to have reported establishes a base rate from which to judge changes in the person's style of reporting that may signal attempts at deception)."

Attentive Silence: The negotiator was quiet while the father reported, "Around noon, I was hanging around the house, not doing much. I had lunch and read the paper—the sports page about the ball scores and the comics. I must have dozed because the phone woke me a couple of times. Once, it was some guy selling newspaper subscriptions. You know, those guys from the paper that want you to take the Sunday paper or something. The second one was a wrong number. I got a couple of beers after that, and about 3:30 or so I turned on the TV. I watched a ball game for awhile. I maybe should have gone to work, but I wasn't feeling good, so I stayed home."

"Sam called about 4:00 or 4:30 from some beer joint. He was mad. Said he hated jail and that he wasn't going back, no matter what. He blamed the girl he was living with for the trouble he was in. I never did like her—told him she was trouble and he had to look out after himself. But no, he knew better. Just like when he was a kid. Never could tell him anything. If she hadn't had the kid, none of this would have happened. He had been drinking pretty good. I got worried 'cause he gets kinda crazy when he's been drinking. That's how come I came over here tonight. The cops were here when I got here and he was in the trailer. You know he keeps all his survival stuff in the trailer. I don't know what he's going to do, but it probably won't be good."

By being quiet and letting the father set the pace of the interview, negotiators got the basics of the afternoon's conversation without raising the father's resistance to a lot of questioning. In avoiding the "third degree" kind of interview, they reinforced the message that they were interested in the people involved in the situation and made their claim of concern for the son's safety more credible. They did not treat people like suspects. In addition, they gathered information about the son that the father might not have been willing to reveal in a more structured, question-and-answer format. They let the father think that he controlled the interview and waited for his discomfort with the silence to motivate him to talk.

Retelling: "Thanks, Mr. _____. Now, can you focus on the phone call from Sam? Tell me again about everything you heard, thought or felt during that call."

"Well, the phone rang. I was a little p____ 'cause it interrupted the game. When I answered, it was Sam. He said something like, 'The b_____ got me arrested.' And I asked what b_____? It could have been his mother. She's done that before. Anyway, he said it was the girl he was living with. That the cops had arrested him for killing her kid, that it was an accident and that he wasn't going back to jail. Too many gays there and too many little s_____ telling him what to do. I could hear the jukebox and noise in the background.

I knew he was drinking. He said he had a good mind to go beat some sense into the b_____. At least he was going to get rid of her. Throw her out or something. I told him to cool it. That he knew how his temper got the best of him and to cool off, 'fore he went home. That just made him mad. He said, 'F_____ you too' and slammed the phone down. I had another beer, thought about it for awhile and came on over."

"I was surprised he let himself get arrested again. After the last time he always said he'd never let 'em take him in. He'd go down in a blaze of glory before he'd do that. I figured he'd put up a good fight. He always said he was a desperado."

By having the source retell his story, more details are filled in about the subject's mental status—angry and drunk; about his potential for violence—had a temper, arrested before for fighting with his mother, saw an aggressive confrontation with police as a solution to current problems; and attitude toward authority. He did not want to be told what to do by either of his parents or by jail personnel. It became clear that he was highly motivated to maintain his freedom and sense of control, that he blamed others for his actions, and that he justified the use of violence. In a relatively short interview, several relevant issues are addressed, without the father even knowing the importance of the information he has provided.

Focusing on Specific Areas After the Initial Report: The negotiators went back after the father made his initial report to focus on areas of particular interest. For instance, to gather relevant tactical information, they asked, "Mr. _____, you mentioned that Sam was a survivalist. Survivalists usually have weapons and others have told us that he has some weapons. Tell us about the weapons you remember him having." To aid with the assessment of the subject's potential for violence, they said, "Mr. _____, you told us earlier about Sam's conflicts with family members. Tell us about those in as much detail as you can remember; again, not leaving anything out." In a similar way, any area of concern could be followed up after the initial interview with questions focused on specific details.

Assessing the Credibility of the Source

In gathering intelligence from human sources, it is important to remember that not all of them are of equal credibility. Some, like police officers, are better trained as observers and generally have less personal involvement in an incident. Their information is likely to be less distorted than the hostage taker's family or friends, who may need to protect the hostage taker. In assessing the accuracy and reliability of an intelligence source, negotiators need to consider:

1. The source's physical condition. Does the source have good eyesight, hearing, sense of smell, memory, and intelligence?

2. The source's psychological condition. Does the source have a permanent or temporary emotional/psychological condition that might distort perception, memory, or recall of significant events?

3. The nature of the source's relationship to the hostage taker. Does the source have a prior history with the hostage taker that would bias his or her report for or against the hostage taker?

4. The proximity of the source to the threat. Is the source directly threatened by the hostage taker?

5. The proximity of the source's "significant others" to the threat posed by the hostage taker. Does the source have friends or family who are still in danger or who are seen as being in danger in the future?

6. The consistency of this source with other sources.

Negotiators need to make a conscious assessment of both the credibility and the accuracy of the source. Include a place on the intelligence summary (see Figure 11.1), because such an estimate will help remind negotiators of the importance of this issue.

Research has shown that there are many clues to lying that may be helpful to the negotiator/intelligence officer. Ekman (1992) has summarized the research on the detection of deceit. Negotiators should familiarize themselves with these clues. He has suggested that there are two general types of clues that a person is lying: clues that suggest the person is poorly prepared for the question and clues that a certain emotion does not fit what the person is saying.

Clues to deception are:

1. *Failure to fabricate well.* People are careless in their lie construction. For instance, in one hostage incident the hostage taker had spread the word that he had a cache of arms, because he kept them for the Mexican Mafia. He claimed to have assault rifles, which, if true, posed a significant threat to the tactical team. The truthfulness of this threat seemed low because he was black and the Mexican Mafia rarely dealt with blacks, especially when it came to holding their weapons.

2. *Slips of the tongue.* People accidentally say things that reveal their lies. For instance, when a hostage taker's brother was asked if he knew anything about his brother's plans to rob the fast food store in which he was trapped, he said that "No, man I haven't even spoke to him since about 11:00. No, I mean 7:00; it was before he left the apartment." As it turned out, he had helped plan the robbery.

3. *Tirades*. People who go into angry speeches that have more force behind them than is justified may provide a clue to deceit. The anger may be a smokescreen behind which the person is masking deceptions.

4. *Pauses*. Pausing for too long or pausing too frequently suggests that the person is giving too much thought to his or her answer, especially if it is to questions that he or she may not have been able to predict were going to be asked. For instance, when the father in the above case study was asked if he thought his son was a threat to others, he paused a long time before replying, "No. He threatens a lot but it's that he just gets frustrated and sometimes it's the alcohol. But when he is sober, he's not going to hurt anybody." This was said in spite of the fact that he had already told negotiators about his son's history of aggression.

5. *A rise in pitch suggests emotional upset*. Raising one's voice is not a perfect predictor of deceit. However, it has been correlated with emotional arousal. An increase in pitch and volume suggests arousal, while a decrease in the person's usual pitch and volume suggests a decrease in arousal, as is seen in depression. Discrepancies between the kind of information the source is reporting and the associated emotional arousal is an indicator of deceit.

6. *Emblems*. There are gestures that have an agreed-upon meaning in a specific culture. For instance, the shrug of the shoulders is generally recognized to mean that the person using it does not know about the topic. A person crossing his or her arms in front of his or her chest is generally seen as a sign of defensiveness. Such emblems will sometimes leak while a person is being interviewed, betraying his attitude about the interview or the interviewee. When this happens, the person's credibility is suspect. For instance, Ekman (1992) reports a study in which nursing students were interviewed after viewing videotape. They saw either a tape of gory medical emergencies or pleasant beach scenes. Then half of them were told to lie about the video they had seen and the other half were told to tell the truth. Both groups were interviewed. One of the questions that was asked during the interview was, "Would you show this film to children?" The group of students that lied about viewing the grotesque film said "yes," but gave themselves away with a slight shrug of the shoulder.

7. *Decrease in illustrators when emotions are aroused*. Illustrators are gestures that accompany speech to emphasize points (an illustrator, for example, would be waving one's arms when making an emotional speech). They are used to explain ideas that are difficult to put into words. Generally, there is a decrease in the use of illustrators when a person is

trying to conceal information or lie. Illustrators are learned culturally, so their use has to be understood in the context of the culture of the person being interviewed. Illustrators should not be confused with manipulators, which are the massaging, rubbing, holding, etc., of one part of the body by another. While a decrease in illustrators is generally a sign of emotional arousal, a change in the frequency of manipulators can mean that the person is either comfortable or uncomfortable with the situation.

8. *Autonomic nervous system arousal is an indicator of emotion.* Autonomic nervous system arousal leads to observable physiological signs that may be inconsistent with the message the source is sending. Arousal includes increased sweating, frequent swallowing, increased blinking, pupil dilation, and changes in facial coloration (reddening or blanching). Careful observation by the negotiator can yield clues of this kind. However, it is important to remember to observe the person being interviewed at a time when he or she is not stressed so that there is a base rate against which to compare his or her later responses.

Case Study Revisited: The Outcome. During three hours of talking to Sam about coming out of his barricaded trailer, the negotiator tried listening to his story, pointing out to him that a lot of people cared about him, and that the trial was his opportunity to tell his story about what had happened to the child. To these strategies, Sam responded that he did not care about others, that he was a survivalist, and that he was not going to be taken alive. He did not plan to go to trial. He began firing at officers. The commander decided to assault the trailer because of the threat the subject posed to others. Tear gas was fired into the trailer. More shots were fired out of the trailer by the subject. More tear gas was fired into the trailer and the SWAT team began their approach to the trailer from the blind side. A shot was heard from inside the trailer. When the officers rushed the door, they found the subject with a single, self-inflicted gunshot wound to the head.

Disseminating Intelligence: Negotiator Position Papers

Intelligence officers should brief negotiator team leaders. Getting intelligence to the members of the crisis response team is the final and essential task in the intelligence process.

The most common way of disseminating intelligence at an incident is the situation board. This is a white board in the intelligence arena where relevant information is organized and summarized. It makes what is known, what has been done, what promises have been made, what hooks and barbs have been discovered, etc. available to the negotiators/commanders, et al. at a

Like any other aspect of the negotiation process, intelligence gathering must be a team function. It is always preferred to have at least two team members gather intelligence so information is not missed, misunderstood, items overlooked, or questions not asked. *(S. Davis)*

glance. In addition, intelligence officers can brief team members, team leaders, and commanders regularly, usually during a break in negotiations. Finally, some form of ongoing review and summary can be prepared.

The FBI has recommended the use of the negotiation position paper to facilitate communications (Dalfonzo, 2003). After each contact with the subject, they suggest that negotiators prepare a summary of the negotiations to date that include: (1) the number of the position papers, to keep track of the flow of the process; (2) the status of the situation based on the most recent intelligence; (3) an assessment section that reflects the team's assessment of the type of incident, the perceived risk level, the motivation of the subject, demands that are being made, and the state of the relationship between negotiators and the subject; and (4) recommendations about strategies the team is using or planning on using, and the desired results.

NPPs have the advantages of assuring that all members of the crisis management team are informed of developments during negotiations. In addition, they can help develop teamwork because all team members are asked for input. They can facilitate briefings of commanders and new team members at shift change by providing a chronological record of events in concise form. They can aid commanders' understanding of incidents when they have to brief their superiors on the status of the incident. And, finally, they provide a written record that can be used during debriefing to assess the actions of the team and their effectiveness (Dalfonzo, 2003)

Summary

One of the keys to success in negotiation is knowledge: information about the goals, needs, techniques, and interests of the hostage taker. Knowledge allows negotiators to establish rapport with hostage takers, to assess their dangerousness, and to generate solutions to the incident that are acceptable to both sides. Knowledge guides the tactical deployment of personnel and resources.

Gathering relevant information requires negotiators to know where to find information, to gather information in an efficient way, to assess its value, and to relay it to people who can use it. Through a thorough knowledge of the kinds of intelligence needed, sources of intelligence information, and methods of gathering and evaluating intelligence, negotiators can be more successful.

References

American Heritage Dictionary (1980). New York, NY: Houghton & Mifflin Co.

Bolton, R. (1984). *People Skills*. Englewood Cliffs, NJ: Prentice-Hall, Inc.

Boltz, F.A. Jr. (2001). "Intelligence Requirements in Hostage Situations." *The Journal of Police Crisis Negotiations*, Vol. 1, No.1, Spring 2001.

Brizer, D. (1989). "Introduction: Overview of Current Approaches to the Prediction of Violence." In Brazier, D. and M. Crowner (eds.), *Current Approaches to the Prediction of Violence*. Washington, DC: American Psychiatric Press, Inc.

Cialdini, R.B. (1984). *Influence: How and Why People Agree to Things*. New York, NY: Quill.

Dalfonzo, V.A. (2003). "Negotiation Position Papers: A Tool for Negotiators." *FBI Law Enforcement Bulletin* October, Vol. 72, No.10.

Ekman, P. (1992). *Telling Lies*. New York, NY: W.W. Norton and Co.

Fisher, R. (1990). "Cognitive Interviewing Seminar." Southwest Texas State University, San Marcos, TX (July).

Fisher, R.P. and Geiselman, R.E. (1992). *Memory-enhancing Techniques for Investigative Interviewing*. Springfield, IL: Charles C Thomas.

———— (1988). "Enhancing Eyewitness Memory with the Cognitive Interview." In M.M. Gruneberg, P.E. Morris, and R.N. Sykes (eds.), *Practical Aspects of Memory: Current Research and Issues*. Vol. I. Memory in Everyday Life. New York, NY: Wiley.

Monahan, J. (1981). *Predicting Violent Behavior*. Beverly Hills, CA: Sage Publications, Inc.

Mount, G.R. (1995). "Assessing and Coping with Violent Behavior." *Journal of Crisis Negotiations* Vol.1, No.1:69-71.

Mullins, W. (1995). "The Role of a First Responder at a Hostage Situation." *Journal of Crisis Negotiations* Vol. 1, No. 1:43-52.

Noesner, G. (1999). "Negotiation Concepts for Commanders." *FBI Law Enforcement Bulletin* 68(1):6-14.

SAPD (1994). "Basic Hostage Negotiations Course." San Antonio, TX (September).

SAPD (1995). "Advanced Crisis Negotiations School." San Antonio, TX (April).

Slatkin, A.A. (2002). Intelligence in Crisis and Hostage Negotiations. Law and Order; Vol. 50, No. 7: April.

Solis, L. (1997). "Advanced Crisis Negotiations Seminar." San Antonio, TX (April).

———— (1999). "Critical Incident Response Planning for Schools." Presented at Texas Association of Hostage Negotiators' Regional Training Workshop. Austin, TX (November).

TCLEOSE (1990). "Texas Basic Hostage Negotiation Course, Course No. 3302." Revised January 1, 1990. Austin, TX: Texas Commission on Law Enforcement: Officer Education and Standards.

Discussion Questions

1. Which type of intelligence do you believe is most important at a hostage situation—incident, person, or tactical intelligence? Why?

2. Discuss how the intelligence officer might decide what information to gather during the crisis stage of the incident? How would he get input from the incident commander, SWAT team leader, and negotiations team leader? What information would he want from them? Where would he go for the information?

3. It has been said that intelligence is the lifeblood of crisis/hostage incident management; and an incident cannot afford an aneurysm or a blockage. What is meant by an "aneurysm" and "blockage" in a crisis incident? Give two examples of each.

4. You are the negotiator team commander and your team is called to the next county to negotiate an incident at a county jail. When you arrive, you are told that a deputy arrested the hostage taker several hours ago for robbery and failure to identify (the deputy, in fact, has not even finished completing the paperwork). All you know about the subject is that he is about 35 years old, Hispanic, apparently has no family in the area, a tattoo on his forearm that says "Death From Above," and is from out-of-state. What could you do to gather intelligence on this person?

5. Your pager goes off at 1030 hours. The dispatcher tells you that there is a call-out at a trailer park involving a man with a gun. What would the location of the call tell you about the potential risk involved and where would you go to gather additional information on risk level?

6. Interview two people who experienced the same event (i.e., a television show, a minor traffic accident, a sporting event, etc.). Interview one using the Structured Cognitive Interview and interview the other by just asking a lot of "yes-no" questions. Who provides the most information? Who has the easiest time recalling information?

7. Think of two friends of yours who know each other. Try to find out seven facts about the background of each (that you do not already know) by interviewing the other. Verify the information by going to the person and getting them to verify the information.

8. Get on the Internet and do a search of your name. How many sources are there and what types of sources are they? How could a negotiation team use the Internet to help resolve an incident?

Unique Incidents:

Negotiating with Special Groups

12

Learning Objectives

1. Understand the value of the developmental perspective in negotiations.

2. Know the biological, cognitive, and psychosocial issues of early adolescents

3. Know the biological, cognitive, and psychosocial issues of late adolescence/young adulthood.

4. Know the biological, cognitive, and psychosocial issues of the elderly.

5. Explain the reasons for joining, in addition to the structure and the risk factors associated with gangs.

6. Explain the negotiation guidelines for dealing with adolescents.

7. Understand the issues that influence negotiating with police officers.

8. Explain the guidelines used in negotiating with officers.

Two teens, a male and a female, shot another teen in an alley at 10:30 P.M. on Tuesday. They were observed running down the alley and into a house at the end of the alley. Patrol officers contained the scene and called the crisis response team. By the time the tactical and negotiating teams arrived, local media were on the scene. A School Resource Officer for the high school in that area was contacted and reported knowing that a 16-year-old male who was in their gang database lived at the address into which the subjects ran. He was considered a minor hanger-on to one of the local juvenile gangs. School records showed that he was in a resource program for a learning disability. The initial demand from the female who answered the phone was to be left alone. She hung up. Negotiators called back right away. The girl answered again. The negotiator asked her not to hang up. He said that the he needed to understand what had happened in the alley earlier, that they were the only ones who knew the whole story. He wanted to hear what they had to say. She explained that the person they ran into in the alley had been one who had given them trouble before and that he had threatened them that night. They had to defend themselves and not let him get away with "the shit he always talks about us." The negotiator stated that it sounded like the other kid was disrespecting them, to which the girl agreed. After listening to a list of grievances, the girl reported about the teen who was shot, the negotiator said that he could understand how frustrating it must be to have to put up with that stuff. He suggested that she they come out and they could work the incident out. She said that she was OK with that but that the boy inside with her was not. He was afraid of having to go to jail. And of what his "homies" would think of him.

The incident above illustrates the importance of being prepared for unique incidents in negotiations. These incidents are low probability but high risk. By that, we mean that they are incidents that do not occur often but have high risk associated with them. Negotiating with youth, gangs, the elderly, and police officers are examples. Data from the national database for the FBI, HOBAS, showed that as of June 2005, only 176 (3.5%) of 4,988 subjects involved in negotiated incidents on record were under the age of 18; 83 (1.7%) of the 4,988 were over 65. These are not events that happen often. However, they are events that have a high risk associated with them. The over-65 group shows a higher risk of suicide than other demographic groups and the most violent crimes are committed by 17- to 25-year-olds.

There are several possible losses to both the subjects and the police department that make these groups especially sensitive. They include: (1) loss of life, (2) bodily injury, and (3) loss of face, reputation, or self-esteem for both the individual and the police department if the incident is not resolved without injury or death. Thomas (2004) reported that juveniles committed 2,000 murders and non-negligent manslaughters, 5,300 forcible rapes,

32,500 robberies, and 72,300 aggravated assaults that year. It is likely that negotiators will deal with adolescents at some point in their career, and the potential losses are high.

Overview of Developmental Psychology

In addition to the usual issues involved in negotiation, a helpful perspective in understanding and managing juveniles, gangs, and the elderly is a developmental perspective. Developmental psychology assumes that people change over their lifetime in ways that influence their behavior, emotions, thinking processes and, most importantly for negotiations, their ability to relate to others. They change biologically, cognitively, and psychosocially. Negotiators who understand what the expected changes are at a given age have an additional tool that will help them resolve incidents with a lower chance of injury and death than negotiators who do not understand.

Nairne (2003) defines development as the age-related physical, intellectual, social, and personal changes that occur throughout an individual's lifetime. He points out that people are genetically programmed to develop in ways that fit them to their environment. They learn to think differently as they grow in order to learn to quickly assess situations, define problems, brainstorm solutions, and plan implementation of solutions, so they can survive in their physical environment and social world. We need to keep this adaptive value in mind in understanding the thinking, emotions, and social behavior we have to deal with. In short, people have developed in ways that have helped them survive and when we challenge these survival skills, we need to expect resistance and we need to be prepared to help people see the value of new skills. For instance, the adolescent who is angry and verbally hostile toward schoolteachers, principals, and the police may be so because it is the way he has learned to survive in an abusive home. His assumption is that verbal aggression and violence is the normal way of doing business and that everyone relates that way.

Scenario and Question

Before reading further, think about the scenario above. What issues do you need to be aware of in negotiating with the two adolescents? What strategies would you use? How would your approach be different from the approach you would use with adults?

Juveniles

The American Heritage Dictionary (1973) defines juvenile as: young, youthful, not fully developed. It has as a secondary definition," intended for or appropriate to children or young persons." The implications of these definitions are that juveniles are not yet grown. They do not function like adults. They think, feel, and behave differently from adults and that these differences need to be understood by negotiators. Without an appreciation of the not-yet-adult qualities of juveniles, it is easy for negotiators to lose patience with them, become judgmental, or break off contact.

Early Adolescents (Ages 13 to 16)

There are several organizations of the stages of development discussed by psychologists. Some of them group all adolescents together, defining adolescents as the age range from 12 to 18. We are choosing to follow the breakdown used by Discovering Psychology, available at: www.learner.org/discoveringpsychology/developmental, which separates early and late adolescents. Further, we are grouping late adolescents and young adults together. We will discuss two age ranges: early adolescents from 13 to 16 and later adolescents/young adults from 17 to 25. We are discussing it this way because we think that there are different developmental issues for these age groups that negotiators need to understand. Risk of violence is different for the two groups, with the older males being the most violent people in our society. Therefore, we will look at the developmental issues experienced by the 13 to 16 age group in this section.

Biological

Biologically, juveniles in this age range are dealing with both physical growth and sexuality. Both sexes are experiencing hormonal changes, and but at different rates Girls are developing more quickly. Estrogen starts in girls between 12 and 13 years of age, while boys generally start producing androgen between the ages of 13 and 14. Sixth-grade boys literally look up to the girls in the class, because the girls have developed faster. However, by the seventh or eighth grade, most boys have caught up or surpassed the girls in height and weight.

Cognitive

During early adolescence, juveniles begin to develop reasoning skills more like adults, what cognitive psychologists call *formal operations*. That is, they begin to be able to gather information, sort it into meaningful categories, and use it to solve problems. Critical thinking develops. They are able to evaluate their own and others' ideas. As a result, their use of irony and sarcasm increases. Many of us have had our eighth-grader point out the flaws in our thinking with a comment like "No duh, Dad," meaning "that's obvious."

The ability to abstract develops. They can think about issues without them having been defined by specific experience. For instance, when asked what "school" means to them, early adolescents are able to define it as an institution that is organized by the community or public that has as its purpose passing along information and preparing children to be good citizens and to earn a living. Children are likely to be more concrete, saying that school is about tests, recess, and Ms. Smith, who is an old witch. This definition is more tied to immediate personal experience, a certain place and time, than the more abstract definitions of adolescents and adults.

Psychosocial

Identity. In early adolescence, questions of "Who am I?" "What do I believe?" "How am I going to act independently of my parents?" begin to occupy a juvenile's thinking. Because of their newfound thinking skills, they are able to see the flaws in their parents, their parents' friends, their way of life, and their values. They start searching for other models in an effort to demonstrate their competence and in an effort to reinforce their new sense of independence. For instance, they may reject the clothes their parents picked out because they are not "in."

Conformity to peer group. In their search for who they are, juveniles look to their peers for standards of behavior. Their choice of dress, language, music, movies, etc. are determined by whether their friends are doing it, wearing it, thinking it. Fitting in becomes of the utmost importance. The irony is that they want to be their own person, just like their friends.

Friendships are defined by loyalty and intimacy. Because fitting in helps define who they are, loyalty to their friends becomes an essential part of their social life. They find people who share their developing ideas about life and about who they are to socialize with—other people who reinforce their thinking, feeling, and behavior. They tend to defend their friends to the death. Any parent who has suggested to their 13-year-old that his or her friends are a bad influence and that he or she should not hang around with them has probably experienced this loyalty firsthand.

Autonomy from family. Family becomes a mixed experience for early adolescents. They sense that their job is to prepare to move away from their family and to become independent people. They are more critical. They want to make their own decisions, yet they want a place of sanctuary when things do not go well. They want to try out their adult skills and they want to be able to run home if it does not work for them.

Sexual orientation develops. As part of their overall identity, juveniles begin to struggle with who they are sexually. They have to learn to manage their sexual urges and identify ways of satisfying them.

Psychological disorders emerge. The issue of independence creates significant stress on adolescents. Consequently, some who have problems navigating the changes or those who had latent emotional, cognitive or behavioral problems begin to come to the fore.

Thomas (2004) has suggested that negotiators have to deal with mood-disordered juveniles and character-disturbed adolescents. Frequently these issues, although present earlier, come to the forefront during early adolescence.

Late Adolescence/Young Adult (Ages 17 to 25)

Biological

Physical development reaches its peak during late adolescence (Nairne, 2002). People change in appearance and strength. During late adolescence, both males and females reach their full height. Motor skills become adult-like and coordination develops to its fullest. The brain reaches its full size and continues to make new connections between neurons. Learning continues even though neurological development seems to stop. The hardware is in place, but the programming continues throughout life.

Cognitive

Problem solving continues to develop in late adolescence/young adulthood. The formal operational period (Nairne, 2002) continues to develop, as does the adolescent's experience base away from home. They can think about imaginary happenings, consider hypothetical outcomes, and come to logical conclusions about places they have never seen or situations they have not experienced.

Psychosocial

Identity. A person's sense of who they are, what they think, feel, and how they are going to act becomes even more defined by their opposition to adults. They believe that they are the first one's that ever had an original thought and that the adults in their life are indifferent, uncaring and frequently, stupid. It is late adolescents/young adults about whom Mark Twain quipped that when he was 17 he thought that his parents were the dumbest people in the world. But, it was amazing when he was 21 how much they had learned in four years.

Dating. Intimacy with another. People learn that intimacy is more than physical during this time. The opposite sex become more important as human being/individuals. Learning to share feelings, thoughts, dreams and plans with another person are skills that need to be developed during this period. Love becomes important, in addition to lust. Intimacy is recognized as involving emotional closeness and intellectual agreement, as well as physical closeness.

Cliques normally decline in importance. As consequence of the need to learn to be close to another person, group affiliation becomes relatively less important than one-to-one relationships. The power if the group diminishes in favor of the power of the "significant other."

Assertiveness increases conflict with parents. Late adolescence/early adulthood sees a refinement of reasoning skills and the move toward independence. Conflicts with parents may increase as the person gets more experience, develops more confidence in himself and learns to assert his or her opinions. Early on, it is difficult for people to distinguish between assertiveness, which requires that a person respect the opinions of others even when they do not agree, and aggression, which is presenting your position without regard to others.

Introduction to work and career. Identity for late adolescents includes developing a sense of what they want to do for a living, how they want to contribute. It requires them to assess their interests, their resources, and the opportunities available to them. Gang members may find their career identity in the gang.

Thomas (2004) suggests that juveniles are motivated by one of three things when they are involved in a critical incident. All of them may be motivating factors for gang members. They are:

1. Attention seeking—Some adolescents become involved because they are looking for recognition from peers, parents, authority figures, or others.

2. Anger—Some juveniles act out in ways that bring them to the attention of the police because they are angry about real or perceived wrongs done to them by the specific person or system against whom they are acting.

3. Revenge—Some are aggressive because they want to get back at people who have humiliated them and caused them to lose face.

Negotiating with Adolescents

The developmental perspective suggests several strategies that negotiators need to consider in dealing with adolescents in addition to the standard crisis intervention approach. They include:

- Check Your Attitude—If you cannot be patient, understanding, and communicate respect, let someone else do the negotiations.

- Rapport and Credibility—Be particularly sensitive to rapport building. Adolescents have attitudes about authority that are part of developing their own identity. However, this makes it difficult for negotiators to find common ground with them. You have to work hard at connecting with them. The rapport building may take longer than you expect, so be patient.

- Active Listening—Active listening helps build trust and rapport—use it.

- Maintain Contact—Even though it may be frustrating, maintain contact. It is the only way to influence other people. This is particularly true of adolescents, because they can be abrasive as they learn to be assertive and others sometimes give up on them.

- Face—Allow adolescents to save face. Be aware of their face statements and help them re-focus on face-affirming statements whenever they are self-critical.

- Recognize the power of the group for early adolescents.

- Suicide potential—Assess suicide potential early and constantly monitor for suicidal intent.

Review your answers to the questions at the beginning of this section. Answer them again, integrating the issues and techniques presented in this section.

Gangs

The *American Heritage Dictionary* (1973) defines a gang as *a group of criminals; a group of people who regularly associate socially*. The second definition points to an important reason for gangs, whether they are criminal gangs or not. That is, people are social animals. We all have a need to be a part of a group, to a greater or lesser degree. We noted the importance of early adolescents having a group of friends that help them define who they are. Social affiliation is a natural developmental stage and it continues to be an issue for most people well into adulthood. In one sense, developing a professional identity is about belonging to a gang. Police officers have initiation rites. It is called the academy and the FTO program. They are tested to see how they will handle themselves on the street, i.e., will they behave in ways that make them acceptable to the group. It is a test to see whether they fit in. All of us belong to some kind of gang. They are just not criminal. However, negotiators do have to deal with criminal gangs. The following section will provide a brief overview of gang issues negotiators may have to deal with.

Reasons for Gang Membership

People become gang members for several reasons, most of them having to do with the developmental issues they are dealing with at the time they are recruited. Sharpe (2002) paraphrases Regan (1996) in suggesting that gangs play a valuable role in socialization as people seek the approval of their peers. Acceptance and identity issues are satisfied through gang membership. It is no accident that juveniles are recruited into gangs as they are making the transition from middle school to high school. Issues of identity and belonging are important to early adolescents. Being approached by a recruiter for a gang speaks to these needs.

In addition, Sharpe (2002) suggests that juveniles who come from families that cannot meet their needs for affection, belonging, loyalty, appropriate supervision, and activities are more likely to join gangs. It is suggested that the gang becomes a surrogate family for these at-risk youth.

Finally, community and school issues play a part in gang membership (Sharpe, 2002). Juveniles who seem to be at high risk for joining a gang live in socially disorganized neighborhoods in which gangs already exist, and that have a high incidence of violence; have friends who are gang members; have difficulty in school; and have a low commitment to school.

In summary, there appear to be four reasons people join gangs:

1. **Affiliation**—people join gangs to belong.
2. **Safety**—people join gangs to feel safe.
3. **Identity**—people join gangs to have a sense of who they are.
4. **Recognition**—people join gangs to feel important.

Gangs are generally organized into levels. Some have suggested that they include: leader, hardcore members, affiliates, fringe members or wanna-bes. In analyzing the terrorist cell structure of the 1970s, Strentz (1981; 1988) has suggested a typology that appears to fit gangs as well, and has utility for negotiators. He suggested that terrorist gangs were composed of leaders, generals, and soldiers. The leaders were obsessive, idealistic thinkers, but not good organizers. The generals were good planners, leaders, and organizers. In addition, they were frequently antisocial. The soldiers were the ones who carried out the plans of the group, were joiners, and depended on the group for guidance, meaning, and affirmation. This typology can be applied to street/criminal gangs as well: the hard-core members can be seen as the generals, leading the troops in the street, and the soldiers are for the most part the affiliates, fringe members, or wanna-bes. This distinction is important for negotiators because the negotiating strategy and tactics will be different, depending on the level of gang membership. Negotiators need to recognize the fact that leaders are obsessive and use appropriate negotiating techniques, while the hard-core people can be approached like antisocial personalities and the soldiers can be dealt with like dependent personalities.

Considerations when Negotiating with Gang Members

There is little research on negotiations with gangs. However, on the basis of his team's experience, Starbuck (2004) suggests that the following issues need to be considered in negotiating with gang members:

- Negotiators' patience will be tested
- There will be a lot of frustration and a temptation to "go tactical"
- Usually, there will be no substantive demands
- The subject will try to goad the negotiator
- Gang members will be familiar with police techniques
- Police are a symbol of authority—what gang members dislike the most
- Gang members will see the event as a way of gaining "respect"

Negotiating Guidelines with Gang Members

- Attitude—As always, the negotiator's attitude toward gang subjects sets the tone and influences the effectiveness of negotiations. Developmentally, juveniles have attitude. Officers need to be careful not to respond in kind. The old maxim, "I treat them the way they treat me" does not apply when negotiating with juveniles. Being "dissed" is reason enough for retribution among gang members and it underlines the importance of negotiators' maintaining a respectful, open, genuine attitude toward gang member subjects.

- Use active listening to get by the expected verbal aggression—Gang members are used to using aggression to get their way—it is their juice. They will try threatening, aggressive, demands because that is what they expect to work. Negotiators can expect an increase in aggressiveness when the threats do not work but are responded to by a reflective statement. Continue to use active listening until they are completely defused.

- Level of membership—As noted above, there are different levels of membership in gangs and there are different personality types that occupy different levels of membership. Negotiators need to be aware of what kind of person they are dealing with and use the appropriate strategy and tactics. Unless they are running a warrant at a gang headquarters, negotiators are more than likely going to deal with the anti-social/narcissistic personality style of the general or the dependent/joiner of the soldiers (see Chapter 7 for negotiating with different personality styles).

- Face—being "dissed" is all about attacking the other person's face. Revenge is all about restoring face for gang members. Negotiators need to track face statements.

- Belonging—A major part of being a gang member is to belong. Membership becomes part of the way people define themselves. Loyalty to the group is as important as loyalty to people. Negotiators need to be aware of this powerful dynamic and not challenge the gang's legitimacy. It is like attacking the individual and will be resisted.

- Take the time—Establishing rapport with someone who belongs to a group that thinks of you as the enemy will take time. Like with the paranoid, the negotiator will have to find ways of separating himself from his own "gang" in the eyes of the adolescent without looking disloyal to his own group. He will have to plan on taking the time to be sure that he is understood by the gang member and the time to find common ground on which to meet.

- Maintain contact—Resolutions can only be reached if you hang in there. Gang members will try to force negotiators to respond like other adults in their life, by getting angry in return or by disengaging. They win if negotiators do either. Continue to use active listening and focus on problem solving.

- Use problem-solving questions—Direct confrontations usually get confrontation in return. Therefore, it is important for negotiators to use indirect methods of getting ideas across to gang members. The use of problem-oriented questions is a particularly good way to get people to evaluate their own ideas without challenging them directly.

Elderly

Incident

He was a 68-year-old man in the early stages of Alzheimer's. He had come to the attention of the police department because he had passed bad checks and there was a warrant out for his arrest. Warrant officers went to his home. He came to the door with a gun in his hand and slammed the door as soon as they identified themselves. During the short time the door was open, the officers saw a living room full of garbage, old newspapers, used dishes, and scattered items such as calculators, and adding machines. They called the crisis response team.

Take a few minutes to think about the issues you may encounter with this man and how you might need to modify your approach to accommodate the age-related issues. Be prepared to review your answers at the end of this section.

Definition: Approaching Old Age

Biological

Smaller brain—After the twenties, people begin to lose brain cells. Their brains begin to shrink. This becomes more rapid as people age. Studies looking at the weight of brains across age show that the weight of the brain decreases with age. It is thought that this change in brain physiology results in changes in brain functioning as well.

Weakening senses—As people age, they lose sensory acuity. Their hearing, vision, and taste decline. They have to rely on sensory aids like glasses and hearing aids. They buy unusually strong mints. Negotiators need to be aware of these issues with the elderly. They may be slow in responding because they did not hear, not because they did not understand or are ignoring what is going on. Always ask the elderly if they wear glasses or use a hearing aid.

Illness—The incidents of illness increase with age. Loss of health is one of the factors that may spark suicidal ideas or actions.

Dementia—Several illnesses in the elder lead to dementia, a neurologically based loss of intellectual ability, memory, planning, or anticipating the consequences of their actions. For instance, Transient Ischemic Attacks, or mini-strokes, in the frontal lobe will diminish the ability to plan, anticipate the consequences of their actions, or follow through with a plan. Negotiators need to ask if the subject has had recent changes in neurological functioning, if they are demented and if they have had a high fever, infection, blow to the head, periods of unconsciousness, or blackouts, to get an idea of how they are functioning neurologically.

Cognitive

Information processing declines—As part of the normal aging process, the ability to take in new information, to categorize it correctly, and to remember it declines. They think more slowly, as a rule.

Short-term memory declines—The ability to remember recent events declines as people age. They have trouble remembering what they went to the kitchen for, even when they decided to go get a drink 10 seconds before. Usually, this memory problem comes and goes, except in cases of severe dementia or diseases like Alzheimer's. Negotiators should also be aware that there are multiple memory paths in the brain. So when an elderly person is having trouble with verbal memory, masking them to visualize or feel an event might get around their verbal problems.

Memory-based language declines—Older people have problems finding the words to express themselves. This creates a couple of issues for negotiators. First, they are slow in answering, making them appear uncooperative. Second, it frustrates them, adding to the stress of having to deal with the police.

Experience based problem-solving increases—One neurological change that appears to work for the elderly is their ability to draw on past experiences to solve problems in the "here-and-now." There is evidence that suggests that as people age, the number of nerves in the brain decreases but the connections between the remaining nerves becomes more complex. That is, the brain seems to compensate for the lose of mass to some degree by connecting things together more. This may be the reason that older people are able to access and use memories of past experiences more readily than younger people.

Psychosocial

Retirement changes social relationships—All of us have seen people retire from the police department and the subsequent reaction of officers who are still on active duty when the "old timers" come around. It is as if they were never a part of the organization. People cannot talk to them about ongoing cases or departmental politics and they cannot talk to people still on the job about grandchildren, their health, or their current part-time job. There are few common interests and relationships grow more distant. The same thing happens to the elderly. Their interests change and they no longer rely on work associates for their social life. In addition, they beginning to lose friends to illness and death.

Family involvement defines satisfaction—For most elderly, the quality of their relationship with their families is the most important factor in their satisfaction with their retirement years. They frequently focus on getting closer to family members they may have neglected for years in favor of their career, hobbies, or other interests. The degree to which their families accept their change in status and interest and make a place for them will determine how satisfied they are with their life. Sometimes the elderly place restrictions on relationships with family, themselves. It is not that their extended family is uninterested. Rather, they find it hard to reach out after years of minimal involvement with family. In addition, when the elderly become depressed as a result of losses of health, relationships, etc., they may tend to withdraw from friends and family.

Well-being is generally higher—Many elderly people make the transition to retirement and change of social status well. They are able to develop a new group of friends that have things other than work in common and they establish more intimate relationships with their extended family. Therefore, their satisfaction with life is generally pretty good.

Coping generally increases—Because of their extensive life experiences, the elderly usually have developed a wide range of coping skills. They are able to bring these skills to bear on current problems. Negotiators can access these coping skills by asking elderly subjects if they have been in similar situations and how they solved them. Another way of capitalizing on the elderly subjects past experience is to ask them if they have had friends who have experienced similar stresses and gotten through them and follow it up with a question about how.

Bereavement issues come to the fore—One of the authors' wife's great-great-grandmother lived to the age of 108. During the last eight years of her life, she stated several times that she was ready to die, because she had outlived her children, her nephews and nieces, and three sets of friends. As people age, they lose friends and family. Grief and mourning and the anger and depression that comes with them increase. They have to learn how to lose people who are important to them. Sometimes, they do not know how to fill the void. Suicide becomes an attractive alternative for some.

Pain management and support become important—In the military, there is a reason you are not charged for equipment that wore out. It was listed as "fair wear and tear." This meant that equipment was only expected to last so long before it wore out and the soldier was not responsible for it no longer being serviceable. In like manner, people wear out. Joints degenerate, discs rupture, rotator cuffs tear, arthritis develops; this creates pain that one did not have before. The elderly have to learn to live with this pain.

Suicide risk increases in the elderly—Slatkin (2003) points out that the depression experienced by the elderly and the increased substance abuse make them an increased risk for suicide. He reported that the suicide rate remains constant until age 65, when it starts to increase dramatically. He reports rates of 25 suicides per 100,000 for people ages 65-69; 30 per 100,000 in people ages 70-74; and a steady increase until at age 85 the suicide rate is 65 per 100,000.

Negotiating with the Elderly

- **Be patient**—The elderly often will need to tell their life story and they may tell it in a rambling way. Their memory and thinking may be slowed. They need to be able to tell their story in their own way and this requires patience. Allowing them the freedom to tell their story their way will help develop rapport and gather intelligence that can be used later to build their self-esteem and validate their feelings (Slatkin, 2003).

- **Slow down**—Given the general slowing of thinking in elderly persons and the problems with short-term memory, it is important for the negotiator to slow the rate of the communication. Elderly who are depressed need more time to understand what they are hearing, to think through their answers, and to respond.

- **Ask them to repeat**—To check to see if the elderly understand the question, the answer, or the points being made; it is helpful to have them repeat what they have heard. Both the loss of their senses and short-term memory problems may limit their understanding.

- **Explore/honor their experience**—Slatkin (2003) suggests that negotiators encourage the elderly to reminisce about their life. He suggests that showing interest in their life helps build rapport and that exploring the positive experiences and accomplishments from an earlier time will help build the subject's self-esteem (restore face).

- **Use imagery/metaphor**—Because some of the developmentally based losses are language related, asking the elderly subject to imagine a time when they were successful, or felt down and survived, or other relevant memory, may facilitate their recall. Metaphors are stories that make a point and usually engage the subject's imagination, making a point indirectly. It encourages visual as well as verbal processing and may be helpful in getting a point across to the elderly.

- **Be aware of suicide potential**—With loss comes depression, and with depression comes suicidal ideas. Be aware and ask.

Police Officers

Incident

After reading the scenario below, stop and ask yourself, "What issues would I need to be thinking about, if I were responding to this incident?" "Would I make the same decisions?" Why or why not?

- At 7:30 A.M. on a Sunday, a deputy sheriff was flagged down by a woman who reported that her husband, a police officer, was barricaded in their home, threatening to shoot himself.

- Eight-year veteran, field training officer, active on streets, no complaints.

- Former deputy with sheriff's office.

- Served with divorce papers on extra job.

- Drinking on way home from his extra job.

- Conflict with wife at home.

- 7:40: Call out of emergency response team.

- 8:45: SWAT, negotiators and command are all on scene. Contact is attempted.

- 10:00: Deputy chief and negotiator sergeant from officer's agency arrive on scene.

- 10:30: Media arrives on the scene and sets up two blocks away.

- 10:30: Deputy chief is on the phone, issuing an order for the man to come out. Response: "How do I know that you are the deputy chief?"

- 11:00: Officer's lieutenant is on phone, assuring him that the deputy chief is for real. The officer refuses to come out, speech is slurred, thinking is slowed, and he wants to go to sleep.

- 1:00: Forward observer reports that the officer is on the porch with a weapon. The officer denies that he has a weapon.

- 1:30: Mentation is much improved, and the officer agrees to meet his lieutenant and doctor in the front yard. Command denies this request for safety reasons.

- 3:15: The officer tries to exit via the back door and is ordered back into the house by SWAT.

- 4:00: Wife is re-interviewed—she says that he wasn't threatening himself or her. She said that to get a response. She did not expect the police to be involved and expressed concern about the officer's job.

- The officer refuses to come out. He expresses concern for his career.

- 7:00: The officer again states that he will come out and meet with his lieutenant and doctor, in a patrol car at end of the driveway. Command agrees, if appropriate safety measures are in place.

- 7:30: The officer meets with his lieutenant and his doctor. SWAT takes the officer down.

This incident, although unusual, illustrates some of the issues involved in negotiating with a fellow police officer. Though the negotiators at this incident were experienced and successful, they did some things that complicated negotiations. For instance, they put a commander on the phone, thinking that the officer had been a good officer and he would respond to a direct order. This section will discuss some of the issues involved in dealing with incidents that are "too close for comfort" (Terhune-Bickler, 2004).

Statistics on the number of incidents that involve police officers is scarce. Terhune-Bickler (2004) reports that 22 incidents involving officers had been reported to HOBAS by 2002. However, they are highly publicized when they happen. A sampling of incidents involving officers that were reported in the media provided to the authors by Max Howard (2005) showed the following:

- **4/03, Nassau County, New York:** NYPD lieutenant climbed into the window of his girlfriend's home resulting in a murder-suicide with gun.

- **4/03, Nassau County, New York:** NYPD lieutenant found dead at home of gunshot wound to head.

- **4/03, Tacoma, Washington:** Police officer killed his wife and himself with his service gun in a parking lot with his two children watching (domestic).

- **5/03, Albuquerque, New Mexico:** Attorney general investigator forced suicide-by-cop when caught robbing a bank (financial issues).

- **7/03, Fayette, Alabama:** Lieutenant was found dead in his yard of a self-inflicted gunshot wound. (health problems and death of son).

- **9/04, Atlanta, Georgia:** A 17-year veteran of the Atlanta Police Department was arrested after third bank robbery (personal business failure).

- **6/02, Waxahachie, Texas:** On-duty Ellis Co. deputy fatally shot himself in the chest while seated in his office.

- **2/03, San Antonio, Texas:** Officer in 12-hour standoff at home (just served with divorce papers).

- **12/03, El Paso, Texas:** U.S. Customs inspector killed his wife at work, took hostages, then killed self.

- **5/04, Dallas, Texas:** Dallas Police Department officer held gun to daughter's head (age 7) and threatened to kill his wife. Later threatened investigators.

It is clear that law enforcement personnel do have crises and that they sometimes have to be managed by negotiators. It benefits negotiators to have thought through their procedures and developed plans for this eventuality, so they are not left without a plan when dealing with a fellow officer. Otherwise, the stresses involved may lead to errors that the experienced negotiator ordinarily would not make. The value of polices and procedures is to provide guidance in the exceptional situation when there are factors that may influence critical decision making.

Considerations in Officer-Involved Crises

Often officers who are in the same agency or who work in an adjacent jurisdiction have a prior relationship with the officer in crisis. In the scenario above, not only did the officers in the subject's agency know him, the negotiators all knew him from his prior employment with their agency. Prior history can work for or against the negotiator, depending on the nature of the relationship the officer had with the negotiators. If they had a good or neutral relationship, the negotiator can probably handle the incident. However, if there were conflicts and unresolved issues, then these issues will flow over into the negotiations.

Media exposure. Incidents involving officers are high-profile events. The media will certainly be there. It will put added pressure on the negotiators and may be an issue to be addressed with the subject. In the incident described above, the officer's real issue—the reason he wanted to surrender behind his garage or after dark—was that he did not want his picture on television. It was shameful and embarrassing. Departments need to be prepared to deal effectively with the media and the media exposure. Negotiators need to be aware of the face issues involved in an incident for an officer in crisis.

Untrained superior as incident commander. Terhune-Bickler (2004) has pointed out that departments are likely to want to avoid embarrassment and exposure, so the supervisor or ranking official at the time an officer is involved in an incident may be reluctant to call out the crisis management team. This leads to relatively untrained commanders and personnel handling the incident.

Pressure to resolve quickly and quietly. To reduce exposure, there is pressure to resolve an incident involving an officer quickly. The hope is that if it is resolved rapidly, it will get less press. So, there is pressure to violate one of the elements needed for successful negotiation—the use of time. Command pressure to resolve the incident quickly will increase the stress on negotiators.

Issues Because They Are Officers

Officers known to team. The first issue that needs to be addressed is: Who will negotiate? Will it be someone from the officer's parent agency or someone from another agency with whom the department has a memorandum of understanding? Will it be someone the officer knows or is there a stranger available? Generally it is better to use negotiators who have no prior relationship with the officer in crisis because they do not bring any unresolved issues into the relationship. However, if that is not possible, as in the incident described above, the primary needs to be chosen on the basis of who had the best relationship with the officer prior to the incident.

Terhune-Bickler (2004) has made the point that one of the issues for an officer in crisis having to deal with negotiators from his own department is that he knows the policies and practices of the department and may not trust the negotiator to have his interests in mind. She recommends have a working relationship and memorandum of understanding with an adjacent department to minimize the impact of this issue.

Assumption of knowledge. Implicit in Terhune-Bickler's point about familiarity with the department is the implication that the officer in crisis not only knows the political tenor of the department, but that they know the department's negotiating style, policies, and procedures. While this may be true, the authors' experience with police-involved incidents has been that officers did not know as much about negotiating as was thought. For instance, one officer who had actually studied negotiations was barricaded and kept telling the negotiators that he knew what they were up to. However, when he heard the SWAT team clearing adjacent rooms in the motel, he shot himself, thinking that they were assaulting him. He assumed that the negotiator was setting him up for a tactical solution. It is important not to assume that officers know what negotiations are about. Officers may need to be educated about the process of negotiations in the same way other subjects need to learn that negotiators are not there to harm them.

Police personality. Historically, there has been much debate about whether there is a "police personality." The general consensus among police psychologists is that a wide variety of people come into police work, but that, over the years, they grow more alike. They are socialized into similar thinking, values, and behaviors, like any tightly knit group. They value discipline, attention to detail, and their reputation. They become perfectionistic and are driven by the threat of shame. That is, their reputation (face) becomes important. This makes incidents that expose them to possible criticism by their peers, administrators, or the public highly stressful for them. This issue has to be taken into account in managing any incident involving a police officer.

Precipitating events. Terhune-Bickler (2004) has reported that the limited research on police-involved suicides involved relationship problems, legal troubles, psychological problems, and work-related stress. Relationship problems in policing are frequently the result of the same things that those in the "real world" find difficult: power and control, saving face, and fear of abandonment. If this is the source, negotiators need to deal with it like any other domestic incident they negotiate. If the source is a legal problem, reputation and self-esteem are likely to be issues. Incidents involving officers who are having psychological problems should include a MHC on the management team to assess the seriousness of the problems, explain the impact of treatment, communicate with treating professionals, and help develop strategies.

Threat to career. Officers will fear the department's reaction to the exposure the incident brings to them. A significant question and issue to be resolved is "what will happen to me now?" The officer in the incident above asked that question multiple times and not without reason. Representatives from his department were pushing early on for a resolution to the incident, even if it took a tactical solution. Administrators were discussing ways of managing the image problems the incident was creating for them, including termination of the officer. Negotiators need to anticipate this issue and have a strategy for responding before it is brought up.

Suicide risk. Being faced with departmental repercussions and the shame of public exposure because of an incident are major stressors. Losses of things in which people invest a lot emotionally, physically, and personally will often result in depression and the risk of suicide. Officers involved in incidents that may end with their being on television and losing their job may feel hopeless and helpless. They may turn to suicide. Negotiators need to constantly evaluate the risk of suicide in incidents that involve officers.

Saving face. To a large degree, being a member of a tightly knit group requires people to value the reputation and opinions of the group. An officer looks to his peers for approval, acceptance, belonging, and safety. His reputation among fellow officers is an important part of his worldview. Being involved in a crisis with fellow officers raises significant "face" problems. The officer who is in crisis may well have difficulty with both the personal embarrassment of having fellow officers know that he had a problem he could not handle and the embarrassment he is generating for the department. Both the officer and department will be interested in saving face and avoiding embarrassment. In the incident above, the officer's real concern was about not appearing on television and having to explain it to his friends and family. Negotiators need to look for ways of helping the officer "restore face."

Negotiating with Police Officers

Several authors (Howard, 2004; Terhune-Bickler, 2004; McMains, 2005) have suggested guidelines for negotiating with police officers who are in crisis. They include:

- Expect rapport to be tricky—Officers do not necessarily trust fellow officers in times of crisis. In fact, Terhune-Bickler (2004) has suggested that rapport may already be established because of the officer's familiarity with the negotiator. On the down side, however, the officer who is in crisis may see the negotiator as a representative of the department and he may consider the department a cause of his problems. Thus, rapport is not automatic, just because the negotiator is known to the officer in crisis.

- Normalize feelings—Because officers generally value action over feelings, they tend to deny their feelings until they are overwhelming. When they get to the point of being overwhelming, officers feel out of control. Therefore, it is important for them to hear that they are responding like a normal human being and it is important to hear it from a fellow officer.

- Allow ventilation but do not spend a lot of time—Because officers tend to devalue feelings, shifting from ventilation to problem-solving needs to be done as quickly as possible. When they have had time to ventilate and they begin to accept the idea that their feelings are "normal," negotiators can begin to focus on problem-solving, emphasizing the officers' prior success in solving others' problems as a "face-restoring" strategy.

- Be respectful and competent—Officers tend to have learned to be perfectionistic and detail-oriented. They expect other officers to be equally competent. They are sensitive to criticism because of the high standard they are expected to meet. Therefore, show them respect and your expertise.

- Stay problem-focused rather than feeling-oriented.

- Use problem-oriented questions and paraphrasing—These active listening techniques minimize feelings and focus the officer who is in crisis on skills they have considerable experience with. Asking them what they would advise someone who was in a similar situation would be an example.

- After rage is defused, the officer is likely to be contrite and cooperative—Police officers are one of two organizations in our society that are sanctioned to use force to solve problems. They are trained on the use of threats and force to control situations and people. When under stress, they use the tools that have worked in the past, so expect them to use threats as a way to try to control their situation. However, they do respect authority and after they have time to get themselves under control, they are likely to respond to the situation by becoming cooperative.

- Provide structure by sharing what "normally" happens in negotiations—To deal with the fact that officers may not know as much as you think about negotiations, share your experiences with them.

- Share experience to establish "expertise"—negotiators can share their experiences of successful negotiations with an officer to establish his competence and expertise. He can say thing like, "I've been involved in X number of incidents and they have generally turned out well." If asked how many involved police officers, he can say something like, "I'm glad you asked. I have studied every incident I could find involving police officers and they generally are resolved peacefully."

- Minimize "fault/blame"—Face is important to officers and if they are in a barricaded or hostage situation, feeling things they have not felt before and doing things they normally would not do, they are likely to have a sense of failure and shame. Minimize their self-criticism and introduce ideas that restore face to them.

- Choose a negotiator carefully—Assess prior relationship.

- Assess risk carefully, especially suicide. The loss of face, the availability of a weapon, and the frequent use of alcohol combine to increase the risk of suicide among police officers.

Review the answers to the questions that were asked before the scenario above was presented. Answer them again, knowing what you know now about issues surrounding incidents that involve police officers. Have your answers changed?

Summary

Negotiations with juveniles, the elderly, gangs, and fellow officers pose unique issues for negotiators. Crisis response teams, negotiators, and commanders need to give thought to how they will manage these incidents before they happen. Procedures need to be developed and skills need to be practiced, so the chances of success increase. Being prepared is the best way to increase chances of accomplishing the mission of saving lives in these low probability/high-risk incidents.

References

American Heritage Dictionary (1973). New York: American Heritage Publishing and Houghton Mifflin Co.

FBI (2005). *HOBAS, Special Response Group.* Quantico, VA: FBI Academy, Crisis Negotiations Unit.

Howard, L. (2005). "Law Enforcement Officers in Crisis." Presented at: ATF Hostage Negotiators Annual Training. San Antonio, Texas.

McMains, M.J. (2005). "Negotiating with Special Groups." Paper presented at Seventeenth Annual Negotiations Seminar and Contest, Texas State University, San Marcos, Texas.

Nairne, J.S. (2003). *Psychology: The Adaptive Mind*, Third Edition. Belmont, CA: Wadsworth.

_____ (2002). *Psychology: The Adaptive Mind.* Belmont, CA: Thomson-Wadsworth.

Slatkin, A.A. (2003). "Suicide Risk and Hostage/Barricade Situations Involving Older People." *FBI Law Enforcement Bulletin* April.

Sharpe, E.G. (2002). "Negotiating with Gang Members: Understanding the Epidemiology and Risk Factors for Membership." *Journal of Police Crisis Negotiations*, Vol. 2, No.2.

Starbuck, D. (2004). "The 'Duece-Duece Crips' Negotiations Incident." Presented at: ATF Conference, Las Vegas, Nevada (January).

Strentz, T. (1981). "The Terrorist Organizational Profile: A Psychological Role Model." In Alexander, Y. and J.M. Gleason (eds.), *Behavioral and Quantitative Perspectives on Terrorism*. New York: Pergamon.

Strentz, T. (1988) "A Terrorist Psychosocial Profile: Past and Present." *Law Enforcement Bulletin* 57(4):11-18.

Terhune-Bickler, S.D. (2004). "Too Close or Comfort: Negotiating with a Fellow Officer." *Law Enforcement Bulletin* 73(4):1-5.

Thomas, B. (2004). "Negotiating with the Juvenile Actor". Presented at the Sixteenth Annual Crisis Negotiations Seminar and Contest. Texas State University, San Marcos Texas.

Discussion Questions

1. How did your approach to the incident involving the juveniles change after reading this chapter?

2. How did your approach to the elderly person change after reading the chapter?

3. How did your approach to the incident involving the police officer change after reading the chapter?

4. Of the four unique groups discussed in this chapter, which would be the hardest and which the easiest to negotiate with? What makes them the hardest and the easiest?

5. During normal development, adolescents switch emphasis from needing to belong to a group to needing to learn to relate to others as individuals. What "hooks" does this give the negotiator in dealing with adolescents? What "barbs" (issues to avoid) does it suggest?

6. The S.A.F.E. model suggests that elderly people may have issues around substance, attunement (relationship with the negotiator), face (self-esteem), and emotional management. Draw four columns on a sheet of paper, one for each heading from the S.A.F.E. model and list each of the negotiation strategies in dealing with the elderly under the appropriate topic.

7. Discuss how your negotiating strategy might be different in dealing with a gang leader, a gang general, or a gang soldier.

8. Your team has to negotiate with a police officer who had been your field training officer because, after an internal affairs complaint of sexual harassment, she is barricaded and threatening suicide. While she was your field training officer, she propositioned you and your wife insisted that you resign from the department. You worked it out with your wife, but never reported the event. Your team leader wants you to be the primary negotiator. What do you tell your team leader about your previous relationship with this officer? Do you negotiate? What issues are important in making this decision?

Crisis Negotiating Equipment

13

Learning Objectives

1. Know what basic equipment each hostage negotiator should have.

2. Know what basic equipment each hostage negotiating team should have.

3. Know how to organize a situation board by topic area.

4. Know what optional equipment each hostage negotiating team should have and what it is used for.

5. Know possible sources for obtaining equipment.

The negotiating team was called out to a possible suicide/hostage situation at approximately 11:00 P.M. on an October evening. One member of the team picked up the negotiating van and drove it to the scene, where she was met by the rest of the team. Team members gathered intelligence and determined that they had a despondent individual who was holding his wife hostage and threatening to kill her and himself. The hostage taker had lost his job that day and when he told his wife, she replied she had had enough and was going to take the kids and leave. The kids were not home at the time and had since been secured with another relative. Negotiators decided to make telephone contact with the hostage taker (Marvin). Using the newly installed telephone system, the primary negotiator attempted to call Marvin, but found the telephone system to be completely inoperable. Members of the team checked the telephone, internal batteries and parts, and tracked the circuits. They could not identify the source of the problem. Putting that telephone away, negotiators got out their old throw telephone system, hooked it up and had the tactical team deliver the hostage taker's handset (which they did by throwing it through a window, irritating Marvin even more). When the primary negotiator attempted to contact Marvin using this system, he found it also to be inoperable. Team members again searched for the source of the problem and finally found it: the fuse servicing that section of the van had blown. Because it was a new van, no one had thought to buy and carry extra fuses and because it was now 1:00 A.M., no service station or garage was open where one of the specialized, oversized fuses could be purchased. Nor were there additional power outlets in other areas of the van. Negotiators finally determined that they were going to have to negotiate face-to-face. Planning on being inside the heated van, team members were not dressed appropriately for spending several hours in the cold October night doing face-to-face negotiations, which later necessitated rotating negotiators. In addition, the tactical team had to change their surveillance and assault plans in order to provide protection to the negotiators. The tactical commander, in fact, had to pull one of her team members and give his protective vest and helmet to the primary negotiator. After approximately 22 hours, Marvin released his hostage and surrendered.

One belief many police departments have when they consider implementing a hostage negotiating team is that the start-up costs will be large. Many departments are familiar with the fictional portrayal in movies and television of hostage negotiators, in which the department has a large budget and the negotiators look as if they just stepped off a Star Wars movie set. The department may have also visited a neighboring agency and been given the "grand tour" of the custom negotiating vehicle, the specialty equipment, and the latest technology for the well-prepared negotiator. The department decides it would have to lay off 90 percent of its force to finance a negotiating team and decides to forget the entire idea.

Simple / Stout

The department has allowed a necessary function to fall victim to technology and has ignored the negotiating team's most valuable asset. All a negotiator needs to do the job is an ability to communicate. Everything else is a luxury. Some of the most successful negotiators are members of small departments. These negotiators (and their small teams) receive very little financial and material support from their departments. Their equipment consists of what the negotiating team brings from home or can borrow from businesspeople and others they know. Other teams, whose departments purchase the latest and best equipment, become overly reliant on this equipment and forget the basic essentials of negotiating—communication and problem-solving between two people.

Every year in San Marcos, Texas, a hostage negotiation "competition" and training seminar is held. It brings in teams from all over the United States (and has even included negotiating teams from other countries). Some teams come with 15 to 20 people, two negotiating vans, an equipment trailer, and enough incidental equipment to open a shopping mall. Other teams have three people and a chalkboard in a patrol vehicle's trunk. Some of the event's best negotiators are those who do not have the benefit of the "fancy" equipment. Although there is no empirical data to support this contention, we believe negotiators who lack the "bells and whistles" often make the best negotiators because they must work extra hard and be extra creative in resolving hostage incidents. Negotiators may become complacent when surrounded by a large assisting team and expensive equipment that rarely malfunctions (and even when it does, there are support personnel to repair the equipment). It is difficult to become complacent when negotiating on one's own with no support, no back-up telephone systems, and no van to provide shelter from the elements.

The authors are not saying that a negotiating team does not need equipment. There is some equipment the negotiating team should have, and there is even more equipment that could be considered a luxury. This chapter will explore the equipment that should be provided to a negotiating team, and equipment that is an asset to the negotiators and that can be purchased, budget permitting. The use, misuse, and pitfalls of that equipment will also be discussed.

Necessary Equipment

Any negotiating team should have some basic equipment. Much of this is equipment the police department probably already has in inventory and can be reallocated to the negotiating team. Other equipment can be obtained from an office supply store.

First and foremost, negotiating teams should have a team uniform that is worn to situations and exercises. The negotiating team is a *team* and should have a uniform to reflect this. The uniform should not be the same

Although not required, it is advisable that negotiators have a team uniform. A uniform helps build team identity and team unity. The uniform should also conform to the environment in which negotiators work. Members here are wearing the summer uniform. *(S. Davis)*

as the tactical uniform. First, negotiators are a separate response unit and the uniform should reflect this. Second, "clothes make the man/ woman" and a tactical type of uniform can reflect a psychological mindset that is not conducive to negotiations.

All negotiating team members should have a briefcase, notebook, pencils and pens, a clipboard, folders, and sundry items such as paper clips, a stapler, and markers. Each person should have a pocket tape recorder to take notes, keep track of conversations, decisions, suggestions, etc. During periods of hectic activity, suggestions will be forgotten, decisions will not be properly remembered, and other details may not be written down. A small pocket recorder can be invaluable for remembering and summarizing important parts of the negotiations. Each team member should have an alphanumeric pager and the dispatcher should have a list of numbers and clear instructions on calling out team members. We know of many cases in which team members were delayed in arriving at the scene due to a lack of clear call-out instructions/policy.

All team officers should have a concealable weapon with holster, windbreaker/jacket and cap with letters identifying them as police or negotiators, raincoat, flashlight, and full body armor. They should wear comfortable and rugged clothing such as jeans, tennis shoes, or boots with heavy socks, and gloves (in cold weather). It is advisable to have a waterproof rainsuit for colder weather, along with torso insulation, polypropylene long underwear, and a wool hat (such as a navy-style watch cap). Many teams are now using heavy-material turtlenecks as their winter shirt because these provide additional protection from the cold. They should have an overnight bag with a washcloth, toothbrush, small towel, toilet paper, aspirin, antacids, and basic foodstuffs. This overnight bag should include a change of clothes. If the negotiator is soaking wet and in the cold, the negotiator will be trying to satisfy his or her needs instead of the hostage taker's needs. In a prolonged negotiating situation, runners bring the team coffee, soda, water, and light meals. Each officer should carry some snacks. Ideal foods include sunflower seeds, jerky, chewing gum, and canned juices. Avoid carrying sweets, spoilable items, or items that need heating or cooling.

Figure 13.1
Sample "Ready Bag" to be Carried by Each Member of the Negotiating Team

Quantity	Item
1 pair	Wool socks
1 pair	Undershirt and underpants
1	Long sleeve shirt (dark, loose fitting)
1 each	Rain coat and rain pants
1 each	"Negotiator" jacket and cap
1	Washcloth
1	Toothbrush
1	Toothpaste
1 roll	Toilet paper
1	Flashlight
4	Extra flashlight batteries
1 bottle	Aspirin
1 bottle	Antacid
5 packs	Chewing gum
2 cans	Canned drink
5	Snack foods (non-spoilable)
5 packs	Jerky

Source: Mullins, W.C.

Figure 13.2
"Ready" Briefcase to be Carried by Each Member of the Negotiating Team

Quantity	Item
1	Pocket tape recorder
4	Extra batteries
5	Cassette tapes
2	Notebooks
5	Pencils
5	Pens
1	Pocket pencil sharpener
1	Mini-light
1 travel pack	Tissues
1	Pocketknife
Assorted	Paper clips and rubber bands
1	Paperback novel, crossword puzzle book, etc. (stress reducer)

Source: Mullins, W.C.

The team should have a dry erase board (and pens) for recording information and intelligence, and for keeping notes of conversations (see following section on situation boards). A dry erase board is preferable to a blackboard (or chalk board) for many reasons, including ease of writing on, ease in reading, and they are much easier to update. The team should have two or three audiocassette recorders (with plenty of extra batteries and a large supply of tapes), with a device that allows them to be attached to a telephone to record conversations. This not only allows the negotiators to go back over a prior conversation, it provides a permanent record should one ever be needed and serves as a training aid for other negotiators. At a hostage situation in a bank in North Carolina, a lone hostage taker had told negotiators that he shot and wounded a hostage. During the course of negotiations, the hostage taker was belligerent, threatening, and repeatedly threatened to kill hostages and the police. During the night, part of the tactical team entered the bank while the other part of the tactical team remained against the outer wall of the bank. From inside came the sounds of "flash bangs" detonating, gunfire, and shouts of "get down, hit the ground." A person ran out the door of the bank and was killed by the tactical team outside the bank. Tragically, it was a hostage. The tactical team members involved in the shooting of the hostage were referred to a grand jury for possible indictment. Tapes of negotiations played a significant role in the tactical team members being exonerated by the grand jury. The audiotape recorder should be of the three-head type, which allows a negotiator to listen to a conversation immediately after it occurs (Leak, 1994b). Negotiators might also want to keep a duplicating tape machine. At the Lewis State Prison incident, for example, negotiators regularly used a duplicating tape machine to make copies of negotiation tapes. These tapes were used for shift briefings, copies were provided to command elements and the tactical team, and to any response personnel who wanted to review past conversations (Dubina, 2005; Dubina & Ragsdale, 2005). At other prison situations and protracted incidents (such as the Branch Davidian siege in Waco, Texas and the Montana Freemen standoff), tape duplicating machines have proven to be valuable assets for negotiators. A telephone lineman's handset is invaluable for checking and tapping into telephone lines (most telephone companies will provide one for police use).

Each agency should check with its legal department or state attorney general's office concerning the legal requirements for intercepting wire and oral communications. In Texas, for example, it is necessary to obtain a court order (Texas Penal Code §§16.02 (c)(5), 16.03; Code of Criminal Procedure §§18.20, 18.21; 1990) to intercept these communications. Title 18 U.S.C. § 2510 *et seq.* allow single-party consent recording, so negotiators talking to a hostage taker can record the conversation without a court order (Leen, 1998). If the hostage taker is on a commercial telephone or cellular telephone and is talking to a person other than the police, and there is no immediate danger of death or serious injury, the police must obtain a court order to record the conversation (if the second party does not consent; 18 U.S.C § 2518[7]). Also, 18 U.S.C § 2511 (1) covers a person's expectations of privacy from listening devices that may be introduced into the situation. People have an expectation of privacy in oral communications. It is recommended that negotiators discuss issues of telephone recording, listening devices, and privacy in communication with local and state prosecuting attorneys prior to using such equipment (and prior to the need arising for using such equipment).

A bullhorn can be valuable for hailing a hostage taker who will not answer the telephone. A bullhorn should be one of the first items obtained by a negotiating team. One negotiating team the authors consult with was once placed in the position of having to write a note on paper, tie it to a brick and have the tactical team throw it through a window (as an aside, the brick hit the hostage taker in the head, knocking him unconscious). The bullhorn enables the negotiator to communicate from a safe distance and can be used for other purposes as well (i.e., warning civilians to stay back or getting the attention of perimeter officers, for example).

The team should have at least one cellular telephone. At many hostage locations, finding a public telephone for prolonged use can be difficult or even impossible. Many businesses will agree to let the police use their telephones until they find out how long their telephones may be tied up. Public telephones have additional problems, as illustrated by an incident related by McClure (1994). In the early 1980s, a hostage taker took over the Atlanta, Georgia, FBI office. During negotiations, the following telephone call and conversation occurred:

> OPERATOR: There is a collect call from "John Smith." Will you accept the call?
>
> HOSTAGE TAKER: No.
>
> OPERATOR: They will not accept the call.
>
> JOHN SMITH: I would pay and talk, but I don't have the money.
>
> HT: No.
>
> JS: It is a matter of life and death.
>
> HT: Okay, we will take the call.
>
> JS: This is John Smith from Rome, Georgia, and I want to speak to someone about some narcotics dealings.
>
> HT: We have no agents on duty today.
>
> JS: You mean to tell me that if someone's life was in danger, you don't have agents on duty?
>
> HT: That's right. You will have to call back on Monday. Call the Georgia Bureau of Investigation. (From McClure, 1994).

Cellular telephones have an added benefit. Cellular telephones are not subject to wiretapping laws, and communications over cellular telephones are not protected by Section 605 of the Communications Act of 1934. Cellular telephone communications can be monitored using a shortwave radio receiver and a scanner radio. The shortwave receiver is used to receive the base transponder side of the cellular telephone (1.705, 1.735, 1.765, or

1.825 MHz) and the scanner radio to receive the handset side of the conversation (46 and 49 MHz bands). The Communications Assistance for Law Enforcement Act of 1994 (CALEA) gives law enforcement the ability to conduct lawfully authorized electronic surveillance over a cell phone. All major cellular providers are CALEA compliant (O'Toole, 2004). Most cell phones today have SMS, or short message service, capability, which allows text messages to be sent via telephone. If an actor is reluctant to answer a phone or verbally communicate with negotiators, it may be that negotiators can establish initial communications using SMS.

The team should consider maintaining a set of pre-paid cellular telephones with a restricted number and restricted access. The situation may arise in which an actor does not have a land-line telephone and it is not possible to insert a full throw phone system. Many people today are removing their land-line phones and using only cell phones. A pre-paid cellular can be given to the actor and limit the actor's ability to use that phone to contact anyone other than the negotiators. Remember to give the actor a charger and extra batteries. Although quite new and its use not widespread, one of the coming technologies is using the Internet and e-mail for phone services. Negotiators should be aware that an actor may have this capability and negotiators may have to negotiate via the computer, or at the very least, disable the actor's computer to restrict outside communications.

Fuselier (1981/1986) has suggested that, in some situations, a bullhorn or telephone may interfere with rapport building and the development of trust. Fuselier pointed out that at times it may be preferable to negotiate face-to-face. Direct contact should be attempted only after some type of rapport has been developed through other forms of communication and should only be attempted in barricade situations. Face-to-face negotiations should only be used as a last (and unavoidable) result. If a phone system or "walkie-talkie" type system cannot be used, it is recommended that negotiators engage in voice-to-voice negotiations. With voice-to-voice negotiations, the negotiator is out of sight of the hostage taker. Voice-to-voice negotiations are somewhat less risky than face-to-face negotiations and have the added advantage of not allowing the hostage taker to watch the negotiators' facial expressions. In addition, in a voice-to-voice situation, the primary negotiator can be supported by a secondary negotiator, mental health consultant, and other team members. This support is virtually impossible in true face-to-face negotiations. If face-to-face (or voice-to-voice) negotiations are attempted, the following guidelines should be followed:

1. Get the hostage taker to agree not to harm the negotiator.

2. Do not negotiate in the face of a gun. Make the hostage taker put the gun down.

3. Never negotiate face-to-face if there is more than one hostage taker.

4. Maintain direct eye contact.

5. Always have a ready escape route.

6. Never turn your back on the hostage taker.

7. Exchange physical and clothing descriptions with the hostage taker before approaching.

8. Give the hostage taker ample body space.

To Fuselier's guidelines, we would add "wear body armor." In a recent incident in which one of the authors was involved, the subject was in an open field waving a .25 caliber pistol, threatening to shoot everyone he saw. Negotiations were conducted from a distance of 10-25 feet and from behind the door of a patrol car. Only the primary negotiator was wearing body armor (and only then because he was on duty that night). After the incident, one negotiator remarked, "we were never in any danger. That guy couldn't have hit the side of a building, much less us." On reflection, one realizes that it does not take skill to hit a person, just luck. In another, similar incident, the actor grabbed his rifle and took a shot at the negotiators before the tactical team could react and their sniper shot the actor.

Negotiators should also be familiar with the type of telephone the hostage taker is using. George Leak, a negotiator with the Alabama State Police, related an incident that almost turned to tragedy because of assumptions the police made concerning the hostage taker's telephone (1994a). Leak reported that negotiators were called to negotiate with a hostage taker who had killed his wife and barricaded himself in his house. Negotiators questioned the man's girlfriend and discovered that his telephone was in the bedroom. Negotiators asked the girlfriend how long the phone cord was. She replied, "From the wall to the night stand, that is as long as the cord is." Negotiators got the suspect on the telephone and the tactical team prepared to assault the bedroom. Just prior to the assault, one negotiator reinterviewed the girlfriend about the telephone. At this point, she said, "Oh yes, it can be used in any of the other rooms or anywhere in the house; it is a cordless telephone." The assault was canceled and several hours later, after the incident was resolved, police discovered the suspect had been using the telephone on a flat part of the roof, along with a shotgun, a 30-06 rifle, and a pistol. Had the negotiator not reinterviewed the girlfriend, the tactical team would have tried to assault the house directly in the suspect's line of fire.

Sidebar: Crisis Negotiator Equipment

Sergeant Rick Shirley currently supervises several units, including the Austin Police Department's Critical Incident Negotiation Team. He is a 20-year veteran of the Austin Police Department and 30-year veteran of law enforcement. Sergeant Shirley has responded to nearly 400 incidents in the 19 years he has been involved with critical incident negotiations. He was assigned to the FBI negotiation team at Waco, Texas, during the Branch Davidian standoff in 1993.

Hollywood movies portray negotiators as having all the latest hi-tech equipment available. Unfortunately, most law enforcement agencies do not have the equipment budget that moviemakers are fortunate to have at their disposal.

On February 28, 1993, I arrived at the ATF Negotiation Center in Waco, Texas. Negotiations were ongoing with members of a group known as the Branch Davidians. The ATF Chief negotiator was on a standard office phone and next to him was a negotiator for the Texas Department of Public Safety. Both looked pretty tired and it quickly became apparent that some different equipment was needed to establish team support.

I plugged in a small homemade blue terminal box that cost about $4.00 to make. Then I connected an inexpensive telephone adaptor plug purchased at the local electronics store to the phone headset and plugged the other end into the blue box. Four sets of headphones and a tape recorder were connected and we were immediately a fully operational negotiation operations center. A day later, technicians from the FBI's International Negotiation Team arrived on the scene and set up the most advanced equipment available at the time. They hooked it into our blue box. I looked up and there was another blue box just like it that the FBI team brought with them from their laboratory in Washington. I was very proud of that blue box. We still use it along with our state-of-the-art equipment.

In this day and age of high-tech equipment, there are many choices available to the negotiation team. Most negotiators I know are like kids in a candy store when the equipment vendors set up their displays at conferences. The boxes with all of the multi-colored switches, plugs, and video displays are very impressive. Most of the equipment displayed is well worth the money when it comes to saving lives, but not every agency can afford nor needs a $20,000 piece of equipment it may never use.

When you start acquiring equipment for your team, start with the basics. Over 19 years of responding to hostage/barricade situations, I have always had to rely at least part of the time on basic equipment I keep with me. Cellular phones, tape recorders, adaptor plugs, and headphones are very basic and can be obtained very inexpensively.

I would suggest getting a very small one-compartment tool box and fill it with inexpensive equipment that you can carry with you at all times. A cell phone, cell phone adaptor, a micro-cassette tape recorder, extra blank tapes, and spare batteries work very well with most situations you will respond to. In the event the suspect doesn't have a phone, electronic megaphones are sold for as little as $50.00 on up depending upon the features and can be easily tucked into the trunk of your car. This gives you a little extra distance and clarity to your voice while at the same time providing a safer distance between the negotiator and suspect. Another very important aspect included in the basics is clothing that identifies you as a negotiator. Unless you live in a very flat community, you are going to be called upon to negotiate with someone threatening to jump off high places to kill themselves. I can't count the number of times I have arrived on the scene with a jumper refusing to speak with officers and as I walk up they see "negotiator" on my shirt and tell the officers they want to talk to me. It's often nearly concluded when they find out you are a negotiator.

So far you are in pretty good shape equipment-wise. This equipment should take care of most situations that last an hour or two. After that you may start experiencing a few problems. You are going to have to find either a larger vehicle or a building to conduct your business from. By now if the suspect has a phone it has probably been ringing off the wall from friends and family who caught the breaking news reports. If the suspect doesn't have a phone you are probably exposed to weather conditions, the public eye, and Murphy's Law. Things start going wrong about that time and you may need more equipment options that will improve your ability to control the negotiation efforts.

This is where the expensive equipment comes in handy. I can only suggest you not run out and buy the first thing someone tries to sell you. Before your department invests in this type of equipment, shop around. Try out several available devices and see what works best for you. Get input from your SWAT team on available options that may help them as well. Choose wisely.

The negotiating team should have a desk telephone and telephone adapter for calls other than those to the hostage taker. Each team member should have a police radio. In larger departments, the team should have dedicated frequencies. Another radio option is to use a cell phone carrier that has radio phones. The team should have a toolbox with small and large wire-cutters, assorted screwdrivers (standard and Phillips head), electrical tape, pliers (long-nosed and standard), a set of open-end wrenches, duct tape, and a hammer. The negotiating team should carry an array of extension cords, portable lights, city plat and topographical maps, traffic cones, and police tape. The team should have one or two pairs of good binoculars for observation (7x35mm or 10x50mm). Finally, the team should have a *Physician's Desk Reference* (PDR) and *The Negotiator's Guide to Psychoactive Drugs* for drug use situations (while EMS may be on the scene, communication may not always be possible in a timely manner), suicides, or hostage needs (DiVasto et al., 1992; Worledge et al., 1997).

Negotiators should have a laptop computer with an Internet connection. One recent situation in the Midwest was negotiated via Internet e-mail. More probable than having to negotiate via the computer, it can be a valuable tool in intelligence gathering. For example, if the hostage taker is a cultist, terrorist, or member of another fringe group, his belief systems can be explored via Web sites on the Internet. Many far-right organizations in the United States have sites that outline and discuss their belief systems. Information can be obtained concerning medical and psychological conditions, demands, area maps, etc. Also, the Internet can be used to locate relatives, friends, and others with a connection to the hostage taker (Mullins, 1995; 1997a; 1997b; 1999). Laptops are also valuable for collating intelligence, keeping a negotiating log, providing situation updates, and carrying case history files. With the addition of a modem, most can be linked directly with the department's mainframe system and dispatch computers for checking criminal histories. Portable fax machines can be invaluable for receiving intelligence, file information, records from outside agencies, and interagency communications.

Situation Boards

It has been our experience in the many years of the negotiator competition in San Marcos that the teams that receive the higher evaluations from the judges tend to be the teams that have complete, well-organized, and understandable situation boards. The need to collect and disseminate intelligence has been discussed previously. It cannot be overemphasized that the collection and dissemination of intelligence information is worthless unless there is a way to clearly, concisely, and completely display that information where the people who need it can see it. It is imperative, for example, that the primary negotiator be able to tell at a glance what demands have been made, the deadlines for those demands, and the disposition of the demands and deadlines. The situation board must be maintained in real time and in a convenient and easily accessible location.

Situation boards can be as simple as single sheets of paper, handwritten and taped to the wall in front of the negotiator. They can be as complex as bigscreen monitors for computer projectors. The most effective situation boards, however, are white dry-erase boards with dark-colored markers. These boards are easy to maintain and change and the high contrast in background and writing make them easy to read. Headings and topic areas should be clearly marked and separated, and the person given the responsibility for maintaining the situation board should have clear, legible handwriting.

The situation board should be divided into topics. Many teams do this and have arrived at topic areas after much experimentation. Duffy (1997) recommended that the topic areas be divided into: (1) subjects, (2) hostages, (3) weapons, (4) medical history, (5) demands, (6) deadlines, (7) positive police actions, (8) delivery plan, (9) site, (10) third-party intermediaries, (11) surrender plan, (12) escape plan, (13) things to know, (14) things to avoid, and (15) important telephone numbers. Vic Bazan (2003) suggests that topic headings be (1) subjects, (2) hostages, (3) victims, (4) demands, (5) deadlines, (6) positive police actions, (7) surrender plan, (8) escape plan,

(9) delivery plan, (10) medical information, (11) weapons, (12) things we need to know, (13) things to avoid, (14) TPI's (third party intermediaries), (15) important telephone numbers, and (16) anticipated concerns/issues. Each topic area should be as complete as possible. The subject topic, for example, should include names, descriptions, clothing worn, motives, association with hostages (if any) health, criminal history, weapons, psychological status, etc. The deadline topic would contain information about the times and dates of deadlines, how the subject set the deadline, response of the authorities to the deadline, etc. The delivery plan topic would have plans for the delivery of any items to the hostage taker, time and date, items actually delivered, how they were delivered, and who accepted the items.

Teams should develop and use situation boards during training scenarios and experiment to find what works best for them. They may discover they need additional categories, or that some can be collapsed and combined. During practice and training scenarios, practice various configurations of the situation board until your team finds a configuration that is preferred. Remember, the situation board has to present information in a visually clear and readily accessible manner.

Optional Equipment

Optional equipment is where the sky is the limit. The only constraints on optional equipment are the department's budget and the team's imagination. What is listed here is the optional equipment most often carried by negotiating teams.

One of the very first purchases a negotiating team should make is a throw telephone with a substantial length (1,000 feet or more) of military-grade field cable. The throw telephone is a portable telephone that operates off an internal battery. It can replace standard telephones during negotiations. Several companies make portable telephone systems specifically for negotiators. These units include headsets for the negotiator with an on/off switch, outlets for additional headsets, jacks for external speakers, and tape-

Negotiator phone systems are self-contained systems that allow negotiators to isolate communications by the hostage taker. Any phone system should have multiple headsets so various team members can listen to both sides of a conversation. Notice in this photo the primary (right foreground), secondary (seated center), team leader (standing) and recorder (far left) all have headsets. *(A. Hanna)*

One of the advantages of self-contained phone systems is that they are portable and can be used anywhere in virtually any type of weather. *(Enforcement Technology Group, Inc.)*

recording capabilities. Some of these systems have an internal, highly sensitive microphone in the hostage taker's unit that allows the negotiators to monitor conversations even when the telephone is not in use. If a system of this type is used, the primary negotiator should not be allowed to listen to the "bug" to prevent him from inadvertently using any information learned from this "bug." Most telephone systems also contain a signaling light so team members can easily tell when the telephone is active. The wire can be marked in measured increments so when the hostage taker is on the telephone, his or her exact position can be accurately determined.

Internal "bugs" in a throw telephone must be used with discretion, as federal law regulates their use. Police are not allowed to conduct electronic surveillance of oral conversations in which there is a reasonable expectation of privacy (notwithstanding a court order—Higginbotham, 1994). If one person in a conversation agrees to monitoring, then the conversation can be monitored. When the hostage taker is talking with the police, the negotiator has agreed to have the conversation monitored. A conversation between a hostage taker and a hostage may be monitored because the police represent the interests of the hostage. However, a private conversation between two hostage takers in a home or business and outside the hearing of any hostages presents a situation in which a reasonable expectation of privacy exists. This is a Fourth Amendment issue and at least one court has ruled that in order for warrantless listening to be legal, there must be an immediate threat to the police or public (*O'Brien v. City of Grand Rapids*). Higginbotham suggests that the department's legal advisors be consulted whenever the issue of privacy is a concern.

Some throw-phone systems now have small, concealed cameras that allow responders to visually monitor events inside the situation. Although there is no case law or legal guideline, it is suspected that the same legal guidelines that apply to listening devices will prevail with visual monitoring devices. As with listening devices, care should be taken with the use of cameras. While a valuable intelligence tool, it would be easy to make a "mistake" during a conversation and say something to the actor that would indicate he is being covertly monitored. It is recommended that the monitors for these cameras be maintained away from the primary negotiator.

Along with a throw phone system, one of the first purchases the negotiating team should make when the budget permits is a negotiating vehicle (Mattman, 1991). This vehicle could be anything from a panel van obtained in an asset seizure case to a custom-ordered van costing hundreds of thousands of dollars. The Austin, Texas, negotiating team, for example, at one time used an old bookmobile. Other teams use a pickup truck with a camper shell. Other teams have vehicles that were donated by private

Negotiators often joke that their equipment (especially phone systems) have to be "SWAT proof." The reality is that SWAT often puts their officers in danger delivering equipment to the hostage taker so negotiators can peacefully resolve a high-threat situation. *(Enforcement Technology Group, Inc.)*

companies. Utility companies may also be willing to donate (or lend) an older vehicle. At the very least, this vehicle should have a small table, telephone setup, and comfortable chairs for the primary and secondary negotiators. Other equipment will depend on what can be purchased or built within budget constraints.

At the January 2000 negotiator competition in San Marcos, Texas, one team brought their new van. One striking feature of this van, which set it far above all other vans present, was the superior quality of the audio speakers. The agency had invested in a high-quality, high-fidelity audio listening system for negotiators. After just a few seconds of listening to the "hostage

taker," it was apparent that this audio system was well worth the cost. The ease in hearing and understanding what was said significantly reduced stress and tension among the negotiators. Rather than struggling to hear and understand what was said, the negotiators were able to focus more on strategy and other aspects of the communication process. The authors strongly encourage teams to spend extra money on a quality audio system. Until this demonstration, we were not

This is a recreational vehicle that was converted into a negotiating van and mobile command post. It has a slide-out room that significantly increases the available space. This van is property of the Friendswood Police Department and was obtained through a grant from the local 100 Club. *(S. Davis)*

aware of the importance of quality audio. Along with quality speakers, obtain quality headphones and noise reducing cords.

Another useful item is a remote-control bullhorn with a listening device. This can be placed close to the location and used in the event that there are no telephones, or if equipment malfunctions (and it will). The team might even consider purchasing video surveillance equipment to use in conjunction with the remote bullhorn. Monitors can be purchased that are no larger than a fat cigar and can be covertly attached to the remote bullhorn. These cameras can also be purchased in infrared and low-light versions.

A video recorder is useful for providing a historical record of negotiations. It can be set up inside the negotiating vehicle to provide a record of all actions and to supplement tape recordings. Team discussions and command decisions can be videotaped as well. Another valuable use teams have discovered for video recorders is to use them as audio recorders for telephone conversations. The videotape can run for up to six hours versus 30 to 90 minutes for audiocassettes, and is of a higher quality than audiocassette recordings.

The team should consider obtaining a closed-loop intercom system. These allow constant communication between team members, allow the entire team to stay in contact, improve communications, and save valuable time. One valuable, but often overlooked, use of a closed-loop system is to link the different response elements. Headsets can provide a communication link between the commander, patrol elements, tactical team, and negotiating team. If the hostage taker has a police-band scanner (not unusual), the intercom system will prevent the hostage taker from monitoring conversations and learning about strategies and tactics.

The negotiating team should also consider purchasing a variety of microphones. A "shotgun" microphone is the best all-purpose microphone for a negotiating team. Shotgun microphones are directional (they receive the most sound energy from one direction), can amplify sounds from a good distance (up to approximately 100 feet), can be covertly inserted, and are fairly inexpensive. The major drawback to shotgun microphones is that they are sensitive to environmental noises, especially wind noise. A "spike" microphone is designed for listening through solid walls. It is "punched" or inserted into a wall and receives sound vibrations through the other layer of wall. It does not receive well if the wall is concrete, block, or brick. The most sensitive and expensive microphone is the parabolic microphone. These microphones can receive extremely low-level sounds from several hundred yards. Parabolic microphones are extremely sensitive to environmental sounds, require a person to keep them properly "aimed," and cannot be used covertly. Body microphones can be useful for face-to-face negotiations.

A Voice Stress Analyzer (VSA) can be used to monitor hostage taker deception. Many departments use the Voice Stress Analyzer in lieu of the polygraph for detecting deception in pre-employment screening, suspect interviews, and internal affairs investigations. The negotiating team could use the Voice Stress Analyzer in a similar manner with the hostage taker, thus obtaining vital information for the negotiator. The VSA will also register deception from an audiotape. Communications can be recorded and analyzed later if it is not possible to monitor communications in real-time.

The team can also use night vision devices. Night vision devices are visual optics that collect and amplify any ambient light. People wearing these devices can see a person dressed in black on a completely moonless night. The danger with these devices is that if any light source is turned on or pointed in the wearer's direction (i.e., flashlight, room light, etc.), the wearer could experience permanent vision damage. If your department is located near a military installation, they will occasionally lend your department night vision devices during crisis situations.

On occasion, some teams have used a robot to deliver equipment, food, or other consumables to hostage takers. In general, use of these robots has not been very successful. For example, a robot was employed to deliver the throw phone at a bank situation in New York City. The hostage takers would not take the phone, believing the robot would disperse a chemical agent that would knock them out. In exercises the authors have conducted with robots, hostage takers refused to allow the robots within range, believing the machine contained various exotic devices that could be used against them. Some of these "devices" included cameras, guns, lasers, chemical agents, and to one hostage taker, radioactive X-rays (for seeing through walls) that would make him sterile. There may be instances in which the negotiating or tactical team could make use of a robot. Technology has improved robots, made them smaller, more operator friendly, and their presence less threatening. Some robots are no larger than a shoe box and resemble a small, remote-controlled car. Even micro, "spider" robots should soon be available. These robots are the size of a spider and can be

Technology does assist negotiators. One recent advance is the use of robots for intelligence gathering, delivering items to the hostage taker, and providing video of the situation. *(Enforcement Technology Group, Inc.)*

inserted into the situation under closed doors, cracks in walls, etc. They have small, fish-eye cameras with excellent resolution. Chances of the actor discovering their presence is very slight, and even if they were discovered, the actor would likely believe them to be a real spider.

A portable generator is a valuable addition for a negotiating team. It can be used to power any electrical needs in the van, such as portable heaters or air conditioners, and any other electrical needs the team might have. On some occasions, the team will not be able to negotiate from their vehicle. The generator can be used remotely to power telephones, tape recorders, and lights. Include a five-to-ten gallon reserve gasoline or diesel supply for the generator.

Ice chests and drinking water, soft drinks, instant coffee, and snack foods are valuable. In most situations, the team will spend several hours in the field. There will not be time or personnel available to run to the local convenience store and buy these items. The primary negotiator, especially, will need plenty of liquids. Most of these items are non-perishable and can be stored in the negotiating vehicle, a team member's vehicle, or at the police department. One team member can be assigned the task of buying ice on the way to the station when called out. Many teams have added a non-negotiation "runner" or "gopher" member whose job is to get food and drinks for the team, hostage taker, and hostages. In many cases, this person also has the technical expertise needed to keep equipment running.

As the team adds equipment, do not overlook the incidentals associated with that equipment. In addition to items such as lights, wire, tape, batteries, plugs, and fuses, the team should keep a small inventory of incidentals, spare parts, and assorted minutiae (screws, nails, connectors, solder, glue, etc.). At any hostage situation, anything can go wrong, and it can go wrong from the least imaginable source.

Following an incident, the team should inventory equipment and supplies, listing any that were used or expended. These items should be replaced immediately. Many teams designate one person to inventory and replace expended items. Any broken equipment should be repaired immediately. The next hostage situation is not the time to realize that the throw phone batteries are bad.

Obtaining Equipment

In today's tight economy, finding the financial resources for obtaining equipment is one of the negotiating team's most difficult tasks. Most police departments do not have the ability to provide equipment funding for everything the negotiating team needs or wants. To fulfill its equipment needs, the negotiating team must become creative.

Some equipment may be purchased through an asset seizure account. Most departments have these accounts and usually allocate these funds for special departmental needs. Asset seizure can also be used for obtaining some equipment. Telephones, microphones, tape recorders, and vehicles are all common items eventually procured by the department from criminal activity. City surplus warehouses can also be used to obtain equipment. All cities maintain an inventory of used equipment. A scavenger hunt can often locate chairs, tables, storage bins, and similar equipment. The city shop can usually provide a multitude of electrical odds and ends and spare portable generators. The key to finding this equipment is to get out and talk to people and find these unused items.

Military surplus sales can be used to purchase almost anything a negotiating team would ever need. With today's military downsizing, the government is selling and auctioning off millions of dollars worth of usable equipment. The procurement office of the nearest military installation will have information on equipment for sale, lists of auction items, and all other necessary information. The General Accounting Office in Washington, D.C. will have information on non-military government surplus.

State and federal grants can be applied for in order to obtain negotiating equipment. Recent anti-crime initiatives have provided numerous sources of funds for personnel, training, and equipment. The team should contact their department or city grant procurement office, the state criminal justice division, or the United States Department of Justice to inquire about these grants.

Many locales have "100 Clubs." These clubs are organized and supported by private citizens, each of whom pays dues of $100 per year. Once per year, departments submit proposals to the club for programs, projects, or equipment. Grants are usually for one-time purchases (salaries or long-term projects would not be within the scope of the grant) and are for items that cannot be purchased any other way. We are aware of several negotiating teams that have obtained vehicles and equipment through these grants.

Many costs can be reduced or eliminated by the team building or "kit bashing" equipment. The team can build storage bins, racks, tables, etc. in the vehicle. Electronic equipment can be modified in-house. Many business organizations will donate equipment or materials. One negotiating team visited construction sites and obtained wood scraps, nails, screws, and other materials to customize their vehicle. The total cost of vehicle modifications was zero. The negotiating team might consider following the example of a fire department that needed a new substation (which the city could not afford to build). Firefighters offered to act as contractors and construction crews on their days off to build the substation. The firefighters talked to building supply houses and got material at cost or just over cost. The city agreed and the facility was built (and custom tailored) for 70 percent less than initial bid estimates. In many areas, equipment can be modified or built using jail or prison inmates. The authors know of many teams that have had jail inmates modify or construct vehicle interiors, telephone systems, etc.

Some equipment can be obtained through loans from other agencies or businesses. Specialized equipment (i.e., night vision glasses) can be borrowed from the military. Local utilities, the telephone company, electronics outlets, and other businesses may all be willing to loan the negotiating team equipment during a crisis. When Pope John Paul II visited San Antonio, Texas, several years ago, the negotiator command post had a large bus loaned by the telephone company, equipment borrowed from four different military installations, food and supplies donated by local businesses, and other equipment from city and state shops. Before needing the equipment, the team should prepare written contracts specifying the equipment to be loaned, uses of the equipment, and damage responsibilities. If operators are needed for the equipment, this should also be included in the written agreement.

At the Branch Davidian siege in Waco, Texas, in 1993, federal authorities and negotiators borrowed equipment from many different sources, including local police departments, state offices, the military, utility companies, private businesses, and even private citizens. Fortunately, the federal authorities had prepared for this eventuality and had the necessary release forms and contracts already prepared. Provisions had also been made for equipment operators where needed.

Summary

Much of the equipment a police department can buy for a negotiating team is not absolutely necessary to the negotiators' basic mission. Much of this equipment will, however, make the negotiators more comfortable, more confident, and better able to physically and mentally withstand a prolonged negotiation situation. Some of the equipment will make the negotiator's job much easier and, in the long run, more efficient. In obtaining the equipment, the negotiating team often must use a great deal of creativity in finding and adapting equipment.

References

Bazan, V. (2003). "Situation Boards." Presentation at the annual Hostage Negotiation Seminar/Competition. Texas State University, San Marcos, TX (January).

DiVasto, P., F.J. Lanceley, and A. Gruys (1992). "Critical Issues in Suicide Intervention." *FBI Law Enforcement Bulletin* 61:13-16.

Dubina, J. (2005). "Lewis Prison Hostage-Taking Incident." Presentation at the Arkansas Association of Hostage Negotiators annual conference. Little Rock, AR (June).

Dubina, J. and R. Ragsdale (2005). "Lewis Prison Incident Debriefing." Presentation at the annual Crisis Negotiation Conference of the National Tactical Officers Association, Nashville, TN (April).

Duffy, J.E. (1997). "Situation Boards." *FBI Law Enforcement Bulletin* 66(6):17-19.

Fuselier, G.D. (1981, revised 1986). "A Practical Overview of Hostage Negotiations." *FBI Law Enforcement Bulletin* 50:12-15.

Higginbotham, J. (1994). "Legal Issues in Crisis Management." *FBI Law Enforcement Bulletin* 63(6):1-6.

Leak, G. (1994a). "Too Dangerous to Be Taken for Granted." *The U.S. Negotiator* (Winter):10.

_____ (1994b). "Should You Record Your Negotiations?" *The U.S. Negotiator* (Winter):11.

Leen, T. (1998). "Legal Issues for Hostage Negotiators." Seminar hosted by the Las Vegas Metropolitan Police Department. Las Vegas, Nevada (August).

Mattman, J.W. (1991). "Creating the Right Command Post." *The Police Chief* 58:20-23.

McClure, F. (1994). "The Takeover of the Atlanta FBI Office." *The U.S. Negotiator* (Winter):2-34.

Mullins, W.C. (1995). "The Changing Nature of Hostage Taking: New Lessons for Negotiating." Paper presented at the Society of Police and Criminal Psychology meeting, Honolulu, Hawaii (October).

_____ (1997a). *A Sourcebook on Domestic and International Terrorism: An Analysis of Issues, Organizations, Tactics, and Responses*, Second Edition. Springfield, IL: Charles C Thomas.

_____ (1997b). "Domestic Terrorism: The Far-Right in the United States." Western States Hostage Negotiators Association. Portland, OR (April).

_____ (1999). "The Current State and Future of Crisis Negotiations in America." Paper presented at the Society of Police and Criminal Psychology meeting, Port Jefferson, NY (October).

O'Brien v. City of Grand Rapids, 23 F.3d 990 (6th Cir. 1994).

O'Toole, P. (2004). "Technical Support for Crisis Negotiations." ATF Negotiator Conference. San Antonio, TX (November).

State of Texas (1989-1990). *Texas Code of Criminal Procedure*. Austin, TX: Department of Public Safety.

State of Texas (1989-1990). *Texas Penal Code*. Austin, TX: Department of Public Safety.

Worledge, J., T.J. Kane, and G.B. Saathoff (1997). *The Negotiator's Guide to Psychoactive Drugs*. Washington, DC: Federal Bureau of Investigation.

Discussion Questions

1. Copy Figure 13.1 and 13.2 for each member of your team. Ask each member to check the items he or she carries and has available. Make a team inventory of the items. What are members not carrying? What can the agency or team leader do to help ensure that each team member has all of the listed items?

2. Design a van for a hostage negotiating team.

3. Talk to the local telephone company and ask them what types of telephone systems they might have for emergency use by a hostage negotiating team.

4. Meet with military personnel in your area. Where can military surplus equipment be obtained? What is the procedure for obtaining that equipment?

5. Go to the library or get on the Internet and identify five grant sources for equipment. Identify grant sources specific to police agencies.

6. Talk to personnel from the local police department hostage negotiating team. Ask about their equipment—where it was obtained, its cost to the department, upkeep and maintenance costs, and replacement schedules.

Overview of the Tactical Team and Operations and Outside Agency Support

14

Learning Objectives

1. Describe the responsibilities of the tactical team.

2. Understand how the hostage negotiation team and tactical team work together to resolve the incident.

3. Understand the selection process for tactical team members.

4. Identify the three major structures of the tactical team.

5. Know the areas of proficiency of tactical team members.

6. Understand the role of the sniper/observer team.

7. Understand the training regimen of tactical teams.

8. Know the intelligence needs of the tactical team.

9. Understand the function and purpose of outer and inner perimeters.

10. Have a basic understanding of assault operations, including the role of each team member during the assault.

11. Understand the debate about combined versus separate hostage negotiation and tactical teams.

12. Understand the debate about whether to tell the primary negotiator that the incident is going tactical.

13. Understand the need for outside agency support, who those agencies are, and how to establish working relations with those agencies.

After drinking 15 beers and taking methamphetamine, Jason began thinking about his ex-wife and children and how his ex-wife prevented him from seeing the kids. He got angry and went to his ex-wife's house to confront her and "make her see the light" and let him have joint custody. At Brenda's (ex-wife) house, he became belligerent, argumentative, and abusive toward Brenda. Jason pulled a pistol and told Brenda that, "If I can't have them, you sure won't." A neighbor who had heard the arguing called the police, who were told upon their arrival to leave. They called the crisis response team, who set up a perimeter, developed an assault plan, and began negotiating. Several hours into the negotiations, tactical officers approached the rear of the house and discovered the two children asleep in a bedroom. Determining they could get in and rescue the children, the tactical commander developed a rescue plan. When ready, the primary negotiator got on the phone with Jason and told him his demand for cigarettes had been met and they would be thrown against the front door. At about the same time, cigarettes were thrown against the front door and tactical officers entered through a rear window into the back bedroom. While Jason was getting his cigarettes, another negotiator engaged in voice-to-voice negotiations, asking Jason if they were the correct brand. After tactical officers removed the children, this negotiator backed off and the primary negotiator dialed Jason on the phone. Negotiations and the distraction were so successful that it was several hours before Jason noticed the children were missing. When he did, he ran into the rear bedroom, angry and emotional, shouting and screaming. When he did, he ignored Brenda (in the front living room) long enough for tactical officers to get her to jump out a side window and get her to safety. When Jason returned and found Brenda gone, he became even more angry and more emotional. The negotiator called him on the phone and Jason refused to talk, calling the negotiator several unkind names and screaming about what he was going to do to the police around his house. The negotiator listened, got Jason to calm down, and then explained that if Jason did not calm down and deal with the negotiator, the tactical team would be forced to make entry and physically "take" Jason. At that, Jason calmed down, began talking to the negotiator, and surrendered a short time later.

The Tactical Team

The tactical team is a necessary component of the police response to a hostage situation. One element that is necessary before a hostage taker will negotiate is containment. Providing this containment is the responsibility of the tactical team (Jacobs, 1983). Another role of the tactical team is to prepare for the use of force, should it become necessary (Crelinsten & Szabo, 1979). As mentioned previously, one requirement for a hostage situation is that the hostage taker know that force can be used against him. Proper positioning of the tactical team makes the hostage taker aware of this. Hostage situations, in fact, are the most frequent type of situation responded to by tactical teams. Stevens and MacKenna (1989), in a national survey of tactical teams, found that 78 percent of teams were used at hostage situations and 74 percent at barricaded suspect situations (the next most frequent call-out was dignitary protection, at 44 percent).

The tactical team must have a close working relationship with the negotiation team and the command post. In addition to forcing negotiations, the tactical team has other responsibilities during a hostage situation. The tactical team has responsibility for maintaining secure inner and outer perimeters. They block and prevent escape or location movement by the hostage taker. Blocking location movement means that the tactical team isolates the hostage taker and hostages to one specific location or one specific area of a building, and keeps them contained at that location so the hostage negotiation team can control and de-escalate the situation.

The tactical team has several responsibilities at the hostage situation. They implement appropriate tactics and provide equipment needed in this high-risk situation. Indirectly, the tactical team motivates the hostage taker to negotiate. The tactical team also provides intelligence and surveillance over long periods. They perform control point missions by securing and commanding positions and keeping desired accesses clear of snipers or other gunmen. The tactical team has the responsibility for making high-risk approaches to the hostage location. If food, drink, or other items need to be delivered, it is the tactical team's role to deliver those items. If hostages are released, the tactical team ensures their safe release and containment until they can be delivered to an intelligence officer. They also ensure that hostages do not attempt to return to the hostage location. Finally, the tactical team assists and protects other police units and non-police units while on the scene at the hostage situation.

In situations in which negotiations must occur face-to-face, the tactical team provides security and cover for the negotiators. This support may be either close-in, such as surrounding the negotiator, or from a distance, such as a sniper providing cover.

Additionally, the negotiating team has the responsibility to provide continuous, updated information to the tactical team (Wargo, 1988). The negotiators must keep the tactical team updated on the hostage taker's activities and location, location of all hostages, physical descriptions and mannerisms of hostage takers, changes in mental status, and any other relevant information. The negotiators must also pass on intelligence gathered from released hostages or civilians outside the situation who have information on the interior (i.e., friends, family, workers from the building, etc.). The negotiating team coordinates the release of any hostages and the surrender of the hostage taker. Coordinating the release of hostages or the surrender of the hostage taker may seem like a simple matter. However, this is one of the more difficult tasks for both teams. For the tactical team, the surrender phase is the most dangerous time of the entire incident (Moore, 2005). The operations of the tactical team are predicated on the instructions given to the hostage taker. Not only must clear and explicit instructions be given to the hostage taker, but the communications and coordination between the negotiators and the tactical team must also be clear and explicit. The tactical team usually determines the exact procedures for the release of hostages. These instructions must be relayed to the negotiating team, who must pass them on to the primary negotiator, who must pass them on to the hostage taker. Once the actual release is in place, this information must follow the reverse path to the tactical team, who perform hostage apprehension. One small mistake, error, or miscommunication could result in harm to a hostage or a major setback to negotiation efforts.

Linear versus Parallel Approach to Crisis Response

It is helpful to think of the tactical team and negotiating team as two legs of a crisis response unit (the third leg being the command element). Negotiators and tactical teams do not operate separately. It requires both to resolve a crisis situation. Negotiators like to think they can resolve a crisis incident without the use or assistance of the tactical element. Likewise, tactical officers like to think they can resolve an incident without the use of negotiators. This type of thinking is linear, in that it is all or nothing. A crisis situation can be resolved through negotiations *or* through the application of force.

The reality is that the successful resolution of a crisis situation requires the parallel application of resources. The tactical team and negotiation team have to work together, applying their assets from both sides of the actor, "squeezing him in a vise" between the two units. The hostage taker has to understand that if he does not talk with the negotiators, he will have to deal with the tactical team. At the same time, if he is talking with the negotiator, the tactical team will not assault or employ other means to forcibly resolve the situation. The hostage taker also has to be made aware that if he becomes violent or harms hostages, the tactical team will quickly resolve the situation (and there are, of course, exceptions to this automatic "green light" rule).

Selection of Tactical Team Members

Careful selection of tactical team members is critical to their later proficiency (Cole, 1989; MacKenna & Stevens, 1989) and to avoid potential liability issues (Mijares & Perkins, 1994). For example, in *Moon v. Winfield* (1974) and *City of Winter Haven v. Allen* (1989), the courts ruled that a department can be found negligent if it fails to reassign an unfit officer to a position in which he or she is not likely to be confronted with situations in which he or she has performed poorly, and that departments can be held liable if high-risk actions are conducted by personnel who are not trained, and if detailed planning and coordination of effort is not established. One of the authors is currently engaged in research to examine selection criteria for tactical officers. One preliminary finding is that there is little consistency across departments in the selection of tactical team members. Some general guidelines, however, can be offered in regard to the selection of team members. Tactical team members must first be volunteers with three to five years of service on the department. They should have a minimum of two years working patrol. The officers should have an exemplary work history with no justified complaints, especially those of unnecessary force. The officers should also have a consistent record of productivity.

The applicants should be in outstanding physical condition. They should have a high level of stamina, be physically strong, and in excellent aerobic shape. Many of the duties of the tactical team require these physical skills. Prospective team members should bring these skills to the team and maintain these skills once on the team.

Supervisor evaluations should be assessed. The applicant should have outstanding marks in all areas of evaluation. The tactical team leader should meet with the applicant's supervisor and discuss the applicant's ability to deal with stress and relate to the public and other officers. The applicant's demeanor,

bearing, and communication skills should also be analyzed. The supervisor should be questioned about the applicant's level of common sense, emotional stability, and self-confidence (MacKenna & Stevens, 1989). The supervisor should be asked whether he or she believes the officer would be a good tactical team member and could maintain perspective on what the job is about (that is, is the applicant likely to become a "John Wayne"-type and use tactical team membership to fulfill a "macho" fantasy?).

Tactical team members must be prepared for and ready to respond to a variety of situations. This includes being familiar with and knowing how to operate a wide variety of weapons and equipment. *(Photograph by Ronald F. Becker)*

The applicant should be given a psychological evaluation (Drovin & Adams, 1992). Many of the issues discussed with the supervisor should also be examined by the department psychologist. Mental stability, stability of personality, interpersonal relations, ability to communicate, and ability to handle stress are areas on which the psychologist should concentrate. The team members should also be given the opportunity to interview the applicants. The ability to be a team player, to communicate, and control stress should be emphasized in this interview.

Finally, applicants should participate in a series of structured role-play exercises, preferably with tactical team members. These exercises should be standardized and the applicant examined for ability to handle stress, think rationally and make decisions, and work as a team member. Ideally, tactical team members should assess the applicant. It is crucial that the applicant work well with the team and that the team work well with the applicant.

Tactical team members must receive training in tactical operations prior to their use in the field. This training should be conducted by experienced, well-trained personnel, and should be specific to their assignment (*City of Canton v. Harris*, 1989; Mijares & Perkins, 1998). The training should include, but not necessarily be limited to, instruction in: equipment, basic operations, legal issues, rappelling, team operation and movement, searches, sniper operations, less-than-lethal technology, entry and crisis-entry techniques, night operations, raids, weapon proficiency, bomb scene management, combat shooting, surveillance techniques, intelligence analysis, dynamic entry, defensive tactics, pyrotechnics, raids, and physical training (Mijares et al., 2000). Additionally, the tactical team should be trained in negotiations and negotiating techniques (Greenstone, 1995). As part of the training, the tactical team should conduct exercises with other elements of the agency that will respond to crises (i.e., negotiators, EOD) (Snow, 1996).

Tactical Team Structure

Three major structures comprise the tactical team. One part of the tactical team is responsible for perimeter control. These team members are responsible for establishing and maintaining inner and outer perimeters. While team members may not actually provide perimeter security, they must arrange to have manpower posted in the proper places with the proper instruction. A second component of the tactical team is the apprehension/assault team. Members of this sub-team make an undetected approach to the location, plan and prepare for the release of hostages, and make an assault if necessary. A third component of the tactical team is the sniper/observer sub-team. The sniper/observer sub-team has two responsibilities. One is to provide intelligence on factors present at the location. These factors may include physical layout, placement of walls, furniture, specific location of hostages and hostage takers, clothing (including any changes in clothing that may be made), and mental state of the hostages and hostage takers. This task has been enhanced by recent developments in technology, such as thermal imaging devices, night telescopes that magnify ambient starlight, and a wide variety of electronic eavesdropping devices. A second responsibility of the sniper/observer team is to prepare for a "shot" on the hostage taker. Greenstone (1998) suggests that EMS personnel be trained in tactical operations and be integrated into the team for tactical emergency medical support. In addition, EMS personnel can be used to provide information on medications and drugs used by hostage takers or hostages, recommendations concerning medical issues, and assessment of released hostages or hostage takers.

To perform the required functions, members of the tactical team need to be proficient in many different areas (Flaherty, 1988; Kolman, 1982; Mattoon, 1987; Miller, 1979). They must be proficient with a myriad of weapons, from specialized weapons like grenade launchers, to rifles, shotguns, and automatic weapons, as well as a wide range of handguns. Most tactical teams train with a large variety of weapons. Not only must they be able to use these weapons, they must know how the weapons operate and the capabilities of those weapons. There is no predicting the type of weapon a hostage taker will have. The tactical team must be prepared for anything—they need to know the dangers to hostages and themselves, and how weapons may be used. An example in the authors' personal experience can illustrate this point. A hostage taker threatened to detonate a hand grenade if his demands were not met. The tactical team assessed the situation and called in an explosive ordnance disposal team (EOD) to advise them. Upon inspection, the EOD team determined the grenade to be a harmless smoke grenade, at which time the tactical team made quick entry and overpowered the subject. Many would argue that there was nothing incorrect in the tactical team's operation. The authors would argue differently. The tactical team unnecessarily prolonged the incident and placed police officers, hostages, and the hostage taker in unnecessary jeopardy by not knowing the weapon the hostage taker was using. A basic understanding of military grenades and proper disarming techniques would have immediately shown the tactical team that the hostage taker had a nonlethal weapon and could be quickly and easily neutralized.

Many less-than-lethal and nonlethal weapons are available to the police and tactical team. The selection and use of these weapons will depend on the seriousness of the offense, the threat to the officers, and the degree of resistance offered by the hostage taker (*Graham v. Connor*, 1989). A failure on the part of the tactical team to not consider the use of less-than-lethal and/or non-lethal weapons may even expose the agency to liability (*O'Neal v. DeKalb County, Georgia*, 1988). Some of these alternatives include CS/CN gas (tear gas), oleoresin capsicum (OC) or pepper gas, "flash-bang" grenades, smoke grenades, shotgun pancake rounds, Taser weapons, and nets. Some of these weapons have only minimal applicability to the tactical team when an assault is necessary. Some, such as the "flash-bang" grenade (which emits a deafening noise at 220 decibels and a blinding light of 20,000 foot-candles, meant to temporarily disorient people within the area of use) and the smoke grenade can help the tactical team when they enter the hostage location. Other diversionary or stun munitions can also be employed.

Starflash grenades (with seven to 12 individual submunition bursts; this disorients the suspect and is similar to a string of fireworks being exploded), smoke and other multiflash grenades, and stun plates (a flat stun device that can be inserted under a door or window) can all disorient the suspect. To make entry, the tactical team can use a variety of devices to blow open doors or windows. For example, Federal Bureau of Prisons tactical teams carry exothermic forced entry torches, which allows them to easily and rapidly cut open metal doors. CS/CN and pepper gas are less useful during an assault. They require the tactical team to wear special equipment (gas masks) that limits mobility and vision, and they may produce illness or death in the hostages or hostage taker. Also, their use is affected by environmental factors that can reduce their effectiveness. The authors have been involved in three incidents in which CS gas was employed by a tactical team. In one case, the wind blew the CS gas back onto the tactical team, immobilizing several team members who were not wearing gas masks. In the second incident, the CS round went completely through the intended house and into a second house not involved in the incident. In the third incident, the gas canister landed on a sofa, burning down the entire structure.

Once inside the suspect's location, the tactical team can use a variety of less-than-lethal and/or non-lethal weapons to overpower the suspect. Less-than-lethal ammunition can be used in standard-issue weapons. Pancake and rubber bullets, dowels fired from 37mm gas guns, and plastic projectiles can

The tactical team performs many dangerous missions during a crisis incident and may have to locate the suspect before negotiations can begin. *(Enforcement Technology Group, Inc.)*

be fired at the suspect. In most circumstances, these will stun and momentarily disable the suspect without causing death. The tactical team can also use a launchable net device, which is fired from a weapon. The net envelopes the suspect, restricting movement and preventing the suspect from reaching for a firearm or escaping. The tactical team can also use a Taser device. The Taser is used by many police departments today. It is a small, hand-held device that, when pressed against a person (some models fire small darts, extending the range), delivers a large electric voltage charge at low wattage to the person, temporarily paralyzing him or her.

Many other less-than-lethal and nonlethal weapons are currently under development and may be available to police tactical teams within the next few years (Pilant, 1993). One is a sticky foam that is under development at

Sandia National Laboratory in Albuquerque, New Mexico. This foam literally "glues" a suspect into immobility. Fired from a special dispenser, the foam entangles the suspect, acting like a super glue. The foam can immobilize a suspect from as far as 35 feet. The foam has been developed and is ready for use. The problem at present is that there is no non-toxic solvent available to remove the foam.

Research is also underway on chemicals that can immediately immobilize a suspect. One promising drug is Lofentanyl, a Fentanyl derivative. Lofentanyl acts as a central nervous system depressant, much like a surgical anesthetic. The current problem with chemicals is the slow onset time (10-20 seconds). The chemical would have to onset within microseconds in order to be useful for tactical team operations.

Other promising less-than-lethal and nonlethal avenues include distraction and disorientation devices such as high-intensity strobe lights, loud noise machines, ionizing and non-ionizing electromagnetic waves, a magnetophosphene gun, and a thermal gun. The magnetophosphene gun would make the suspect "see stars" by "delivering what would feel like a blow to the head" (Pilant, 1993) The thermal gun would instantly raise the suspect's body temperature to 107 degrees, incapacitating him or her. Although these devices are still in the developmental stages, they do hold promise for future tactical team use at hostage situations.

Devices that can be used by the tactical team to assist in locating the suspect inside a structure include thermal imaging devices such as FLIR (Forward Looking InfraRed, which detects a heat signature) and low-range radar that can detect people through solid walls. The team could also use various resonance-type devices that help identify the composition of walls and other structural material.

Possibly the most difficult function of the tactical team is that of sniper/observer. Sniper/observers work as two-person subunits. Both members of this subunit are trained snipers and they alternate roles, one as sniper, the other as observer. Not all tactical team members will be trained in sniper/observer functions, as this is a specialized function within the tactical team.

The tactical team will be trained in making rapid, safe, and disorienting explosive entries using diversionary devices. This involves expertise in explosive ordnance, structural integrity, shape charges, and blast effects. The tactical team must also be familiar with a variety of explosive ordnance the hostage taker may employ, including the differences between high and low explosives, home-made explosives, detonators, initiators, and booby-trap devices.

Tactical team members must be experts in close reconnaissance/scouting operations. They must be able to approach the hostage location undetected, remain in a secure and safe position, and provide intelligence on interior aspects of the location (i.e., placement and construction of walls, doors, windows, partitions, furniture, etc.). Training should include surveillance techniques, ambush operations, and counter-ambush techniques.

Finally, tactical team members must be experts in stealth and dynamic entry techniques. In most hostage situations that are not peacefully resolved, the tactical team must physically assault the location. Unlike military assaults, the tactical team must be able to make the entry, rescue hostages, secure the hostage taker, and make an exit without endangering themselves, the hostages, bystanders, or the hostage taker. This requires specialized skills that military assault teams are not prepared to utilize.

The tactical team should be outfitted with pistols, machine pistols, shotguns, and rifles. Each team member should carry a pistol (semi-automatic) and, depending upon their function within the team, one other weapon. Each member should wear a bulletproof vest and have a protective shield. The vest should be a level IV vest with ceramic or metal insert plates. Members should have gas masks, nylon web gear, and other specialized equipment as the mission demands (Hansen, 1988; Pilant, 1992).

Intelligence Needs

The tactical team must have accurate, reliable, timely, and complete intelligence in order to perform their tasks (Hillman, 1988). While the intelligence needs of the tactical team are no more important than the needs of the negotiating team, the tactical team needs more intelligence than the negotiating team. The negotiating team needs intelligence on the hostage taker and hostages and, in some cases, intelligence on the location.

Without proper intelligence, the tactical team operates in the dark. If the tactical team operates without relevant, timely, accurate, and complete intelligence, people die. Many police departments could open their own files for "locker room tales" of operating without complete intelligence. Three military operations illustrate the point. On March 27, 1945, Task Force Baum, 294 men and 53 vehicles operating on the orders of General George S. Patton, crossed enemy lines to rescue 1,500 German-held American prisoners of war. Following the liberation of the American prisoners and on return to Allied lines, the Germans caught the raiding party. All 1,500 prisoners of war, and all but one of the rescue party, were killed or captured (McGeorge, 1983). Task Force Baum lacked accurate intelligence—on German deployments, weapons, and strength. On November 21, 1970, a Green Beret-led rescue effort was launched to free American prisoners of war at Son Tay, North Vietnam. The raiders encountered an empty camp. On May 15, 1975, United States Marines stormed Koh Tang Island and attempted to rescue American seamen held aboard the Mayaguez, a U.S. merchant shop, by the North Koreans. Fifteen Marines were killed, three disappeared, and 50 were wounded. No seamen were rescued. Both the Son Tay and Koh Tang Island rescue attempts lacked timely and accurate intelligence (McGeorge, 1983; Moorer, 1982; Rowan, 1975).

Sidebar: Negotiating for SWAT

Sergeant Donnie Manry is a 23-year veteran of the Bryan, Texas, Police Department. He has served in many capacities, including uniformed patrol, vice/narcotics, sergeant of the personnel services unit, accreditation manager, and with the internal affairs unit. He is trained in SWAT tactics and was part of the entry team for three years while assigned to narcotics enforcement. He has served with the emergency response unit since 1998 as team leader of the eight-member crisis negotiation team.

Emergency response units have come a long way since their inception during the early 1970s. In their infancy, conflicts could often be found within the tactical and negotiations subunits, which prevented either from achieving maximum effectiveness. Some conflicts were caused by the opposing paradigms of team commanders, each thinking that the situation needed to be resolved by their team and not the other. It was this type of thinking, usually fueled by strong egos, that had a propensity to create "turfism" and bitterness between the two teams. Each team often believed that an incident could be resolved by their team independently of their counterpart.

Emergency response teams of today have evolved into highly technical, highly trained units with a symbiotic relationship. Each team recognizes the need for the other and the necessity to train and work together to resolve an incident. There are many ways the two teams can complement each other when working to resolve an incident. Negotiators depend on tactical coverage for security, which allows them to concentrate solely on negotiating with the subject. Negotiators can also use tactical personnel to apply pressure to a subject who may not want to talk with negotiators. Oftentimes requesting movement of tactical personnel or equipment outside of the target will cause the subject to initiate contact with negotiators in order to find out "what is going on."

While the primary mission of the negotiator is to safely resolve an incident without tactical intervention, there are incidents that clearly dictate that tactical intervention is necessary. In those cases, the primary mission of the negotiation team shifts to that of tactical support, providing intelligence, and distraction for the tactical team.

Negotiators can be a great asset to tactical officers. Barricaded or suicidal subjects provide several good examples of how negotiators are able to support tactical operations during an incident. Establishing a secure inner perimeter utilizing tactical personnel is obviously critical for the safety of all involved. Once the perimeter is secured, negotiators can safely move personnel closer to the objective where they are able to deploy bullhorns or loudspeaker systems. Quite often the bullhorn or loudspeaker system is needed to establish initial communication, but just as important, the continuous loud noise from these systems can be used to hide any noise created by tactical operations, such as team movement or installation of monitoring equipment, such as video or audio surveillance devices. Negotiators can also use a combination of loudspeakers, cellular phones, throw phones, and phones already at the target location to create timely diversions/distractions allowing for tactical movement or tactical operations. Careful choreography, enabling all of the above items to simultaneously activate, can create quite a distraction inside the target location.

Once initial communication/rapport has been established with a subject, the negotiator may be able to re-establish contact with the subject with ease. This can also be very beneficial to tactical operations because the negotiator has the ability to distract the subject with dialogue while tactical operations are performed. This causes divided attention on the part of the subject and thereby increases the subject's reaction time to any tactical entry.

While most incidents nationwide are resolved through negotiations, there are incidents that are deemed non-negotiable or due to exigency require an immediate tactical resolution. Negotiators can be of great value to tactical operations in these cases as well. Many negotiation teams have specialized equipment with sound amplification capability and the ability to monitor any sounds inside the target location. Many times negotiators are able to determine where the subject is located within the target location. This information can be extremely beneficial to a tactical team that has decided to make entry. Negotiators, for example, can advise when the subject is in the front portion of the target, thereby allowing tactical officers to make entry at the rear of the target.

By using their expertise with telephone systems, negotiators may also be able to guide the subject into a particular area of the target location. For example, negotiators are able to determine that a cordless phone, a cellular phone, and one wall-mounted telephone are inside the target area. In addition, they have also deployed their "throw phone" into the target. Negotiators have the knowledge to shut down both the cellular phone and the cordless phone independently of the wall-mounted phone. Most negotiation teams also have their throw phone cables marked in a manner that enables them to determine how many feet inside the target their throw phone is located, i.e., five feet inside the target. Given this scenario, negotiators may be able to identify where the subject is located within the target area by which phone the subject used. Negotiators are also able to monitor the sound amplification equipment (mentioned earlier) in order to pinpoint an area of the target occupied by the subject.

As a last resort, negotiators may be directed to manipulate the subject into an area where a scout/sniper team has a clear view of the subject. These cases are rare in negotiations; however, they do occur. Negotiators have the skills and training to accomplish this mission as well. A properly trained and equipped negotiations team can be the most valuable asset available to tactical operations. Experienced commanders recognize this and rely upon the recommendations of the negotiations team to formulate their strategies as well as notifying negotiations prior to tactical action. This interaction between negotiations and tactical commanders ensures that the teams are working in unison and ensures that the actions of the teams do not negatively affect the other team. We have come a long way in 30 years—I wonder what we'll say 30 years from now.

The tactical team needs intelligence on the hostage taker, just as the negotiating team does. Many of the intelligence needs for the tactical team are more critical than for the negotiating team. The tactical team needs intelligence on the hostage taker's criminal history. An old psychological maxim is that the best predictor of future behavior is past behavior. Knowing the criminal history of the hostage taker is vital for determining how the hostage taker might be armed, his potential for violence, and what actions he might take if assaulted. Likewise, the tactical team needs to know of any military, survivalist, or special forces training the hostage taker might have received. This information indicates the hostage taker's level of expertise in resisting an assault as well as his or her determination to fight if assaulted. A 1984 FBI incident in Dade County, Florida, is a prime example of this point. FBI agents attempted to stop two armed suspects and became involved in a gun battle. Two federal agents were killed and several others were wounded. These casualties were caused by two men who had received military special forces training and were determined to survive. One remarkable aspect of this incident was that one of the suspects received a fatal round in the first seconds of the incident, yet remained alive for another four minutes and was the suspect responsible for killing the two federal agents. Had the FBI agents had intelligence on the suspects, such as prior military training and psychological profiles, the agents would probably have used different tactics and there would have been no agent deaths. This example is not presented to second-guess or criticize the actions of the agents—it is presented merely to show the value of intelligence for the tactical team. The tactical team needs to know all weapons and ammunition available to the hostage taker. The armament of the hostage taker plays a large role in determining assault tactics. It also allows for a measure of safety when the incident is resolved and people are exiting the location.

The tactical team needs to have complete and accurate descriptions of the clothing worn by the hostage taker and hostages. This intelligence has to be updated continually, because the hostage taker and hostages sometimes change clothing. In the past, several hostages have been inadvertently killed after being forced to trade clothes with the hostage taker. During the assault or sniper operations, the tactical team, operating on the intelligence they had, killed hostages instead of hostage takers. Continuous updates can help prevent these tragedies. The tactical team should not be allowed to conduct an operation unless they receive last-minute updates confirming the identities of all parties inside the situation.

The tactical team should know the mental condition of the hostage taker, his emotional state, and his stress level. The hostage taker's physical condition is also valuable intelligence. A hostage taker who is physically worn down will not be as alert and prepared as a hostage taker who is fresh and rested. The mental condition of the hostage taker is important for many reasons. First, the paranoid schizophrenic or antisocial hostage taker may resist more than other hostage takers. Second, the depressed hostage taker may desire "suicide by cop" and do something to get the police to kill him while having no intention of doing any harm to the police. Third, a highly emotional hostage taker may let his anger influence his actions, or he may not follow directions given by the tactical team.

Knowledge of medical and employment history is also beneficial to the tactical team. Medical conditions and relations with supervisors and co-workers can indicate how the hostage taker will respond if assaulted. Family history and known associates are needed by the tactical team. Personal and social relationships can provide information on possible reactions of the hostage taker if assaulted.

In addition to detailed information on the hostage taker, the tactical team needs complete information on the hostage taker's location. The more complex the structure, the more detailed information the tactical team must have. Assaulting an office complex is much more difficult than assaulting a house or convenience store. Stairways, halls, partitions, and egress routes that could be used by the hostage taker must all be considered.

The tactical team needs, if possible, complete up-to-date blueprints of the hostage location. They need to know the structure's construction; location of power, water, and gas cutoffs; interior construction; location or presence of burglar bars, steel doors, etc.; location and height of fences or other obstacles; and fire doors and fire stops. Blueprints should be augmented by residents or workers. Many instances have been reported of a tactical team assaulting a target location using available blueprints, only to discover that the structure had been changed considerably since they had been made. Residents and workers can supplement the blueprints and provide updated information. Many assault teams use tape and lay out a full-scale model of the assault operation before entering. A model requires complete and accurate information.

Another valuable piece of information that residents and workers can provide is the location of portable walls, furniture, plants, and other obstacles that could hinder the tactical team and help the hostage taker. Furniture and other portable objects can be as formidable as any permanent part of the structure. Blowing a door for a quick entry is useless if the tactical team cannot enter and clear the room because metal desks are in the way. Organizations are becoming more concerned than ever about internal security in regard to attacks on their employees. Many of these organizations arrange furniture and portable walls, to make it difficult for people to walk through the facility unimpeded. Temporary obstacles, such as those mentioned above, in addition to providing a degree of security for organizational personnel, will also hinder tactical team efforts to assault the location. In some instances, they may assist the tactical team by providing concealment and cover. In any event, however, the tactical team must know the location of these obstacles.

The team must locate any security systems (internal and external) and dogs or other noise-making animals. Security systems must be disarmed or neutralized, especially those that activate and automatically lock doors and windows. Animals will make noise, alerting the hostage taker to the tactical team's presence. While dogs are the primary concern, other animals can be equally volatile. Chickens, ducks, pigs, other livestock, and other animals can make enough noise to alert a hostage taker (for example, in various parts of the world such as China and Costa Rica, geese and ducks are used as "burglar alarms"). In addition, animals can attack the tactical team as it prepares for the assault and interfere with the assault. Friendly animals may be curious or want to play. In rare instances, some animals can be used to the tactical team's advantage. Livestock (horses and cows), for example, can be used to provide concealment and cover during an approach. At the Branch Davidian compound in Waco, Texas (February 1993), the initial assault team approached the compound in pick-up trucks and livestock trailers. Had Koresh and the Davidians not had prior knowledge of the assault, this tactic might have worked effectively.

Situation Security

One responsibility of the tactical team is to provide security for the entire incident (Maksymchuk, 1982). Tactical team members might not physically provide the security, but they will assign patrol officers to these functions based upon tactical team recommendations.

A hostage incident typically has two perimeters—an outer perimeter and an inner perimeter. The outer perimeter is the incident's controlled, outermost boundary. The purpose of this perimeter is to restrict vehicle and foot traffic into the incident. The outer perimeters should be established far enough from the incident that no traffic or citizens are in danger (Biggs, 1987). Only approved members of the police, media, or other response personnel are allowed past the outer perimeter. The area between the outer and inner perimeters contains the command post, negotiators, media, EMS, fire department, and utility workers. This perimeter is usually well out of the hostage taker's sight and, if space permits, is out of range of any firearms the hostage taker may possess. Figures 14.1 and 14.2 illustrate the arrangement of two common situation perimeters and command post locations.

The inner perimeter is usually maintained by the tactical team and is close to the hostage location. This perimeter is designed to control ingress and egress to the target area. The only persons allowed inside this perimeter are the assault and apprehension teams. Depending on the hostage location, the inner perimeter can be as close as the walls of a house, or as far as a city block. At the incident's outset, the inner perimeter may be rather large and then shrink in size as the incident progresses, as the tactical team gathers intelligence, or as the tactical team prepares for an assault.

Figure 14.1
Location of Elements at a Hostage Situation with a Fixed Command Post

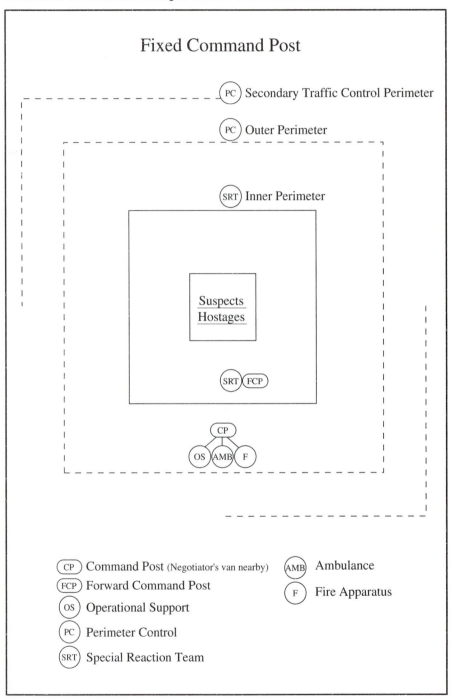

Source: Mullins, W.C.

Figure 14.2
Location of Elements at a Hostage Situation with a Mobile Command Post.

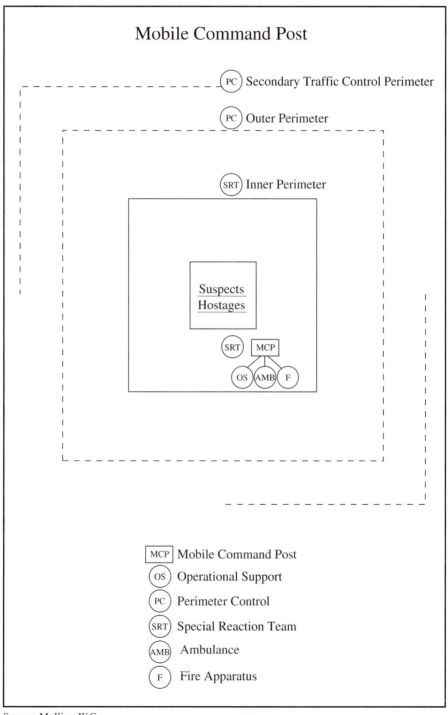

Source: Mullins, W.C.

Assault Operations

If the tactical team is called upon to resolve the hostage incident, the most likely course of action is a physical assault on the location. An assault operation is one of the most dangerous operations in which the tactical team can engage (Hudson, 1989), and next to sniper operations, is a last resort (Whittle, 1988). The assault team must physically confront and gain control of the hostage taker, while at the same time ensuring the safety and security of the hostages (Kaiser, 1990). An assault is also the most complex operation for the tactical team. It requires careful planning and split-second execution. Although there are many things that can go wrong during an assault operation, the courts (in *Taylor v. Watters*, 1987) have provided support for assault operations. In this case, the court said, "It is in the nature of police work that the pressure becomes intense and decisions must be made quickly. . . . Such mistakes made in the best judgment of the trained police officer should not be the province of constitutional tort suits." An assault by the tactical team requires a minimum of six team members.

One of the specialties of the tactical team is effecting the rescue of released hostages or hostages who manage to escape. *(Enforcement Technology Group, Inc.)*

One member is the team leader. This person commands and controls the assault team and assault operations. His or her job is to implement tactics and organize the assault, communicate intelligence to the command post and tactical team commander, and make on-scene tactical decisions. He or she must constantly be prepared to change assault operations if the situation changes or if intelligence is inaccurate.

A second team member is the point man. This person leads the team in the assault. His responsibilities include team movement and forward search. He is responsible for the entire assault team's security. He must determine precisely the location of all hostage takers and hostages, and check for booby traps, obstacles, and other obstructions the assault team might face.

The third assault team member is the point cover man. His role is to provide backup for the point man. If the point man becomes incapacitated, the point cover assumes point responsibilities. As point cover man, his responsibilities include communicating between point and the rest of the team, providing cover for the point man, and relaying information from the team leader. This officer should possess adequate strength and agility to carry the point man in the event of a wounding or other injury.

The fourth assault team member is the observer/cover man. He provides backup for the point cover man and his responsibilities include assuming point cover if the point cover man has to take over point, covering the point cover man, and taking control of the apprehensions.

The rear guard, the fifth member of the assault team, provides security for the entire team. He must provide close fire support for the team and transfer prisoners and hostages.

One of the most dangerous jobs performed by the tactical team is making a forced entry when a suspect refuses to negotiates or if they begin injuring hostages. *(Enforcement Technology Group, Inc.)*

The final team member is the marksman. He provides intermediate and long-range defense for the entire team. One important role the marksman provides is target intimidation. If the hostage taker is aware that the marksman is prepared to shoot, the hostage taker may not resist when assaulted, or may even surrender should an assault begin.

Sniper Operations

The loneliest job on the tactical team (and the entire police force) may belong to the sniper/observer unit. The sniper must keep the hostage taker in his crosshairs for several hours at a time and be ready to fire on a moment's notice. If the sniper is employed, there is only one possible outcome to the situation: a human being is killed.

The media is full of fictionalized accounts of snipers shooting targets at ranges of several hundred to several thousand yards. While these may occur in the minds of fiction writers, the police sniper usually operates at a range of fewer than 100 yards. Any distance over 100 yards makes the probability of a take-down shot unrealistic. Most excellent sniper rifles are accurate to within one-half to one inch at 100 yards (Plaster, 1993). Any greater distance has too much room for error. Even the advances in ammunition technology (e.g., the new "long-range projectiles") do not resolve the distance problem. There still remain too many variables that can affect the long-range shot. The longer the range, the more difficult it is to account for environmental variables such as wind drift (movement of the air that pushes the projectile off-course). Also, the longer the range, the greater the possibility of the target moving during projectile travel time. Even though we are talking about milliseconds, even the slightest movement of the target can significantly alter the shot. Finally, and perhaps most crucially, the longer the range, the greater the probability of sniper mistakes. Basic physiological processes, such as heartbeat, cause imperceptible movements in the sniper rifle. As range increases, these slight movements become magnified in terms of shot placement. In one case, the hostage taker had taped himself to the hostage (using duct tape), including taping his gun hand to the hostage's head so that if the police attempted to shoot him, involuntary muscle contractions would cause the gun to fire, killing the hostage. The sniper had to make the "perfect shot," hitting the suspect in the brainstem, immediately stopping any neural transmissions to the lower body. The sniper made this shot from approximately 60 yards away. Improvements in weapon and ammunition technology do not account for, nor offset, these other issues in sniping. Most snipers use a .308 caliber bolt-action scoped rifle, although a few use a heavier caliber weapon. Ammunition is match grade, manufactured to extremely close tolerance. Each bullet in a batch is almost identical in weight, powder load, and size to every other bullet in that batch.

The sniper's most difficult job is not in making the shot, but in waiting to make the shot. The sniper will get in position when the tactical team arrives at the hostage situation. He will then have to wait in position for several hours, constantly watching the target, ready for the command to shoot. Many police officers have the inner resolve to make the shot when ordered, yet few have the inner resolve to remain in one position for many hours waiting to take the shot. Because of the tasks required of the sniper, police snipers should have excellent marksmanship skills, be in top physical condition, have excellent vision (without glasses), be emotionally stable, and possess excellent decision-making skills (Gnagey, 1984).

An incident that occurred several years ago in Georgia illustrates the difficulties faced by a sniper. In this incident, negotiators talked with a barricaded suspect for several hours. At one point, the suspect wanted his pet dog placed in the yard. Officers tied a rope around the dog's collar and "pitched" the dog near the suspect's house. The suspect called for the dog, but the dog ran back toward the police. Upon seeing that, the suspect burst out of the house unexpectedly and began firing at officers. Two of the rounds missed the primary negotiator and a tactical team member by inches. Before the suspect could fire any more rounds, the tactical sniper located across the street shot and killed him. For several hours the sniper had been patiently "sighting" on the house for the possibility of just such an action by the suspect. Had the sniper not been prepared, several officers could have been injured or killed (McClure, 1994).

The training of police snipers should include a multitude of high-stress shooting exercises. Plaster (1990) reported that in a moderate-level stress shooting exercise, one in 12 police snipers failed to make a simple shot. Without high-stress training, a greater number than one in 12 could be expected to miss the shot in an actual situation. No room for this type of mistake exists for the police sniper.

The second member of the sniper unit is the observer. He is armed with a pair of binoculars (7x35mm or 10x50mm) and a spotting scope (30x). The observer has many responsibilities during the hostage situation, including watching the hostage taker, giving intelligence to the tactical team commander, determining engagement priorities, announcing target indicators, estimating wind, range, and angle, operating communication equipment, identifying target priorities, and observing and reporting bullet impact. One important observer duty is to update intelligence to the tactical team commander. The observer and commander must be in constant contact on intelligence matters. The observer is one of the few people who can verify physical and structural intelligence, report changes in the situation, and provide constant updates on specific locations. During an assault, the observer must be in a position to give continual updates to the assault team. Without his input, the assault team will be operating blind. During protracted incidents, the observer and sniper will alternate duties to reduce fatigue.

Special Issues

Historically, there have been two issues concerning the operations of the tactical and negotiations teams that received a great deal of debate, both academically and practically. Both of those debates have been resolved informally, but are important enough to deserve attention here. They concerned first, whether the tactical and negotiation team should be one integrated unit or two separate units and second, whether the primary negotiator should be told when a tactical resolution was going to occur.

The negotiating and tactical teams should be independent entities with different personnel and different commanders. The duties, responsibilities, and goals of each team are different. These differences go beyond the basic duties each performs, and involve a difference in the psychological and emotional approach team members take to a hostage situation (Olin, 1980; Roberts, 1988; Mullins, 2000; 2003). Most crisis response units have two separate teams. There are, however, a few agencies that still combine personnel into a single crisis response team.

The tactical team prepares for a physical resolution to the incident. Team members train, prepare, and respond to a hostage situation anticipating a physical confrontation. Their approach is to use force to bring resolution. The negotiating team, on the other hand, trains, prepares, and responds for a non-physical resolution. Each team mentally prepares for a different type of resolution. It is unrealistic to expect a person to spend hours negotiating and then tell him to physically go and get the hostage taker. Likewise, it is unrealistic to expect a person to talk a hostage taker out in one situation and then in the next situation tell that person he will be point man on the assault team.

Similarly, is it unrealistic to expect one team (even if responsibilities are set and do not change) to perform disparate functions. The attitude of the team must be to resolve the incident with or without force. It cannot successfully do both. The training requirements for each team are different. With limited training hours, team members do not have time to adequately cross-train for both teams. The most serious drawback, however, concerns actual negotiations. The negotiator attempts to develop trust with the hostage taker. If the hostage taker suspects that the negotiator is one of the tactical team members "setting him up," the negotiator cannot possibly develop this trust (Miller, 1980).

The other debate concerned whether to inform the primary negotiator when the tactical team is going to use force to resolve the incident. For years, it was thought best to not tell the negotiator because the negotiator might possibly tip off the hostage taker. The negotiator might subconsciously put the hostage taker on alert by changing his inflection, tone of voice, or mannerisms. The negotiator is a trained professional who should be informed when the incident goes tactical. The negotiator, in fact, should be used to assist the tactical team (Fuselier, 1986; Wargo, 1988). The negotiator can get the hostage taker on the telephone before the assault, thereby giving the tactical team knowledge of the hostage taker's exact location (public phone or marked wire on the throw phone). The negotiator can also verbally distract the hostage taker during the assault. He or she can largely control the hostage taker's emotions and attention. The negotiator can agree to a major "concession" just before the assault, causing the hostage taker to psychologically let down his defenses. The negotiator can also "position" the hostage taker for a sniper shot.

A final issue that needs to be examined is the growing trend of combining personnel from several agencies into a tactical team (Mijares et al., 2000). For example, a sheriff's department and two cities within the county may each supply personnel to form a joint team. While these joint teams make a great deal of sense from several perspectives (cost, manpower usage, equipment sharing), several issues need to be addressed in the formation of a joint team. First to be decided is the type of arrangement the agencies are going to enter into. Agencies can participate in a task force, in which equipment and people from different departments are combined under a common command structure. This is the most common type of arrangement and has been used successfully for years in the area of narcotics enforcement. Agencies can also provide direct assistance, in which agencies agree to provide services to one another. The agency with primary jurisdiction provides the command structure. The authors argue against this type of arrangement due to the differing command structure across incidents. That is, if the incident occurs in City A, personnel from City A assume command, and if the incident occurs in City B, City B assumes command. We believe that it is better for tactical teams to have a stable command structure.

Agencies that form a joint tactical team (or negotiation team) should develop mutual assistance pacts (MAPs) (Mijares, et al., 2000) that govern the use and operation of these teams. The mutual assistance pact should address several issues relevant to the operation of the team. First, agencies should establish that there is legal authority to support the formation and operation of a joint team (Perkins & Mijares, 1996). The local government code should provide for the support and validity of such an arrangement. Second, arrest powers and arrest authority should be established. Third, responsibility for managing the agreement should be addressed and clarified. Mijares, McCarthy, and Perkins argue for a board of governors composed of the heads of each agency as an oversight committee to manage the agreement. Fourth, the MAP should clearly address and answer issues concerning the administration of the team (i.e., overtime pay, medical expenses, court time compensation). Finally, the MAP should cover issues of civil, criminal, and vicarious liability.

Outside Agency Support

Frequently, the resolution of a hostage situation requires the cooperation and assistance of many divisions within the police department and many non-police agencies. Many functions performed by these divisions and agencies are beyond the capabilities and training of the negotiating and tactical teams. Many negotiating teams and tactical units hesitate to call on these outside agencies because of pride, dilution of authority, and other reasons. The negotiating or tactical team should never hesitate to rely on the expertise and assistance these agencies can provide.

The negotiating team should rely on other divisions within the police department to help resolve the hostage situation. The intelligence unit can help with intelligence needs. In fact, many negotiating teams use intelligence-gathering officers selected from the agency intelligence unit. These officers gather intelligence for a living and do it full time. If possible, it is recommended that the intelligence gatherer be selected from an intelligence unit.

Traffic control officers may be used to maintain the outer perimeter. They can control crowds, media, and "rubberneckers," as well as secure the perimeter. The public relations division should be used to deal with the news media. Public relations deals with the media on a daily basis; they know the media representatives and usually have their respect. They can give invaluable assistance simply by being the media liaison. The K-9 unit should be used during the negotiating situation. Should the hostage taker escape confinement, the K-9 unit can usually track and locate the hostage taker. Many people resist the police but surrender when they see a dog.

If it is suspected that the hostage taker has explosive devices, the explosive ordnance disposal (EOD) unit should be called in. If the department does not have an EOD unit, federal agencies such as the Bureau of Alcohol,

Tobacco, and Firearms (ATF) can be called upon to assist. Military installations also have EOD units that will assist. The EOD unit can also work with the tactical team to plan an assault. Following the resolution of the hostage incident, the EOD team can search for explosives and booby-trap devices.

Other government agencies that may be needed are the fire department and medical services, such as EMS. Many negotiating teams train with these units because they are usually notified when a hostage situation occurs. Fire and EMS can provide auxiliary services at a hostage situation. Fire department equipment can be used to help maintain perimeter and crowd control. EMS can assist with hostage debriefing and stress management.

Aerial support may be necessary during a hostage situation. Most departments do not have their own helicopter. Helicopters and other air support elements can be obtained from the state police, National Guard, television and radio stations, military installations, and private companies.

The local telephone company is usually notified when a hostage situation occurs. They can hook up direct phone lines, isolate telephones, change telephone numbers, limit phones to allow only incoming calls, and provide specialized equipment. Many telephone companies will even loan equipment for the negotiators' use.

Public utility companies will turn off gas, electricity, and water. They can also be a valuable source for building blueprints and recent modifications. They can help locate and isolate incoming utility lines and provide valuable information for the tactical team.

Specialized agencies that may be utilized include building engineers and security personnel, locksmiths and other skilled craftsmen, foreign language consultants, disability experts (i.e., signers for the deaf), mental health professionals and medical doctors the hostage taker may have had contact with in the past, the Red Cross, victims' services personnel, and counselors. The military may provide specialized equipment and personnel (i.e., night vision goggles, specialized surveillance equipment, etc.). As an example of the latter, the federal agencies at the Branch Davidian siege at Waco used military personnel carriers. What most people do not realize is that the federal agencies also needed drivers for those vehicles. If arrangements are made for the equipment, make sure the arrangements provide for operators for the equipment.

All of the above-mentioned agencies will readily provide assistance when asked. However, it is important to prepare for their assistance before a hostage incident occurs. Written and signed agreements should be prepared and completed by all parties. Written directives for the call-out and use of these agencies should be prepared and discussed with these agencies. These outside agencies should have primary responsibility for preparing these agreements. They know their capabilities better than the police department does. Their responsibilities should be delineated and a clear chain of command specified. Agreements on expenses should be developed. A police department may be surprised when they use the telephone company's multi-million dollar command post and then receive a bill for several thousand dollars. Resolve these issues before they become a conflict that affects working relationships.

Finally, training situations should be developed utilizing these agencies. Training and debriefing standards should be developed and practiced. Department units and outside agencies should periodically meet and train with hostage response units. At least once per year, a mobilization exercise should be conducted utilizing these agencies. Many departments include these agencies in training scenarios and have them verbally relate what they would do at a hostage situation. They should be allowed to practice just as the police do—booby-trap buildings for the EOD team, have the telephone company reroute and isolate telephone lines, have EMS and the tactical team work together to "rescue" injured hostages, let a civilian mental health professional work with the primary negotiator, make the tactical team responsible for security, and have the negotiators use a disability expert and conduct a face-to-face negotiating session. Prepare everyone—not just the negotiators and tactical team.

Summary

The tactical team is just as necessary as the negotiating team at a hostage situation. Without the threat of force, the hostage taker can simply walk away. The specialized functions of the tactical team work to ensure the safety and security of the hostages and, if well-trained, can perform high-risk operations with minimal danger to police, hostages, and the hostage taker. If a situation requires force in order to resolve it, the tactical team should be able to effectively neutralize the hostage taker before the hostage taker is aware of their presence or before he or she has time to injure hostages. As a last resort, the tactical team sniper can neutralize the hostage taker to prevent the loss of hostages' lives.

Outside agencies will be an integral part of the hostage situation response effort. Identify these agencies, prepare written agreements with them, and involve them in practical scenarios. When an incident occurs, they will be valuable only if they are prepared.

References

Biggs, J.R. (1987). "Defusing Hostage Situations." *The Police Chief* 54:33-34.

City of Canton v. Harris, 489 U.S. 378, 109 S. Ct. 1197 (1989).

City of Winter Haven v. Allen, 541 So. 2d 128 (Fla. Dist. Ct. App. 1989)

Cole, D. (1989). "Tactical Unit Personnel Selection in San Diego County." *The Tactical Edge* 7:4-6.

Crelinsten, R.D. and D. Szabo (1979). *Hostage Taking*. Lexington, MA: Lexington Books.

Drovin, J. and J. Adams (1992). "Skokie's Tactical Intervention Unit: Ready for the Challenge." *The Police Chief* 59:17-19.

Flaherty, M.J. (1988). "I've Got Hostages." *The Police Chief* 55:48-50.

Fuselier, G.D. (1986). "What Every Negotiator Would Like his Chief to Know." *FBI Law Enforcement Bulletin* 55:12-15.

Gnagey, J.M. (1984). "Selection of a Police Countersniper." *FBI Law Enforcement Bulletin* 53:2-6.

Graham v. Connor, 109 S. Ct. 1865 (1989).

Greenstone, J.G. (1995). "Tactics and Negotiating Techniques (TNT): The Way of the Past and the Way of the Future." In Kurke, M.I. and E.M. Scrivner (eds.), *Police Psychology Into the 21st Century*. Series in Applied Psychology. Mahway, NJ: Lawrence Erlbaum Assoc., Inc.

_____ (1998). "Tactical Emergency Medical Support for Hostage and Crisis Negotiations." *The Police Chief* 65:38-41.

Hansen, K.A. (1988). "A Successful Composition of SWAT/Hostage Teams for Medium to Small Cities." *The Police Chief* 55:32-33.

Hillman, M. (1988). "Tactical Intelligence Operations and Support During a Major Barricade/Hostage Event." *The Police Chief* 55:18-30.

Hudson, R.A. (1989). "Dealing with the International Hostage-Taker: Alternatives to Reactive Counterterrorist Assaults." *Terrorism* 12:321-378.

Jacobs, J. (1983). *SWAT Tactics*. Boulder, CO: Paladin Press.

Kaiser, N.F. (1990). "The Tactical Incident: A Total Police Response." *FBI Law Enforcement Bulletin* 59:14-18.

Kolman, J. (1982). *A Guide to the Development of Special Weapons and Tactics Teams*. Springfield, IL: Charles C Thomas.

MacKenna, D. and J. Stevens (1989). "Selecting and Training Police Tactical Officers." *The Police Chief* 56:12-15.

Maksymchuk, A.F. (1982). "Strategies for Hostage-Taking Incidents." *The Police Chief* 49:58-65.

Mattoon, S. (1987). *SWAT: Training and Deployment*. Boulder, CO: Paladin Press.

McClure, F. (1994). "The Last Day of Hugh Johnston." *The U.S. Negotiator* (Winter):13-14.

McGeorge, H.J. II (1983). "Plan Carefully, Rehearse Thoroughly, Execute Violently: The Tactical Response to Hostage Situations." *World Affairs* 146:59-68.

Mijares, T.C., R.M. McCarthy, and D.B. Perkins (2000). *The Management of Police Specialized Tactical Units*. Springfield, IL: Charles C Thomas.

Mijares, T.C. and D. Perkins (1994). "Police Liability Issues: Special Concerns for Tactical Units." *Police Liability Review* 6:1-9.

_____ (1998). "Just Like a Swiss Army Knife: The Many Roles of The SWAT Trainer." *Command* (Summer):8-10.

Miller, A.H. (1979). "Hostage Negotiations." In Alexander, Y. and A. Kilmarx (eds.), *Political Terrorism and Business—The Threat and Response*. New York, NY: Praeger.

——— (1980). *Terrorism and Hostage Negotiations*. Boulder, CO: Westview Press.

Moon v. Winfield, 388 F. Supp. 31 (N.D. Ill. 1974).

Moore, R. (2005). "The Tactical Dance." *Crisis Negotiator Journal* 5 (Winter):12-13.

Moorer, T.H. (1982). "A Personal Insult to Each of Us." *Washington Post*, Jan. 16:A19.

Mullins, W.C. (2000). "Hostage Negotiator Selection." Presentation at the annual meeting of the Texas Association of Hostage Negotiators. San Antonio, TX (November).

——— (2003). "Selection of Crisis Negotiators." Presentation at the annual Hostage Negotiator Seminar/Competition. Texas State University, San Marcos, TX (January).

Olin, W.R. (1980). "Tactical Crisis Management—The Challenge of the 80s." *FBI Law Enforcement Bulletin* 49:20-25.

O'Neal v. DeKalb County, Georgia, 850 F.2d 653 (11th Cir. 1988).

Perkins, D.B. and T.M. Mijares (1996). "Police Liability Issues Associated With Interagency Mutual Assistance Pacts." *Police Liability Review* 8(1):8.

Pilant, L. (1993). "Less-than-Lethal Weapons: New Solutions for Law Enforcement." *IACP Executive Brief*. Washington DC: International Association of Chiefs of Police.

——— (1992). "Equipping Your SWAT Team." *The Police Chief* 59:36-39.

Plaster, J.L. (1990). "Police Sniper Training." *FBI Law Enforcement Bulletin* 59:1-6.

——— (1993). *The Ultimate Sniper: An Advanced Training Manual for Military and Police Snipers*. Boulder, CO: Paladin Press.

Roberts, J.R. (1988). "S.W.A.T.: Special Weapons and Tactics Teams in Policing." *Law and Order* 36:62-69.

Rowan, R. (1975). *The Four Days of Mayaguez*. New York, NY: W.W. Norton & Co.

Snow, R.L. (1996). *SWAT Teams*. New York, NY: Plenum Press.

Stevens, J.W. and D.W. MacKenna (1989). "Assignment and Coordination of Tactical Units." *FBI Law Enforcement Bulletin* 58:2-9.

Taylor v. Watters, 655 F. Supp. 801 (E.D. Mich. 1987).

Wargo, M.G. (1988). "The Tactical Use of Negotiators." *The Tactical Edge* 6:39-40.

Whittle, R.A. (1988). "Hostage Negotiations: A Situational Motivational Approach for Police Response." In Palmiotto, M.J. (ed.), *Critical Issues in Criminal Investigations*, Second Edition. Cincinnati, OH: Anderson Publishing Co.

Discussion Questions

1. Select a single-story business in your area. The business should be housed in a stand-alone structure. Plan a tactical assault on this location.

2. Select a multi-story office or business structure in your locality. Visit and inspect the structure. Afterward, assume that a hostage situation occurred in the structure. Where would be the best place to confine the hostage taker in terms of an assault? For sniper operations? Make a plan to move the hostage taker from the best place for an assault to the best place for a sniper operation.

3. Assume that a hostage situation occurred in your town in the downtown business section on a weekday. Plan and establish (on paper) outer and inner perimeters. How could you reroute traffic and business to cause the least disruption in the working day for the citizens?

4. Visit a local county jail or prison. Based upon the layout of that facility, prepare tactical plans for the possibility of a hostage situation. What specialized equipment would your team need? What would you do with the prisoners who are not part of the incident?

5. Visit with local EMS personnel. What issues and considerations are important to them during a hostage situation? During a tactical team operation? What types of support could they provide you?

6. Talk to a representative of the local electric utility company and telephone company. What support would they be willing to give during a hostage incident? What support could they give?

7. Call or visit the nearest military base and meet with the military or security police. What equipment and support could the military provide during a hostage incident? What are the conditions and regulations governing their support and assistance?

Post-Incident Debriefing

15

Learning Objectives

1. Understand the purpose of conducting an operational debriefing.

2. Understand the value of maintaining a standard record of information like HOBAS in debriefing an incident.

3. Understand the purpose of the critical decision point method.

4. Understand how to conduct a debriefing using the critical decision point method.

5. Explain the value of "best practice" standards in assessing teams.

6. Understand the purpose of conducting an emotional debriefing.

7. Understand how to conduct an emotional debriefing.

8. Understand the effects of the "triple whammy" of isolation on negotiators.

9. Understand the basics of a critical incident debriefing.

10. Understand the reasons that therapies that have been shown effective in intervening in ASD and PTSD may be more effective than an emotional debriefing.

The man's distraught mother called the Sheriff's Office at 9:30 P.M. Her 28-year-old son was barricaded in their mobile home with "bombs," a weapon, and gasoline, threatening to kill himself. The mother had found out that her son had gotten his girlfriend pregnant, and because the mother had been supporting him since his discharge from the service, she wanted him out of the house so she wouldn't have to support both of them. He only wanted to be left alone. The smell of gasoline permeated the trailer home in which the man was barricaded. A patrol sergeant tried to talk with the man, only to have him throw a light bulb at him, cutting him. Deputies tried talking him into coming out through a broken window. He was angry with his mother for "starting" the incident. He had been drinking and may have been taking drugs. His brother was in the mobile home with him. He asked to talk with his girlfriend. The man was a veteran who had been released from the service for harassing women. Before he was discharged, he had barricaded himself in the barracks for eight hours. Since his return home, he had had difficulty keeping a job. He was depressed and agitated when deputies arrived. The brother left the residence at 2:30 A.M., stating that he was never really a hostage. He confirmed the mother's report that the man had a history of arrests for assault before he went into the service and that he had not been gainfully employed since his discharge. At 8:30 A.M., the emergency response team, including the negotiators, arrived at the scene. They found deputies standing by their patrol cars, smoking and joking. Negotiators sent in a throw phone, which the individual ignored for the first hour. When he did answer, he demanded to see his girlfriend, and kept saying he wanted to commit "copicide." His affect was flat and he spoke in a monotone. The ERT opened the back door to air out the house. The subject went to close it and confronted the tactical officers. After yelling at them for several minutes, he slammed the door himself. The negotiator described in detail what it was like to be severely burned. At 1:40 P.M., the subject went to the back porch to retrieve a pizza that the ERT had placed there. When he opened the door, he was hit with a beanbag round that did not immobilize him. He scrambled back into the house and drenched the place with more gasoline ands taped a "bomb" to himself. He kept yelling at the ERT to stay away. The negotiator denied any knowledge of the tactical move, acting outraged by "those bastards." The negotiator tried offering the subject a soft drink, to help with the fumes. The subject observed a change of shift at 3:00 P.M. He started talking to the negotiator about how the ERT wanted to kill him. With the scene commander's permission, the negotiator played up his ability to protect the subject. He suggested that the subject could defeat ERT at their own game by coming out, not giving them the chance to "kill" him. They emphasized his child's need for him as he or she grew up by asking him to remember how it was for him to grow up without a father. The subject surrendered at 4:00 P.M.

Incidents like the one above have many points where they could go wrong. If they go wrong and someone dies, they generate strong feelings in negotiators. They need to be debriefed. The entire crisis management team, commanders, tactical team members, and negotiators need to review each incident to improve and refine their skills. Negotiators need to review the incidents in two ways: operationally, to identify the reasons for the injury or death, and emotionally, to defuse the impact of the trauma on the negotiators. The former needs to examine the details of the incident: how it was managed, what negotiating strategies and tactics were used, and how the situation can be improved. The latter needs to start the process of helping the negotiator accept the fact that he or she did the best job possible, given the circumstances.

Operational Debriefing of Hostage Incidents

Kidd (2005) has suggested that negotiations has come far enough as a profession to develop "best practices," which are criteria against which a specific negotiation can be measured. He suggests a set of standards that can be used to "audit" a team's performance, so they can refine and improve their performance. He states, "These standards provide some tools to enable us to move closer to peak performance. They provide a set of guidelines by which we can assess our individual skills, and the performance level of our teams."

Operational debriefings using such a set of standards serve two purposes: (1) they are a tool for refining the art of crisis management, and (2) they are effective ways of documenting the actions taken by police during the incident. Noesner (1999) has pointed out that incident commanders are going to be expected to explain their decisions more frequently in the future. Having a systematic way of reviewing the incident will help put departments in the best position for defending their actions. Incidents in which hostages are taken deserve close scrutiny after the incident, so that negotiators can learn from their experience what works—when, how, why, and for whom. The purpose of operational debriefings is to identify and solve potential problems, not to place blame. It should be done in an atmosphere of respect for the participants and with an eye toward solving problems.

An issue in debriefings is "What information needs to be collected and evaluated?" There have been several databases that have collected information about incidents over the years. After the incident in Waco, the FBI established HOBAS, a national database for collecting data after incidents that can be used to standardize the information reviewed in a operational debriefing. HOBAS represents the most extensive nationwide source of information about negotiator activity and it has the largest existing sample of negotiations incidents from which to learn. It provides a summary of the nature of incidents and the data collected is the minimum amount needed by teams in reviewing their functioning. It is recommended that teams begin their debriefing by gathering the data needed by HOBAS, which includes:

1. Information about the incident itself, including: the type of incident; the date and time of the incident; the location of the incident; when violence occurred during the incident, if it did; and who the violence occurred against.

2. Nature of the contact with the subject, including: who initiated communications; what types of communication were used during the incident; whether or not a TPI was used; the type of TPI; whether or not the TPI was helpful; whether a mental health consultant was used.

3. How the incident was resolved, including: type of resolution; type of tactical actions taken, if any; time and date of assault, if any; CNT's role in tactical resolution, if any.

4. Post-Incident information, including: injuries; deaths; property damage; language in which negotiations were conducted.

5. Data on the subject, including: age; sex; marital status; race; language fluency; employment; education; military experience; criminal history; prior suicide attempts; mental health problems; substance abuse history; substances used during incident; explosives used during incident; weapons used during incident; restraining order on subject; status of subject at the end of the incident.

6. Hostage/victim data, including: age, sex, race, English fluency (language), how victim was treated during incident, mobility allowed during incident, subject manipulated by victim, Stockholm Syndrome, type and timing of release, subject's use of victim to talk for him, victim talked to law enforcement, was victim injured or killed during the incident.

Critical Decision Debriefing: A Methodology for Debriefing Crisis Intervention

After the basic information is summarized, crisis management teams need to review their decisions and actions. Negotiators should debrief every incident, whether or not the crisis management team does. Incidents that are primarily crisis intervention can be debriefed using an intensive case-study method that focuses on critical decision points during the incident. Every negotiation incident has critical decisions that must be made if the situation is to be resolved peacefully. How these critical decision points were reached and how the decisions were made should be reviewed. The focus on what information was available at the time the decision was made, how the information was used, and what the impact of that use was. Recommendations for training and operational changes can be made on the basis of a critical decision review (McMains, 2000). The decision points usually occur sequentially as the incident unfolds over time. They include:

1. Was the type of incident assessed and what did that tell you about strategy and tactics?

2. Was appropriate intelligence gathered, analyzed, and disseminated?

3. Was the incident negotiable or was it made negotiable?

4. Were the demands recorded and what did they tell you about the person?

5. Was the subject's emotional, behavioral, and cognitive status assessed and how did that help develop strategies and tactics?

6. Was the subject's suicide potential assessed?

7. Was the subject's risk of aggression assessed?

8. Were witnesses, family members, and bystanders managed?

9. Was an opening planned with safety and security in mind?

10. Were communications skills appropriate for the crisis stage used?

11. Were persuasion techniques used? How did they work?

12. Were open, clear, and timely channels of communication with command and tactical maintained?

13. Was there a review of the subject's behavior and a plan developed for responding to the behavior between calls?

14. Were backup plans developed in the event that the first one was not received well?

15. Were basic guidelines used?

16. What worked and what did not work?

17. What recommendations are there for next time?

Case Study: The call at the beginning of this chapter will illustrate critical decision debriefing.

1. **What type of incident?** The incident was primarily a spontaneous incident between family members. It was planned in the sense that the subject had prepared to some degree for the arrival of the sheriff's deputies. He had spread gasoline around the mobile home and had built "bombs," in part to keep deputies from entering the house. It was spontaneous, in the sense that it involved people who knew one another, the subject's motivations were personal, there was little preparation, weapons were readily available, the subject's state of mind was generally emotional, and the use of crisis intervention skills was the appropriate strategy. The subject was using the incident to gain concession, staying in house and, more importantly, to express his anger at his mother for trying to put him out. There were no hostages.

2. **Was appropriate intelligence gathered, analyzed, and disseminated?** Intelligence was needed on the location, on the precipitating incident, and the type of person the deputies were dealing with. Site intelligence that was needed included a floor plan. The incident intelligence developed over time and was helpful to the negotiators in deciding on the subject's motivation: he was being dispossessed and had no place to go. Person intelligence was needed to develop a profile of the actor, to assess suicide risk, and estimate his dangerousness. Little was done on this until ERT arrived eight hours into the incident.

3. **Was the incident negotiable or was it made negotiable?** When negotiators arrived on the scene, several things needed to be done to make the above incident negotiable. The subject had mixed feelings about living. On the one hand, he said he wanted to die. On the other, he asked for his girlfriend and he was externalizing his anger toward his mother. The threat of force was not available: they had to establish a perimeter. They appeared to have time to negotiate because the incident had been going on for 10 hours before the ERT was mobilized and it had not deteriorated. Reliable and safe communications had to be established by getting him to accept a throw phone. Containment was established by ERT's perimeter. However, none had really existed prior to their arrival. This subject was the only one in the house when negotiators arrived, so it was reasonable to assume that the subject was the decision maker.

4. **Were the demands recorded and what did they tell you about the person?** His initial demand to be left alone suggested that he might be depressed and suicidal. Later, his demand to talk to his girlfriend suggested that he might be backing off his suicidal position. His demand that the ERT get back, and his threats to blow the place up if they entered the trailer suggested that he was afraid of a violent encounter with the police, perhaps out of concern for his personal safety.

Negotiations can have an emotional impact on responders, including negotiators. It is important that teams debrief following incidents (especially extremely traumatic incidents) to minimize any impact on team members, hostages, and other responders. *(B. Miller)*

5. **Was the subject's emotional, behavioral, and cognitive status assessed, and how did that help develop strategies and tactics?** A formal assessment of the subject's personality was not made. Had it been, the following analysis would have been valuable in developing strategies and tactics: His history of relative success for several years in the

military, elite units like the SEALS, and then his inability to keep a job after his discharge; the neighbors' reports that he "talked a good game but never did anything"; his reliance on his mother for support; his use and abuse of alcohol to manage stress; and his poor decision-making in getting his girl-friend pregnant when he could not keep a job all suggested an inade-quate/dependent person who would have trouble with abandonment. Being on his own without anyone to make decisions for him would terrify him. The good news is that he might develop a dependency on the negotiator that would help resolve the incident peacefully. His slowed speech, monotone, and suicidal ideation suggested moderate depression. Instilling hope would be a strategy the negotiator could use.

6. **Was the subject's suicide potential assessed?** Even though the sub-ject was threatening suicide, the risk was assessed to be moderate because there was no history of prior attempts, and the plan seemed to be only par-tially developed. It reflected a moderately lethal method, although it was not one that was private, and it allowed for significant intervention by authori-ties. The longer the incident went on, the less likely the subject was to com-mit suicide. He made a point of using the gasoline threat to keep police at bay and he asked on several occasions for his girlfriend. In conjunction with his personality profile, it was likely that the request for his girlfriend was moti-vated by his dependency on her, rather than his need to have an audience.

7. **Was the risk of aggression assessed?** No, because the subject seemed angry with himself and his mother more than anyone else. There was some minor aggression in his history.

8. **Were witnesses, family members and bystanders managed?** Par-tially. The neighbors, the mother and the brother, after his escape from the house, sat across the street from the subject in lawn chairs. They were not contained until ERT arrived on the scene.

9. **Was an opening planned with safety and security in mind?** Yes, the subject was reassured that the deputies did not want to harm him; they wanted to help him find a solution to his problems. After the abortive assault attempt, the negotiators were able to calm the subject by reassuring him that they would not let anything else like that happen.

10. **Were communications skills appropriate for the stages of crisis used?** Yes. Active listening techniques, and particularly reflection of feel-ings, were used to help defuse his anger in the early stages and after the bean-bag crisis occurred. An attitude of caring and concern was established by the negotiator by his efforts to get the subject to accept a telephone, so "we can work this out, together," and by the negotiator's concern for the subject's com-fort and health when he suggested that the subject might want to open the windows to air the place out. Persuasion techniques were used to get him to buy into defeating the ERT at their own game and to tacitly accept that his child would be better off with him rather than without him. Vivid descrip-tions of the effects of burns on the negotiator's friend made the conse-quences of the subject's plan real. It helped bring home to the actor the fact that his best alternative to a negotiated solution was not good.

11. **Were open, clear, and timely channels of communication with command and tactical maintained?** Yes. The on-scene commander supported building up the protector role. Negotiators were part of the planning, including the plan to get the subject out where he could be hit with a bean-bag round.

12. **Was there a review of the subject's behavior and a plan developed for responding to the behavior between calls?** Yes. Both the primary negotiator and the secondary negotiator brainstormed approaches and issues between calls. They developed the idea of giving the subject a face-saving way out of the situation after the incident was defused, by focusing on how much more experience he had than tactical and how he could defeat them by surrendering with honor. If that failed, the fallback position was to re-emphasize how important it was for his child to know his father. Not like his experience growing up, when he did not know his father.

13. **Were backup plans developed, in the event the first one was not received well?** Yes. Pleading ignorance, being outraged at the tactical team, siding with the subject in designing a way to defeat the tactical team "at their own game," and emphasizing the importance of the subject being there for his child were all alternate plans.

14. **Recommendations for the future.** Two major recommendations came out of this review: (1) The ERT performed well once they were mobilized. However, it took all night for them to be mobilized. When they got to the scene, several things had to be done to make it safe and negotiable. First responder training and supervisor training focused on management of critical incidents would help alleviate this situation and help set up the transfer to ERT. (2) Negotiators could make better use of personality profiling in both assessing risk and developing interventions. An accurate assessment might have made it less stressful for the negotiator, because the systematic assessment would have reduced the perceived threat level.

Sidebar: Post-Incident Debriefing

London "Max" Howard served as a Special Agent with the FBI for 33 years. He has taught hostage/crisis negotiation to U.S. and foreign law enforcement since 1981. He served on the FBI negotiating teams at the Branch Dividian siege at Waco, Texas, and the Montana Freemen standoff in Jordan, Montana. Max was the training and negotiation coordinator for the FBI's Dallas division when he retired in 1998. In addition to teaching, he has assisted local law enforcement by developing and judging practical scenarios and served as a consultant during hostage incidents. He is an active member and former office-holder in the Texas Association of Hostage Negotiators and assisted in forming the Louisiana Association of Crisis Negotiators. Upon retiring, Max formed his own business, Crisis Management Training of Arlington, Texas, and continues to teach negotiation locally and abroad.

Most crisis situations end too soon. Once the immediate danger presented by a hostage taker or person in crisis is past and someone satisfies the media's appetite, we often make a hasty retreat, with a goal of

---

resuming normalcy. If we consider the incident closed at this point—we have done our professions and ourselves a disservice—and possibly great damage. There was no recognition of those who performed well and the procedures that led to success or safety. There was no critical evaluation of the personal or departmental practices that need to be improved in future incidents. There was no opportunity for individuals to release emotional baggage (positive and negative) that now must be carried alone. The crisis situation should not be over until a post-incident debriefing (PID) has been successfully completed.

There are few things in life that are more rewarding and reaffirming than to have a co-worker compliment your performance. "Good job" or "He/she is a good (officer, agent, negotiator)" is great to hear. Besides the personal satisfaction, this type of reinforcement is part of all teaching/learning principles. Obviously, the sooner after the event the affirmation comes, the stronger and more long-lasting the impact. Because teams handle crisis responses, most of the positive feedback should be directed at and shared by all teammates. Similarly, procedures that contributed positively to a safe outcome should be recognized, reinforced, and documented. Doing so anchors them in the minds and habits of all members of the response group, and makes them more resistant to arbitrary change.

PIDs should not used to point fingers or make excuses, but we must honestly evaluate the performances of all teams. Sometimes this means identifying and admitting mistakes that were made or acknowledging that deviations from established policy occurred. This may be difficult for some, especially when the excitement of the event is still fresh in their minds. By not identifying and examining an area in need of change, we confirm its current status. This is true not only for team performances, but also for policies and procedures employed during the incident. Crisis response has been a constantly evolving science/art since the days we used rocks as our primary assault weapon. Most positive changes developed only when we recognized shortcomings and applied appropriate remediation. Our policies and procedures serve as a beacon, but have never been etched in stone. They should not be changed arbitrarily, but sometimes significant trends indicate that a different approach can be beneficial. Identifying those trends is one of the objectives of a critical, but professional PID.

One of the most used quotations is "Those who cannot remember the past are doomed to repeat it" by George Santayana. This is certainly true of law enforcement's responses to crisis events. It is the duty of some outsiders to identify our mistakes and address them as a means of legitimate oversight. It is the desire of others to exploit our shortcomings for personal gain. When errors are repeated we lose a valuable asset—our credibility. It is in our best interest to identify and correct procedures that can be improved in order to avoid the embarrassment of having others do it for us—or providing our adversaries with an easy opening.

> Finally, we negotiators encourage people in crisis to realize their elevated emotions and then share them with us. We invite and encourage them through active listening and empathy to release their tensions to understanding, non-threatening, and non-judgmental people who care—us. We apply these skills equally on suicidal individuals, murderers, and perverts—yet we often do not practice this essence of our own process. My personal experiences, and those others have shared with me, confirm that law enforcement negotiating can present great rewards—and it can also send one to the depths of despair and self-doubt. In either case, the recognition of our emotions, the opportunity to vent them to an understanding, non-judgmental person, and to receive feedback, are things we owe each other and ourselves.

A definition of a professional is a person who has a unique body of knowledge that he or she applies to life problems and a set of standards that govern the application of that knowledge. Kidd (2005) has suggested that negotiators have reached a level of professionalism that requires that they look critically at their organization, performance, training, and skills so they can continually improve their performance. In addition to the operational debriefing discussed above, he has suggested that there is value in negotiators and teams assessing themselves using a set of "best practices" so they can identify problems that need to be corrected as they can come closer to the goal of "zero defects" in their managing critical incidents. He has compiled the following list of "Best Practices"[1] as standards for individuals and teams that want to evaluate their performance to improve their professionalism:

1. Organizational issues: negotiators are a part of an organized and trained crisis management team that is recognized and supported by their agency.

2. Negotiators are selected using a standard process that is available to department personnel and that are consistent with guidelines set by NCNA.

3. Policies are in place that cover the team's mission.

4. All team members have successfully completed a basic negotiations course.

5. The majority of the team members attend update training outside the department.

6. All negotiators attend in-house training four times a year and one training is a joint exercise with tactical and command.

7. The agency has a written call-out procedure.

8. The agency is able to deploy at least one negotiator to the scene of an incident within one hour, and a full team within 90 minutes.

9. The negotiating team is able to utilize the appropriate communication equipment for the incident.

10. Clear guidelines are in place and understood covering face-to-face communications.

11. The CNT has a protocol for employment of "up front" negotiators who are to facilitate the transition from officers to the primary negotiator.

12. Negotiators are trained in interviewing skills that will allow them to gather information about person, place, and incident intelligence that can be used to plan the negotiating approach.

13. Intelligence collection and analysis is done at a central location.

14. Intelligence is disseminated from the central point to all elements that need it.

15. CNT will continue to evaluate and modify plans on the basis of the changing situation and intelligence.

16. Primary negotiator will identify himself to the subject and reassure him that the goal is to work together toward a peaceful resolution.

17. The primary maintained patient and un-hurried approach.

18. The primary built trust and rapport utilizing the appropriate non-judgmental, non-threatening, sincere, and concerned attitude.

19. CNT used appropriate active listening skills to defuse emotions, encourage the person to ventilate, draw the subject out.

20. The primary used active listening.

21. The negotiator handled demands appropriately.

22. The CNT worked effectively as a team, showed competence, communicated effectively, stayed within accepted guidelines, brainstormed between contacts.

23. All CNT are trained in selection, scripting, and monitoring third-party intermediaries.

24. CNT maintains effective communications with tactical.

25. CNT maintains effective communications with command.

26. The team made appropriate use of mental health resources.

27. The agency has an established surrender procedure worked out by CNT leaders and tactical commander and all team members are trained on it.

28. The agency has the capacity to provide post-incident debriefing to mitigate the emotional impact of an incident on negotiators and has written policies governing the use, attendance, and procedures to be used during such a debriefing.

29. The agency has a written protocol for written documentation of incidents.

As is evident, many of the best practices overlap the issues to be assessed in an operational debriefing. However, they include organizational, training, and policy issues that are important for excellence in negotiations and that reach beyond the negotiator's or the CNT's performance at a single incident. One way these "best practices" can be of benefit to negotiators is that they can provide departmental administrators standards against which to assess the quality of their teams and provide guidance for what needs to be done to do the best possible job, thus reducing the department's liability exposure. Kidd has suggested that departments can use the best practices as a tool to audit themselves.

Emotional Debriefing

Like other traumatic situations, a negotiating incident that ends in death has an emotional, cognitive, and psychological impact that can stay with a person for weeks, months, or years. At best, it disrupts the lives of the negotiators, and at worst, it changes them permanently. Negotiators must understand the emotional impact of a death during negotiations, be prepared for the emotional impact, have developed a method of intervening that reduces the impact, and practice this method like any other negotiation skill. The following reprint illustrates the issues negotiators have to deal with when a situation ends badly.

Post-Incident Stress for the Negotiator
Officer C.J. Ricketts
San Antonio Crisis Police Department

Nineteen of my 20 years as a veteran of the San Antonio Police Department have been spent as a street officer. Fifteen of those years were on concurrent assignment as a crisis negotiator. During my 15 years as a negotiator, I responded to more than 200 critical incidents. During one of these incidents, I learned some important lessons that I would like to share with you.

As in any line of police work, all of our experiences are not positive ones. Oftentimes, officers do not receive emotional support to help them cope with difficult experiences, nor do they have the necessary knowledge to support themselves. Post-Incident Stress for the crisis negotiator is an area which many times is not recognized or dealt with by negotiation units. Because of this, some crisis negotiators who have had to deal with Post-Incident Stress have not had the proper support. I have experienced Post-Incident Stress, and perhaps you have also. The following should help you recognize and deal with Post-Incident Stress, should it happen to you.

In 1988, a street transient gunned down two San Antonio police officers, working in the Foot Patrol Division. After the gunfire, the transient barricaded himself in a building, not far from the incident. Our Negotiation Unit was activated at this time. I was the primary negotiator at the scene, and after a period of negotiations, and after considerable communication, the transient surrendered. This process is what negotiators spend their time training for, and the outcome was what was expected or hoped for based on that training.

After the surrender, other members of my unit and I went to the Homicide Unit. An officer I had known for 15 years, a friend, approached us and told us we should have killed the transient. Never before in my career had I been met by such negative feelings from a peer. As time went on, I discovered that this officer's feelings echoed those of many officers in the Department.

The day after the shooting, because I was the primary negotiator, I was ordered into a press conference by my chain of command. The press conference caused my picture to be shown on television news stations, and it was also pictured in the newspaper. This publicity caused me to be identified as the negotiator who had successfully negotiated with the transient who had shot two police officers. I did not ask for any recognition in connection with this incident, but because of the publicity, I became associated with the incident, and it put me in the forefront for negative reactions from my peers. They were angry and trying very hard to deal with the shooting. In the past six months, six San Antonio police officers had been shot, and officers were looking for some "street justice," and I had not provided that for them.

One of the officers had been released from the hospital; however, the other was in critical condition. We all knew that he probably would not live. His dying became my greatest fear and I started perceiving myself as the police officer (negotiator) that had saved the life of a "cop killer." For the next four months the officer remained in a coma until his death.

During those four months, I began to question my work as a crisis negotiator. At the time, I had successfully resolved a conflict based on eight years of experience as a negotiator; however, it was contrary to the beliefs of a lot of the officers around me. The officers believed something else should have been done. I no longer had confidence in myself and my part as a negotiator in this incident. Nor could I justify the job I had done, either to myself, or to my peers. I began to have trouble sleeping at night and had some dreams about the incident. My feelings would range from anger to depression. I would wake up each morning fearing that today was the day that the officer would die. I isolated myself from everyone in my unit and from everyone in the Department, by not talking about how I felt. The only person I talked to during this time was my future wife, Valerie. I did express my feelings to her concerning the incident and she was very comforting and understanding. Without her support during this time, I probably would have resigned from the unit and police work altogether.

The day the officer died was one of the worst days I have ever experienced. On that day I tagged myself as the police officer that had saved the life of a "cop killer." This was a tag that I thought I would never wear, and because of my beliefs, I felt I had no right to attend the officer's funeral. I did not attend the funeral and this caused me to feel even more isolated from my Department. This was a very painful time for me, because I would not allow myself to grieve the loss of the officer with my own police family. I felt like I was no longer a member of that family.

Sometime after this incident, I discovered that other members of my unit felt some of the same feelings I had felt. We talked about how we felt. From these conversations, I began to accept what I had done as a crisis negotiator. Members of my unit and I have formulated the following guide to help crisis negotiators who experience similar feelings.

First, let's talk about who we really are and where we come from. When we first became police officers, we probably had no intention of ever becoming a Crisis Negotiator. When we talked to brother officers about officers being shot, it went something like this: "Man, if you ever get shot, you can bet I'll make sure the guy never makes it to the jail." When you made the scene of a critical incident, where a guy was held up, you wondered why they just didn't go in and get him. Then somewhere down the line we matured and developed the ideas of a Crisis Negotiator. We respond to critical incidents and talk people out, people who are suicidal, trapped criminals, and so on. Officers on the outside probably have made the comment, "I don't understand why they talked them out instead of just going in and getting them." We just kind of shrug these messages off and keep on successfully operating as a crisis negotiator within our normal work environment. Officers on the outside don't really give us any big hassles over it, because we haven't really crossed the line. What I mean by that, is that no officer or civilian that they really care about all that much has really been hurt during an incident. Then, we make that one critical incident where someone has been injured or killed that they do really care about. Now, we may really face the heat. It happened to me, and I was no longer able to feel comfortable about my work environment or myself. For that reason, we have to be able to justify why we are negotiators to others and ourselves.

There are some hard facts about crisis negotiators that you should remember. As regular law enforcement officers, we are isolated from the understanding of the general public. As crisis negotiators, we are not only isolated from the understanding of the general public, but also isolated from the understanding of most law enforcement officers. In some cases, the crisis negotiator who is experiencing Post-Incident Stress may become isolated from his own negotiation unit members. He begins to question his own existence as a crisis negotiator and isolates himself from everyone. This is what I did to myself. I call this the "Triple Whammy." Whatever you do, don't isolate yourself. Talk to your unit members about how you feel. We are an elite group and have to depend on each other for support.

There are some policies in place for dealing with and reducing Post-Incident Stress.

1. First, recognize and identify incidents that may produce that stress. Put yourself on the alert.

2. Have good team support within your unit for fellow negotiators and use debriefings to talk about the emotions you and your team members are feeling.

3. Have a person trained in debriefing present during the debriefings. He should direct the debriefing and it is very important that he was not involved in the actual critical incident being debriefed.

4. Don't allow a crisis negotiator to be singled out to his peers after a critical incident that may receive critical response from fellow officers. This is what occurred to me at my press conference. I became the target of officers angry about the incident.

5. Start educating your department concerning the responsibilities of a crisis negotiator. This can be done through a First Responder Training Program provided to fellow officers.

6. Last, have mental health support available for your crisis negotiators, should it become necessary.

It is important that you recognize as a crisis negotiator, that there are normal signs and symptoms of Post-Incident Stress following a critical incident where you receive: (a) negative feedback from fellow officers; (b) there has been a loss of life; or (c) you feel you didn't do your job the best it could have been done. The signs and symptoms of post-incident stress can be one or more of the following: (a) Heightened sense of vulnerability, (b) Anger, anxiety regarding future situations, (c) Intruding thoughts or flashbacks, (d) Isolation, (e) Withdrawal, (f) Emotional numbing, (g) Sleep difficulties, (h) Alienation, (i) Depression, (j) Problems with authority, (k) Nightmares, (l) Family problems, (m) Alcohol or drug abuse, (n) Sexual dysfunction, (o) Just flat denial that anything is wrong with you, (p) Significant physical problems such as: tension headaches, stomach problems; digestive problems, and aching bones.

Don't think you're going crazy. All these signs and symptoms are normal, and you're really doing okay. You're just feeling stress. I felt a lot of these signs and symptoms after my critical incident. Just realize you need to recognize the situation, talk about the situation and these problems should take care of themselves within six to eight weeks, at the most. If they don't, professional help may be necessary.

There are other things that you can do to help reduce the stress of being the crisis negotiator with post-incident stress. Moderate exercise and relaxation exercises will help. Maintain a balanced diet and do not increase alcohol intake. Recognize that signs and symptoms of stress are normal and that it is okay to have these feelings. Most important of all, accept what you did as a crisis negotiator.

Finally, justify to others and yourself why you do the job of a crisis negotiator. It is not hard to recognize that after the onset of a critical incident, at the time of an assault, is when it is most likely that an officer will die. Even if it is the worst case scenario, and one officer has already been shot and critically wounded as a result of the critical incident, such as the situation I dealt with, why make it possible for another officer to die on an assault, instead of negotiating. In short, we do the job as a crisis negotiator to save the lives of fellow officers. Every time my unit successfully negotiates a critical incident, I know we may have saved a police officer's life. Remember you're the professional who is the "calm" during the storm. You are the one who makes sense out of a bad situation and brings it to a successful resolution without loss of life. Remember that we do the best that we can do, and if it doesn't work out just the way we wanted it to, remember what we were working with. Human nature is unpredictable.

The incident that I went through has only made me a stronger and better crisis negotiator. I only wish I had known then what I know now so the pain and confusion I was experiencing would not have lasted so long. I hope some of the ideas that my unit has come up with for dealing with post-incident stress will help you if you are dealing with it or may deal with it in the future.

Reprinted with permission from *Journal of Crisis Negotiations*, Vol. 1, No. 2, October, 1995. Reprinted with permission.

Emotional Impact on the Negotiator

The above article poignantly illustrates the impact on a negotiator when an incident does not go as expected. It is important to note that the incident was handled by a well-trained, experienced officer who did his job well. Still, the emotional impact was profound. Other authors (Bohl, 1997; Lanceley, 1999) have described the potential emotional impact of critical incidents on negotiators. They describe officers who feel excessive responsibility for the outcome of the incidents. They describe symptoms of depression, including insomnia and preoccupation with their responsibility, second-guessing and rumination. Officers have reported intrusive thoughts in the form of both nightmares and uncontrolled images and thoughts about the incident. Bohl (1997) has reported officers' replaying the incident in their minds and making the outcome worse than it was originally. To deal with the emotional impact of these incidents, debriefings need to be established as a regular procedure for negotiators.

Debriefing Negotiators

The *Encyclopedia of Psychology* (Eysenck et al., 1972) defines psychic trauma as: ". . . any painful individual experience, especially if that experience is associated with permanent environmental change(s). As a rule a psychic trauma involves a loss of possible motive gratification." Figley (1988) goes on to say that a traumatic event is "an extraordinary event or series of events which is sudden and overwhelming and often dangerous, either to oneself or significant others." Nielsen (1984) points out that traumas are characterized by four things:

1. A sudden and unexpected onset;

2. A threat to life;

3. A loss of some kind, usually to the person's sense of self;

4. A disruption of values.

An event that has a sudden and unexpected onset is traumatic because it gives people a sense of unpredictability and uncontrollability. It is like walking into your bedroom and having someone jump at you from behind the door, yelling, "Boo!" You are startled and feel an immediate sense of arousal. You were not expecting to be jumped at in your own room (it was unpredictable) and you could do nothing to stop it or to prepare yourself for it (it was uncontrollable). Research has shown that tension, anxiety, and stress rise when an incident that is unpredictable and uncontrollable occurs.

A hostage incident in which a life is lost is sudden and unpredictable because of experience. Experience shows that 95 percent of hostage incidents are resolved without loss of life (FBI, 1984). This means negotiators go into situations expecting to be successful and that the odds are in their favor. When a life is lost, it violates expectations of success. It is sudden and unexpected because it does not go along with the script we have in our head.

Hostage incidents are always a threat to life. They threaten the hostages, the police, bystanders, and even the hostage taker. The stakes are high, the cost of failure extreme. If the negotiator fails, someone dies. This makes the stress high and failure a trauma. Most police officers are people who were

Although negotiations can be stressful and emotional, the dynamics of the crisis situation often lead to close bonds and friendships among team members that can last a lifetime. *(S. Davis)*

taught the value of life before they put on the uniform, the badge, and the gun. Loss of life is a serious issue for them.

Additionally, the loss of life reminds us of our own vulnerability and mortality (NOVA, 1991). The threat to another person's life is a threat to our own. It underlines the lack of permanence and the fragility of life. It raises questions about life's ultimate meaning and purpose. It gives us a sense of powerlessness and purposelessness. To be successful, negotiators have to believe in their goals. They must value life, respect others, and have a wish to help. They need to see themselves as helpers.

The loss of a human life is the ultimate failure for negotiators. It strikes at the heart of their mission. It threatens their professional identity and their sense of self, to the degree that negotiators accept their job to be the preservation of life. There is a loss of self-esteem. This is the third characteristic of a trauma.

Finally, a trauma involves the disruption of values. Values are things that are important to a person. They involve clusters of feelings, thoughts, and behavior that are focused on goals and are normative in character. They prescribe the appropriateness of behaviors, thoughts, and feelings, what is acceptable and what is not. The value of human life is one that people in our culture learn long before they become police officers. The just-world hypothesis is another. The meaningfulness of life is yet a third value that is accepted by most on faith. Traumas challenge all three of these values because they are uncontrollable, unpredictable, life-threatening, and self-esteem destroying. They challenge the assumptions of meaningfulness, fairness, and value in life. What is left are some basic questions about life at best, and nihilistic meaninglessness at worst.

Stages of a Trauma

As early as 1958, Tyhurst suggested that most traumas follow a similar pattern. They can be thought of as having three stages:

1. Impact stage

2. Recoil stage

3. Adaptation stage

The impact stage begins with the realization that there is a threat to the person's well-being and ends when the person no longer experiences that threat. For a negotiator this could be a matter of minutes, hours, or days, depending on how long the incident lasts, how long the review of the incident lasts, and how long the negotiator needs to relive the incident in his mind. The specific threat for a negotiator is usually the threat to self-esteem and to values. Unlike a physical threat, this sense of failure is something a negotiator does to himself. It is in his or her thoughts. Therefore, it is not over as soon as the incident is over. Rather, it is over when the negotiator quits thinking about it.

The recoil stage of a trauma begins when the precipitating stressor ends and lasts until the time the negotiators' normal life resumes. This stage is characterized by a hypersensitivity to others. Negotiators will seek support from friends, family, and others. During this stage, they may need to go over the incident repeatedly to help resolve their feelings of failure, guilt, frustration, and anger. This stage may last days or weeks after the incident.

The adaptation stage begins when negotiators are no longer preoccupied with the incident and when they return to their normal functioning. If they have not successfully resolved the incident, negotiators have intrusive thoughts about the incident or they have periods of emotional numbing in which they just do not feel anything. If they have accepted the incident, they will be able to think and talk about it without excessive emotion.

Goals of Debriefing

If officers move through the stages of a trauma without incident, all is well and good. However, sometimes negotiators become preoccupied with the incident. When this happens, they may experience a number of the symptoms described above. Debriefing is a process that is designed to help keep officers from getting stuck. Bohl (1997) outlines three specific goals of debriefings: (1) to alleviate pain associated with the incident; (2) to prevent subsequent Post-Traumatic Stress Disorder from developing; and (3) to return the officer to his pre-incident level of functioning.

Debriefing the Impact

To help negotiators who have been involved in a traumatic incident, a critical incident debriefing (Mitchell & Bray, 1990) may be helpful. Critical Incident Debriefing (CID) is a group process designed to start officers talking about what they did and how they reacted to their actions during an incident. It is usually done by a combination of professionals and peers who have been trained in CID. It assumes that the people the debriefer is working with are normal people who are dealing with an abnormal situation, that people have the resources to support each other and to resolve their own problems, that early intervention can facilitate their ability to move beyond their emotional arousal before it becomes a chronic problem, and that peers are a credible resource in beginning their resolution of the emotional impact of a crisis (McMains, 1986).

There are several models of debriefing (Mitchell & Bray, 1990; NOVA, 1992; McMains, 1986; Bohl, 1997; Hatcher et al., 1998), but they all have three elements in common:

1. They all review what happened to the person and to others during an incident.

2. They all review how people felt about what happened to them.

3. They all educate by providing information about the usual reactions to a trauma.

Generally, a debriefing is done in a group setting by a team of debriefers. The group is told that the purpose of the debriefing is to provide a setting in which it is safe to talk about how they have reacted to the incident. To help establish the safety of the situation, it is explained that the group is not an operation debriefing, that there is no rank in the room, and that they all must agree not to talk about anyone else's experience outside the debriefing room. Then, a debriefer asks each person to describe what he or she did during the incident. Each person has a turn at describing his or her part of the operation so an overall picture is developed of what happened to whom and when. Next, the debriefer asks each person how he or she reacted to the incident and to his or her part in it. These accounts are reported and listened to without criticism by the group members. Finally, the accounts are used as examples to summarize the impact of a traumatic incident on people. There are several points that need to be made about typical reactions (Nielsen, 1986):

1. During the impact stage, it is normal to feel stunned and bewildered, to go about life like they are on "automatic pilot." Emotions are contained by rigid denial and isolation. The person can not allow the intensity of emotions to interfere with functioning. Compliance with authority and rules is frequent.

2. During the recoil stage, people can expect to continue to function with a sense that things are not real. They will need to go over the incident in an almost compulsive way. They will be preoccupied. They may be oversensitive to criticism from others. They may withdraw from their usual activities and interests.

3. During the adaptation stage, people may feel alternating periods of depression and anxiety. They may be troubled with nightmares. Unwanted memories of the incident may intrude on the negotiators. They need to know that as they come to terms with the trauma, these experiences will abate.

4. It is important to continue to talk about the incident with accepting, caring, and understanding friends.

5. It is important to know that:

   a. Judging themselves on the basis of the results is self-defeating. Rather, people need to be able to believe that they did the best with what they had to work with.

   b. The cataclysm of emotions they felt is the same as how most people feel in a crisis. Their feelings are OK.

   c. Trauma by definition involves incidents that are out of control and that people who take hostages have a mind, plan, and goals of their own. It is OK not to be in complete control all the time.

   d. By nature, people are limited in their knowledge, skills, and abilities. They are subject to feelings of anger, frustration, rage, fear, panic, and confusion. It is OK to be human.

The goals of debriefing are to:

1. provide an intellectual understanding of both the incident and its emotional impasse;

2. start to develop an acceptance of the negotiator's thoughts, feelings, and actions during the incident; and

3. desensitize the person to the excessive emotional arousal that frequently accompanies a traumatic incident.

By doing this, it is hoped that the impact of a trauma can be reduced to manageable levels, negotiators who are involved can put their performance into perspective, and the harmful impact of the trauma can be eliminated much in the same way that it has been for officers involved in shootings.

The effectiveness of debriefings has been suggested by Allen et al. (1990) in a study of personality characteristics of successful hostage negotiators. The authors tested 12 experienced hostage negotiators who had responded to a total of 500 incidents. One of the purposes of the study was to explore the possibility of Post-Traumatic Stress Disorders in these officers who had been exposed to multiple traumatic incidents. No officers showed the typical PTSD profile as described by Keene et al. (1984). The authors suggested that the lack of symptoms may have been the result of immediately debriefing negotiators at the scene. They thought that an on-the-scene debriefing may provide for an exploration of the negotiator's actions and feelings in a setting that provided social support and that facilitated desensitization of excessive arousal.

An alternative interpretation of the data is that officers were more likely to be experiencing an Acute Stress Disorder that is like PTSD, but shows fewer symptoms and lasts for a shorter period. In 1990, ASD was not recognized as a diagnostic category in the *Diagnostic and Statistical Manual* of the American Psychiatric Association.

In the general population, there is little evidence to support the effectiveness of debriefings alone in the reduction of PTSD. In fact, there are controlled studies that suggest that under certain conditions and with certain populations, debriefings may lead to an increase in PTSD symptoms. What debriefings seemed to do is bring groups who have experienced life-threatening events closer together as a group.

Several interventions have shown to be effective in reducing ASD/PTSD symptoms among the general public. Friedman (2001) reports that the cognitive behavioral therapies such as Exposure Therapy, Cognitive Therapy, Cognitive Processing Therapy, and Stress Inoculation Therapy have proven the most effective interventions in reducing symptoms of PTSD. One reason for the efficacy of these treatment modalities is that they intervene at behavioral, cognitive, and emotional levels. Many of these therapies have the same elements as the debriefing model. The major difference is that they take place over a period of time, rather than at one time. It may be that more than one session is required for people who are experiencing PTSD/ASD symptoms to reduce the physiological arousal and change the self-evaluative/self-critical statements they associate with a traumatic incident.

One of the neurophysiological effects of being threatened by uncontrollable events is that the nervous system becomes more "irritable." The receptor sites on the nerve endings increase in number up to 300 percent after a traumatic experience (Everly, 1989). It is this neurological change that makes people irritable and jumpy after a trauma. In addition to an understanding of this fact, people are benefited by methods of returning the nervous system to normal levels. Systematic relaxation exercises have the advantage of giving people an activity that effectively reduces the reactivity of the nervous system.

Another issue is the self-evaluative statements people are likely to make at the time of a traumatic event. If an officer thinks that he or she has somehow failed to meet a standard during the trauma of a life-threatening event, he or she may think of him- or herself as a poor police officer or an inadequate human being. These self-evaluative thoughts may become fixed in the officer's head, leading to the need to avoid situations that challenge his or her sense of "efficacy." Therefore, interventions that focus on restructuring the self-critical statements need to be part of an intervention for PTSD.

Hogewood (2005) has suggested that debriefings alone are not enough in dealing with the impact of traumatic stress in policing. Rather, he argues that policing itself leads to cumulative stress that can affect functioning, morale, and the mental health of officers without their realizing it. In addition, he argues (along with others) that police officers are reluctant to use mental health resources. Therefore, he recommends that debriefings be a part of a larger peer counseling program. Using peers who are readily available to officers who have experienced the impact of traumatic stress and who "know the job" has the advantage of instant credibility without the stigma of being seen as a "shrink."

The authors' experience has been that by far the majority of officers who are involved in traumatic incidents, including negotiators, experience an acute stress disorder and that they benefit from having understanding, accepting, and caring people to whom they can turn for support when they are questioning themselves. For officers, this is usually other officers, because they do not believe that people outside the job understand the job. Having trained peer support officers is a valuable resource because they have the attitude, the listening skills, and the knowledge to know when an acute stress reaction is developing into something more serious and when to refer to the professionals.

It is the authors' opinion that there is a place for knowledgeable mental health professionals in policing. Although not common, PTSD does occur among police officers. Over the years, the authors have intervened with officers who were beaten 18 years before and were starting to develop PTSD symptoms, with officers who were involved in a shooting 18 months before and were experiencing PTSD symptoms, and officers who had to shoot and kill teenagers who were shooting other officers and were experiencing PTSD symptoms, as well as a negotiator who was the first to find the body of six-month-old baby who was killed by the subject with whom the negotiator had been talking for six hours and was experiencing PTSD. They had all been debriefed, talked with their peers, their families, and their chaplains about the events without any relief. Professional intervention was required to return them to the level of functioning at which they worked before.

The authors have long believed that negotiators are the best and brightest in policing. As such, they deserve the best from policing. That best includes debriefing, peer counseling, and dedicated professionals who are there to support and care for those who support and care for people in crisis.

Summary

When an incident "goes bad," someone dies. Both the police and the hostages need to be able to manage the aftereffects of such a trauma. Even when no one dies, hostages are frequently traumatized by the experience of losing control of their lives. They need to deal with the emotional impact of the incident. Both the negotiators and the hostages need to start the process of dealing with the aftereffects by debriefing, peer support, and appropriate mental health support. Negotiators will debrief both the operation (to gain a better understanding about what can be improved) and the impact (the emotional effects) of the incident. The hostages will debrief the impact. Both can minimize the long-term consequences of a life-changing event by immediately starting to understand that everyone did the best they could with what they had. Success has to be measured by the quality of the effort, not by the results.

Note

1   The list of best practices above is a summary of the "best practices" that are currently being developed. Negotiations teams and police departments should contact Deputy William Kidd, Sonoma Sheriff's Office, for a complete version of the standards.

References

Allen, S.W., S.L. Fraser, and R. Inwald (1990). "Assessment of Personality Characteristics Related to Successful Hostage Negotiators and Their Resistance to Post-Traumatic Stress Disorder." In Reese, J., J. Horn, and C. Dunning (eds.), *Critical Incidents in Policing*. Washington, DC: U.S. Department of Justice.

American Psychiatric Association (1994). *Diagnostic and Statistical Manual*, Fourth Edition. Washington, DC: APA.

Bohl, N. (1997). "Post-incident Crisis Counseling for Crisis Negotiators." In Rogan, R.G., M.R. Hammer, and C.R. Van Zandt (eds.), *Dynamic Processes of Crisis Negotiation*. Westport, CT: Praeger.

Everly, G. (1989). *A Clinical Guide to the Treatment of the Human Stress Response*. New York, NY: Plenum Press.

Eysenck, H.J., W. Arnold, and R. Meili (1972). *Encyclopedia of Psychology*. New York, NY: Herder & Herder.

Federal Bureau of Investigation (1984). *Basic Hostage Negotiations Seminar*. Quantico, VA: Federal Bureau of Investigation.

Figley, C. (1988). "Post Traumatic Family Therapy." In Ochberg, F.M. (ed.), *Post Traumatic Therapy in Victims of Violence*. New York, NY: Bruner-Mazel.

Friedman, M.J. (2001). *Post-Traumatic Stress Disorder*. Kansas City, MO: Dean Psych Press Corp.

Hatcher, C., K. Mohandie, J. Turner, and M. Gelles (1998). "The Role of the Psychologist in Crisis/Hostage Negotiations." *Behavioral Science and the Law* 16:455-472.

Hogewood, William (2005). "Post incident Debriefing: Emotional Survival for Negotiators." Presented at: Hostage/Crisis Negotiations 201. Olatehe, KS (August).

Keene, T.M., P.F. Malloy, and J.A. Fairbanks (1984). "Empirical Development of an MMPI Subscale for the Assessment of Combat-Related Post-Traumatic Stress Disorder." *Journal of Consulting and Clinical Psychology* 52:888-891.

Kidd, W. (2005). "peak performance 'Best Practice" Standards for Negotiators/CNT. Presented at: Hostage/Crisis Negotiations 201. Olathe, KS (August).

Lanceley, F.J. (1999). *On-Scene Guide for Hostage Negotiators*. Boca Raton, FL: CRC Press.

McMains, M.J. (1986). "Post-Shooting Trauma: Principles from Combat." In Reese, J.T. and H.A. Goldstein (eds.), *Psychological Services for Law Enforcement*. Washington, DC: U.S. Government Printing Office.

_____ (2000). "Critical Decision Points in Crisis Negotiations: An Intensive Case Study." Presented at the 10th Annual Crisis Negotiators' Seminar and Competition, San Marcos, TX (January).

Mitchell, J. and G. Bray (1990). *Emergency Services Stress*. Englewood Cliffs, NJ: A Brady Book.

Nielsen, E. (1986). "Post-Shooting Trauma in Police Work." In Reese, J. and H. Goldstein (eds.), *Psychological Services for Law Enforcement*. Washington, DC: U.S. Government Printing Office.

Noesner, G. (1999). "Negotiation Concepts for Commanders." *FBI Law Enforcement Bulletin* 68:6-14.

NOVA (1991). *Community Crisis Response Team Training*. Ft. Sam Houston, TX (April).

Ricketts, C. (1995). "Post Incident Stress for the Negotiator." *The Journal of Crisis Negotiations* (October), Vol. 1, No. 2.

Tyhurst, J.S. (1958). "The Role of Transition States—Including Disasters—in Mental Illness." In *Proceedings of Symposium on Preventive and Social Psychiatry*. Washington, DC: U.S. Government Printing Office.

Discussion Questions

1. Review the incident described at the beginning of this chapter and draft a report utilizing the HOBAS data as a guide to what information you need on the incident. If information is not available, mark it N/A. Discuss with the class the importance of the missing data. What would it add, if you had it? How could you use it to improve team performance?

2. Think about the most traumatic incident you have experienced. Identify one person with whom you would be comfortable talking with about incident and one with whom you would be least comfortable. What is the difference in these two people and what do those differences tell you about debriefing an incident?

3. Discuss the importance of Kidd's "best practices," identifying the elements in them that were not in the HOBAS data or the Critical Decision Review. How are these additional elements important in increasing negotiator skills and in protecting the police department from liability?

4. If you were the officer described in Officer Ricketts' article, what would you have done before, during, and after the incident to protect yourself from the long-term emotional impact of the incident?

5. When should an officer who has been involved in a negotiation incident in which a person dies be required to attend a debriefing, be approached by a peer counselor, and be referred to the department mental health professional?

6. What are the similarities and the differences between an emotional debriefing and the counseling/therapies that have been shown to be effective with PTSD/ASD.

Name Index

Subject Index